South University Library
Richmond Campus
2151 Old Brick Road
Glen Allen, Va 23060

D1793331

JUN 0 4 2012

Deep Learning

HOW THE MIND OVERRIDES EXPERIENCE

Stellan Ohlsson
University of Illinois at Chicago

CAMBRIDGE UNIVERSITY PRESS
Cambridge, New York, Melbourne, Madrid, Cape Town, Singapore,
São Paulo, Delhi, Dubai, Tokyo, Mexico City

Cambridge University Press
32 Avenue of the Americas, New York, NY 10013-2473, USA

www.cambridge.org
Information on this title: www.cambridge.org/9780521835688

© Cambridge University Press 2011

This publication is in copyright. Subject to statutory exception
and to the provisions of relevant collective licensing agreements,
no reproduction of any part may take place without the written
permission of Cambridge University Press.

First published 2011

Printed in the United States of America

A catalog record for this publication is available from the British Library.

Library of Congress Cataloging in Publication data
Ohlsson, Stellan.
Deep learning : how the mind overrides experience / Stellan Ohlsson.
p. cm.
Includes bibliographical references and index.
ISBN 978-0-521-83568-8
1. Learning, Psychology of.   2. Cognitive learning theory.   3. Mind and
body.   4. Experience.   I. Title.
BF318.O45   2011
153.1′5–dc22   2010030593

ISBN 978-0-521-83568-8 Hardback

Cambridge University Press has no responsibility for the persistence or
accuracy of URLs for external or third-party Internet Web sites referred to in
this publication and does not guarantee that any content on such Web sites is,
or will remain, accurate or appropriate.

DEEP LEARNING

Although the ability to retain, process and project prior experience onto future situations is indispensable, the human mind also possesses the ability to override experience and adapt to changing circumstances. Cognitive scientist Stellan Ohlsson analyzes three types of deep, non-monotonic cognitive change: creative insight, adaptation of cognitive skills by learning from errors and conversion from one belief to another, incompatible belief. For each topic, Ohlsson summarizes past research, re-formulates the relevant research questions and proposes information-processing mechanisms that answer those questions. The three theories are based on the principles of *redistribution* of activation, *specialization* of practical knowledge and *resubsumption* of declarative information. Ohlsson develops the implications of those principles by scaling their consequences with respect to time, complexity and social interaction. The book ends with a unified theory of non-monotonic cognitive change that captures the abstract properties that the three types of change share.

Stellan Ohlsson is Professor of Psychology and Adjunct Professor of Computer Science at the University of Illinois at Chicago (UIC). He received his Ph.D. in psychology from the University of Stockholm in 1980. He held positions as Research Associate in the Robotics Institute at Carnegie-Mellon University and as Senior Scientist in the Learning Research and Development Center at the University of Pittsburgh before joining UIC in 1996. His work has been supported by the Office of Naval Research, the National Science Foundation and other organizations. Dr. Ohlsson has published extensively on computational models of cognition, creative insight, skill acquisition and the design of instructional software, as well as other topics in higher cognition.

CONTENTS

Preface — *page* vii

PART ONE   INTRODUCTION

1 The Need to Override Experience — 3
2 The Nature of the Enterprise — 24

PART TWO   CREATIVITY

3 The Production of Novelty — 53
4 Creative Insight: The Redistribution Theory — 87
5 Creative Insight Writ Large — 130

PART THREE   ADAPTATION

6 The Growth of Competence — 169
7 Error Correction: The Specialization Theory — 205
8 Error Correction in Context — 255

PART FOUR   CONVERSION

9 The Formation of Belief — 291
10 Belief Revision: The Resubsumption Theory — 329

PART FIVE   CONCLUSION

11 Elements of a Unified Theory   363
12 The Recursion Curse   389

Notes   393
References   455
Name Index   515
Subject Index   519

PREFACE

The theme of this book is that human beings possess cognitive processes that enable them to override the imperatives of past experience and to act and think in novel ways, and that these processes differ from the types of cognitive processes usually envisioned in psychological theories of learning. The capability for what I call *deep learning* – or, more precisely, *non-monotonic cognitive change* – constitutes a distinct aspect of mind that follows its own laws and hence requires its own theory. The book develops this theme by summarizing and extending prior research by me and others with respect to three specific types of non-monotonic change: the creation of novelty; the adaptation of cognitive skills to changing circumstance; and the conversion from one belief to another, incompatible belief. The book offers novel theories of the mental processes operating in each of these three types of cognitive change, as well as a unified theory that captures the abstract principles that they share.

My interest in creativity, adaptation and conversion preceded my awareness that these topics are variations on a theme. As a graduate student at the University of Stockholm in the late 1970s, I tried to relate the Gestalt view of insight to the information-processing theory of problem solving proposed by A. Newell and H. A. Simon. My first attempt at such a synthesis was published in 1984, and over the years it morphed into the theory of insight in Chapter 4. I thank my Ph.D. advisor, Yvonne Waern, for her constant encouragement and strong support for this as well as other oddball activities, and for managing a weekly cognitive seminar where her students could argue about cognition. I fondly remember discussions with Yvonne herself and, among others, Ove Almkvist, Göran Hagert and Susanne Askvall. Swedish psychologists interested in cognition formed a small community at that time and I learned from my interactions with, among others, Carl Martin Allwood, Berndt Brehmer, Anders Ericsson, Henry Montgomery, Lars-Göran Nilsson, Lennart Nilsson, Rolf Sandell and Ola Svensson.

Modern work on skill acquisition began with a 1979 article by Y. Anzai and H. A. Simon at Carnegie-Mellon University (CMU). They reported a computer simulation model of a single subject learning a new problem-solving strategy. As a graduate student, I had the opportunity to visit CMU in the fall of 1978, at the very moment when this line of work began. Anders Ericsson, a fellow graduate student from Stockholm, was already at CMU as a post-doctoral Fellow, and I thank him for his generosity in letting me stay at his house for several months. I appreciate the willingness of CMU faculty members John R. Anderson, David Klahr, Allen Newell, Lynn Reder, Robert Siegler, Herbert A. Simon and their students and associates – including Patrick Langley, David Neves, John Laird and Paul Rosenbloom – to engage intellectually with a student visitor. Pat in particular took me under his wing. We spent many hours debating computational models of skill acquisition, and our collaboration continues to this day. The multiple-mechanism theory of adaptation presented in Chapter 6 is a descendant of those discussions.

My work acquired an educational aspect during my years as Senior Scientist at the Learning Research and Development Center (LRDC) at the University of Pittsburgh. I continued work on insight in collaboration with Jonathan Schooler, which resulted in a widely cited paper on the relation between insight and language. During those years my work on skill acquisition led to the theory of learning from error that is the centerpiece of Chapter 7. I also branched out into research on intelligent tutoring systems. Pat Langley and I had previously investigated the application of machine learning techniques to the problem of online diagnosis of student errors, but my understanding of tutoring systems was much improved at LRDC by discussions and collaborations with Jeffrey Bonar, Bruce Buchanan, Alan Lesgold, Johanna Moore and Kurt VanLehn. My collaboration with Bruce and Johanna on the automatic generation of explanations for medical patients strengthened my long-standing interest in the philosophy of explanation. The reader will encounter this topic in Chapter 2.

The focus on explanation led in turn to an interest in the nature of declarative knowledge generally. My understanding of this topic owes much to interactions with Michelene ("Micki") Chi, James Greeno, Lauren Resnick, James Voss and others. The years at LRDC touched other aspects of my professional development as well. From Glynda Hull I learned that the prose of scholarly texts does not have to be dull and boring, and I hope the reader can see the effects of this lesson in the present book. From Gaia Leinhardt I learned to respect the skills of classroom teachers. Robert Glaser and Lauren Resnick taught me the elements of grantsmanship. There was a steady stream of visitors passing through LRDC. Andreas Ernst, a student from Germany, now professor of environmental systems analysis at the University of Kassel, spent a year with me teaching cognitive skills to the HS simulation model that stars in Chapters 7 and 8. My interactions with Erno Lehtinen provided an opportunity to think through the function of abstraction in declarative knowledge. Similarly, I benefited from my conversations with David Perkins, then and in later visits with his group at Harvard University. During the LRDC years, I was privileged to have Nancy Bee, Ernest Rees and James J. Jewett working with me in their various capacities. I thank John Anderson, Micki Chi, Susan Chipman and Lauren Resnick for their assistance at a crucial moment in my career.

When I moved to the University of Illinois at Chicago (UIC) in 1996 I continued all three lines of research. Guenther Knoblich, then a graduate student at the Max Planck Institute in Munich, Germany, spent the better part of a year with me in Chicago. We pushed the theory of insight beyond what I had been able to do in previous publications, and we conducted experiments to support it. The theory in Chapter 4 is a revised version of the cognitive mechanisms we identified. Our experimental work benefited from our collaboration with my UIC colleague Gary Raney, who contributed his expertise in eye-tracking methodology. I thank Guenther for arranging an opportunity to continue this work during a six-week visit to the Max Planck Institute in the spring of 1998, and Institute Director Professor Wolfgang Prinz for his support and hospitality.

My work on the design of intelligent tutoring systems for cognitive skills has advanced in two important ways at UIC. The first advance occurred when I was contacted in 1996 by Antonija ("Tanja") Mitrovic, a computer scientist who was in the process of escaping strife in her former homeland and re-settling herself and her family in New Zealand. Tanja wanted to use the theory of constraint-based learning from error that the reader finds in Chapter 7 to guide the design of intelligent tutoring systems. Tanja is now a leading researcher in that field, and I thank her for the thrill of seeing the ideas we talked about become real in the series of intelligent tutoring systems that she and her co-workers and students have produced at Canterbury University in New Zealand. The second important advance was the arrival at UIC of Barbara Di Eugenio, a computational linguist with expertise in tutoring whom I already knew from LRDC. We have studied tutorial dialogues in order to base the design of tutoring systems on a solid empirical basis. The all-too-brief statement about the application of the constraint-based approach to tutoring in Chapter 7 summarizes a few of the insights gained through my collaborations with Tanja and Barbara and their students.

At UIC, I have had multiple opportunities to develop my interest in the nature of declarative knowledge. Andrew Johnson, Jason Leigh and Thomas Moher are three UIC computer scientists who specialize in virtual reality and related technologies. Together we built and field tested a learning environment for teaching children that the Earth is spherical rather than flat. The instructional intervention was not as powerful as we had hoped, but the design and data collection stimulated our thinking about the nature of declarative knowledge and belief. My interest in the philosophy of explanation has also benefited from discussions with Nicholas Huggett, Jon Jarrett and Colin Klein, colleagues in the philosophy department at UIC. Micki Chi invited me in 2004 to co-author a review paper that summarized the cognitive mechanisms behind the acquisition of complex declarative knowledge. That effort stimulated me to develop a new theory of belief revision. I thank Gale Sinatra for encouraging me to put that theory in writing, and for making room for it in the pages of the *Educational Psychologist*. The reader will find the current version of that theory in Chapter 10.

Like many other cognitive scientists, I often find it difficult to explain to people in other professions what I do for a living. One defense against such social embarrassment is to talk about the implications of cognitive science for everyday life. The question arises as to what those implications are. How do the consequences of cognitive processes scale up to long periods of time and across levels of complexity? Do the details of individual cognition matter for the groups, teams and organization in which human beings normally operate? These questions have stimulated my interest in computer simulation of the connection between individual and social cognition. Two UIC colleagues stand out as sources of inspiration in this regard. Siddartha Bhattacharyya and I have collaborated on a computer model of social creativity using a technique called agent-based modeling. My understanding of this enterprise has been greatly advanced by interactions with my colleague James Larson, a social psychologist whose experiments are as elegant as his simulation models of group decision making and problem solving. What I have learned from these colleagues has informed my treatment of the relations between the individual and the collective in Chapters 5 and 8.

Throughout my years at UIC, I have had the privilege of working with a large group of graduate students: Bettina Chow, Andrew Corrigan-Halpern, David Cosejo, Thomas Griffin, Joshua Hemmerich, Trina Kershaw, Timothy Nokes, Justin Oesterreich, Mark Orr, Shamus Regan and Robert Youmans. The reader will see glimpses of their work here and there throughout the book. I thank each and every one of them for our many stimulating discussions.

Pursuing the three topics of insight, skill acquisition and belief revision in parallel over multiple years inevitably led to the question of how these three types of cognitive change are related. In the 1990s, I became fascinated by the complex systems revolution that swept through both the natural and the social sciences, and it dawned on me that this new view of reality directly impacts my own work: If both nature and society are chaotic, complex and turbulent, then how must the mind be designed to enable people to function in that kind of world? The question led to a different synthesis of my three interests from any that I had envisioned previously.

A 2004 sabbatical year at the Computer Science Department at Canterbury University in New Zealand provided the opportunity to attempt a synthesis. I thank the Erskine Foundation for the fellowship that made this visit possible. I thank my friend and colleague Tanja Mitovic, department head Timothy Bell and the staff of the Erskine Foundation for bearing the burden of the paperwork and the other practical arrangements associated with my visit. As befitting the laptop lifestyle of the contemporary era, this book was written in coffee shops rather than in offices. The first draft was hammered out in a charming café in the Cashmere Hills, just southwest of the Canterbury plain, called, appropriately enough, The Cup, while the inevitable rewriting was done in Starbucks and Barnes & Noble coffee shops in the Gold Coast neighborhood of Chicago. I thank the staff at these places for their friendliness, their patience with a customer who never leaves, and their diligence in keeping those cappuccinos coming. In the course of my writing, colleagues at UIC and elsewhere who have helped by responding to various questions and requests for comments and materials include John Anderson, Tibor Bosse, Daniel Cervone, William Clancey, Stephanie Doane, Renee Elio, Susan Goldman, David Hilbert, Ben Jee, Jim Larson, Michael Levine, Matthew Lund, James MacGregor, Clark Lee Merriam of the Cousteau Society, Thomas Ormerod, David Perkins, Michael Ranney, Steven Smith, Terri Thorkildsen, Jan Treur, Endel Tulving, Jos Uffink, David Wirtshafter and Beverly Woolf.

The specific investigations that underpin the theoretical formulations in this book were made possible primarily by grants from the Office of Naval Research (ONR). Very special thanks to Susan Chipman, who as program officer dealt with 20 years' worth of grant proposals with analytical acumen, broad knowledge of the field, much good advice and some mercy. In addition, I have been the grateful recipient of grants from the National Science Foundation (NSF) and the Office for Educational Research and Improvement (OERI). Seed grants from UIC helped get some of these investigations under way.

Throughout the six years of writing this book, the staff at Cambridge University Press has been patient, to say the least, with my repeatedly postponed deadlines. I thank the editors, the copy editor and the members of the production department for their work in bringing the manuscript through the production process. I have Deborah Roach to thank for the jacket photo.

Although an author of this kind of book has many people to thank, writing is a solitary endeavor for which all the rewards arrive well after the work is done. As the work stretches over multiple years, moments arrive when it is difficult to sustain belief in the enterprise. I thank my wife, Elaine C. Ohlsson, for her upbeat encouragement and her unwavering belief that the book would one day be done, and that it would be worth the sacrifice of the many hours we could have spent together if I had not been glued to my keyboard.

I have benefited from my interactions with all the individuals mentioned here and with many others. I am solely responsible for the use I have made of what I have learned, and any errors and mistakes, conceptual or technical, are entirely my own.

This book can be read in different modes. It can be read as a review of research in the three areas of creativity, skill acquisition and belief revision. The reader in this mode should be forewarned that Chapters 3, 6 and 9 are not neutral summaries. They are designed to lead the reader to the conclusion that existing theories are insufficient to answer the relevant questions, and thereby prepare the ground for my own theoretical proposals. That said, I have tried to mention every good idea that I have encountered in 35 years of reading the cognitive research literature, and I believe the book could serve as the text for a graduate seminar on cognitive change. Readers in this mode are encouraged to pay attention to the notes; I put most of the history and background material there. Regarding issues in human cognition, I cite original research articles. Regarding matters outside my specialty, I allow myself to cite secondary sources. I believe that a newcomer to the study of cognitive change has no need to repeat my extensive idea mining of the cognitive literature, but can take the present book as his* starting point and move forward, but perhaps that is an author's conceit.

A second reading mode is to focus on the technical contributions, that is, the three specific theories proposed in Chapters 4, 7 and 10, and to evaluate each on its own terms as a contribution to the relevant research area. This

---

* For brevity and elegance of expression, I use "he," "his" throughout as synonyms for "he or she," "his or her." This is a stylistic choice and not a statement about gender.

mode will be natural for cognitive psychologists. Readers in this mode will find that I emphasize the theoretical ideas themselves and use the broader canvas of a book to discuss them in more detail than can be fitted into the standard research article. My goal throughout has been conceptual clarity and deep explanation, not coverage of laboratory findings.

In a third mode, the reader would focus on the goal of understanding non-monotonic change as a category of cognitive change that poses unique theoretical puzzles and therefore requires its own principles and explanatory schemas. In this reading mode, the synthesis of the three theories into a unified theory in Chapter 11 is the most important contribution of the book.

The core contributions are necessarily technical in nature, but I have tried to write in such a way that an educated layperson can read this book as an extended reflection on the turbulence of the human condition. My ambition has been to write the kind of book I enjoy reading: A serious contribution to science that spells out the broader implications of the research for everyday life. Readers in this mode might want to skim the central sections of Chapters 4, 7 and 10, but I hope they enjoy the rest of the book.

For very busy people, there is yet another way to approach this book: Read the first sentence of Chapter 1 and the last sentence of Chapter 12, and postpone the stuff in between until after retirement.

The Gold Coast, Chicago
May 2010

DEEP LEARNING

PART ONE

INTRODUCTION

1

The Need to Override Experience

> *Upon those who step into the same stream ever different waters flow.*
> Heraclitus[1]

> *Nothing so like as eggs, yet no one, on account of this appearing similarity, expects the same taste and relish in all of them.*
> David Hume[2]

Life is change. Natural forces continuously knead our material environment as if it were so much dough in the cosmic bakery, and few features of our social environment remain constant for even one generation. How do human beings live in ubiquitous change? How do we cope with, and adapt to changes in our environment? How do we initiate change and create novelty? Due to late 20th-century advances in the natural sciences, these questions are more difficult to answer than they once seemed.

Few changes are so beguiling to children, poets and whomever else has the good sense to stop and look as a change of season. In four-season climes, the visual transformation of the landscape as the dominant color moves from green to red and on to white is stunning. The spectacle of an early autumn snowstorm must have overwhelmed the first band of hunter-gatherers to push north into a temperate climate zone and convinced them that their world was coming to an end.

Yet, children, poets and hunter-gatherers are wrong; striking as it is, seasonal change is no change. Winter displaces summer, true enough; but after winter, summer returns, and all is as it was. The change is cyclic, hence stable; hence not a change. The world remains constant; it is merely going through motions. According to this view, change is an illusion because the fabric of reality is a weave of eternal laws of nature.

It follows that creatures who can remember, reason, imagine and plan can respond to the superficial changes by accumulating experiences, extracting the underlying regularities, projecting them forward in time and acting accordingly. To survive, the hunter-gatherers only needed to see through the transient snowstorm to the repeating sequence of seasons, predict the return of summer and stockpile food. This picture of the interlock between world and mind has dominated Western intellectual traditions since the beginning of written scholarship.

As it turns out, this picture is a mirage. We live in a world in which change is no illusion. Adaptation to this world requires cognitive capabilities over and beyond those implied by the traditional view.

A CLOCK SO TURBULENT

Since the scientific revolution of the 17th century, the natural sciences have scored astonishing successes by viewing nature as an unchanging machine, a kaleidoscope that generates shifting appearances.[3] Searching behind the complex appearances of the night sky, astronomers found a simple geometric system of spheres traveling around the sun in elliptical orbits that are fixed by eternal laws and universal constants.[4] The changes in the night sky from dusk to dawn, from day to day and from month to month are clearly visible and yet no changes at all, merely the way the stable planetary system looks from the limited perspective of an earthbound observer.

On the surface of the Earth, pendulums, projectiles and pulleys turned out to be understandable as instances of a single category of mechanical motion.[5] All such motion is shaped by the constant force of gravity. Over time, physicists came to realize that an observer has a choice of reference frame and that an object that appears to be in motion within one frame appears to be at rest in another. Hence, motion – a change of place – is not a genuine change, but the way an object appears from certain points of view. Reality is captured in the mathematical equations that specify the translation from one frame of reference to another, and those equations are invariant.

Astronomy and physics are not the only success stories in the search for unchanging regularities. Looking behind the multitude of material substances, each with its own color, melting point, smell, taste, texture, weight and so on, chemists also found a simple system consisting of a short list of building blocks, the atomic elements, and a handful of mechanisms – the co-valent bond, Van der Waals forces – for combining them into larger structures, molecules, that determine the observable properties of material substances.[6] A chemical reaction might transform its reactants into very different substances and yet there is no fundamental change, only a rearrangement of the eternal building blocks.

 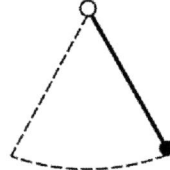 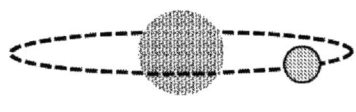

FIGURE 1.1. For clockwork systems, past behavior can be extrapolated into the future.

In these and other scientific breakthroughs, Nature appears as a clock, a machine that endlessly repeats the same movements. Figure 1.1 illustrates the analogy. The movements drive superficial events like the successive displacements of a clock's hands or the successive phases of the moon, but the underlying machinery does not change. Quoting science pioneers Robert Boyle, René Descartes and Johannes Kepler, historian Steven Shapin writes: "Of all the mechanical constructions whose characteristics might serve as a model for the natural world, it was the *clock* more than any other that appealed to many early modern natural philosophers."[7]

Scientists found that they could describe clockwork nature with linear differential equations, a mathematical tool for deriving the future state of a system, given two pieces of information: the current state of the system and the equations that describe how each property of the system is related to its other properties. Time plays an important role in such equations, but it is symmetrical between past and future. The physicist's equations can be used to calculate the position of the moon a hundred years ago as easily as to predict its position a hundred years hence. Because nothing truly changes in a clockwork world, past and future are mirror images.

The success of this approach to nature compelled scientists to regard natural systems that can be understood from within the clockwork mind-set as prototypical models of nature. Systems with a transparent link between the changing appearances and the underlying mechanism became scientific showcases, dooming generations of schoolchildren to the study of pendulums, projectiles and batteries hooked up to lightbulbs. The clockwork model was so successful that little importance was attached to the fact that not every natural system conforms. A system that did not behave like a clock was assumed to represent either a temporary state of ignorance about how to analyze it or an unimportant or peripheral part of nature.

In the last two decades of the 20th century, scientists surprised everyone, including themselves, by formulating a fundamentally different view of material reality. Consider a mountain river. The waters along its banks are forever shifting. The appearance of eddies and whirlpools cannot be predicted with the linear differential equations of clockwork physics. A hydrologist might try to describe the action of the river waters in terms of the movements of small, imagined cubes of water, but such a description does not predict when and where eddies will form. It does not help to appeal to probability. Descriptions in terms of statistical aggregates only work when the underlying system is random, and river water fails to conform. The scientist labors over his description, but the river rages on, spraying water in his face; its turbulence is irreducible.[8]

Mountain rivers exemplify a class of natural systems that scientists have come to label chaotic, complex, dynamic and nonlinear; for brevity I will use the single term *complex*.[9] Examples of complex systems include anthills, earthquakes, epidemics, forest fires, storms and volcanoes. As a group, complex systems are characterized by properties that do not fit, or can only be made to fit with great difficulty, into the clockwork model.

Instead of cycling through a fixed orbit forever, complex systems come into being, run their course and cease. That is, they have a *history*. A tree sprouts, grows, matures, topples and rots; a storm gathers, releases its energy and abates. The historical character of a system is difficult to establish when the system is so large that it cannot be encompassed in a single glance and when it lasts considerably longer than a human life, but scientists have found that climate zones, continents and ecosystems are historical entities. According to the Big Bang theory favored by some cosmologists, the universe itself might have a history.[10] It began as an incomprehensibly dense kernel that exploded and expanded rapidly, creating both space and materia in the process. The universe is still expanding, but it might one day reverse direction and contract, eventually ending in a Big Crunch.

In historical systems, past and future are not mirror images. Changes are *irreversible*, not repeating or cyclic. A river, once it reaches a plain, meanders.[11] It slowly and patiently alters its course, becoming more serpentine over time. A meandering river might be altered by a variety of processes, but it will not spontaneously straighten itself again. The ever more pronounced bends do not represent a phase in the life of the river that alternates with a phase of ever shallower bends. Likewise, a volcano rumbles, erupts and becomes dormant again. The resulting changes are not mere appearances. An eruption can fragment a mountain and replace it with a crater, an event that might have consequences for the biology, geology and weather of the surrounding area. Those consequences can be further modified by subsequent geological processes but not reversed; once the mountain has exploded, it does not come back together again. Unlike the cyclic processes of clockworks, such changes are directional with respect to time; they progress or unfold from past to future.[12]

In complex systems, changes are not illusory, no mere surface appearances driven by a constant causal machinery hidden behind the appearances. Instead, change is *thoroughgoing*. The turbulence of a river is not *caused* by the behavior of the water; it *is* the behavior of the water. Wind gusts are not *indicators* of a storm in the sense in which the hands of clock are indicators of the clock's internal state; they *are* the storm. There is no stable reality underlying the ceaseless movements; there are only the movements themselves.

If the changes appear regular, we have no guarantee that those regularities are themselves stable over time. Even in the strongholds of the clockwork mind-set, astronomy and mechanics, scientists discuss whether the laws of nature are the same everywhere in the universe and at all times.[13] Is the gravitational constant – the celebrated $g = 9.81$ m/s^2 that plays a central role in Newtonian physics – one of the eternal constants of the universe or a variable that slowly drifts from value to value as the universe expands? If changes in constants and laws are themselves regular, we have no guarantee that those second-order regularities are stable. Reality might be turbulent all the way down.

Complex systems have to be understood in terms of multiple *system levels*. At each level, system components exhibit characteristic properties and interact in characteristic ways to determine the properties of the next higher system level. The prototypical examples are the particle-atom-molecule-substance sequence of material science and the cell-organ-organism-species sequence of biology. Each system level is associated with a characteristic *scale* of complexity along size, time or some other dimension. The interactions among the components and processes at system level N propagate upward to shape the components, processes and system properties at level $N+1$. The propagation process can operate in different modes and exhibit different properties, depending on the characteristics of the system.

Some systems consist of components of qualitatively different types, interacting in qualitatively different ways. Typically, there are only a few, perhaps only a single component of each type. The human body and a car engine are examples. There are only two kidneys, one heart and one stomach, and the kidneys interact with the heart in a different way than with the stomach. Similarly, there are only a few cylinders in a car engine, and they interact differently with the fuel injector than with the differential. In systems of this type, the fine-grained details of one level seldom matter at higher levels. It does not matter *how* the heart pumps blood. Some individuals have lived for some time with artificial hearts that operate very differently from an organic one. But it matters greatly *that* the heart pumps blood. Similarly, if we replace the combustion engines in our cars with electrical engines, the internal structure and functioning of the cars will change radically, but there will be little effect on the traffic system. We will still have traffic jams, rush hours, speeding tickets, parking shortages, teenagers wanting to reserve the family car for Saturday night and so on. It does not matter from the point of view of the traffic system *how* an engine makes the car go, but it matters greatly *that* it makes the car go. In general, only gross properties of system level N punch through to become causes at higher system levels. I refer to this flavor of scaling as *direct impact*. It appears primarily when the operation of the higher-level system is dependent on a single, unique component at a lower level.

Systems with many components often exhibit *cascading causation*: Properties at system level N cause phenomena at level $N+1$, which in turn propagate upward to determine system characteristics at yet higher levels. The cascade can be *dampened*, so that the effect is smaller and smaller at each successive level. The accidental death of a single fox will have some effect on the local prey population, but at the level of the entire ecosystem, Mother Nature takes the fox's demise in her stride. The important cases are those in which the causal cascade is *amplified*, so that the consequences grow in magnitude from level to level. Even a minor change in, for example, the average global temperature can trigger processes of climate change: melting of polar caps, alterations in the flow of the ocean currents and so on. Amplified propagation of minor perturbations is popularly called a "butterfly effect," but is technically labeled *sensitivity to initial conditions*. Amplified cascading causation makes systems *massively contingent* on the exact properties and interactions of their components, one source of unpredictability.

Cascading causation can create patterns at a higher system level that are *emergent* – that is, impossible, at least in practice, to predict from a description of the lower system level. The meandering of a river can once again serve as example.[14] What makes a straight river develop ever more loopy bends? A river carries sediments – silt, sand and gravel – and the rate of sedimentation depends on the speed of the river. Where the river turns around a bend, the waters along the inner bank slow down and the sediments sink and become deposited on the bottom, extending that bank. At the same time, the rapid passage of the waters along the outer bank excavates that bank. As a result of these simultaneous processes, one riverbank will become thicker and grow toward the middle of the river, while the opposite bank is being scooped out and hence recedes in the same direction. The combined effect of these two processes is to

The Need to Override Experience

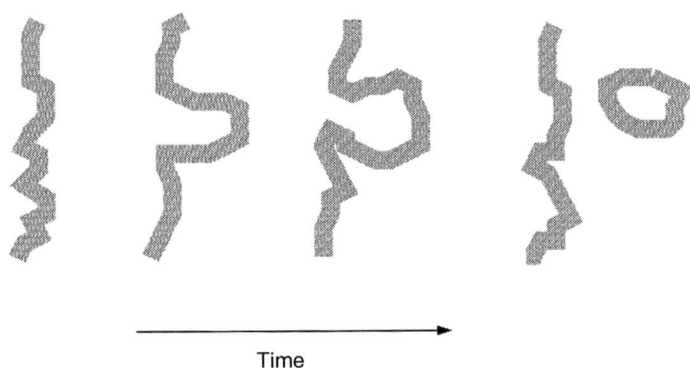

FIGURE 1.2. Successive views of a meandering river and the creation of a circular lake.

move the river sideways. Repeat this process at any point along the river where the two banks are such that the waters flow at different speeds, and the result is the snake-like shape we see in an aerial view of a meandering river. The river might spin off a small circular lake where a bend becomes so pronounced as to reconnect with itself; see Figure 1.2. Standing on the bank where a mountain river meets a coastal plain, a wanderer can observe these component processes without any other instruments than a pair of eyes hooked up to a brain. Nevertheless, the concept of *a small, circular lake with an island in the middle* does not fall out of statistical manipulations of immense numbers of water molecules. It is an emergent feature of rivers.

Direct impact and cascading causation contrasts with a third flavor of scaling called *self-organization*.[15] This concept applies to a system that consists of a large number of similar components and the components interact according to local rules that are the same for each pairwise interaction. Self-organization also produces emergent characteristics. Under certain rules, the components fall together into structures that are stable and exhibit properties that differ from the properties of their components. An anthill is the prototypical example.[16] The intricate social organization of the hill does not follow any master plan but is created by the interactions among the individual ants. The latter interact pairwise in accordance with relatively simple rules which, when followed by thousands of ants, generate complex patterns that we, the observers, recognize as *defending, foraging, nesting, tending the young* and so on, none of which exist at the level of the individual ant.

A fourth flavor of scaling is *level-invariance*. Some patterns are independent of the material constitution of the relevant system, so they recur at multiple system levels.[17] Sometimes this is referred to as *self-similarity*; the system looks like itself at each level of scale. On a map, a small tributary to a larger river looks the same as the river: a gradually widening band of water winding its way through the landscape. It is difficult to tell how big a waterway we are looking at without consulting the scale on the map. Famously, a map of the coast of Britain looks much the same regardless of its scale.[18] More abstract examples have been proposed by both natural and social scientists. Evolutionary biologists debate whether natural selection scales across levels.[19] Organisms, species and perhaps even taxa might be units of selection. Scaling in the other direction, some biologists argue that individual genes are subject to natural selection. In economy, the interaction between supply and demand applies to a village souk as well as to the global economy, or so economists claim.[20] In this scaling flavor, the units at system level N exhibit some property P such that when multiple units are combined into a larger-scale unit, that unit also exhibits P. Two generations ago, Arthur Koestler anticipated the centrality of level-invariance in contemporary systems theory by proposing that in most hierarchical systems the laws of behavior are the same at each level in the hierarchy.[21]

Most material systems interact with their environments and their trajectories are significantly influenced by events outside their own boundaries. Economists have coined the convenient term *externalities* to refer to events that are not themselves economical in character but that nevertheless have significant economic consequences (droughts, technical inventions, wars, etc.) and the concept is useful outside economics. A famous example of an externality is the meteor that might have slammed into the Earth some 65 million years ago, spelling the doom of the dinosaurs and perhaps thereby giving mammals a chance.[22] The emphasis on sensitivity to externalities in complex systems research is in stark contrast to the strategy of clockwork science to identify material systems that are so decoupled from their environments that their state variables can be expressed as mathematical functions of each other. Table 1.1 summarizes the key properties of complex systems.

The implication of historicity, irreversible, thoroughgoing change, propagation across multiple system levels, emergence and sensitivity to externalities is, in the words of Nobel laureate Ilya Prigogene, that "the laws of physics, as formulated in the traditional way, describe an idealized, stable world that is quite different from the unstable, evolving world in which we live."[23] This conclusion extends to the core paradigms of clockwork science. Science writer Ivars Peterson summarizes the developments in astronomy: "Long held up as a model of perfection and the symbol of a predictable mechanical universe, the solar system no longer conforms to the image of a precision machine. Chaos and uncertainty have stealthily

TABLE 1.1. *Key properties of complex systems.*

Property	Description
Historicity	No cyclic behavior; unidirectional unfolding from past to future. The past and the future are not mirror images.
Irreversibility	Changes are not reversible. Effects can be undone by further changes, but the system cannot return to a previous state.
Thoroughgoing change	The laws of change are themselves changing. There are no eternal change constants or laws, no fixed building blocks.
Multiple levels	A system must be described in terms of multiple levels of analysis. A property or a change at level N may or may not project upward, and determine system properties or changes at level $N+1$.
Multiple modes of projection	Events at level N can be related to events at level $N+1$ through direct impact, cascading causation or self-organization.
Emergence	The consequences of projections onto higher system levels are not always predictable.
Externalities	Systems are not decoupled from their environments, so a system trajectory can be radically influenced by events that follow other laws and principles than the system itself.

invaded the clockwork."[24] Natural systems are, by and large, unpredictable. Although clockwork science proudly designated successful predictions as the arbiters of scientific controversies, predictions about natural systems outside the laboratory are in fact rare. This insight is not new. In the early 20th century, the philosopher Charles Sanders Peirce wrote, "There is no greater nor more frequent mistake in practical logic than to suppose that things which resemble one another strongly in some respects are any the more likely for that to be alike in others."[25] What is new is that scientists now realize that unpredictability is not the exception but the typical case.

The lack of predictability is not due to a lack of regularities. But the regularities exhibited by complex systems are of a different kind from those that support the predictions of clockwork science. Earthquakes are, unfortunately, not predictable; that is, there is no known technique of deriving a conclusion of the form *there will be an earthquake of magnitude M at time t on such and such a day, with epicenter located at geographic coordinates x and y*.[26] Nevertheless, earthquakes exhibit regularities. For example, their frequency and size are inversely related: There are many small earthquakes but few large ones. This relationship follows a simple and elegant mathematical form. It is a regularity, not in the individual earthquakes, but in their statistical distribution and so provides no basis for predicting the occurrence, location, size or unfolding of any one earthquake. Similarly, meteorologists cannot now and have no hope of ever being able to predict the local weather with precision over long periods of time. The weather is not the kind of system that allows such predictions. Abrupt and unpredictable changes might characterize the weather in the long run – the climate – as well.[27]

We all know that we cannot rely on weather forecasts, but in the past we put this down to insufficient resources or perhaps to the competence of the forecasters. Among scientists, lack of predictability was blamed on insufficient information, the probabilistic character of the relevant system, the practical impossibility of collecting the relevant data, or, as a last stand, flaws in the theory used to generate the predictions. All material systems were assumed to be predictable in principle. But the complex systems revolution teaches us that lack of predictability is a real and central feature of the world. Evolutionary biology cannot predict which species will evolve next, or even how a given species will change in the next period of time. Evolutionary biology is nevertheless one of the most successful of sciences. The response to the lack of predictability is to give up predictability as a defining feature of science, not to give up the claim to be a science.

The shift to acknowledging the complex nature of most material systems should not be taken to deny the successes of clockwork science. The lawful dampening of the swings of a pendulum is not illusory. Clockwork science works well in *tight contexts*. The classical strategy of clockwork science to define the system under study in such a way that it is nearly de-coupled from its environment and hence relatively safe from externalities is perhaps the main source of tight contexts. A chemical reaction vessel that is tightly sealed to prevent any impurities from entering the reaction is an iconic instance. Tight contexts are local in space and last for a brief period of time, where these boundaries should be understood at the scale appropriate for the system under study. Allow externalities and extend the context in space and time and even the most well-behaved material system will become unpredictable: How does a pendulum swing when its rope begins to rot?

Complex systems have always attracted attention, but they were regarded by scientists as recalcitrant cases that would yield to a clockwork analysis eventually.[28] In the last two decades of the 20th century, the complex system was promoted from fringe exception to central case.[29] The situation is the opposite of what the natural sciences taught for 300 years: The systems that fit the clockwork model are special cases, unusual and rare. Even in those cases, the clockwork model is an approximation that holds only under special conditions, epitomized by the frictionless, inclined planes of high school physics.

Almost all natural systems are of the complex, unpredictable sort. To adapt to this reversal in perspective, natural scientists might want to choose some artifact other than the clock as their model of a prototypical material system. A loaf of bread would serve: The many ingredients interact to form an emergent, hard-to-predict structure that exists for some time, undergoes thoroughgoing changes and eventually ceases to exist.

If scientists surprised us, and themselves as well, by moving beyond clockwork science, historians were no doubt more surprised than everyone else. History was the first science, and it will be the last.[30] Long after we have learned everything there is to know about nature, human beings will continue to love and work, squabble and scheme, form and break alliances and somebody will feel the itch to chronicle and interpret. History is also the quintessential science of change. In the past, history and clockwork science have had little to say to one another. However, the conceptual vocabulary that scientists have developed for complex systems is eminently suitable for talking about aspects of society that are of intense interest to historians, economists and social scientists.

Organizations, governments, nations and entire civilizations have a life cycle; they emerge, unfold and collapse. Although the ancient Greeks hypothesized a repeating cycle of ages, modern historians assign time a direction.[31] The past and future are not mirror images. The Vikings shall never again row their boats across the Atlantic to conquer Britain for lack of entertainment at home, and samurai swords shall forever gather dust in art exhibits. Historical changes are not only irreversible but thoroughgoing. There have been attempts to discern laws underlying historical change – progressions through stages of perfection, movements toward ever more efficient modes of production and so on – but the majority of historians write as if the turbulence of human affairs is irreducible.[32]

Historical analyses necessarily move back and forth between the level of the individual and the social systems – armies, civilizations, firms, governments, markets, nations, organizations – within which he functions. Emergent phenomena are commonplace. Political economy began with the question of how the economic system that we now refer to as the Industrial Revolution appeared in Britain in the period of 1780–1830. It was not the product of a plan but emerged as a consequence of the interactions among the individual economic agents.[33]

Instances of other complex system features are equally obvious in history. There is no better example of a butterfly effect than the determination of British Prime Minister Winston Churchill in the spring of 1940, when France fell to the invading German armies and all seemed darkness, that England should continue to resist Nazi expansion, whatever the cost.[34] The consequences of this stance and Churchill's ability to transform it into a national policy cascaded through the war years and beyond, however unlikely Mr. Churchill may seem in the role of butterfly. From a complex systems perspective, there is no conflict between levels of description, no contrast between attributing historical change to societal movements or to the actions of Great Persons. It is true that the Allies won World War II by outproducing the fascist states, but it is equally true that the Allies won because Winnie was stubborn. All social systems are sensitive to externalities; economic markets are thrown into disarray by inventions and wars, and entire civilizations can become destabilized by climate changes. In *The Landscape of History*, historian John Lewis Gaddis writes that the focus on complex systems in the physical and biological sciences has "brought those disciplines closer than they once were to what historians had been doing all along."[35]

Our ability to predict the trajectory of social and political systems is widely acknowledged to be limited. Even in the two most analyzed types of social systems, elections and stock markets, prediction is notoriously difficult and imprecise. Anybody who could predict the future course of the market would gather riches without limit, but the only people who make money on this possibility are the authors of books that advocate systems for how to make such predictions. In *The Box*, a history of the standardized shipping container, Marc Levinson writes: "Perhaps the most remarkable fact about the remarkable history of the box is that time and again, even the most knowledgeable experts misjudged the course of events. The container proved to be such a dynamic force that almost nothing it touched was left unchanged, and those changes often were not as predicted." Political analysts have fared no better. When the Berlin wall came down on November 9, 1989, it came as a surprise to everybody in the West, including intelligence analysts, policy experts and social scientists. The rise and fall of popular movements, social practices, religious commitments and fashions are not predictable to any interesting degree in spite of the ambitions implicit in the term "social science."[36]

My purpose is not to deny the successes of predictive social science. Like natural systems, a social system can be locally predictable over short periods of time, but even then only if the system is not seriously impacted by an external event. Instances of predictability in social systems are not unreal, but they are rare. Turbulence is the normal state of human affairs.

The lesson of the complex systems revolution is that we live in and through complex, unpredictable and irreducibly turbulent systems. This statement is as true of our natural as of our social environment. Fires and wars; earthquakes and market crashes; global warming and global trade; the connections go deeper than mere analogy. The systems of which we are the parts unfold forever in novel ways. There is nothing old under the sun.

LEARNING IN A TURBULENT WORLD

Sometime during hominid evolution, our species – more precisely, a hominid species in the phylogenetic lineage that eventually produced *Homo sapiens* – came to adopt an uncommon survival strategy. Unlike other animals, they, and hence we, came to rely more on learned skills than on innate dispositions. Certain aspects of human behavior have a genetic basis, but our behavior on a typical day nevertheless consists primarily of actions that we had to practice before we could do them – driving a car, using a telephone, sending e-mail – and very few actions that we did not have to learn: smiling, blinking and little else.[37] Other animals learn as well, but we are more effective learners by far. Even dolphins and chimpanzees, generally regarded as the smartest among animals, cannot match the ease with which a human toddler soaks up new information and acquires new skills.[38] Most important, we easily learn to use tools and symbols, two keys to the astonishing progress of the naked ape we once were; without stone axes, no space shuttles; without scratches on bone, no mathematics.[39] We are not merely different from other animals in these respects; we are orders of magnitude different.

The advantage of learned over innate skills lies in the speed of adaptation. Both learning and biological evolution are mechanisms for tracking change in the environment.[40] When the material environment changes, it exerts novel selective pressures on any species that was adapted to that environment, and over time such a species is molded by natural selection to fit the altered environment. The change in the species mirrors the change in the environment, and its phylogenetic lineage records the successive changes. Similarly, when a person confronts changes in a familiar task, he prevails by adapting prior skills to the new circumstances. The change in the skill mirrors the change in the environment, and a person's learning history records the challenges he has faced throughout life. The similarities notwithstanding, these two mechanisms for tracking change operate at different time scales: Evolution requires tens of thousands of years, often more, to create a new anatomy and its associated lifestyle, while learning operates over much shorter time periods, from minutes to years. Species that rely primarily on innate skills and hence track change at evolutionary rates become extinct eventually, victims of some environmental change that was too rapid for this type of adaptation. Learners, on the other hand, can deal even with rapid change.

Our superior ability to learn is arguably our species-specific characteristic, so a theory of the human mind requires a learning theory as one of its components. As long as psychologists conceptualized the environment within the clockwork mind-set, it was clear in principle how learning works: Because change is an illusion and reality consists of stable regularities, a person can learn by accumulating experiences, analyze them to identify the regularities, project those regularities onto the future and act accordingly.

This requires certain cognitive capabilities. To accumulate experience requires memory. Each event or experience must leave a trace of some sort – Richard W. Semon suggested that we call it an *engram* but it is now more often called an *episodic memory* – which can be reactivated later to inform action at some future time.[41] Although early efforts by Karl Lashley and others to locate individual engrams in the brain were unsuccessful, the existence of such traces is not in doubt.[42] Every person can recall any number of events and situations that have happened in his own past, and textbooks in cognitive psychology require multiple chapters to describe the many experiments that investigate our capacity to form, retain and retrieve episodic memories.[43]

Memories of individual events are not very useful in themselves, but, according to the received view, they form the raw material for further learning. By extracting the commonalities across a set of related episodic memories, we can identify the underlying regularity, a process variously referred to as *abstraction*, *generalization* or *induction*. The output of this supposed process is a knowledge structure that summarizes a regularity that was present in a person's past experience.[44] There is little doubt that people are capable of identifying patterns in sequences of experiences. People obviously form general concepts like *food, kin* and *tool*, and the march of the seasons, the phases of the moon and the cycles of the tide must have been identified by early humans long before the systematic investigations we now call science began.

In the clockwork view, general knowledge is useful because the regularities in past experience are also the regularities that will control future experiences. We can form more or less precise expectations about what future situations will be like on the basis of what the past was like. Indeed, the past is our only source of information about the future. The process of applying a regularity from the past to future situations is traditionally called *transfer* by psychologists and *induction* by logicians, but the philosopher Nelson Goodman suggested the more descriptive term *projection*.[45] Under any name, this process is useful to the extent that regularities in past experience continue to operate in the future.

Finally, to reap the benefits of our abilities to remember, process and project past experience, a person has to be able to use the resulting expectations to plan and act accordingly. People maintain complex systems of goals and multiple alternative plans for reaching them, and although we often have occasion to react on the spot to unexpected events, most of our actions throughout a normal day are parts of some plan or another. Like memory, generalization and transfer, the process of planning has been extensively studied by cognitive psychologists and the reality of this cognitive process is not in doubt.[46]

In short, the received view of our cognitive system in general and our capability for learning in particular is tightly interlaced with the clockwork view of reality; see Figure 1.3. Because past experience provides clues to the regularities that underpin the appearances, we can handle future situations by storing episodes in memory, and then process them to extract the underlying regularities, project those regularities onto the future to generate specific expectations, and plan and act accordingly. I suggest the term *empirical inductivism* for this view of the how mind and world interact, to distinguish this psychological theory from work on induction in artificial intelligence, mathematics and philosophy.

Empirical inductivism runs like a subterranean river under the landscape of cognitive research, watering not only studies of learning but almost all other subfields as well. It is the perfect partner for the clockwork view of nature. As seemingly perfect partners sometimes do, these two bring out the worst in each other. An inductive learning theory justifies the self-understanding of the clockwork scientist, and the findings of the latter in return confirm the

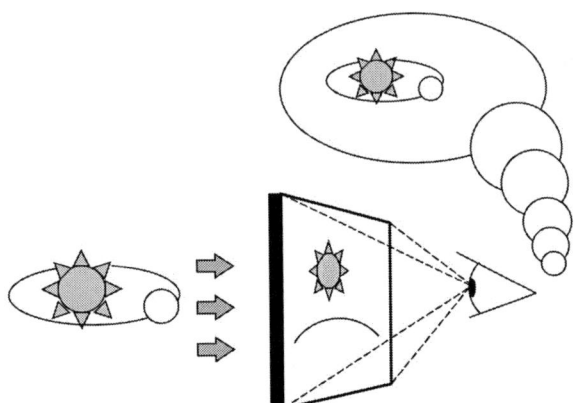

FIGURE 1.3. The clockwork interpretation of the epistemological situation.

view of the world that is assumed in inductive learning theories. The details of memory, induction, transfer and planning remain to be worked out, psychologists say, but the type of account sought is clear. Hundreds of experiments are conducted every year in psychology departments around the world to fill in those details.[47] Empirical inductivism thus acts as an implicit meta-theory for the study of cognitive change, a set of broad principles that do not by themselves explain any particular psychological phenomenon but specify what kind of explanation psychologists should seek.

If reality – material as well as social – does not operate like a clockwork but instead is complex, turbulent and unpredictable, empirical inductivism cannot be the whole story of learning. Adapting to a turbulent world is not like figuring out how a clock works. It is more like playing Meta-Chess. This difficult game looks exactly like an ordinary chess game. It is played with the same board and the same pieces. Unlike the case in ordinary chess, when a player moves a piece in Meta-Chess, he changes not only the location of that piece, but also the rules that control how the pieces move. When a player moves a rook forward the rules change so that pawns can only go backward, queens can only move three steps in any one direction and knights travel only in straight lines. Each type of move changes the rules in a different way. To select a move, a player has to think through not only the changing relations between the pieces, but also how the associated changes in the rules will affect the relative strengths of his own and his opponent's positions. To make matters worse, the set of rule changes associated with a move depends on the number of moves made so far in the game. At intervals determined by the decimal digits of the number *pi*, the rule changes change. The point is not that this hypothetical game would be difficult to play, but that one could not learn to play it via the processes envisioned in empirical inductivism. Change is not confined to the arrangement of pieces on the board, but reaches all the way down. There are no stable features that could form the basis for an inductive theory of the game. Strangely, Meta-Chess is a well-defined game and yet turbulent through and through.

If reality is more like Meta-Chess than like a clock, if living is like playing a game in which the rules change in ways that are themselves forever changing, then this fact must be reflected in the cognitive mechanisms that evolved as humans marched down the evolutionary pathway to cognitive flexibility. One might object that discoveries about complex systems in the late 20th century could hardly have affected pre-human hominids or archaic hunter-gatherers 150,000 years ago. Surely the self-organizing nature of climate change or the possibility of a slowly drifting value for the gravitational constant would not have troubled them.

This objection inverts the true relation between the turbulent material and social systems in which we live and the clockwork systems studied in classical natural science. It is the latter that are hard to find outside the laboratory, not the former. Most of the classical showcase systems, from pendulums to electrical circuits, share with clocks an element of artificiality; they are constructed rather than found. Systems that fit the clockwork mind-set have to be invented, built in special rooms called laboratories and studied under deliberately contrived conditions. Even then they can only be observed with the help of scientific instruments, themselves artifacts. As many laboratory scientists discover during their doctoral apprenticeship, to make a material system conform to the expectations of the clockwork view can be a challenge. In spite of multiple experimental controls – actions taken to reduce the number of relevant variables and the influence of externalities – confounding variables, randomness, impure samples or even the trembles produced by a nearby subway train can ruin an experimental setup and make the system under study fail to conform to the rules of the clockwork game.

In contrast, the turbulent character of complex systems is and always was ready at hand: The life history of a flower is visible in the garden, the unpredictability of the weather is proverbial, the irreversibility of volcanic action is obvious to anyone who has heard of Pompeii and Herculaneum[48] and cascading causation is not news to victims of severe floods: One small breach in the dam and your village is gone. Human beings suffered forest fires long before they suffered pendulums. In everyday experience, complex, turbulent and unpredictable systems are pervasive and clockwork systems are rare.

Was this also the case in early hunter-gatherer society, the context in which human beings evolved?[49] Consider three hypothetical vignettes. Imagine a hunter-gatherer band that lives in a valley where a particular prey constitutes a significant proportion of their diet. A newly arrived predator is likely to upset the predator-prey relations in the valley, possibly causing a drastic contraction of the prey population. Such effects can occur quickly, certainly within the lifetime of the band's members. Prior experience might not be very useful in reacting to a perturbation of this sort. How should the band respond? Past experience might suggest a gradual and smooth variation in abundance of prey from year to year. Projecting this experience onto the unprecedented situation caused by the new predator might lead to the unproductive decision of sitting out what the band's members expect to be a temporary dip in prey availability, chew roots and wait for better times. A more constructive response might be to develop techniques for hunting a different prey, or even to pack up and leave the valley. The latter decisions might be unprecedented in the experience of the current members of the band.

Although climate shifts most often occur over a long period of time compared to a human lifetime, they occasionally happen abruptly. "Dramatic alterations between cold and warm, steppe and forest, glacial and interglacial, occurred time and again in the late phases of humanity's descent, and when they happened, the change was measured on a scale from decades up to a few centuries."[50] Also, migration can move a hunter-gatherer band from one climate zone to another, perhaps in a decade of migration. Within the living memory of its members, a hunter-gatherer band might experience a shift from a wet-dry, two-season climate to a temperate, four-season climate. Such a shift requires a response that goes beyond past experience. Whereas the response to a wet season might be to move temporarily to higher altitudes, the appropriate response to autumn is to stockpile food; to move to higher ground will only increase the hardship of winter.

In a period of plenty the children in a hunter-gatherer band might survive more often than normal. The result might be an unprecedented population explosion, a strain on the band's resources and a subsequent splitting of the band. Each of the descendant bands now operates in an environment that includes another and potentially competing band, perhaps an unprecedented situation. Competition might lead to warfare, and then as now, inventions in military technology might create novel situations.[51] The first hunter-gatherer band to go into battle carrying shields must have bewildered their opponents; how do you fight an enemy you cannot reach?

We do not know that these hypothetical vignettes ever occurred in exactly this way, but they are plausible. My purpose in presenting them is not to claim that they happened at some specific time or place but to give concretion to the idea that the historical and experience-defying character of the environment was a living day-to-day reality for proto-humans and archaic humans, as opposed to an intellectual curiosity of interest primarily to philosophically disposed scientists at the end of the 20th century. Over the hundreds of thousands of years of human evolution, perturbations in the material, biological and social environments that changed the rules of survival must have occurred over and over again; if not these exact perturbations, then others. The turbulent and unpredictable character of reality was always directly experienced; it was the clockwork character of some material systems that required systematic investigations to be seen.

We arrive at a paradox: Prior experience is our only guide to the future. There is no other source of expectations. But in a world characterized by complexity and turbulence, change is the only constant. Furthermore, change is thoroughgoing, and the rules that control change are themselves changing. In this kind of world, prior experience is guaranteed to be misleading most of the time, although it might provide a good enough approximation in local contexts or over short periods of time. Learning in this kind of world requires cognitive capabilities other than those implied by empirical inductivism.

DEEP LEARNING

If prior experience is a seriously fallible guide, learning cannot consist solely or even primarily of accumulating experiences, finding regularities therein and projecting those regularities onto the future. To successfully deal with thoroughgoing change, human beings need the ability to override the imperatives of experience and consider actions other than those suggested by the projection of that experience onto the situation at hand. Given the turbulent character of reality, the evolutionary strategy of relying primarily on learned rather than innate behaviors drove the human species to evolve cognitive mechanisms that override prior experience. This is the main theme of this book, so it deserves a label and an explicit statement:

The Deep Learning Hypothesis

In the course of shifting the basis for action from innate structures to acquired knowledge and skills, human beings evolved cognitive processes and mechanisms that enable them to suppress their experience and override its imperatives for action.

The Deep Learning Hypothesis does not deny the existence of cognitive mechanisms that operate on the basis of experience. Inductive learning works in tight contexts and people obviously do possess the processes for encoding episodic information into memory, inductive reasoning, projection and planning that are described in cognitive psychology textbooks. The type of learning supported by those processes generates new knowledge that is consistent with what was known before. Borrowing a useful term from logicians, I refer to such additive cognitive growth as *monotonic*.[52]

The claim of the Deep Learning Hypothesis is that monotonic learning is at most half the story. The other half describes how we abandon, override, reject, retract or suppress knowledge that we had previously accepted as valid in order to track a constantly shifting and fundamentally unpredictable environment and thereby indirectly create mental space for alternative or even contradictory concepts, beliefs, ideas and strategies. A complete theory of human learning must complement inductive mechanisms with a second set of *non-monotonic* learning mechanisms that allow experience to be overruled.

The hypothesis that we possess cognitive mechanisms for overriding the imperatives of the past does not imply that doing so is effortless. Everyday life requires a balance between projecting and overriding past experience – what philosopher Thomas S. Kuhn has called "the essential tension" – and there is no reason to believe that evolution provided us with a perfect solution to this balancing problem.[53] To explain cognitive change is to explain both the possibility and difficulty of non-monotonic change.

Situations in which the environment is the source of change and the person has to follow suit are interesting cases of non-monotonic change, but people are also agents of change. The astonishing developments in art, business, science and technology since the dawn of civilization some 12,000 years ago measure our capacity to instigate change and create novelty. People sometimes create something novel in order to fill a need, sometimes because they have a vision of how things ought to be and sometimes for no other reason than that they desire change. Changes instigated by one person or group of persons frequently create a need in others to adapt to those changes.

Adaptation to the changes imposed by the environment – typically referred to as *learning* – and the deliberate initiation of change – often referred to as *creativity* – might seem like distinct cases and are usually treated as such, but closer examination reveals a deep similarity. When people instigate change by acting differently, something must have changed in their minds. The Spanish painter Pablo Picasso changed the art of painting when he initiated the cubist movement by painting *Les Demoiselles d'Avignon*.[54] To produce that painting, Picasso must have created a new concept about what a painting should be, or could be, or should or could accomplish. We need not believe that he worked out the complete composition before setting brush to canvas, nor need we assume that the ambition to paint in a new way was fully conscious at the start. However, something must have changed in Picasso's mind or else the work could not have turned out so different from anything painted before.

The Deep Learning Hypothesis suggests that the processes that produce the cognitive changes required to track environmental change will turn out to be the same processes that produce the cognitive changes that enable us to create novelty. The working assumption that these two cases will eventually fall under the same theory unites two fields of research – creativity and learning – which have been kept separate by accidents of historical origin and differences in conceptual foundations, methods and vocabulary, to the detriment of both.

The Deep Learning Hypothesis is a high-level principle, a perspective on cognitive change. It does not in and of itself explain any behaviors or psychological phenomena, any more than the principle that materia consists of atoms explains any particular chemical reaction. The purpose of this book is to articulate the Deep Learning Hypothesis into specific theories for three types of cognitive change, called *creativity, adaptation* and *conversion*. The three theories postulate different mechanisms to account for these three types of change, but they share a focus on the non-monotonic aspect of cognitive change.

Before embarking on this enterprise, it is useful to rehearse the fundamental working assumptions and reflect on the criteria of success. What does it mean to explain cognitive change? Indeed, what does it mean to explain any kind of change?

2

The Nature of the Enterprise

In psychology, we are overwhelmed with things to explain, and somewhat underwhelmed by things to explain them with.
                                                                Robert Cummins[1]

At [the information processing] level of theorizing, an explanation of an observed behavior ... is provided by a program of primitive information processes that generates this behavior.
                                    Allen Newell, J. S. Shaw and Herbert A. Simon[2]

A theory of change must be rooted in some initial conception of the thing that is changing, some working assumption, however incomplete and preliminary. This has been so in other sciences.[3] Chemists had to describe material substances in terms of atoms and molecules before they could explain chemical reactions in terms of the rearrangement of atoms. The description of the double helix structure of DNA paved the way for a deeper understanding of genetic mutations and biological evolution, and the discovery that the crust of the Earth consists of continental plates floating on a molten core was a prerequisite for the plate tectonics theory of geological change. Likewise, the principles about the nature of mind set forth in this chapter serve as a backdrop for the study of cognitive change. They are not new, and they are not mine but represent a collective achievement of the cognitive sciences. Although the principles are unlikely to be entirely accurate, they constitute the best available framework for the study of deep learning. In a mature science, a chapter like this would be unnecessary, but as things stand, disagreements go deep, so a theorist needs to declare his intellectual commitments.

The second task of this chapter is to address the question of what does and does not constitute a satisfactory explanation of cognitive change. This question has not been a target of much discussion in the psychology of learning or in the cognitive sciences in general. The floor of the cognitive theorist's workshop is strewn with debris from past theories, including the behaviorists' stimulus-response connections and Jean Piaget's developmental stages.[4] These theories turned out to be less than explanatory, everyone now agrees, but so, I suggest, are most other explanations for cognitive change, including those proposed since the cognitive revolution in the 1950s.[5] If so, what should a satisfactory explanation be like instead?

The first task is to establish that mind is the proper subject matter of psychology. There have been multiple attempts to escape.

CLOSING THE ESCAPE ROUTES

Psychology is the science of mind. Nevertheless, some psychologists have tried to replace the task of describing how the mind works by the task of describing something else. Different schools of thought have proposed different replacements.

According to the phenomenological approach, to describe mind is to describe *subjective experience*; that is, to state what a person is consciously perceiving, feeling, remembering and thinking.[6] Once the contents of consciousness have been described, there is yet more to say, but what is left to say falls within the scope of neuroscience. Phenomenologists do not deny mind but limit its scope. Psychology's responsibilities end at the edge of consciousness; the rest is neurons.

The emphasis on subjective experience is useful. Cognitive processes are expressed in subjective experience as well as in action and discourse. For example, we are all familiar with the frustration of trying to recall a name or a fact that refuses to be recalled, the elation associated with a sudden insight into a recalcitrant problem and the satisfaction of performing a complex skill thoroughly mastered. If psychology is to be a tool for understanding ourselves, our theories must explain the flow of subjective experiences as well as the streams of action and discourse.

But basic facts about cognition reveal as fallacious the idea that the mind can be reduced to nothing but subjective experience. Consider trying to recall a name, failing to do so but spontaneously succeeding a short while later. There cannot be a phenomenological explanation of this type of cognitive event. The subjective experience consists of the effort to recall, the blank mind that accompanies failure to recall and the slight surprise and relief of tension that accompanies the subsequent success. But this remains a description, not an explanation. The process that produces these conscious experiences – retrieval from long-term memory – is not itself conscious. An account of the subjective experiences, no matter how accurate, does not suffice to explain the regularities associated with retrieval failures, tip-of-the-tongue feelings and similar mental events.[7] This and many other observations force the conclusion that there are mental processes that are not conscious. The weakness of the phenomenological approach does not lie in its descriptions of conscious experiences but in the unwarranted add-on claim that there is nothing but conscious experience for a psychologist to describe.

Other researchers deny mind by equating it with the brain.[8] This approach is the more attractive, the less a person knows about psychology. It is a perennial favorite among computer scientists, members of the medical profession and particle physicists with philosophical aspirations. According to this view, all psychological phenomena are to be reduced to descriptions of neurons, modules, pathways, transmitter substances, axons, dendrites and synapses – in short, the material anatomy and physiology of the brain considered as a cause-effect machine. Once the brain has been completely described, all the questions of psychology will also have been answered, or so the claim goes.

This reductionist approach ignores the fact that we need multiple levels of description to understand any complex system. A description of human cognition at the level of individual brain cells would not only be impractical in its overwhelming complexity but it would also be uninteresting. To see the need for another level of description, consider questions like the following: *Why did person X succeed in solving task Z while person Y failed? Why did X take twice as long as Y to solve problem Z? Why did Y fail at time t_1 but succeed at time t_2? Why does a sample of performances on tasks of type Z exhibit such-and-such a regularity?* These are among the types of questions that cognitive psychologists want to answer. But an answer in terms of brain cells and neural processes (e.g., *because neurons N_1, N_2, N_3, ..., N_n were active in such-and-such a way*) is not explanatory. To understand why the person performed the task at hand in the way he did, we need to know what he was thinking. That is, we need an explanation in terms of his beliefs, capabilities, concepts, decisions, memories, perceptions, skills, thoughts and so on. Neuroscience is a fascinating science and it has made great progress in explaining the workings of the brain, a most worthwhile goal. No value is added to this science by the unwarranted metaphysical claim that a complete description of the brain will answer all questions about mind.

Perhaps the most persistent denial of mind locates the driving force behind our behavior outside ourselves, in the material environment. In the first half of the 20th century, adherents of behaviorism denied that any significant processes occur in people's heads and asserted that very simple processes, in combination with the structure of the environment, suffice to explain human behavior.⁹ The disposition to think that the structure of mind mirrors the structure of the environment and that the former is therefore explainable in terms of the latter appears in several forms throughout history and continues to be recycled.[10]

The fundamental mistake of the environmentalist approach is that it replaces the goal of explaining mind with the goal of explaining behavior. This move confuses means and ends. The end goal of psychology is to understand how the mind works; proposing explanations of overt and hence observable behavior is the method psychologists use to subject their theories of mind to the test of evidence. It is not an end in itself. Even if it were, reduction to the environment is not possible. The environmentalist approach is refuted by the observation that people are guided by goals as well as by the situation at hand. A goal is a mental representation of some desired, future state of affairs. Goals are cognitive constructions, not events in the world. Furthermore, a person changes his response to the environment over time, and different individuals react differently to one and the same environment. Such basic facts cannot be understood without postulating significant internal processing.

A related form of escape is to replace the description of mind with a description of the social environment or the surrounding culture. This approach has long flourished in social anthropology and related sciences, and in the last two decades of the 20th century the members of the so-called situated cognition school gave it a particularly radical formulation: We act in the context of groups of different kinds, and we carry out the actions that are considered appropriate in those groups. According to the situated cognition view, to learn is to adopt a set of related behaviors – a *practice* – that is valued in some community of practitioners.[11] So far, so good. The radical claim is that the process of passing from peripheral participation in a group to being a central member of that group can be described without reference to the novice's mind. There are no mental processes; no internal mechanisms need to be described to explain the adoption of a new practice. Once the interactions within the relevant community of practitioners have been fully described, there is nothing left to describe.

The error in the sociocultural approach is once again the failure to acknowledge that complex systems like people need to be understood at different levels of description. Consider a car. There are many questions one can ask about the relations between cars. For example, *how will the traffic flow in city X change when the new motorway opens up?* The traffic analyst's answer takes the car as the unit of analysis and describes the impact of the new highway in terms of the density of cars on a given road over time. The question is posed and answered at the level of the traffic system. On the other hand, we can also ask, as children do, *what makes a car go?* To answer this question, we need to deconstruct the car into its parts (engine, wheels, etc.) and their connections. This type of description does not answer questions about traffic flow and questions about how the engine works are not answered by a description of the traffic flow. The answers are not mutually exclusive or competing because they are answers to different questions.

Similarly, questions about how minds work and questions about how groups work are equally valid and interesting, but answers to the former question do not answer the latter or vice versa. The answers are not alternatives because they refer to different levels of description. Researchers in the sociocultural approach have contributed interesting studies of the cognitive aspects of groups and teams, and their emphasis on the fact that cognitive practices are embodied in communities is useful.[12] But the claim that we can replace descriptions of mind with descriptions of social interactions and cultural systems is absurd. How does the mind work, such that a person can create and participate in social and cultural systems?

In short, mind cannot be reduced to conscious experience, the brain, the material environment or sociocultural factors. Scholars working within those approaches have made, and continue to make, significant contributions to cognitive psychology, but they err in adorning those contributions with the unnecessary and unwarranted metaphysical claim that their research programs will answer all the questions of psychology. They escape rather than tackle the central question: How does the mind work? The answer has to be cast in terms of mental entities and processes. Nothing less will satisfy. In the words of Zenon W. Pylyshyn: "There are many reasons for maintaining that explanations of behavior must involve cognitive terms in a way that does not serve merely as a heuristic or as something we do while waiting for the neurophysiological theories to progress."[13] The name for this stance, if it needs any other name than common sense, is *mentalism*. One difference between mentalism and other approaches is that mentalism runs the risk of being comprehensible to nonpsychologists; so be it. It also suggests a particular specification of what a theory of human cognition should look like.

THE ARCHITECTURE OF COGNITION: THE BASICS

Mind is a system, but what kind of system? Scientists are familiar with ecosystems, electrical systems, mechanical systems, weather systems and many others. Different types of systems differ in what kinds of stuff they are made of, and what kinds of processes and transformations that stuff

TABLE 2.1. *Summary of background principles presupposed throughout this book.*

Key concept	Statement
Mentalism	Explanations of human behavior require a level of description that is distinct from descriptions of the behavior itself, and also from descriptions of the brain and of the environment.
Representation	Representations are structures that refer to something (other than themselves).
Functionalism	Cognition is to be analyzed in terms of processes that implement the main cognitive functions (acting, learning, perceiving remembering and thinking).
Multiple processes	Each function is implemented via a repertoire of basic processes, as opposed to a single process.
Multiple levels	Cognition has to be understood at multiple levels of description.
Projection	Interactions among the processes at system level N create the properties and processes that occur at system level $N+1$.
Central executive	Although mental processes occur in parallel, they are coordinated in the service of particular intentions or goals; the latter are pursued sequentially.

undergoes. In the case of human cognition – or the *intellect*, as it would have been called in the 19th century – the relevant stuff consists of *representations*. Cognitive *functions* like seeing, remembering, thinking and deciding are implemented by *processes* that create, utilize and revise representations. The processes are coordinated by a *control structure*. Table 2.1 summarizes the central concepts. The elaboration of these concepts provides a sketch of human cognition that is unlikely to be entirely accurate but nevertheless is the best available.

The Centrality of Representation

Few buildings in the world are as well known and recognizable as the Eiffel Tower in Paris. Visualize the Eiffel Tower; try to see it in your mind's eye! An attempt to comply with this exhortation creates a transient state of mind of a special sort, usually called a *visual image*. The image stands in a special relation to the Eiffel Tower itself: It is an image *of* the Eiffel Tower. Borrowing a term from linguistics, the image *refers* to the Eiffel Tower; it does not refer to, for example, the three-crowned City Hall in Stockholm or the Sears Tower in Chicago. The opposite is equally true: Images of the latter do not refer to the Eiffel Tower.

The exercise of visualizing something that is not present proves that mind is representational.[14] The visual image – the state of mind that endures during visualization – is a representation. The subjective experience of the image is real to the person whose experience it is and so cannot be argued away or declared nonexistent. Something that refers to some other thing is by definition a symbol or a representation of that other thing. If there were no mental representations, the exhortation to visualize the Eiffel Tower would be meaningless and impossible to follow, but it is not. When I ask a hundred students in a lecture class to close their eyes and visualize a peacock on a lawn, none of them raises his hand to ask what I mean by this. The conscious experience of visualizing, of deliberately representing something in the mind's eye, is familiar to all but a few. The latter usually say they think "in words." They do not mean by this that they do not represent, but that they think with a different type of mental representation that is closer to language than to pictures. Laboratory experiments have confirmed the ancient claim that visualized information is remembered better than information represented in silent speech, so the choice of representation has measurable consequences.[15] Representation is no mere epiphenomenon.

The ability to represent underpins many characteristics and powers of our cognitive system. Our perceptual representations – representations of the immediate present – constitute a buffer between the impact of physical stimuli on our sensory organs and our decision making. Moths fly into flames because their eyes are connected to their wings in such a way that when one eye receives less light than the other, the wing on the shadowed side flaps faster, thus causing a course adjustment that leads the moth toward the light and its own destruction.[16] If moths were conscious, they would presumably scream in agony as they inexorably flap themselves into a flame, unable to override the causal connection between their eyes and their wings. Human beings are not wired in this way; physical stimuli do not cause our actions. Instead, physical stimuli give raise to perceptual representations. Our decisions, and hence our actions, are determined by processes over those representations. The ability to represent rather than react to perceptual input provides us with a certain level of stimulus independence, a central characteristic of human cognition emphasized by such otherwise different thinkers as Donald O. Hebb and Jerome S. Bruner.[17]

Representations are equally necessary for dealing with the past and the future. Without representation, we could not have memory, because the past cannot be present – a paradox – but only represented in the present. A memory representation exists in the present, although that which is represented by it is in the past. There is no other way for the past to act in the present than through our representation of it. Similarly, a prediction is a representation of something future, something that has not yet become actual. We sometimes act in response to a prediction – if the forecast says rain, we pack an umbrella – but the future could not possibly cause our decisions or actions, because it does not yet exist and cause comes before effect. Like the past, the future can only act in the present via our representation of it.

The power of cognition is greatly increased by our ability to form abstractions. Mathematical concepts like *the square root of 2* and a *four-dimensional sphere* are not things we stumble on during a mountain hike. They do not exist except in our representations of them. The same is true of moral concepts like *justice* and *fairness*, as well as many less moral ones like *fraud* and *greed*. Without representation, we could not think with abstractions of any kind, because there is no other way for abstract entities to be available for reflection except via our representations of them.[18]

The necessity of postulating representations is even more obvious when we consider goals, desires and intentions. A goal is not a representation of something that exists; if we have it in hand already, it is no longer a goal. A goal is a representation of something that does not yet exist, so it is a subspecies of representations of the future, but with a twist: Goals represent some *desired* aspect of the future. The property of being desired is not a physical attribute. It does not inhere in an object or a state of affairs but is assigned to it by somebody, so it can exist only as part of the person's representation of that object or state of affairs.

Finally, representation enables imagination: We can fantasize about things that have only a thin connection to reality. Counterfactual reasoning has been developed to a fine art in what is known as alternate history (*if Germany had won the Battle of the North Atlantic, then …*). We can even represent to ourselves events, objects and states of affairs that we firmly believe to be impossible. Santa Claus visiting every child in a single night is one example; time travel – a staple of science fiction – is another. We do not believe that these things are possible, but we can invent stories about them and so represent them to ourselves as well as to each other. In short, our ability to mentally manipulate the present, the past, the future, the abstract and the fantastical highlight and prove the representational nature of mind.

Cognitive scientists frequently refer to the mind's representations as *knowledge representations*.[19] In doing so, they use the term "knowledge" in a different way than philosophers. The latter have had a hard time with the concept of knowledge. What does it mean for a statement to be true? What conditions guarantee truth? How can we reliably distinguish between truth and falsehood? The effort to answer such questions has kept epistemologists busy for at least two and half millennia.[20] Progress has been modest. As long as we deal only with statements about the present, as in *the cat is on the rug*, we can be tempted into believing that the truth of the statement can be specified in terms of its similarity with or correspondence to that which it represents. A statement is obviously not literally similar to a situation, so the relevant concept of correspondence is not easy to define. Once we move to general statements, this approach becomes so intractable as to no longer deserve our attention. Consider the assertion that ice ages are caused by variations in solar radiation due to cyclic astronomical events. How could this statement be similar in any sense whatsoever to the state of affairs to which it refers? But if correspondence to reality is not the hallmark of truth, then what is? Mere coherence with other truths is too weak a criterion, as is usefulness in practice. Philosophers struggle to create other theories of truth, but none has so far won general acceptance. Unworkable answers sometimes indicate a misconceived question.

Cognitive scientists ignore the epistemological questions and study knowledge as a natural phenomenon. The difference between traditional epistemology and the cognitive approach is highlighted by how they handle differences among beliefs. For example, children see many aspects of the world differently from adults. To a child, clouds might be alive and the Earth might be flat. In the philosopher's usage of the term "knowledge," these beliefs are not knowledge. In the cognitive science usage, these beliefs constitute the child's knowledge of these matters, however inaccurate those beliefs might be. This way of talking is justified by the fact that there is no way to distinguish between truth and falsity of a piece of knowledge in terms of its psychological function. A false belief is not composed of different types of concepts than a true belief, and those concepts are not related to each other in qualitatively different ways. The person who maintains an inaccurate or false belief does not know that it is inaccurate or false (otherwise he would presumably change it), so it enters into his cognitive processes in the same way as a more accurate representation. In this naturalistic approach, the task for the study of knowledge is not to seek a criterion of truth but to describe what knowledge representations are like, how they are created and how they function; that is, how they enter into the cognitive processes of the person whose knowledge they encode.[21] The laws of mind apply equally to truth and falsehood.

We cannot say with certainty when and how the ability to form mental representations arose, but the archeological and paleontological records contains one suggestive clue: There are no traces of physical representations – cave paintings, bone carvings, stone sculptures, wood models – before the appearance of our own species.[22] For example, *Homo erectus*, widely believed to be one of our ancestor species, existed for over a million years without leaving any physical representations behind. The archeological remains of the Neanderthals, our enigmatic relatives and co-existents, are similarly bereft of pictures and statues. But the archeological remains of our own species are replete with multiple forms of physical representations. Both the famous cave paintings in the Chauvet and Cosquer caves in the south of France and the oldest known carved figurines are approximately 30,000 years old. Archeological finds in southern Africa push the beginnings of representation perhaps as far back as 100,000 years ago, close to the emergence of modern humans.

It is tempting to hypothesize that the ability to represent mentally and the ability to represent overtly evolved in parallel. After all, how could someone draw a bison on a cliff face inside a pitch black, torch-lit cave unless he had the ability to visualize the bison? If internal and external representations evolved in parallel, the lack of pre-human representational artifacts might indicate that other hominid species, including the Neanderthals, did not represent, and the capability to represent thus emerges as a decisive evolutionary advance. The human species might have been born on the day when a person for the very first time deliberately created a likeness, a physical object that was not valued for what it was but for its capacity to stand for something else. Once the ability to create representations, internal and external, was established, it came under strong selective pressure to better support memory, reasoning, planning and other cognitive functions, perhaps providing *Homo sapiens* with a decisive competitive advantage over the now conspicuously extinct Neanderthals.[23]

Functions and Processes

The traditional form of scientific analysis aims to understand a natural system – the circulatory system, say, or an ecosystem – by picking it apart and figuring out how the parts are related. Because minds are not physical entities, it has always been unclear how to apply scientific analysis in psychology. How do we decide what the parts are? Once upon a time, psychologists hoped to be able to identify the parts of the mind by rolling their eyeballs 180 degrees inward and introspect, but this method turned out to be unworkable; researchers could not agree on what they saw in there. One might expect the parts of the mind to correspond, one-to-one, to parts of the brain, but this turns out not to be the case. Phrenology is no longer considered a viable theory,[24] and results from brain imaging studies show that every complex activity draws on multiple areas of the cortex, and that many areas contribute to multiple types of activities.[25, 26] Psychometric research attempted to analyze the mind into distinct abilities or factors, defined by the correlations among different kinds of psychological tests.[27] Examples include numerical, verbal and visual abilities. However, the concept of an ability has limited explanatory power, because the definition of a psychometric ability does not describe how people go about performing test items.

An approach that has enabled at least some progress is to begin with the *functions* of our cognitive system and then hypothesize specific processes that carry out those functions.[28] Common sense suggests that there are at least five major cognitive functions: perceiving, remembering, thinking (including reasoning and decision making), acting and learning, each of which is implemented by multiple cognitive mechanisms and processes. To turn this list into a theory of cognition is to be more precise about the cognitive mechanisms and processes that implement each function.

Perception creates representations of the immediate present – the *here-and-now* – and requires processes that allocate attention, identify colors, recognize objects, estimate relative distances and so on. Remembering requires that representations are encoded into long-term memory and maintained over time. For the information to be useful, there must also be a process for retrieving a representation when needed. Thinking draws new conclusions from existing information, and the relevant processes determine which conclusions can be reached. Deductive reasoning requires processes for selecting premises and applying inference rules, while analogical reasoning requires processes for selecting an analogue and for mapping that analogue onto the case at hand, and so on. Decision making requires processes for generating alternative options, for evaluating their likely utility and for choosing among them. Action – planning and execution – requires processes that expand goals into subgoals, call upon actions and apply them to the situation at hand. Learning, finally, is a meta-function; it produces changes in the other cognitive functions.

A sequence of mental processes can generate three streams of events: a succession of subjective experiences, a stream of actions and a sequence of utterances; see Figure 2.1. Any one process might be expressed in one, any two or all three streams. For example, my memory representation of the spatial layout of the university campus where I work allows me to visualize a bird's-eye view of the campus (a subjective event), to find my way to a particular building across campus (action) or to give directions to someone else

The Nature of the Enterprise

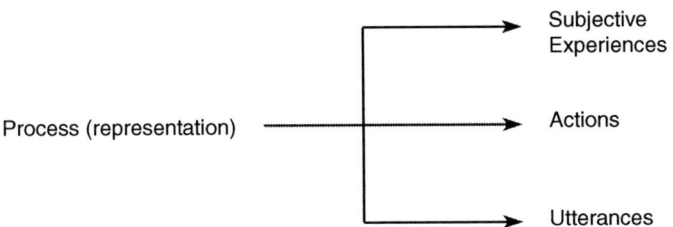

FIGURE 2.1. The application of cognitive processes to representations generates three streams of events to be explained by a general cognitive theory.

(discourse). Applied to a paper map (another representation) some of the same processes can be used to guide myself around an unfamiliar city. The main point is that the three streams of subjective experiences, actions and utterances are produced by cognitive processes that operate on the person's stock of representations.

The parts of the mind thus turn out to be dynamic entities – processes – rather than things. In this respect, the mind is more like the weather than like a clock or a kidney. This explains why mind has an ethereal quality. Every state of mind exists only long enough to transition into the next state of mind.

The Necessity of Control

At any one point in time, multiple processes are happening in a person's mind: The focus of attention moves continuously from one point in the environment to another, perceptual representations are created anew for every shift in attention, what is seen and heard serve as reminders of information stored in memory, recalled memories trigger reflections or choices among options and so on. How are these multitudinous processes coordinated? Although neuroscientists have been able to map many functions onto different areas of the brain, they have not found any Neural Self, nothing analogous to the central processing unit in a computer, no center of operations from which the workings of all other brain modules are controlled. This suggests a view of mind as a distributed system in which processes occur in parallel but independently of each other, without any overarching organization.

In addition to the subjective experience of having a self – of being a person, not an aggregate of interacting but separate processes – two related observations limit the accuracy of a purely distributed model of mind. First, processing is selective. The processes that occur at any moment in time constitute a small subset of the infinitely many processes that could have occurred at that time. The memories that are retrieved in some period of time constitute a small subset of all the memories that could have been retrieved during that period, and the inferences drawn are few compared to the many inferences the person could have drawn. A pure distributed view implies that what is selected in one area of cognition is independent of what is selected in another, because there is no center to coordinate the different selections. But when we are engaged in a task, our cognitive processes work in concert, with attention being allocated in such a way as to select the information in our environment that enables our memory processes to retrieve exactly the knowledge that our reasoning processes need to decide which action to perform next.

Furthermore, the parallelism that invites the distributional view is limited. It is true that perception, memory retrieval, reasoning and decision making are intertwined and happen in parallel, but it is equally true that I, as a person, do one thing at a time: make breakfast, get dressed, teach a class, answer e-mail, revise a book chapter and so on. Although cognitive *processes* occur in parallel, intentional *actions* are, by and large, carried out sequentially. Even when we appear to be doing two things at once, as in using a cell phone while driving, careful measurements show that such situations are better understood in terms of rapid switching back and forth between the two tasks rather than in terms of true parallelism.[29] Only when two simple, repetitive perceptual-motor tasks have been practiced over and over again can they be carried out in a truly parallel manner. Such rare exceptions aside, intentional action is sequential.

Action is also organized over long periods of time. Consider a plan for a vacation trip or for attending college. Plans of this sort coordinate hundreds or even thousands of actions, each underpinned by multiple cognitive processes, in the service of a goal – a college degree, a comfortable retirement and so on – that might be several years into the future. It strains credulity that such sustained projects happen as side effects of nothing but local interactions and distributed processes.

The conclusion is that something coordinates the various cognitive processes in the service of purposeful action. The main task of this *control structure* is to resolve conflicts. At each moment in time, there are multiple processes that could run, multiple memories that could be retrieved, multiple inferences that could be drawn, multiple goals that could be set and multiple actions that could be carried out next, so the flow of cognition requires ongoing evaluation of options and continuous choices as to which processes to execute. This is known as *conflict resolution*.

The term "control structure" is borrowed from the computational sciences. Some psychologists prefer the term "the central executive" while others prefer "executive functions" or "the global workspace"; a closely related term is "cognitive architecture."[30] This cognitive entity is a conceptual cousin to the psychoanalytic concept of the Ego.[31] Given the absence of any Ego Module in the brain, exactly how, by which processes, the mind implements a coordinating function in its distributed, center-less neural substrate is a fundamental but as yet unsolved problem of neuroscience. While awaiting the solution, we can make progress by describing the control structure in terms of how it works instead of how it is made.

The Turing-Newell Vision

The insight that an intelligent agent – be it animal, human, robot or space alien – can be modeled in a precise way by specifying its representations, its basic processes and its control structure independently of their material embodiment was first formulated explicitly by the British mathematician and World War II code breaker Alan Turing in the 1930s.[32] It is one of the foundational insights of the cognitive sciences and the basis for the design of general purpose, programmable computers like the laptop on which this book was written.

The transfer of this type of theory into psychology was the collective achievement of the founding generation of cognitive psychologists, including, among others, Donald Broadbent, Jerome Bruner, Noam Chomsky, Allan Collins, George A. Miller, Ulric Neisser, Allen Newell, Donald A. Norman, Zenon Pylyshyn, Roger C. Schank and Herbert Simon. In a pioneering 1958 paper, quoted at the beginning of this chapter, Allen Newell, J. C. Shaw and Herbert A. Simon turned Turing's insight into a radical and novel concept of psychological explanation: To explain a behavior (or a regularity therein) is to specify a *program*, that is, a control structure, a set of processes and a stock of representations, that generates this behavior (or regularity).[33] To verify that the program does indeed generate the explanatory target, implement the program, run it on a computer and observe whether the behavior or the regularity is, in fact, produced. Explanation is reenactment. This intellectual move created modern cognitive psychology as a distinct discipline.

In two papers published in 1972 and 1973, Newell developed this idea into a vision for cognitive psychology.[34] The end goal of cognitive psychology is not a long list of representation-process-control triplets, one for each phenomenon that we want to explain, but – and this is Newell's radical idea – a *single*

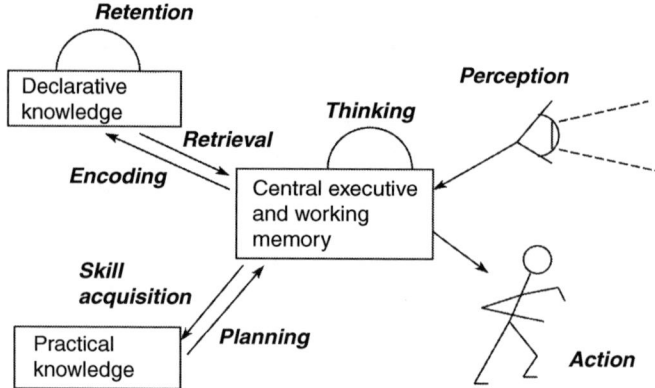

FIGURE 2.2. An overview of the cognitive architecture as currently understood.

system that explains *all* behavioral regularities and phenomena. We specify the mental representations, the repertoire of basic processes and the control structure once and for all. The only component that varies from explanation to explanation is the content of the representations; that is, exactly what knowledge we hypothesize that the person or persons brought to bear in the course of the cognitive performance to be explained. Ten years after Newell's proposal, John R. Anderson coined the label "cognitive architecture" for such a specification and the term stuck. The ACT-R theory proposed by Anderson, arguably the most influential theory in 20th-century cognitive psychology, is a sustained attempt to carry out Newell's theoretical program.[35] Figure 2.2 is a sketch of the cognitive architecture as understood by most cognitive psychologists. The trick in the cognitive architecture game is to specify exactly the right system. A specification is correct if the resulting system solves cognitive tasks in the same way (or ways) as people, and if it exhibits the same behavioral regularities and phenomena as people. Newell's vision was, and remains, the only clear, complete and coherent concept of what it means to have a unified theory of human cognition, analogous to the Final Theory of Everything that some physicists suspect might be within their reach.[36]

Representation-process-control explanations differ radically from other forms of psychological explanation such as behaviorist, dynamicist, Gestalt, Freudian, Piagetian or psychometric explanations. A comparative study of strengths and weaknesses of these different explanatory programs would require too many pages. The main reasons to prefer the Turing-Newell conception over its competitors are its clarity and the specific guidance it provides for building models of particular cognitive processes. Due to these strengths, the Turing-Newell conception dominates contemporary cognitive psychology. Information processing concepts are used up and down the pages of cognitive psychology textbooks. Few of the experiments reported in psychological research articles make sense unless we assume that there is a cognitive architecture that remains stable across tasks and content domains; after all, the tasks performed by the subjects in those experiments are seldom of any intrinsic interest.

Nevertheless, the Turing-Newell conception is unlikely to be correct.[37] It is not plausible that representations and processes are as neatly separated in the brain as they are in a computer. It seems more plausible that the medium of mind will ultimately turn out to be representations that are also processes, or processes that also represent. We do not know how to model such strange entities. Also, the assumption of a fixed, presumably innate control structure might have to yield to a more fluid notion of control that emerges through self-organization at the neural level. But such developments are in the future, so the following chapters adopt a Newell-inspired view of the cognitive architecture as a conceptual platform from which to pursue principles of cognitive change.

EXPLAINING CHANGE

If the mind is a system for processing knowledge representations in the service of action and discourse, how does it change over time? What form should an explanation for cognitive change take? What are the criteria of a satisfactory explanation and what issues arise in the construction of such explanations? It is informative to consider successful explanations for other types of change. Cognitive psychologists need not imitate other sciences or assume that their own theories must, in the end, look like those of any other science, but neither is it wise to assume that other sciences have no lessons to teach. Natural scientists, social scientists and humanists have grappled with the concept of change and their successes provide calories for psychological thought.

Componential Explanations

To extract the general features of scientific explanations of change, consider contagion and electrolysis, two seemingly different phenomena. How do contagious diseases like yellow fever spread such that we suffer epidemics?[38] It required considerable research to identify all parts of this complicated process. Although a specialist on yellow fever could add innumerable details, a mere outline suffices here: The disease is caused by a germ that multiplies in a person's body, causing the symptoms. The sick person is bitten by a mosquito, which sucks up blood that contains the germ. The mosquito flies to another person and bites again, at which point some of the germs are inserted in that person's body and begin to multiply there; and so on. This narrative makes understandable several otherwise inexplicable aspects of yellow fever, such as the timing and geographical location of epidemics and the pattern of diffusion within each epidemic.

Consider next the explanation for the electrolysis of water: Pass electricity through water and the water turns into hydrogen and oxygen gases.[39] How does this chemical transformation happen? As every chemistry student knows, water molecules consist of two hydrogen atoms and one oxygen atom connected via co-valent bonds, H_2O in the standard chemical formula. The electrical current dissolves the bonds, causing the hydrogen and oxygen atoms to drift apart. When two hydrogen atoms bump into each other, they bind, forming one molecule of hydrogen (H_2). Likewise, two oxygen atoms bind to form one molecule of oxygen (O_2). So two water molecules turn into two hydrogen molecules and one molecule of oxygen.

These two explanations differ in content but share certain structural features. Both explain by breaking down the observed change – the spread of the disease, the transition from water to gas – into a succession of changes of smaller scope or duration. I refer to the latter as *unit changes*. A unit change is brought about by a process that we are willing to accept as given for the purpose of explanation. In the medical example, the unit changes are the reproduction of germs inside the body and the abilities of mosquitoes to penetrate human skin and to fly from person to person. In the chemistry example, the unit changes are to dissolve and to form bonds between atoms. In this case, the effects of the basic processes accumulate over large numbers of molecules to produce the visible change that we call electrolysis of water. Briefly put, such *componential explanations* break down a change of large scope into a succession of changes of smaller scope, each brought about by a different process. The unit changes are components of the greater change to be explained, and they produce that change as a cumulative result of their combined and repeated action. Although the unit changes are taken as given for the purpose of explaining some particular observed change, they are not atomic in any absolute sense. Each can in turn be subject to analytic breakdown into processes of yet smaller scope or duration (*How do atoms share electrons in a co-valent bond? How does the proboscis of a mosquito penetrate human skin?*).

The second key feature of the two example explanations is that they specify the *triggering conditions* under which the unit changes occur. In the disease example, the triggering conditions include the conditions that enable mosquitoes to breed, especially the availability of freshwater ponds. Another set of triggering conditions pertains to timing: A person is not contagious until some time after being bitten, and the germs cannot live indefinitely in the mosquito before being transferred to the next victim. The triggering conditions for the dissolution and formation of atomic bonds are even more precise, turning on energy levels, the number of electrons in an atom's outer shell and the so-called ideal gas configuration. The specification of triggering conditions differentiates a disciplined, generative explanation from an ad hoc one. Without triggering conditions, the theorist has too much freedom to postulate whatever sequence of basic processes will yield the observed outcome.

Sometimes a scientific debate is more about the triggering conditions than about the processes themselves. Evolutionary biologists all agree that natural selection is the mechanism of speciation – the appearance of a new species – but they have never stopped debating the triggering conditions. A key proposal, *allopatric speciation*, says that speciation happens in small, geographically – and hence reproductively – isolated populations that are subject to different selective pressures in their different areas.[40] After having evolved in different directions, members of the two populations can no longer interbreed if the geographic barrier eventually comes down. Allopatric speciation is not an alternative to natural selection but a specification of the conditions under which natural selection might produce a new species. Other biologists also embrace natural selection as the key mechanism but argue for different triggering conditions for speciation. The small size of so-called founding populations, mutations that directly affect reproductive behavior and extreme selective pressures at the edge of the species' normal range have all been proposed as factors that contribute to the reproductive isolation that natural selection needs to be able to push two or more populations in different directions. The important lesson is that a change mechanism and its triggering condition are two distinct parts of an explanation. A hypothesized change mechanism predicts different consequences, depending on how its triggering condition is formulated, so the accuracy of an explanation can be improved by revising the triggering condition for a given change mechanism.

In short, componential explanations explain a change of large scope as the cumulative result of multiple changes of small scope, produced by basic processes controlled by particular triggering conditions.[41] I suggest that this is how we understand change generally: We break it down into a sequence of smaller changes.

What is the nature of the unit changes in the case of cognitive change? We infer that cognitive change has occurred on the basis of changes in what a person says or does. If he is asked to name the capital of New Zealand at some point in time t_1, and answers "Auckland," and if he answers that same question at some later time t_2 by saying "Wellington," we infer that sometime between t_1 and t_2 he learned that Wellington is the capital. The situation is similar with respect to skills. If a person cannot drive a car at time t_1, but turns out to be a skilled driver at time t_2, we infer that he learned how to drive a car in the meantime. Evidence for learning is essentially comparative, consisting of differences between two or more behaviors (actions, utterances) occurring some time apart. But the change in behavior is not in and of itself learning.

If behavior is generated by processes operating on knowledge representations, then a change in action or discourse must have been preceded by some change in the underlying knowledge. It is the act of revising the representation of New Zealand by replacing *the capital is Auckland* with *the capital is Wellington* that constitutes learning. The change in behavior – the different answer given to the question *what is the name of the capital?* – is an overt expression of that internal change. The distinction between a change in knowledge and its overt expression is necessary because the person might learn the correct name of the New Zealand capital but live the rest of his life without ever using that piece of knowledge; nobody ever asks him, New Zealand never comes up in conversation and so on. The situation is similar with respect to a skill such as driving a car. The change of interest is a change in the person's representation of the skill; any observable change in his driving behavior is a consequence of that internal change. The relevant unit changes are changes in knowledge, not changes in behavior.

The Repertoire of Learning Mechanisms

Sciences differ in an interesting way with respect to their repertoires of unit changes. Some fields of research attribute all their phenomena to a single type of change.[42] Adherents of the mechanical world view in the 17th and 18th centuries tried to explain all of physics through the motions of physical bodies and the forces they exert on each other. Chemists explain all chemical reactions in terms of the rearrangement of atoms through the breaking and forming of atomic bonds. Earth scientists, in contrast, draw upon a rich and varied repertoire of change mechanisms: glaciation in response to astronomical cycles, plate tectonics, erosion caused by water freezing in cracks, the actions of wind and water on soil and sand and so on.[43] Whether a science will turn out to need a sparse or a rich repertoire of change mechanisms cannot be known ahead of investigation.

Tradition has handed down a long list of suggestions about the basic processes of knowledge change. I refer to them as *learning mechanisms*. Perhaps *association*, the idea that knowledge changes by the creation of a link between two previously unconnected ideas or concepts, is the oldest learning mechanism of all. The notion of *generalization* (abstraction, induction) – the idea that the mind extracts commonalities from sets of instances – has likewise been with us since antiquity. Over time, psychologists have coined a wide variety of terms to refer to what are ostensibly different types of cognitive change: *association, automatization, belief revision, categorization, chunking, conceptual change, concept learning, conditioning, cognitive development, discrimination, equilibration, generalization, habit formation, implicit learning, maturation, memorization, perceptual learning, induction, knowledge acquisition, list learning, skill acquisition, schema extraction, stage transition, strategy change* and *theory change*.

This plethora of technical terms implicitly claims that cognitive change is a heterogeneous phenomenon and intuition provides some support. It is certainly plausible that, for example, conceptual knowledge and skills are acquired via different mechanisms. Furthermore, knowledge can change both by becoming more abstract and by becoming more specific, two processes that are each others' opposites and hence difficult to explain with a single mechanism. We should not expect a final theory of learning to pull together all of cognitive change in a single law of learning to take its place next to Isaac Newton's law of gravitation as one of the triumphs of science.[44]

On the other hand, the proliferation of terms is to some extent an artifact of the sociology of research psychologists. Several of the terms label a distinct field of research, complete with its own pioneers, laboratory techniques, phenomena, concepts, theories, controversies, authoritative reviews, heroes, villains and in some cases its own conference and scientific journal. The preference for developing one's own concept is often rooted less in empirical evidence than in dislike for the philosophical assumptions that lurk in the terminology of others, and it is sometimes easiest to do cutting-edge research by moving that edge closer to one's own work with a deft terminological invention. In the race for research grants, the appearance of doing something novel might be decisive. It is also easy to confuse topic with approach and to regard, for example, work by Gestalt psychologists on insight as a different field of research from information-processing research on heuristic search, even though they study the same phenomena.[45] Another example is the work on cognitive consistency from the 1950s and 1960s, which is all too easily dismissed as either old, mere social psychology or both, even by those who study conceptual change, a field that keeps itself too busy rediscovering what was learned back then to access the original texts.[46] To the extent that the proliferation of purported types of change is driven by such sociological forces, it overestimates the heterogeneity of cognitive change.

A second observation that warns against overestimating the heterogeneity of cognitive change is the fact that the brain is a relatively homogeneous computational medium. All parts of the brain contain neurons, and all neurons receive input signals from a large number of other neurons, integrate those in some complicated and as yet only partially understood manner and respond by sending a signal forward to another large set of neurons. Neurons in different parts of the brain vary in size, the number of connections and in other ways, but they function in fundamentally the same way. This observation suggests that there might only be a small number of types of changes at the neural level, or *modes of plasticity* in the terminology preferred by neuroscientists.

In short, it is implausible that all cognitive change can be explained by the operation of a single learning mechanism, be it analogy, association, chunking, equilibration, or restructuring. Instead, theory construction should aim for a repertoire of diverse mechanisms that jointly suffice to explain the behavioral phenomena associated with cognitive change. In this respect, a cognitive psychology of learning will be more like geology than like chemistry. On the other hand, intuition rebels against the idea that the mind employs hundreds of qualitatively distinct change mechanisms. Steering clear of the extremes, the investigations reported in this book assume that a unified theory of cognitive change will list a handful of learning mechanisms. This is an imprecise guess, but the best guess.

Triggering Conditions

To describe a change in a knowledge representation in terms of a combination of basic processes is clarifying, but for an account to be truly explanatory, it has to be augmented with a specification of the relevant triggering conditions: When, under which mental circumstances, does the mind apply or execute any one learning mechanism? For example, when does the mind create a new link between two nodes in a conceptual network? Classical accounts of association claim that links are created when the referents of the relevant nodes are either very similar, occur adjacent to each other in space or time (contiguity) or stand in a cause-effect relation to each other, but there might be other conditions as well.[47]

The question of triggering condition is relevant for every change mechanism. When, under which mental circumstances, does the mind invent a new subgoal, revise a strategy, restrict the application of a concept or schema or lower or raise the activation level of a representation? Robert M. Gagné identified the question of triggering condition as central by putting it in the title of his 1965 book *The Conditions of Learning* and it remains central.[48] Unless the relevant triggering conditions are specified with some precision, the claim that such-and-such a learning mechanism was operating on such-and-such an occasion is an ad hoc reconstruction instead of an explanatory account.

Patterns as Explanatory Targets

Sometimes the target for a cognitive explanation is a single *learning event*, a change in knowledge that a person underwent on a particular occasion. For example, we might want to explain why a student failed to learn a piece of subject matter in a given learning scenario. This type of detailed analysis of single events has precedents in other sciences: Evolutionary biologists might attempt to explain the evolution of a particular species, while economic analysts might try to explain the rise and fall of a particular company.[49]

However, the more significant explanatory targets are *patterns of change*. A pattern is not a theory or an explanation, but a description of the general character of the change a system undergoes over time. To take an example from paleontology, the temporal pattern in the fossil record is one of relatively short periods of speciation followed by much longer periods of stasis during which a species does not change, which in turn are followed by relatively short periods of decline, ending in extinction; this pattern is known as *punctuated equilibrium*.[50] In economics, another well-known pattern is the existence of *business cycles*, the regular succession of booms and busts in the market. In the Earth sciences, the pattern of advance and retreat of the world's glaciers is a major explanatory target.[51] In human cognition, the best-documented pattern of change is the learning curve: If the time to complete a practice problem is plotted as a function of how many practice problems the person has solved already, the result is a smoothly decelerating curve.

Patterns are important in part because they are more difficult to explain than individual learning events. Any single learning event can be explained if we are free to include any representation and any repertoire of basic processes among our premises. But an explanation for a pattern must show not only how the change can come about but also why it recurs. If geologists had found only a single meandering river on the entire planet, they could have attributed it to unique local conditions, but because rivers meander all over the Earth, the explanation for meandering draws upon recurring factors such as silt deposit and bank erosion.[52] Patterns are powerful clues to the mechanisms that produce them.

Patterns of change often unfold over a period of time that is significantly longer than the duration of a single unit change. A pattern is a cumulative outcome of multiple applications of the basic change mechanisms. A focus on patterns forces the theorist to consider how the effects of the basic mechanisms accumulate and how the multiple mechanisms interact in shaping action, discourse and the stream of consciousness. That is, a theory of change is necessarily concerned with *scale*, both across time and across system levels.

Theory Articulation

Abstract specifications of learning mechanisms do not by themselves explain anything. To explain is to *articulate* general principles vis-à-vis a case at hand – that is, to work out how the abstract principles apply to the event, pattern or phenomenon of interest.

Articulation typically requires chains of reasoning that rely on extensive factual knowledge. Examples from the domain of biology include the explanation for the evolution of flight, the large egg of the Kiwi bird and altruism in social insects.[53] The principle of natural selection applies in each case, but it is articulated differently. The explanation for flight proposes that wings evolved in two distinct stages. They grew as temperature regulators until they had the size required to support flight, at which point a new set of selective pressures were brought to bear. The large egg of the Kiwi bird might have come about by a shrinking of the body of a larger bird. Because the slope of the regression of egg size onto body size is lower within a bird species than between species, evolving a smaller body tends to leave the bird with a larger than average ratio of egg size to body size. Altruism in social insects can only be understood in terms of natural selection once we know that the conspecifics for which soldier ants sacrifice themselves carry many of the same genes as the soldier ants themselves. The general lesson of these examples is that explanations for particular speciation events require not merely the general principle of natural selection but also a database of facts specific to each case, and the particular way in which the general principle of natural selection is applied to each case depends on those facts.

Similarly, to explain cognitive change requires that the relevant learning mechanisms and their triggering conditions are spelled out with respect to the specific case or pattern that the explanation is supposed to explain. The articulation of a general principle vis-à-vis a particular case is typically complex and depends on multiple auxiliary assumptions and often requires considerable creativity on the part of the theorist.

Challenges for Componential Explanations

The construction of componential explanations for cognitive change encounters a variety of issues and challenges. These include the distinction between existence and prevalence, interactions, scaling and transition to practical applications.

It is important to distinguish between two types of empirical support for a hypothesized learning mechanism. A laboratory experiment might demonstrate that a particular learning mechanism *exists* – that is, that people do possess such a process and they can be induced to execute it by the right experimental manipulation. The process might nevertheless be unimportant because it is rarely triggered in everyday life and so does not explain a large number of cognitive changes occurring outside the laboratory. Existence does not guarantee *prevalence*. A laboratory experiment – an artificial situation specifically arranged to enable observation – is in principle unable to provide information about prevalence. As a result, information about prevalence is almost always missing, complicating the evaluation of hypothesized learning mechanisms.

The duration of individual learning events vary from a fraction of a second to a few seconds. To explain large patterns in cognitive change (learning curves, developmental patterns, the life-time growth of expertise, etc.), a theory has to show how such events combine to generate the observed effects at longer time scales. If there is a basic process that creates new links in memory (under some set of triggering conditions), then what kind of memory network does the repeated application of that process create over time? For example, does it produce hierarchical structures? If not, it might not be a good hypothesis about the acquisition of conceptual knowledge. If the mind composes cognitive operations that repeatedly occur in sequence into a single operation, what type of structure does that process produce in the long run? Deriving the cumulative effect over time is difficult, but proposed mechanisms must produce realistic results over days, years and decades to be plausible.[54]

Scaling over time is closely related to scaling across system levels. If a basic change process produces such-and-such an effect at the level of individual knowledge representations, what are the implications for the behavior of the cognitive architecture as a whole? For example, if an association process creates, say, 10,000 new associations over, say, 20 years of living, what is the effect on the person's cognitive functioning? If every new link is a potential retrieval path, will working memory be continuously flooded by retrieved information items of dubious relevance for the task at hand? For learning theories that postulate multiple basic change processes, scaling to the cognitive system as a whole also requires attention to how these processes interact. If there is more than one learning mechanism, observable behavior is to be explained as the composite outcome of the simultaneous operation of these multiple interacting mechanisms. For example, if a learning theory postulates separate mechanisms for generalization and specialization, what is the long-term outcome of their interaction?

The issue of scale across system levels can be pursued to the social level. Groups, teams, organizations and communities are cognitive systems, and they change over time. Do the properties of cognitive change impact change at the level of such collectives, or is the latter an independent system level, where change is decoupled, or nearly so, from the nature of change at the level of the components, the individual persons? Psychologists tend to treat cognitive psychology as one discipline and social psychology as another, but given that social systems consist of individuals, this is not productive.

Finally, we can ask how a learning theory handles the transition from a descriptive mode (What is true of learning?) to a prescriptive and applied mode (How can we support learning in real contexts?). We would expect an accurate theory to generate workable practical applications.

In short, an attempt to explain cognitive change has to address the issues of existence versus prevalence, interactions among multiple mechanisms, scaling across time, scaling over system levels and practical usefulness. These issues are intrinsic to componential explanations of any type of change.

Criteria of Adequacy

To summarize, a satisfactory explanation for cognitive change consists of at least the following components:

1. A description of the *explanatory target* itself. The latter can be a unique *learning event*, a particular change that happened for a person at some point in time and place, a *type* of change (belief revision) or a recurring *pattern* of change (the learning curve).
2. A *background theory* of the relevant aspect or aspects of the cognitive architecture. It will include a specification of the types of mental representations assumed; the repertoire of basic cognitive processes that create, manipulate and utilize these representations; and the mechanism that passes control among those processes. This background theory serves as a processing context within which the postulated change mechanisms are assumed to operate.
3. A repertoire of *learning mechanisms*. The change produced by a learning mechanism is typically small in scope compared to the explanatory target. The micro-theories proposed in this book distinguish mechanisms for *monotonic* learning from mechanisms for *non-monotonic* learning.
4. A specification of the *triggering conditions* under which each learning mechanism tends to occur.

5. An *articulation* of the mechanisms and the triggering conditions vis-à-vis the explanatory target. An explanation is a demonstration that (a) the relevant triggering conditions held in the situation in which the target change is supposed to have happened, and (b) the specified learning mechanisms, if triggered under those conditions, would in fact produce the observed change. If the explanatory target is a pattern of change, then the articulation needs to show why that type of change tends to recur.
6. An explanation is the more satisfactory if it comes with an argument to the effect that the postulated change mechanisms scale up, that is, produce observed or plausible outcomes over long periods of time and across system levels.
7. Last, but not least, an explanation is more satisfactory if it comes with a demonstration that the postulated learning mechanisms can support successful practice.

In the terminology of the philosophy of science, these seven points are *criteria of adequacy*. Their satisfaction does not guarantee the truth of a theory. They constitute a test that a purported explanation has to pass in order to be a viable candidate. Bluntly put: If a theory or hypothesis lacks these features, it is not worth considering.

THE PATH AHEAD

The research strategy behind the investigations reported in this book is to study specific types of non-monotonic change and propose micro-theories to explain them. Once the micro-theories have been clearly formulated, they can be mined for deeper principles, if any. In this approach, theory construction does not proceed in an inductive, bottom-up or top-down fashion. The choice of phenomena to be studied is guided by the prior decision to focus on non-monotonic change, itself a theoretical concept. On the other hand, theory construction does not proceed by pushing a single concept or principle into every corner and crevasse of the cognitive landscape. Instead, the principles of each micro-theory are designed to provide understanding of the case that inspires them without regard for their applicability elsewhere. The deeper theory, if any, is to emerge from the conceptual analysis of the micro-theories. In this layered approach, the degree of unification to be sought is itself an outcome of the investigation rather than something given at the outset. Figure 2.3 shows the overall structure of the enterprise.

Following this strategy, Parts II–IV investigate three cases of non-monotonic change: the *creation* of novelty, *adaptation* to an unfamiliar or changing task environment, and *conversion* from one belief system to another.

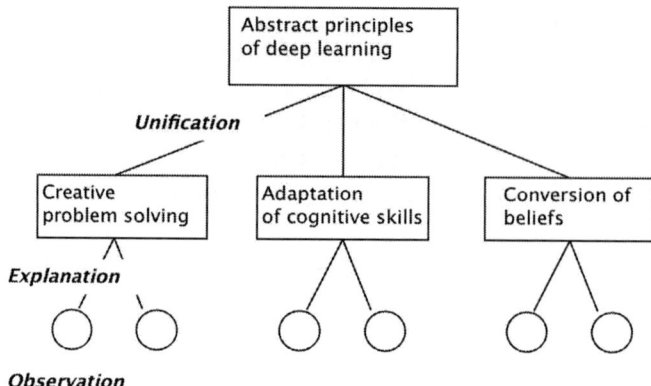

FIGURE 2.3. The layered theory approach encompasses empirical patterns, explanations of the latter derived from micro-theories and unifying abstract principles.

The factor that unites these three types of cognitive change is that they require the learner to overcome some part of his prior knowledge, the distinctive feature of non-monotonic learning. They are separated by the key phenomena, the learning scenarios and experimental paradigms in which we can observe those phenomena and the intellectual traditions within which past explanations for those phenomena have been embedded.

Parts II and III consist of three chapters each. The first chapter in each part frames the theoretical problem to be solved, anchoring it in everyday experience as well as in prior research. The latter includes any work that addresses the relevant problem, regardless of age or disciplinary label. In the second chapter, I state a micro-theory for the relevant explanatory target. In the third chapter, I develop the broader implications of the micro-theory, especially in regard to its interactions with other processes, the accumulation of changes over time and the projection of its effects across system levels. Part IV follows the same schema, except that the third chapter is absent.

In Part V I ask how the three micro-theories relate to each other and propose a unified theory of non-monotonic cognitive change in terms of a set of abstract principles that are instantiated by each of the three micro-theories. The book ends with a brief reflection on the implication of the unified theory for the human condition.

PART TWO

CREATIVITY

3

The Production of Novelty

> *Indeed, it is obvious that invention or discovery ... takes place by combining ideas.*
> Jacques Hadamard[1]

Western culture recognizes three fields of activity as particularly devoted to the exercise of originality. Artists aim to create original works, scientists seek to discover previously unknown phenomena and technologists strive to invent new devices and techniques. The three verbs *create, discover* and *invent* jointly triangulate the application of mind to the production of novelty.

Novelties are diverse in character and consequence. In 1935, when war in Europe seemed unavoidable, Arnold F. Wilkins, a junior scientific officer of the British National Physical Laboratory, was asked by his superior, superintendent Robert Watson Watt, to calculate whether radio waves could be emitted with enough force and precision to boil the blood of the pilot of an approaching enemy aircraft. Watson Watt had in turn been asked this question by a member of the Committee for the Scientific Study of Air Defence. When Wilkins's calculations showed that this death ray concept was not workable, his superior asked how radio technology could be used to defend Britain instead. In a momentous act of inspiration, Wilkins proposed that *perhaps we can detect enemy air planes at a distance by bouncing radio waves off them.*[2] Calculations showed that a detection device, unlike the death ray, could work. Five years later, when the bombers of the German Luftwaffe attacked, a string of radar stations along Britain's east coast gave the British Royal Air Force (RAF) advance warning of their approach. Without this advantage, the RAF might not have been able to fight off the Luftwaffe and Germany might have invaded Britain, in which case World War II would have unfolded differently. Seldom have so many benefited so greatly from so simple an idea.

The battle context for the invention of radar contrasts sharply with the serene elegance of mathematical physics. At the end of the 19th century, James Clerk Maxwell discovered a phenomenon – the electromagnetic field – that turned out to unify large parts of physics by showing that both light and radio signals, among other types of radiation, can be thought of as a wave that propagates through space.[3] While Maxwell mathematized the physics of radiation, some of his French contemporaries worked and lived in a rather different atmosphere. In 1860–1880, a group of French artists, including Paul Cézanne, Edgar Degas, Édouard Manet, Claude Monet, Camille Pisarro and Pierre-August Renoir, began painting in a novel way.[4] Instead of representing the details of people and objects as they are known to be, they put paint on canvas in ways that were calculated to create particular visual experiences in the viewer. This shift from a referent-oriented to a viewer-oriented conception of painting was enduring. A century later, exhibits of French impressionists invariably draw large crowds to art museums.

The invention of radar, the discovery of electromagnetic waves and the creation of the impressionist style of painting illustrate the wide spectrum of human creativity. Technologists, scientists and artists work under different conditions, with different tools and with different aims. Nevertheless, all their projects ultimately rest on novel ideas: *Perhaps we can detect airplanes at a distance by bouncing radio signals off them; electromagnetic radiation might propagate like a wave; we could paint things the way they look instead of the way we know they are.* The task for a theory of creativity is to explain how such ideas arise in the mind and become articulated into novel techniques and products in the course of creative work.

THE CREATIVITY QUESTIONS

Creativity is a complex phenomenon, so what is sometimes called the creativity question needs to be expanded into a list.[5] Theories of creativity can be evaluated by how well they answer the questions on that list.

How Is Novelty Possible?

How can anything new come into the world? If the universe is lawful, then how can anything novel ever appear? Where does it come from? Specifically, how is it possible for people to formulate novel ideas or concepts? The material world rolls along in its causal groove, and the human brain is a material system. How can it jump to a new groove? We learn concepts on the basis of experience and we cannot think without concepts any more than we can see without eyeballs or talk without words, so how can we think about an event or a situation in ways that go beyond experience? If the mind is a system for processing experience and projecting it onto future situations, then the very possibility of novel ideas requires explanation.

Formal analyses deepen this puzzle. Logicians have developed a formal calculus called *predicate logic*.[6] Some areas of human knowledge can be expressed in this system, and it possesses a certain generative power. Given a set of initial assertions – axioms – formal logic enables mechanical deduction of the consequences of those assertions. Consequences can be remote and surprising: Pythagoras's famous geometry theorem about the squares of the sides of a right-angled triangle does not automatically come to mind when one contemplates Euclid's axioms for plane geometry, even though it follows logically from those axioms.[7]

Nevertheless, the generativity of deduction is limited. A chain of logical deductions from given axioms cannot lead to new or better axioms. Deduction spins out the perhaps infinitely many implications of a given set of axioms but cannot override those axioms. Worse, a famous proof by Kurt Gödel shows that there is no set of axioms that enables the derivation of all true statements, even within a narrowly defined domain of knowledge.[8] Gödel proved this for arithmetic. No matter how a mathematician chooses his axioms about numbers, there will always be some true statements about numbers that cannot be deduced from those axioms. If the axioms are altered, some of the previously unreachable conclusions become derivable, at the cost of losing the ability to derive others. There is no set of axioms from which every true statement about numbers can be derived. Logicians believe that Gödel's principle holds for more complex domains of knowledge as well, only more so. Any axiomatic, deductive system necessarily operates within a bounded perspective that makes certain potential insights unreachable.

In *The Language of Thought*, Jerry A. Fodor argued the closely related thesis that a symbol system – a *language of thought*, in his terminology – cannot contain within it the possibility of constructing a new system that is more powerful than itself.[9] The gist of his argument is that if the meaning of a new concept can be represented in a person's mental symbol system, that is, if it can be defined in terms of concepts already known, then learning that concept does not significantly alter the expressive power of the person's symbol system. Every thought that the person can think with the help of the new concept he could have thought with the help of his prior concepts, albeit perhaps in a more clumsy and long-winded way. Every thought that one can think with the concept *uncle* one can think with the concepts *male sibling to parent*. The new concept unpacks without residue into the concepts used to define it, so it is not truly novel and there is no genuine increase in conceptual or expressive power. On the other hand, if the meaning of the new concept cannot be represented in the person's existing system, he could not represent its meaning to himself; that is, he could not learn or acquire that concept. The implication is that the system of symbols (concepts) with which a person is equipped at the outset of life defines and circumscribes the space of all thoughts that he is capable of thinking and ever will be capable of thinking.

Although Fodor's purpose in constructing his argument was different from Gödel's in constructing his, its implication is similar: A formal symbol system can, in principle, only generate a subset of all possible truths and that subset is implicitly specified in the definition of the system. There is no way to bootstrap into a more powerful system. But breaking out of initial frameworks, moving between perspectives and stepwise ratcheting up the power of cognitive representations is precisely what human beings somehow do. The bounded generativity that inheres in deductive symbol manipulation is insufficient to model human creativity.

The neuroscience framework for understanding the mind is equally unhelpful on this point. Consider the kidney, that prerequisite of good health. Day in and day out, it clears out chemical junk from a person's bloodstream. It is a physiological system that evolved to perform a specific task within the overall configuration of human physiology. It performs that task with high reliability across the life span. No physician has observed a kidney changing the way it operates. How could it? After all, the kidney is merely a physiological system specified in the person's genetic blueprint and governed by the causal laws of chemistry and physics.

Now consider the human brain. Day in and day out it carries out the task of interpreting perceptions and coordinating motor actions. It is a physiological system that evolved to support the individual's survival within the overall configuration of human physiology. It performs this task with a high degree of reliability. We would not expect it to ever change. How could it? After all, the brain is merely a physiological system specified in the person's genetic blueprint and governed by the causal laws of physics and chemistry.

The analogy between the kidney and the brain shows once again that the capability to produce novelty is in need of explanation. If every organ in the body, the brain included, goes about its business in accordance with the laws of cause and effect, life ought to be an endless repetition of the same cycle of events. But even on days when life feels that way, it is not, in fact, that way;

novelty is ubiquitous. When one is striving to understand the production of novelty, a focus on the brain as a material system is unhelpful.

In short, neither empiricism, formal logic nor neuroscience explains how and why the production of novelty is possible. If the mind is a device to process experience, how does it go beyond experience? If cognition is like a formal symbol system, how does it transcend its axioms? If the brain is a physiological machine governed by cause and effect – and what else could it be? – how does it change its operation? The first and most basic task for a theory of creativity is to specify a cognitive mechanism that is sufficient to produce novelty.[10]

What Is Creative About Creativity?

Fish do not need a concept of water. Concepts make distinctions and fish have no opportunity to distinguish water from anything else. If we need a concept of creativity, it is to contrast that which is creative with that which is not. A theory of creativity should specify the features that distinguish the two. There is a prior question: To what are we to apply the distinction between creative and noncreative? Some scholars differentiate between creative and noncreative *products* while others distinguish between creative and noncreative *individuals*. Both approaches are less useful than distinguishing between types of cognitive *processes*.

Products
It is irresistible to talk about products as more or less novel, and (therefore) as more or less creative. An invention that is similar to an already existing device is a mere improvement. Putting a wooden handle on a cast-iron pan to avoid frying the cook's hand is an example. A device that is further away in the space of possible designs is more novel and hence more creative. Replacing the frying pan with a microwave oven is a case in point. A new device has to be sufficiently far away from its starting points if it is to qualify as creative. Creativity researchers have experimented with different methods of measuring the creativity of products.[11]

There are at least two conceptual difficulties. If degree of creativity is a matter of similarity to prior products, then there is a point somewhere along the similarity scale such that if a product is closer to its origins than that point, it is not creative; if it is further away, then it is. But any such cutoff point is arbitrary. Two products close to the cutoff point but on different sides of it are similar to each other, but, according to the product-oriented view, one is creative while the other is not. This is not reasonable or helpful.

The point is not idle. Controversies about significant inventions sometimes turn on the claim that some proposed novelty is nothing but a minor improvement on prior devices, and hence – so we are supposed to infer – not creative. In 2003, the Nobel Prize in Physiology or Medicine went to two researchers, Paul C. Lauterbur at the University of Illinois at Urbana-Champaign and Sir Peter Mansfield at Nottingham University, United Kingdom, who had figured out how to make images of the inside of a human body with nuclear magnetic resonance (NMR).[12] They built upon the prior work of Raymond Damadian, a medical doctor who had built an NMR device and proposed ways of using it in medical diagnostics, but who had not taken the next step of analyzing the resonance signal into separate slices through the body, the feature that makes NMR imaging such a powerful instrument. Dr. Damadian was so incensed at not being awarded the Nobel Prize that he tried to pressure the prize committee into changing its decision – something unheard of in Nobel Prize contexts – by arguing his case in whole-page advertisements in major newspapers like the *Washington Post* under the title, "The Shameful Wrong That Must Be Righted." In his view, the steps taken by Lauterbur and Mansfield did not move the NMR technique far enough beyond his own work to be creative; in the view of the Nobel Prize committee, they did.[13] Such controversies are intractable because every cutoff point is equally arbitrary.

A second difficulty with the product-oriented view is that any product can be either creative or uncreative depending on the circumstances. A simple example is the use of a clever metaphor or turn of phrase that already exists as a common idiom in the language. The first time someone used the phrase, *to soar like a lead balloon* it was a creative joke; the *Nth* time, it was not. But it is the same utterance; the same joke; the same product. To assign it a degree of creativity, we have to know whether it was generated de novo at the time of speaking or recalled from memory. There can be no metric of creativity that applies to products per se, because the creativity of a product is a function of how it was produced.

Products do of course differ in distance to their origins. The difficulties arise only when we try to equate that distance with degree of creativity. There might be a modest correlation between the two, but occasionally noncreative thinking produces something that is very different from its origins. A pile of bricks is very different from a brick building and putting one brick on top of another is hardly an act of creation, but repeated execution will nevertheless lead from one to the other. On the other hand, sometimes it requires an act of creation to think of a minor but crucial alteration. Consider the electronic mouse. A computer with a mouse is not very different from a computer without one. The operating principle of the computer and almost all of its components are the same in both cases. Nevertheless, few would deny that the computer mouse was a creative invention. The question, *how similar is this product to its origins?* is distinct from the question, *did this product come about through an act of creation?*

Individuals
Creativity research and common sense emphasize differences between individuals with respect to creativity. Some individuals create more than others and there is a natural temptation to attribute to them a higher degree of something called "creative ability." Researchers have tried to measure this supposed ability but it is unclear what those measures are supposed to quantify: Which property of a human mind is such that if a person has more of it, he is better able to create?[14]

There are plausible candidates. The cognitive processes involved in creative thinking might operate at different levels of effectiveness in different individuals. For example, memory retrieval might be quicker in one brain than in another, giving its owner an advantage in situations that require intense use of prior knowledge. Individuals certainly differ in how much information they can keep active at any one moment of time, a quantity psychologists call *working memory capacity*.[15] One or more variables of this sort might singly or jointly constitute creative ability.

This view is plagued by difficulties. First, cognitive effectiveness, unlike a trait or ability, is not a stable attribute of an individual but is strongly influenced by training and practice. Psychological investigations have documented that experts decide faster, recall more, hold more information in working memory and so on than nonexperts.[16] This increase in cognitive efficiency due to training is domain-specific rather than general. That is, the expert's advantage holds only in his field of expertise. This contradicts the idea that creativity is an ability because abilities are, by definition, stable characteristics. Second, levels of effectiveness apply to noncreative thinking as well. Some people are better at mental arithmetic than others; some people find it easier to memorize the lines of a play than others; and so on. If stable individual differences in cognitive effectiveness – collectively referred to as *intelligence* – were the source of differences in creativity, then measures of intelligence should correlate perfectly with measures of creativity, but they do not.[17] Third, measures of cognitive effectiveness suffer from the same difficulty as measures of the distance between products: Exactly where on the scale of effectiveness is the cutoff point that separates creative from noncreative persons? Every such point is equally arbitrary. A person who is immediately below a proposed cutoff point functions similarly to someone who is immediately above it, a fact that denies the proposition that the cutoff implements a significant distinction.

These observations notwithstanding, it is a fact that some individuals create more than others and this fact cries out for explanation. But variation in the frequency of creative acts is a better explanation than the amount of creativity expanded in each such act. We do not all live equally creative lives. Some life trajectories provide more opportunities to undertake creative projects than others, and individuals differ with respect to their disposition to respond to such opportunities, the amount of time they devote to them and the passion and persistence with which they pursue them.[18] A would-be creator has to be willing to work every day on tasks that he does not know how to do, to be driven by goals that he cannot reasonably hope to achieve and to live with the realization that the products of his best efforts are likely to be declared failures at the very moment they are completed. As a consequence of differences in the willingness to suffer these burdens, some individuals attempt a larger number of creative projects than others, and this is a sufficient explanation for the differences in their accomplishments. He who hammers more often drives more nails, even though his blows are no harder than anyone else's.

To explain how opportunity and disposition intertwine in the life story of a creative person is a complicated enterprise, better executed with the tools of biographers and novelists than with those of cognitive psychologists. Much has indeed been learned from such studies.[19] The important point for present purposes is that the question of how opportunity and disposition enabled someone to produce more than his share of novelty is distinct from the question of what distinguishes creativity from its opposite.

Processes
The conceptual pains associated with the attempts to measure creative products or creative individuals are relieved if we assume that there are distinct types of cognitive processes with different properties and patterns of unfolding, generating different types of outcomes. One set of processes corresponds to what we intuitively recognize as routine, normal or *analytical* thinking, possibly brilliant and worthwhile along some dimension (rigor, systematicity, usefulness, etc.) but not creative. The contrasting set contains processes that are essential ingredients in acts of creation. The question of what is creative about creative thinking is to be answered in terms of the differences between the two types of processes.

Merely labeling the hypothesized processes *analytical* and *creative* is not in and of itself explanatory. To say that what is creative about creative thinking is that it employs creative processes is to prattle in a circle. The mechanisms must be described in some detail and their properties related to their outcomes in such a way that we understand why the processes we choose to call *analytical* generate one type of outcome and the processes we choose to call *creative* generate outcomes of another sort. Only then have we earned the right to so label them.

Empirical investigations support the notion that some problems engage different cognitive processes from problems that are generally regarded as requiring nothing but analytical thinking. One striking set of studies was conducted by Janet Metcalfe and co-workers.[20] They asked subjects to estimate how close they were to the solution for diverse problems. They found that people can accurately estimate how close they are to the solution to analytical problems but not to solutions of problems that require an act of creation. A second source of empirical evidence is provided by neuroscience studies by Mark Jung-Beeman and others that demonstrate that different parts of the brain are engaged when a person is solving analytical problems as compared to problems that require a creative response.[21]

If we locate creativity in a set of to-be-specified cognitive processes, then the attribute *creative* refers to a category, not to a quantitative dimension. The category is genealogical. Just as a fruit is a lemon if and only if it grew on a lemon tree, an idea is creative if and only if it was generated by, or with the help of, the specified processes. A product is creative if its production engaged those processes, otherwise not, irrespective of its distance or similarity to prior products and irrespective of how much cognitive strain its production required. Individuals are creative when they execute the relevant processes, noncreative otherwise. The factors that determine the probability that the relevant processes will occur and hence the frequency of acts of creation vary in strength from situation to situation, life story to life story, but there are no degrees of creativity; a person either drew on the creative processes in the course of performing a task or did not.

This view recognizes that creative acts abound in everyday life. After buying a mountain bike, I discovered that my jeans leg threatened to catch in the complicated gear mechanism. Using an office binder clip to keep the fabric on the outside side of the leg is a modest example of the many minor creative acts that people perform as they muddle through their day. In this case I used a familiar object in a novel way, a key type of creative act. The working assumption that the same mental processes are operating in creative acts both momentous and mundane obligates a theory of creativity to explain both, and not lose itself in the adoration of the history-changing works of the great creators.

What Gives Direction to an Act of Creation?

Why does a person engaged in a creative project create whatever he ends up creating? If the creative process moves beyond experience, then there is an infinitude of possible outcomes. Staring with dismay at a badly functioning device, the inventor contemplates the infinite space of possible improvements. Which factors shape his path? Having decided that his current theory is unsatisfactory, a scientist enters an infinite space of possible novel theories. Why does his research meander through the labyrinth of nature's secrets along one path rather than another? Having decided not to paint the same old painting once again, the painter enters an infinite space of possible novel paintings. What factors control the direction of his exploration?

According to a proverb, necessity is the mother of invention, but this cannot be the whole truth of the matter. Perhaps our caveman forebears invented the hearth as protection against ice age colds, but this type of explanation is limited. The brilliant architectural inventions of the medieval cathedral builders can hardly have been driven by the need of the community, because those cathedrals served no practical purpose; on the contrary, they were a drain on the community, leaving the members with less resources to attend to their needs. The originators of the French impressionist movements might have felt an inner need to paint differently, but this is a different kind of need from the caveman's wish for temperature control and it strains credulity that they needed to paint in the particular style that they invented. The history of science is dotted with examples of need-independent inquiry. Nobody needs to know exactly how the universe began, but cosmology fascinates. If necessity is the mother of invention, perceived possibility is the father. Individuals who operate at the edge of what is known discern unexplored possibilities and they pursue them because they desire to pursue them.

The principles of need and possibility only go so far. They are too general to answer specific questions about direction. There are many needs and many possibilities. Why does this or that creative project unfold along one path rather than another? A theory of creativity should explain the direction of creative processes at the level of particular projects.

Why and How Is Creativity Limited?

To be stuck on a problem that is solvable is the most common of experiences. We are confronted with some obstacle or difficulty; we struggle; we reach an impasse; eventually we think of something that works. The fact that we succeed in the end proves that the problem was solvable. But if it was solvable, why were we stuck? Why did we not find the solution right away? Limits on creativity operate in all areas of life, and they require explanation. If a person creates once, that proves that he possesses the cognitive mechanisms required to do so; what prevents those mechanisms from operating continuously?

A satisfactory theory of limitations should help explain why problems that require a creative response are not all equally difficult for one and the same person. Laboratory studies show that even problems that look very similar and have very similar solutions in terms of the complexity of the actions they require can vary drastically in how easy or difficult they are to solve.[22] What are the factors that cause the right solution to come to mind sooner or with higher probability in one case than in another?

Theories that propose mechanisms of creativity without specifying any limiting factors implicitly predict that everyone is creative all the time, and theories that specify limitations but no mechanism for overcoming them imply that nobody ever succeeds in creating anything. A satisfactory theory must address both the difficulty and the possibility of creating. It is plausible that difficulty and possibility are two aspects of the same process. The limitations are intrinsic to the cognitive processes that make it possible to create.

Four Creativity Questions

A satisfactory theory of creativity should, first, explain how the production of novelty is possible in principle by proposing cognitive processes that are sufficient to generate novelty, and, second, explain what is creative about those processes by contrasting them with the processes behind noncreative, analytical solutions to problems. Third, such a theory should explain what gives direction to the creative process. Fourth, it should explain not only how it is possible to produce novelty but also why it is difficult to do so. These four questions are criteria of adequacy against which theories of the production of novelty can be evaluated.

THEORIES OF NOVELTY PRODUCTION

The creativity questions have attracted much attention but remain unanswered, so the field of creativity research is a graveyard of unworkable answers. The purpose of the rest of this chapter is to honor the fallen with epitaphs that acknowledge their contributions. I discern in the seemingly diverse creativity literature three principled answers to the question of how novelty is possible. Each principle captures one aspect of the truth; none, the whole truth. Each has generated a family of concepts and hypotheses that has grown in clarity and explanatory power over time, and these advances need to be extracted from their original contexts and brought forward to inform the next generation of creativity theories. The rational reconstructions in this section are selective, partly chronological and partly systematic. Because it is commonplace to encounter multiple formulations of the same idea by authors who do not acknowledge each other, this approach overestimates the orderliness of intellectual history in order to facilitate critical examination.

Novelty Through Combination

One can produce something novel by combining entities in some way in which they have not been combined before. Neither the things combined nor the type of combination need to be novel for the result to be novel. The familiarity and ordinariness of this principle veil its depth and importance. The explanatory power of combinatorial processes resides in the disparity between the simplicity of their inputs and the magnitude of their outputs.[23] Five components chosen among no more than 10 potential components and related pairwise via any one of three distinct types of connections – a rather modest generative mechanism – can produce more than 1.7 billion possible combinations. In general, combinatorial processes generate vast *possibility spaces*. The size of such a space increases rapidly with increases in the number of potential components and potential connections, a phenomenon known as *the combinatorial explosion*. The phenomenon is more familiar than the unfamiliar term suggests. The 26 letters in the alphabet suffice to spell the approximately 100,000 words in the English language, as well as the many thousands of words yet to be invented. The generativity of combination is also the secret behind the infinite diversity of the material world, with atoms playing the role of parts and molecules being the combinations. Billions of possibilities might suffice to encompass even such ill-defined but vast possibility spaces as all possible paintings and all possible machines.

A combinatorial theory of creative thinking must specify, at a minimum, the cognitive elements that can enter into combinations and the process by which they are combined. The generative power that makes combination an attractive principle for explaining the production of novelty also poses a conceptual puzzle. An educated adult knows some 50,000 words, and hence approximately that many concepts.[24] He is capable of producing many billions of conceptual combinations, only a few of which would stir anyone's interest. A satisfactory theory must specify how the mind tames the combinatorial explosion by giving direction to the creative process, lest the interesting combinations be lost among the rest.

The French 19th-century mathematician and scientist Henri Poincaré proposed a combinatorial theory of creativity in mathematics, based on his own experience.[25] He suggested that conscious work on a problem activates ideas and concepts related to the problem. When the problem is set aside for lack of progress, unconscious processes form random combinations of the activated ideas. The combinations vary in their aesthetic qualities. Combinations with higher mathematical beauty pass into consciousness and become objects of deliberate reflection. Poincaré claimed near-infallibility for this process. The most beautiful combination almost always turns out to contain the solution to the problem at hand, although he did admit the occasional exception. The key feature of Poincaré's theory is that it breaks down the creative process into two structural components: an unconscious combinatorial process that generates new idea configurations and an equally unconscious evaluation process that selects those that are to be subject to conscious reflection. In computer science terminology, this is called a *generate-and-test* process, with the unconscious processing playing the role of generator while conscious reflection plays the role of evaluator. The generation and testing are related to the transition between the unconscious and conscious levels of mind, so this is a form of projection from one system level to the next; see Figure 3.1.

The structure of Poincaré's theory recurs in later proposals, albeit with different articulations of the generative and selective components. In *Psychology of Science*, Dean Keith Simonton also claimed that new ideas come to mind as chance combinations of mental elements (sensations, concepts, schemas, etc.); "… the fundamental generating mechanism in scientific creativity involves the chance permutation" of mental elements.[26] As in Poincaré's theory, a small number of the new combinations are retained, but configurations are selected on the basis of their *stability* instead of their mathematical beauty. A stable configuration functions as a single cognitive unit and therefore can enter into yet more complex configurations; Figure 3.1 illustrates this concept. Simonton

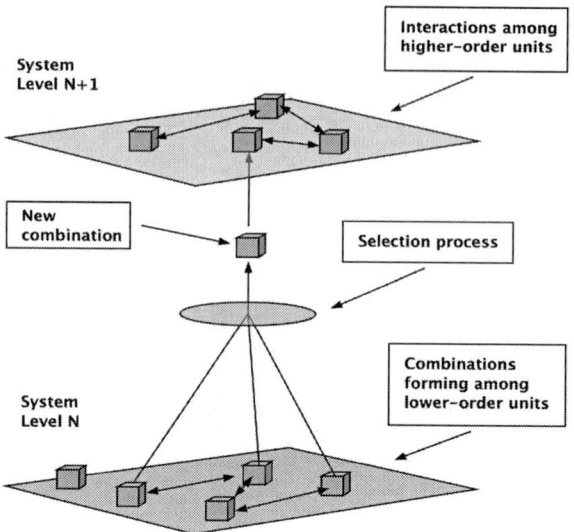

FIGURE 3.1. A combination of multiple cognitive elements at system level *N* creates a single element at level *N+1*.

also emphasized that much conscious and deliberate cognitive work might be needed to articulate a new, conscious idea for the purpose of communication to others.

The GenePlore theory proposed by Ronald A. Finke, Thomas B. Ward and Steven M. Smith emphasizes conscious and deliberate thought in both generation and evaluation.[27] It was formulated in the context of the invention of novel gadgets. The creative person begins with a set of basic forms and deliberately manipulates these, perhaps in the form of visual images.[28] The authors do not specify any constraints on the combination process, but the new forms, called *preinventive forms*, are evaluated and selected on the basis of whether they are "appealing," "interesting" or "intriguing." Useful functions are then sought for the selected forms and the end result might be a novel design.

Although these three articulations of the combination principle differ in how they conceptualize the generating and testing processes, they are not contradictory or mutually incompatible. Nothing prevents the mind from containing both unconscious and conscious generate-and-test mechanisms. A more fruitful view embeds one mechanism within the other. The subjective experience of a new idea coming unbidden to mind – unconscious generate-and-test – can be understood in terms of self-organization at the subsymbolic, neural level. Once an idea has come to mind, it can participate in further,

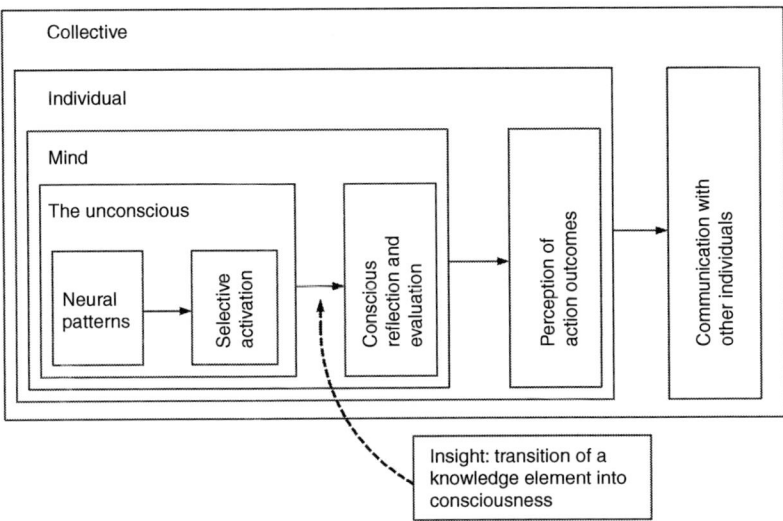

FIGURE 3.2. The four envelopes of selection in generate-and-test. Each envelope contains a generator and an evaluator, which together constitute the generator for the next envelope.

conscious processes of combination and selection. Such a nested generate-and-test mechanism is more powerful than a single-level mechanism; see Figure 3.2. At each level, the combination process works with elements that have already been subject to selection at the lower levels. Evaluation is carried out by successively more encompassing *envelopes of selectivity*: In the first envelope, unconscious ideas pass into consciousness as a function of hard-to-describe mental filters like beauty, stability, interestingness and so on; in the second envelope, new conceptual combinations are evaluated via conscious reflection; and in the third envelope, a new thought is articulated into a discourse, prototype, sketch or other type of product that is subject to evaluation by the judgments of peers or teammates and, when relevant, by its material consequences.

The articulations of the combination principle proposed by Poincaré, by Simonton, and by Finke, Smith and Ward share some similarities, but they also differ from one another in some respects; see Table 3.1 for a comparison. This type of theory answers two of the four creativity questions: Novelty is possible because cognitive elements can be combined in for all practical purposes infinitely many different ways. Creative thinking differs from noncreative thinking in that the former results in novel cognitive combinations while the latter works with previously produced combinations.

TABLE 3.1. *Overview of three creativity theories that emphasize the principle of combination.*

Theoretician/year	Types of elements	Type of combination process	Type of output	Constraints on generation	Source of evaluation
H. Poincaré 1908	Prior ideas	Blind, unconscious combination	New ideas	Relevance to task; goal directedness	Affinity with aesthetic sensibilities
D. K. Simonton 1988	Mental elements: sensations, cognitions, emotions	Blind, unconscious combination	New configurations	None on blind generation; some configurations are based on experience, some on conventions	Stability of the configuration; information-processing efficiency
R. A. Finke, T. B. Ward and S. M. Smith 1992	Geometric, 3D forms	Deliberate, conscious combination	Preinventive forms	Aims for forms that are interesting or intriguing	Can the new form be interpreted as a novel device?

The ways in which these theories provide direction by taming the combinatorial explosion leave something to be desired. The first issue is how the mind selects the set of concepts, ideas or mental elements that should be considered as potential ingredients in a new combination. Poincaré's appeal to the preparatory phase of deliberate problem analysis as a source of constraints on the unconscious generator is more problematic than helpful: The claim that conscious work on a problem tends to activate a set of relevant concepts is plausible, but it poses the puzzle of how we ever come to apply a concept that we did not anticipate to be useful for the problem at hand. This hypothesis does not help explain how the unconscious idea generator can produce a combination that goes against the expectations created by prior experience.

The alternative is to place no restrictions on the cognitive elements that can participate in new combinations, but this aggravates the problem of direction. How, given some set of initial elements, are new combinations generated? Terms like "blindly," "randomly" and "by chance" claim that the combination process proceeds without direction. This hypothesis is tempting because it frees the combination process from prior experience and hence promises to help explain how people go beyond experience. It also frees the mind – and hence the theorist – from having to solve the unsolvable problem of how to compute exactly which idea combination will turn out to be the solution to any one problem. But without any restriction on the set of components, a random combination process provides no protection against the combinatorial explosion.

The particular evaluation processes proposed by these combinatorial theories are even more problematic. Poincaré's idea of selection by beauty is difficult to generalize to other areas than mathematics. The invention of the computer certainly ranks as a creative project, but it is difficult to see beauty in those early roomfuls of vacuum tubes and crisscrossing wires. A deeper problem is how, by what process, the unconscious measures mathematical beauty. The sophistication of this process makes its attribution to the unconscious implausible. There are no reasons to believe that there exists an evaluation function that unerringly selects the right constellation of ideas for any problem, and none to believe that evolution has endowed our brains with the capacity to compute such a function. Similar concerns apply to evaluation based on stability and interestingness. Perfect evaluation filters contradict the fact that human beings are fallible; sometimes the evaluation process picks a promising new combination that turns out not to be the solution. A closely related weakness is that generate-and-test mechanisms do not explain how the direction of a creative project is impacted when an idea that is not in fact useful nevertheless slips through the successive envelopes of selection and leads to failure.

The question of limitations is also unanswered. If the mind can generate novel combinations indefinitely, there is no reason why a problem that requires a creative response should be hard. All it takes is to keep generating new combinations until one is found that passes the relevant test. The only limitation on creativity according to generate-and-test theories is the time it takes to find the desired new idea. Along the way, the mind is frantically busy generating and testing endless combinations, or so this type of theory implies. There is no explanation for the experience of being at an impasse; that is, of being stuck, of having exhausted all possibilities and not knowing what to do next.

In short, the principle of combination of cognitive elements cannot answer the creativity questions as long as it is embedded in a generate-and-test mechanism with a random generator, so the three combination theories are unsatisfactory. However, the combination principle itself is powerful, and the notion of nested envelopes of evaluation resonates with the concept of multiple system levels. Both play central roles in Chapter 4.

Novelty Through Accumulation

Novelty can arise through the accumulation of work. When a familiar step is executed as part of a sequence of steps, it might interact with other steps in such a way that the final outcome is novel. Chess provides an example. The individual moves in a chess game are guaranteed to be familiar, because the legal moves are specified by the rules of the game. Nevertheless, every chess match unfolds differently from any match played before it, and the particular sequence of moves played in a particular match might be called creative by chess experts. Similarly, a mathematical theorem can be novel even though every step in its proof consists of a familiar algebraic transformation. Each step along the solution path contributes some small amount to the gradually widening gap between the product under construction and prior products of the same type. Cognitive psychologist Robert W. Weisberg puts this position as follows:

> On the whole, it seems reasonable to conclude that people create solutions to new problems by starting with what they know and later modify it to meet the specific problem at hand. At every step of the way, the process involves a small movement away from what is known, and even these small tentative movements into the unknown are firmly anchored in past experience.[29]

The accumulation-of-work principle has the advantage of concurring with two of the most salient facts about the production of novelty: Creative individuals tend to work hard and invest enormous effort into their projects. Furthermore, it is a matter of historical record that many famous novelties in the areas of art, science and technology emerged out of processes that lasted orders of magnitude longer than the time it takes to have a new idea. (The duration of creative processes is discussed in Chapter 5.)

An accumulation theory of creativity has to specify the repertoire of steps that are available to the creative agent, the mechanism for choosing each successive step and the principle by which the outcomes of the steps accumulate. These components can be articulated in different ways, not all equally viable. Unlike generate-and-test theories, accumulation theories emphasize that creative solutions consist of long sequences of coordinated actions. The questions of what is creative about creative thinking, about direction and about limitations acquire somewhat different flavors when applied to the individual steps.

Accumulation Through Variation-Selection?

When an idea initially assessed as promising turns out to be a dead end, there are only two responses: Give up or try again. The possibility of failure coupled with the willingness to persist implies that a creative process necessarily exhibits a *cyclic structure*: generate; evaluate; repeat as needed. The ability to execute the generate-and-test cycle repeatedly relieves the process from the need to be infallible, or even nearly so. But running it again is of no use if it produces the same output as before. The point of trying again is to try something different, to vary the approach.

Inspiration for a theory based on cyclic processes, variations and stepwise accumulation was provided by Poincaré's contemporary, Charles Darwin. According to his *natural selection* theory of how novelty emerges in the living world, genetic processes produce offspring that vary in minor ways from their parents and the environment acts as a selective filter, allowing some variations to reproduce more often than others, which alters the relative frequencies of the relevant genes by some amount from one generation to the next.[30] It takes many generations – that is, many cycles of genetic variation followed by environmental selection – to accumulate enough genetic change to bring forth a novel adaptation.

The temptation to draw an analogy between biological and mental evolution is strong, in part because natural selection has the advantage of being a proven mechanism for the production of novelty.[31] In an influential review published in 1960, social scientist Donald T. Campbell documented applications of the variation-selection principle to different aspects of psychology, including perception, decision making and problem solving.[32] After the appearance of his review, the application of Darwin's theory of variation and selection to cognitive phenomena became an academic growth industry.[33] By the end of the 20th century, the trickle of such applications had grown into a flood that cannot be contained in a review.

The various articulations of the variation-selection principle exhibit less fidelity to their source of inspiration than their advocates would have us believe. One would expect a variation-selection theory of human creativity to specify cognitive analogues to differential reproduction rates, environmental selection among phenotypes, genes, genetic variation, ontogenesis, organisms, populations and species. As evolutionary biologists tirelessly point out, although the organism is the unit of selection, the species (or the population) is what evolves, so a Darwinian variation-selection theory must recognize at least three system levels: gene, organism and species (or population). A key component of the Darwinian mechanism is reproduction, the multiplication of those organisms whose genes give them the advantage in the struggle for survival.

The various applications of the variation-selection idea to cognitive processes do not fit this theoretical schema with any precision: What are the cognitive analogues to the three system levels? What is the population that evolves in creative thinking? What are the cognitive counterparts to ontogenesis and reproduction? Critical analyses by David N. Perkins and others show that variation-selection theories of cognition are not Darwinian in any precise sense, and so cannot draw strength from the proven ability of biological evolution to produce novelty.[34]

Two key issues in formulating a variation-selection theory of cognition are how the variations are generated and how the successive variation-selection cycles are related. With respect to the first issue, Campbell argued that random generation is sufficient. As in generate-and-test theories, the notion of a random generator frees the mind, and hence the theorist, from the need for an informed generator.

Anticipating resistance, Campell launched an energetic defense of random generation as an explanation for creative achievements. First, the density of useful novelties in a typical possibility space is indeed low, but we tend to overestimate the success rate of attempts to create. If we take into account the number of failures in creative fields like art, science and technology, the ratio of success to failure will turn out to be consistent with a random search through the space of possibilities, he claimed. But as long as no calculation or estimate of this ratio is presented, this pseudo-quantitative argument remains a promissory note. It also fails to explain why some individuals, studios, research and development teams and laboratories consistently create more than others. On the assumption of random generation, one would expect the hit rate to be uniform across creative agents within a field of activity.

Campbell's second argument is that creative thought is serendipitous. Creative people often search without any specific goal in mind, he claimed, and there are a good many things to create, so although the probability is low of finding the particular thing that the person intended to find, the probability of hitting upon something of interest might be much higher. This is yet another quantitative claim unsupported by any calculations. Autobiographical accounts in which artists claim that they occasionally engage their medium without a clear goal or purpose suggest that there is a grain of truth in this.[35] But the stronger theme in creative work is the deliberate pursuit of goals. Darwin's decades-long struggle to understand the organization of the living world was no meandering through the conceptual landscape on the chance that some interesting ideational specimen might turn up.[36] The Wright Brothers did not tinker without forethought, and neither Mozart, Beethoven nor Ravel stumbled on this or that composition by combining notes without purpose.[37,38] To the extent that creative processes are goal-directed, the generative process cannot be random, because such a process, by definition, is unbiased and so cannot be guided by a goal.

The application of the variation-selection schema to creativity is rediscovered and reformulated time and time again because it is easily observed and it is intuitively compelling. But variation-selection, as applied to creativity, is not an explanatory principle but a logical necessity. If a solution does not work, the problem solver only has two choices: Generate another solution – that is, vary the approach – or give up. The variation-selection pattern is a logical consequence of fallibility, and it is necessarily the mode of operation of any agent who persists in the face of failure. The variation-selection schema, extracted from its biological content, is neither explanatory nor in need of explanation. What needs to be explained is how, by which processes, new variations are generated and selected in the search for a creative outcome or product.

Accumulation Through Heuristic Search

A creative person at work on a complex problem does not typically try this or that approach haphazardly. The successive variations have sensible relations to each other and constitute a development rather than a random series. As a biological analogy, ontogeny would be closer to the mark than natural selection. There is a logic to the unfolding, an internal organization that provides direction. What is generated in cycle $N+1$ depends on what was generated and evaluated in cycles 1 through N.

Theorizing about this dependency began with the work of Edward L. Thorndike, another of Poincaré's contemporaries. His advisor was William James, co-founder of the pragmatist school of philosophy. The collaboration between one of the last scions of the philosophical era in psychology and one of the founders of the experimentalist tradition produced one of the most influential doctoral dissertations in psychology.[39]

Thorndike studied how cats, dogs and chickens solved problems, with the purpose of laying a foundation for understanding the higher cognitive functions in people. His method was to shut the animals into problem boxes. The boxes were not comfortable or inviting and the animals were typically observed when they were hungry, so they tried to escape. This required some action the animal was physically able to perform – pull a string, press a bar, and so on – but which was unfamiliar. Thorndike observed that the animals went through their repertoire of actions until they happened to hit upon the one that opened the box. Over multiple trials, the animals came to execute the correct action sooner and with more precision, until they performed it effectively and immediately upon being shut in the box. Although the term *trial and error* had already been used by others and occurs only once in Thorndike's dissertation, his study has become the iconic illustration of this concept.[40, 41]

Thorndike's work was an important stimulus for psychological research on learning; the behaviorist school was the response. Although the behaviorists' theoretical concepts proved insufficient to explain human cognition, their focus on observable behavior provided a useful corrective to prior theorizing. Poincaré and other theorists assumed that the relevant cognitive unit for explaining creativity is an *idea*. This view is plausible in mathematics. Elsewhere, the production of novelty is often better thought of as a matter of *action*; the issue is what to do about a problem or how to proceed in an unfamiliar situation. The novelty produced by Thorndike's animal subjects was not a concept but a behavior, the action that got them out of the box. Trial and error is generate-and-test applied to action instead of ideas.

Thorndike's main contribution was to formulate an enduring principle about the links between successive actions. He claimed, and later formalized in his Law of Effect, that the choice of action is molded by what he called *aftereffects*. If an action is followed by a *satisfier* – a reward – the animal's inclination to perform the action grows stronger. If an action is followed by an *annoyer* – punishment – the inclination diminishes. By blocking the action that caused them, annoyers provide an opportunity for other actions to be tried, as long as the individual persists in his efforts. A sequence of actions is a sequence of generate-and-test cycles, but with the twist that the generation is not random because the failure of one action informs the selection of future actions.

Thorndike's interest in aftereffects, or *reinforcement* in the behaviorist terminology foreshadowed a major intellectual development at mid-century. During World War II, psychologists and technologists worked shoulder to shoulder on many difficult and unfamiliar problems, including how to aim (or train someone to aim) an anti-aircraft gun.[42] If the gunner aims at a moving target but misses, how should he correct his aim? Interdisciplinary work on this and other problems was the origin of *cybernetics*, the science of control systems – the human mind among them – that was launched by the mathematician Norbert Wiener and his associates in the 1940s.[43] Although the cybernetic approach faded with the postwar spread of digital computers, it left behind a three-part legacy. First, the cybernetic term *feedback* was generally adopted to describe information about the outcome of an action that can be used by the acting agent – man or machine – to guide future behavior. Second, in the transition from "reinforcement" to "feedback," the modifiers "positive" and "negative" lost their motivational flavor. Machines know naught of pleasure or pain, so feedback is neither reward nor punishment but merely information. Technically, feedback is positive when it implies that the agent should repeat the action that caused it, negative when it implies that the action should cease.

The third advance was a shift to a more fine-grained analysis. Wiener's feedback systems continuously compared the effects of their actions with their intended effects. An attempt to perform a task – a single trial in the trial-and-error schema – might require multiple elementary actions, each of which can generate feedback. This shift played a central role in *Plans and the Structure of Behavior*, the 1960 attempt by G. A. Miller, E. Galanter and K. H. Pribram to specify what we now would call a cognitive architecture by replacing reflex arcs with feedback circles.[44] A similar project was undertaken by W. T. Powers in *Behavior: The Control of Perception*.[45] When cybernetics faded, so did these theories, but the concept of feedback, the use of outcome information to guide future action, remains as Norbert Wiener's permanent contribution to the cognitive sciences.

Both behaviorism and cybernetics focused on overt behavior. Navigating a maze, tracking a moving target like an airplane and hammering a nail were prototypical examples of the kinds of behaviors these theories attempted to explain, unpromising starting points for the study of creative thinking. In the 1960s, Nobel Prize–winning economist H. A. Simon and computer scientist A. Newell put thinking and problem solving front and center by moving the idea of a succession of choices between alternative actions, guided by action

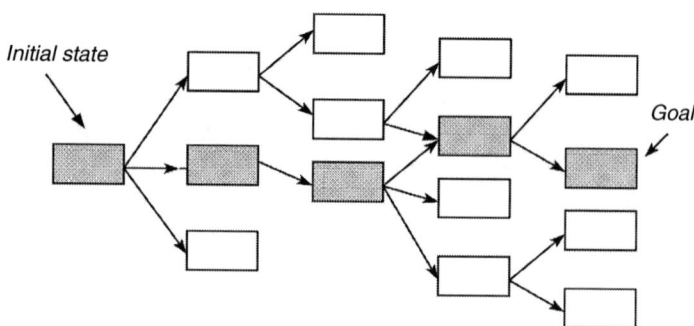

FIGURE 3.3. Heuristic search solves a problem by finding a path through the space of possible actions that leads from the initial state to the goal state.

outcomes, inside the head. In their theory, presented in their monumental 1972 volume on *Human Problem Solving*, a problem solver's mental representation of a problem has three main components: First, the *initial problem state* is, approximately, the perception of the situation at hand. Second, there is a set of *operators* which in their effects on the problem representation mimic the effects of physical actions on the material problem situation. The operators enable the problem solver to simulate in the mind's eye the effects of actions. Third, there is the *goal*, the problem solver's concept of what it means to solve the problem. The set of possibilities defined by the initial state, the operators and the goal defines the *problem space*, the space of possible solutions that the person is considering.[46]

To solve a problem is to identify a *path* through the problem space that leads from the initial problem state to the goal state. This can be done by applying an operator, evaluate the outcome, apply another operator and so on; this process is called *search*. It can be visualized as in Figure 3.3.

The key difficulty is that search, like generate-and-test, is subject to combinatorial explosion. Even when the number of relevant operators is modest, the number of possible paths is astronomical. For most problems, a problem solver can only explore a small proportion of the possible paths before running out of cognitive capacity, time or some other resource.

How, then, do problem solvers succeed? Newell and Simon's answer is based on three central concepts: heuristics, look-ahead and evaluation functions. Even if a problem is unfamiliar and requires a creative response, it is unlikely to be completely and utterly unfamiliar. (If it is, we are unlikely to make much progress: How would we begin to build a time travel machine?) We can always bring some prior knowledge to bear on the ever-branching alternatives and reduce their number to a smaller set of promising options. Sources of selectivity – which Newell and Simon called *heuristics* – can be derived from the goal (*how does the current situation deviate from the desired one?*), task instructions, background knowledge and other sources. In general, a heuristic is a piece of knowledge that can be used to select among the options in a problem state. A collection of heuristics forms a *strategy* for how to navigate the problem space.

Problem-solving steps are not only tentative but also *anticipatory*. Problem solving alternates between the problem space in the head and the physical task environment. To decide what to do next, the problem solver tries this or that action tentatively in the mind's eye (*what would happen if I did this?*). By anticipating outcomes, the person can think through and evaluate a course of action before executing it. Such *look-ahead* has multiple advantages. Searching in the head is faster and cheaper (and sometimes less dangerous) than searching in the flesh.

The evaluation of an action outcome – real or anticipated – can be thought of as mapping an anticipated problem state onto a value on some quantitative dimension, hence the term *evaluation function*. For example, chess players evaluate chess positions in terms of what they call "material." Each chess piece is ranked with respect to usefulness for winning the game, and a board position can be evaluated with respect to which player has the stronger set of pieces left. If one move leads to a stronger position than its alternatives, perhaps it should be preferred. As the example illustrates, evaluation functions tend to be task specific. They can be derived from goals, task instructions and background knowledge. Like strategies, evaluation functions provide selectivity and hence help tame the combinatorial explosion; indeed, in Newell and Simon's works, the term "heuristic" refers both to tactics for choosing among options and to evaluation functions.

The selectivity provided by heuristics – in both senses – is a matter of degree. If a problem is truly unfamiliar, the problem solver will, by definition, not possess any applicable heuristics, so the search will be random and unselective, or nearly so (e.g., find the jar of tea bags in someone else's kitchen). If the problem is well known, the person already possesses an applicable strategy and the search process collapses into a confident walk down the correct path, as if produced by an infallible generator (e.g., multiply two 4-digit numbers). For unfamiliar but solvable problems the process will fall somewhere between these two extremes.

The heuristic search theory is a powerful theory of analytical thinking. It explains the nature of the mental effort that goes into solving problems. It explains why problem solving is possible even though success is not guaranteed.

Most important, it specifies with precision the interaction between a general cognitive mechanism (the choose-act-evaluate structure of the search process) and task-specific knowledge (strategies and evaluation functions). The function of the latter is to tame the combinatorial explosion and provide selectivity, either by reducing the number of options or by enabling evaluation of outcomes. Nevertheless, the heuristic search theory, as applied to creativity, shares weaknesses with other articulations of the accumulation principle.

Evaluation of Accumulation Theories

Accumulation theories in general and the heuristic search theory in particular explain how novelty is possible by showing how it can arise out of a succession of steps: If elementary actions are executed in a novel sequence, their ultimate result might be novel. The crucial advances over generate-and-test is that evaluation happens continuously, to each individual step along the way, so each generate-and-test cycle is informed by, and builds on, the results of prior cycles; see Table 3.2 for a comparison of the essential features of some prominent accumulation and variation-selection theories.

But accumulation theories cannot explain what is creative about creative thinking. If every thought process is a search through some problem space, then

TABLE 3.2. *Four theories of creativity based on variation and selection.*

Theoretician/year	Unit of variation and selection	Source of variability	Basis for selection
E. Thorndike 1898	Physical actions	Unspecified; iteration through the behavioral repertoire (?)	Aftereffects; satisfiers and annoyers
D. T. Campbell 1960	Any cognitive process; memory, perception, thinking, deciding, etc.	Random choice	Performance outcomes
A. Newell and H. A. Simon 1972	Steps during problem solving, mental or physical	Search heuristics; task-specific knowledge	Evaluation functions
W. G. Vincent 1993	Design features	Wish to improve; results of experiments	Flying characteristics

novel products or solutions can emerge only because someone searches longer or deeper than anybody else. This is indeed how some famous chess-playing computer programs win over their human opponents.[47] They search the space of possible moves and countermoves to a greater depth than human beings can do. In this view, there is no distinction between analytical and creative processes. For example, Simon and Craig A. Kaplan claimed that creative problem solving is heuristic search as usual; a creative solution is distinctive merely in that it depends on the use of particular heuristics.[48] For example, noticing invariants might be particularly important in solving a puzzle known as the Mutilated Checker Board Problem.[49] This is clearly too specific a hypothesis to apply to a wide range of creative projects – which invariants had to be noticed to invent radar? – and hence fails to provide a principled explanation of what is creative about creativity.[50]

The notion of heuristics appears to provide a strong answer to the question of direction. Empirical studies of creative problem solving both inside and outside the laboratory have verified that the problem-solving heuristics used by both novice and expert problem solvers can be specified with some precision.[51] However, because heuristics are task specific, they must have been learned through prior experience. Their application in guiding search in an unfamiliar problem space is thus a case of projecting past experience onto a new situation. But the central task for a theory of creativity is to explain how creative thinkers go beyond experience.

The principle of accumulation also fails to explain why the production of novelty is limited and difficult. If search were the whole story, there would be no reason to ever experience an impasse: search, back up, search some more, and so on, until the solution is complete. Indeed, if all it takes to be creative is to plug along until enough advances have accumulated, then why can we not be consistently creative? Why do so many garage tinkerers fail to invent anything useful? Why do so many scientists retire without ever having published a consequential paper, and why do so many painters who paint all their lives produce nothing but mediocre works? If all it takes to produce a masterpiece is to keep working, then the production of masterpieces would be routine, unremarkable and a function of nothing but amount of effort, contrary to all experience.

In short, the accumulation idea explains why novelty is possible but provides no insight into what is creative about creativity, the direction of creative projects or the limits on creativity. So-called variation-selection theories of creativity make no substantive claims but merely rehearse the logical point that failure must be followed by a renewed attempt. Heuristic search is a powerful theory of analytical thinking but cannot explain creativity. The central weakness is that Newell and Simon never proposed a theory of the origin of problem spaces.⁵² Cycles of selection, look-ahead and evaluation occur in the context of a well-defined search space. How does the problem solver construct that space? Even more important, how does the problem solver move from one problem space to another? This question was considered in a third tradition with a very different focus.

Novelty Through Restructuring

Novelty is possible because an object, event or situation does not uniquely determine its own representation. Every representation is an interpretation, and there are always alternative interpretations. Moving sideways from one representation to another might activate dormant but useful knowledge, suggest unheeded action possibilities or reveal previously unsuspected connections. Representational change theories have to specify the kind of representation that is changing, the nature of the change process and the relevant triggering conditions.

In the final years of the 19th century, the German psychologist Max Wertheimer – yet another contemporary of Poincaré – and two of his students, Wolfgang Köhler and Kurt Koffka, formulated a representational change theory based on the observation that a person's perception of a situation is not a collage of perceptual features but can be said to have a *Gestalt*.⁵³ The difficulty of translating the German word "Gestalt" – neither "structure" nor "configuration" is entirely satisfactory – has been avoided by each generation of English-speaking psychologists by assimilating the word itself into English. To a first approximation, the Gestalt of a situation is the totality of the relations between its parts. A Gestalt is neither entirely subjective nor entirely objective, but resides in the *perceptual field*, a phenomenological construct that is best understood as the interface between the mind and the world. The organization that a Gestalt imposes on perception is subject to laws of organization that belong to the perceptual field itself. The latter include completeness, proximity, symmetry, good continuation and several others that can be found in most psychology textbooks.⁵⁴ Their insistence that any object, event or situation must be understood as an integrated whole earned Wertheimer and his colleagues the label *Gestalt psychologists*.

The holistic nature of Gestalts is illustrated by the well-known reversible figures that often appear in psychology textbooks.⁵⁵ The Necker Cube is an example; see Figure 3.4. If a person looks intently at this picture, his perception flips back and forth between seeing the cube in one or another spatial orientation. Such reversals are neither entirely objective nor entirely subjective. The material picture remains unchanged but the possibility of reversal depends on its properties. Not every picture flips, but those that

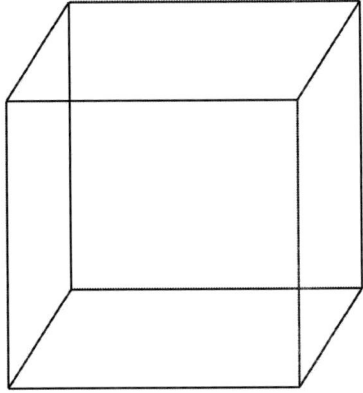

FIGURE 3.4. The Necker Cube. Sustained attention causes the cube to flip between two possible spatial orientations.

do alternate between the same two possibilities for every viewer. In a reversal, every part acquires a new meaning within the figure. A reversal is also non-monotonic: It is not possible to see the two spatial orientations of the cube simultaneously. We see the figure one way or the other, and when it flips, the previous view temporarily disappears from consciousness. We can only access it by waiting until the figure flips back. The reversal happens in a subjective instant and we have no introspective access to the mechanism. The Gestalt psychologists called this process *Umstrukturierung*, a word that has been rendered into English as both *restructuring* and *reorganization* by different translators.

A central but peculiar aspect of the Gestalters' theory is that some Gestalts are *better* – better balanced, more harmonious, more stable – than others. The introduction of a value judgment into a supposedly descriptive theory of how the mind works was natural within the 19th-century German philosophical tradition in which Wertheimer, Köhler and Koffka were trained but runs counter to the naturalistic stance of contemporary cognitive psychology. This aspect of their theory cannot be purged because the striving for a better Gestalt gives the restructuring process its direction. Reversible figures move back and forth between equally good Gestalts but they are atypical. In the normal case, the mind moves up the goodness gradient, from worse to better Gestalts.

The Gestalters developed these concepts in the course of their studies of perception but then turned around and cast them as a theory of thinking. A problem is a problem because its Gestalt is incomplete or imbalanced; it suffers from gaps and tensions; the problem solver has not parsed the situation into the most fruitful structure of part-whole relations. To solve the problem is to let its structure collapse into a different and better Gestalt which is complete and balanced, or at least more so. In the words of Wertheimer, the tradition's senior member:

> Before the thought process takes place, or in its early stages, one often has a certain whole-view of the situation, and of its parts, which is somehow unsuited to the problem, superficial, or one-sided.... On the other hand, when the change [i.e., the restructuring, S.O.] has occurred, and the problem has thereby been solved, one is sometimes astonished to see how blind one has been ... what matters here, and what is characteristic of intelligent processes, is the transition from a less adequate, a less proper structural view to a more sensible one.[56]

The new representation is typically accompanied by a feeling of *insight*, the standard translation into English of the German word *Einsicht*; the latter could equally well be rendered as *comprehension* or *understanding*. Subjectively, the problem solver perceives the problem situation differently. Difficulties are not so much resolved as dissolved or left behind: Köhler wrote, "How must we change the situation so that the difficulties disappear and our problem is solved?"[57] Behaviorally, the problem solver might express a certain surprise and rouse himself from a state of frustrated inactivity to resume work on the problem. A moment of insight – sometimes called an *Aha*-experience – can be accompanied by a feeling that the new view was, or should have been, self-evident all along. Restructuring is something that happens to a person rather than something he chooses to do. We cannot will ourselves to see a problem differently, but the probability of restructuring is a function of multiple triggering factors, some of which can be influenced by voluntary action. For example, the Gestalters insisted that it helps to analyze the given situation and the goal carefully. The better one's grasp of the structure and requirements of the problem, the more salient the gaps, and the greater the probability that the situation will collapse into a better Gestalt.

The fact that any problem or situation can be interpreted in multiple ways answers the question of how novelty is possible, but we are left wondering what is distinctive about creative thinking. The Gestalters' interest in good thinking – in various senses – made them neglect not-so-good thinking. Analytical thinking is only present in their writings as a somewhat repulsive contrast case. Wertheimer wrote about "blind" problem solutions and contrasted good and bad errors. The former are those that foreshadow an insightful solution. Bad errors, on the other hand, are discussed as if they were embarrassments of manner, like picking your nose at the dinner table. The Gestalters had no theory of how people think throughout the long stretches between the insights, and hence only half an answer to the question of distinctiveness. Creative thinking essentially involves insight, but what effective analytical thinking consists of, they did not say.

The most interesting but also most problematic aspect of the Gestalters' theory is their answer to the question of what gives direction to the creative process. The Gestalters claimed that restructuring moves toward better, more balanced representations. By *better* they meant more responsive to the task demands, but also more intelligent and sometimes even aesthetically and morally better. They refused to separate fact and value. A better structure is not only more effective or useful vis-à-vis the problem at hand, but also more proper and harmonious, more in touch with the true nature of things. Like Poincaré's claim about the power of intellectual beauty to guide mathematical discovery, the Gestalters relied on differences in the goodness of the relevant Gestalts to select the right representation for the problem at hand.[58]

The obvious question is how this is supposed to work. If the material situation confronting the problem solver is compatible with a set of possible representations, and the restructuring process is a lateral move from one of those representations to another, then why cannot the restructuring process move from better to worse, from a modestly helpful representation to a useless one? What guarantees that restructuring moves up the goodness gradient and what guarantees that a Gestalt that is better, in the aesthetic, almost moral sense, is also more useful for solving the problem at hand?

Köhler provided a surprisingly contemporary answer.[59] He claimed that Gestalts were consequences of the laws that govern the electromagnetic fields generated by electrical activity in the brain. He hypothesized that Gestalts arise as a result of the interactions among local electrical processes such as the discharges of individual neurons. He anticipated many of the observations in later studies of self-organization in nature by highlighting physical systems that tend to spontaneously organize themselves into patterns and regular structures. Flames and soap bubbles were among his examples. Restructuring of a problem representation is analogous to the redistribution of tension over the surface of a soap bubble when disturbed. The brain's electrical activities, like other material systems, move toward states of lowest energy. The Gestalt of a problem situation moves toward a better structure in the same way and for the same reason that water flowing downhill invariably collects in the lowest point. No psychological theory before or since has linked the mental and the physical in quite this way.

Unfortunately, this interesting and elegant theory – so 21st century in both its emphasis on self-organization and its attempt to explain cognitive phenomena with neurophysiology – cannot be true. The behavior of individuals vis-à-vis complex cognitive tasks is strongly influenced by prior knowledge and practice. Training effects are large in magnitude and they can make the production of a novel solution either more or less likely. The Gestalt theory cannot accommodate this commonplace observation. What is the locus of training effects if restructuring is a predetermined tumble down a minimal energy curve to a stable end state specified by the laws of self-organization, operating on the electrical activity of neural matter? The Gestalters formulated their theory in conscious opposition to the behaviorist claim that human beings are infinitely malleable in response to experience. As a consequence, they produced a theory that goes too far in its denial of prior experience, as Jean Piaget, Robert Weisberg and other critics have pointed out. [60]

Köhler's hypothesized connection between self-organization in the cortex and creative thinking is not explanatory but itself in need of explanation. Why must a structure that is determined by the laws of self-organization in neural matter correspond precisely to the mental representation of a situation that is most helpful in solving the problem that the situation poses? Without further principles about the relation between the brain, the mind and the world, this intrinsic harmony appears as mysterious as Poincaré's claim about the relation between beauty and mathematical truth. Indeed, the claim that the direction of a creative process is dictated by the laws of material nature is strangely incompatible with the open-ended character of creative work.

The Gestalt theory of restructuring has no deep answer to the question of why creativity is limited. Why do we not flip instantaneously and effortlessly, as soon as we encounter a poor Gestalt? Why does the flipping act require cognitive work, even sustained effort in the face of an impasse? The Gestalters sometimes wrote as if there is resistance to representational change. For example, Koffka wrote, "We know from the testimony of great thinkers that in order to solve difficult problems, they persevered in concentrating on them. But this concentration is effective only inasmuch as it supplies the problematical external situation with sufficient energy to make reorganization possible."[61] However, they never specified why restructuring requires "sufficient energy."

A satisfactory explanation for creativity should break down the creative process into component processes that are simpler than the target process itself, preferably so simple that we feel no need for further breakdown. The Gestalt theory fails on this point. The holistic flipping to a better Gestalt is a so-called homunculus, a supposed component that is so complex that it is no easier to understand than the process of creative thinking itself.

The Gestalt theory of productive thinking cannot answer three of the four creativity questions and it should be abandoned. It nevertheless teaches several important lessons: Novelty is possible because problem situations do not uniquely determine their own representations. Acts of creation come about via changes in representation. A change to a different representation is holistic in character and the new representation may or may not preserve the prior division into parts and wholes or between figure and background. The restructuring process is non-monotonic in that the previous representation fades from consciousness. We lack introspective access to the machinery of restructuring and its triggering conditions are such that its occurrence is only indirectly under voluntary control. The triggering conditions include careful analysis of the problem situation and of the requirements of the goal. These ideas are useful and should be carried forward into the next generation of creativity theories.

A REPERTOIRE OF IDEAS

Progress is a bloody affair. There would be no biological evolution if the environment did not kill large numbers of organisms before they reproduce. If every organism passed on its genes, there would be no change and no new species. In intellectual history, the destruction of ideas is equally necessary. Let every theory flourish and we are stuck with the same bad old theories forever. Progress requires selective pressure in the form of critical analysis.

The conceptual lineages that began in the late 19th century with works by Darwin, Poincaré, Thorndike and Wertheimer have not resulted in a theory that provides satisfactory answers to the creativity questions and the plethora of theories their works have inspired should be abandoned. However, those theories fail less due to what they say than to what they leave unsaid. Being incomplete is less of a sin than being false, and a failure of this lesser sort does not imply that a theory or a program of research made no contribution.

There is only a handful of fundamental answers to the question of how novelty is possible: Reality is layered, and everything, including ideas, problem solutions and products, is made of parts, and the parts can be combined in different ways. The effects of successive actions accumulate over time, so a sequence of actions can have a novel outcome, even if every action in the sequence is familiar. Finally, the mind is representational and a representation is always an interpretation. Objects, events and situations do not uniquely determine their own interpretation, so novelty can arise by moving sideways from one representation to another.

The notions of combination, accumulation and restructuring are good ideas that should not be thrown out because the theories in which they were originally embedded do not measure up to the challenge of answering all the creativity questions. Each represents a sliver of truth. The puzzle of creativity is hard, so we need to make use of every good idea. The concepts and principles proposed since the end of the 19th century need to be extracted from their original contexts, reformulated and incorporated into a better theory. To state such a theory is the task for the next chapter.

4

Creative Insight: The Redistribution Theory

> ... *under the stress of our wish to solve a certain problem – and after our thorough consideration of various parts of the given material – sometimes brain processes tend to assume new forms or structures which, when reflected in our minds, suddenly make us see new relations and thus give us new insights which tend to bring about the solution.*
>
> Wolfgang Köhler[1]

An inventor, scientist or artist might work on one and the same project for a day, a week, a month, a year or many years.[2] The thought processes associated with such extended activities are not equally creative throughout. Even when the work results in a creative product, much of what occurs along the way is analytical thinking or even habitual or routine behavior. What distinguishes creative from analytical processes is that the former are punctuated by *insights*, mental events in which new ideas come to mind. An extended project is likely to require more than one insight before completion. Projects vary with respect to the density of insight events, but each such event is of short duration compared to the duration of the project as a whole. I call this the *Raisins in the Dough Principle*.

To explain creativity is therefore to carry out three theoretical tasks: Describe analytical thinking, explain what happens in moments of insight and clarify how insight expands the power of analytical thinking. To explain insight is, in turn, to decompose insight events into processes that are so simple that we feel no need to decompose them further, and to show how those simple processes combine to produce mental events in which new ideas come to mind. The purpose of the present chapter is to propose such a theory, the first of the three micro-theories that are the technical contributions of this book. The first step in developing the theory is to specify which aspects of insight need to be explained. A second preparation is to formulate a theory of analytical thinking that is sufficiently complete and detailed to serve as a context for the explanation of insight events.

FRAMING THE PROBLEM OF INSIGHT

To study insight, researchers need a technique that allows them to reliably produce such events. Historical and biographical studies of the Edisons, the Einsteins and the Michelangelos of human history are limited by the fact that there are only a few of them and their appearance is unrelated to the investigator's needs. We cannot whistle up a creative genius whenever a hypothesis about creativity is ready to be tested. In addition, the historical records of great achievements seldom allow us to follow the thought processes at fine enough a temporal grain. If a scientist writes in his laboratory notebook three times a week, and a new idea forms in the course of a few minutes, then that notebook is too blunt an instrument with which to grab hold of the creative act. It is possible but impractical for an observer to follow the activities in, for example, a chemical laboratory for a year or a decade, in the hope that a Lavoisier or a Pauling will emerge in that place during that time.[3] Another problem is that field studies of creative projects do not allow the psychologist to study creativity under systematically varied conditions, a powerful investigatory technique.

The alternative is to conduct experiments. I use the word broadly to refer to any study in which the researcher deliberately arranges for certain events to take place for the purpose of observing them. To conduct an experiment on creativity is to ask a person to solve some problem that requires a novel response under conditions that allow his behavior to be recorded for later analysis. The key step in conducting such an experiment is to choose a suitable problem.

The Case Against Insight Problems

The Gestalt psychologists, whose approach to insight was discussed in Chapter 3, had a knack for identifying problems that intuitively seem like good tools for eliciting creative insights in ordinary people. These problems tend to share the following features: (a) They can be stated concisely. The given materials encompass only a few simple objects, if any at all. The task instructions and the goal can be summarized in a handful of sentences. (b) The solutions, once thought of, take only a few seconds to complete, and they consist of no more than a handful of actions or inferences. They require no exotic skills but only actions that any normal adult is familiar with, such as drawing a line on a piece of paper, cutting something with a pair of scissors, tying a knot, multiplying a number by a small integer and so on. Some insight problems require no physical actions at all, merely an inference or two. The difficulty lies solely in thinking of the right action or inference. (c) The problems are difficult in the sense that the time required by adults of average intelligence to think of the solution is out of proportion to the time it takes to execute the solution, once thought of.

For example, the Two-String Problem poses the task of tying together two ropes hanging from the ceiling at such a distance that a person cannot reach the second rope while holding on to the first.[4] The solution is to tie some heavy object to the second rope and set it swinging, walk back to the first rope and grab it, and grab the second rope at the end of its swing. The Hat-Rack Problem requires the problem solver to build a hat rack out of three 2-by-4 wooden boards and a C-clamp.[5] The solution is to wedge two boards between floor and ceiling, keep them in place with the clamp and hang the hat on the clamp handle. Other problems are more geometrical than practical. For example, the Nine Dot Problem poses the task of drawing four straight lines through nine dots, arranged in a square, without lifting the pen and without retracing.[6] Yet others are verbal riddles. The B.C. Coin Problem is an example: *A man enters a rare coin shop proposing to sell what appears to be a Roman coin with an emperor's head on one side and the text "150 B.C." on the other. The store owner immediately phones the police. Why?*[7] It usually takes a couple of minutes before a college student spots the anomaly that a coin maker could not have known himself to be living in the year 150 B.C. (Before Christ). Yet others are numerical puzzles. In the Lily Pond Problem, the question is this: *If the lilies on a pond cover 1.6% of the pond surface and grow so fast that they double the area they cover every 24 hours, and the pond surface is 1.2 acres, how much of the surface of the pond do they cover the day before they cover the whole pond?*[8]

Researchers have inherited a list of such problems, designated as *insight problems* by previous generations of researchers. To some critics of insight research, the relevance of the results obtained by observing people solve such artificial tasks and puzzles is questionable.[9] But the distinction between artificial and natural tasks does not survive scrutiny. Human beings engage in an infinite variety of activities and practices, few of which are natural in any deep sense. If *artificial* means *socially constructed* or *invented*, then the set of artificial tasks includes chess, computer programming, mathematics, painting, scientific discovery, technological invention and most other tasks commonly seen to require creativity, so cognitive research on all those tasks would lack relevance for the study of creativity. The set of natural tasks would be reduced to eating, gathering berries, procreating, sleeping and escaping from cold winds by huddling in a crevice – an unpromising set of activities to study when searching for a theory of creativity. If the criticism of artificiality is not to be reduced to this absurdity, those who issue the charge of artificiality need to explain how "artificial" is to be defined instead. Until they do, the charge of artificiality has no meaning, and the artificial versus natural distinction is not useful for judging the relevance of particular tasks for the study of creativity.

There are nevertheless difficulties with the idea of labeling problems as insight problems. The first is empirical. For some of these problems, empirical studies support the claim that they engage other cognitive processes than problems that are not designated as insight problems.[10] However, for other problems on the received list, there exists no empirical demonstration that they do, in fact, elicit insights in experimental subjects. Many are designated as insight problems on no other basis than that they seem to be insight problems to the researchers who use them. As research continues, the list of problems anointed as insight problems grows by an undisciplined mixture of received but unexamined opinion, implicit appeals to readers' intuitions and willingness to mindlessly follow prior practice.

A second difficulty cuts deeper. Labeling a problem as an insight problem is questionable because a problem is unlikely to elicit insights in everybody who tries to solve it. Being an insight problem is not an objective property of a problem in the same sense in which having a certain weight is an objective property of a bowling ball. Insight is an event that arises in the interaction between a person and a problem, and that interaction is determined by the person as much as by the problem. Individuals differ with respect to which ideas and concepts they have become familiar with throughout prior learning, so even though one person needs a new idea before he can see the solution to a certain problem, somebody else might be able to solve the same problem through analytical thinking. For example, the Two-String Problem might not be an insight problem to someone who works with pendulums, because he thinks *pendulum* as soon as he sees a hanging rope. For him, the problem does not require an act of creation and the problem is not an insight problem; for others, it is.

To label particular problems as insight problems creates the temptation, widely succumbed to in an implicit way, to assume that every time someone attempts to solve one of the problems on the received list, his performance is an instance of something called "insight problem solving." This label, in turn, suggests that all such solutions are of a kind, and therefore should be explained by one and the same theory. The purpose of a theory of insight then becomes to account for data from all experiments in which the participants solved one or more of the designated insight problems. This way of proceeding conjures a supposed theoretical category – insight problem solving – out of the labels psychologists assign to certain problems. But there is no reason to believe that all such solutions come about through similar processes and hence can be subsumed under one and the same theory. The task for a theory of insight cannot be to account for all experiments in which researchers asked subjects to solve so-called insight problems but must be defined otherwise.

The Insight Sequence

A successful problem solution is not in and of itself remarkable. If a person is competent to solve a problem, we do not need a theory to explain why he solved it. Likewise, a failure to solve a problem is no great mystery if the person lacked the knowledge or competence necessary for solving it. For example, we need no psychological theory to explain why nobody is marketing a time travel machine; engineers do not know how to build one. The puzzling and interesting feature of creative problem solving is success following failure.

More precisely, creative thought processes sometimes unfold according to the following pattern:[11]

1. *Search*. The problem solver explores the problem materials, develops an understanding of the goal and tries out the options and possibilities that come to mind right away. His grasp of the problem improves. Progress appears to be steady.
2. *Impasse*. The person no longer generates previously unexplored solution types. If solution attempts are costly in terms of effort or time, problem-solving activity might cease altogether. If solutions are cheap to generate, he might continue to re-execute solutions already found unsatisfactory. Subjectively, the person experiences himself as "stuck," out of ideas, unable to think of a new approach; his mind is "blank." An impasse is *warranted* if the person lacks the competence, capacity or knowledge that is necessary for the solution. Failure is then inevitable.
3. *Insight*. If the impasse is *unwarranted* – that is, if the person is, in principle, capable of solving the problem – and he persists in the effort to solve it, a new idea might come to mind. Insight is not a deliberate, conscious process that a person decides to carry out, but a mental event. Indeed, insight

is not guaranteed to occur. Even unwarranted impasses sometimes remain unresolved within the limits on patience, time or other resources.

4. *Aftermath.* The consequences of insight vary. Sometimes the solution is achieved quickly and unhesitatingly, and the person subjectively experiences himself as having seen the entire solution in the mind's eye at once. This is the proverbial *Aha*-experience; I refer to it as *full insight*. At other times, success is achieved only after further analytical problem solving; I refer to this as *partial insight*. Sometimes analytical problem solving resumes but ultimately ends in failure because the new idea was not, in fact, helpful; I refer to this as *false insight*.

This four-part pattern is called *the insight sequence*. Its main feature is the successive alterations in mode and tempo, from steady initial progress to a state of slow progress or no progress at all; this is interrupted by a short moment of rapid, qualitative change, which in turn might be followed by a second period of steady progress; see Figure 4.1. The existence of the insight sequence is not in doubt, because we experience it in everyday life, we can sometimes observe it in the laboratory, we can catch it in brain images and we can find it in autobiographical and historical accounts of creative projects.[12-14] The claim is not that creative thought processes always or necessarily exhibit such alterations in mode and tempo, but that they sometimes do. Although the existence of this pattern is not in doubt, we have almost no information about prevalence. We do not know how often problem solving in real life conforms to this pattern, nor do we have much data on what proportion of solutions to so-called insight problems observed in laboratory studies conforms to this pattern.[15]

Even if rare, the insight sequence cries out for explanation. The paradox is that a person sometimes enters an impasse that is unwarranted in the sense that he does in fact possess all the knowledge and competence required for the desired solution. If he is capable of solving the problem (as proven by his eventual success), then why does he experience an impasse? If the relevant cognitive resources are available, then why are they not brought to bear? What causes impasses? The second half of the insight paradox is that unwarranted impasses, once entered, can be resolved. If something is blocking the productive application of the person's knowledge and competence to the problem at hand, then why does he not stay in the impasse until limits on time and resources force him to give up? Why does the blockage not persist?

The main purpose of a theory of insight is to explain the sequence of alterations in mode and tempo that defines the insight sequence. To do so,

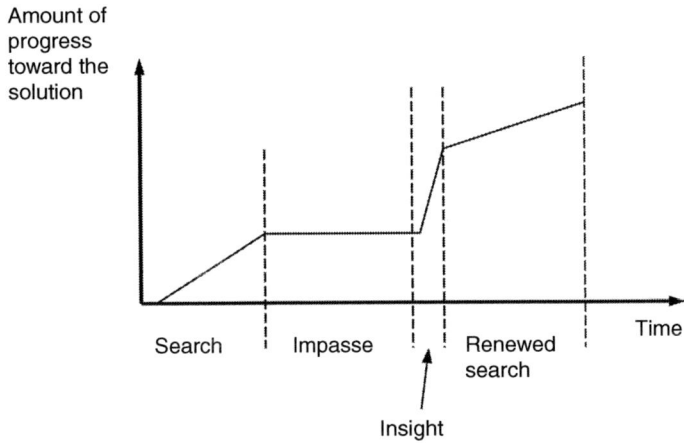

FIGURE 4.1. Alterations in mode and tempo during the insight sequence.

the theory must specify both the causes of unwarranted impasses and the processes by which they are resolved. Insight theories that propose causes of impasses without specifying their resolution fail to explain why insight is possible, while creative mechanisms unaccompanied by impasse-producing processes fail to explain why insights are infrequent. The triggering conditions for the hypothesized processes should be such as to answer the question of direction and hence of the aftermath: Why does one insight occur rather than another? What determines whether an insight is full, partial or false? Insight events occur in the context of analytical problem solving, so their explanation has two parts: a mechanism for analytical thinking and the set of additional hypotheses needed to account for insight.

ANALYTICAL PROBLEM SOLVING

When explaining change, it helps to have a description of the system that is changing. Analytical thinking unfolds through interactions among three main processes: problem perception, knowledge retrieval and heuristic search. The initial perception of the problem serves as a probe for retrieving relevant knowledge elements from long-term memory, which in turn are applied to the current state of the problem to constrain the search for the solution. This component of the theory of insight is not new but a synthesis of well-established concepts and principles.

Problem Perception

Before someone can be said to be thinking about a problem, he must have grasped the problem and formed at least a preliminary idea of what it means to solve it. These two components are called the *initial problem state* and the *goal*. For brevity, I focus on situations in which the problem solver encounters the problem through visual perception, through language or through some combination of the two. The theory of insight need not wait for a complete theory of either visual perception or language comprehension, but it needs to incorporate some of their principled features.

Visual perception
When a person's eyes alight on an object, the percept appears to be constructed instantaneously, without complex processing and without cognitive effort, and what the person sees appears to him to be determined by the object itself: You see a chair because there is a chair there. The speed, lack of subjective effort, high veridicality and intersubjective validity of perception trick us into believing that perception is a passive recording of reality. Philosophers and psychologists tirelessly repeat that this is not so.[16] Perception is a constructive, selective process of considerable complexity and a percept is an interpretation, not a recording, of the physical situation in front of the eyes.[17] The machinery of interpretation has several properties that play key roles in insight.

Perception is layered. The layers are both anatomical – layers of neurons in the visual cortex – and functional.[18] Each layer consists of *processing units* that receive input from the layer below, operate on what they receive and pass on their outputs to the next layer. A processing unit corresponds to what we for lack of a better term might call an *encoding rule* or a *feature detector* that reacts to constellations of features and creates a higher-order feature that is passed on to the next layer. The encoding rules can be conceptualized as having the general form

$$\{f_1, f_2, ..., f_i\} \rightarrow g$$

where $f_1, f_2, ..., f_i$ are features identified in layer N, while g is a feature at layer $N+1$. A processing unit can pass its result – the higher-order feature g – onto multiple units in the next layer. To the extent that the processing unit transmits its output selectively, along some of its outbound links but not others, it constitutes a *choice point*.

The units in the bottom layer of the visual system detect very simple perceptual features. The latter are elaborated by the intermediate layers. The top layer writes the final output of the perceptual system into working memory. For example, the perception of an object at the very least passes through layers that (a) identify boundaries between light and shadow, (b) determine the object's shape and (c) assign the object category membership. Those tasks are likely to be accomplished in that order (presumably with yet other layers in between). The orderliness of the sequence of layers should not be overemphasized – the brain is a messy system – but it is a useful idealization.

A complex visual scene causes many parallel, simultaneous streams of processing to travel upward through the successive layers. Color is not processed in the same place in the brain or in the same way as either shape or spatial location.[19] Exactly how the parallel strands of information come together into the subjective experience of seeing a single, integrated physical object of a particular type, located in a particular place, is still unknown. However this is accomplished, the implication is that mental representations are combinatorial structures with distinct constituents.

At each layer, different interpretations of the inputs from the preceding layer are possible. The choice of which interpretation to pass on to the next layer is assumed to happen via a version of the *construction-integration process* hypothesized by Walter Kintsch for language comprehension.[20] This type of process requires horizontal links among the processing units within each layer. Such links can be either *excitatory* or *inhibitory*. An excitatory link between units A and B has the effect that if A is found in the stream of perceptual input, the system is biased toward also finding B in that stream, and vice versa. The two features "yellow" and "banana shape" are examples. The identification of the color of an object as yellow increases the probability that the visual system will conclude that the shape of the object is that of a banana and vice versa. The identification of either feature causes the other feature to be *activated*. An inhibitory link has the opposite effect. Seeing "blue" would bias the perceptual system away from "banana shape" by lowering its activation level, because we rarely see blue bananas. Horizontal links can be thought of as *constraints* on processing. They limit the set of possible interpretations of the visual input to the most plausible ones. The mutual excitatory and inhibitory interactions continue within each layer until the activation levels settle and the processing units that were stronger than their competitors pass on their processing products and their activation to the next processing layer, where they enter into new combinations.

The hypothesis of a sequence of layers should not be taken to imply that processing is bottom-up. Information from layers further up in the stack is fed back down to preceding layers.[21] For the purpose of explaining insight, the

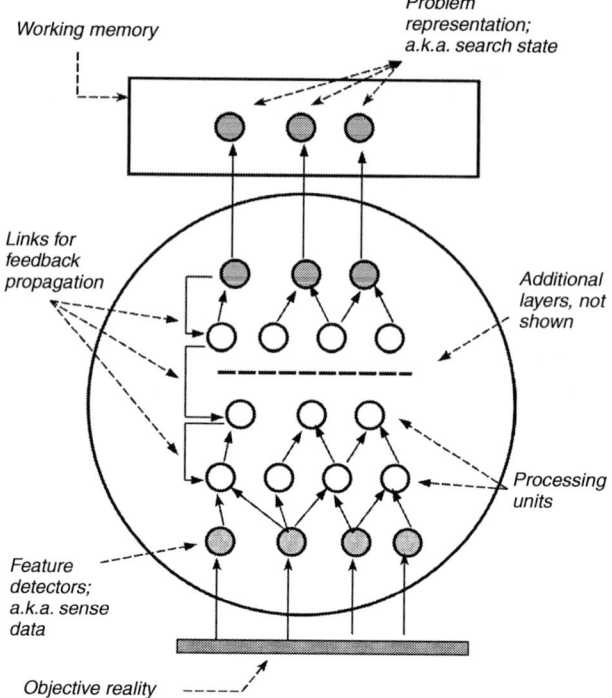

FIGURE 4.2. The layered structure of problem perception and discourse comprehension.

exact nature and detail of this feedback mechanism is less important than its existence. Figure 4.2 illustrates how the various components are connected.

In daily life, the information in ambient light is rich enough that the visual system can rapidly resolve the conflicts between alternative interpretations of a visual scene. We remain unaware that choices are made. But the constructive nature of perception is revealed by displays that fool the visual system into inaccurate representations or prevent it from making a single, stable choice. Visual displays of this sort include illusions like the Ames' Room, a room of odd proportions and shape that tricks the eye into seeing other people as changing in size as they walk through it.[22] Reversible figures like the Necker Cube are atypical stimuli in that the visual system never resolves the conflict between the two most plausible interpretations.[23] These figures keep flipping between the alternatives for as long as the person keeps looking. Illusions and reversible figures are intriguing because they so clearly demonstrate the constructive nature of perception.

For the purpose of explaining insight, the key point is that the subjective experience of seeing an object or a situation is the result of a number of rapid and unconscious but nevertheless real choices, constrained and biased by the prior experience encoded in the relative strengths and activation levels of the vertical and horizontal links. The existence of an outgoing link from processing unit U in layer N to unit W in layer $N+1$, the activation of that link, the activation of excitatory and inhibitory links within a layer and the activations of the feedback links from higher to lower levels are determined by prior experience as well as by current perceptual input. The biases residing in the relative strengths and activation levels jointly produce the visual system's best guess as to the nature of the perceived situation. The final percept – the working memory content – is a projection of prior experience onto the situation at hand.

Language comprehension
Research in psycholinguistics and cognitive psychology has established that comprehension is no less an interpretive and constructive process than is visual perception. It requires choices, although we are usually unaware of them. For example, a pervasive feature of English as well as other languages is that words are polysemous, that is, they have multiple meanings. For example, my dictionary lists 14 distinct senses for the word "line." Laboratory studies show that the process psychologists call *lexical access* activates a word's meanings in parallel and settles on the right one for each context through a complex series of excitatory and inhibitory interactions among the possible meanings of the words in a sentence.[24] The word "wire" is interpreted differently when it occurs in a sentence that also contains "electrical circuits" than in a sentence that also contains "circus act." Words mutually constrain each other's meanings. Walter Kintsch originally proposed his construction-integration process for the case of language.

Like visual perception, discourse requires multiple layers of processing (lexical access, syntactic parsing, implicit inferences, etc.) before the language processing system arrives at what psycholinguists call a *situation model*, that is, a mental representation of what the text refers to or is about.[25] Once again, each processing layer executes choices, however implicit and unavailable for conscious inspection. The construction-integration process operates within each layer. Processing, although it passes through the successive layers in sequence, is not bottom-up. On the contrary, each layer provides a context for the previous layer and influences the processing at those layers via downward feedback links. The sentence, *they are washing pans* is parsed differently in the context of gold digging (a type of pan) and in the context of a field hospital (a type of activity).

Discussion

The key principles of combinatorial, layered processing, mutual constraints within each layer due to horizontal excitatory and inhibitory links and context effects implemented via downward feedback links are shared between visual perception and discourse comprehension, and presumably by perceptual processing generally. The application of these basic principles to problem solving is straightforward. Whether in the psychologist's laboratory, in school or in work situations, people are confronted with situations and problem materials that require visual inspection and interpretation.

For a situation or a set of materials to constitute a problem, it must be paired with a *goal*, a mental representation of a desired (but, by definition, not yet realized) state of affairs. If the goal is posed and communicated by someone else, the constructive nature of comprehension has similar consequences as the constructive nature of vision: Goal comprehension is not uniquely determined by the verbal input. The problem solver's representation of that goal is an interpretation based on prior experience.

The representations of the initial situation and the goal constitute the starting points for analytical problem solving. One might object that this perspective applies only to material problems, such as a flat tire, or to problems posed by someone else, such as an employer or a teacher. But many important problems are found and posed by the problem solver himself. Also, many problems do not seem to refer to any concrete situation. Problems in mathematics and other formal domains are examples. However, it remains true that to have a problem is to entertain some initial representation of some state of affairs, even if it is found rather than imposed and even if it is abstract and imagined instead of concrete and situational. Also, to be engaged in problem solving, a person must have posed some goal. It might be abstract, vague or incomplete, but it has to contain enough information so that the person can tell when he or she has solved the problem.

Knowledge Retrieval

A person's knowledge store is vast.[26] At any one moment, only a small number of all the knowledge elements in long-term memory are active. When a person is faced with a problem, particularly an unfamiliar one, every piece of his prior knowledge is potentially relevant. To be applied to the situation at hand, a knowledge element has to be retrieved through *spread of activation*.[27] To visualize this process, it is useful to conceptualize long-term memory as a network in which knowledge elements are nodes and the relations between them are links. Each node is associated with a level of activation that fluctuates over time. At each moment in time, a small subset of the nodes have activation levels above a threshold. Those elements are immediately available for processing; they form the current content of working memory. Activation is passed along the links from elements that are currently above threshold to other, related but not yet active nodes. If a knowledge element receives enough activation to rise above threshold, it "comes to mind" as we say. "Retrieval" is a label for the event that occurs when the activation of a knowledge element rises above threshold. As activation spreads from a source node N, it is passed along its outbound links. A certain amount of activation is lost in each step of the spreading process, so the amount that is spread from a given source node N decreases gradually with increased distance from N. There are several variants of this theory that differ in the quantitative details of the spreading process, but those details need not concern us here.

Memory retrieval is selective. A person can keep only a small amount of information in an active state at any one time – working memory has a limited capacity – but the knowledge store is vast, so the retrieval process necessarily makes choices, however implicit and unconscious, about what to retrieve. Retrieving an element X constrains which other elements can also be retrieved at the same time. In a problem situation, activation initially spreads from the problem representation and the goal. The initial encounter with the problem thus determines the knowledge elements that are initially marshaled to solve it, and those elements in turn become sources from which activation spreads. Retrieval is a cyclic, iterative search through memory for those knowledge elements that are most likely to be relevant for the problem at hand.

Memory links are acquired in the course of experience, so the structure of the memory network mirrors the structure of experience. Reaction time studies reveal, to no one's surprise, that the two concepts of *chair* and *table* are more closely linked in people's heads than *chair* and, for example, *parachute*.[28] The strengths of memory links are influenced by a variety of factors, including frequency of use, recency of use, estimated capacity demands and past usefulness. The structure of the knowledge network – the set of links – and the strength of the links serve to project the accumulated prior experience onto the current situation. In conjunction, the relative strengths determine what knowledge is retrieved on the initial encounter with a problem, and what is retrieved constitutes the memory system's best guess as to what knowledge is relevant for the problem at hand.[29]

Psychological research on memory has focused on information communicated via pictures, texts or observations of events. For the purpose of understanding problem solving, it is more useful to focus on the retrieval of knowledge about the actions and the cognitive operations by which the problem might be solved. There are at least three types of cognitive operations, fulfilling three distinct functions: anticipation, inference and subgoaling.

Anticipation
When we perceive an object, we register certain actions that we can perform vis-à-vis that object and certain functions that the object can perform for us. Seeing a chair, the thought of sitting down is not far away; seeing a soccer ball on a lawn, the thought of kicking it not only comes to mind but is hard to resist. Children need no instruction to figure out that pebbles on a beach can be thrown into the sea. In general, the mere perception of an object is sufficient to activate certain actions and dispositions vis-à-vis that object. The opportunities for action associated with an object are called the *affordances* of that object.[30] We can think about overt actions without performing them, so we must possess mental representations of them.

Goals likewise suggest to us actions that accomplish them. The need to fasten two things to each other prompts us to think about gluing, nailing, taping and tying. The need to reach something on a high shelf makes us look for a box that is sturdy enough to stand on, a chair, footstool, ladder or some other means of increasing our height. Failing to find one, we might look for a broom handle or some other way to increase our reach. In short, both the current state of affairs and the goal can serve as memory probes that retrieve actions – more precisely, to retrieve mental representations of actions.

In their 1972 treatise on analytical thinking, *Human Problem Solving*, Herbert A. Simon and Allen Newell emphasized that thinking is *anticipatory*.[31] The representation of a familiar action contains knowledge that enables a person to execute it but also to anticipate its effects. To think about a problem is to imagine the outcomes of the possible actions before they are carried out: *If I do this or that, the result, the new state of affairs, will be such-and-such*. This mental *look-ahead* process allows us to evaluate the promise and usefulness of actions ahead of time. For example, in playing a board game like chess, a player will imagine making a move, anticipate how the relations on the board would change if he were to make that move, and use that anticipated outcome to evaluate the move before deciding what to do. Another commonplace example is to think through the effects of moving the sofa in one's living room to the other side of the room before taking the trouble of moving it physically (*if we put the sofa there, there is no place for the end table*). Look-ahead is quicker, requires less effort, allows us to explore mutually exclusive options (buy house X vs. buy house Y) and saves us, when consequences are costly, from having to pay the price of our poor judgment. To think analytically is, in part, to carry out actions in the mind before we carry them out in the flesh.

Inference
Many cognitive operations do not have counterparts among physical actions. If somebody is told that some object O_1 is smaller than O_2, which in turn is smaller than O_3, he immediately knows that O_1 is smaller than O_3. This mental operation is better thought of as an inference than as a mental simulation of an action. The relevant inference rule is, *if X is smaller than Y, and Y is smaller than Z, then X is also smaller than Z*. Exactly how people draw such inferences is a matter of controversy.[32] There is widespread belief that the laws of logic as explicated by logicians is a poor theory of how people reason, but agreement stops there.[33] Some researchers have proposed psycho-logics they claim fit data from human reasoning, while others have suggested nonlogical reasoning mechanisms. The theory of insight need not wait for the resolution of this controversy. People possess cognitive elements of some sort – which I will call *inference rules* or *reasoning schemas* – by which they can spell out what follows, given certain starting points. To be applied to a problem, these rules and schemas have to be retrieved from memory. The set of inference rules activated at each moment in time is a projection of past experience, the mind's best guess as to which parts of prior knowledge are needed to reason about the situation at hand.

Subgoaling
People can analyze a goal into components that can be attacked one at a time. It is useful to distinguish between two types of subgoals. Some subgoals correspond to nearly independent components of a larger problem. The task of making tea includes putting tea in the tea strainer and boiling water. The top goal – make tea – and the two subgoals are related hierarchically via part-whole relations. In this case, there are no constraints on the order in which the two subgoals are to be achieved, but there are also subgoals that form a temporal sequence, typically because each is a *prerequisite* for the following one. To fly somewhere, you have to get yourself to the airport, clear security, locate the right gate and board the plane. These actions cannot be performed in any other sequence; each one sets the stage for the next. We know little about how people analyze goals into subgoals, but the reality of the subgoaling process is not in doubt.[34]

To summarize, spread of activation through long-term memory serves to activate at least three types of prior knowledge: mental representations of actions, schemas for reasoning and processes that break down goals into subgoals. This list is not exhaustive but highlights important and well-documented types of operations in analytical thinking. For the purpose of explaining insight, it is essential that retrieval is selective. Due to the limited capacity of working memory, not everything can be retrieved at once; only memory nodes that rise above an activation threshold enter working memory.

Heuristic Search

The problem solver's initial mental representation of the problem (the situation and the goal) and the set of cognitive operations initially retrieved from memory define the space of solutions that can be reached via analytical thinking, "the sector of exploratory activity" in Robert S. Woodworth's phrase.[35] A. Newell and H. A. Simon called this a *problem space*, but their term suggests a space of problems while what is meant is a space of potential solutions. I prefer the term *solution space*. The solution space is a theoretical construct; it does not exist in any explicit sense. It is a way of referring to all the solutions that are possible, given the problem solver's initial perception of the problem and the repertoire of actions and operations initially retrieved.

A problem solution consists of a path through the solution space, a sequence of cognitive operations that transforms the initial situation into a situation in which the goal is satisfied. In a familiar task environment, the person already knows which step is the right one at each successive choice point. However, in unfamiliar environments, the person has to act tentatively and explore alternatives. Analytical problem solving is difficult because the size of a solution space is a function of the number of actions that are applicable in each situation – the *branching factor* – and the number of actions along the solution path – the *path length*. The number of problem states, S, is proportional to b^N, where b is the branching factor and N the path length. S is astronomical for even modest values of b and N, so solution spaces can only be traversed selectively. By projecting prior experience onto the current situation, both problem perception and memory retrieval help constrain the options to be considered to the most promising ones.

The search through the solution space is a cyclic process. The problem solver considers the current situation, thinks of one of more promising steps, chooses one of them, performs the chosen one and evaluates its outcome; the cycle repeats. Anticipating the outcomes of actions, drawing inferences and posing subgoals are usually deliberate and capacity-demanding processes, and they tend to occur sequentially rather than in parallel. The set of options considered at each step along the way is called the *conflict set* and the process of choosing an option is called *conflict resolution*. If the chosen step turns out to have a negative outcome, the best response might be to *back up* to an earlier state of affairs and do something different from what was done before. This is often easier to do in the mind's eye than in the material world.

Knowledge elements that decide choices among rival actions and operations are called *heuristics*.[36] Like inhibitory links in perception and memory, heuristics constrain the set of options. There are two types of heuristics. *Strategies* focus attention on the most promising actions available in a particular situation or problem state. Some strategic heuristics apply generally because they abstract from the task content. For example, if one action appears to be more promising than its rivals, it makes sense to explore it first. As the example illustrates, general methods are not very helpful. Most effective heuristics are specific to a task or a type of situation. For example, a locked door might trigger a search for a key, while a swollen mountain creek might trigger a search for a bridge. *Evaluation functions*, a second type of heuristic, support comparisons between outcomes. For example, a chess player can calculate the relative strengths of his own and his opponent's positions after a move, and thereby evaluate the usefulness of the move. The application of evaluation functions presupposes the application of strategic heuristics, because some cognitive operation or action has to be executed before there is some outcome to evaluate. Strategies and evaluation functions are retrieved from memory through the same process of spreading activation as other types of knowledge elements.

The Power and the Limit of Experience

Analytical thinking proceeds by projecting past experience onto the situation at hand. The initial interpretation of a problem situation is determined by the biases laid down in the visual and verbal systems by prior experience. The retrieval of affordances, inference rules and potential subgoals is determined by the relative strengths of memory links, another repository of past experience. The choices of which steps to take, which paths through the solution space to explore is determined by heuristics – strategies and evaluation functions – acquired in prior experience. Each of the main processes – perception, retrieval and search – helps contain the combinatorial explosion inherent in solution spaces by constraining the set of options to the most promising ones. In tight contexts, this is effective. The more knowledge that can be brought to bear, the better. In a completely familiar situation, the search process is so constrained that there is only a single option to consider in each successive problem state. We then say that the person knows what to do; he has mastered the task. The successes of chess-playing computers against the best human players illustrate how effective analytical problem solving can be in stable task environments, particularly when backed by the memory and speed of electronic hardware.[37] Analytical thinking is nevertheless limited in ways that are unrelated to processing capacity. As mathematical derivations from a set of axioms cannot lead to a theorem that contradicts those axioms, so analytical thinking cannot find any solution that is not included in the search space in which it moves. To reach all possible solutions, the mind must be able to jump over its own axioms and move sideways from one search space to another.

THE THEORY OF INSIGHT

If the theory of heuristic search through a solution space is at least approximately accurate as a theory of analytical thinking, how do the alterations in mode and tempo in the insight sequence arise? Why do people encounter impasses on problems which they are, objectively speaking, capable of solving? Once they have entered an impasse, by what processes do they break out?[38]

The Causes of Unwarranted Impasses

If a person is faced with an unfamiliar problem, he cannot know with certainty which interpretation of it will turn out to be most useful. In a turbulent and imperfectly known world, there is no guarantee that the biases laid down in the course of experience are predictive of which knowledge elements are most useful for solving a current problem. The perceptual encoding rules acquired in past experience will nevertheless execute and construct some initial representation of the problem. An unfamiliar problem might give rise to an initial representation that accidentally activates knowledge elements that are not, in fact, useful for constructing the solution. Once activated, those knowledge elements constrain further retrievals from the knowledge store via inhibitory links as well as by hoarding the available activation. Consequently, activation might not spread to those knowledge elements that are crucial for the solution. The result is an unwarranted impasse; the problem solver possesses the knowledge needed to solve the problem but fails to retrieve it. This explanation was already formulated by Woodworth in 1938: "When, as must often happen, the thinker makes a false start, he ... falls into certain

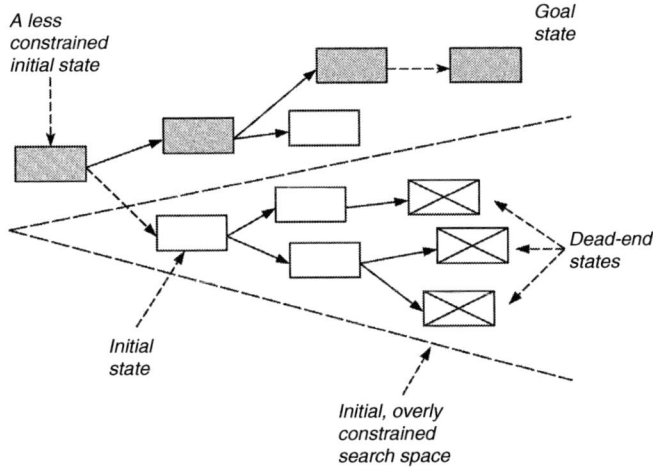

FIGURE 4.3. The relation between insight and search: Insight requires drawing back to an initial state that generates a less constrained search space.

assumptions which restrict his sector of exploratory activity ... and as long as he continues actively at work in this section he does not escape from these assumptions."[39]

Problems that end up on the psychologist's list of insight problems have a high probability of triggering an initial representation that in turn has a low probability of activating those knowledge elements that are needed for the solution, even when those elements are present in memory. A problem becomes an insight problem for a person if it is misleading. The person's prior knowledge accidentally matches the features of the problem so as to suggest that the problem should be understood in one way, whereas it would be more productive to think of it some other way. The resulting solution space is overly constrained and excludes the desired solution; see Figure 4.3.

Constraining contacts between prior experience and particular visual or verbal problem features are indeed common in the classical insight problems.[40] Consider once again the Hat Rack Problem: *Construct a hat rack out of 2-by-4 wooden boards and a C-clamp.* The wedge solution to this problem consists of two boards that are wedged between floor and ceiling and held in place with the clamp; the hat is hung on the handle of the clamp. Why might this solution be hard to think of? Everyday experience provides few examples of constructions that rely on the ceiling as a source of support, but many examples where 2-by-4s are used to prop something up. This leads most people to attempt a stable construction that stands on the floor. Visual attention is rarely directed toward the ceiling of a room, so the concept *ceiling* might not be highly active and actions directed toward the ceiling are unlikely to receive enough activation to pass the threshold of retrieval. Also, outward tension is more often used to push two things apart than to achieve stability. Finally, the handle of the clamp is likely to be categorized as a tool, or part of a tool, a view that is likely to interfere with seeing it as a functional part of the hat rack.

In unfamiliar situations, the mind cannot predict with any certainty which interpretation of a discourse will turn out to be most useful. There are multiple examples of classical insight problems in which the goal description can be understood in different ways, and in which the less useful interpretation is likely to come to mind before the more useful one. Consider the Inverted Pyramid Problem: *There is a steel table in a room; there is a $100 bill on the table; a steel pyramid is perfectly balanced, upside down, with its tip resting on the bill. The goal is to remove the bill without upsetting the precarious balance of the pyramid.*[41] The phrase *remove the dollar bill* can send activation down slightly different paths, depending on the exact meaning assigned to the verb "remove." This word might be understood to mean *transport the bill to another location*. In this case, it might evoke a representation in which the goal state contains both the pyramid and the dollar bill, physically separated from each other. This interpretation suggests that the dollar bill is to remain intact; a change of place is not typically associated with a transformation of the object. This interpretation of the goal constrains the possible actions in such a way that an impasse is unavoidable. On the other hand, if "remove" is interpreted to mean *make the bill disappear*, then the goal is consistent with the destruction of the dollar bill and actions like *burn it, pour acid on it, smear it with honey and let ants eat it* and *wait until it rots* have a higher likelihood to come to mind.

The time to impasse depends, in part, on the size of the search space.[42] Prior knowledge might affect the size of the search space in such a way as to delay the solution. A person who is knowledgeable about the relevant domain might be able to think of more options to explore within the unhelpful solution space, while a less knowledgeable person might quickly run out of things to try and hence move sooner into the process of impasse resolution.

In short, the possibility of unwarranted impasses on unfamiliar problems follows from the facts that perception and comprehension are interpretive processes, that interpretations are constrained by prior experience and that an interpretation constrained in the wrong way might fail to trigger retrieval of the crucial knowledge elements, so the problem solver creates an inappropriately constrained solution space. The occurrence of an unwarranted impasse is massively contingent on the exact structure of a person's knowledge network. In principle, every person has a unique life trajectory and hence a unique knowledge network, but subjects in experiments on insight – mostly college students in Western universities – share enough cultural background that there are in practice enough similarities across individuals for some problems to reliably trigger impasses. This is the source of the persistent but erroneous intuition that some problems are insight problems in some intrinsic sense.

How Impasses Are Resolved

The cause of unwarranted impasses is half the explanation for the insight sequence. The other half is the mechanism by which impasses are resolved. If the initial representation of the problem constrains the search space in unproductive ways by not retrieving the most useful knowledge elements, how can this state of affairs ever change? The problem solver is trapped in a circle: Because he thinks about the problem in a particular way, he retrieves certain concepts, schemas, strategies and so on. Because he retrieves those particular knowledge elements, he thinks about the problem in the particular way that is consistent with them. To explain how impasses are resolved is to specify a mechanism that enables the mind to break out of this unproductive circle.

Only change begets change, so the problem appears intractable: If we attribute an insight to some cause C, then we have merely moved our focus one step backward in the causal chain. To complete the explanation, we have to explain why C happened when it did rather than earlier or later; this is presumably due to some prior cause C'; and so on. All explanations of insight that postulate special insight processes are undermined by this regress. A genuine explanation has to terminate the regress, preferably by showing that impasse and insight are two sides of the same coin.

Impasses cannot be resolved by pushing forward, searching deeper in the inappropriately constrained space. Instead, the problem solver must draw back to the initial problem representation to leap in a new direction. In the words of Newell, Simon and J. C. Shaw: "What is needed in these cases [that require an unconventional response] is not an elimination of the selective power of a solution generator, but the replacement of the inappropriate generator by an appropriate one."[43]

The triggering factor for this change is the problem-solving effort itself. Persistent but unsuccessful solution attempts cause negative feedback to be passed back down the layers of processing units. The experience of failure – more generally, a negative evaluation of the outcome of a problem-solving step – causes activation to be subtracted from the processing units that were instrumental in producing it. If a unit P is involved in generating a result or outcome R through option O, and R is evaluated negatively, then the activation of O is decreased. If alternative options O', O'', ..., are available in P, and if the person continues to attend to the problem, the balance among the options is altered. O will eventually lose out to some competing option even though O was preferred initially.

The change in P propagates upward through the layers of processing, potentially causing a qualitative change in the problem representation in working memory. This in turn alters the distribution of activation over memory, which might cause potentially useful but hitherto unheeded knowledge elements to be retrieved. The ultimate consequence is that the heuristic search process moves through a different solution space.

The core of this *redistribution theory* of insight is a specification of the exact conditions under which the process of responding to negative feedback with gradually lowered activation levels will produce a qualitative change in the problem representation. Consider a choice point (processing unit) in the visual system with, for example, three different outbound options. The argument proceeds through six hypotheses that jointly constitute sufficient conditions for insight; that is, for the involuntary and unexpected passage of a previously unheeded option into consciousness after a period without progress.

First, each choice point is associated with a certain amount of activation. To a first approximation, the amount of activation can be thought of as the sum of the activations contributed by the inputs to the unit. This assumption is familiar from network theories of all kinds.

Second, the activation associated with a choice point is distributed across its outbound links (options) in proportion to their relative strengths. The strength of an option measures past experience; more precisely, it is proportional to the frequency with which that option has been executed, how often it has been associated with success or failure, the expected payoff if it is executed, the estimated cost or effort of execution and perhaps other variables as well. The strength determines the proportion of activation allocated to an option when the choice point is active.

Third, there is a *threshold* such that when the activation associated with a choice point is distributed over the outbound options, some options might rise above threshold, while others remain below. Options that are above threshold pass activation and information – the result of whatever computation the processing unit performs – onto the next processing layer. Options that receive a level of activation less than the threshold remain dormant or unheeded. That is, neither activation nor information is passed along those links, nor is excitatory or inhibitory activation passed sideways from them to other units within the relevant layer. Unlike most network theories, the present theory assumes that forward propagation is selective.

Fourth, when an option is executed, its activation level is affected by subsequent events. A negative outcome can be either an internal evaluation of a problem state in the mind's eye (*this is not going to work*) or the perception of a physical or undesirable outcome (*that didn't work*). This outcome is fed back to all choice points that were instrumental in producing it. The effect of the negative feedback is to subtract a certain amount of activation from the relevant option or options. Presumably, the amount of activation lost is a function of multiple variables, including the importance of the problem and the severity of the negative feedback. We would expect a painful outcome in a matter of great importance to have a greater effect than a minor annoyance with respect to something trivial. The structure of the present argument is not dependent on the exact function that determines the activation decrement. It is sufficient that the activation of an unsuccessful option is lowered by some amount.

Fifth, the activation subtracted from one option is *redistributed* over all other options associated with that option. The redistribution process can operate in different ways, but the simplest assumption is that the activation subtracted from an unsuccessful option is redistributed in proportion to the relative strengths of the other options at the same choice point. The result is that the option that was already tried now has a lower level of activation and the others a higher, by some amount.

Sixth, a processing unit that receives negative feedback passes that feedback down to the layer that precedes it. Its antecedents might thereby be pushed below threshold, in which case the unit loses its own inputs. The effect is that the unit turns itself off. This restricts the solution space, because fewer options are considered. But cognitive processes and structures are always competing against their alternatives. A processing unit represents options, but it also places constraints on its rivals via inhibitory, within-layer links. If a unit becomes dormant, its inhibitory activity ceases. Turning off a choice point relaxes whatever constraints it imposed on the alternatives to the options it represents. This gives other, competing choice points a chance to become active and propagate activation and information along their outbound links, so the overall effect can be to widen the search space.

A processing unit that implements the six redistribution principles will exhibit alterations in mode and tempo like those that define the insight sequence. To demonstrate this, I embedded the redistribution principles in a computer model of a single processing unit with two input links and three

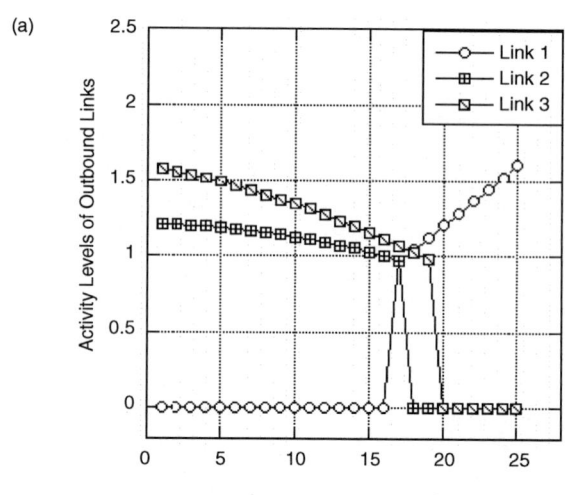

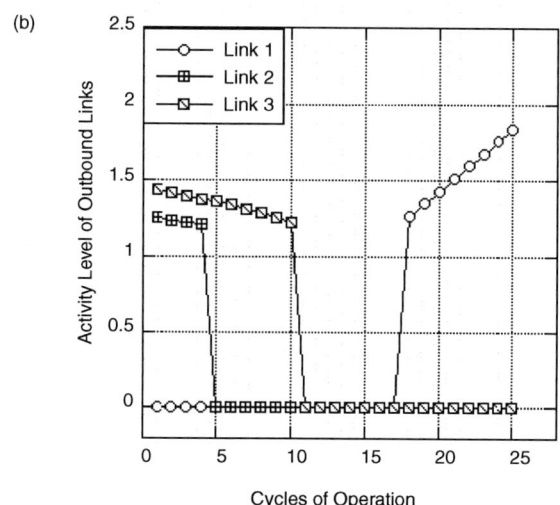

FIGURE 4.4. Results from a simulation of a single processing unit. Panel (a) shows analytical, routine processing. Panel (b) shows an impasse followed by an insight event.

output links.[44] Figure 4.4 shows some results obtained with the model. In all cases, all the output links but one produced negative feedback. Panel (a) shows a case of routine problem solving; no impasse. Panel (b) shows the insight case: A previously dormant option suddenly rises above threshold after an impasse and the previously explored options fall below threshold and cease to be considered.

A key feature of this explanation is that nothing extra or unusual is happening at the moment of insight. Both perseverance and insight are produced by the same redistribution process. In every cycle of operation, some option is tried, its outcome evaluated, and feedback is propagated down through the system. In each choice point, negative feedback causes a certain amount of activation to be subtracted from the unsuccessful option and redistributed across all other options. This is what is happening when the person perseveres with an unsuccessful approach, and also what is happening when a person has an unexpected insight that leads to the solution. There is no difference in the nature of the processing that occurs at those two qualitatively different types of mental events. The difference between perseverance and insight is not due to different cognitive processes but depends on the relative initial activation levels, the threshold, the amounts of positive and negative feedback, the decay rate and other factors. That is, the difference emerges out of the interactions among the structure of the processing system, the current strengths and activation levels, the location of the threshold and the evaluations of the outcomes. The punctuated nature of insight is not built into these processes, but emerges in their interactions.

The computer model simulates the behavior of a single processing unit. The hypothesis is that our perceptual systems comprise tens of thousands, perhaps hundreds of thousands, of processing units, each of which functions in accordance with the six redistribution principles. The behavior of the overall system is a function of the structure of the network – which nodes are linked and by which type of link – and the exact strengths and activation levels. In some cases, subtracting and redistributing activation in one of the choice points will have no effect. The option with the highest activation might still be the most active option even after negative feedback has caused some of its activation to be lost. If so, then the result is perseverance; that is, the problem solver keeps pursuing the same approach to the problem, although the approach is known not to work. Perseverance is often observed in laboratory studies of insight.

Another possibility is that the rank order of the activation levels of the above-threshold options is revised when activation is subtracted and redistributed. If the most-active option in the new rank ordering was above threshold to begin with, no novel option comes to mind, but the person's behavior changes. He pursues another of the options that came to mind initially. If the second option is also unsuccessful, control might pass to yet another of the above-threshold options. Behaviorally, this appears to an observer as a deliberate, heuristic search.

If the problem solver persists in the face of failure, the activation levels of the above-threshold options will gradually approach the threshold, and the below-threshold options will rise correspondingly. Eventually, one or more of the previously dormant or unheeded options available in some processing unit will rise above threshold and pass information and activation along to the next layer. The change at that processing unit is *propagated* onto the next layer of processing, which in turn will alter the processing at that layer; and so on.

As the wave of changes propagates from layer to layer, different outcomes are possible. The change might be *dampened*. That is, the alteration at layer N might have little impact on layer $N+1$ and the change might eventually fade without causing a change in the top layer, that is, in the person's problem representation. On the other hand, the change might be *amplified* as it passes from layer to layer, ultimately affecting the problem representation and possibly direct the problem-solving effort down a novel path. The subjective experience that accompanies such an event is likely to include relief at being freed from the impasse and a corresponding enthusiasm for exploring the new option (*wait a minute, I can do this ...*). Which outcome will occur in any one situation is massively contingent on the exact structure of the person's knowledge network and the exact strengths and activation layers as determined by prior experience.

If a representational change is ultimately triggered by a change in a single processing unit, why is the change holistic in character? Why do problem representations not change the way a digital screen picture would change if a single pixel were changed? Within each layer, the mutual excitation-inhibition links between the units in that layer keep the different parts of the interpretation consistent with each other. As the wave of changes travels upward, it is subject to integrative and synthesizing processing within each layer. The result is that, as the Gestalt psychologists insisted, the entire problem representation undergoes change.[45] Each part is reinterpreted or understood differently; furthermore, each part is reinterpreted in such a way that the parts fit together in a coherent, qualitatively different whole. Reversible figures such as the Necker cube provide a model: When the Necker cube flips for the observer, each part of the figure – each corner, edge and side – is reinterpreted and the parts are all interpreted in such a way that they fit together and make up a coherent perception of the cube. The holistic nature of the change is, in part, why a representational change can be subjectively striking to the person to whom it happens.

Once the representation in working memory has been revised, additional changes follow. The elements of the new representation serve as new retrieval probes, nodes from which activation spreads through memory. As a result, previously dormant but potentially useful knowledge items – cognitive operations – are retrieved; they suddenly "come to mind," as we say. Newly retrieved actions, reasoning schemas and subgoals will in turn trigger the retrieval of previously unheeded heuristics to control their application. The upshot is that the heuristic search mechanism is operating within a different search space. The cognitive system has leaped sideways to override the imperatives of its own prior knowledge. The new search space is also constrained, but constrained in a different way and hence might include a workable solution. In summary, unit alterations in problem perception caused by the downward propagation of feedback cause changes in the problem representation, which in turn causes the retrieval of previously unheeded knowledge elements from long-term memory; the latter define a different search space.

This hypothesis explains why problem solvers sometimes cease overt activity, including concurrent verbalization, during an impasse. A person trapped in an impasse is not in the same mental state as someone who has disengaged from problem solving. The thinker is absorbed in the problem; he is concentrating. His brain is busy propagating negative feedback down the processing layers, recomputing the balance between options in individual processing units and propagating the consequences back up to working memory, where changes will trigger knowledge retrieval by altering the distribution of activation over long-term memory, which in turn will trigger look-ahead in the new search space. These processes conspire to create a false impression of passivity, for two reasons. First, representational change processes do not correspond to any particular overt behaviors. One does not spread activation with a shovel. Second, representational processes tend to occur outside consciousness. Immediately before an insight, the problem solver does not know any better than an observer what is going on in his mind. He feels compelled to concentrate on the problem, but he has little to say about what he is doing, much to the chagrin of the psychologist who wants to know what happens as an impasse is resolved.

Aftermath: Pursuing the New Option

What happens after the insight event? If breaking an impasse produces a change in representation that triggers a change in what is retrieved from memory, why does the problem solver sometimes feel as if the complete solution suddenly came to mind at the moment the impasse was resolved?

According to the redistribution theory, this subjective experience is illusory. The solution is always constructed piecemeal, but under some circumstances the construction is so rapid and effortless that it leaves little or no trace in consciousness. It is possible to specify those circumstances with some precision.

If a problem solver could extend his look-ahead – his mental search through the space of possible solutions – all the way to the goal, then there would be no further uncertainty, no more false starts and no dead ends. If he can see the entire path to the goal in his mind's eye, he merely needs to carry out the actions on that path in the physical solution space. Trial and error thinking – look-ahead – preempts trial and error action.

But mental look-ahead is limited by working memory capacity.[46] Cognitive psychologists have not yet reached a consensus about the nature of this capacity limit.[47] The alternatives include a finite amount of activation, interference, rapid decay, small storage space and an inability to inhibit distracting information. From the point of view of the theory of insight, the important point is that capacity is limited (somehow). Mental look-ahead cannot illuminate a large region of the solution space; it only reveals the immediate vicinity of the current problem state. For novices working in an unfamiliar solution space, the *horizo*n of mental look-ahead is likely to be only a few steps away.

What happens when one or more previously unheeded options come to mind depends on the distance between the state in which the insight occurred and the goal state, taken in relation to the horizon of mental look-ahead. The variable of interest is the number of steps required to reach the goal from the problem state in which the impasse is resolved. If working memory capacity allows look-ahead to extend a maximum of n steps into the search space, and the goal is more than n steps away, then mental look-ahead cannot reveal the entire solution. In this case, the insight is followed by continued analytical problem solving, complete with backups, errors, search, uncertainty and perhaps further impasses. In this case, there is no subjective feeling of seeing the entire solution in the mind's eye, only relief at being able to think of a new approach. This is *partial insight*.

If, on the other hand, the goal is fewer than n steps away from the state in which the impasse was resolved, then the remaining path to the goal fits within the horizon of mental look-ahead. Because n is small – at most half a dozen steps – the construction of the new path in the mind's eye can happen quickly. The problem solver will experience the resolution of the impasse and the construction of the path to the goal as a single event. This is *full insight*. The illusion

Creative Insight: The Redistribution Theory

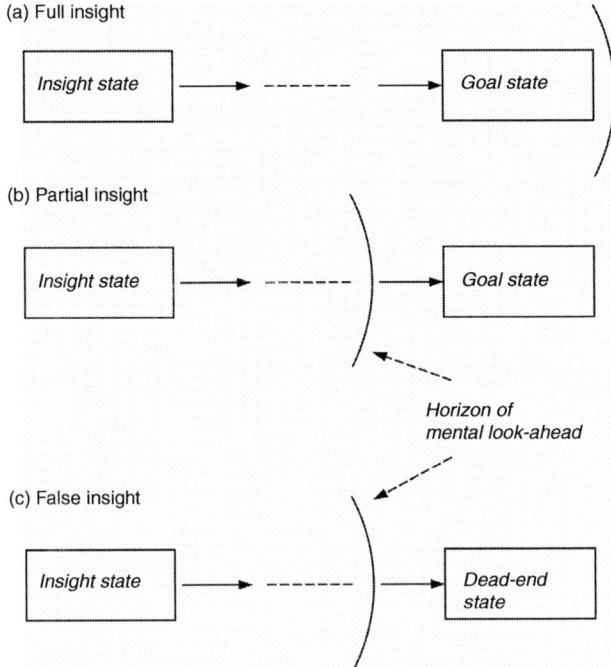

FIGURE 4.5. The relations among full, partial and false insight.

that the entire solution presented itself to consciousness is caused by the lack of introspective access to the process of look-ahead. This hypothesis makes the strong prediction that the subjective experience of suddenly seeing the entire solution in the mind's eye will accompany only those insights that occur when the problem solver is close to the goal state. This is consistent with the fact that the problems that are traditionally designated as insight problems have short solutions.

Finally, it is possible that the insight event and its consequences create a new search space that is as inappropriate or unproductive as the previous one. Analytical problem solving in the new space has two possible outcomes: Either the problem solver leaps to yet another search space, or the problem-solving effort eventually fails. This is *false insight*. See Figure 4.5 for the relation between full, partial and false insight.

It follows that insight events, especially full insights, are massively contingent. They depend on the fine-grained details of the problem solver's prior knowledge. To predict whether a person will experience an insight if he tries to solve a certain problem, we would have to know the exact biases that will shape his initial representation of the problem. We would have to know the exact content and structure of his memory network, including the strength of each link along which activation might spread. To predict the point in the heuristic search at which he will encounter an impasse, we would need to know which heuristics he is likely to apply. It is impossible to know the content of another person's mind at this level of detail, so the occurrence or nonoccurrence of individual insight events is in practice unpredictable. Mind is as massively contingent as other complex systems.

ANSWERS TO THE CREATIVITY QUESTIONS

Alterations in mode and tempo of creative problem solving are caused by complex interactions among multiple cognitive processes. The initial perception of a problem serves as a retrieval probe and the retrieved knowledge elements shape the initial solution space. For analytical thinking to proceed without being blown up in a combinatorial explosion, knowledge has to be brought to bear on the current problem to constrain the set of possibilities considered. Certain options appear more likely to lead to the solution than others and hence are tried first. If prior experience – the biases embedded in the relative strengths and activation levels of perceptual processing units and the links that connect them – does not extrapolate to the problem at hand, the initial solution space might not contain the desired solution and an impasse results. The only cure for this is to draw back to leap: The constraints imposed by prior knowledge must be relaxed, so as to open up a wider space of possibilities. Continued attention to the problem generates feedback that eventually shifts the balance among one or more links. If a previously dormant link rises above threshold, the change might propagate upward through the processing layers and alter the contents of working memory. This might lead to the retrieval of previously unheeded but potentially useful knowledge elements, including actions and inference rules. Heuristic search resumes in the revised search space. Once again, the trick to progress is to constrain the set of options in the new search space so as not to get lost in the maze of possibilities. But every constraint threatens to exclude the desired solution from the set of paths considered, and every time an impasse is encountered, some constraint or constraints have to be relaxed. Creative problem solving oscillates between imposing and relaxing constraints.

How does this theory answer the four creativity questions posed in Chapter 3? First, how are novel ideas possible? Human cognition operates with representations, and representations have parts. They are structured combinations of simpler representations, and they can be revised by reordering and replacing their parts. A representation is an interpretation, not a recording of objective reality, so a problem does not determine its own representation; alternative interpretations are always possible. A system that is able to represent is thereby also able to represent differently.

Second, what are the key features that distinguish creative processes and justify calling them creative? In analytical thinking, the initial solution space contains the desired solution, so the latter can be found by heuristic search through that space. In creative processes, the analytical processing is punctuated by one or more representational changes that revise the search space. Creativity is a categorical dimension; any one thought process either contains at least one non-monotonic representational change or it does not.

Third, what gives direction to the creative process? According to the present theory, the main determinant is the structure of the person's processing network. The amount of negative feedback and how it is propagated downward through the processing layers will determine which links are suppressed, and the content of the network will determine which options come to mind instead. The direction of an insight event is massively contingent and for all practical purposes unpredictable.

Fourth, what are the limiting factors? Why is it difficult to create? Our brains are wired to constrain the options we consider by projecting prior experience onto the present. Due to our evolutionary history, our disposition to push forward, to apply prior knowledge more energetically or with more care, is stronger than our disposition to draw back to leap. This bias is effective within tight contexts – that is, in stable, local situations of short duration. For the mind to override its own bias, it must feed information back down the processing layers to tip the balance among the options at some choice point or another. But the relevant information might not be available. Not all task environments are transparent with respect to the effects of actions. Negative feedback might also be lacking because the motivation for persistence in the face of failure is not present. Even if the person persists, the feedback might not be strong enough to overcome the built-in bias to push forward instead of drawing back to leap. Finally, no amount of feedback will help, if the person's mind is not prepared. It must contain the knowledge needed to construct the alternative representation. Representational change can only resolve *unwarranted* impasses. The redistribution theory thus answers the four creativity questions.

EVALUATION

The evaluation of a complicated scientific theory is a multifaceted affair that includes assessments of the conceptual clarity and internal coherence of the theory, its explanatory power, completeness, simplicity, support from empirical studies, relations to other theories, practical usefulness and other factors as well. The evaluation process sometimes takes decades, and widespread acceptance of a theory is rarely due to the work of a single person or laboratory. The evaluation of the redistribution theory has hardly begun. The previous sections implicitly argue for its clarity, internal consistency and explanatory power. The present section discusses completeness, simplicity, empirical support and relations to other theories.

Completeness and Simplicity

The redistribution theory reduces the insight sequence to cognitive processes that are so simple that they can be completely explained in mechanistic terms. All of the basic processes and structures postulated by the theory (layered perceptual processing, memory retrieval via spread of activation, heuristic search, limited working memory capacity, mental look-ahead, feedback propagation, etc.) have been modeled by running computer simulations.[48] Breakdown into processes of yet smaller scope would take us into neurophysiology. Raising or lowering the activation of a memory link cannot be analyzed further at the cognitive level, but has to be explicated in terms of neural matter. The task of analyzing insight into processes that are so simple that they do not cry out for further analysis has therefore been completed. There is no homunculus waiting to be discharged in the redistribution theory, no black insight box in the flow diagram and no leftover component to be explicated another day.

Furthermore, the theory is innocent of exotic claims. None of the processes presupposed by the theory were postulated specifically to explain insight phenomena. On the contrary, cognitive psychologists routinely draw upon them to explain a variety of phenomena, many of which have little to do with the production of novelty.[49] That perception and comprehension are constructive, interpretive processes guided by prior experience is the standard view, supported by countless studies and a variety of phenomena from visual illusions and priming effects to perspective shifts during reading.

Also, there is nothing controversial about the claim that information in memory might fail to come to mind when needed. The everyday experience of trying to recall a person's name, failing to do so but then spontaneously succeeding a few minutes later is a case in point. This phenomenon has been documented in laboratory studies under the label *the tip-of-the-tongue phenomenon*.[50] In studies of list learning, Endel Tulving and co-workers noticed that successive attempts to recall a list, first without and then with retrieval cues, often resulted in better recall on the second, cued, attempt.[51] If an item on the list is recalled in attempt *N+1* it must be encoded in memory, so if it was not recalled on some previous attempt *N*, then the retrieval process failed to access it and deliver it to working memory on that occasion, even though the item was in fact available in memory. Failure to retrieve previously stored information in the course of problem solving is also commonly observed in educational research, where it is called *inert knowledge*. The existence of retrieval failure is so uncontroversial as to be a standard topic in textbooks in cognitive psychology.

The hypothesis that cognitive structures are associated with different levels of activation is also a standard component of theories of human cognition. It plays a central role in theories of memory, decision making and perception. That working memory, and hence mental look-ahead, is limited with respect to capacity is perhaps the most basic of all cognitive principles. The psychological reality of mental look-ahead and heuristic search is supported by think-aloud studies of problem solving. Finally, the notion of a threshold is neither exotic nor ad hoc. Neural matter exhibits such a threshold: Individual neurons respond to incoming stimulation by passing on the signal, but only if the incoming stimulation is strong enough. The relation between a single neuron and a cognitive processing unit is at the present time unclear, but it is plausible that a processing unit that is built out of elements that operate with a threshold will itself exhibit threshold behavior. In short, the redistribution theory of insight relies entirely on concepts and principles that have independent support in cognitive research.

The theory explains insight as a side effect of the same processes that are involved in analytical thinking. The cognitive processes that are executing in the mind of the person who experiences insight are the same as those running in the mind of the same person a minute earlier, or of another person who is unable to think of a new idea. At each moment, feedback is propagated through the system and activation is redistributed over all available options in each relevant processing unit. This point cannot be stated strongly enough: *According to the redistribution theory, the experience of creative insight is a consequence of the same cognitive processes as the experience of being at an impasse; the processes that generate a novel approach are the same processes that produce perseverance in an unsuccessful approach. No additional process is assumed to be executing at the moment of insight over and above those that execute at any other moment during problem solving.* The difference in outcome is entirely a function of differences in the amount of activation, the amount and content of the feedback, the activation and strength levels associated with the various knowledge elements and their relations to the activation threshold. For some values on those parameters, the interactions among the basic processes will generate an insight; for other values, those same processes will produce an analytical solution or a terminal impasse.

As did the Gestalters, the present theory claims that insight during problem solving is rooted in perception, even though the relation is conceptualized differently. According to the present theory, a change in problem perception affects problem solving indirectly, by affecting the problem representation. This starts a cascade of changes: New working memory elements alter the distribution of activation over long-term memory, which leads to the retrieval of unheeded knowledge elements, which in turn opens up new options, so the heuristic search mechanism faces different choices. The contemporary understanding of the cognitive system provides precise causal links that replace the inexplicable goodness gradient of the Gestalt theory.

Experimental Grounding

The redistribution theory provides an in-principle explanation of the insight sequence. If it is accurate, it should help us understand results, regularities and patterns in the data from particular insight experiments. Articulating an abstract theory vis-à-vis a specific instance often requires auxiliary principles that mediate between the general mechanism and the specific situation in which its operation is observed, similar to the way in which the effects of air resistance mediate between the Newtonian principle of constant gravitational acceleration and the observable fact that feathers fall slower than marbles. Two such auxiliary principles have emerged in the work of myself and my associates and collaborators. Both principles address the most striking property of the classical insight problems: the gap between their objective simplicity and their subjective difficulty.

The first principle addresses the question of why two problems with very similar solutions can vary drastically in their difficulty. The *Principle of Scope* claims that the larger the scope of the representational change that is required to solve a problem, the lower the probability that the change will be achieved in a given time period. The term "scope" refers to the proportion of the mental representation that needs to be revised to bring the productive options to mind. The larger the required change, the lower the probability that it will occur.

(a) An easy Match Stick Arithmetic problem

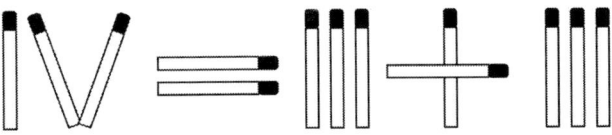

(b) A difficult Match Stick Arithmetic problem

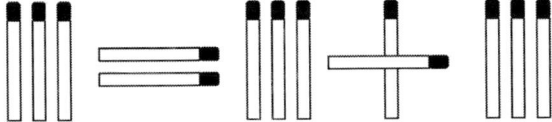

FIGURE 4.6. Two examples of Match Stick Arithmetic Problems.

This idea was put to the test by Guenter Knoblich and myself in a series of experiments with so-called Match Stick Arithmetic Problems, puzzles that exhibit a strong mismatch between prior experience and the requirements of the problem.[52] In such a problem, the goal is to correct an incorrect arithmetic equation, written in Roman numerals made out of match sticks, by moving exactly one match stick to another place in the equation. Figure 4.6 shows two examples of this type of problem. The solutions to all Match Stick Arithmetic Problems used in our studies consist of exactly one step. There is little doubt that an average educated adult in Western culture will spontaneously activate his arithmetic knowledge when confronted with such a problem. But to solve it, he has to override the constraints normally followed in arithmetic. The solution requires actions that are not valid in arithmetic.

Consider the differences between problems 1 and 2 in Figure 4.6. Each problem requires a single step and so has the same objective difficulty. Nevertheless, we found in a series of experiments that the second problem is more difficult than the first. The general principle of mismatches to prior knowledge does not suffice to explain this difference, because both problems will activate unhelpful arithmetic knowledge.

Guenther Knoblich and I hypothesized that the differentiating factor is the scope of the representational shift that has to take place. To solve the top problem, the person only has to override the constraint on altering the numbers in an equation, while leaving the structure of the equation intact. To solve the bottom problem, the structure and meaning of the entire equation have to be revised. Precise analysis of exactly which constraints have to be relaxed to solve a given

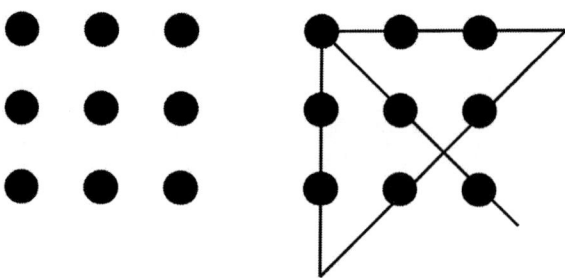

FIGURE 4.7. The Nine-Dot Problem and its solution.

problem allowed us to predict with precision the rank order of the difficulty of such problems, the effects of repeated exposures and even the distribution of visual attention over different components of the problem, as well as changes in that distribution over time. These findings strongly support the theory, because there is no other obvious explanation for these differences in difficulty.

The second principle also addresses the gap between subjective and objective difficulty. Why do college students stare for minutes on end at a problem that only requires a short sequence of actions that they are entirely capable of carrying out? Trina Kershaw and I explored this question in the context of the Nine-Dot Problem: The goal is to draw four straight lines that go through all nine dots, without backtracking or lifting the pen from the paper.[53] Figure 4.7 shows the problem and its solution. Kershaw proposed the *Principle of Multiple Difficulties*, which says that the subjective difficulty of an objectively simply puzzle is caused by the combined action of multiple cognitive constraints, each representing a small representational change that is required before the most productive option comes to mind.

Specifically, we hypothesized that the Nine-Dot Problem, though simple, contains three distinct sources of difficulty: that lines should be drawn outside the square; that lines should turn in a place where there is no dot; and that the solution requires diagonal lines. In each case, we could identify prior experiences that would bias thinking away from the useful option. If this is the right analysis, then providing help on one of these aspects of the problem should help a little, but only a little. To boost the solution rate in a group of subjects to the vicinity of 100%, it is necessary to provide help on all three aspects. These predictions were supported in a series of experiments.

Although the consistency between theory and these experiments is positive, the experiments constitute only a weak test of the theory. The expectations that shaped these experiments are consistent with common sense.

The *Scope* and *Multiplicity* principles are explications of the intuitive ideas that a representational change is more difficult to achieve, the larger it is, and that relaxing several constraints is more difficult than relaxing a single constraint. More stringent experimental tests have to await the derivation of yet other predictions from the theory. The main strength of the theory is that it improves on prior theories.

Relations to Prior Theories

Experimental psychologists tend to believe that scientific progress is served by pitting theories against each other in a race for the best account of the data. Although philosophers and historians of science agree that competitive comparison is an important part of scientific method, psychologists' advocacy of this procedure is overdone. Theories are only in competition with one another when two conditions are satisfied: Both theories aim to explain the same phenomena, and the two theories are mutually exclusive in the strong sense that if one theory is true, the other cannot also be true. In practice, these two conditions hold less frequently than philosophers have assumed, and they hardly ever hold in cognitive psychology. The more common case is that two or more theories address different phenomena or make different but compatible assertions. Research articles that present two or more equally plausible but mutually exclusive theories and compare their relative fit to data are in fact quite rare.

I see the task of theory building differently. There is no possibility that any single principle or process will turn out to explain every aspect of human cognition, or even every feature of insight, so we should hesitate to throw away potentially useful principles and instead make the most of each one. Principles proposed by different researchers are sometimes synonymous once we look behind differences in terminology; they are more often complementary than contradictory; and they are occasionally related as special case to general principle. Researchers should identify those relations and assemble a repertoire of explanatory principles that enable us to understand as many aspects of creative insight as possible. Theory building should proceed through critical analysis and conceptual synthesis rather than through selection by competition.

Alternative explanations for impasses?
The idea that impasses are caused by unhelpful prior knowledge has been rediscovered multiple times. The Gestalt psychologists advanced two principles to

explain why people fail to make progress on a problem that they are capable of solving. In his 1935 monograph *Zur Psychologie des productiven Denkens*, Karl Duncker, one of the Gestalt psychologists, advanced the idea that familiar objects are encoded in memory in terms of their common functions, as opposed to (or in addition to) their physical attributes.[54] A hammer is encoded as something to strike a nail with as well as something that is heavy, long and metallic. When we perceive an object, we automatically retrieve from memory its familiar function and we spontaneously think about it in terms of that function. This hypothesis became entrenched in the English research literature as *functional fixedness*. The reality of functional fixedness is not in doubt; it can easily be produced in the laboratory.[55] But many problems that produce unwarranted impasses do not involve the use of any objects, familiar or otherwise, or do not require that those objects are used in any novel way. In solving the Nine-Dot Problem the person uses a pen or pencil in its standard function of drawing lines on paper. Functional fixedness is not an alternative explanation of unwarranted impasses, but merely a special case of the general principle that impasses are caused by the activation of unhelpful prior knowledge, applicable only when the relevant prior knowledge pertains to the common uses of familiar objects.

Abraham H. Luchins demonstrated that training can make a person blind to possible solutions.[56] In the Water Jar Problem, a person starts with a water supply and three unmarked beakers of known volume, and the goal is to end up with a certain amount of water in the largest beaker.[57] Luchins showed that if subjects are given a sequence of problems that require a long solution S, and then a problem that can be solved by the long solution and also by a shorter solution S', they will as a rule overlook the shorter solution. This effect has entered psychology under the German term *Einstellung*; the English word *set* has a very similar meaning. Like functional fixedness, Einstellung is merely a special case of the general principle that activation of unhelpful biases – in this case, biases acquired as a result of training deliberately contrived to mislead – causes unwarranted impasses.

More recent rediscoveries of this principle include the concept of a mental rut and the constraining effects of expertise on problem solving.[58] In research on skill acquisition, the same idea is discussed under the terms *automaticity*, *capture errors*, *negative transfer*, *negative priming* and *task switch costs*, as if every generation and every group of researchers feel a need to make the phenomenon their own by giving it a new name. Because the data gathered to document the specific cases lend support to the general principle, the latter has a broad basis and can be considered established.

Edward P. Chronicle, James N. MacGregor and Thomas C. Ormerod have advanced an explanation for unwarranted impasses that contributes something new.[59] They propose that subjects in insight experiments, and problem solvers generally, translate their understanding of the problem at hand into a sense of what it means to make progress. What does a productive step look like? In the N-Balls Problem there are, for example, 9 indistinguishable balls, 8 weighing the same and one weighing slightly more, and the task is to find the heavier one with two, and only two, uses of a balance scale.[60] A plausible notion of progress is to weigh as many balls as possible in the first round, to have as few left to process with that single remaining round. In the 9-Balls Problem, this will cause an impasse, because a 4-against-4 weighing could leave the problem solver with 4 balls to choose among, a situation that cannot be resolved with the single remaining weighing. There is no a priori reason to doubt the progress criterion principle, and the experiments reported by Chronicle, MacGregor and Ormerod provide strong support. The maximal progress explanation for impasses emphasizes decision heutistics while the unhelpful knowledge explanation emphasizes problem perception and memory retrieval. The relative prevalence of situations in which an impasse is rooted in the activation of unhelpful prior knowledge and situations in which it is better described as rooted in an inappropriate progress criterion is unknown.

Resolving impasses: A role for forgetting?
There are multiple alternative explanations for the resolution of impasses. A popular idea is that it helps to "sleep on it." More precisely, the claim is that the probability of finding the solution is higher after setting the problem aside for a period of time, as compared with continued efforts to solve the problem for the same amount of time. This notion is often ascribed to the Gestalt psychologists, but it was first named by Graham Wallas, who in 1926 suggested that creative problem solving follows a sequence of four phases called *preparation* (studying the problem to grasp its requirements and the goal), *incubation* (temporarily setting the problem aside), *illumination* (the spontaneous transition into consciousness of the problem and the solution, typically in some unrelated context) and *verification* (executing the solution).[61] Wallas's 1926 theory is sometimes cited as if it were the latest word on creativity.[62] His four-stage formulation has become so firmly entrenched in the culture of creativity studies that it has become common sense, and the concept of incubation and even the four stages are sometimes mentioned without acknowledging Wallas.

Wallas's four-stage sequence is similar to the insight sequence in that it is also a pattern of alterations in mode and tempo, but with the crucial difference that an impasse is not an incubation period. During an impasse, the problem solver is passive in the sense that he is not making progress, but this passivity is enforced rather than voluntary; he does not know what to do next. During an incubation period the problem solver decides to set the problem aside. While it is true that people sometimes resolve impasses in the course of continued attention to a problem, it can also be true that the probability of resolving an impasse sometimes increases after a rest period. We lack data on which of these two patterns is most prevalent but as long as both occur at least sometimes, both require explanation. But principles proposed to explain incubation effects are not in competition with principles that explain the resolution of impasses; the two sets of principles are complementary.

The literature on incubation is not extensive.[63] C. A. Kaplan reviewed 18 studies, 12 of which provided positive evidence for incubation. The support is not overwhelming but sufficient to make it more likely than not that a pause can help. Why might it help to pause? It is paradoxical that doing nothing can be more productive than doing something. One repeatedly rediscovered possibility is that the pause allows the problem solver to forget the unproductive approach. In the words of R. W. Weisberg:

> ... forgetting is what is needed. A person may be unable to solve a problem because he or she is approaching it in the wrong way. If so, a break might enable them to forget the incorrect approach, thereby making it easier to think of a different, potentially more successful approach.[64]

The problem with the forgetting explanation is that it does not explain why the incorrect representation is not re-activated after the pause. If a problem activates a certain representation when it is first encountered, then why would it not activate that same representation when the problem solver returns to the problem after the rest period? If the initial encounter with the problem is a race between an unhelpful and a helpful representation, the forgetting that occurs during the rest period will affect both representations equally. Forgetting, by itself, does not explain how or why the balance between the two representation shifts during the rest period. The forgetting hypothesis must be supplemented with an auxiliary hypothesis about differential rates of forgetting to be a viable explanation.

Simon proposed an explanation of this sort.[65] He postulated that control information, including subgoals, decays at a faster rate than factual information about a problem. In addition, he assumed that factual information is only accessible in the context of the subgoal that was in effect when the information was learned, but becomes generally accessible when that subgoal fades from memory. These assumptions yield two predictions: First, a person might persist in following an unsuccessful approach to a problem, because factual information learned in the course of exploration might not be accessed when it is most needed. Second, when a person returns to a problem after a rest period, he is able to access all the factual information learned in the course of prior explorations and as a consequence constructs a different search space. These hypotheses are entirely ad hoc and have no independent support in psychological research. It is nevertheless possible that some version of the differential forgetting idea will turn out to be true.

Resolving impasses: The role of externalities
The oldest explanation for how an impasse is broken is embedded in the ancient story of the philosopher Archimedes' efforts to measure the volume of an elaborately wrought gold wreath without destroying it.[66] After several fruitless attempts, he decided to take a break and lowered himself into the classical version of a jaccuzzi. Seeing the water level rise, he realized that the volume of a body, no matter how irregular, is equal to the volume of the water that it displaces when submerged. The perception of the rising water level, an event seemingly unrelated to the problem of measuring the volume of irregular solids, triggered the activation of a previously unheeded but crucial fact.

Although the story is unlikely to be true, it is useful as a striking symbol for the general principle that fortuitous events in the environment might activate knowledge elements that are crucial for a problem solution, but which were nevertheless not activated by the problem solver's perception of the problem. Archimedes already knew, in some implicit sense, that a submerged body displaces a volume of water equal to its own volume, but this piece of knowledge was not activated by his initial, geometric approach to the problem.

Like many other ideas in the study of creativity, the principle of fortuitous reminding has been rediscovered multiple times since Archemedes. For example, Michael I. Posner wrote in 1973 that a pause provides an opportunity for "the chance occurrence of an external event which completes the solution. The external event might retrieve the incomplete solution and provide the missing association to complete it, leaving the subject aware only of the solution and not the event."[67] Colleen Seifert and co-workers have called this opportunistic assimilation or opportunistic reminding.[68] Ilan Yaniv and David E. Meyer added the twist that the initial attempts to solve the problem partially activate the required knowledge structures in memory, making the problem solver more prone to react to an accidental hint, should it happen to appear in the environment.[69] They called this *the memory-sensitization hypothesis*.

Patrick Langley and Randolph Jones have specified a computational mechanism for fortuitous reminding that adds yet another twist.[70] In their version of this idea, an impasse is particularly likely when the components of the problem representation have many connections in memory that go off in many different directions; this is called a *high fan* or a large *branching factor*. A high fan rapidly dissipates activation as it spreads and thereby lowers the probability that activation reaches the crucial knowledge elements. Fortuitous reminding might remedy this situation if the fan is smaller in the opposite direction, from the crucial knowledge elements toward the problem representation. Activation then might spread all the way, with the consequence that the concepts crucial for the solution and the problem appear simultaneously in consciousness. This *differential fan hypothesis* has not been tested empirically but was found to work well in computer simulations.

Paradoxically, fortuitous reminding explains the beneficial effect of a pause in a way that makes the pause itself irrelevant. The fortuitous event could happen in the very first second of the pause, and it would be as helpful as if it happened the next morning. Nothing happens during the pause except that attending to other matters and engaging in other activities provide opportunities for events that were not part of the initial representation of the problem to influence the distribution of activation over long-term memory. There are many sources of potentially relevant events: changes in the environment, remarks by co-workers, and so on.

There is no reason to doubt that fortuitous reminding can affect problem solving in the manner described. However, this principle is not a general theory of incubation effects, because it cannot explain those cases of incubation in which no such fortuitous event occurred. The prevalence of this type of incubation effect in real life is not known.

Resolving impasses: Laterality in spread of activation?
M. Jung-Beeman and co-workers have advanced a hypothesis about impasse resolution that relies on differences in how the two halves of the brain encode information, and consequent differences in the spreading of activation.[71] The basic idea is that if nodes are densely connected, there is a large fan, and activation does not travel very far from its source node. In a conceptual network, this means that a source node will very quickly activate many other nodes, but only closely related ones. If nodes are sparsely connected, activation will travel farther and activate more remotely associated nodes, albeit with a slight delay.

This idea explains why responses that require remote associations are delayed compared to responses that only require closely associated concepts. It has the disadvantage that it presupposes that knowledge is duplicated in the two brain hemispheres and encoded differently in each. The hypothesis explains well what happens in remote association tasks, but it is not clear how it applies to complex problem-solving tasks.

Assembling a Complete Theory

The redistribution theory proposed in this chapter emphasizes the constraining effects of unhelpful prior knowledge as the cause of unwarranted impasses. The two Gestalt principles of functional fixedness and Einstellung are not competing explanations but special cases of the prior knowledge principle. The idea of a progress criterion adds a new twist but is compatible and complementary rather than competing. Likewise, the present theory emphasizes the power of negative feedback to resolve impasses by affecting the balance between competing options. Impasses are not incubation periods, but the two are similar enough to make explanations for positive incubation effects relevant for a theory of insight. The two principles of differential rates of forgetting and of fortuitous reminding do not assume any other effect of failure than to convince the problem solver to take a pause. The pause, in turn, allows forgetting and fortuitous events to occur. If we construe these principles as rivals to the redistribution theory, we risk causing a battle about which theory is best. But the redistribution explanation for the resolution of impasses and the various explanations of incubation are not mutually exclusive and hence not in competition. In conjunction, they can explain a broader swath of creative thought processes than either principle by itself. In due time, we will possess a set of principles by which we can explain all such processes.

5

Creative Insight Writ Large

> *The Eureka act proper, the moment of truth experienced by the creative individual, is paralleled on the collective plane by the emergence ... of a new synthesis, brought about by a quick succession of individual discoveries.*
>
> Arthur Koestler[1]

The millennium A.D. 1000–2000 brought mind-boggling changes to the life of the average person. The French might insist that the more the human condition changes, the more it remains the same, but from the point of view of the average person, the change from farming with a handheld plow – a common activity in what was not yet Europe in A.D. 1000[2] – to trading stocks on the Internet is not superficial. Historical change is driven by the production of many different kinds of novelty. People change what they believe; improve their mastery over material processes; try different forms of economic, political and social organization; and struggle to formulate moral dictums by which they can live more happily. Considered at the millennial scale, the production of novelty is larger than life and mightier than the individual. The river of conceptual, technological and organizational inventions sweeps people along, sometimes to the tune of ineffectual protests about the loss of this or that value supposedly inherent in tradition.

The gap between laboratory studies of insight and historical change looks like the Grand Canyon of cognitive theory. The prospect of bridging it is daunting, and the construction will require more than the modest beginning attempted in this chapter. The purpose is to investigate to what extent the theory of insight is relevant for human affairs and to clarify how the production of novelty unfolds in realistic contexts. What and how much of what happens in significant creative projects can be explained by the principles about individual insight events proposed in Chapter 4? Which features cannot be so explained? Do additional features and change mechanisms, unrelated to those principles, emerge at higher system levels? The traditional strategy for how to build this kind of bridge is sterile, but the complex systems perspective provides an alternative.

GENERALIZATION VERSUS SCALING

Philosophers and psychologists often discuss the relevance of results from laboratory studies in terms of a hypothetical process called *generalization*. When generalizing, a person supposedly takes a statement that turned out to be true in one or a handful of situations and asserts that it is also true of other, similar situations. A simple example is to conclude that *golden retrievers are friendly* after meeting a few and finding them friendly. The notion of generalization has its roots in empiricist philosophy and it is deeply embedded in the culture of academic psychology.

Like other types of projections from past experience, generalization carries epistemic risk: How can we know the set of situations in which a particular assertion holds? The fact that a handful of golden retrievers turns out to be friendly does not, after all, guarantee that all golden retrievers are friendly; there could exist, somewhere, a retriever that is miserable and snaps at babies.[3] This much is common sense. The problem is that not even 10,000 friendly retrievers warrant the conclusion that *all* golden retrievers are friendly; a miserable one might nevertheless be lurking somewhere. N. Goodman and other philosophers have tried to pinpoint the conditions under which a projection from the observed to the not-yet-observed is warranted, without having produced a satisfying explanation of how such projections are supposed to work, and without producing a technique for generating valid generalizations in practical contexts. The root of the problem is that generalization is defined in terms of the size of the reference set; the concept "dog" is said to be more general than "retriever" because there are more dogs than retrievers. But this is only true at a single moment in time. Over infinite time, all reference sets are infinitely large, so this concept of "more general than" is incoherent.

Systems theory implies that the central concept in projecting knowledge gained from the study of simple situations onto more complex ones is not generality but *scale*. Everyday situations extend further in space, last longer and have more components than simplified laboratory situations. The question is how the processes that operate at small scale influence systems that are orders of magnitude greater along one or more dimensions.

Different sciences scale along different dimensions. One remarkable aspect of Newton's theory of mechanical motion is that it applies across levels of size and mass. It is equally applicable to the stone I throw in a creek and to a planet orbiting a star; indeed, to entire galaxies. Today this is so well established that we tend to forget how surprising it is. Before Newton there was no good reason to expect the physics of small objects to scale to the physics of the heavens, but it did.[4] Chemical regularities, on the other hand, do not scale with respect to temperature: A substance changes radically at its melting and boiling points, creating new chemical phenomena and hence forcing a division of chemistry into the study of solids, liquids and gases. The General Gas Law is precisely what the label claims, a law about gases; it does not apply to liquids.[5] Scaling moves along different dimensions in different types of systems. For each dimension some properties scale, others do not.

Scale is important because complex systems must be understood at different levels of description. But the properties of one level seldom matter at higher levels. Only gross properties of the units and processes of level N impact level $N+1$ directly.[6] Consider the limitation on our working memory capacity. It does not matter exactly *how* working memory capacity is limited (amount of activation? interference? storage space?), but it matters greatly *that* it is limited. This feature of our cognitive system constrains which cognitive strategies we can reliably execute without external memory aids and hence directly impacts higher-level thought processes.

As spelled out in Chapter 1, direct impact is one of four flavors of scaling.[7] In amplified, *cascading causation* – popularly known as butterfly effects – a property at system level N propagates upward to have a greater effect on level $N+1$, which in turn propagates so as to have an even greater effect on level $N+2$, and so on. A contrasting flavor of scaling is called *self-organization*. This concept applies to a system that consists of a very large number of similar components that interact according to rules that apply to each pairwise interaction. The components fall together into structures that are stable and exhibit properties that differ from the properties of their components. Self-organization is presumably what brain cells do in response to experience. A fourth flavor of scaling is *level-invariance*. The determinants of some patterns are independent of the material constitution of the relevant system, so the patterns recur at multiple system levels. Sometimes this is referred to as self-similarity; the system looks the same at each level of scale. Sometimes level-invariance comes about because the units at system level N exhibit some property P such that when multiple units are combined into a larger-scale unit, that unit also exhibits P. Direct impact, cascading causation, self-organization and level-invariance are not competing or mutually exclusive principles. The task is not to choose between them but to discern which flavor best explains any one phenomenon. A complex system is likely to be characterized by multiple potential scaling variables and we cannot know before we conduct the relevant analysis which scaling flavor is operating for a particular system and a particular variable.

Regardless of which flavor applies in a particular case, there is no reason to expect processes at level N to explain all patterns at $N+1$. Novel phenomena and patterns are likely to emerge at the higher levels, limiting the explanatory power of events at the lower levels and requiring explanation in terms of processes and mechanisms that are unique to the higher levels. Applied to the production of novelty, these observations generate three questions: Which characteristics of insight project onto higher levels of scale? What are the mechanisms of projection? Which novel characteristics and mechanisms emerge at the higher levels?

The production of novelty in significant projects differs from problem solutions observed in laboratory studies along at least three dimensions: the complexity of the tasks undertaken, the time required to complete them and the number of people engaged. For lack of a better term, I will refer to the third dimension as *collectivity*. The upper levels of time and collectivity merge in history, which in turn is a single event on the evolutionary time scale.

SCALING ACROSS TIME AND COMPLEXITY

There is no widely accepted metric of cognitive complexity and no natural levels of complexity present themselves to intuition. Was the invention of radar more or less complex than the discovery of the structure of DNA? Perhaps cognitive psychologists will one day specify system levels that are as distinct as the cell-organism-species levels in biology or the atom-molecule-substance levels in chemistry, but they have not yet done so. However, by whatever measure, insight puzzles are less complex than significant creative projects. If so, to what extent are the principles introduced in Chapter 4 helpful in understanding the unfolding of creative projects? Do the postulated processes scale up from laboratory tasks with few components and short solutions to scientific discoveries, technological inventions and works of art? Because the theory of insight is built on top of the theory of analytical problem solving, the natural approach is to verify that the latter is relevant, document the occurrence of impasses and insights and then inquire into the mechanisms of scaling.

Complexity: Analytical Problem Solving

The two central concepts in the theory of analytical problem solving are heuristic search and subgoaling (see Chapter 4). Historical case studies leave little doubt that both concepts apply to creative projects. Although most of the cases cited in this chapter are taken from the history of technological invention, analogous cases could be cited from the history of art or science.

Search

The initial concept of a desired device is sometimes functional, as in *a machine for flying*, sometimes a mix of material and functional ideas, as in *use radio waves to detect enemy airplanes at a distance* and sometimes a special case of an existing device, as in *a clock that is accurate enough under sea conditions to enable the determination of longitude*. The initial concept is not a blueprint and even less a prototype, or else invention would be easy and anyone could invent a time travel machine. Between the concept and the working prototype is the space of possible designs.

Engineers can sometimes calculate in advance what will and will not work, but at the cutting edge of technology such predictive knowledge might not be available and possibilities have to be evaluated by material tests. Three classical instances are Thomas Alva Edison's work on the telephone, the lightbulb and the electrical battery. In *Edison: Inventing the Century*, Neil Baldwin writes, "… Edison, with [his assistant] Batchelor at his side, pressed on intermittently with the 'speaking telegraph' throughout the next two years … testing the electronic resistance properties of more than two thousand different chemical compounds.…" In the case of the lightbulb, there was an issue of which substance to use for the filament. For over a year, the Edison team explored filaments made out of platinum. They proceeded by trying one type of platinum filament after the other. This search took place after the concept of the lightbulb was already well articulated: a glass-enclosure with electricity being led through a glowing filament. What was varied in this search was the exact composition, thickness and so on of the filament. After a year with only partial progress Edison changed the direction of the search to focus on carbon compounds instead of platinum ones, a space in which success came rapidly. Finally, Edison's research team spent three years working through possible designs of the first working battery. Baldwin writes, "For three years, Edison set his chemical research team at West Orange to work testing thousands of different permutations for the variety of elements within the structure of the battery, to find the right interaction of an alkaline (i.e., nonacidic) solution with a noncorroding plate, and to establish a constant chemical reaction that would not wear down the components...."[8]

Resorting to unselective search was not a peculiar feature of Edison's work habits. Consider how Robert H. Wentorf, the inventor of synthetic diamonds, describes that process:

> About a year and a half later, after hundreds of experiments and grinding tests, we found a process that produced a well-bonded mass of sintered diamond.... we tried ... all the possible processes we could think of. Viewed from the goal end, the route seems almost obvious, but viewed from the starting end, it is just one of myriads of routes....[9]

In these cases, the problems were solved by searching the relevant possibility spaces as originally conceived, bringing available knowledge and experience to bear but resorting to exhaustive search when no selective heuristics were available. Search – successive cycles of tentative action followed by evaluation – is a basic component of significant creative work.

Subgoaling
A second key component of analytical problem solving is subgoaling, the partitioning of a problem into a hierarchy of nearly independent parts that can be attacked separately. It is common to attribute the success of the Wright Brothers in inventing a workable airplane to, among other factors, their encouraging mother, their partnership and the mechanical skills developed in their bicycle repair shop. Gary Bradshaw's cognitive analysis dismisses these factors as incapable of explaining the difference between the Wright Brothers and other teams working on the same problem.[10] Members of those teams no doubt had encouraging mothers as well – most mothers are – they worked in teams and in some instances they had more advanced mechanical and engineering skills and greater resources. These factors, although likely necessary for the Wright Brothers' success, are insufficient to explain why they succeeded ahead of the other development teams.

Bradshaw's analysis shows that the main difference lay in their manner of working. Everyone who attempted to build a workable aircraft assumed that there would be a fuselage, wings, a power source and some arrangement for steering, but these features can be varied in many ways and along several dimensions, defining a gigantic space of possible airplane designs. Some of the competitors in the race toward a flying machine searched this space design by design: settle on a particular design, build it, try to fly it, notice that it does not fly, dispose of the debris and go back to the drawing board. In the case of a possibility space with thousands of nodes, this process is too laborious, costly and time-consuming – not to forget dangerous – for rapid progress. The problem of flight remained unsolved for two centuries after it was first formulated in terms of its three main components.

According to Bradshaw's analysis, the Wright Brothers proceeded differently. They separated the overall design into the three subproblems of lift, propulsion and steering, and worked on each problem separately. They did not attempt to build an airplane until they had developed solutions to each subproblem, and they adopted their methods to the demands of each subgoal. They investigated lift by building a wind tunnel in which they could measure the lift provided by different wing shapes, and also by building and testing large kites. They investigated propulsion by, among other methods, making a large number of model propellers and measuring the drag achieved with each one. In this way, they could search the space of possible propeller shapes faster than if they had tried to build full-scale airplanes and fly them. When they went to Kitty Hawk in 1903, they understood their three subproblems and had some confidence in their solutions. Although much work was needed to make the design practical, there was little doubt that their machine would fly. Subgoaling, the partitioning of the overall problem into nearly independent parts, won the race for mastery of the air.

The list of examples could be extended, but these instances already demonstrate that the theory of analytical thinking that underpins the theory of insight is applicable to complex creative projects. It is not surprising that search reappears at higher levels of complexity. The structure of heuristic search is rooted in the basic facts of uncertainty and fallibility; in an unfamiliar possibility space, steps at any level of complexity are necessarily tentative, so the generate-evaluate-backup-vary pattern is bound to be level-invariant along the dimension of complexity. Hierarchical organization is a technique for managing complexity, so it is even less surprising that subgoaling plays a role in complex projects.

Instances of a theoretical principle provide an existence proof but say nothing about frequency of occurrence. Data on prevalence – what proportion of significant creative projects exhibit search and subgoaling – are not available. For present purposes, the existence proof is sufficient.

Complexity: Impasse and Insight

If inventors search and subgoal, do they proceed at a steady pace or do they experience successive alterations in mode and tempo? Accounts by historians of technology and autobiographical accounts by inventors suggest the latter.

For example, James Hillier, the inventor of the electron microscope, worked on the device between 1937 and 1945, almost eight years. However, progress was not smooth during that period. In his autobiographical account, Hillier pinpoints three insight-like breakthroughs.[11] The first came about because the prototype microscope did not at first provide a sharp enough focus to make the instrument useful. In the inventor's own words:

> We began to realize that the [trouble with the focus] was due to the relative coarseness of the grain structure of the iron and, frequently, to nonmagnetic inclusions in the iron, probably close to the lens opening. We then went through the exercise of searching for better iron and better annealing processes. This led only to frustration. Then came the "eureka." Late one night, my subconscious suddenly made me aware of what immediately became obvious: If crystal structure and impurities were responsible for the distortions of the lens field, why not deliberately introduce a controllable distortion that could be adjusted to counteract the existing distortion? … within eighteen hours from the time the idea germinated, we were getting consistent results that were better than the average for the days before by a factor of 10.…

The impasse was unwarranted because once the crucial idea – *let the user adjust the focus each time he uses the instrument* – had come to mind, its implementation posed no serious obstacles, although fine-tuning continued for some time. Why was Hillier operating in the wrong solution space to begin with? When a device is not working properly, the natural tendency is to improve it by removing the cause of the problem. It is likely that he had encountered the idea *remove the cause of the problem* more often than the idea *let the problem persist and adjust to it while using the device*. In this case, searching the original space for better, that is, magnetically more uniform, iron did not work, and the solution was instead to live with the problem. That is, to accept that imperfections in the iron would continue to interfere with the focus and give the user a tool for adapting to the problem in the course of using the device, a nonstandard approach to fixing an unsatisfactory device. It is difficult to know with any certainty how the moment of insight came about, but there was obviously negative feedback produced by the persistent lack of success in replacing the iron (*"This led only to frustration."*). It is plausible that the feedback eventually suppressed the *remove the cause* strategy to the point where other ideas could come to mind.

The invention of the telephone provides a second example of an expert searching the wrong possibility space.[12] Edison and Alexander Graham Bell are generally credited with bringing out the first workable telephones. In Germany, someone else worked on the problem before them: Philipp Reis, an electrical engineer. Once again, we have to explain a difference in outcome: Why did Reis fail where Bell and Edison succeeded? According to the analysis by Bernard Carlson and Michael E. Gorman, Reis was familiar with the telegraph and assumed that the human voice would be transmitted the way signals were transmitted in the telegraph: in small, discrete packages like dots and dashes. This limited the space of designs Reis considered. In this case, the impasse was terminal. Reis did not produce a workable device. Bell was not constrained in this way and found a solution using undulating, continuous electrical current instead; Edison's telephone worked on the same principle.

A third example of the insight sequence in a complex project is the first formulation of the periodic table of chemical elements. At the end of the 19th century, enough elements had been identified that chemists began to suspect they followed a system. Substances could be ordered in a sequence by their atomic weights, but there were also qualitative similarities that begged to be systematized. The Russian chemist Dmitri Ivanovich Mendeleyev tried to organize groups of chemical substances for the purposes of writing a textbook for his students. As P. Strathern tells the story, Mendeleyev struggled with this task, trying various organizations, postponing a trip, exhausting himself until he fell asleep at his table.[13] Upon waking, he wrote down what we now recognize as the first version of the periodic table. The history of science is dotted with such stories. The general lesson is clear: To create, a person benefits from failure, because failures generate the feedback that suppresses unproductive approaches and enables the emergence of a novel solution.

The examples show that the bridge from insight problems to significant creative projects holds up. Creatives do experience alterations in mode and tempo; see Table 5.1 for additional self-reports of creative individuals engaged in complex projects in art, mathematics, science and technology. In the words of cognitive psychologists Matthew I. Isaak and Marcel A. Just: "During design generation, the inventor often must recognize and release or reformulate implicitly held constraints on the nature of the invention."[14] In short, the hypotheses that impasses are caused by the activation of inappropriate prior knowledge and that insights are caused by the feedback generated by multiple unsuccessful solution attempts apply at high levels of complexity.

Individual examples only prove existence; they do not measure prevalence. I do not claim that every creative project progresses through mental events of this sort, only that some of them do.

Nor do I claim that a single insight suffices to complete a novel device, theory or work of art, a claim sometimes attributed to experimental psychologists by those who study creativity with biographical methods. If not one, then

TABLE 5.1. *Retrospective self-reports by individuals engaged in creative projects.*

Source	Report
J. L. Alty (1995), p. 219.	"Composers struggle for days with 'acceptable' material and then, suddenly a really good solution will present itself and there will be no doubt as to its worth."
T. R. Cech (2001), p. 14.	On the discovery of catalytic RNA: "... the progress one makes is not linear with time. For any given amount of time spent, you often get nothing in return. And then, all of a sudden, the breakthrough comes, the flash of inspiration, and the problem is solved in a relatively short time."
T. A. Edison, quoted in Baldwin (2001), p. 104.	"The first step is an intuition, and comes with a burst.... It has been so in all of my inventions."
G. Gould, quoted in Brown (1988), p. 310.	"In the middle of one Saturday night in the fall of 1957, the whole thing ... suddenly popped into my head, and I saw how to build a laser."
H. von Helmholz, quoted and translated in Woodworth (1938), p. 818.	"Often enough ['happy thoughts'] crept quietly into my thinking.... But in other cases, they arrived suddenly, without any effort on my part, like an inspiration."
G. Polya (1968), p. 54.	"The solution of a problem may occur to us quite abruptly. After brooding over the problem for a long time without apparent progress, we suddenly conceive a bright idea, we see daylight, we have a flash of inspiration."
C. Thacker, quoted in Smith and Alexander (1999), p. 92.	Regarding the invention of multitasking computers: "The solution just came to me. It was an 'ah ha' experience."

how many? Hillier continues his description of the invention of the electron microscope in terms of two additional "breakthroughs" over and beyond the one quoted above: analyzing a very thin sample by shooting a beam of particles through it, and using information about how particles scatter to develop the so-called scanning microscope.[15] How typical is the number three? Shamus Regan and I analyzed the discovery of the structure of DNA into eight novel conceptual steps.[16] For example, the molecules that form the ladder steps in the double helix – the so-called base pairs – combine in a complementary rather than a like-with-like manner. That is, molecules of type A (*adenine*) pair with molecules of type T (*thymine*), while molecules of type G (*guanine*) pair with molecules of type C (*cytosine*) Both types of pairs have the same length and thus form ladder steps of the same width. This feature of the DNA molecule was quite unfamiliar at the time, as were the other seven features, and so had to be discovered in the course of the work.

Identification of key steps on the basis of autobiographical memory or historical materials is fraught with difficulty and uncertainty. Regan and I attempted an experimental validation of our analysis of James D. Watson and Francis N. C. Crick's achievement into eight key conceptual steps by constructing a laboratory version of the DNA structure discovery problem. We compared the time to task completion for experimental subjects who received hints on these eight points with subjects who did not receive those hints. The effect on the solution time was strong and directly related to the number of hints the subjects received; see Figure 5.1. Our results support the hypothesis that the double helix concept can be approached along a trajectory that is dotted with those eight conceptual inventions, but they cannot prove that Watson and Crick did in fact move along that particular trajectory. We can be certain that, whatever their trajectory, it required multiple insights.

To conclude with an example from art, Herschel B. Chipp has analyzed the painting of *Guernica* into 10 phases, each of which is marked by a distinct change in the concept of the composition.[17] At one point, Picasso repainted the head of a screaming horse so as to turn it from upside down to right side up, drastically changing the character of the horse's scream from pitiful to defiant. The three examples of the electron microscope, the structure of DNA and the painting of *Guernica* illustrate the lower boundary on the number of insights in significant creative projects.

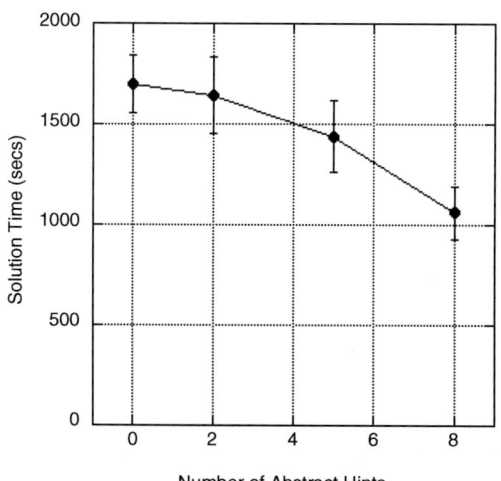

FIGURE 5.1. The effect of priming eight key insights on the time to solve a simplified version of the DNA structure problem.

What is the upper boundary? Howard E. Gruber reports an unpublished diary study by the psychologist Herbert Crovitz that produced an estimate of two to three insights per week over multiple years.[18] Gruber estimated, based on his analysis of Charles Darwin's notebooks, that Darwin might have had as many as two or three insights per day. If we consider that each of these creators worked on their problems for months or even years, the number of insights behind their accomplishments is in the hundreds. An open question is whether the upper boundary is set by the finite lifetime of human beings or by some limit on the number of insights that can be integrated into a novelty.

In short, there is no magic number of insight events, nor do we know that the number of insights measures the importance or novelty of an invention or a discovery, although this is a possibility that might reward attention. But the claim that the insight theory applies to significant creative projects should not be confused with the obviously inaccurate claim that such a project requires only a single insight. The important conclusion is that creativity scales across complexity through the accumulation of multiple insights, not via some different or unknown cognitive mechanism or mysterious "creative ability."

Scaling Across Time

How long do significant creative projects last? Picasso worked on *Guernica* for approximately six weeks, from May 1 to mid-June, 1937, and on *Les Demoiselles d'Avignon* just under a year, from the autumn of 1906 to July, 1907.[19, 20] Watson and Crick worked for almost two years to identify the double helix structure of the DNA molecule, counting the work as having begun when Watson and Crick met in the fall of 1951 and ending with their first publication on April 25, 1953.[21] Charles Darwin opened a notebook labeled the "Transmutation of species" in July, 1837, and stated the theory of natural selection in his notebooks a year later, in late fall of 1838; empirical work and deliberate postponing followed until the *Origin of Species* was finally published in 1859.[22] The invention of the airplane took the Wright Brothers more than three years, from 1899, when they began practical work on the problem, to the flight at Kitty Hawk on December 17, 1903, that most historians of technology regard as the birth of controlled, heavier than air flight.[23] The brothers then spent a couple of years improving the details of their design. Antoine Lavoisier worked on the oxygen theory of combustion for at least three years, beginning no earlier than 1774 and publishing it for the first time in 1777; the mature theory did not appear until 1783.[24] Hillier spent approximately seven years, from late 1937 through

1945, to construct the electron microscope.²⁵ Andrew Wiles spent eight years, from 1986 to 1994, inventing the first valid proof of Fermat's Last Theorem.²⁶

These examples support the statement by Gruber, "It seems safe to say that *all* examples of creative insights occur within protracted creative processes."²⁷ Specifically, the examples suggest that significant creative projects stretch over approximately two orders of magnitude on the time scale, from 0.10 to 10 years. It is plausible that they cluster toward the middle of that range. Estimation is complicated by the fact that a person sometimes puts a project aside, perhaps for years, before completing it. In such cases, the sum of the periods of active engagement might fall within the .10 – 10 range. The range is a rough approximation, but it will serve.

If significant projects only require a dozen or so insights, and if an insight can occur in a few seconds or minutes, why do creative projects take .10 to 10 years? The principles of *Accumulation* (see Chapter 3) and *Raisins in the Dough* (see Chapter 4) provide the answer. A complex project generates multiple subproblems, each of which might require a creative response. From the point of view of the overall project, the solution to one subproblem is only a partial insight, a step forward but not the entire solution. In addition, there is the analytical or noncreative work. Inventing a device, formulating a scientific theory or completing a work of art involves many processes and activities other than generating novel ideas. A product has to be made, not merely thought of, and making is a complicated affair. Creative products require the accumulation of work of both the creative and the noncreative sort, and accumulation takes time.

If we observe the rate of progress across months or even years, the slowdowns and speed-ups associated with single insights might disappear in the aggregating process. Adjectives like *slow* and *sudden* are relative to a time scale. A squall might seem like a sudden change in the weather during a walk in the park, but that same squall will not appear as a distinct event in a chart of rainfall per year; the daily ups and downs of the stock market disappear in a graph of the increase in economic output over the last century; the death of a single mosquito makes a big difference to the mosquito but little difference to a hiker; and so on. But if events of small magnitude or scope disappear from view as we zoom out to a longer time scale, then the properties associated with those events are not necessarily replicated at the higher level.

However, there are two scaling mechanisms that make alterations in the rate of progress almost unavoidable at the significant time band. The first mechanism is that although a single insight usually does not suffice to complete a creative project, a single impasse is sufficient to hold up a project of any complexity. This is a consequence of hierarchical organization. If a subgoal cannot be obtained, then its superordinate goal cannot be obtained, so its superordinate goal is unreachable, and so on, up to the top goal.

In his classic tale of underwater exploration, *The Silent World*, Jacques-Yues Cousteau describes the invention of the SCUBA diving equipment that is now used by millions of recreational and professional divers.[28] Spear fishers along the Mediterranean coast had invented the rubber fins, the mask and the snorkel in the 1930s, but they had not invented a lightweight breathing apparatus that allowed them to stay down longer than the time they could hold their breath. Experiments that nearly killed him convinced Cousteau that carrying compressed air in a tank on his back was safer than breathing through a hose connected to a compressor on the surface. The problem was that a diver's depth varies throughout a dive. If the tank feeds air to the diver at too low a pressure, the water pressure will squeeze him, and if it delivers air at too high a pressure, precious air is wasted in bubbles. The subgoal of delivering the air at just the right pressure held up the development of a practical device, which in turn was the key to the program of underwater exploration that eventually became Cousteau's lifelong project. The adaptation of a valve originally developed to feed household gas to car engines during the gasoline shortage of World War II resolved this impasse. The adaptation was simple in engineering terms, but because it was a subgoal at the bottom of a high stack of superordinate goals, it had major consequences for recreational and professional diving, marine biology, the tourist industry and, let us not forget, popular television. Although a single clever idea seldom suffices to produce a significant novelty, a single impasse suffices to hold up its production, creating a slowdown that is visible at the higher scale. Impasses punch through to directly impact significant creative projects.

A second mechanism that contributes to alterations in mode and tempo at the significant time band is that insights are unlikely to appear at even intervals; there is no mechanism to ensure that they do. If impasses are massively contingent on the details of what a person knows and how that knowledge is organized, they are more likely to appear at random intervals. The time it takes to resolve any one impasse is also a random variable, massively contingent on the details of each particular instance. Consequently, impasses and their associated insights are likely to form clusters in time. Viewed from the perspective of a project as a whole, a temporal cluster of impasses, each of which requires a lengthy effort to resolve, will appear at higher system levels as a mega-impasse, a period during which progress was slower than average. In contrast, a cluster of quickly resolved impasses will appear at the higher

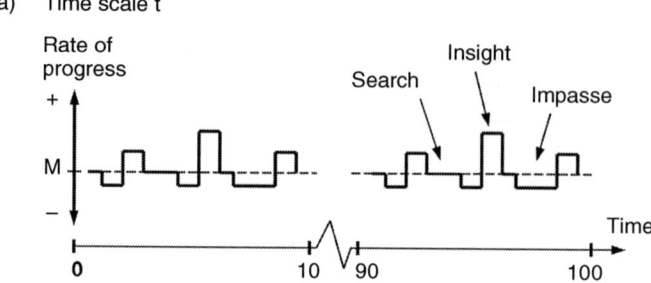

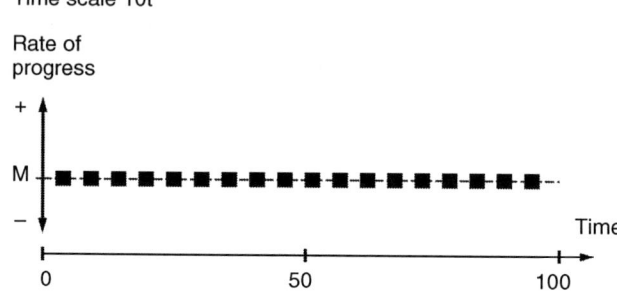

FIGURE 5.2. Rate of progress when insight sequences are evenly distributed over time. Panel (b) shows the same process as Panel (a), but at an order of magnitude lower temporal resolution.

time scale as a period when progress was more rapid than average. Figure 5.2 graphically illustrates the (unlikely) case of even distribution of impasses with respect to onset, severity and resolution. Panel (a) shows the process at a level of temporal resolution at which the variations in the rate of progress over time are visible. In panel (b), which depicts the same process at a lower temporal resolution, the evenly spaced variations disappear from view and the process looks smooth, as if it were progressing at a constant pace.

Figure 5.3 exhibits a case in which the severity of impasses varies over time. For simplicity of exposition, it only covers two cases: a series of impasses of low severity, followed by a series of impasses of high severity; see panel (a). As in Figure 5.2, panel (b) shows the same process at a temporal resolution that is an order of magnitude lower. Once again, the local variations in tempo fade from view, but the average differences in rate of progress over a period of time stand out. A casual observer might conclude that the initial 50 time units constitute "a creative period" or an "annus mirabilis," while the last 50 time units constitute a "period of stagnation" during which something interfered with

(a) Time scale t

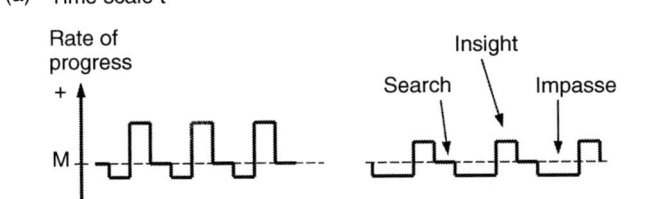

(b) Time scale 10t

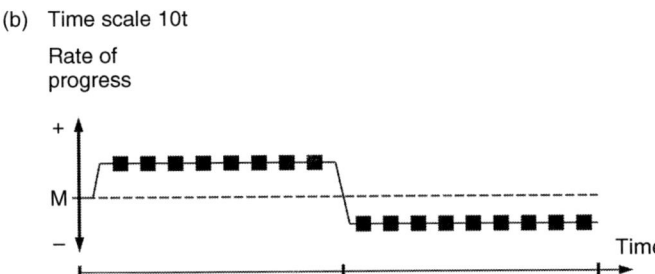

FIGURE 5.3. Rate of progress when insight sequences are unevenly distributed over time. Panel (b) shows the same process as Panel (a), but at an order of magnitude lower temporal resolution.

the creative process. Conclusions of this type are unwarranted because the observed average variations might be caused by random clumping of insight sequences of higher or lower severity of impasses and by a coarse-grained record of the overall process such as would be produced by, for example, an analysis of the creative person's notebooks and by successive views of the creative product, common methods in the study of significant creative projects.

In short, the existence of impasses, the fact that there is no mechanism to distribute them evenly in time and the fact that the severity of an impasse – the time it takes to resolve it – is a random variable conspire to ensure that creative processes will exhibit alterations in mode and tempo at the significant time band. When biographers and historians ask why a creator made much or little progress during such-and-such a period of his life, they might be asking a misconstrued question. To the extent that the quantitative variations in rate of progress reflect the massively contingent clustering of insight events, they do not have a cause or an explanation, at least not the type of explanation that biographers and historians seek.

The scaling principles at work in replicating the alternations in mode and tempo at longer durations are quite general: As a chain is no stronger than its weakest link, so a stack of subgoals is no more realizable than its most intractable element. A process composed of multiple events that are randomly distributed over time, and each of which exhibits alterations in mode and tempo, will itself exhibit such alterations.

Other Properties That Scale

If a creative project requires multiple insights, each of which is massively contingent and hence unpredictable, the progress of the project as a whole becomes unpredictable. This contributes to the open-ended flavor of creativity. It also has three specific consequences that are consistent with what is known about creative work: First, the uneven rate of progress is an incentive to work on multiple projects in parallel. While there is a temporary lack of progress on one project, it might be possible to make progress elsewhere. Creative people engage in a network of semi-independent but related enterprises.[29]

Second, creatives are unable to keep deadlines. If they cannot predict when impasses will appear or how long it will take to overcome them, they cannot promise to have a product or solution ready by a given date. Past experience might have taught them that there is a high likelihood *that* current and future impasses will be overcome, but this expectation does not provide a way to predict *when* a particular breakthrough will come – hence, the apparent lack of ability to keep deadlines.

Third, creative individuals are unlikely to flourish in bureaucratic organizations with top-down goal setting and scheduling. All three features are so commonly noted that they are part of both folklore and systematic studies of creativity. The important point for present purposes is that all three features follow directly from the massive contingency of impasses and the random distribution of the time to resolution, principled consequences of the cognitive processing principles laid out in Chapter 4.

If impasses are caused by the activation of knowledge that will constrain the solution space inappropriately, then the role of expertise in creativity acquires a double edge.[30] On the one hand, more prior knowledge will help constrain the search space for the analytical part of the work. On the other hand, more extensive but inappropriately activated prior knowledge might constrain the search space in a way that interferes with the solution. The implication is that expertise exhibits a particular relation to success in creative endeavors: At low

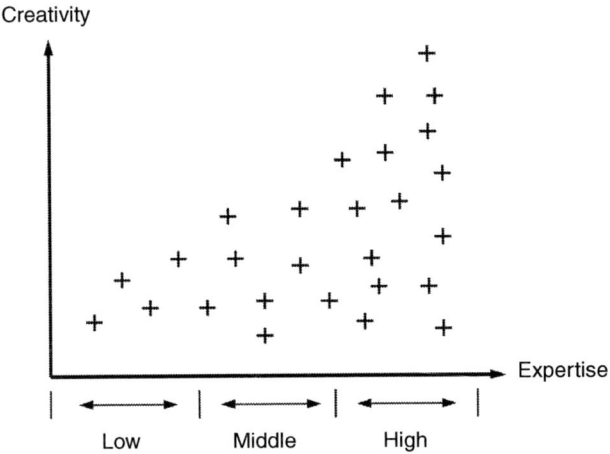

FIGURE 5.4. The triangular correlation hypothesized to relate expertise and creativity.

levels of expertise, the person does not have enough background knowledge to carry out the necessary analytical work, and hence is almost guaranteed not to succeed. However, at high levels of expertise, the outcome is contingent on the content and representation of that knowledge. If the inventor's understanding of his problem tends to activate helpful knowledge elements, the probability of success is high; but if that knowledge is encoded in such a way that the initial problem representation activates unhelpful knowledge elements, the probability of success decreases. This state of affairs should create a particular empirical pattern, known as a *triangular correlation*. In research on the related question of the connection between creativity and intelligence, the expectation to find this type of pattern is sometimes referred to as the *threshold hypothesis*.[31] The key idea is that a person has to be above a minimal threshold to able to succeed; but being above that threshold does not guarantee success; it only makes it possible. This state of affairs implies that if we could measure and plot expertise versus creative achievement for a large number of individuals, the result would resemble Figure 5.4. The evidence for a triangular correlation between intelligence and creativity is weak and somewhat inconsistent; evidence regarding the predicted triangular correlation between expertise and creativity is not available. The important point for present purposes is that the hypothesis that impasses are caused by the constraining effects of inappropriately activated prior knowledge has a definite and testable prediction at the significant time band.

The fact that impasses are resolved by passing negative feedback down through the cognitive system creates a need for persistence. Paradoxically, a creative person is likely to try a variety of unsuccessful solutions, because failed efforts create feedback that might eventually alter the distribution of activation over memory and initiate restructuring of the search space. At the significant time band, this will create a pattern of trying again and again. From the point of an observer, the voluntary exposure to negative feedback makes the creative person appear to have character traits like tolerance for ambiguity, flexibility, persistence and tolerance for frustration.[32] But psychologists find that character traits are less general and less stable than common sense would have us believe, so the patterns of behavior that give rise to these labels is better seen as strategic instead of constant.[33] Creative people know that repeated attacks on a seemingly unsolvable problem can result in progress eventually, so they keep at it. It does not follow that they exhibit those same characteristics in other areas of life. The important point is that anxious avoidance of failure should be negatively correlated with success in creative enterprises, and this commonly noted feature of creative work follows directly from the theory of insight as stated in Chapter 4.

Summary and Discussion

Insights are raisins in the dough of significant creative work. Some properties of the cognitive processes and mechanisms specified in the micro-theory of individual insight events laid out in Chapter 4 scale up to the significant time band and explain at least the following patterns and phenomena: (a) the 0.10 – 10 years' duration of significant creative projects (*accumulation of analytical work; need for multiple insights*); (b) the replication of the alterations in mode and tempo at the higher time band (*impasses punch through directly; uneven temporal clustering of impasses and insights*); (c) the unpredictability of creative work, which in turn has multiple consequences (*unpredictability of insights punches through directly*); (d) the triangular correlation between expertise and creative achievement (*impasses are caused by the constraining effects of prior knowledge*); and (e) the impression that highly creative people have certain personality traits such as tolerance for ambiguity and frustration (*need for exposure to negative feedback*). Further analysis of the cognitive mechanisms behind insight might yield additional effects at the significant time band.

The claim is not that all properties of the processes and mechanisms postulated in the micro-theory of insight scale up to higher levels of complexity and time. The fine details of the cognitive processes have little or no impact. For example, it does not matter at the 0.10–10 years' time band whether memory retrieval is accomplished by spreading activation or through some other mechanism. What matters is that retrieval failure is a possibility. Nor can it matter exactly how activation is redistributed at a single choice point. The principle of redistribution of activation in a single processing unit – the central contribution of Chapter 4 – does not have any consequences at the significant time band. There are no regularities in the production of novelty at the higher levels of time or complexity that owe their existence and shape directly to the fact, if it is a fact, that activation in a single processing unit is redistributed in the particular way specified by that principle. What matters is that activation is capable of being redistributed. Only the gross characteristics – problem perception determines knowledge retrieval; knowledge constrains search; feedback affects the distribution of activation – punch through to higher levels of scale.

Conversely, the micro-theory of insight does not explain all phenomena and patterns at higher levels of time and complexity. New mechanisms emerge. For example, consider problem finding.[34] It is often claimed that creative people have a superior ability to spot a fruitful problem or a promising opportunity. Case studies provide examples. John J. Wild, the inventor of ultrasound diagnosis, accidentally discovered that a cancer growth gave a different ultrasound echo than the surrounding healthy tissue, opening up the possibility of using ultrasound to diagnose cancer.[35] He recognized that this problem was more significant than the one he was working on at the time, so he set it aside to explore the ultrasound technique. Serendipity, to accidentally stumble on a solution to a problem that one is not working on and nevertheless recognize it as a solution, is a closely related and well-established phenomenon.[36] Both problem finding and serendipity rely on a special type of sensitivity to the environment that allows a person to be simultaneously goal-driven and interruptible. This phenomenon is not captured in the theory of analytical problem solving and it does not seem amenable to an explanation in terms of representational change.

The long duration of significant projects also exposes them to the impact of externalities. The role of externalities is discussed in Chapter 4 in relation to fortuitous reminding and incubation, but their importance increases at the higher levels of time and complexity. Events in the environment that either distract the problem solver or trigger cognitive change are not accounted for in the micro-theory of insight. But even a quick scan of the history of some creative projects indicates a strong causal impact for events that are independent of the internal dynamics of the creative work. If Darwin had not been invited, through family connections, to participate in the voyage of the *Beagle*, would he nevertheless have been stimulated to think about the transmutation of species? Without World War II and the resulting influx of refugee European scientists desperate to stop Nazi Germany from taking over the world, would the atom bomb have been invented? If Watson had not been assigned a desk in Crick's office at the Cavendish Laboratory, would their collaboration have been delayed or prevented? The role of externalities grows even more prominent when we scale along the dimension of collectivity.

SCALING FROM INDIVIDUALS TO COLLECTIVES

Discoveries, inventions and works of art are often associated with single individuals. It is common knowledge that Edison invented the electric lightbulb, Darwin thought of natural selection and Picasso founded cubism. Some creativity researchers argue that these single-name attributions are inaccurate and that they obscure the collective nature of creative achievements. Many seemingly lone geniuses will on closer examination be found to have interacted intensively with at least one other person, even in cases where posterity has found it convenient to elevate one member of such a couple over the other.[37] Scientific discoveries are often made by large research teams and technical inventions are products of industrial research and development laboratories with many workers. Edison employed hundreds.[38] Likewise, a style of painting is not created by a single person. The 19th-century French impressionists painted, talked and traveled together, exchanging techniques, ideas and aesthetic judgments in their search for a new art.[39] Groups, teams, organizations and communities are the true agents of creativity, or so the claim goes.

Although the focus on the collective aspect of invention is a useful corrective to the past tendency to overemphasize lone geniuses, the contemporary prevalence of teamwork is not an intrinsic or universal feature of creative work but a historically recent trend. Before the modern era, artists, inventors and scientists often worked in relative isolation. They were few and scattered. Travel was difficult and dangerous, postal communications slow and unreliable and there was no system for publishing preliminary results. The life of Gerardus Mercator, the cartographer who invented the mapping technique that we now call Mercator's projection, illustrates this situation.[40] Dissemination of his revolutionary cartographic invention depended on whether he could travel from his home town, on horseback and in winter, to book-and-map fairs elsewhere on the European continent. Bandits, floods, famine, religious strife and warfare were potential obstacles to this primitive form of dissemination. Even Martin Luther had to publish his revolutionary religious theses by nailing a single handwritten copy to a church door. The contrast to attaching a document to an e-mail message could not be greater. In general, between the fall of the Roman Empire in the fifth century and the beginning of the first stirrings of the scientific revolution in the 13th, European science is better described as a scattering of nearly unrelated geniuses than as a community of collaborators. The same is true of art and technology. Yet, creative works appeared.

Even in collaborative enterprises, every new idea or concept arises in a single mind for the very first time. As told in Chapter 3, there was a moment in January 1935 when A. F. Wilkins formulated the thought that *perhaps we can detect enemy airplanes at a distance by bouncing radio waves off them*. That moment did not give us radar, but it was one event on the path to radar, and a very interesting one. There is no contradiction between saying that, on the one hand, the idea of detecting airplanes with radio waves came to one person at a specific moment in time, and, on the other hand, that the development of a working radar took a good many people the better part of a decade.[41] These statements do not contradict each other because they pertain to different questions: *How, by what mental processes, did this or that idea arise in such-and-such a person's mind?* versus *How did the members of such-and-such a group interact to solve their problem?* At the level of the individual, ideas, concepts, perceptions, hypotheses, schemas and other cognitive units interact within a single mind to form the individual's view of the problem at hand. At the level of the collective, the individual persons are the units, and their interactions constitute the problem-solving approach of the collective, the latter considered as a cognitive agent in its own right. Collectives can in turn interact to form systems of yet greater scope, as when multiple research groups pursue the same field of research while interacting through conferences, peer review, personal contacts and so on.

In short, groups consist of individuals, so the question of whether novelties are produced by individuals or groups is misconstrued. The theoretical task is not to choose between the individual and the group or to prove that one system level is more real or interesting than the other, but to investigate how events at one level affect events at the other. Scaling along the dimension of collectivity has different consequences from scaling along time and complexity.

Stagnation and Breakthroughs in Collectives

A group, team, population or organization – any collective of 10 to 10^3 individuals – engaged in the production of novelty can be said to search and pose subgoals. In unfamiliar task environments, collectives, like individuals, have to take tentative steps, evaluate outcomes and try again in the case of failure. Search is a necessary consequence of uncertainty and fallibility, and those factors affect collectives no less than individuals.

What we call subgoaling at the level of the individual reappears as *division of labor* at the group level. The analogy between subgoaling and division of labor is precise from the point of view of task analysis. As the individual identifies subgoal X as a piece of the overall task that can be attacked in relative isolation – as the Wright Brothers did with the problem of lift – so an organization can package task X and assign it to a group, section or division. Division of labor does not by itself add anything qualitatively new to problem solving. If all subtasks had to be solved in temporal succession, a group would be no faster than an individual. However, from the point of view of task execution, there is a major difference: Division of labor enables *parallelism*, the simultaneous pursuit of multiple subgoals. This speeds up search. Edison's lifetime would not have sufficed to invent the telephone, the electric lightbulb *and* the electric battery if he had not been able to assign different members of his staff to different tasks, to be pursued simultaneously. Parallelism is an emergent feature that has no counterpart at the level of the individual, and it has major consequences for the shape of impasses and insights at the collective level.

An equally fundamental difference between an individual and a collective is that the latter introduces the necessity to *communicate*. Individuals have to interact to form a collective. This feature also lacks any counterpart at the level of the individual mind. Communication is relatively free of friction in small teams with few individuals who know each other well or work closely together. The Wright Brothers and the Watson and Crick collaboration are good examples. In larger collectives, communication acquires characteristics that have major effects on the nature of impasses and insights.

Collectives no less than individuals can suffer periods of stagnation. The fundamental reason is that the same mechanism that produces impasses at high levels of complexity and duration is also operating in collectives: A single recalcitrant subgoal, no matter how small in scope, can hold up a collective enterprise, no matter how large.[42] The scaling mechanism is simple in principle: If each member of a group is at an impasse with respect to some component of the shared task, then the group as a whole is at an impasse. If a subgoal cannot be reached, its superordinate goals are likewise out of reach. Nothing in the nature of collectives invalidates this law.

For example, the large research organization that created the first atomic bomb at the Los Alamos research facility during World War II needed not only to figure out how to enrich the uranium but also how to detonate the bomb.[43] How could they bring subcritical pieces of enriched uranium together into a single, critical mass in an instant? The group of researchers who worked directly on this problem had the idea of arranging subcritical pieces of uranium around a hollow core, surrounded by conventional explosives. When the latter were set off, the hollow sphere imploded, bringing the uranium pieces into nearly instantaneous contact. Because the entire project rested on being able to detonate the bomb in a controlled manner, this solution, which was but one component of a vast enterprise, was essential. Without a reliable method of detonation, there could have been no atomic bomb.

The role of prior knowledge in causing impasses also scales, in principle, to collectives. If each member of a collective adheres to a particular constraining presupposition, then the possibility space searched by the collective will be constrained accordingly. For example, the assumptions that the Earth is in the center of the solar system and that the heavenly bodies move in perfect circles held up progress in astronomy for almost two millennia.[44]

It might seem as if this situation ought to be common. If every group member has the same knowledge as every one else, organized in the same way, there is no reason to expect one person to say something that causes the others to see the shared problem differently. But if the members of the group or organization approach the problem from diverse backgrounds, communication should preempt impasses at the level of the collective. Even if one team member begins by searching the wrong solution space, some other member with qualitatively different prior knowledge might nevertheless happen to activate the relevant knowledge and hence work in a more useful search space. The implication is that a group whose members have widely varied backgrounds should, on average, be more creative than one in which all members represent the shared problem in the same way, not because diversity promotes idea generation per se, but because such a group is less likely to encounter impasses. This is indeed a commonly claimed advantage for collaborations.

However, research on group problem solving has failed to strongly support this prediction. Problem-solving groups sometimes perform as well as their most creative member, but it is rare that a group works better than its most creative member.[45] What happens to the supposed advantage of bringing multiple perspectives to bear? The phenomenon that the expected advantage of collaboration is seldom realized in practice is known as *process loss*. There are multiple sources of process loss lurking in group dynamics, most of them side effects of the need to communicate. In a particularly elegant analysis, social psychologist James R. Larson has shown in a series of decisive studies that groups tend to spend more time rehearsing *shared* information, that is, information that each group member already knows, than pooling the unique – *unshared* – pieces of information that each individual brings to the joint effort.[46] Larson's explanation is simple: For a concept to become a topic of conversation, somebody has to mention it, which in turn means that they must think of it. The probability that a concept is retrieved, thought of and mentioned is higher, the more group members know of it. The pieces of knowledge that have the highest probability of being talked about are therefore those that everybody already knows. Larson's studies show that as discussion continues, a group might exhaust their shared information and move onto unshared information. The creative power of groups might not be realized unless the members keep interacting for some time.

Common sense suggests other sources of process loss. The sheer difficulty of understanding what a speaker is saying about a difficult topic or problem might blunt the possibility of his jolting the other team members out of their mental ruts. Furthermore, the most helpful and relevant communications tend to be few and far between, embedded in streams of information in which most items are neither. Attending to communications takes time and effort, and the balance between resource drain and utility can be negative. When everybody receives 300 e-mail messages a day, nobody will have time to create anything. The main effect of process loss is to negate the potential advantage of diverse backgrounds in preempting collective impasses.

Siddharta Bhattacharyya and I explored communication effects in a simulation model of a creative collective. We used a computational technique known as *agent-based modeling* to create a collective of simple, simulated cognitive agents who all worked on the same problem and communicated partial results along the way. The question of interest was which factors determined the rate at which the model reached the solution to the shared task. The model demonstrated clearly that increasing the number of communication links among capacity-limited cognitive agents causes process loss. The result of one such simulation run is shown in Figure 5.5.

Further out along the collectivity dimension, the formal structure of a large organization can cause impasses. The operative knowledge of a collective is not always exhaustively defined by the sum of the beliefs of the participating individuals. Organizations have a formal structure and, typically, a center of authority. The knowledge of an organization includes pronouncements and policies by leaders and authorities. The point of view of the chief executive officer (CEO) impacts the search space of a firm's research and development team, the battle plan of a commanding officer constrains the tactics of his

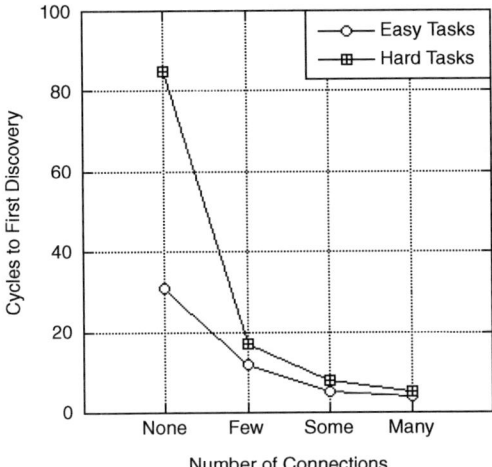

FIGURE 5.5. Process loss in a computer simulation of a creative collective.

subordinates and the doctrine of a religious leader can affect the space of solutions to community problems considered by the members of his church.

One example of the effect of top-down constraints is the failure of the Xerox corporation to exploit the revolutionary advances of its own research and development team at its Palo Alto Research Center (PARC).[47] Early in the development of the computer, the team moved away from the prevalent conception of a computer as a large mainframe, located in a computer center, used primarily for number crunching and operated by specialists that reported directly to the management. In its stead, the researchers at PARC envisioned the system that is in place today: distributed, networked and ubiquitous personal computing, applied to every conceivable information-processing activity. The PARC researchers stacked up an impressive array of hardware and software inventions to support their vision, including a digital mouse inspired by a prior device by Douglas C. Engelbart, bit map displays, separate processing circuits for input and output to off-load the central processor, multitasking, the Ethernet technology, the first laser printer and a user-oriented text editing program. As Douglas K. Smith and Robert C. Alexander tell the story in *Fumbling the Future*, the top management at Xerox was so entrenched in the mainframe conception of computing that they were incapable of grasping the notion of distributed, personal computing. The conception of the management prevailed against the vision of the researchers and Xerox left the greatest business opportunity in a century to be exploited by companies like Apple, Data Corporation, Hewlett and Packard, IBM and Microsoft. In general, pronouncements by authority, explicit codification or inclusion in an incentive system might serve to entrench unhelpful assumptions and create impasses that are unwarranted in the strong sense that the collective contains individuals who are not at impasse, or have already overcome an impasse, but who are not allowed by the authority structure of the organization to act on their insights. From this point of view, communication within an organization can act as an additional cause of impasses. That this possibility is more than idle speculation is shown by the extensive literature by business thinkers about how to create an institutional atmosphere that fosters and sustains creativity.

If groups have unwarranted impasses, do they also have insights? The scaling mechanism once again appears simple in principle: It is enough that a single member of a collective has an insight for that collective to have that insight, or "breakthrough" as they are often called in this context. It required Mercator's genius to invent the cartographic technique that bears his name, but almost every map that we look at utilizes that technique. From the day that Watson and Crick published their description of the double helix structure of DNA, the entire disciplines of biochemistry and genetics possessed that insight.[48] Once Walter Reed and his co-workers and associates had described the mosquito path for the dissemination of yellow fever, the entire medical profession knew.[49]

Such cases suggest a straightforward application of the mechanisms behind individual insight to collectives. However, they mislead by being too clear-cut. Parallelism and communication introduce processes and phenomena that have no analogues in the individual mind and complicate the picture

The parallelism inherent in collectives can be utilized to conduct parallel searches – that is, to launch multiple search processes that explore different regions in a search space, or different search spaces, in the service of the same subgoal. This is a different mechanism from division of labor as ordinarily conceived. The latter pertains to different members of a team attacking different problems, or different parts of a problem; in the present case, the focus is on different individuals working on one and the same problem, simultaneously and independently of each other.

The discovery of the structure of DNA provides an example.[50] There were at least three different research teams who took an interest in the problem in the early 1950s. In addition to Watson and Crick at Cavendish Laboratory in Cambridge, UK, and Maurice Wilkins and Rosalind Franklin at King's

College, London, there was the research group led by Linus Pauling at the California Institute of Technology. Each team explored different assumptions about the molecule's structure. For example, it was not known with certainty how many backbones, strands that held the molecule together lengthwise, the DNA molecule had. Nor was it known how the backbones were arranged. Did they form a central core, as the label "backbone" suggests, with the information-bearing elements attached to it (the "outside" solution), or did they form a shell, with the information-bearing elements on the inside? Wilkins proposed a single-strand model, Pauling a three-strand model, while Watson and Crick began with an alternative three-strand model but soon homed in on the two-strand, outside model that turned out to be correct. The possibility space may seem small ($2 * 3 = 6$ possibilities), but evaluating any one of them required much empirical and theoretical work. The relative speed with which this fundamental scientific problem was solved was in part due to the parallel explorations of that space. It bears repeating that this effect is not due to the division of labor as ordinarily understood (different teams attacking different components of an overall problem), but to multiple teams exploring different solutions to *one and the same* problem simultaneously.

The micro-theory of insight claims that an insight can appear only if there is relevant feedback, more commonly called *criticism* when the topic is collective problem solving. It follows that groups that allow and tolerate mutual criticism will be more creative than groups in which criticism is rare or considered inappropriate. This accords with the common observation that open sharing of information and the practice of subjecting claims and proposals to public scrutiny are key determinants of scientific progress. Unlike the prediction about the power of diversity, the prediction about criticism is well supported by available data.[51] Kevin Dunbar and co-workers have conducted field studies in chemistry laboratories that pertain to this point. They found that critical comments were common in laboratory meetings, and that the most common response is methodological: An unexpected finding is initially attributed to an error or to some undesirable or previously unattended feature of the laboratory procedure. However, when unexpected effects persist, researchers seek a substantive, theoretical explanation that can involve a revision of the relevant hypothesis. The culture of science does not allow publicly stated criticisms to be ignored; they have to be answered. From this point of view, communication is a powerful source of feedback.

Like individual creators, creative collectives are sensitive to externalities. A well-documented example occurred in the discovery of the structure of DNA. Watson and Crick were at an impasse in part because they worked with the wrong structural forms of the molecules that form the horizontal connections, the ladder steps, in the double helix. Watson and Crick learned about the correct structural from of these molecules in conversations with the American crystallographer Jerry Donohue who was visiting the Cavendish Laboratory for reasons independent of Watson and Crick's quest. Without that communication, the problem of the structure of DNA would have been unsolvable. Continued work might have pinpointed the structural formulas of those molecules as sources of trouble and so triggered the subgoal of finding out their true structure, a research enterprise in its own right. Communication of the correct structures preempted the need for such a subproject. Once the correct structures were known, it soon became obvious that one way of pairing the four types of molecules was more plausible than its alternatives.

Perhaps the biggest difference between the individual and the collective pertains to the consequences of insight. In the individual, a new idea enters consciousness accompanied by a certain conviction as to its rightness. The person feels no hesitation to act on it. In the collective, the emergence of a new idea has no immediate effect. The originator has to convince at least some others of the worth of the idea. This creates a need for *dissemination*, a process that has no counterpart within the individual mind. The process of dissemination is complex. In particular, the sheer difficulty of applying language to abstract matters, the negative balance between effort and utility in attending to the daily steam of communications and the formal structure of an organization can all get in the way and prevent the inventor from convincing others about the value of his invention.

An Emerging Change Mechanism: Replacement

The fact that the processes and mechanisms specified in the theory of insight have consequences at the collective level should not be taken to imply that those processes and mechanisms explain all patterns at that level. A new system level is likely to exhibit change mechanisms that are rooted in different processes.

A collective exhibits at least one emergent change mechanism: The individuals that make up the collective come and go. Replacement of group members opens up possibilities for change that have no obvious counterpart at the level of the individual. Over time, the individuals who hold the constraining assumptions resign, move away, retire, die or are thrown out, as the case might be. New individuals with different learning histories and contrasting backgrounds join. If a constraining assumption is less prevalent among the joiners than it was among those who left, the collective undergoes a change that might lead it out of an impasse. In the words of Max Planck: "A new scientific truth does not triumph by convincing its opponents and making them see the light, but rather because its opponents eventually die, and a new generation grows up that is familiar with it."[52]

Impasse-breaking through replacement shares none of the specific properties of insight at the individual level. It is more gradual than punctuated, and it does not require feedback. Instead, the collective gradually outgrows its unhelpful constraints as it attracts individuals who do not share them. This idea deserves a label; I will refer to this as the *Principle of Replacement*. It is not a consequence of the redistribution of activation in individual insights but is rooted in the essence of a collective – the fact that it consists of multiple individuals – and the mortality of membership. A complete theory of creative collectives should encompass the mechanisms of individual insight as well as the change mechanisms that emerge at the collective level.

Summary

Collectives like individuals suffer ups and downs, periods of stagnation alternating with periods of rapid progress. There are features of problem solving that reappear at the group level for principled reasons, including heuristic search, goal hierarchies and alterations in mode and tempo due to unwarranted impasses and insights. The same mechanisms are operating: An impasse, no matter how small, can block the progress of a collective project, no matter how large. Inappropriate assumptions are potential causes. An insight of a single individual can punch through like a butterfly effect and radically impact collective problem solving. These scaling mechanisms preserve the massively contingent and hence unpredictable nature of progress.

The theory of insight makes two specific predictions at the group level: Groups whose members have diverse prior knowledge and groups whose members accept mutual criticisms have a greater probability of avoiding and resolving unwarranted impasses than homogenous groups and groups in which criticism is considered bad form. The validity of the first prediction is obscured by the possibility of process loss, but the second is supported by empirical observations. As with scaling along the time dimension, scaling along the dimension of collectivity only depends on a few gross features of the relevant cognitive processes. It matters little how inappropriate presuppositions act to constrain the search space, but it matters greatly that presuppositions can have that effect. It matters little exactly how negative feedback acts to relax constraints and thus allow a person to draw back to leap, but it matters greatly that feedback can have that effect. However, group problem solving also exhibits emerging mechanisms: the parallelism of search that becomes possible in a collective, the contributions of diverse backgrounds, the imposition of inappropriate presuppositions by authority, the impact of public feedback and the replacement of group members. These have no counterparts at the individual level.

MERGING TIME AND COLLECTIVITY

Only so much can be accomplished in a few years; indeed, only so much can be accomplished in a lifetime. Creative processes extend beyond that limit. In the 300 years since Newton, physics has been a highly cumulative enterprise, producing a stack of experimental techniques, findings and theories in which each new layer of knowledge rests upon and synthesizes the previous ones. The entire advance from pre-Newtonian to post-Einsteinian physics could not have been completed in the course of a single lifetime; the cognitive distance is too great. Similar observations hold for mathematics, technology and other creative fields. Music is perhaps the most cumulative of all the arts, with an unbroken tradition that extends back into pre-history.[53] Humanity could not have advanced from an absence of music to Mozart's compositions in the course of a single lifetime.

A team can only be so large if it is to be held together by person-to-person communication. But the production of novelty might require yet larger collectives. There are more than 100,000 aerospace engineers in the United States alone, many of them involved in the invention of novel technologies for, among other activities, space exploration.[54] The total number of U.S. biologists exceeds 80,000, U.S. chemists number more than 100,000, and U.S. physicists top 150,000. The arts are not far behind in numbers. More than 200,000 individuals in the United States state their occupation as "artist," more than 30,000 as "actor," and as many as 170,000 as "musician or singer." The corresponding numbers for the world as a whole would obviously be significantly greater. The production of novelty transcends the boundaries of creative collectives.

The upper levels of time and collectivity merge in history. There are many types of creative collectives that are too large to be called organizations and exist longer than a single generation. An example is the *academic discipline*, a community of researchers that overrides geographical and cultural boundaries, counts thousands of members and accumulates work on a set of shared problems over centuries. Philosophy is the undisputed grand old dame in this company. Contemporary philosophers are almost annoyingly articulate about how their own work relates to the works of their predecessors 2,000 years removed. Art historians prefer the term *school*, a loosely connected population of artists or writers who paint or write in a particular style, explore a particular technique or – more seldom – adhere to a shared manifesto about the purpose of art. A different type of historical unit is the *market*, a population of producers and consumers. Although usually regarded as an economic rather than cognitive entity, a market can be a locus for the production of novelty. The explosion of electronic consumer products in the period 1950–2000 is an example. A popular unit among historians is the *nation*, a population with a geographic location and a shared culture. Historians and social scientists also think in terms of armies, religions, social classes and other types of historical entities, each of which might be a locus for the production of novelty. The important observation for present purposes is that these units of analysis are larger or last longer than the collectives that we call groups, teams or organizations.

What are the characteristics of the production of novelty in historical systems? Examples of alterations in mode and tempo are ready at hand. The rate of technological invention in, for example, Western Europe from A.D. 500 to the year 1000 was obviously lower than the corresponding rate in A.D. 1500 to 2000.[55] The rate of innovation in the information technology industry in the period 1975–2000 was higher than the rate of innovation in, say, automobiles, buses and trains over the same period. This year's car is different from the 1975 car, but the year 2000 laptop computer was not merely different from the computer of 1975. The personal computer did not exist in 1975; we were still working on time-sharing machines. In the words of technology historian N. Rosenberg, "One of the central historical questions concerning technical progress is its extreme variability over time and place."[56]

In science, we might compare the relative stability of physics in the period 1790–1830 with the turbulent emergence of relativity and quantum mechanics in 1890–1930.[57] As for nations, the increase in economic growth that produced the Industrial Revolution in Britain in the period 1780–1830 was more rapid than during any preceding period.[58] The economic policy of New Zealand changed at a more rapid rate in the 1980–2000 period than in the 1960–1980 period.[59] Such differences in rate of change are difficult to quantify with any precision, but when considered in conjunction they nevertheless convince. Alterations in the mode and tempo of novelty production recurs at historical time scales.

Can impasses at the historical level – *periods of stagnation* as a historian might call them – be caused by the constraining effects of prior knowledge? In principle, the constraining effect of unhelpful presuppositions scales in a straightforward way: If every member of a historical system embraces a particular belief, this will affect the space of possibilities explored by that system. Within the sciences, the assumption that the heavenly bodies, being perfect, necessarily move in perfect circles locked astronomy into the Ptolemeian paradigm for a millennium and a half, and Empedocle's idea that the four ultimate constituents of matter, the elements, are water, fire, air and earth, kept chemistry back for even longer.[60, 61] The assumption that a painting is supposed to be a picture *of* something constrained Western art (but not Islamic or Australian aborigine art) from its stone age inception to the early years of the 20th century.[62] Western Europe during medieval times is often depicted as an era in which the production of novelty was prevented by the constraining influence of church dogma.[63] In the middle of the 19th century, Japan found itself scrambling to catch up with Western inventions after two centuries of adherence to the axioms of samurai society.[64]

But the relation between what individuals believe and what a historical entity like a scientific discipline, an army or a market "believes" is not straightforward. No community is so homogenous that all its members share one and the same belief system. The official position of a large collective is a complex function of its mode of organization and the individual participants' beliefs; simple majorities seldom prevail. Of the many organizational factors that can contribute to stagnation, entrenched interest is perhaps the most powerful. When concepts and principles are embedded in the very design of institutions and practices, including accountability and incentive systems, they become obstacles to creative change. The severity of this kind of impasse is, in part, a function of the degree of authoritarianism that characterizes the system. Enforcement of religious or political axioms can slow the production and dissemination of new ideas.

The blocking of modern genetics in the Soviet Union is the classical example.[65] Trofim Denisovich Lysenko proposed agricultural practices ("vernalization," changing plant characteristics by operations like heating, watering, planting early or late, etc.) that contradicted established facts and principles of plant physiology and claimed a greater degree of malleability for agriculturally important plants like wheat than could be accommodated by the principles of genetics. Lysenko's vernalization concept appealed to the Soviet political leadership, both because it fit thematically with the Marxist principles that everything in both nature and society is dynamic, changeable and shaped by its environment, and also because it implied that it was possible to obtain practical results in agriculture and elsewhere that went beyond the results of Western agriculture. The political support for Lysenko's false ideas and useless practices created an impasse for Soviet biology in general and agriculture in particular that lasted from 1929, when the Soviet regime officially elevated Lysenko to a leadership role, to 1964, when Lysenko died. Societies with monolithic ideologies invent less than those in which the right to dissent is recognized in principle and protected in practice, because creativity essentially depends on being able to adopt another perspective, another representation of the matter at hand.

Although centralized power structures are perhaps more often agents of stagnation, they can also facilitate change. The historical analogue to the relaxation of constraints is the repeal of regulations and laws. Although lawmakers are more prone to create laws than to cancel them, there are examples to the contrary. During a short period in the middle 1980s, the government of New Zealand overhauled an entire set of economic practices, institutions and regulations, including deregulation of the labor market, elimination of agricultural subsidies, privatization of state assets and revision of monetary policy to focus on preventing inflation.[66] The triggering factor was a gross case of negative feedback: Economic indicators showed that the New Zealand economy was not working and the situation became so dire that the government fell. Multiple reforms were executed in quick succession by those who took over. Two decades later, New Zealand's economy was still changing rapidly as various economic agents – banks, firms, individuals – expanded into the new possibility space.

In short, forward projection of past concepts, principles and practices can cause unwarranted periods of stagnation in historical systems, and the relaxation of constraints in response to internal or external events can prepare the way for a period of rapid change. But the explanatory power of these concepts is limited at the historical level by the complexity of the mechanisms that produce and maintain the official stance of the historical entity.

The situation is parallel with respect to the scaling of insights. In principle, if a single member of a historical system has an insight, that system is in possession of that insight. In some cases, an individual event punches through in the manner of a butterfly effect, causing consequences that are larger than itself, as when the loss of a shoe means the loss of a horse, which in turn means defeat in battle and the loss of a kingdom. Examples are ready at hand. Consider once again the idea that *perhaps we can detect enemy airplanes at a distance by bouncing radio waves off them*. This insight initiated work on radar, and radar had a decisive effect on the outcome of the Battle of Britain in particular and of World War II in general, with worldwide consequences for the postwar world, as fine a butterfly effect as ever flitted through the pages of history.[67] World War II is a breeding ground for butterflies of this sort: the novel code-breaking techniques that allowed the Allied forces to listen in on German military radio traffic; the high-frequency, long-range direction finding that allowed the Allies to locate German submarines in the North Atlantic on the basis of their radio transmissions; the development of the Norden bombsight that allowed the Allied bomber fleets to hit their targets from high enough an altitude that they were almost out of range from the anti-aircraft batteries on the ground; the insight that a nuclear chain reaction could be made into an atomic bomb; and so on. The consequences of these inventions depended on the authoritarian structure of the military. It did not matter that the majority of pilots who flew in the Battle of Britain did not understand how radar works, nor was the battle won because a majority of Britain's population shared the belief that enemy airplanes could be detected at a distance with the help of radio waves. The war effort provided a machinery by which creative achievements in science and technology were translated into collective action. Commanders issued orders and men and machines moved.

In other types of historical systems, novelties scale up via other types of processes. For example, a revolutionary change in a scientific discipline requires widespread adoption of a new theory by many individual researchers. The scaling mechanism that connects the individual insight with a scientific revolution is in this case more like diffusion than top-down execution. When the Russian chemist D. I. Mendeleyiev produced the first version of the periodic table of the chemical elements, other chemists recognized its importance and the new theory spread.[68] (The innocent-looking word "spread" glosses over the complexities of the evaluation of evidence, peer review publication and the training of graduate students.) Popular fads and fashions also diffuse in a bottom-up manner. Analysts like Susan Blackmore, Aaron Lynch and others have suggested that small pieces of popular culture, so-called memes, are analogous to genes and diffuse via Darwinian processes of variation and replication. In markets, the equilibrium mechanisms of micro-economics predict that a new product or mode of production will spread through competition.[69] The many producers and consumers in the market might have very different internal structure depending on the market and the individual agent's role, but they self-organize into an equilibrium state by interacting according to simple rules of maximizing benefit, or so micro-economics claims. For present purposes, the important point is that the mechanism by which insights diffuse vary from one type of historical system to another.

But the complexity of the mechanisms that maintain historical systems obscure how the production of a single-point breakthrough can affect the entire historical system in which it appears and cause an increase in its rate of change. It cannot matter for the outcome of the Battle of Britain how

A. F. Wilkins came up with the basic idea for what was then not yet radar; it does not matter for chemistry exactly by what cognitive processes Mendelyiev produced the first version of the periodic table; and it does not matter for the computer industry example how the personal computer was first thought of. It is the very ability to have novel ideas that has the power to trigger a causal cascade upward though the system levels. The only property of insight that punches through to the historical level is the very ability to create.

We should expect novel change mechanisms that have no counterpart at the lower levels to appear at higher system levels. Maintaining a society requires *transmission across generations*, a process that can either facilitate or hinder change. Parenting and schooling are powerful ways of controlling the perspective of the next generation, and to the extent that parents, teachers and recognized authorities speak with a single voice, transmission will tend to suppress rather than disseminate novelties. Social mores and practices cover all aspects of life, so there is no locus at which change could start, because everything is subsumed under the status quo. Indeed, there are striking examples of such continuity: Classical Egyptian civilization, medieval Europe and samurai Japan replicated themselves over centuries, even millennia.

However, intergenerational transmission has a fatal twist: The members of the transmitting generation eventually die. The important consequence is that they lose control over what they transmitted. Texts that attempt to regulate life – the Bible, the U.S. Constitution, Emily Post's *Etiquette* – are forever reinterpreted. The larger the transmission slippage, the more the replacement of one generation by another opens up possibilities for change. To mention a single, arbitrarily chosen instance: To the generation of 1870, a union between France and Germany would have seemed beyond unthinkable; today, the European Union is a fact. As the members of each generation explore the wiggle room left them by transmission slippage, society morphs.

To summarize, the pattern of alterations in mode and tempo recurs at historical scales. Impasses due to the projection of past concepts, principles and practices onto a current situation recur at every level of collectivity. An impasse can take the form of a problem solver with a blank mind, an engineering project stalled by a series of obstacles, a team wasting time in meetings that are as endless as they are fruitless and a political stalemate that causes one parliamentary crisis after another. The explanation of any particular period of stagnation must describe the cultural, social, economic and political mechanisms by which individual concepts, principles and practices are translated into collective practices, and these mechanisms vary from one type of historical system to another. The explanation of how such a period ends must similarly describe the mechanisms by which an invention at the cognitive level is translated into change at a higher system level. This is a brain-straining exercise that the cognitive psychologist with relief hands back to his colleagues in the economic, social and historical sciences.

THE ULTIMATE SYSTEM LEVEL

Beyond history, at the evolutionary time band, the unit of analysis is the species. Our evolutionary ancestor *Homo erectus*, although superficially similar to ourselves, moved from one type of stone tool to a slightly more sophisticated type of stone tool in approximately one and a half million years, a rate of invention that compares rather unfavorably with the technological advances of our own species over the past 2,000 years.[70] The ability to produce novelty on a regular basis is itself a novelty, one of the raisins in the hominid phylogeny. The record from our pre-history strongly suggests that this novelty coincided with the emergence of the representational mind.[71] Once human beings could represent, they could thereby also re-represent. This novelty came about through mutation and natural selection. These change processes differ utterly in their operation and material implementation from the mechanisms of novelty production at the cognitive, collective and historical levels. Nevertheless, biological evolution also proceeds through punctuated equilibria, alternating periods of stasis and change: "The history of evolution is not one of stately unfolding, but a story of homeostatic equilibria, disturbed.... by rapid and episodic events of speciation."[72] Biological species spend most of their life in a state of stable adaptation to their environment. Speciation and extinction occupy periods of time that are short, relative to the total lifetime of the species. Alteration in mode and tempo is the ultimate pattern in the production of novelty, perhaps the only pattern that recurs at every level of time and complexity and at every system size.

PART THREE

ADAPTATION

6

The Growth of Competence

Skilled activity is a programme specifying an objective or terminal state to be achieved, and requiring the serial ordering of a set of constituent, modular subroutines.
Jerome S. Bruner[1]

From [the] naturalistic viewpoint, it will be possible to show that there are eight kinds of learning, not just one or two.
Robert M. Gagné[2]

On March 18, 1965, the Soviet astronaut Alexei Leonov exited from the airlock on the Voskhod 2 space shuttle and floated in orbit above the Earth for 20 minutes.[3] This was the first space walk and the endpoint of a process that started approximately 200,000 years ago, when members of *Homo sapiens* migrated out of Africa and into what we now call the Fertile Crescent.[4] The move out of Africa was the beginning of the colonization of Earth by humans. By the middle of the 20th century, the ocean depths and outer space were the only habitats as yet uninhabited.

In the course of this giant dispersal, human beings colonized environments so different from one another that they might as well have been on different planets. South of the Fertile Crescent lies what we now call the Arabian Peninsula, sand dune upon sand dune promising nothing but dehydration and heat stroke between here and the horizon. Yet the ancestors of the Arabs lived successfully there, figuring out how to tame the bad-tempered camel, protect themselves against the sun with layers of cloth and locate what little water there was. At the opposite end of the Earth, ecologically speaking, the ancestors of the Polynesians learned to build oceangoing sailing vessels – misleadingly called "canoes" in popular accounts – which eventually took them thousands of kilometers across the open waters of the Pacific to Aotearoa, the place Westerners call New Zealand. Wandering off in a different direction, the Inuits and other Eskimo nations survived by hunting from sealskin kayaks and building houses out of snow. In this diversity of habitats, neither the ocean floor nor outer space stand out as especially hostile or complicated, merely different.

The migration of humans into diverse environments happened in such a short period of time that their genetic adaptations were limited to minor variations in metabolism, skin color and body shape. Geneticists and anthropologists agree that there is a single human species.[5] But the different environments placed different demands on those who wished to survive. To hunt the North American buffalo with bow and arrow required different skills from those needed to bring down a kangaroo with a boomerang. To build an igloo required a different technique from that required to build a tree shelter in the Papua New Guinea rain forest. If the speed of colonization was too quick for genetic change, people must have adapted to each new environment by learning rather than evolving the relevant skills and survival techniques.

This point is particularly well illustrated by cases in which a population mastered a novel environment within a single generation. When the Polynesian ancestors of the contemporary Maoris arrived in New Zealand, they found an environment that differed radically from a tropical island, the type of environment from which they set out.[6] Clubbing giant moa birds in the evergreen high-altitude forests and spearing fur seals from open boats in the cold waters off the coast of the South Island bore little resemblance to food production on a coral atoll with its jungle, lagoon and shoreline coconut trees. The old food production skills must have been suppressed and new ones developed in the course of a single generation – indeed, in the time it took the Polynesian settlers to consume what little foodstuffs remained on their sailing vessels after the approximately 3,000 kilometer sea journey from the launching point somewhere in Eastern Polynesia.

The closure of the colonization process provides examples of even more rapid mastery of novel environments. On September 6, 1962, off the coast of Villefranche-sur-Mer, a Belgian diver by the name Robert Sténuit descended 60 meters to the bottom of the Mediterranean inside a 1 by 3.5 meter metal cylinder designed, built and operated by the American aviator and undersea explorer Edwin Link.[7] With support from the U.S. Navy, Sténuit, who was breathing a helium-oxygen mixture to combat depth narcosis, was to stay on the sea floor for two days, exiting the cylinder to perform submarine work in its vicinity. Due to accidents and bad weather, the experiment was cut short after one day, but Sténuit was nevertheless the first person to spend 24 hours on the bottom of the sea. Only a few days later, on September 14, and a few kilometers away, off the coast of Marseilles, two divers, Albert Falco and Claude Wesley, entered Conshelf I, an undersea habitat designed and operated by the French research organization Office Française de Recherches Sous-Marins under the direction of Captain J. Y. Costeau. Conshelf I was a two-person dwelling, 17 feet long and 8 feet high, anchored a few feet above the sea floor at a depth of 40 feet near the island of Pomègues. Falco and Wesley lived and worked at a depth of 10 meters for seven days. In conjunction, these two pioneering efforts demonstrated that human beings could live and work underwater.

A decade later, space explorers made the same point for the very different environment of near space.[8] On May 14, 1973, the National Aeronautics and Space Administration (NASA), the U.S. space agency, launched Skylab, the first successful, manned space station. The three astronauts Charles Conrad Jr., Paul J. Weitz and Joseph P. Kerwin stayed in Skylab between May 25 and June 22, thus becoming the first humans to live and work in space and to return safely to Earth.

Our hunter-gatherer ancestors cannot have bequeathed to us any genetic adaptations for flipping around 30 meters below the ocean surface with SCUBA tanks, and none for exiting from an airlock to repair a telescope in freefall. Although the human species is subject to natural selection, the speed with which we colonize unfamiliar environments shows that people do not primarily adapt via alterations in the genome. Skills are learned, not inherited. Our species-characteristic adaptation is not any particular behavior, or repertoire of behaviors, but our superior ability to change our behavior.

The cost of this survival strategy is that each new generation has to acquire the necessary skills anew. Human babies are born with almost no capacity for effective action, but a normal day in the life of, for example, a white-collar worker in a Western city requires an astonishing range of skills: cook breakfast; drive to work; use cell phones, word processors and copiers; communicate via e-mail and fax; transform numerical data into graphs and figures; master the tango or the violin; arrange a successful birthday party; care for the fish in the tank and keep upright on the mountain bike. Although the execution of an acquired skill might be quick and effortless, the acquisition of that skill requires both time and effort. Alone among mammals, a human being requires 15–20 years to become a competent member of the species, and a 20-year-old future professional faces yet another decade of training before he has mastered the skills needed to excel in a complicated, typically high-technology work environment.

Once mastered, skills remain in flux. Task environments change due to their own internal causal dynamics as well as in response to externalities and thereby force modifications of already acquired skills. After you have been driving the same route from home to work for years, the transit authority closes down a portion of that route for pothole therapy, throwing you into discovery mode: What is the best detour? Likewise, new versions of software systems are released on a schedule that seems calculated to ensure that the associated skills become obsolete the moment they are mastered. Household appliances change, tax laws change and work places change. Reality is turbulent through and through, so habits, methods, operating procedures and techniques constantly need to be adapted to new circumstances. The central concept for understanding this aspect of human nature is practice.

QUESTIONS ABOUT PRACTICE

Novices sometimes have no choice but to perform a task that they have not quite mastered in a situation in which the outcome matters, a scenario which we call *learning on the job*, or, jokingly, *being thrown into the deep end of the pool*. If this had been the only option, relying on acquired skills might not have been the successful survival strategy it turned out to be for proto-humans. The moment when a wounded animal turns in rage on the hunter is not the time to learn how to wield a spear.

Instead, skills are typically learned through *practice*. That is, the learner repeatedly attempts to perform a task that he has not fully mastered, not for the sake of the results of his performance but for the sake of improving. Practice is ubiquitous in every sphere of human activity, from arts and crafts to music, sports and the professions. Although we often take *studying* to mean *reading*, practice is also important in academic learning. Many subjects, although taught in a lecture format, contain elements of practice. In physics and mathematics, students practice solving problems; in English composition, they practice writing; in laboratory subjects like chemistry and psychology students practice experimental design, data collection and data analysis. Practice is the most prevalent mode of learning, in and out of school.

Practice requires a situation that is set aside for the purpose of learning. The notion of a training environment recognizes the conflict between the fact that mistakes and failures are unavoidable during learning and the fact that failure in real situations often has unacceptable consequences. Training environments resolve this dilemma by allowing a learner to fail without having to suffer the consequences. Better practice with the spear before going on a hunt lest your tribe goes hungry because you missed your throw; better crash a flight simulator than an airplane. The practice of practicing, of executing mock performances as a preparation for the real thing, must have had a strong impact on the survival rate of a species that relied on acquired rather than innate competence. But practice requires no genetic mutations, no changes in brain or body – the person who practices a task performs the same actions as the person who performs that task for the sake of its results – merely a change in how the activity is labeled by the surrounding community. The practice of practicing is perhaps humankind's greatest invention.

Practice is extraordinarily effective.[9] Repeated attempts to perform a task automatically produce improvement. Consider the following thought experiment: Imagine a pretext for asking some person to fill out an unfamiliar, made-up but official-looking form that requires the insertion of various pieces of information here and there, simple arithmetic operations on certain numbers, the results to be inserted in the appropriate boxes (inevitably located on a different page), conditional rules as to which part of the form to fill in next – in short, an unfamiliar version of the kind of bureaucratic product that is all too familiar. After laboriously filling out the form, our unwitting experimental subject is asked to wait a few minutes. He is then informed that the experimenter's dog ate the form; would he kindly fill it out again? We repeat this charade 10 times. In this situation, the person has no reason to learn, but we need conduct no study to know what will happen: The time it takes him to complete the form the 10th time will be a fraction of the time it took him the first time, his behavior will be less hesitant and he will make fewer mistakes in following the instructions. That is, he will be on his way to mastering the task of filling out our nonsense form. The repeated execution of a coordinated series of actions is sufficient to trigger change, at least in the early stages of learning. Improvement is an almost automatic side effect of activity.

In terms of the magnitude of the improvement, practice is the most powerful manipulation of behavior known to cognitive psychologists.[10] In the long run, it brings about changes in behavior that are much greater than the typical effects caused by other types of manipulations such as alterations in the task itself or in the task instructions, if any. Extended practice can generate a level of performance that is not merely superior to initial performance, but orders of magnitude superior. Some chess masters can play blindfolded against as many as 30 average players simultaneously and win almost every match. The precision of a world-class violinist or bass player in hitting exactly the right note at the right time is a source of admiration by even professional musicians. Performance improvements of several orders of magnitude are routinely observed in training experiments.

The familiarity of practice makes its causal efficacy seem self-explanatory: A learner practices in order to improve, and he improves because he practices.

But this verbal circle is not explanatory. Mindful scrutiny rends the veil of familiarity and reveals a paradox.

The novice cannot know how to behave vis-à-vis an unfamiliar task, except in a very general way. If he needs to practice, he has not yet mastered the task well enough to perform it appropriately, correctly or successfully, or at least not to his satisfaction. But if his performance is flawed or incomplete, why does practice not engender a flawed or incomplete skill? If the learner repeatedly generates an incorrect sequence of actions, why does that sequence not become a habit, entrenched in memory in such a way that the learner is doomed to repeat it forever? If a novice car driver pulls out of a driveway in front of another car 50 times, surviving by the grace of other drivers' short reaction times, why does this not produce the habit of pulling out of the driveway without looking? If the diligent piano pupil repeatedly plays Mozart's Piano sonata no. 14 incorrectly, why does this behavior not wear smooth the corresponding path in the brain, ensuring that every future performance will depart from the composer's intention in equal measure? Why does the repetition of an incomplete and erroneous performance result in improvement?

Practice is not only sufficient but also necessary for the mastery of skills of even modest complexity. A person cannot learn a new skill by first listening to a verbal description of how the task is to be done, and then perform it in a competent manner the very first time. If this were possible, driving schools would soon go out of business, because teaching a novice to drive a car would take 15 minutes. Airline companies would rejoice in cheap pilot training, and the military could save on boot camp. But even when a novice has studied the relevant task instructions to the point of being able to recite them verbatim, he cannot therefore perform the target task perfectly and unhesitatingly the first time he attempts it. English is not a programming language for the human mind. A satisfactory theory of skill acquisition should explain why this is so.

A satisfactory theory must also explain why improvement during practice is gradual. On each attempt, each *practice trial*, the performance improves by a small amount, and many trials are typically required before a new skill has been mastered. Observe a novice driver operating a stick shift. He handles the car jerkily; the individual actions are uncoordinated, sometimes with audible effects on the gearbox; his attention is located on the road in front when it should be on the rearview mirror and vice versa; and so on. In general, novice behavior is characterized by bad timing, clumsiness, errors and mistakes, frequent need to backtrack, hesitation, poor spatial coordination, repetitions and slow and inaccurate task completion. In the course of practice, the task comes to be performed with fewer errors and

The Growth of Competence

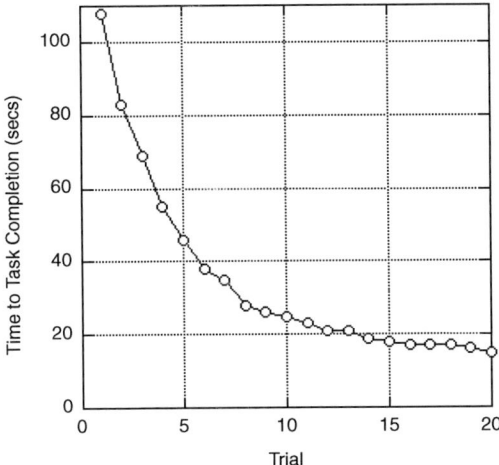

FIGURE 6.1. Mean task completion times for 106 students practicing an unfamiliar symbol manipulation task as a function of the number of trials.

less need to backtrack; the performer hesitates less and completes the task faster; and he can achieve more finely specified outcomes (*come to a full stop five feet before the stop sign*). As he performs the task over and over again, his actions gradually shape themselves to fit the contingencies and causal laws of the task environment (*when the roadway is wet, it takes longer to stop the car, so start braking earlier*).

Improvement is not only gradual but follows a particular form. When performance is plotted as a function of amount of practice, the result is a well-documented temporal pattern called *the learning curve*.[11] Learning curves are invariably negatively accelerated. That is, the rate of improvement is high initially but gradually diminishes, producing a concave curve. Figure 6.1 shows a learning curve for a group of college students practicing a simple symbol manipulating exercise.[12] The curve drops sharply in the beginning, but the rate of change decreases smoothly. After 20 practice trials, improvements have almost ceased and the curve approaches a stable level, referred to as the *asymptote*. Our familiarity with such practice effects veils a conceptual puzzle: Why is skill acquisition gradual? Why is a skill not fully mastered at the moment the target task has been completed correctly for the first time? Why does the rate of improvement follow a decreasing (negatively accelerated) curve?

Practicing in a training environment would be pointless unless the skills acquired there can be executed in the real task environment. We expect a training course for novice drivers to engender competent behavior on the street and a flight simulator to engender competence in a real cockpit. A training environment will differ in some respects from the real task environment, so the skill will need to be adjusted during the transition, but the effort to adjust should be small in proportion to the overall learning effort. The case of adapting an already mastered skill is similar. Tracking changes in a task environment would be prohibitively costly in terms of cognitive effort if every change triggered the construction of a brand new skill. It is more plausible that we deal with environmental change by re-using and modifying what we have already learned. An experienced driver who visits a country where the inhabitants drive on the opposite side of the road need not learn to drive from scratch but adapts to the changed task environment in a few hours. In a vast knowledge base containing skills for hundreds, possibly thousands, of tasks, how do our brains know exactly which components of a skill can be re-used and how the skill should be revised to fit an altered task environment? This is traditionally known as the problem of *transfer of training*.[13]

A coach, instructor or tutor can assist the skill acquisition process in various ways: He typically ensures that the learner tackles problems of gradually increasing complexity, stretching his growing competence bit by bit, but also provides helpful comments. Enormous sums of money are invested in the belief that such assistance is effective. When a sports team performs poorly, fans might call for the resignation, not of the players, but of the coach, a rather flattering assessment of the latter's importance for the team's ability to win. Ambitious parents of high school students sometimes pay as much as $200 per hour for tutoring to ensure the academic success of their offspring. Belief in the power of one-on-one instruction to abet skill acquisition is not misplaced. Measures of learning show that one-on-one tutoring is indeed more effective than other forms of instruction such as lectures and independent practice.[14]

Our familiarity with instructional situations veils the underlying conceptual puzzle: How does instruction work? How can words spoken by another person enter the learner's mind and, once there, change his mental representation of the relevant skill so as to enable faster and more accurate execution? How, by what cognitive processes, does the learner's mind compute exactly which revision in the skill is indicated by any one instruction? A theory of skill acquisition should explain how and when, under which circumstances, instruction helps, and enable us to improve the design of instruction in general and computer-based instruction in particular.

In short, the familiar act of practicing a cognitive skill raises six fundamental questions:

1. *Mechanism.* How, by what cognitive processes, does practice exert its effects? What is the internal structure of a single, local mutation in a cognitive skill?
2. *Sufficiency of practice.* How can practice be sufficient to produce improvement?
3. *Necessity of practice.* Why is practice necessary to acquire a skill?
4. *Gradual improvement.* Why is improvement gradual? Why does it exhibit a negatively accelerated rate of change?
5. *Transfer effects.* How are acquired skills applied and re-used – transferred – to novel or altered task environments?
6. *Efficacy of instruction.* Why is instruction possible? How does it work? What are the factors that determine its effectiveness?

The approach to these questions developed in this and the two following chapters is analogous to the approach to creativity employed in Part II of this book: First, I develop a theory of stable, competent behavior. It specifies cognitive processes for the execution of an already mastered skill. A theory of skill acquisition extends the latter with specifications of the cognitive mechanisms by which skills change and improve. Due to a century of cumulative scientific progress, we now possess a repertoire of hypotheses about those mechanisms. The weakest component of that repertoire is the explanation of how people learn from their errors. In Chapter 7, I propose a micro-theory of learning from error, the second of the three technical contributions of this book. Chapter 8 develops the implications of the micro-theory for higher levels of scale.

RULES AND THE STRUCTURE OF ACTION

To describe change, we need a description of the system that is changing. A theory of how skills change presupposes a theory of how skills are represented and executed in the normal, routine case when no change is needed. How, by which processes, are actions and cognitive operations selected and performed when the relevant skill is already mastered and the environment is stable? One of the great ironies of psychology is that the behaviorists, who for 50 years aggressively argued that psychology is not the science of mind but the science of behavior, never tried to describe human behavior as we see it all around us. The broad strokes of the theory presented here are uncontroversial and shared across the cognitive sciences; most of it is mere common sense. The purpose of stating this theory is not to assert something new, but to assert that what everybody knows *is* the theory of behavior that the behaviorists failed to bequeath us, or a first approximation thereof. The task of this theory is not to predict behavior but to describe what human behavior is like. It complements the theory of analytic thinking in Chapter 4 by fleshing out the action side of the cognitive architecture.

The Units of Behavior

In physical terms, a person's behavior is continuous and, if sleep counts as a behavior, lasts from birth to death, but we spontaneously parse the stream of movements into discrete and qualitative units: *pour the water, push the button, open the window, slice the loaf*, and so on. An action is a unit of behavior that has a relatively well-defined beginning, unfolds in a certain manner and has a relatively well-defined end. Strictly speaking, a phrase like *pour the water* references an action *type*, and each event in which someone pours water is a *token* of that type. The ease with which both adults and children refer to action types in ordinary conversation implies that we possess mental representations of such types. Verb phrases like *pour the water, pass the butter* and *open the door* are overt expressions of those representations.

Complex actions break down into recognizable parts. Consider *make tea*, which is made up of, at least, *boil the water, fetch the tea leaves, fetch a cup, fetch a strainer, place tea leaves in strainer* and *pour the water through the strainer*. The breakdown into parts can be pursued further. *Boil the water* is composed of, for example, *fetch the pan, fill the pan with water, turn on the stove*, and so on. If we continue the analysis, we reach a point at which the actions are so simple that we cannot discern any meaningful parts. The action *turn the faucet* is a case in point. Cognitive theory shares with common sense the inclination to accept units like *push the button* and *turn the faucet* as *elementary actions*, atoms of behavior that cannot be further divided.

In cognitive analyses, the individuation of elementary actions abstracts from the physical aspects of movements. Consider the domain of chess. An elementary action in this task domain is to move a chess piece from one square to another. The move has to follow the rules that apply to that piece, different rules for different pieces. But it does not matter, from the point of view of chess, by which physical movement a chess piece is moved. A piece can be moved with the left hand, the right hand, the mouth or even grasped by a foot. In Kungsträdgården, a park in downtown Stockholm, Sweden, there is a giant chessboard painted on the ground and the park service supplies wooden chessmen four feet high. These are moved by walking onto the chessboard, lifting them up and waddling them over to their destination squares, very different physical movements from those used to make the same move on a traditional board or on a chess-playing computer. The physical movements involved in moving a piece can vary along any number of dimensions such as speed, degree of extension, the angles of the shoulder and elbow joints, the number of fingers extended, the stiffness of the fingers, and so on, and these quantitative variations are of great interest to those who study motor coordination.[15] But as long as the chess piece ends up in the same square, it is nevertheless the same action, from the point of view of chess, as the movement of a chess piece by hand on a tabletop board. The intuitive distinction between tasks that are cognitive (algebra, chess, programming, writing, etc.) and tasks that are physical (baseball, dancing, hammering, pottery, etc.) can be defined in terms of whether the success of an action depends on the physical properties (amplitude, force, speed, etc.) of the associated movements or is independent of those aspects.

Goals

Action is purposeful. Water might be poured in the service of making tea, and a button is typically pushed to make some machine do what is desired of it. A goal is a mental representation of a future state of affairs, be it that I have a cup of tea in my hand or that the elevator arrives. Although goals are like descriptions, they are neither true nor false. If a goal were true, it would be accomplished already. To say that a goal is false is technically accurate but peculiar. Unlike a false belief, a goal description is intentionally formulated to differ from the current state of affairs; no use wishing for things you already have. Goals are neither true nor false but *desired*.

Goals and actions need to be distinguished because people can pursue one and the same goal through different actions. If the kitchen in your new home has an unfamiliar layout, the actions needed to make a cup of tea might change – the tea is now in a cupboard to the left instead of to the right, forcing you to make a change in motor behavior – but the goal, the cup of tea, remains the same. Unless goals are represented separately from the relevant actions, goals cannot remain constant while actions vary. Flexible behavior requires that we can pursue a goal through different actions depending on the circumstances, and this in turn requires distinct mental representations for goals and actions.[16]

Goals vary with respect to the amount of time they control a person's behavior. To make a cup of tea takes a few minutes, but to fill the cup of life takes longer. Andrew Corrigan-Halpern and I refer to the duration of the behavior controlled by a goal as the *scope* of that goal.[17] A goal that controls behavior over a long time period is likely to be accomplished by calling upon goals of smaller scope rather than by calling on elementary actions directly. Such subordinate goals are called *subgoals*, and the dominant goal is their *superordinate goal*. A superordinate goal can be either a *top goal* or a subgoal to some other goal of yet greater scope. Tracing the relations upward, *make tea* might turn out to be part of *throw a dinner party*. There is no upper limit on the scope of goals; consider *achieve world peace*. The goals that are involved in performing a given task jointly form a *goal hierarchy* or *goal tree*.[18]

Typically, all the subgoals to a given goal have to be accomplished for that goal to be accomplished. To make tea, you have to boil the water *and* put tea in the strainer *and* pour the water through the strainer. These subgoals are linked by *conjunction* ("and"). From the point of view of the superordinate goal, it might not matter exactly how any one subgoal is accomplished. A subgoal can be associated with different ways of achieving it; you can boil water over an open fire *or* on an electric store *or* in a microwave oven. These methods are alternatives. There is no need to boil the water three times; once will do. Similarly, *go to dinner* might entail *tell X that we"ll meet him at the restaurant*, but success in this part of the dinner project does not depend on whether X is told face-to-face or via fax, phone, pigeon post or texting; all that matters is that X is told, somehow. Alternative methods for achieving a goal are linked by *disjunction* ("or"). A goal tree consists of alternating conjunctive and disjunctive layers; multiple subgoals, each reachable by alternative paths, each of which in turn poses multiple sub-subgoals, and so on. In everyday parlance, we refer to such a structure as a *plan*; see Figure 6.2. The claim is that battle plans, business plans, lesson plans and travel plans all share these structural features. The computer science term *AND/OR tree* is awkward but descriptive of these complex structures.

Task Environments

When a person decides to pursue a particular goal he is in the *initial state* of his performance. A situation in which the criteria or constraints that define the goal are satisfied is a *goal state*. Although some tasks can be accomplished with a single action – *to turn on the light, flip the switch* – it is more common that a task requires a sequence of actions. *To open the window* might require us to *draw the curtain, lift the latch, push the window outward*, and *secure the latch* again. Each action changes the material situation in some respect. A sequence of actions $A_1, A_2, A_3, ..., A_n$ creates a sequence of situations, $S_1, S_2, S_3, ..., S_n$. Each

The Growth of Competence

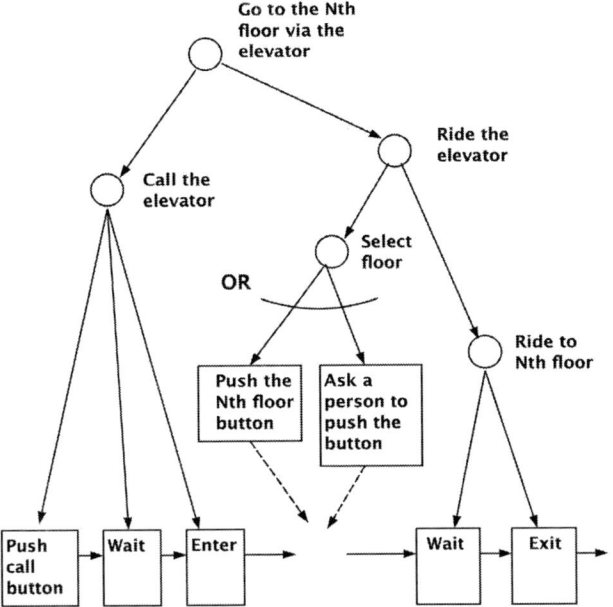

FIGURE 6.2. A goal-subgoal hierarchy for using an elevator. Goals are symbolized by circles and actions by rectangles. This plan is implemented by the rules in Table 6.1.

situation is the output of the action applied to its predecessor and serves as the input to the immediately following action. A situation in which the goal has not been satisfied but the person must stop pursuing it anyway due to lack of time or other resources is a *dead-end state*.

In each successive state of affairs, the person has to choose which action to perform. The initial state and the person's repertoire of actions define a *situation tree*. The latter includes all the situations that can be accomplished by applying some action to the initial state S_o; then all the situations that can be reached by doing the same to each of its descendants; and so on. A situation tree is neither objective nor subjective but emerges in the interaction between a person and his material environment. The person contributes the set of actions and the objective environment contributes the set of causal laws that determine the consequences of those actions and hence the possible successors to each situation.

It is convenient to depict situation trees graphically. A graph of a situation tree has a single *root node*, the initial situation, and paths branching off from each other, ending in *leaf nodes* that are either dead-end states or goal states; see Figure 3.3. Such a graph is a description of the task environment in terms of the action possibilities it affords. To describe the person's behavior as a path through a situation tree is to describe it in the context of the ensemble of possible behaviors (by that particular person, in the given situation). The situation tree is analogous to the solution space in the theory of analytical thinking proposed in Chapter 4, but the moves from one state (situation) to another are actions rather than mental operations or inferences.

Practical Knowledge

As chemists distinguish between organic and inorganic chemical compounds, so cognitive scientists have settled on a broad distinction between declarative and practical knowledge. *Declarative knowledge* is knowledge about the way the world is. *Practical knowledge*, on the other hand, is knowledge about what to do.

The distinction was originally stated in terms of declarative and *procedural* knowledge.[19] However, the term "procedural knowledge" is unfortunate, because it is too easily misunderstood as referring to knowledge of more or less explicit, codified or fixed procedures, which is not the intended concept. As used in this book, the term "practical knowledge" refers to knowledge about how to perform tasks, reach goals or produce desired consequences and effects.[20] This usage has natural links to the verb *to practice*, the logician's concept of *practical logic*, the anthropologist's notion of *a cultural practice* and the common distinction *theory versus practice*, all of which are relevant for the topic of skill acquisition.

Declarative knowledge and practical knowledge differ in multiple interlocking ways. The units of declarative knowledge are variously called *assertions*, *propositions* or *statements*. *The Earth is round* is a prototypical example. Assertions are typically thought of as either true or false, although these concepts have caused more trouble for philosophers than common sense would anticipate. Two millennia of debate aside, it makes sense to ask about a declarative statement whether it is accurate with respect to the part of reality that it purports to describe. Practical knowledge, on the other hand, is neither true nor false but more or less effective.

Descriptions are neutral with respect to task and purpose. The assertion that *the Earth is round* is not intrinsically related to any particular task, but it might be useful in reasoning about a wide range of tasks. By itself, it does not specify any particular action. If you are in Europe and your task is to get to India, the knowledge that the Earth is round makes you wonder if it is better to sail east or west, an issue that does not arise in the absence of this proposition, but it does not specify which way is best. If you like camels, take the path of Marco Polo; if you like fish, go the way of Christopher Columbus. If your task is to draw a map of the world, that same proposition forces you to choose some projection of the spherical surface of the Earth onto the flat surface of the map, a problem that does not arise for people who believe in a flat Earth, but it does not specify which projection is best. If you want your map to exhibit geographic areas in their correct proportions, use a Sylvanus projection, but if you, like sailors, want your rhumb lines – courses of constant compass bearing – to appear on the map as straight lines, use Mercator's projection. The belief that the Earth is round does not specify or recommend any particular action, but it can be used to reason about action in an infinitude of situations, most of them not contemplated at the time in life when this belief is adopted.

Practical knowledge, in contrast, specifies which action or actions to perform to solve some task. *If you want the elevator to come, push the button* is a prototypical example. Actions must be adapted to the situation at hand if they are to be effective, so practical knowledge must include knowledge of the conditions under which an action should be performed and the conditions under which it should not. If you are at an intersection and the traffic light is red, you are supposed to stop; if the light is green, to keep going. In most cases, the contingency of action is more intricate and complex than this example, but the principle is the same: An action is appropriate under some conditions but not under others. To be competent, to know what to do, is to know when, under which conditions, to do what.

These observations imply that the smallest unit of practical knowledge is a three-way association between a goal, a situation (or a class of situations) and an action (or action type). For historical reasons, such three-way associations between goals, situations and actions are called *production rules*, or *rules* for short.[21] The term "rule" inconveniently confuses implicit knowledge in a person's head with explicitly codified entities like traffic laws, but the usage is too entrenched in cognitive science to escape. We can represent a rule in the following schematic way:

Rule: Goal, Situation → Action,

which is a shorthand for the hypothesis that the person whose rule it is, when pursuing the specified goal and finding himself in a situation of the specified type, will consider the action mentioned in the right-hand side of the rule. The situation is assumed to be specified as a conjunction of features (*the water is boiling and the tea leaves are in the strainer and the strainer has been placed in the cup* ...). A three-way association is an atom of practical knowledge that cannot be split into smaller parts that themselves are meaningful units of practical knowledge. The hypothesis that practical knowledge is represented in terms of goal-situation-action triplets is known as the *Production Systems Hypothesis* and it was first proposed by H. A. Simon and A. Newell.[22]

Unlike a proposition, a rule is neither true nor false. A rule of action is like a piece of advice or an exhortation, with the difference that rules are typically known only implicitly and hence not available for introspection. A rule is more or less useful, more or less appropriate in that the action it recommends may or may not lead to the goal, or may lead to the goal with greater or lesser cost or effort, under the given circumstances. We can talk about the correctness of rules only in the sense of efficiency vis-à-vis goal attainment, and efficiency is a matter of degree. Unlike declarative knowledge, practical knowledge is goal and task specific. Techniques for sailing a ship are not much use when drawing a map, and vice versa.

A single production rule does not suffice for even the simplest task.[23] The strategy for making a cup of tea, for example, might contain as many as a hundred rules. The set of all rules that are relevant for a task constitutes the person's practical knowledge of how to do that task. If a rule is an atom of practical knowledge, a *rule set* is a molecule. There are many words in English that refer to cognitive units of this latter sort: algorithm, heuristic, know-how, method, plan, procedure, program, recipe, strategy, tactic, technique, trick, and so on. For consistency, I will use the word "strategy." Table 6.1 shows a hypothetical strategy (rule set) for the everyday task of using an elevator.

Strategies are of various types. There are highly general but vague strategies like, *if you don't know how the device works, just push any button and see what happens*. Others are very specific: *if you need to use an ATM, look for a bank*. Some strategies are codified and learned explicitly. The standard procedures for arithmetic taught in primary school are perfect examples. Other methods are implicit and more flexible. Cooking is a good example. Recipes are explicit but cooking skills are nevertheless largely implicit. Sometimes implicit knowledge is said to be *tacit* or *intuitive*. Some strategies, like the rules for using an elevator, are simple and small in scope, while others, like the management skills needed to run an international company, are complicated and vast in scope. Unfortunately, there are few naturalistic studies of strategies and there is no widely accepted classification.[24] A rule set is an idealization, but a useful idealization. The next question is how a set of independent rules generates coherent and organized task behavior.

Strategy Execution

For a set of rules to produce overt behavior, some goal must be posed, the current situation assessed, the most promising option (rule) selected, and the

TABLE 6.1. *Goal-situation-action rules that implement the plan in Figure 6.2.*

Goal	Situation	Actions
Go to Nth floor via the elevator	Standing by elevator door & elevator is at some other floor & call button is not lit	Set goal to "Call elevator"
Call elevator	Standing by elevator door & elevator is at some other floor & call button is not lit	Push call button
Call elevator	Standing by elevator door & elevator is at some other floor & call button is lit	Wait
Call elevator	Standing by elevator door & elevator is at the current floor & elevator door is open	Enter elevator; goal is satisfied; set goal to "Use elevator"
Use elevator	Is inside elevator & floor button is not lit	Set goal to "Select floor"
Select floor	Is inside elevator & button for Nth floor is not lit & button is within reach	Push button for Nth floor; goal is satisfied; set goal to "Ride to Nth floor"
Select floor	Is inside elevator & button for Nth floor is not lit & button is not within reach	Ask a person to push the button; goal is satisfied; set goal to "Ride to Nth floor"
Ride to floor	Is inside elevator & elevator is moving & button for Nth floor is lit	Wait
Ride to floor	Is inside elevator & elevator is at the Nth floor & elevator door is open	Exit the elevator; goal is satisfied
Go to Nth floor via the elevator	Is on Nth floor & outside elevator	Goal is satisfied

action of the selected rule performed. Each turn through this *perceive-decide-act cycle* results in some change in the current situation, and the cycle repeats. A task performance normally consists of a long sequence of perceive-decide-act cycles, each cycle ending with either a motor action or a cognitive operation such as an inference or the setting of a subgoal. In programming terminology, execution is *iterative*.

Because practical knowledge is hierarchically organized, execution is also *recursive*. That is, the top goal is unpacked into a set of subgoals and the latter are processed and unpacked in turn by the same processes. Eventually, the process of unpacking encounters elementary actions, which are carried out without further breakdown. If the relevant subgoal is thereby satisfied, control reverts to the next goal upward, where the process repeats itself. In the terminology of computer science, this is called *top-down, left-to-right execution*. This pattern is familiar to writers who use outlines.

At each decision point, the situation at hand is evaluated by testing all relevant rules – that is, all rules that share the currently active subgoal – for the satisfaction of their conditions. If there are no relevant rules that match the current situation, then the person's practical knowledge is incomplete; he has not yet mastered the task. If there is a single rule that matches, the action of that rule is executed. If there are multiple rules that match, they are entered into a temporary memory structure called the *conflict set*. A single rule is chosen from that set by a process called *conflict resolution*, and the action of the selected rule is performed. There are various conflict resolution schemes.[25] A specific scheme will be described in Chapter 7.

In short, a set of rules is executed by four main processes: First, a *matching* process compares all relevant rules against the person's perception of the current situation to determine the available options. Second, a *conflict resolution* process selects a single rule from the set of matching rules. Third, the action of the chosen rule is *performed*. Finally, a *control process* moves the locus of control from node to node in the goal tree. The mental machinery that performs these processes is called the *cognitive architecture*.[26] The distinction between a task-independent architecture and a pool of task-specific rules neatly slices cognition into its invariant and changeable aspects. The former is possibly innate, the latter certainly acquired.

PROCESSES FOR SKILL ACQUISITION

If practical knowledge consists of a collection of goal-situation-action associations – production rules – then to master a novel task or to adapt to changing task demands is to extend or revise such a collection. A process that takes one or more rules as input and generates an improved rule as output is a *learning mechanism*. Like other change mechanisms, a skill acquisition mechanism can be partitioned into a triggering condition and the change process proper. A situation in which the triggering condition for some learning mechanism is satisfied constitutes a *learning opportunity*. The execution of the corresponding change process is a *learning event*.

Learning events are brief compared to the time it takes to master a skill, so the *Raisins in the Dough* principle applies (see Chapter 4). The majority of the cognitive processes that occur during practice participate in the execution of the learner's current version of the strategy-to-be-learned. Only a few operations, irregularly distributed across time, revise the rules. In one analysis, Kurt Van Lehn identified 11 strategy changes in a problem-solving effort that lasted 20 minutes, a rate of 1 learning event per 2 minutes.[27] A single learning event might take between 1 second and 1 minute. Each learning event tweaks the current version of the relevant skill, but the magnitude of the change is small. Observable effects on the time to solution, the probability of error and other aspects of behavior are cumulative consequences of many minor changes in the underlying strategy. The rate of change during a practice period is a function of the density of learning events, and the latter depends on the task environment, the difficulty of the target task, the learner's current level of mastery and other factors.

The central theoretical task is to specify the number and nature of the learning mechanisms. The growth of a cognitive skill is a complex type of change and it is highly unlikely that it is due to a single mechanism. For example, learning from instruction is quite different from learning in the course of independent practice, and learning by adapting an already mastered skill to a new task is obviously a different process from learning from error. A successful skill acquisition theory needs to postulate a repertoire of distinct learning mechanisms, or *modes of plasticity* in neuroscience terminology. For ease of reference, I call this the *Multiple Mechanisms Principle*. The question is how large a repertoire to expect. If not a single mechanism, then how many? Intuition rebels against the thought that there are a hundred distinct ways in which practical knowledge can change. More than 1, but less than a 100; so 10 appears to be the right order of magnitude. As it turns out, most skill acquisition theories proposed over the last century are indeed multimechanism theories with less than 10 distinct mechanisms. The complexity of the hypothesized mechanisms and the rigor with which they are specified have increased over time.

A Century of Progress

The beginning of systematic research on the acquisition of cognitive skills can be specified with precision. William James's comprehensive *Principles of Psychology*, published in 1890, did not include a chapter on skill acquisition, but the Ph.D. thesis of his student E. L. Thorndike, begun in 1896 at Harvard University but issued a few years later from Teachers College at Columbia University, reported experimental studies of how various species of animals learned to escape from cages with nonobvious door-opening mechanisms.[28, 29]

Thorndike displayed the time it took individual animals to escape from a box as a function of trial number. He proposed a two-mechanism theory known as the *Law of Effect*, which says that organisms weaken their disposition to perform an action if that action is followed by negative consequences, but strengthen it if the action is followed by positive consequences. At the same time, William L. Bryan and Noble Harter's analysis of training data for Morse code operators stimulated interest in the acquisition of complex, real-world skills.[30] Although Hermann Ebbinghaus had already published curves for the memorization and forgetting of lists of syllables, Thorndike and Bryan and Hartner were the first to plot what we now call learning curves for skills. Table 6.2 highlights select milestones since this beginning.[31]

Learning became the major theme of the behaviorist movement, conventionally dated as beginning with John B. Watson's 1913 article, "Psychology as the Behaviorist Views It."[32] During the 1913–1956 period, "experimental psychology" and "learning theory" became almost synonymous in the United States, but the dominant experimental technique was to study the memorization of lists of letters, syllables or words. R. S. Woodworth's 1938 review of experimental psychology included a chapter on practice and skill that summarized a mere 27 studies that tracked learning in complex tasks like archery, telegraphy and typing.[33] Woodworth discussed the shape of the learning curve and stated the idea that skill acquisition goes through phases: "... it appears that the typical process of learning a complex motor act proceeds from whole to part and back to whole again." He did not propose a rigorous theory.[34]

World War II prompted psychologists in Britain and the United States to focus on complex skills.[35] The war posed novel psychological problems, such as how to train anti-aircraft gunners. A second transforming influence was that psychologists came to work alongside engineers, mathematicians and scientists who were in the process of creating new information technologies. Code breaking, long-range direction finding, radar tracking and other information-processing problems led researchers to realize that information can be measured and processed in objective and systematic ways and that it is possible both to build information-processing systems and to view humans and animals as examples of such systems.

After the war, Norbert Wiener at the Massachusetts Institute of Technology envisioned an interdisciplinary science to be called *cybernetics*, which was to study complex information-based systems, encompassing humans, machines and animals, in terms of *feedback circles*.[36] Like Thorndike's Law of Effect, the principle of feedback describes how behavior changes in response to positive and negative action outcomes. The idea of replacing the stimulus-response

TABLE 6.2. *Milestones in a century of progress in skill acquisition research.*

Year	Event	Reference
1896	E. L. Thorndike's dissertation shows practice curves for animal problem-solving skills.	Thorndike (1898)
1913	John B. Watson proclaims that behavior, not mind, is the proper subject matter for the psychology of learning.	Watson (1913)
1935–1945	Psychologists work alongside the founders of the information sciences and information technologies in the war effort.	Baars (1986); Mandler (2002)
1948	Norbert Wiener publishes *Cybernetics*, a proposal for a unified theory of information processing based on feedback circles.	Wiener (1948); Conway & Siegelman (2005)
1945–1955	Discovery of probability matching; statistical learning theory becomes a separate subfield.	Estes (1950); Grant et al. (1951)
1958	A. Newell, J. S. Shaw and H. A. Simon publish the Logic Theorist, the first symbolic simulation of a complex cognitive skill.	Newell, Shaw and Simon (1958)
1960	G. A. Miller and co-authors publish *Plans and the Structure of Behavior*, a unified theory of cognition based on the notion of plans.	Miller, Galanter, and Pribram (1960)
1960–1970	Applied psychologists R. Gagné and P. M. Fitts propose the notions of multiple mechanisms and of distinct phases of practice.	Gagné (1965); Fitts (1964)
1965–1975	E. A. Feigenbaum and B. G. Buchanan launch the study of expert systems in Artificial Intelligence. Such systems provided a model of expertise, the end point of cognitive skill acquisition.	Buchanan & Feigenbaum (1978); Davis et al. (1977)
Early 1970s	A. Newell creates the first computer implemented production system architecture for the simulation of human cognition.	Newell (1972, 1973)
1979	Y. Anzai and H. A. Simon publish the first symbolic simulation of skill acquisition.	Anzai & Simon (1979)
1983	J. R. Anderson publishes the first version of the ACT model, with six learning mechanisms.	Anderson (1983)
1985–1995	Anders Ericsson launches the empirical study of expertise as a product of deliberate practice.	Ericsson et al. (1993)
1980–2000	Symbolic learning mechanisms proliferate.	Ohlsson (2008a)
1990–2010	The symbolic (explicit) and statistical (implicit) modes of learning are re-united in hybrid models.	Anderson (2007); Schneider & Oliver (1991); Sun et al. (2001, 2005)

reflex with the feedback circle as the key building block of human cognition received much attention in the 1950s and 1960s.[37] Unfortunately, Wiener focused on continuous feedback, which is more relevant for sensorimotor than cognitive skills and which can only be analyzed with the help of complex mathematics. These and other factors reduced the influence of the cybernetic approach.[38]

Cybernetics was overtaken by the digital approach, variously called *complex information processing* and, eventually, *artificial intelligence*, launched by A. Newell, J. C. Shaw and H. A. Simon with a 1958 article describing the Logic Theorist, the first symbol-processing computer program that performed a task, logical deduction, that is recognized as requiring intelligence when done by people.[39] The program formalized the notion of *heuristic search*, an enduring concept. Significantly, the article was published in *Psychological Review* rather than in an engineering journal, and the authors offered speculations on the relation between their program and human cognition. The article thus simultaneously initiated the field of artificial intelligence and introduced psychologists to computer simulation as a theoretical tool.

Paradoxically, the success of the digital symbol manipulating approach had a detrimental effect on the study of learning. In the period 1958–1979, no leading cognitive psychologist conducted basic research on the effects of practice or other problems related to the acquisition of complex cognitive skills. Success in simulating human behavior – any behavior – was recognized as an achievement in and of itself, even if a model did not simulate changes in that behavior over time.

Progress toward understanding skill acquisition was instead driven by the goal of contributing to education and training. Educational psychologists like David Ausubel and Robert Gagné developed the educational implications of the concepts developed in basic research on learning.[40] In his 1965 book *The Conditions of Learning*, Gagné summarized research up to that time in a multimechanism theory that specified eight different modes of learning, including motor and verbal chaining of actions, two types of discrimination, concept learning and learning by saving the results of successful problem solving. He also argued for the importance of specifying the triggering conditions for the different modes of learning. Focusing on training rather than academic learning, applied psychologists like Paul M. Fitts and Alan T. Welford continued to accumulate empirical data on the learning of complex skills.[41] In the 1960s, Fitts developed the notion of a small number of phases that are characterized by the types of changes occurring, another enduring contribution. The distinction between sensorimotor and cognitive skills was not emphasized in this line of work.

The hiatus in theorizing came to an end with a 1979 *Psychological Review* paper by Simon and Yuichiro Anzai.[42] They presented a computer program that modeled the successive strategy changes of a single person who solved a problem-solving task multiple times. The paper demonstrated the feasibility of simulating the acquisition and not only the execution of cognitive skills. The paper was soon followed by the initial versions of J. R. Anderson's ACT model and the Soar model proposed by Newell, Paul S. Rosenbloom and John E. Laird.[43, 44] The 1983 version of the ACT model included six different learning mechanisms (proceduralization, rule composition, rule generalization, rule discrimination, strengthening and weakening). The success of the initial models established computer simulation as a useful theoretical tool.

The story since 1979 is one of proliferation. A wide variety of theories have been proposed and embodied in computer simulation models. Typically, a model consists of a cognitive architecture that follows some theory of stable behavior like the one presented earlier in this chapter, plus a repertoire of learning mechanisms. Models differ in the details of their performance mechanisms, but, more important, they incorporate different learning mechanisms. The fact that theories are embedded in computer programs have the peculiar linguistic consequence that they tend to be known by the proper names of those programs instead of descriptive titles. Almost all serious models are multimechanism models. For example, Ron Sun's *CLARION* model learns through both bottom-up generation of rules and rule generalization, while VanLehn's *Cascade* model learns from solved examples as well as by analogy.[45, 46] All in all, the emergence of computer simulation as a theoretical tool triggered an unprecedented explosion of the theoretical imagination. More new hypotheses about the mechanisms behind the acquisition of cognitive skills were proposed in the period 1979–1999 than in the previous century.[47]

The journey from the Law of Effect to *Cascade* and *CLARION* represents a century of scientific progress. Theories of skill acquisition are more precisely formulated, more responsive to the complexity of human skill acquisition and more explanatory than they were a century ago. Nevertheless, the historical trajectory through the space of theories looks in retrospect like a drunkard's walk. The choice of mechanisms to include in any one model is not grounded in any principled argument about which repertoire of mechanisms is most likely to be the one that has in fact evolved in the human brain. For example, why did the ACT model of 1983 vintage not include any mechanism for learning from examples, and why does *Cascade* lack a discrimination mechanism?

Computer simulation of skill acquisition resembles work on heavier-than-air flight before the Wright Brothers: Would-be aeronautical engineers would design an airplane, build it, try to fly it, sweep up the debris and build another one.[48] When confronted with the huge space of possible airplane designs, this mode of operation made for slow progress. The Wright Brothers succeeded because they worked separately on the three subproblems of lift, propulsion and steering, and combined the solutions. The study of skill acquisition also needs a principled way to guide the search through the space of possible repertoires of learning mechanisms.

The Information Specificity Principle

Hypotheses about skill acquisition can be organized in terms of their inputs. Improvements in a task strategy cannot arise out of nothing; structure has to come from somewhere.[49] If a learning mechanism produces rules that are better adapted to the target task than the learner's current rules, that mechanism must have incorporated additional information about the target task into those rules. A learning mechanism can therefore be conceptualized as a process that takes one or more rules plus some additional information as inputs and delivers an improved rule as output. The new rule is better adapted to the task environment precisely because it incorporates the additional information.

The question of the number and nature of the learning mechanisms can therefore be approached by considering the number and nature of the sources of information that are available to a learner in a practice scenario, and the types of information they provide. The processes needed to make use of one type of information typically differ from the processes needed to make use of some other type. For example, learning from a solved example requires different processes from learning from an error, and learning from an analogous task requires different processes from learning from positive feedback. This *Information Specificity Principle* postulates a mapping between types of information and types of learning mechanisms. It attributes the multiplicity of learning mechanisms to the existence of multiple types of information.

Multiple Mechanisms and *Information Specificity* are abstract principles and they do not by themselves explain any one instance of skill acquisition or any regularity therein. They are meta-principles in that they specify the kind of explanation psychologists should seek. Together they suggest that we can make an informed guess about the repertoire of skill acquisition mechanisms

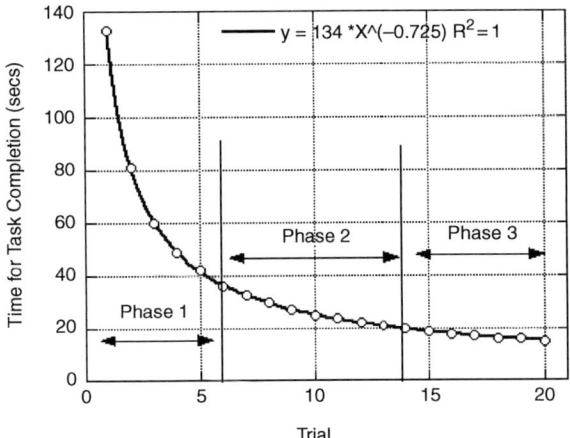

FIGURE 6.3. The three phases of skill acquisition proposed by Paul M. Fitts superimposed on a learning curve.

by first identifying the relevant types of information that might be available to a learner in the course of practice. The second step is to specify, for each information type, how the mind might use it to improve an existing rule set. The possible inputs constrain the possible mechanisms, because no mechanism can learn unless there is information to learn from.

This view suggests that theories and models of skill acquisition can be organized by slicing each model into its learning mechanisms and sorting the mechanisms by type of input. Furthermore, it is clarifying to group the various types of information and the associated learning mechanisms by the stage during practice in which they are most important. Building on the formulation of Fitts, I distinguish three main phases, which I call *getting started*, *mastery* and *optimization*; see Figure 6.3.[50] As Fitts emphasized, the stages are idealizations. "It is misleading to assume distinct stages in skill learning. Instead, we should think of gradual shifts in ... the nature of the processes ... employed, as learning progresses."[51] That is, there are no sharp boundaries between the stages and no big switch in the head that determines which stage a learner is in. The appearance of stages is created by gradual shifts in the relative abundance of different types of information, with consequent changes in the relative frequencies with which the different learning mechanisms are triggered. The mix of mechanisms that is responsible for most of the change in any one practice period gradually changes as competence grows. The division into three distinct stages superimposes artificially sharp boundaries on this gradual shift but the division is nevertheless a useful device for organizing a review of mechanisms for skill acquisition.

Stage 1: Getting started
The first stage begins when the learner encounters the practice task and ends when he completes the task correctly for the first time. In this stage, the main theoretical problem is to understand how the leaner can start practicing. How does he know what to do before he has learned what to do? There are five distinct types of information that might be available at the outset of practice: direct instructions; declarative knowledge about the task; strategies for analogous tasks; demonstrations, models and solved examples; and outcomes of unselective search. Consequently, researchers have hypothesized five different types of learning mechanisms that operate primarily in this stage.

A coach, teacher or tutor who already knows how to perform the target task can tell the novice how to perform the target skill. For example, a parent might tell a child: *If you want the elevator to come, then press the button*. The cognitive processes that operate on such instructions are presumably the same as for discourse comprehension generally, with a twist: To benefit, a novice must not only understand the utterance in the linguistic sense but also turn it into a piece of executable practical knowledge. That is, the instruction has to be transformed into one or more rules. Anderson and David M. Neves introduced the convenient term *proceduralization* to refer to the mechanism responsible for this step.[52] In the elevator example, proceduralization is straightforward: The "if" part becomes the rule condition and the "then" part becomes the action. For other instructions, proceduralization is less straightforward (e.g., *be cautious!*). Language is notoriously elliptical, so the resulting rules are likely to be incomplete (*which button?*), but they nevertheless constitute a kernel for the strategy-to-be-learned, to be improved by other mechanisms.

A second hypothesis claims that people might be able to figure out what to do if they possess sufficient *declarative knowledge* about the task.[53] This view is often heard among mathematics educators. For example, if a teacher tells a student that two triangles in which all three sides are congruent are themselves congruent, he would want the student to infer that one way to prove two triangles congruent is to prove that all their sides are pairwise congruent, thus deriving a proof procedure from a descriptive statement. A good term for this type of process is *practical reasoning*. The most consequential practical inference in history is perhaps that *if the Earth is round, you can get to the Far East from Europe by sailing west*. The prevalence of reasoning from first principles is likely to be limited by the complexity of the required inferences.

A third source of information available to a novice learner is his or her stock of *prior practical knowledge*. Novel tasks are never completely novel; there are always similarities to already mastered tasks. Edward Thorndike suggested that already acquired "elements" of practical knowledge can be re-used on a novel task.[54] Thorndike did not define what he meant by "elements," but we can identify them with rules.[55] If a rule was learned in the course of mastering task X and that very rule also applies to another task Y, it need not be re-learned. No particular learning mechanism is needed to revise or edit the rule. Identity is a strong requirement. A weaker criterion is that the current task is *analogous* to some already mastered task. To use analogical information, the learner has to retrieve a useful analogue from memory, map the two tasks to each other in a consistent way and then use the strategy for the already mastered task as a template for the strategy-to-be-learned. Researchers have proposed several different ways in which this type of learning mechanism might be implemented in the human brain.[56]

In real-world contexts, a person can learn by observing others performing the target task, as when a novice barista observes an experienced coffee shop employee whip up a couple of complex espresso drinks (*modeling*).[57] In a training environment, the competent person might carry out a *demonstration* that is specifically designed to help a novice see how the target task is to be done, as when a drill sergeant shows the recruits a rifle maneuver. In academic settings, lectures and textbooks often provide *solved examples*, canned demonstrations that the novice can study in order to see how a particular type of problem is supposed to be solved. A major difficulty with this type of information is that models, demonstrations, and solved examples require the learner to generalize the presented solution, and it may not be obvious what or how to generalize.

If there are no helpful instructions, if the task situation is too opaque to handle via practical reasoning, if the target task is not analogous to any prior task, and if no model, demonstration or solved example is available, then the learner can nevertheless act vis-à-vis the task. People possess general heuristics that apply to almost any task (*if you have no idea what to do, do something*), and those heuristics can at least generate task-relevant behavior. Acting generates new information in the form of observable outcomes. This source of information becomes more extensive and important in the second phase of skill acquisition.

Stage 2: Mastery
The second stage of practice begins when the learner completes the task for the first time and it lasts until he can reliably perform the task correctly. During this stage, the main theoretical problem is how the learner can improve his incomplete and possibly incorrect version of the strategy-to-be-learned. The most important source of information during this middle stage consists of the outcomes of the actions generated by the current version of the target skill. To act tentatively in an unfamiliar environment is to ask questions of that environment. Pushing a button is to ask, *what does this button do?* and the machine's response is the answer; poking a piece of coral with the tip of a diver's knife is to ask, *what is this?*; if it scampers off, the information gained is that this a well-camouflaged fish. In general, the relation between action and outcome contains information. Since the emergence of cybernetics in the 1940s, information to the effect that the learner's action was appropriate, correct or useful is called *positive feedback*. The source of such information can be an instructor or a peer (*good job; that's the right answer;* etc.), but it can also be the material task environment (*oh, I see; this button does turn on the red light*). Information to the effect that the learner's action was erroneous, incorrect, inappropriate or unhelpful in some respect is called *negative feedback*. It, too, can come from a tutor (*perhaps you should double-check that answer*) or originate in the material environment, as when a novice driver fishtails when trying to drive on ice for the first time.

Different mechanisms are required to learn from these two types of information. In their 1966 review of learning theories, Ernest R. Hilgard and Gordon H. Bower stated this point succinctly, using *Right* to refer to positive feedback and *Wrong* to refer to negative feedback:

> There is a logical difference between responding in the intelligent direction to *Right* and *Wrong*. The intelligent response to *Right* is to do again what was last done. This makes possible immediate rehearsal; the task is clear. The intelligent response to *Wrong* is to do something different, but what to do is less clear. It is necessary both to remember what not to do and to form some sort of hypothesis as to what to do.[58]

The main conundrum regarding learning from positive feedback is what there is to learn: To elicit positive feedback, the learner must have done the right thing. But if he already knows what to do, then how does the positive feedback help? It almost certainly has some role to play, because giving positive feedback is a common move by experienced tutors.[59] One possibility is that many actions taken during skill acquisition are tentative. The learner does not know the right step with any certainty but moves forward anyway. In some proportion of such situations, the step taken will, in fact, turn out to be appropriate, correct or useful. In those situations, positive feedback helps to reduce the uncertainty about that step. This type of effect can be modeled with *strengthening*, a learning mechanism that was formulated by Thorndike and constitutes the first half of his Law of Effect: When a rule generates a positive outcome, increase its strength.[60] The consequence is that the rule will win against its competitors more often, thus being executed more often. In Thorndike's own words: "The one impulse, out of many accidental ones, which leads to pleasure, becomes strengthened and stamped in thereby, and more and more firmly associated with the [relevant] sense-impression. ... [Learning curves] represent the wearing smooth of a path in the brain."

However, positive outcomes invite other, more generative processes as well. If the learner tentatively performed action A in situation S in pursuit of goal G, the outcome turned out to be positive and there is no prior rule that would have recommended that step, then it is reasonable to create the new rule

$$G, S \Rightarrow A,$$

which will recommend the successful action in future encounters with S; this is sometimes called *bottom-up rule generation*.[61] One complication is that the situation S is history by the time the positive feedback arrives and will not recur, so the rule needs to specify *situations like S*, rather than S itself. Bottom-up learning requires a *generalization* process that can determine, given the example situation S, in which class of situations, $\{S\}$, the action A will produce a positive outcome.[62] It is not obvious how such a generalization process might work. If I see a movie by director X with story line Y and I like the movie, it makes more sense to conclude that I should see more movies by director X than to conclude that I should see more movies with story line Y. The right conclusion is obvious in each specific case, but it is less obvious how it can be computed by a general mechanism.

One possible technique is to extract shared features across multiple situations. For example, users of word-processing software learn to select text by double clicking on a paragraph, and also to select graphical elements by double clicking. It is plausible that the similarities between the corresponding rules result in a more general rule of the form *if you want to select any object on a computer screen, double click it*. This rule is more general than its parents and hence might come into play in other contexts, such as programming. In rule notation, if the learner has already acquired the two rules

$$R_1: G, S_1 \rightarrow A$$

and

$$R_2: G, S_2 \rightarrow A,$$

it might be useful to create the new rule

$$R': G, (S_1 \cup S_2) \rightarrow A,$$

where $(S_1 \cup S_2)$ is a symbol for whatever S_1 and S_2 have in common. This mechanism produces a new rule that is more general than either R_1 and R_2 and hence might apply in situations not covered by either of those two original rules. In such situations, action A might turn out to be correct, because that situation shares some features with S_1 and S_2. Strengthening, bottom-up rule creation and various rule generalization mechanisms have been incorporated into several computer models of skill acquisition.

Feedback can be negative as well as positive. When a person is acting in an unfamiliar or changing task environment, his repertoire of rules will fit that environment to some extent, but not completely. Consequently, some of his actions will have their intended outcomes, but others will either be impossible or irrelevant or they will produce unexpected outcomes. In everyday parlance, we call deviations between expected and observed outcomes "errors," and we are used to regarding errors as undesirable. But in the context of skill acquisition, errors provide information. It may seem obvious how to learn from this type of information: Do not repeat the action just taken. But the problem of learning from error is more complex than it first seems. It is discussed in depth in Chapter 7.

Stage 3: Optimization
The optimization stage begins when the target skill has been mastered, that is, when it can be executed reliably, and lasts as long as the person keeps practicing. Improvements can continue for a very long time. What improvements are possible, once a learner knows how to perform the task correctly? What additional types of information become available after mastery? As practice progresses, the stock of memories of past actions, answers and solutions grows. Mechanisms that can make use of this type of information include shortcut detection and optimization on the basis of statistical regularities in the task environment.

A task strategy might yield a correct answer and yet be inefficient. Well-documented examples can be found in children's arithmetic. At a certain age, children respond to simple addition problems like 5 + 3 = ? by counting out five fingers and then continuing to count out three more to arrive at the right answer (*one, two, three, four, five, six, seven, eight – eight is the answer*). At a somewhat later age, children discover that counting out the first addend is unnecessary, and they begin with the larger addend and count up (*five; five, six, seven eight – eight is the answer*). This shortcut can be discovered via analyses of *execution traces* of past task solutions: Every solution that begins counting at unity passes through the larger addend along the way. A mechanism that detects and deletes repetitious and redundant steps is sufficient to detect such shortcuts. Shortcut detection only applies when there is a shortcut to be detected.[63]

Even in cases when there is no shortcut to be detected, strategy execution can be optimized by extracting *statistical regularities* from the environment.[64] The latter are typically learned implicitly. For example, reaction times to words that occur with high frequency in normal discourse are shorter than reaction times to low-frequency words. This helps optimize reading, because the high-frequency words, by definition, need to be accessed more often. This type of optimization occurs late during practice, because the extraction of statistical regularities requires large amounts of experience. Estimates of word frequencies cannot be stable until the person has been reading for a while.

If a person is called upon to answer a question or solve a problem many times, he will eventually remember the answer.[65] This form of optimization replaces computation with information storage. Like other forms of optimization, it requires extended experience. Implicit information about frequency of occurrence is needed to identify tasks for which it is more efficient to memorize the answers than to compute them as needed. Shortcut detection and optimization via statistical regularity extraction and memory-based responding probably account for much of the speed-up that occurs after a task has been mastered.

THE NINE MODES THEORY

To summarize, there are nine different types of information that might be available in practice scenarios: verbal instructions issued by a coach or tutor; prior declarative knowledge about the task environment; already mastered strategies for analogous tasks; models, demonstrations and solved examples; outcomes from unselective search; positive feedback; negative feedback; execution histories; and statistical regularities in the environment. Each type of information can be used to adapt, improve or speed up a cognitive skill.

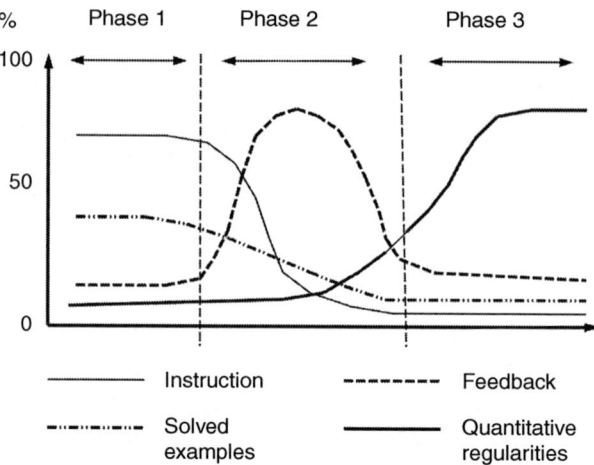

FIGURE 6.4. A hypothetical case of how the relative importance of four learning mechanisms might shift across the three phases of skill acquisition. The *y*-axis represents the percentage of overall improvement within each phase that is accounted for by each mechanism. To avoid clutter, the figure assumes that there are only four mechanisms, so their contributions sum to 100% within each phase.

The relative prevalence of each information type is likely to vary across the course of learning. In the beginning stage, instructions, examples, prior strategies, practical inferences and outcomes of tentative steps are likely to be the most available sources of information and the mechanisms that make use of them hence must account for much of the initial improvements. In the middle stage of learning, those types of information will typically fade because their usefulness has been exhausted. Instead, the information generated by acting vis-à-vis the task – feedback – and the mechanisms that utilize feedback dominate. Eventually, the task environment is so well understood and explored that there is little that can be learned from yet more feedback. In this stage, additional speed-ups and error rate reductions are possible only because execution histories enable the learner to discover shortcuts, and statistical regularities in the environment enable the learner to optimize his decision making. The nature of the changes that take place is itself gradually changing as practice progresses; see Figure 6.4 for a simplified illustration with four types of learning.

In principle, there could be other types of information that are not yet included in the preceding list, but to date no such addition has come to mind. The possibility that the nine constitute the complete list raises the question of how we should interpret the learning mechanisms proposed to date.

The fact that there are multiple theories and models of skill acquisition should not fool us into conducting experiments with the purpose of selecting one of them as the better theory. Competitive comparisons of goodness of fit to experimental data are only meaningful when two hypotheses are mutually incompatible in the strong sense that if one is true the other cannot be. But this condition does not hold for hypotheses about individual skill acquisition mechanisms because nothing prevents human beings from learning in multiple ways. The theoretical task is not to pit different learning mechanisms against each other in a race to account for this or that phenomenon, but to assemble a repertoire of mechanisms such that we can explain as many aspects of skill acquisition and skill adaptation as possible.

Human beings are efficient learners, and reliance on a protracted period of learning is a species-characteristic trait, so it is plausible that we have evolved to be *maximally efficient* learners. As our eyes are maximally efficient in the sense that the retina can react to a single photon, so our ability to learn might have evolved to make use of every bit of information.[66] To be maximally efficient is to make maximal use of all information that might be available to a learner during practice. This *Principle of Maximally Efficient Learning* is an example of what cognitive scientists call a rationality principle.[67] It is an idealization, but it is close enough to the truth to anchor the search for an empirically adequate theory. The implication is that to propose a theory of skill acquisition is to assemble a repertoire of nine different learning mechanisms to make use of the nine types of information.

The pool of hypotheses proposed and formalized in simulation models already contains one or more well-specified mechanisms to make use of each of the nine information types. The surprising conclusion is that *we already possess a first-approximation, multimechanism theory of skill acquisition*. More precisely, we possess a family of such theories in which the members vary slightly, depending on exactly which variant of each mechanism we select from the smorgasbord of proposals. Abstracting over those details for a moment, the Nine Modes Theory claims that people acquire skills through nine different learning mechanisms: (a) *Proceduralization*, or translating verbal instructions into executable practical knowledge, perhaps in the form of a set of production rules. (b) *Practical reasoning*, or reasoning from prior declarative knowledge about the task environment to a conclusion about what to do. (c) *Analogy*, or mapping the current task onto an analogical task in memory and using the strategy for the analogue as a template for the strategy-to-be-learned. (d) *Internalization* of demonstrations or solved examples. (e) *Caching* outcomes of unselective search (trial and error). (f) *Generalization* of tentative steps that produced positive outcomes. (g) *Learning from error*, or revising rules that produced negative outcomes so as not to generate such outcomes in the future. (h) *Shortcut discovery*, or identifying redundancies and repetitions in execution histories and deleting unnecessary steps. (i) *Optimization*, or anticipating processing demands on the basis of statistical regularities extracted from the environment.

The point cannot be stated strongly enough: *The theory of stable behavior and the list of proposed learning mechanisms, sorted by the nine types of information, constitutes a scientific theory of how skills are learned during practice.* Although this is stated as a theory for the first time here, it is not my theory. It is a collective accomplishment of the community of skill acquisition researchers. The steady growth of this theory over a century of research is one of the great success stories of cognitive psychology. It remains for cognitive psychologists to claim it.

The theory does not only answer the question of mechanism, but it also answers the questions about sufficiency, necessity and gradual change. Practice is sufficient for learning in the sense that practice automatically engenders improvement, at least in the beginning of practice. The reason is that the learning mechanisms, like most cognitive processes, are not under voluntary control but run outside consciousness. To practice is a conscious and deliberate activity that one can choose to engage in, but a mutation in a production rule is caused by a mental process that occurs at a particular moment in time because its triggering conditions are satisfied, not because the person has an intention or volition to improve. Improvement in skill is a side effect of intentional activity. Practice is sufficient to cause cognitive change in the same sense that ingestion is sufficient to cause digestion.

Practice is necessary because improvements cannot arise out of nothing. Learning incorporates new information into the strategy-under-construction, and that information has to come from somewhere. The paradox of learning by practicing is that the learner generates that information himself by attempting to perform the target task. Action triggers the construction of initial rules, and the execution of those rules produces positive and negative feedback. By performing the target task repeatedly, the learner produces an execution history that might reveal shortcuts, accumulates information about statistical regularities in the environment and stores solutions and answers in memory. In short, practice is necessary because the response of the task environment to the learner's actions is the ultimate source of information about the task; no action means no information and no improvement.

Why is improvement gradual? The *Raisins* principle introduced in Chapter 4 provides the answer: Each learning event, each application of a learning mechanism like those described previously, produces a single mutation in a single rule within a large rule set. The effect of a single application of a learning mechanism to a single rule is necessarily minor. To master a complex task requires many such mutations, multiple revisions of each one of a large number of rules.

These answers cover the first four of the six questions about practice stated at the beginning of this chapter. The fifth and sixth questions, about transfer of training and the efficacy of instruction, are answered in Chapter 7.

The fact that the Nine Modes Theory provides in-principle answers to the fundamental questions about skill practice does not prove that it is the best possible theory, because some other theory might be able to provide even more satisfactory answers. One way to improve the theory is to try to improve on the three meta-theoretical principles that shape it: Multiple Mechanisms, Information Specificity and Maximal Effectiveness. But it is more plausible that there are multiple mechanisms than that all aspects of skill acquisition can be explained by a single change mechanism. To question Information Specificity is to claim that learning mechanisms can operate on any type of information, but no such mechanisms have ever been proposed and it is not clear what this means. The potentially weak point in the meta-theory is the assumption of Maximal Effectiveness. The latter sounds too optimistic to be true. But which of the nine modes of learning could a critic plausibly deny? Even casual observation of everyday behavior would quickly yield examples of each of the nine learning modes. All in all, to try to improve the meta-theory is an unpromising line of attack.

A more plausible approach is to accept the meta-theory and to question the particular mechanisms proposed for each type of information. The theory might be improved by developing psychologically more plausible mechanisms for one or the other mode of learning, or by increasing the empirical support for one or the other mechanism. For example, a particularly weak component of the theory is the pool of hypotheses for learning from errors, failures and other types of negative feedback. For beings who constantly deal with novel and changing task environments, errors and unexpected outcomes are facts of life, so it is likely that we have evolved a more sophisticated mechanism for making use of negative feedback than those proposed in past research.

Even if the mechanism for a particular mode of learning is well developed and motivated, the question remains of whether it is the right mechanism – that is, whether it is equivalent in its input and output to how the brain operates when changing in the relevant mode. How well grounded is the mechanism in empirical observations? On this dimension, each of the nine modes does as well as any hypothesis in psychology. All nine modes are supported by systematic empirical studies as well as by common sense. Some mechanisms, such as learning by analogy and learning from solved examples, have been supported in dozens of studies. From this perspective, the Nine Modes Theory is as empirically grounded as any theory in cognitive psychology.

The methodological implication of multiple mechanisms is that observable changes in performance are not due to any one mechanism but to the interactions among the different change mechanisms. We should not expect to derive empirical phenomena from any one mechanism by itself, even though the majority of research studies attempt precisely such single-mechanism tests. The more telling test would compare data with predictions derived from a model that learns in all nine ways. The question is what to use as a baseline. What counts as a good versus unsatisfactory fit to the data? We do not have several nine-mechanism theories to compare; as long as we accept that different implementations of a mechanism cannot be reliably differentiated with the kinds of behavioral data currently available, then we have only a single ninemode theory. Estimates of goodness of fit are then meaningless. One partial solution is to compare the full nine-mode theory with models that lack one or the other mechanism. The issue is whether each of the nine mechanisms adds predictive power to the model, that is, whether it does a better job of accounting for data than a model without that mechanism. If this is true for all nine mechanisms, then the complete theory is supported. James J. Jewett and I made a modest move in this direction by building a simulation model that could learn from either positive or negative feedback or both simultaneously.[68] Simulation runs with the model did indeed show that having both mechanisms operating at the same time produced better fit to human learning curves than either mechanism by itself. A serious test of the full Nine Modes Theory requires a simulation model that can learn in all nine ways. Developing such a model is a task for the future. The first century of skill acquisition research prepared the ground and put the main conceptual support in place, but finalizing the theory might take a second century. A reasonable first step is to improve the theory of learning from negative feedback. This is the task of Chapter 7.

7

Error Correction: The Specialization Theory

For a slip to be started, yet caught, means that there must exist some monitoring mechanism of behavior – a mechanism that is separate from that responsible for the selection and execution of the act.

Donald A. Norman[1]

The crucial issue in the regulation of intentional action is the opportunity to compare what was intended with what in fact resulted, using the difference between the two as a basis of correction.

Jerome S. Bruner[2]

The world is not a stable, repetitive clockwork that travels forever in the same orbit, but a nonlinear, turbulent and complex system, continuously transformed by forces both material and social. The laws of change are themselves changeable. A person knows this complex world only through a small and necessarily unrepresentative sample of situations. Consequently, prior knowledge will fit some aspects of the person's environment but not others. Even if the world were to stay still, we do not. Every time we colonize a new task environment, we turn into novices once again. The novice struggling to master an unfamiliar task and the competent performer working in a task environment that is changing under his feet differ in some respects, but both scenarios undermine the projectability of prior experience. Attempting to perform the task at hand by methods and strategies that worked well until yesterday, we unavoidably act inappropriately, incorrectly or unproductively part of the time. The turbulent character of the material and social worlds, the limitations on prior experience and the recurring need to acquire new skills imply that the occurrence of unexpected and undesired outcomes is an intrinsic aspect of action.

In everyday parlance, we label such outcomes "errors." Although errors can be disastrous and we do what we can to eliminate them, they are informative.

Every action is a probe that bounces off the environment like a sonar signal, returning with the outlines of otherwise unseen causes, objects and processes. Deviations between expected and observed returns tell us that the world is not as we assumed and hence provide an opportunity to correct our assumptions.

The prevalence of error must have been one of the factors that exerted selective pressure on early humans once they set out on the unique evolutionary pathway of relying more on acquired than innate skills. As the hunter-gatherer bands moved through habitat after habitat on their great migration across the globe, their survival strategies were forever becoming maladaptive.[3] It is plausible that they evolved a special-purpose cognitive mechanism for making use of the information that resides in errors, failures and other undesirable outcomes to improve the fit between their strategies and their environments. If so, errors are not merely eliminated as a side effect of successful adaptation. Errors play an active role in their own elimination; we unlearn errors by learning from them. The theoretical questions are these: What information resides in erroneous outcomes? How, by what cognitive processes, can that information be extracted and utilized? What behavioral implications follow from those processes?

FRAMING THE PROBLEM

The old proverbs *burnt child dreads the fire* and *once bitten, twice shy* suggest that learning from error is straightforward: The cure is to refrain from performing whatever action produced the bad outcome.[4] Edward Thorndike codified this idea in the second half of his Law of Effect: What he called an "annoying aftereffect" (i.e., an undesirable outcome) lowers the probability that the learner – adult, animal or child– will perform that same action in the future.[5] Repeated negative outcomes cause the erroneous action to disappear from the learner's behavior. In Thorndike's colorful terminology, the "futile impulse" is "stamped out."[6] In the terminology introduced in Chapter 6, this effect can be modeled by reducing – *weakening* – the strength of the rule that produced the offending action. That rule will then lose to competing rules during conflict resolution and hence apply less often and therefore generate fewer errors. Learning a skill is to a considerable extent a matter of learning what not to do.

This *don't do it again* response to error works with respect to sticking fingers into flames, but it does not work as a general explanation. Unlike burning one's fingers, most actions are not intrinsically correct or incorrect. For example, if an absent-minded professor tries to open the door to his home with the key to his office, the lesson cannot be *never use the office key*, lest he lock himself out of his office forever. The more plausible lesson is not to use the office key in the apartment door. Actions are only correct or incorrect in relation to some situation. To learn from an error is to distinguish the situation in which the action is an error from those in which it is correct. Adjusting the strength of an action or rule downward does not accomplish this, because the adjustment lowers the probability of the relevant action in every situation.

William James devoted four pages of his *Principles of Psychology* to an explanation of how a child who is burned by a flame avoids being burned by that flame again.[7] According to James, "… we know that 'the burnt child dreads the fire,' and that one experience usually protects the fingers forever."[8] The perception of the flame, the reflexive action of reaching for it, the sensation of pain and the equally reflexive retraction of the arm become associated in the child's mind, in that sequence. The next time the child sees the candle flame, the action of reaching for it is initiated by the same lower, reflexive neural pathways that made the child reach for the flame the first time, but it is inhibited by the higher brain centers due to the chain of associations from the sight of the flame to the retraction of the arm. This pseudo-neural mechanism does not suppress the disposition to reach out and grab interesting objects, only the tendency to perform this action with respect to the candle flame. James's explanation has the peculiar implication that errors are never truly corrected. Error-producing response tendencies remain after learning. We commit fewer erroneous actions over time because we spend more and more of our waking time inhibiting those tendencies. A better theory of learning from error should describe how the disposition that led to an erroneous action is altered so that the action is no longer triggered in the situation in which it causes the undesirable outcome, thus relieving the higher brain functions from the need to monitor and inhibit.

James's explanation is an attempt to capture the intuition that the cure for an error is to avoid repeating the same action *in the same situation* in which it caused trouble. But the phrase "in the same situation" overlooks the fact that situations, once past, are history. If we perform action *A* in situation *S* and experience a negative outcome, in which future situations should we avoid doing *A*? It is not enough to say *in S*, because by the time the learner knows the outcome of doing *A* in *S*, that situation is past and will never recur. We can say, *in situations that resemble S*, but situations resemble each other to varying degrees along different dimensions. The better answer is, *in situations that resemble S in the relevant aspects*, which immediately leads to the question of how our brains know which aspects are relevant. If the candle hurts, what is the relevant class of situations? The blue flame on a gas stove does not look like a candle flame, but a picture of a candle does. Similarly, if a chess player loses a match, what is the lesson? A useful answer cannot refer to the specific moves made in that match, because the match is over and will never be played again. Exactly which change in the player's strategy is implicated by the disappointing checkmate? In general, if action A generates an erroneous or undesired outcome in situation S, how can the person's brain compute the class of situations $\{S\}$ in which A should be avoided? We are demonstrably capable of learning from our errors, so our brains must be able to carry out a computation of this sort. The micro-theory of learning from error presented in this chapter specifies such a computation.[9]

ERROR DETECTION

The triggering condition for learning from error is the occurrence of an error, so the first two questions are what we mean by error and how people detect their own errors. A third question is what information an error provides that the learner's brain can use to compute the indicated revision of the relevant practical knowledge.

Objective Versus Subjective Errors

A driver approaches an intersection and makes a left turn; his intended destination required a right turn. We recognize this as a mistake, but there are complexities. It cannot be the case that the action type *turn left* is erroneous in any absolute sense. There are a good many intersections at which *turn left* is correct. Rather, it was the occurrence of that particular token of *turn left* in that particular intersection that was mistaken. The fact that the driver's destination lay to his right is one of the facts that made the left turn erroneous. Another relevant fact is that the driver approached the intersection from the south. If he had approached the same intersection from the north, with the same destination in mind, a left turn would have been correct. Whether the left turn is an error also depends on the availability of alternatives. It was a mistake in part because the driver made a left turn *instead of* a right turn. If the other roads at the relevant intersection were blocked by roadwork so that the left turn was the only action available, then it would not have been an error. It might be the start of an undesirable detour, but if the left turn was the only physically possible action, it was nevertheless not a mistake. The possibility of error is a consequence of the fact that most situations present a person with multiple options, only some of which are on any path to the desired goal.

The phrase *the left turn was an error* must therefore be understood to mean *turning left instead of right at that intersection, approaching from the south with destination X in mind, was a less effective way to get to X than one of the alternative turns available at that intersection*. An action token is a mistake when it is performed in a situation in which it does not serve the goal of the person performing it, at least not as well as some other action. An error is an action that does not lie on the (shortest) path to the goal.

Like common sense, this view defines errors as deviations from a normative standard (the best or correct solution). This concept of error belongs to an omniscient observer who can access the entire situation tree and evaluate every action in relation to its alternatives. Although the objective view is a useful analytical tool, it does not explain how people detect their own errors. The concept of a deviation from a standard might capture the essence of errorhood, as it were, but it does not provide someone who has not yet acquired that standard with a cognitive mechanism for detecting errors. To be informative during learning, errors must be recognizable by the learner himself. A theory of error detection requires a shift from an objective to a subjective view of errors.

Situations produced by erroneous actions typically contain features that reveal that an error has been committed. In everyday task environments the features can be perceptually intrusive, as when the learner smells something burning while cooking or hears grinding noises from the gearbox while learning to drive with a standard transmission. In technical task domains, error detection might be less direct. A chemistry student might detect an error in a laboratory procedure by comparing the weight of the reaction products with the weight of the reactants and observe that they differ. In symbolic task environments, error signals tend to be subtler. A statistics student might suspect that the magnitude of a quantity is unreasonable, and a programmer might recognize unbalanced parentheses as a syntax error.[10]

The recognition of such *error signals* typically requires task-specific knowledge. For example, a driver trying to find a location north of his or her current location who encounters a road sign saying *Route 60 south* knows that he or she has made a wrong turn. To recognize this traffic sign as an error signal one must know that roads are labeled according to their directions and that south and north are opposites. In other situations, the knowledge required to recognize an error signal might be more extensive. To recognize the answer to a statistics problem as unreasonable one must have some knowledge about the range of reasonable answers. To recognize syntax errors in computer code one has to know something about the correct syntax. To check a laboratory procedure by weighing the reactants and the reaction products one has to know that mass is conserved in chemical reactions.

In general, prior declarative knowledge about the task environment is the learner's main resource for judging the appropriateness of the situations he or she creates or encounters in the course of performing a task. Learners monitor their own actions by comparing what they observe with expectations based on what they know. *Errors appear subjectively as conflicts between what the learner knows ought to be true and what he or she perceives to be true.* Prior knowledge implies that such-and-such should be the case, but the actual situation fails to conform; hence, some action taken en route to that situation was incorrect.

Dissociation Between Action and Judgment

The hypothesis that learners detect errors through prior knowledge is paradoxical: If the learner has enough knowledge to recognize a particular action as incorrect, then why did he or she perform that action in the first place? Why not apply that knowledge so as to select the correct action? On the other hand, if the learner does not have sufficient knowledge to produce the correct action, how can he judge his action as incorrect? The ability to catch ourselves making errors points to a duality in our relation to the environment.

The dissociation between execution (action) and evaluation (judgment) can be understood in terms of the distinction between declarative and practical knowledge. This *Dual Knowledge-Base Principle* is a well-established aspect of human cognition.[11] The function of practical knowledge is to generate action in the service of goals. The function of declarative knowledge is less obvious. The functions most frequently proposed are to enable people to describe and explain phenomena, infer new conclusions and predict future events. Declarative knowledge is said to consist of *propositions*. A proposition is the meaning of a statement or an assertion. It is meaningful to ask whether a proposition is true or false, even though establishing the answer is sometimes difficult. This view of declarative knowledge was invented and developed by philosophers, linguists and artificial intelligence researchers for their various purposes.

However, this view leads to conceptual riddles that have befuddled thinkers in all those disciplines. After two millennia, there is no widely accepted theory of what it means for an assertion to be true.[12] We can understand the truth of a specific proposition like *the cat is on the mat* in terms of a correspondence between assertion and reality, but this interpretation of truth is already problematic with respect to such innocent-looking assertions as *all swans are white* and *the sun will rise tomorrow*, and it becomes hopelessly inadequate when confronted with counterfactual assertions (*if we had more money, we could afford a car*), probabilistic statements (*there is only a 50–50 chance that this stock will increase in value*) and abstract principles about theoretical entities (*two electrons cannot occupy the same orbital shell*).

There is no good evidence that the propositional view is psychologically accurate. Nothing is more commonplace than the casual cocktail party comment that *people don't always reason logically, do they?* – a comment that wraps the speaker and the hearer in a shared mantle of superior rationality. Cognitive snobbism apart, this attitude is supported by systematic inquiry. Laboratory experiments have demonstrated several types of illogical behavior on the part of experimental subjects: atmosphere and framing effects (the wording of an argument influences its acceptability), confirmation bias (people tend to accept as valid arguments that end with conclusions that coincide with what they believe), difficulties in processing negated statements and a disposition to accept certain fallacious argument patterns as valid.[13] The hypothesis that people reason by applying truth-preserving inference rules to propositions is contradicted by a large body of empirical evidence. If the propositional model is not correct, it is possible that the function of declarative knowledge is not primarily to support description, explanation or reasoning.

The question arises as to what the function of our vast database of declarative knowledge might be instead. A novel departure is to cast declarative knowledge as *prescriptive* rather than descriptive. The cognitive function supported by declarative knowledge might not be deduction, description, explanation or prediction but *judgment*. Declarative knowledge enables a person to assess an object, event or situation. In particular, it enables him to guess whether his current situation lies on the path toward his goal. While practical knowledge enables the generation of action, declarative knowledge enables the evaluation of action outcomes.

This view invites the idea that action and judgment are dissociated because they rely on distinct knowledge bases. Consequently, a person might possess the (declarative) knowledge required to judge a performance as incorrect but lack the (practical) knowledge required to perform better. In the words of D. N. Perkins in *The Mind's Best Work*:

> A fundamental fact – maybe even the fundamental fact – about making is that critical abilities are more advanced than productive abilities. We can discriminate differences we can do little to produce. ... For many reasons, the test for a certain property requires much less of us than producing something with that property.[14]

The dissociation between action and judgment is well supported by everyday experience. For example, an athletic coach is not necessarily a world champion; a good editor is not necessarily a successful author; and so on. The ability to judge a performance or a product benefits from some level of skill in the relevant domain but does not require superior performance. On the other side of the coin, superior performance is not necessarily accompanied by connoisseurship. An artist or an inventor may or may not be able to recognize genius in others. The dissociation between action and judgment is also supported by different types of experimental evidence.[15] For example, young children can accurately judge the performance of someone else on numeric tasks as either correct or incorrect, even though they might be unable to produce the correct performance themselves. There is neuroscience evidence for specific brain areas that deal with internal conflicts, error detection and error correction.[16]

In short, a person might possess the declarative knowledge required to judge a performance as inappropriate, incorrect or unhelpful, but nevertheless lack the practical knowledge required to perform better. This is not an exotic possibility but the normal case. The distinction between practical and declarative knowledge resolves the paradox that people can detect their own errors but it raises the question of how declarative knowledge can be represented in memory so as to serve this evaluative function.

Error Signals as Constraint Violations

If the function of declarative knowledge is to support judgment, then it is helpful to conceptualize the smallest unit of declarative knowledge as a *constraint* rather than a proposition. A constraint is not an assertion about the world but a prescription. It states what *ought* to be the case rather than what *is* the case. The set of all constraints that apply in a particular task environment – the *constraint base* – defines what is meant by a correct performance in that environment. A task performance that does not violate any of the constraints in the relevant constraint base is appropriate or correct. Errors – conflicts between expected and observed outcomes – appear as *constraint violations*. For example, the set of all traffic laws is the constraint base for the traffic environment. A speed limit is a constraint on a driver's performance, as is the rule to drive on the right-hand side of the road. The traffic laws do not specify how people in fact drive; they specify how they ought to drive. A driving performance that does not violate any of the traffic laws is correct in the sense of being legal.

To develop this view of declarative knowledge, we need a formal theory, a logic of constraints to rival the logic of propositions.[17] This requires assumptions about how constraints are represented in memory and how they are processed. I propose that a constraint can be represented as an ordered pair

$$< C_r, C_s >,$$

in which C_r is a *relevance criterion*, that is, a specification of the conditions under which the constraint is relevant, and C_s is a *satisfaction criterion*, that is, the conditions that have to be met for the constraint to be satisfied. Each part of the constraint is a conjunction of expressions that refer to situation features. If the features specified in C_r hold in a particular situation, then the features specified in C_s ought to hold in that situation as well, or else the constraint is violated. If C_s does not hold, then it is irrelevant whether C_r holds.

Many familiar instances of declarative knowledge can be reinterpreted as collections of constraints. To continue with the traffic example, my knowledge that ABC Avenue is a one-way street constrains how I drive on that street. If I drive in the approved direction, my action satisfies the constraint; if I drive in the opposite direction, my action violates the constraint. Expressed in the formal representation, the knowledge that ABC Avenue is one-way in the easterly direction becomes this: *If you are driving on ABC Avenue, you ought to be driving in the easterly direction.* In this example, *driving on ABC Avenue* is the relevance criterion and *driving in the easterly direction* is the satisfaction criterion, so this constraint can be formalized as

(Driving x) & (On x ABC-Avenue) ** (Direction x East)

The "**" symbol stands for the connective "ought to." If I am walking or if I am not on ABC Avenue, the direction in which I am traveling is of no importance from the point of view of this particular traffic regulation; that is, the constraint is irrelevant. But if I am driving and, furthermore, driving on ABC Avenue, that is, if the conjunction

(Driving me) & (On me ABC-Avenue)

is the case, then I had better be driving east rather than west, meaning the expression

(Direction me East)

ought to hold as well. If I drive westward, I violate the constraint, which implies that I made a wrong turn.

A *constraint base* – the set of constraints a person believes hold in a domain of activity – is processed by matching the relevance patterns of all constraints against the situation at hand. The satisfaction patterns of those constraints that have matching relevance patterns are also matched against the current situation. If no constraints have matching relevance patterns or all constraints that have matching relevance patterns also have matching satisfaction patterns, then the situation is consistent with the person's declarative knowledge. If at least one constraint with a matching relevance pattern has a nonmatching satisfaction pattern, then the new situation violates that constraint and this tells the person that he has made an error. The set of constraints serves as a self-monitoring device by which the mind can judge the correctness of the solution path constructed by its (possibly incomplete or incorrect) practical knowledge. For example, cognitive psychologist Carl Martin Allwood concluded from a detailed study of errors in statistics problem solving that error detection occurs "when the problem solver perceives a discrepancy between the activity or result he or she has produced and one or more of his or her expectations."[18] In general, errors appear subjectively as constraint violations, mismatches between the satisfaction conditions of one or more constraints and the actual properties of the situation at hand.

Constraints generate expectations. When a relevance pattern is satisfied, there is an expectation that the corresponding satisfaction condition will be satisfied as well. In the normal course of everyday events, we are not aware that we anticipate effects and events. The fact that our minds are always one step ahead of the current state of the world becomes obvious when an expectation is violated. Imagine someone opening what looks like the front door of a house only to find a brick wall two feet from his nose. The resulting reaction shows that his mind was not neutral with respect to the unknowns on the other side of that door; if no hypothesis, expectation or prediction was unconsciously entertained, why the surprise? We are constantly applying knowledge about the world to anticipate the outcomes of our actions, even when we are not aware of doing so.[19] The machinery for executing a constraint base is a hypothesis about how this is done. The totality of the satisfaction conditions for all the constraints with matching relevance conditions is the person's set of expectations about the current situation.

How wide a swath of declarative knowledge can be reconceptualized as consisting of constraints rather than propositions? Not only traffic laws but also other types of conventions, from punctuation rules, Robert's Rules of Order and table manners to the rules for tic-tac-toe and the seating protocol for state dinners, fit the constraint format. Less obviously, at least some mathematical principles can also be expressed as constraints. Consider the concept of a one-to-one mapping: If object X is mapped onto object Y, and Z is some third object, different from Y, then X had better not be mapped onto Z as well (or else the mapping is not one-to-one). All these examples pertain to artificial, invented task environments.

Surprisingly, the constraint concept also applies to material reality. Many natural laws and scientific principles can be reinterpreted as constraints. Consider the laws of conservation of mass and energy. The function of these laws is to constrain theoretical calculations and laboratory work. The fact that neither mass nor energy can be either created or destroyed constrains the possible reactions between chemical compounds: Chemist Walter J. Gensler wrote, "There is so much trust in the mass conservation law that an experimental result ... that does not conform is automatically treated as false and rejected."[20]

It is not surprising that this is true centuries after the discovery of the law, and after the collection of large amounts of data in support of the law, but surely this natural law was regarded as a description rather than a prescription for the chemists who first discovered it? Some historians of chemistry disagree: "These [data] did not provide an independent confirmation of ... the principle of the conservation of mass. Rather Lavoisier relied on what was for him the axiomatic truth of the principle to adjust one result through another ..."[21] So even for Lavoisier, who was the first to formulate the mass conservation law and use it in his laboratory practice, conservation of mass functioned as a constraint on the interpretation of his experimental results.[22] The law is as much a constraint on the analysis of chemical data as it is a description of the material world.

Although the interpretation of declarative knowledge as prescriptive rather than descriptive reaches further than one might expect, there is no need to assume that all declarative knowledge is of one kind or that all pieces of declarative knowledge have the same form and function. For the constraint concept to play a role in a theory of learning, it is enough if a significant subset of the learner's declarative knowledge consists of constraints.

ERROR CORRECTION

Error detection is not yet learning. A detected error is a *learning opportunity*, but learning has not occurred until the error has been corrected. What this means is not self-evident because an erroneous action, once carried out, is history and so cannot be changed. The effect of an incorrect action on the person's

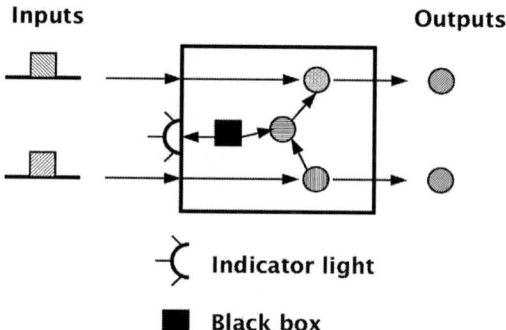

FIGURE 7.1. The difficulty of inferring the appropriate rule revision, given a falsified expectation. The top light is "off" although it is expected to be "on." The required diagnostic inference that the two conditions *indicator light is on* and *bottom light is on* should be added to the relevant rule.

environment can sometimes be altered or reversed through further action. This is often what is meant in everyday contexts by correcting an error. An example is to edit a misspelled word. The person reacts to the undesirable outcome – a complaint from the spell-checking software – by taking further action. If that is his only response, he might misspell that word again in the future. This meaning of "error correction" is not central for the theory of learning from error.

An action is the overt expression of a (not necessarily conscious or deliberate) decision. If the action is incorrect, then the practical knowledge on which the decision was based is erroneous. The *overt error* (the erroneous action) must be distinguished from its cause, the flaw in the underlying practical knowledge. Since the seminal study of arithmetic errors by John Seely Brown, Richard R. Burton and Kurt VanLehn, flaws in practical knowledge are often called *bugs* in analogy with mistakes in computer code; science education researchers use the term *misconception*; I prefer the term *fault*.[23] To learn from an action that generates an undesirable outcome is to eradicate the fault (or faults) in the practical knowledge that recommended that action. As a consequence, the learner has a lower probability of committing further errors of the same type. To correct an error in this sense is to improve future action, as opposed to revising the undesirable outcome of an action already executed.

The difficulty of inferring the underlying fault (or faults) in a complex system from observations of system behavior is well known among computer programmers, electricians and physicians; see Figure 7.1 for an illustration.[24] The square symbolizes a device with two input buttons, an indicator light and, on the other side, two output lights. The natural expectation is that the top button controls the top output light, while the lower button controls the bottom light. This leads to a rule such as *to turn on the top light, push the top button*. However, as the device is configured internally, a component is on only when all its inputs are on, so both the indicator light and the lower output lamp have to be on for the top button to switch on the upper output light. If the black box component is on or off due to factors the user cannot observe, this conclusion is difficult to draw. The diagnostic problem is no easier when the system consists of knowledge and the error is an inappropriate, incorrect or unhelpful response to some situation. How does the brain know which revision of the underlying practical knowledge to choose out of the infinitely many logically possible revisions? Something must give direction to the revision process if the faulty strategy is to be revised in such a way that the fitness between action and task environment improves. But what is the lesson that is embodied in an error? How, by what process, can the brain use the information residing in a constraint violation to infer the best, or at least a good or useful, revision of the faulty rule? One approach to this problem is to consider the origin of errors.

The Origin of Errors

The commonplace observation that things can go wrong in different ways suggests that there are distinct sources and types of errors. Different types of errors might need to be corrected in different ways, by different processes. For example, James Reason and Donald Norman have proposed a useful distinction between slips and mistakes.[25] *Slips* are errors that occur because the person does not do what he intended to do. They are due to some glitch in the execution of the person's strategy – a momentary lapse of attention, for example – and they are not informative with respect to the correctness of his relevant practical knowledge. *Mistakes*, on the other hand, result from the (faithful) execution of a faulty strategy. A child who intends to write "3" in an arithmetic problem but writes "5" instead makes a slip; a child who consistently borrows without decrementing makes mistakes. Slips are not the focus of attention here.

Are there different types of mistakes?[26] James Reason divided mistakes into rule-based mistakes and knowledge-based mistakes, whereas Heinz Heckhausen and Jürgen Beckmann distinguished implementation, initiation and termination errors. In fact, so many taxonomies of errors have been proposed that John W. Senders and Neville P. Moran felt compelled to propose a taxonomy of such taxonomies! The proliferation of error taxonomies does not inspire confidence in the proposed divisions of mistakes into types.

A plausible approach is to divide errors into types based on their origins. The concept of general problem-solving methods suggests a particular hypothesis about the origin and hence the correction of errors.[27] At the first encounter with the target task, a learner is not so much practicing as solving the problem of how to perform the practice task. In the earliest stage of practicing – the very first training trials – he cannot yet have a strategy that is adapted to the specific task (or else the task is not unfamiliar). But if he is acting, he is, by definition, executing some strategy or another. General methods are not adapted to the particular structure of any one task environment. They are widely applicable, but inefficient. Their function is not to produce solutions but to enable the learner to generate task-relevant behaviors vis-à-vis an unfamiliar task.

Like other strategies, general strategies can be described as collections of rules. The latter serve as templates for task-specific rules. For example, the general heuristic, *if you want to switch on an electrical device, then push its power button*, when applied to a particular device such as a computer projector, might generate the specific rule, *if you want to turn on a computer projector of brand X, then push the red button to the right*. The conditions on such rules (i.e., the part between *if* and *then*) are likely to be incomplete because the general rules do not contain any knowledge about the specific situation to which they are applied. Consequently, a rule has some probability of matching situations in which the action it recommends is not, in fact, appropriate, correct or useful. To continue the projector example, perhaps the projector works only if it is switched on *after* being hooked up to the computer, so a more complete rule is, *if you want to turn on a computer projector of brand X, and the projector has been hooked up to the computer, then push the red button to the right*. Without this additional condition, the rule will recommend pushing the power button even in situations in which the projector and the computer are not yet connected, perhaps causing a communication problem between the two devices. I refer to errors caused by overly general rules as *displacement errors* because they arise when an action was recommended even though it should not have been and thereby displaced whatever action would otherwise have been performed in that situation.[28] The claim that a significant proportion of errors in real situations is due to displacement is the *Displacement Hypothesis*.

Evidence that errors are generated because rules and strategies are overly general at the outset of learning has been found in multiple task domains; see Table 7.1. Overregularization in language acquisition is a classical example.[29] Children at a certain age apply linguistic rules to cases that constitute exceptions to those rules. An example is the overregularization of past tense formation. That is, the tendency to use the suffix "*-ed*" even in the case of irregular

TABLE 7.1. *Examples of overly general rules in four task domains. The underlined parts of the correct rules are the conditions that have to be learned.*

Past tense of verbs	
Overly general rule:	If the root of a verb is V, then its past tense is V+ed.
Example symptom:	"goed," "runned," "speaked," etc.
Correct rule:	If the verb is V and <u>V is not one of {go, run, speak, ... }</u>, then its past tense is V+ed.
Multiplication	
Overly general rule:	OP(X + Y) = OP(X) + OP(Y), where "OP" is any operation.
Example symptom:	$\sqrt{34} = \sqrt{25+9} = \sqrt{25} + \sqrt{9} = 5 + 3 = 8$
Correct rule:	<u>If "OP" is multiplication</u>, then OP(X + Y) = OP(X) + OP(Y).
Highway lane changes	
Overly general rule:	If you want to switch into the left lane, then turn left.
Example symptom:	Cutting in front of a car in the left lane.
Correct rule:	If you want to switch into the left lane and <u>the left lane is empty</u>, then turn left.
Cell phone volume control[a]	
Overly general rule:	If you want to increase the sound volume, push the volume button.
Example symptom:	Pushing the button before making a call.
Correct rule:	If you want to increase the sound volume and <u>a call is in progress</u>, then push the volume button.

[a] This example applies to a particular cell phone brand for which the volume control button works only when a call is in progress.

verbs (e.g., *comed* and *runned*). A large corpus of such events can be explained by the hypothesis that children have a single general rule for all regular verbs and many specific rules, one for each irregular verb. Overregularization occurs when the rule for regular verbs is applied to an irregular verb. That is, overregularization errors are a type of displacement error, caused by an overly general past tense rule. Table 7.1 shows additional examples from three other task domains.

The Displacement Hypothesis explains incorrect actions in terms of the normal functioning of the cognitive system. It is common for practical knowledge to be overly general. Only when we perform exactly the same task over and over again do we develop rules that are specific to that very task. This view of error contrasts with the assumption that performance errors are caused by some malfunction in the cognitive architecture such as lack of attention, loss of information from working memory due to processing overload or too much noise in the activations and strengths of knowledge structures.[30] We lack information about the prevalence of the different causes of error in everyday life.

Constraint-Based Specialization

If the main cause of errors is that the initial rules for a task tend to be overly general, then to adapt a strategy to a task is to gradually specialize those rules by incorporating more and more information about the task environment into them. As learning continues, the condition side of each rule becomes more and more restricted and the rules will consequently become active in fewer and fewer situations. As this process continues, a rule is eventually activated only in those situations in which its action is correct. According to this *Specialization Principle*, the direction of change during practice is from general but ineffective methods toward methods that are specific to a particular task. To adapt is to incorporate information about the task environment into the knowledge that controls action.

Given these concepts, the problem of learning from errors can be stated with precision: If a rule R with goal G and situation S as its conditions and action A as its right-hand side,

$$R: G, S \rightarrow A,$$

is activated in some situation S_1, and if the execution of A leads to a new situation S_2 that violates constraint $C = <C_r, C_s>$, then what is the appropriate specialization of R? That is, which conditions should be added to the condition side of R so as to prevent the rule from violating C in future situations?

For example, suppose that a novice car driver has discovered that driving behind a bus makes for slow progress on the highway and consequently acquired the rule, *If I am trying to get ahead, I am in the right-hand lane, another vehicle* x *is also in the right-hand lane,* x *is ahead of me, and* x *is a bus, then I switch to the left lane.* Formally, this rule can be written as

R: Goal = (Make progress)
Situation = [(In me rightlane) & (In x rightlane) & (Ahead x me) &
  (Isa bus x)]
$\Rightarrow$ SwitchLeft(me),

where the SwitchLeft action has the effect of changing *(In me rightlane)* to *(In me leftlane)*, while leaving everything else unchanged. This driving heuristic is overly general, because reckless moves between lanes are dangerous.

This state of affairs violates the constraint that one should not switch into the left lane when there is a faster car coming from behind. This constraint – call it C – can be formalized as

$$C = \{C_r = [(\text{In me leftlane}) \,\&\, (\text{In } y \text{ leftlane}) \,\&\, (\text{Behind me } y)]$$
$$** \; C_s = \text{not-}(\text{Faster } y \text{ me})\},$$

in which the double asterisk once again symbolizes the connective "ought to." C says that if there is a car coming up behind me, it had better not be faster than me (or else I am in trouble). Activating rule R when a faster car is coming up from behind in the left lane creates a constraint violation, which becomes obvious to the novice when the other driver honks his annoyance at the former's amateurish driving. When the novice switches lanes, the relevance criterion is suddenly satisfied by the situation at hand while the satisfaction criterion is not. What might the novice learn from this mistaken action? How should the novice driver revise his rule for driving?

When we encounter an unexpected and undesired outcome, we react in two ways. We infer that we should do A only when the constraint is irrelevant *(I should turn left only when the left lane is empty)* or when it is satisfied *(I can turn left when any vehicle in the left lane is slower than I am)*. The first response constrains the rule to situations in which C is irrelevant. The second response constrains the rule to execute only in situations in which C is guaranteed to be satisfied.

Consider the first of these two responses. If there is no vehicle in the left lane, the constraint is irrelevant and hence cannot be violated. In the driving example, the criterion for relevance is that there is a vehicle coming up in the left lane. The first specialization of the rule is achieved by negating that relevance condition and adding it to the situation part of the rule. (The precise algorithm for computing the conditions to be added is available in technical publications.)[31] The revised rule is

R': Goal = (Make progress)
Situation = {(In me rightlane) & (In x rightlane) & (Ahead x me) &
(Isa bus x) & **not**-[(**In y leftlane**) & (**Behind y me**)]}
$\Longrightarrow$ SwitchLeft(me).

The added condition elements are shown in bold face. The rule condition now says that it should not be true that there is a vehicle behind me in the left lane. More colloquially, the revised rule says, *switch to the left lane only if there is no car coming up from behind in that lane*. This rule recommends switching lanes only when the constraint is irrelevant. The procedure by which the new restriction on the rule is identified is general and well-specified: Negate the relevance condition of the violated constraint and add it to the situation part of the rule.

The second response to the constraint violation avoids future violations by creating a second version of the original rule that applies only when the constraint is guaranteed to be satisfied. This is done by adding both the relevance and satisfaction conditions (without negating them) to the rule. In the driving example, the relevance condition is once again that there is a vehicle coming up from behind in the left lane and the satisfaction condition is that this vehicle is moving more slowly than the driver's vehicle. If those conditions are added, the second revised rule becomes

R'': Goal = (Make progress)
Situation = {(In me rightlane) & (In x rightlane) & (Ahead x me) & (Isa bus x) & **(In x leftlane) & (Behind me x) & not-(Faster x me)**}
$\Longrightarrow$ SwitchLeft(me),

where the added conditions are once again shown in bold face. This second new rule says, approximately, *if there is a vehicle in the left lane, switch to that lane only if that vehicle is moving more slowly than your own*.

When these two revisions are completed, the initial disposition to switch into the left lane as soon as there is a bus ahead has given rise to two specialized versions of itself. The first new rule says that one can switch into the left lane if that lane is empty; the second says that one can switch into the left lane if any vehicle in that lane is slower than oneself. Between them, these two new rules exhaust the possibilities. The rule revisions identify the weakest conditions under which the original rule will violate the constraint, and then constrain the rule so as not to be active under those conditions. The result of these revisions is that the wisdom encoded in the learner's declarative knowledge is incorporated into his practical knowledge for how to drive. In A. Newell's terminology, structure has been moved from the evaluator (the constraint base) to the generator (the rule set).[32]

The learning algorithm works because constraint violations are informative. Mismatches or deviations between expectations and observations do not merely signal that an error as been committed; they also provide information about the exact nature and cause of the error. Merely designating an outcome as undesirable or inappropriate does not provide much information about how to correct it. The frequency of error is likewise void of useful information. The information that resides in an erroneous action can only be extracted by paying attention to the qualitative nature of the error – that is, to what the learner knows, what the constraints say and what the learner is seeing.

Rule Genealogies and Conflict Resolution

The mechanism described so far specifies the internal mechanics of a single learning event, a local modification of a single rule in response to a self-detected error. A rule typically needs to be revised multiple times on its path from being overly general to being correct. In addition, a strategy of even modest complexity consists of a large number of rules. For both reasons, acquiring or adapting a skill necessarily requires a sequence of rule revisions. Three additional principles are needed to understand how a single learning event affects an entire rule set.

When a rule R is revised, its two descendants R' and R'' are added to the stock of rules in the person's memory but they do not replace R. Instead, all three rules remain in memory. When either of the descendant rules is revised in turn, it also produces two descendants, grandchildren, as it were, to R. In this way, the specialization process generates a *rule genealogy*, a tree of descendants of R. The original rule R is a *root rule* and the rules that have not yet generated any errors and hence have no descendants are *leaf rules*; the versions between the root and the leaves are *intermediate rules*. As the genealogy grows, it becomes deeper; that is, the number of levels between the root rule and the leaf rules increases. The tree also grows wider; that is, each level contains more rules than the one preceding it. The root rule is the most general rule in a genealogy and the leaf rules are the most specific. If we trace a path from the root node to some leaf node, the set of situations to which each rule on the path applies – its domain of application – gets smaller and smaller from level to level; see Figure 7.2.

If a situation falls within the domain of application of one of the leaf rules, it is guaranteed to also fall within the domain of application of any of its ancestors, including the root rule. The question arises as to which version of the rule should be entered into the conflict set to compete with alternative rules for the control of action in that situation. The theory asserts that the most specific rule within a genealogy is the only one entered into the conflict set. This might turn out to be one of the leaf nodes, but it might also be one of the intermediate rules or even the root rule.

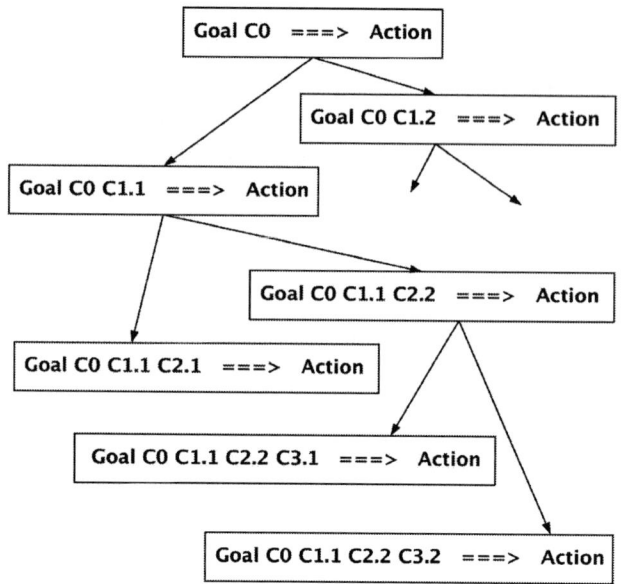

FIGURE 7.2. A schematic rule genealogy. The top rule recommends its Action when condition C_0 is satisfied. In Learning Event 1, two new versions are created by adding conditions $C_{1.1}$ and $C_{1.2}$. In Learning Event 2, the first of these new, more constrained variants is in turn specialized by adding conditions $C_{2.1}$ and $C_{2.2}$; and so on.

If the root rule is entered into the conflict set and if it wins against alternative rules, it will control action in that operating cycle. This is counterintuitive. The root rule was revised because it generated errors. How can the cognitive architecture eliminate errors if an erroneous rule remains in memory and retains the possibility of grabbing control of action? The answer requires a more careful analysis of what happens to the domain of application of a rule in the course of specialization.

If a rule R that recommends action A applies in some set $\{S\}$ of situations, and if that rule is specialized, $\{S\}$ is functionally speaking split into three subsets: one subset in which the descendant R' applies, a subset in which the other descendant R'' applies and a third subset that contains all other situations. We know that some of the situations in the third subset are those in which A generates an error, but it might also contain some situations in which it is as yet undecided whether A is correct or erroneous. To keep the parent rule R in memory after it has been revised is to retain the option of doing A in the latter class of situations. If A once again generates an error, it will be specialized again but in a different way, generating a different pair of descendants and hence starting a new genealogy from the same root.

Because A is known to be an error in some of the situations in the third subset, it is also necessary to consider actions other than A in those situations. This will occur because rules from other rule genealogies, recommending other actions, will also be entered into the conflict set. Within the conflict set, the same conflict resolution scheme applies: A more specific rule is preferred over a less specific rule. If a leaf rule R_2 is the result of multiple revisions and it recommends action B, it will be preferred over the root rule R_1 that recommends action A. The rule that has been revised a greater number of times is guaranteed not to cause certain types of errors, so it makes sense to prefer it over any general rule. If the situation falls within the domain of application of one of R_1's descendants, then that descendant will enter the conflict set instead of R_1, and there will be competition between two specific rules recommending different actions. The conflict resolution scheme has additional features as well, but the details are not important for present purposes.

In short, when a rule triggers a constraint violation, the relevant rule set is augmented with two specialized versions of that rule, but the rule itself is also kept in memory. In each operational cycle, the most specialized version of a rule that matches the current situation enters the conflict set. Within the conflict set, more specific rules are also preferred over less specific ones. The effect of this conflict resolution scheme is to consider action A in situations in which it is known to avoid certain types of errors, and at the same time give alternative actions greater priority in situations in which A's correctness is still unknown.

Relation to Alternative Mechanisms

According to the specialization theory, the acquisition and adaptation of a cognitive skill begins with general problem-solving methods. The rules that implement such methods generate errors precisely because they are general; that is, they put minimal restrictions on the actions they recommend. Consequently, those actions are sometimes executed in situations in which they are not appropriate, correct or useful. To detect such an error, the learner has to have sufficient knowledge about his task environment to evaluate the outcomes of his actions. An error is recognized as a constraint violation. To correct the fault in the responsible production rule is to specialize that rule by adding conditions that restrict its application to situations in which the relevant constraint is not violated. During conflict resolution, more specialized rules are preferred over less specialized ones.

An unexpected or undesirable outcome is sufficient to show that the responsible rule needs to be revised, but it is not by itself sufficient to determine the direction of the change, and the number of logically possible changes is large. The rule specialization process extracts the information that resides in the particular way in which the outcome of an action deviates from the outcome specified by the constraint for the domain and uses that information to decide how the faulty rule should be revised. The content of the constraint and the manner in which the observed outcome violates it – that is, the nature of the error – contains information that can be used to compute exactly which restrictions should be placed on the rule. In effect, we say to ourselves, *I guess it is only okay to do* A *when such-and-such is the case*; for example, *I guess it is only okay to switch to the left lane when that lane is empty*, or *I guess it is only okay to turn on the projector when it is already hooked up to the computer*. The added condition elements ensure that the revised version of the rule will not violate the particular constraint that triggered the revision, but there is no guarantee that the revised rule is correct in other respects. It might violate other constraints and so have to be revised again. Eventually, it will only apply in situations in which it does not cause errors.

Are there alternative mechanisms for learning from error that are equally consistent with standard cognitive concepts but that make significantly different assumptions about the error-correcting process? Although the unlearning of errors is both interesting theoretically and of considerable practical interest, the majority of learning mechanisms incorporated into cognitive simulation models capitalize on successes. For example, analogy and generalization both require a correct step as input. There is little point in building an analogy with a past problem that one failed to solve, or to generalize over one's mistakes. The same point applies to most of the mechanisms proposed in theories of skill acquisition.

The core problem in learning from error is to distinguish the set of situations in which an action or a rule has positive outcomes from those in which it has negative outcomes. One long-standing line of thought proposes that learners accomplish this by comparing particular situations of either type. A rat might be trained in a laboratory to jump to the left when it sees a star-shaped pattern and to the right when it sees a circular pattern, thus proving that it can discriminate between the two shapes. Computational mechanisms that operate on the comparison principle have been explored by P. Langley and other theorists.

Langley's version of discrimination utilizes the information in the execution history of a rule to compute the appropriate revision of that rule.[33] Suppose that action *A* is recommended by some rule *R*,

$$R: G, S \rightarrow A,$$

and that R applies in a sequence of situations. Suppose further that A turns out to be the right thing to do in some of those situations but not in others. Its execution history then contains a set of situations, $\{Sp\} = Sp_1, Sp_2, Sp_3, \ldots$, in which action A generated positive outcomes, and other set of situations, $\{Sn\} = Sn_1, Sn_2, Sn_3, \ldots$, in which the same action generated negative outcomes.

The natural inference is that there is some factor that distinguishes these two sets of situations. The condition of the rule needs to be augmented by some feature that discriminates between $\{Sp\}$ and $\{Sn\}$. The question is how to identify the relevant feature or features. The latter should be true of all members of $\{Sp\}$ but not of any member of $\{Sn\}$. It can be identified by first extracting the list of all features that are shared by all the members of $\{Sp\}$. The second step is to delete from that list every feature that is also true of at least one member in $\{Sn\}$. The features that remain differentiate the situations with positive outcomes from those with negative outcomes. Call that set of features $\{f\}$. Finally, add those features to S to produce a new rule R':

$$R': G, S, \& \{f\} \rightarrow A$$

This rule recommends action A only in those situations that exhibit the differentiating features. There is no guarantee that the new rule will never generate errors, but there is some probability that it will avoid the type of error produced in the past.

There are multiple difficulties with this model of learning from error. If there is more than one discriminating feature, this mechanism provides no systematic way of choosing among them. The options are to add all discriminating features to the condition side of the responsible rule, as in the schematic example earlier, or to create multiple new rules, each including one of the discriminating features. Given that two sets of situations might differ with respect to hundreds of features, these are unattractive options. In addition, discrimination, computed this way, makes implausible demands on memory. The learner's brain has to encode into long-term memory every application of every rule. There is no way of knowing in advance which features of a situation will turn out to be crucial for future discriminations, so each memory trace has to be quite detailed. Like all other inductive processes, discrimination lacks a criterion for deciding how much evidence is enough. How many situations of either type have to be in memory before the discrimination process is triggered? When it is triggered, the learner must retrieve all applications of the relevant rule from memory and compare them with respect to shared and unshared features to identify the potentially discriminating ones. Finally, the presence or absence of a particular feature does not by itself prove causation. The comparison process is unable to determine whether the presence of a particular feature is accidental or related to the outcome. For example, if a person rents three red cars of brand X and all three break down, while three yellow rental cars of brand Y do not, then the discrimination mechanism is as prone to form the rule "do not rent red cars" as "do not rent cars of brand X." These problems reduce the psychological plausibility of discrimination mechanisms that are based on the idea of comparing rule applications with positive and negative outcomes.

In contrast, the process of constraint-based specialization – apply the constraints, notice constraint violations and specialize the relevant rule according to the algorithm specified previously – does not require extensive memory storage or the retrieval of episodic information, it is computationally cheap and it does not require decisions that are necessarily based on insufficient information. The reason is that it operates on a richer type of information. Thorndike's weakening mechanism operates on the action that produced the negative outcome, while rule discrimination operates on the situations that appear in the execution history of the relevant rule. In contrast, constraint-based specialization operates on the information that resides in the relation between the observed and the expected outcomes of an action. A single constraint violation contains sufficient information to uniquely determine the appropriate revision of the relevant rule.

At a higher level of abstraction, the constraint-based specialization theory bears a family resemblance to a wide range of theories centered around the action-conflict-change principle.[34] The latter has been articulated in many different ways by different theorists. Jean Piaget's disequilibrium, Leon Festinger's cognitive dissonance, Roger Schank's expectation failures and Karl Popper's falsified predictions are different conceptualizations of cognitive conflict. Different types of conflicts imply different types of processes for overcoming them. For example, cognitive dissonance supposedly triggers changes that restore consistency to the learner's belief system (see Chapter 10), while expectation failures might trigger so-called tweaking of the explanation patterns that generate failed expectations. Although the theory of constraint-based specialization proposes novel conceptualizations of both conflict and change, it is similar to other conflict-driven theories in that it builds on the principle that intelligent action must be guided by the information residing in the relation between expected and observed outcomes of actions.

The Anatomy of a Single Learning Event

Evaluation of a complex scientific theory is necessarily a multifaceted affair that covers a variety of dimensions. In particular, a learning mechanism must prove its worth by passing two basic tests: It must be *sufficient* to aquire ecologically valid cognitive skills. Also, it must be *robust* in the sense that it works in multiple task domains. A theory that fails either of those tests cannot be the right theory, regardless of how it fares along other dimensions. Another important test is that the theory is *fruitful*, both in the sense that it answers the relevant theoretical questions and that it supports practical applications.

The constraint-based specialization theory describes the internal mechanics of a single error-correcting event. But a rule is likely to suffer from multiple faults and hence to need repeated revisions and a task strategy of even modest complexity consists of multiple rules. A theory of what happens in a single learning event is interesting only if it can be shown that the cumulative effects of multiple such events suffice to construct the kinds of cognitive skills that people learn. But it is almost impossible to predict with mere brainpower the cumulative effects of a sequence of rule specialization events. A powerful technique for deriving those effects and to demonstrate sufficiency and generality is to implement the theory as a computer simulation model and apply it to multiple task domains.

Ernest Rees and I programmed a model that we called *Heuristic Self-Improvement* or HS for short. The HS model consists of two parts. Its performance mechanism is a cognitive architecture that implements the theory of stable behavior put forth in Chapter 6. When faced with an unfamiliar task, the performance mechanism proceeds through forward search. The learning component consists of a constraint base and the rule specialization mechanism described earlier in this chapter. To run a simulation, the user gives the model a search space, defined in terms of an initial problem state, a goal and a set of primitive actions. In addition, the user supplies a set of initial rules with minimal conditions, and a set of constraints that encode correctness for the task. The model learns by doing. It acts vis-à-vis the target task, makes errors, detects them and corrects them by specializing the offending rule.

The following sections describe three applications of the HS model to three different task domains, exemplifying learning from error in elementary science and mathematics. For all three task domains (chemistry, counting, subtraction) the model had to work through multiple practice problems, making many minor corrections to the rules in response to multiple errors. The final learning outcomes – the correct procedures for these tasks – are the cumulative results of multiple learning events. In this sense, the model shows that the learning mechanism is sufficient to acquire ecologically valid skills through practice. The three skills are very different in character, which provides modest confidence in the robustness and content-independence of the learning mechanism. Besides providing snapshots of constraint-based learning in ecologically real task domains, the three applications provide novel perspectives on transfer of training and the nature of instruction, thus answering the fifth and sixth questions about practice posed in Chapter 6. In science education, students often acquire problem-solving skills in two steps. First, the student studies the relevant theory, its concepts and principles, presented in a declarative format. Second, the student attacks some class of problems for which the theory specifies correct solutions, and the student practices until he has mastered a relatively well-defined strategy for this class of problems. Textbook chapters often implement this two-punch scenario.

To simulate this scenario, HS learned to construct Lewis structures, a routine problem-solving skill in high school and college chemistry. Chemists use several different symbolisms for representing atoms and molecules. The most basic is the *sum formula*, which states how many atoms of each type a molecule contains. For example, the sum formula for ethanol (commonly known as ethyl alcohol or just alcohol) is C_2H_5OH, indicating that 1 molecule of ethanol contains 2 carbon atoms, 1 oxygen atom and 6 hydrogen atoms. Sometimes chemists need to know which atom is connected to which other atom. This is represented in a *structural formula*, also called a Lewis structure. The structural formula for ethanol is shown in Figure 7.3.

To construct a Lewis structure is to derive the correct structural formula, given the sum formula. The Lewis structure for a molecule is constrained by the theory of the co-valent bond, the type of chemical bond symbolized by the horizontal and vertical lines.[35] Basic principles of this theory include that each bond requires the sharing of 2 electrons; that only the valence electrons, the electrons in the outermost electron shell, can participate in such bonds; that

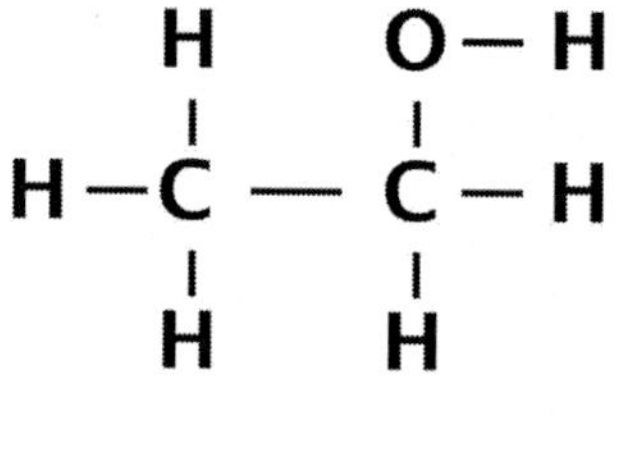

FIGURE 7.3. The structural formula for ethanol (C_2H_5OH) as it might be presented in a college textbook. Each line between two atoms stands for a shared pair of electrons.

each atom strives to have a certain number of electrons in its outer shell, its so-called noble gas configuration; and that the total number of valence electrons in the molecule cannot differ from the sum of the valence electrons of the component atoms. Only a few of the logically possible arrangements of the atoms will satisfy the constraints imposed by this theory.

The cognitive skill of deriving the structure of a molecule from its sum formula is typically taught at the beginning of an advanced high school or college course in organic chemistry. Many textbooks teach the derivation of Lewis structures by giving students (a) an exposition of the theory of the co-valent bond, (b) a verbal recipe for a weak, radically underspecified derivation procedure, (c) one or two solved examples, and (d) practice problems.[36] This learning scenario was simulated with the HS model.[37] The principles of the theory of the co-valent bond were encoded as constraints. The hints about how to proceed typically given to students were encoded as initial rules. Finally, the model was given a sequence of practice problems corresponding closely to the problems posed in college textbooks. The model successfully learned a general strategy for constructing Lewis structures.

For example, at one point the model had constructed for itself the rule:

If the goal is to *balance the Lewis structure*,
if *there are 2 carbon atoms in the molecule*,
and if *the 2 carbon atoms have a single bond between them*,
then *double that bond*.

To balance a Lewis structure is to make sure that the number of valence electrons of the molecule equals the sum of the valence electrons for the component atoms. If this is the goal, and if there are 2 carbon atoms that have only a single bond between them, then consider creating a double bond between them. This is a standard move in deriving Lewis structures. The hypothetical rule shown above is representative of the kinds of rules that one would expect a novice to possess halfway through mastering the target skill: It is sensible but not completely correct. The context in which doubling a carbon-carbon bond is appropriate and useful has not been fully specified. Consequently, the rule creates double carbon-carbon bonds in many situations in which this move creates an incorrect Lewis structure.

For example, consider a situation in which 2 carbon atoms have a single bond between them but one of them already has 8 valence electrons, which is the ideal gas configuration for carbon. If the rule above is executed in this situation, then the bond is doubled, so the atom with 8 electrons acquires one more, for a total of 9. Doubling the bonds between two carbon atoms is the right action in some situations, but it is an error in this situation. The reason is that carbon atoms strive toward the noble gas configuration, which means that they strive to have 8 valence electrons. In this case, the carbon atom already had 8 valence electrons, so creating one more bond overshoots the goal of achieving the noble gas configuration by giving the atom 1 valence electron too many.

The HS model can discover this error by inspecting the resulting problem state and noticing that the number of valence electrons is too large. To do this, the model has to have some prior knowledge of the fact that there is a maximal number of valence electrons for each substance and that an individual atom cannot have more valence electrons than indicated by that number. That is, it must already possess the following constraint:

If X *is an atom in a Lewis structure,* X *belongs to element* M, *and atoms of* M *have at most* N *valence electrons, then the current number of valence electrons for* X *is equal to or lower than* N *(or else the Lewis structure is not correct).*

The meaning of this constraint is that if the current number of valence electrons for a particular atom is V and the maximum number of valence electrons for atoms belonging to that substance is N, then it had better be the case that V is smaller than or equal to N (or else some error has been committed). More colloquially: An atom cannot have more valence electrons than the maximal number of valence electrons for its type.

Having detected that the constraint is violated, HS proceeds to revise the responsible rule. The computations described previously will in this case produce three possible new conditions:

Atom X *belongs to element* M.
The maximum number of valence electrons for atoms of element M *is* N.
The current number of valence electrons for X, V, *is less than or equal to* N-1.

The first of these three conditions can be eliminated because it is identical to an expression that is already part of the rule and hence is redundant. Adding the remaining two expressions to the existing rule produces the new rule (new conditions in bold font):

If the goal is to *balance the Lewis structure,*
if *there are 2 carbon atoms in the molecule,*
if *the 2 carbon atoms have a single bond between them,*

if the maximum number of valence electrons for atoms of element **M** *is* **N**, *and*
if the current number of valence electrons for **X**, **V**, *is less than or equal to* **N-1**.
then *double that bond*.

After the two new conditions have been added, the rule will execute only when the relevant atoms have space left, so to speak, to add another valence electron. For carbon, it will execute only when the current number of electrons is less than or equal to $8 - 1 = 7$. In this situation, the constraint of a maximum of 8 valence electrons will not be violated, because after the addition, the number of valence electrons could at most be 8. The rule has been cured of the tendency to make this particular error.

The new rule is not completely correct. It can lead to other types of errors. For example, there are many situations in which the remaining valence electrons have to be disposed of in some other way than by doubling the bonds between carbon atoms. The rule has not been miraculously transformed from incomplete to perfect in a single step. Instead, it has been cured of the tendency to causing one particular type of error. There is no guarantee that it does not cause other types of errors. If it does, additional conditions might be imposed on the action of doubling bonds between carbon atoms. In addition, revising this one rule does not preclude other rules from generating other types of errors. After modest amounts of practice, HS's set of rules for constructing Lewis structures made only occasional errors.

Three Central Concepts

The constraint-based theory of learning from error breaks with past thinking about learning from error in three ways. First, it reinterprets declarative knowledge as prescriptive rather than descriptive and as consisting of constraints rather than of truth-bearing propositions. Philosophers, logicians and, more recently, artificial intelligence researchers have assumed that the function of declarative knowledge is to support description, inference, explanation and prediction, and the formal notion of a proposition was designed to support those functions. The constraint-based view instead claims that the function of declarative knowledge is to support judgment, and that the unit of declarative knowledge is the constraint. The notion that declarative knowledge is more normative than descriptive explains how we can catch ourselves making errors, why there can be art critics who cannot paint and how it is possible to coach someone else to perform better than oneself. It implies that when we adapt to new circumstances, we lead with our ability to evaluate outcomes rather than our ability to infer new conclusions.

The second contribution of the constraint-based theory is the principle that practical knowledge starts out general and becomes more specific in the course of learning. There is a long-standing tradition, with roots in the beginnings of Western philosophy, of viewing learning as moving in the opposite direction, from particulars to abstractions.[38] Particulars are given in perception while abstractions are human constructions, or so the ancient story goes. The hypothetical process that supposedly transforms particulars into abstractions is called *induction* and it is often claimed to operate by extracting commonalities across multiple particulars. If the first three swans you ever see are white, the idea *swans are white* is likely to come to mind. However, the notion of induction is riddled with problems. How are experiences grouped for the purpose of induction? That is, how does the brain know which experiences are instances of some abstraction *X*, before that abstraction has been learned? How many instances are needed? Which features are to be extracted? How are abstractions with no instances in human experience such as *the infinite, the future* and *perfect justice* acquired?

The notion of induction has even less plausibility as an explanation for the acquisition of practical knowledge. We do not learn to tie our shoelaces by observing multiple instances of shoelace tying and extracting what they have in common. Skills are learned via practice, not induction, and what happens during practice is that initial, vague and underspecified action tendencies and dispositions become better adapted to a task environment by incorporating information from that environment. The end point of practice is not abstraction but competence, a collection of tactics for operating effectively in a particular environment. According to the specialization principle, the acquisition of practical knowledge thus moves in the opposite direction to what is often assumed in education, philosophy and psychology.[39] The concept of specialization resonates better with basic themes in the biological sciences: Both evolution and ontogenesis proceed from general, undifferentiated structures to more differentiated and specific ones.

Third, the theory focuses attention on the information in negative rather than positive outcomes. It is natural to expect a target strategy to be learned primarily from correct and positive information. Indeed, it is an axiom in Western culture in general and the culture of U.S. education in particular that positive feedback is more helpful than negative feedback. This is undoubtedly so when feedback is interpreted as praise or punishment. But it is not obvious that the information contained in positive outcomes is richer or more useful than the information contained in negative outcomes.

The successful acquisition of problem-solving skills at the level of high school or college science supports the sufficiency of the constraint-based specialization mechanism. Applications to other task domains provide evidence for robustness as well as answers to two of the main problems to be solved by a theory of skill acquisition: the problem of transfer and the problem of instruction.

THE PROBLEM OF TRANSFER

Competence grows in two seemingly distinct scenarios. On the one hand, the learner sometimes appears to be faced with an entirely unfamiliar task and has to construct a brand-new skill. Parents and teachers are constantly introducing the young of the species to novel tasks (*today we are going to start with algebra*). Adults also experience such cases. The members of the post–World War II generation had to learn, among many other skills, how to use Internet search engines, a task that bears little resemblance to any prior task. In this *acquisition* scenario, the learner appears to pick up a piece of mental chalk and write the code for a new cognitive strategy on his own blank slate. On the other hand, a learner sometimes masters a skill only to see the task environment change due to its own internal causal dynamics or due to externalities, forcing him to adapt his strategy to the changed circumstances. The switch from landlines to cell phones is an example; some features of phone use remained the same, others changed. This *adaptation* scenario highlights the fact that practical knowledge often needs to be used in situations other than the one in which it was acquired.

These two scenarios – acquiring a brand-new skill and adapting an existing skill to a new task – are discussed separately in the cognitive research literature under the two labels "skill acquisition" and "transfer of training." Research studies are typically conceptualized as being about one topic or the other. The implicit assumption is that acquisition is the fundamental case. A strategy has to be acquired before it can be transferred, or so it seems. In this view, transfer must be accomplished by some additional cognitive mechanism, over and above those needed to acquire a cognitive strategy in the first place. Identifying the mechanism of transfer is a long-standing research problem in cognitive psychology.[40]

There is no doubt that people can transfer what they learn in one situation to another. I prove this every time I eat in a restaurant where I have not eaten before: I smoothly transfer the relevant parts of a typical restaurant script (*be seated, order, eat, pay*), and I do not get confused if the tablecloth has a novel color scheme or the items on the menu are different from any I have seen before. Everyday life suggests that transfer of prior skills to altered or novel situations is ubiquitous and nearly automatic. Empirical evidence for powerful transfer mechanisms should therefore be plentiful.

But when cognitive psychologists conduct experiments to measure transfer, they tend to find less transfer than they expect.[41] Even when experimentalists set up a sequence of problem-solving experiences that is ideal for transfer, their experimental subjects can appear peculiarly obtuse in their inability to apply what they learned in the beginning of the sequence to the challenges at its end. Teachers and educators report frustrations that mirror those of the psychologist. Students are forever disappointing their teachers by not applying the knowledge they have learned – or seem to have learned – to novel problems for which that knowledge is relevant. Educators speak in despair about *inert knowledge* and some have proposed that knowledge acquired in one situation applies to future situations only if it is processed at the time of learning so as to prepare for those very situations, a rather pessimistic view of human flexibility.[42, 43] In short, transfer of practical knowledge works smoothly and successfully in everyday life, but when we try to put it under the microscope or enhance it, it turns fickle.

A theory of skill acquisition should resolve this puzzle, but the Specialization Principle that is at the heart of the theory of learning from error appears to make transfer more rather than less difficult to understand. If skills are morphing from higher levels of generality to greater specificity in the course of practice, the end result should be even less transferable than the starting point. High performance depends on a close fit between skill and task, but better fit to one task necessarily lowers fit to another, different task. To be effective, practical knowledge has to be specific; to transfer, it has to be abstract.[44] We cannot have it both ways, or so it seems.

The Constraint-Based Theory of Transfer

The rule genealogies and conflict resolution scheme introduced previously provide a resolution to this dilemma. Recall that when new, more specialized versions of rules are added to memory, the previous versions are kept in memory but downgraded in priority. A task will be processed by the most specific rule (or rules) that matches the situation at hand. In the case of a highly familiar task, the most specific matching rules will be the leaf nodes in the relevant genealogies. A completely unfamiliar task will only match against the root rules (i.e., the rules that encode general methods). Between these two extremes lies the succession of rules of intermediate generality that were created in the learning events that lead from the root node to the current leaf node.

Consider what happens when a person encounters a task that bears some relation to an already mastered task without being identical to it. By hypothesis, the leaf rules in the relevant rule genealogies will not match. However, less specific rules in those genealogies might nevertheless match, precisely because they are less specific. Conflict resolution by specificity causes the novel task to be filtered through the rule genealogies until it encounters intermediate rules that do match. Those rules constitute the initial rule set for the transfer task. Conflict resolution by specificity will automatically pull the most specific prior rules that match out of the total set of rules available. Prior practical knowledge will hence be re-used precisely to the extent that it is applicable to an altered or novel task.

How useful the prior rules will be depends on the relation between the set of prior tasks and the transfer task. If the two are utterly different, only the root rules might match the transfer task and the learner is then indeed in a blank slate situation. If the task is not entirely unfamiliar, the matching rules will be some distance from the root rule and hence embody some prior learning, but they might require more or less additional revisions before they stop violating constraints in the novel task. If the intermediate rules are close to the leaf nodes, then the learner almost knows the transfer task already and he will master it with little cognitive work, corresponding to the ease of adaptation that characterizes everyday life. If this transfer mechanism works, it should enable the HS model to exhibit transfer.

Simulating Successful Transfer

Ernest Rees and I explored the problem of transfer in the context of the task of counting a set of objects, a task that preschool children master so early and so well in the face of haphazard adult instruction that developmental psychologists suspect that the relevant constraints – called *counting principles* by Rochel Gelman, C. R. Gallistel and their co-workers – might be, if not innate, at least supported by some preparatory neural structures that make their acquisition highly probable in the presence of relevant stimuli.[45] An example of a counting principle is that each object in the set to be counted is assigned exactly one number (One-One Mapping Principle). The case of counting thus provides a

TABLE 7.2. *Summary of the initial HS model of children's counting skill.*

<u>Ontology</u>
Entities: X, Y, Z, ..., of types *object, number, set*
Objects: $O_1, O_2, O_3, ...$
Numbers: N = 1, 2, 3, ...
Sets: $\{O_i\}$, i = 1, 2, 3, ...
Properties: *first*(X), *current*(X), *origin*(X)
Relations: *associate*(N, O), *member*(O_i, {O}), *successor*(N, M), *after*(O_j, O_i)
Counting tasks: *count*({O})
Answers to counting tasks: *answer*(N, *count*({O}))

<u>Actions and operators</u>
FirstObject (O) ==> *first*(O)
NextObject(O_i, O_j) ==> *after*(O_j, O_i)
FirstNumber (N) ==> *first*(N)
NextNumber(N, M) ==> *after*(M, N)
AssNumObj(N, O) ==> *ass*(N, O)
Answer(N, *count*({O})) ==> *answer*(N, *count*({O}))

<u>Initial, overly general skill:</u>
R1: *count*({O}) *object*(O_i) ===> FirstObject(O_i)
R2: *count*({O}) *current*(O_i), *object*(O_j) ===> NextObject(O_j, O_i)
R3: *count*({O}) *number*(N) ===> FirstNumber(N)
R4: *count*({O}) *current*(N) *number*(M) ===> NextNumber(M, N)
R5: *count*({O}) *current*(N) *current*(O) ===> AssNumObj(N, O)
R6: *count*({O}) *current*(N) ===> Answer(N, *count*({O}))

Based on Ohlsson and Rees, 1991a, Tables 2 and 3.

case of skill acquisition for which there are strong empirical reasons to believe that there is a prior declarative knowledge base. Children can learn to count with minimal and haphazard instruction because they have prior knowledge of a small set of counting principles that constrains counting behavior.

HS can duplicate the acquisition of this skill, given the same knowledge that children start out with.[46] HS was programmed with the basic competence of pointing to objects and saying numbers. In addition, we gave HS the actions that are specific to the counting domain, primarily to select an object, point to an object, retrieve a number, speak a number and declare the answer. HS was given an initial competence that consisted of six rules, one to control the application of each of the six key cognitive operations; see Table 7.2. These rules were overly general and hence error prone. The prior declarative knowledge consisted of constraints that represented a version of the Gelman and Gallistel counting principles. The five constraints are stated conceptually in Table 7.3.

Error Correction: The Specialization Theory 239

TABLE 7.3. *Declarative knowledge in the HS model of children's counting skill.*

Label	Content
A	*One-One Mapping Constraint*: If a number N is associated with object O_j, O_i ought to be the only object that N is associated with.
B	*Cardinality Constraint*: If object O_i is the last object to be associated with some number N, and N has been designated as the answer to *count*({O}), then every object in {O} ought to be associated with some number.
C	*Regular Traversal Constraint*: If each number from 1 to N has been associated with some object, and M is the current number, then M ought to be the successor to N.
D	*Order Imposition Constraint*: If O is chosen as the current object, O should not already be associated with a number.
E	*Coordination Constraint*: If O is the current object and O is associated with number N, then N ought to be the current number.

Based on Ohlsson and Rees, 1991a, Table 4.

We then gave HS repeated practice on counting sets with two to five objects. In the beginning, the model made the same types of errors that children do: skipping numbers, skipping objects, counting one object more than once and issuing a seemingly arbitrary number as the answer. However, the constraints that encoded the counting principles enabled the model to detect its errors, and the specialization mechanism gradually restricted the conditions of its rules. Even when practice was limited to small sets, the model, like children, learned a general strategy for how to count sets of any size. If the initial rules and the constraints are stated in general terms so that they apply to any type of object, then the model learns a counting procedure that applies to any type of object.

Consider a particular run with the counting model, summarized in Table 7.4.[47] The model acquired the correct counting procedure in 22 trials, performing correctly on trial 23. The path illustrates several properties of the model's behavior. The third column shows the constraint that was violated, that is, which type of error was committed, on each trial. Some constraints were violated several times, like *D* (trials 2, 3 7, 9, 10, 14, 15, 17, 18, 19 and 20), while others were violated less often, like *C* (trials 4, 6 and 21) and *A* (trials 1, 5 and 16). Sometimes constraints were violated again and again on adjacent trials, like *D* on trials 17 through 20, while others were violated on trials separated by other trials on which they were not, like *E* on trials 13 and 22. The model did not work on one type of error until it was completely eradicated, and then turn its attention to the next error type. Instead, it responded to errors as they occurred in the course of

TABLE 7.4. *A run by the HS counting model depicted in Tables 7.2 and 7.3. Each trial represents one attempt at counting one and the same set of objects. In the right-hand column, the rule that was revised is underlined.*

Trial number	Cycles before first constraint violation	Constraint violated	Rule revised on each trial
1	1	A	1 2 **3** 4 5 6
2	1	D	**1** 2 3 4 5 6
3	2	D	**1** 2 3 4 5 6
4	2	C	1 2 **3** 4 5 6
5	2	A	1 **2** 3 4 5 6
6	3	C	1 2 3 **4** 5 6
7	3	D	1 2 3 **4** 5 6
8	3	B	1 2 3 4 5 **6**
9	4	D	1 **2** 3 4 5 6
10	4	D	1 **2** 3 4 5 6
11	4	E	1 2 **3** 4 5 6
12	4	B	1 2 3 4 5 **6**
13	4	E	1 2 3 **4** 5 6
14	5	D	1 2 **3** 4 5 6
15	5	D	1 2 **3** 4 5 6
16	5	A	1 2 3 4 **5** 6
17	6	D	1 2 3 **4** 5 6
18	6	D	1 2 3 **4** 5 6
19	7	D	1 **2** 3 4 5 6
20	7	D	1 2 **3** 4 5 6
21	9	C	1 2 3 **4** 5 6
22	10	E	1 **2** 3 4 5 6
23	11	None	None

Based on Ohlsson and Rees, 1991a, Table 5.

its actions. Nor was there a one-to-one mapping between constraints and rules such that each constraint informed the revision of a single rule. The fourth column in Table 7.4 shows the rule that was revised on each trial. Some constraints led to improvements in multiple rules. The two violations of constraint *D* in trials 7 and 9 led to improvements in rules 4 and 2, respectively. Some rules violated more than one constraint. For example, rule 2 violated constraints *A* (trial 5), *D* (trial 9) and *E* (trial 22). There was no one-to-one mapping between constraints and rules such that each constraint was translated or transformed into a particular rule. Some rules, like rule 2, required multiple revisions, while others, like rules 1 and 6, required only two revisions each.

These details of how learning progressed in this particular simulation run are not interesting in themselves, but they illustrate the complexity of the interaction between the knowledge embedded in the constraints, the initial rule set, the particular errors encountered during practice and the resulting sequence of learning events. All constraints apply at each moment during practice, and a learning event is massively contingent on the state of the current practice problem, the current version of the relevant rules and exactly which constraints the learner knows. The learning of the HS model is lifelike.

The counting application provides a natural test of the HS transfer mechanism because Gelman and co-workers not only investigated how young children acquire the competence to perform the *standard* counting task (*count how many teddy bears there are*), but also the kinds of modified counting tasks they are able to perform.[48] In a series of studies, they confronted children with several such tasks. In one of these, *ordered counting*, the child is asked to count a set of objects in a particular order. For example, the child might be asked to count from left to right, or to count yellow objects before blue ones. Ordered counting thus imposes a constraint that is not a normal part of counting. In a second modified counting task, the child is asked to count a set of objects in such a way that a designated object is assigned a designated number (*count these but make sure that the yellow bear is number five*). Gelman called this task *constrained counting*, but as the term "constraint" is used in this book, both modified tasks are constrained, but in different ways. I will call this second modified task *targeted counting*, because the counting process has to land on a particular target, the designated object, at a particular point in the counting sequence. The results of the studies by Gelman and co-workers show, contrary to the results of many other transfer studies, that young children are capable of adapting their knowledge of the standard counting procedure to both of these modified counting tasks.

What about HS? Rees and I put the model through the complete set of transfers for the three counting procedures (standard, ordered and targeted).[49] That is, it first learned one of the three counting methods from scratch and then transferred the acquired strategy to each of the other two counting tasks; then it learned another of the three from scratch, and transferred to the other two; and so on. There were thus six different simulation runs in all. The two modified counting tasks were defined by giving the model the obvious constraints to define ordering and targeting (*if* X *is counted after* Y, *it should be after* Y *in the ordering*; *if* X *is assigned the designated number, it should be*

TABLE 7.5. *Amount of transfer among three counting tasks, measured as percent savings, for each of three performance variables.*

Training task	Dependent variable	Transfer task		
		Standard counting	Ordered counting	Targeted counting
Standard counting	Rule revisions	–	81	83
	Operating cycles	–	58	72
	Search states	–	60	72
Ordered counting	Rule revisions	92	–	8
	Operating cycles	78	–	34
	Search states	79	–	34
Targeted counting	Rule revisions	100	73	–
	Operating cycles	81	41	–
	Search states	81	35	–

Based on Ohlsson 2007a, Table 11.3.

the designated object). The criterion for success was that the model achieved correct performance on the transfer task.

It turned out that HS, relying only on rule specialization, could transfer from any one of the three counting procedures to each of the other two. Table 7.5 shows the quantitative transfer results from the counting simulations. There are huge transfer effects from standard counting to both ordered and targeted counting. Having first learned standard counting saves more than half of the learning effort on any of the three dependent variables. Although ordered counting and targeted counting differ from standard counting in different ways – one affects the selection of objects, the other the assignment of numbers – the transfer effect from standard counting is huge in both cases. With respect to rule revisions, the prior training saves more than 80% of the effort of mastering either of the modified counting tasks. That is, if you know how to do standard counting, you almost know how to do modified counting, consistent with the observations by Gelman and co-workers that children can switch from one type of counting to the other with relative ease. The explanation for this phenomenon is a straightforward application of the specialization principle: Both ordered and targeted counting are more constrained than standard counting. That is, almost all of the learning required to do standard counting is also needed to do either of these modified counting tasks. The unique cognitive work needed to master the latter is to further specialize the rules to fit the additional constraints that define the modified tasks. That is why transfer is not 100%.

The explanation for the high transfer from standard to modified counting makes a counterintuitive prediction: that transfer in the opposite direction, from a more constrained to a less constrained task, should be even higher. If the strategy does not need to be more constrained, it might not require any modifications at all. This is indeed the case. Transfer from either of the modified counting tasks to the standard task is even higher than in the opposite direction. In one case, switching from targeted to standard counting, no rule revisions are required, so transfer is 100% in that case.

Finally, moving from a task that is constrained one way to a different task that is constrained in some other way should be the hardest transfer task of all. This is indeed the case, as Table 7.5 shows. The transfer from ordered to targeted counting is only 8%. If the rules have been constrained in a different way than required, then the model needs to back up further in the rule genealogies and there will be much work required to re-specialize the rules and hence a small transfer effect. In general, *the constraint-based specialization theory predicts that the magnitude of a transfer effect is a function of the number of learning events needed to revise the prior (intermediate) rules to fit the transfer task.* The theory predicts large transfer effects when a strategy only needs to be further specialized, lesser effects when it needs to be re-specialized.

The fact that the constraint-based specialization mechanism predicts asymmetric transfer effects is noteworthy because it differentiates this hypothesis from the identical rules hypothesis. Recall that the latter claims that rules are re-used when the identical rule appears in the strategy for a training task and the strategy for a transfer task. This formulation predicts that the magnitude of the transfer effect when moving from task X to task Y is directly proportional to the overlap between the two rule sets; that is, to the number of rules needed to perform X that are also required to perform Y. This measure is necessarily symmetrical, so the identical rules hypothesis implausibly predicts that the amount of transfer from task X to task Y is always and necessarily equal to the amount of transfer from task Y to task X. This strong prediction is falsified by empirical studies by Miriam Bassok and others.[50] The constraint-based transfer mechanism claims that symmetrical transfer effects are accidents and that the principled regularity is that transfer effects are proportional to the number of learning events (not the number of knowledge elements) that are required to adapt the prior rules to the transfer task. Hence, effects are large when the transfer task is consistent with but more constrained than the training task; because "more constrained than" is asymmetric, so are transfer effects. The empirical data in the literature are not sufficient to evaluate this prediction, but it is consistent with the results of Bassok and others. In general, skill acquisition theories that predict asymmetric transfer effects are more likely to be psychologically accurate than those that predict symmetric transfer effects.

The Primacy of Adaptation

It is unlikely that skills are ever constructed from scratch. A computer programmer can "teach" a computer a new procedure by typing code into a blank file, but skill acquisition by a human brain is more likely akin to growth, differentiation and specialization and to recycling existing structures to serve new functions, one of Nature's favorite tricks. Even in situations that we intuitively conceptualize as learning a brand-new skill, many prior competencies provide small pieces of the target competence. Learning to use SCUBA gear is a case in point. The equipment and the procedures are all unfamiliar. Yet, fastening the regulator on the air tank means fitting one metal piece over another and tightening a screw with a rotating movement of the wrist – surely not entirely unfamiliar; putting on a buoyancy compensator is somewhat similar to putting on any other kind of vest; the dive mask is similar to a pair of ski goggles; a diver moves underwater with almost the same kicking motion he uses to swim on the surface; and so on. There are many precursor tasks, but each contribution to the new skill set might be so slight and so implicit as to escape conscious notice.

The theory of learning from error builds on this observation. It claims that human beings can adapt to novel environments because we can both specialize general strategies to particular environments and fall back on slightly more general strategies when the specialized ones become obsolete because the environment shifts under our feet. The slightly more general strategies are guaranteed to be available in memory, because, according to the principle of specialization, they are intermediate products generated on the path to the more specific strategies. Conflict resolution by specificity guarantees that the most specific strategy available will be used as the initial strategy for the changed circumstances, that is, that the cognitive architecture will make maximal use of past learning. In conjunction, constraint-based specialization, rule genealogies and conflict resolution by specificity resolve the conflict between the fact that highly general strategies, although widely applicable, provide too little guidance for action, and the fact that highly specialized strategies, although effective, are guaranteed to become maladaptive as the environment changes.

This explanation for cognitive flexibility implies that the question of how learners acquire new skills and the question of how they adapt and transfer already established skills from one task or set of circumstances to another are one and the same. Contrary to long-standing concepts in cognitive psychology, there is no separate problem of transfer; more precisely, there is no separate problem of acquisition. People learn new skills *by* transferring their prior skills to new situations. A successful transfer theory is therefore also a successful theory of acquisition, but the reverse is not true. Theories that explain transfer by adding a transfer process to an acquisition theory are unlikely to be correct. Adaptation, not blank slate acquisition, is the primary case.

THE PROBLEM OF TUTORING

The natural sciences have taught us to expect accurate scientific theories to generate successful practical applications. For theories of learning, the obvious domain of application is instruction. The fact that instruction can work is so familiar as to seem self-explanatory, but it poses the question of how utterances from one person can enter the mind of another person and, once there, facilitate learning. How does instruction achieve its beneficial effect? A related question is how unassisted learning is related to learning from instruction.

All mammals learn, and, as a group, mammals learn better than other animals.[51] Primates, in turn, learn even more effectively than other mammals. If the genetic basis for neural plasticity dates from the point in time at which hominids branched off from other primates, then the hominid evolutionary lineage emerged with a genetic basis for superior learning already in place some 5 million years ago. If our capacity to learn is so ancient, then it is plausible that unassisted learning is the primary mode and that learning from instruction emerged later.

How much later? It is plausible that instruction did not begin to make a difference for human survival until the emergence of language. One can instruct by example, gestures and nonverbal feedback, but the full power of instruction is not realized unless instructor and pupil can talk. We do not know with certainty at which point hominids began to talk, but the archeological and paleontological records provide one suggestive clue: There are few if any traces of representations and symbols – carvings, graphic signs scratched on bone, paintings, statues – by members of any hominid species before our own.[52] It is possible that the use of articulated symbol systems, including language, became possible as a result of a small number of evolutionary changes in the brain of archaic *Homo sapiens* or its immediate predecessor. If so, language, and therefore effective instruction, is not much older than the oldest cave paintings. Our genome has changed little since then, so this line of thought implies that learning from instruction does not have a genetic basis of its own. If so, instruction is not an adaptation in the biological sense but a cultural practice. We might not have any brain structures that evolved in response to any selective pressure toward learning from instruction. Instead, instruction works by abetting the operation of learning mechanisms that evolved for unassisted learning. I refer to this as the *Piggyback Hypothesis*.

Piggyback raises a paradox: If assisted learning makes use of the same learning mechanisms as unassisted learning, why is it more effective? The answer must be that instruction makes those mechanisms do more, or different, work. As a didactive example, consider the hypothesis that learning proceeds, at least sometimes, through generalization. It is widely believed that we group our experiences on the basis of similarities, extract those similarities and encode them in general concepts. If our brains are indeed wired to carry out such a generalization process, then how might instruction help? In the unassisted mode, the number of general concepts acquired per unit of time is determined by the density of generalizable events in the stream of experience. But an instructor can make the generalization mechanism do more work by arranging events that trigger the formation of a particular concept within a shorter time period than would have been the case in the natural sequence of events. A geometry teacher does precisely this when he teaches the concept *equilateral triangle* by showing students a series of examples on the blackboard, such triangles being somewhat scarce in the woods and on the streets. Although one might question the idea that we form concepts in precisely this way outside geometry class, the example illustrates how a deliberately designed sequence of experiences can abet a cognitive mechanism that did not evolve to learn from instruction.

This situation is not unique. Consider an analogy to vaccination: Our immune system did not evolve to create antibodies in response to a shot in the arm. Nevertheless, by receiving a weak form of a virus before an encounter with the real thing, the immune system can be boosted to handle an otherwise overwhelming virus attack. Cooking provides a second analogy: The time since we began to heat our food is too short for there to have been many genetic changes to our digestive system, so the latter is primarily designed, as it were, to process raw food. Cooked food nevertheless nourishes us better, improving health and longevity. Vaccination and cooking are both examples of Father Artifice helping Mother Nature make the most of biological systems that evolved before the relevant artifices were invented.

I propose that the relation between instruction and learning is similar.[53] According to the *Information Specificity Principle* introduced in Chapter 6, the learning mechanisms in a person's brain take particular types of information as input. Assisted learning is more efficient than unassisted, not because there are dedicated brain mechanisms for assisted learning, but because the instructor arranges for information of the relevant types to be more abundant than they otherwise would be, thereby making the learning mechanisms in the students' brains do more work, or different work, in a given period of time.

Simulating Learning From Tutoring

If this line of reasoning is correct, a model of unassisted learning is also a model of assisted learning and it should be possible to turn the underlying learning theory into a set of design principles for effective instruction. But in the computer simulations of constraint-based error correction discussed previously in this chapter, the relevant constraints were assumed to be acquired before practice began. In the counting simulation, the constraints are hypothesized to be part of the child's innate cognitive structures. In the case of college chemistry, the constraints must be acquired while the student studies the relevant textbook chapters. In both simulations, the entire set of constraints was available to the model at the outset of practice. In those scenarios, the HS computer model acted as a model of unassisted skill acquisition.

According to the Piggyback principle, the HS model should not need to be extended with any additional learning mechanisms to model assisted learning. When the learner does not know all the relevant constraints, he cannot recognize all of his constraint violations. Learning opportunities are missed. But a tutor can recognize the constraint violations that the student overlooks and alert the learner to them. By calling attention to an error and supplying the learner with the information that is needed to correct it, a tutor makes the constraint-based specialization mechanism do more, and different, work than it would have done otherwise. The interaction with the tutor allows the learner to operate as if he knows more than he does, because his own constraint base is augmented, functionally speaking, with the more extensive constraint base of the tutor. All that is needed to model learning from tutoring with HS is to reinterpret the constraints as feedback messages provided by a tutor in the course of problem solving instead of knowledge structures retrieved from the learner's long-term memory.

To verify that the HS simulation model passes this test Andreas Ernst, Rees and I tutored HS in subtraction with regrouping, an instructional topic that has received much attention in educational research.[54] We began by defining the basic cognitive capabilities that are needed to do subtraction. These include the ability to allocate visual attention as well as motor skills like writing and crossing out digits. The initial rules for subtraction were sufficient for canonical subtraction problems in which the subtrahend digit is greater than the minuend digit in each column, for example, 678 − 234 = ?. Regrouping (popularly known as "borrowing") was not necessary to solve the canonical problems. We then taught the model to perform correctly on problems that require regrouping as well. This two-step instructional sequence – canonical problems followed by problems that require regrouping – corresponds to the one observed in classroom teaching.[55]

We tutored the subtraction model in two different methods for noncanonical problems, the *regrouping method* taught in most American schools and the *augmenting method* preferred in some European schools. The two procedures differ primarily in how they handle noncanonical columns, either by decrementing the subtrahend in the column with the next higher place value or by incrementing the minuend in that column. This difference was once thought by mathematics educators to be of pedagogical importance.[56] We tutored each of these subtraction methods in two ways that we referred to as procedural and conceptual. In procedural (rote) arithmetic, the learner sees an arithmetic problem as a spatial arrangement of digits on a page. In this version, the constraints referred to that arrangement, for example, *the answer should have a single digit in each column*. In contrast, a conceptual arithmeter thinks about subtraction mathematically instead of typographically. The characters are symbols for numbers. In this version, the model's internal representation explicitly enoded the place value of each digit, and the constraints encoded mathematical relations, such as *if the value of a digits* D *in column* N *is* $D * 10^m$, *then the value of a digit* E *in column* N+1 *should be* $E * 10^{m+1}$. Mathematics educators regard the conceptual approach to arithmetic as pedagogically superior.

The distinction between procedural (rote) versus conceptual learning combined with the two different algorithms, regrouping and augmenting, to define four different learning scenarios. We tutored HS until mastery in each scenario with the same procedure we would use to tutor a student: We watched the model solve a problem until it made an error. We interrupted the model and typed in a constraint that we thought would allow the model to correct that error. The constraint was added to the constraint base in the model, and the model was restarted. This cycle continued until the model performed correctly. Mastery was assessed by running the model on a test set of 66 subtraction problems that were not used during training.

It required two training problems to learn augmenting procedurally, five to learn augmenting conceptually. It required four training problems to master regrouping in both the procedural and the conceptual conditions. The number of tutoring messages required for correct performance varied between 20 and 31 in the four conditions. Given that children do worksheets with hundreds of problems, these numbers seem low, but the model was learning in a one-on-one tutoring scenario, it learned from tutors who caught every error and, being a machine, suffered no distractions, lack of motivation or working memory limitations. The number of learning events (rule revisions) required for mastery varied between 16 and 32. Interestingly, the regrouping method is easy to learn when there are no blocking zeroes, that is, zeroes that force the learner to borrow from the next column. Mastery required only 16 learning events. However, the model required 32 learning events to learn the conceptual version of the regrouping procedure for problems with blocking zeroes. For both the conceptual and procedural versions, the regrouping method, but not the augmenting method, was strongly affected by the presence of blocking zeroes. How realistic are these numbers?[57] Gaea Leinhard has shown that mastery of subtraction might require six classroom lessons. Six lessons represent 4.5 hours of instruction. The HS model required 32 learning events in the conceptual regrouping condition, the approach used in most American classrooms. Thirty-two events per 4.5 hours comes to one learning event per eight minutes. Empirical estimates of the rate of learning are hard to come by but this learning rate is of the right order of magnitude.

The tutoring simulation illustrates the idea that learning from instruction is embedded within unsupervised learning. The very same computational mechanism that was invented to learn from error in the presence of declarative principles such as the counting principles or the laws of chemistry can also learn when the constraints arrive in a succession of tutoring messages. No additional cognitive machinery was required for HS to be able to learn from tutoring instead of from prior declarative knowledge.

Constraint-Based Tutoring

The question arises whether it is possible to use the constraint-based theory to design instructional software systems that tutor human students in the same way that we tutored the HS model. Instructional software systems that attempt to mimic human tutors are called *intelligent tutoring systems*.[58] The key features of this class of instructional systems are that the target skill is represented explicitly, the student's incomplete and possibly erroneous knowledge of the target skill is inferred from his task behavior and, finally, the system uses artificial intelligence techniques to compute when (at which moments during practice) to intervene, what information to convey and how to convey it. It is widely assumed that one-on-one instruction is superior to classroom instruction because a human tutor adapts on a moment-to-moment basis to the needs of the individual student, especially to the gaps and faults in his or her representation of the target skill. Consequently, much research on tutoring systems aims to invent programming techniques that allow a computer to similarly individualize its instruction in general and its response to student errors in particular.

The constraint-based theory implies a particular blueprint for intelligent tutoring systems that is known as *constraint-based modeling* (CBM). The correct knowledge of the target domain is to be implemented as a constraint base. A student is represented by the subset of constraints that he has violated. Learning opportunities are identified as constraint violations. A tutoring message should state the violated constraint, formulated in colloquial but general language, highlight the specific features of the student's answer or solution that cause the constraint to be violated and explain how those features violate the constraint. Constraint-based modeling is an elegant and practical recipe for computer-based tutoring in response to student errors.

The proof of a recipe is in the pudding. In this case, the pudding was cooked in New Zealand, but it is enjoyed worldwide. Computer scientist Antonija Mitrovic at Canterbury University in New Zealand and the members of her research team have implemented, deployed and evaluated multiple constraint-based tutoring systems. The performance of these systems constitute a test of the constraint-based blueprint for tutoring systems, and, indirectly, of the underlying learning theory.

The first constraint-based tutoring system was SQL-Tutor.[59] It teaches students to formulate queries in SQL, a database query language. The task of the student is to fill in fields in a query schema in such a way that the resulting query poses a meaningful and answerable question with respect to a particular database. The student fills in the fields and submits the query. The system evaluates it and provides feedback; the student has the opportunity to revise the query; and so on. The task of formulating SQL queries is quite difficult. The mature version of the system contains more than 600 constraints. The SQL-Tutor was followed by two other constraint-based systems that teach other database skills: database design (KERMIT) and database normalization (NORMIT). The three tasks of designing, normalizing and querying databases are quite different from one another.[60] Normalization is a multistep, sequential choice task, similar to the tasks traditionally investigated by tutoring researchers in domains such as algebra, physics and programming. The database design tutor KERMIT presents the student with a complex graphical interface that requires multiple actions but does not impose any particular sequence on the steps. The task of formulating database queries is different from either of these. The second generation of constraint-based systems to come out of the Intelligent Tutoring Systems Group at Canterbury broke out of the computer science domain to encompass such varied instructional topics as the rules of capitalization in English and group interaction skills. The variety of topics taught by these systems demonstrates the versatility of the constraint-based modeling philosophy.

There is no doubt that students learn effectively while interacting with these systems. Multiple empirical studies carried out in Mitrovic's laboratory have shown that the probability of violating a constraint decreases as a function of the number of past opportunities to violate that constraint.[61] In particular, studies that compared tutoring messages based on intuition with messages that were in strict accord with these theory-based prescriptions have found a small advantage for the latter.

The most impressive demonstration of the usefulness of these systems is that several of them have entered the commercial educational market, an unusual success in the field of intelligent tutoring research. Web access to the Canterbury suite of database tutors – SQL-Tutor, KERMIT and NORMIT – was packaged with a commercially successful series of textbooks in computer science. Figure 7.4 shows the growth of the online user population. Thousands of students worldwide have benefited from the advantages of constraint-based tutoring systems.

From CBM to Multiple Tutoring Modes

The success of constraint-based tutoring systems demonstrates the usefulness of the design principles derived from the theory of learning from error. However, that theory only describes one learning mechanism. But as argued in Chapter 6, there is no reason to believe that every learning event that occurs during skill acquisition can be attributed to one and the same learning mechanism. Instead, there are good reasons to believe that people learn in multiple ways during skill practice. Students can benefit from verbal instructions, especially at the outset of practice; they can reason from their declarative knowledge about the task; they can draw analogies to already mastered skills; they can make good use of solved examples; and they can learn from the outcomes

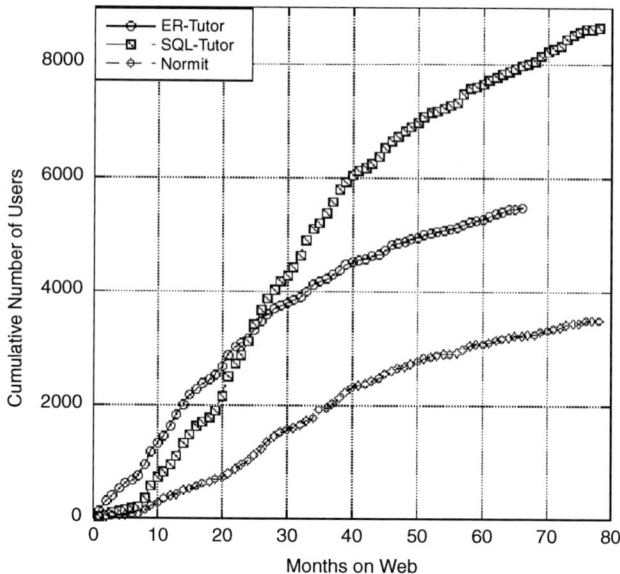

FIGURE 7.4. Growth of the user pool for constraint-based tutoring systems.

of trial and error behavior. Once practice is under way, students learn primarily from the information residing in the outcomes, positive or negative, of their own actions. In the long run, information laid down in memory during the execution of a learned strategy supports the discovery of shortcuts and multiple forms of strategy optimization.

Each mode of learning is a potential target for tutoring. The research and development process used in the case of learning from error potentially applies to every mode of learning: select a psychologically plausible learning mechanism; specify the type of information that mechanism needs to receive as input; identify the conditions that mark a learning opportunity; specify how to compute what information to convey and how to convey it; implement the tutoring system; and evaluate. The full pedagogical power of intelligent tutoring systems will be realized when those systems become capable of supporting all nine modes of learning described in Chapter 6. Eventually the production of effective tutoring systems will become routine. Educators will develop systems for every conceivable topic and make them available electronically, thereby providing individualized instruction for every person on the planet at virtually no cost, over and above the initial development costs. The race between the need for citizen training and society's ability to pay for it is on, and we can still win.

NORBERT WIENER'S INSIGHT

The acquisition of practical knowledge is shaped by the facts that we necessarily operate on the basis of a small and unrepresentative sample of experiences, that our material and social environments are turbulent and that we frequently move to colonize unfamiliar task environments. Under those conditions, prior experience is a limited guide to action, and errors and failures are unavoidable. The error rate can only be reduced locally, in tight contexts and over short periods of time.

According to the constraint-based specialization theory, errors are not merely passively eliminated as a side effect of the acquisition of the correct knowledge. Errors play an active part in their own elimination by providing information that gives direction to the adaptive process. People have always understood that errors are learning opportunities – witness proverbs like *burnt child dreads the fire* – but they did not know how to conceptualize the information that resides in errors. A negative outcome is not, by itself, informative, and neither is the frequency with which a particular type of error occurs or the type of situation in which it tends to occur. Comparisons between multiple situations that produced positive and negative outcomes are informative but they require psychologically implausible computations.

It was not until the cybernetics movement in the 1940s and 1950s that it became clear that the information provided by errors resides in the deviations between expected and observed outcomes.[62] In his book *Cybernetics*, published in 1948, the mathematician Norbert Wiener argued for an interdisciplinary science centered on the concept of feedback circles.[63] Wiener's genius was to realize that intelligent, purposeful action, whether by animal, human or machine, needs to be guided by the information provided by the deviations between the intended (or expected) action outcomes and the observed (or realized) outcomes. In engineering applications, outcomes are typically values on quantitative variables, so the deviation between an intended and an observed outcome can be expressed quantitatively. The desired correction is achieved by feeding the magnitude of the deviation back into the system, which then adjusts its operation so as to bring the actual outcome closer to the intended one. For example, the operation of a thermostat is controlled by the difference between the set temperature and the actual temperature in the room.

The idea of a comparison between the projected and observed outcomes of an action is more general than Wiener's strictly quantitative definition of negative feedback. The constraint-based specialization process described in this chapter generalizes Wiener's idea to cases in which the deviation must be described in qualitative terms. Constraints provide the expectations against which the observed outcomes are compared, and the specialization process translates a deviation between expectation and observation – a constraint violation – into a revision of the learner's knowledge about how to perform the task at hand. This theory may or may not turn out to be psychologically accurate, but any explanation of learning from errors requires a cognitive mechanism that operates on the information that resides in the difference between expected and observed outcomes, Wiener's enduring contribution to the study of cognition.

8

Error Correction in Context

> *The question is not so much how to prevent [errors] from occurring, as how to ensure that their adverse consequences are speedily detected ...*
>
> James Reason[1]

> *... the real question is why only some societies proved fragile, and what distinguished those that collapsed from those that didn't.*
>
> Jarred Diamond[2]

The actions of hunter-gatherers have limited causal reach. A shot that misses its target might mean sudden death for the hunter or warrior whose shot it was, but the consequences of that particular error for the tribe or troop are likely to be absorbed into the flow of events and make only a small difference to the outcome of the hunt or the battle. With the advent of large-scale social and technical systems like airlines, container shipping, global financial markets, irrigation agriculture, power grids and research hospitals humans came to know man-made disasters. A single erroneous action can be the starting point for a butterfly effect that propagates upward through the levels of the relevant system until it makes the difference between cure and death, between ubiquitous electricity and power blackout, between wealth and bankruptcy or between victory and defeat; in general, between normality and disaster. The unacceptable consequences of disasters make it imperative to understand the dynamics of error correction in individuals, social systems and entire societies.

The constraint-based theory of learning from error put forward in Chapter 7 describes the inner mechanics of a single learning event, the correction of a single fault in a single person's cognitive skill. Such an event might last anywhere from a couple of seconds to a couple of minutes. Expertise in operating a complex social or technical system, on the other hand, consists of skills that are likely to execute over days, weeks or even months, that are learned over several years and that are distributed over multiple operators. The gap between the time scale of a single learning event, on the one hand, and the time scale of expertise in the context of a complex system, on the other, raises the questions whether the constraint-based theory of learning from error applies at the longer time band and the higher levels of complexity, and what implications, if any, it has at the level of collectives. At the longest time band and highest level of collectivity, the question is whether the fall of seemingly successful societies can be understood in terms of identifiable errors.

SCALING ACROSS TIME AND COMPLEXITY

Simple skills can be acquired by practicing for a few minutes or at most an hour. To learn how to tie a bowline knot, to master a new cell phone and to find one's way around an unfamiliar shopping center are examples. But how much practice is required before a person is competent to diagnose medical cases, pilot a passenger jet or manage a multinational business? Thanks to empirical studies by Anders Ericsson and other expertise researchers we know the answer: Top-level performance in any field of skilled activity requires approximately 10 years of practice, if we assume that the learner practices approximately four hours per day.[3] Unexpectedly, the order of magnitude of these numbers is relatively constant across such otherwise different fields of activity as athletics, games, music and the professions (e.g., business, engineering, medicine and the military).

The claim is not that this amount of practice automatically produces expert performance, but that expert performance cannot be reached with less than this amount of practice. The 10-year estimate should not be interpreted to mean that learning stops after 10 years. On the contrary, the growth of competence is a lifelong affair, beginning in the 15-year period that we refer to as the period of cognitive development, progressing through the adult years, which for many include a decade or two of achieving expertise in a profession or vocation, and continuing into late adulthood. It slows down only when further improvements in cognitive performance are counteracted by cognitive aging.

The question of interest is how learning mechanisms that execute in a few seconds or at most a couple of minutes relate to the growth of competence at the time bands of cognitive development, expertise and life-span learning. The constraint-based theory of learning from error presented in Chapter 7 is based on five principles: (a) Errors are caused by overly general (underspecified) skills, or components of skills. (b) Errors are detected as deviations from observed outcomes of actions from the outcomes expected on the basis of declarative knowledge about the task environment. (c) Declarative knowledge is normative rather than descriptive in nature; it consists of constraints rather than propositions. (d) Errors are unlearned by incorporating violated constraints into the applicability conditions of faulty knowledge elements. (e) The conditions to be added are identified through the particular computations described in Chapter 7.

What kinds of long-term effects should we observe if the mechanism of constraint-based specialization is executed many times over? How does a skill change as it is mastered? What are the cumulative effects? Do the five key features of constraint-based specialization punch through to higher system levels and influence changes that unfold over 10 years or more, a stretch across five or six orders of magnitude? If so, which empirical regularities at the higher levels of time and complexity can be explained with their help and which are driven by other factors?

The Patterns of Skill Acquisition

The acquisition or adaptation of a skill through practice is necessarily gradual. The learner's initial representation of the target skill consists of rules – goal-situation-action associations – that are incomplete and possibly incorrect. To learn a skill is to revise the initial rules by incorporating more information about the task environment into them. A rule undergoes only a minor change in the course of any one learning event, so every rule requires multiple revisions before it ceases to generate errors. Complex skills consist of large collections of rules, so the target skill as a whole is necessarily reached through a long sequence of learning events. What little empirical evidence is available suggests that learning events occur relatively infrequently, perhaps one event per 5 or 10 minutes, on average. Hence, a skill that requires 20 learning events to master cannot be learned with less than 1.5–3 hours of practice. If change is necessarily gradual, what pattern or patterns does it exhibit?

The short-term learning curve

Improvement due to practice is not only gradual but it also follows a well-documented temporal pattern: If performance, measured in terms of the time to complete the target task, is plotted as a function of the amount of experience with the task, usually measured by the number of training trials (attempts to perform the task), the result is a *negatively accelerated* curve.[4] That is, the rate of improvement is fastest in the beginning and gradually diminishes as mastery is approached. The curve eventually approaches a horizontal line, the *asymptote*, which represents the best possible performance. Figure 8.1 shows an example. The top panel reproduces the curve from Figure 6.1; the data are average task completion times, measured in seconds per trial, for a group of college students who practiced an unfamiliar symbol manipulating task 20 times. The negatively accelerated improvement is obvious, as is the regular nature of the data.

Why does change in the time to task completion follow a negatively accelerated curve rather than, for example, a linear, positively accelerated, S-shaped

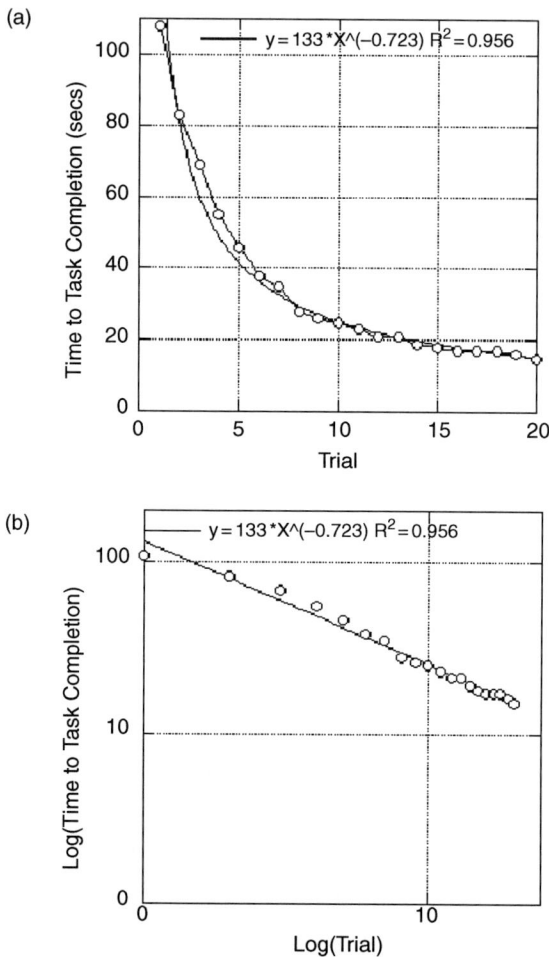

FIGURE 8.1. Learning curve for 106 students solving a symbol manipulation task. Panel (a) shows the mean task completion time in seconds as a function trial. Panel (b) shows the same data plotted with logarithmic coordinates on both axes.

or irregular curve? The consequence of a fault in practical knowledge is floundering, that is, backtracking, hesitation and repetitions. Faulty practical knowledge produces unnecessary steps and to learn is, to some extent, to excise those steps. Performance speeds up when a fault is corrected because the amount of floundering decreases. The unnecessary cognitive work caused by a faulty strategy or skill varies in magnitude from fault to fault, but performance measures such as solution time refer to entire performances and hence effectively average the savings produced by individual error correction events. At the outset of practice the learner makes many errors in each practice trial, so there are many learning opportunities per trial. As the learner approaches mastery, the number of errors per trial decreases because the faults in the underlying rules are successively eliminated. Consequently, there are fewer learning opportunities and hence fewer error-correcting events per trial, so the rate of improvement slows down.

This qualitative argument is consistent with the results of computer simulations. Figure 8.2 shows a simulation result achieved with the HS simulation model described in Chapter 7. The model learned to construct structural formulas, so-called Lewis structures. In this particular simulation, the model worked on nine different Lewis structures taken from a college chemistry text. The problems were presented to the model multiple times in random order until each one had been mastered. The values shown in the figure are averages across multiple simulated students. (Empirical learning curves are typically constructed by aggregating data from multiple human learners.) The model's learning curve exhibits the same gradually declining rate of improvement as do the learning curves of human learners. No aspect of the constraint-based error-correcting mechanism was specifically designed to achieve this result. The shape of the resulting learning curve emerges out of the interactions among the processes postulated in the model.

Since the beginning of the 20th century, researchers have debated whether the shape of the practice curve follows a particular mathematical form and, if so, which one. The leading hypothesis is that it conforms to the shape described by power laws – equations of the general form

$$P(t) = A + Bt^{-a}$$

where P is a measure of performance, usually the time to perform the target task, t is the amount of practice, usually measured in number of training trials and $P(t)$ is the performance on trial t. The parameter A is the asymptote, the best possible performance, while B is the performance on the first trial. The

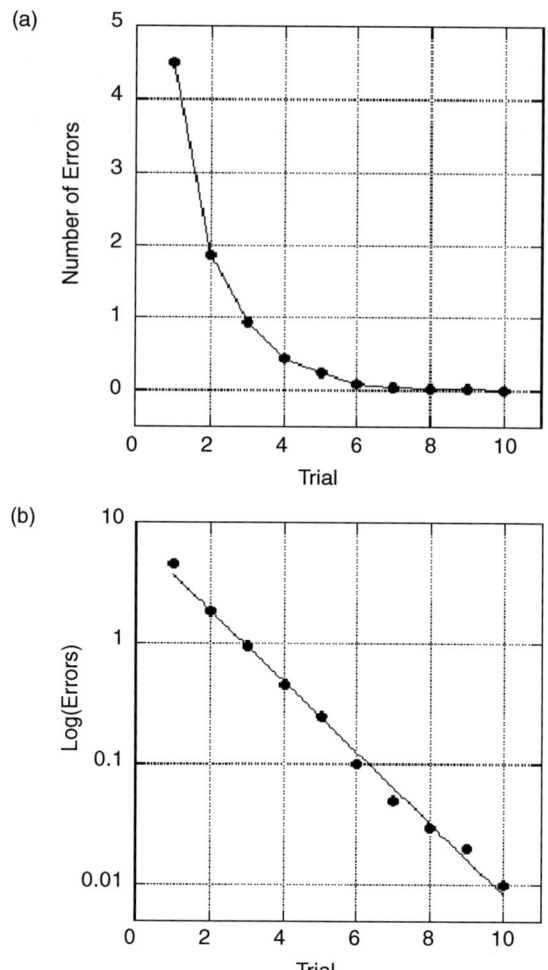

FIGURE 8.2. Error reduction curve for the HS simulation model in the chemistry task. Panel (a) shows the normal plot, while panel (b) shows the same data plotted with logarithmic coordinates on the *y*-axis (but not the *x*-axis).

exponent, *a*, referred to as the *learning rate*, is sometimes interpreted as an individual difference parameter.[5] The fit between empirical data and power laws is consistently high across a wide range of tasks and subject populations, and it is present in both individual and group data. As Figure 8.1 shows, the power law fit for this particular data set is better than 0.96. Power law curves have the peculiar mathematical property that if the values on both axes are replaced by their logarithms, the curve becomes a straight line. To decide whether a particular data set conforms to a power law it is sufficient to plot it with logarithmic coordinates and verify that the data points cluster along a straight line. Panel (b) in Figure 8.1 shows the same data as in panel (a), plotted with logarithmic coordinates on both axes. What appears as a curve in panel (a) appears as a straight line in panel (b).

Some researchers have claimed that empirical learning curves exhibit better fits to exponential equations, that is, equations of the general form

$$P(t) = A + Be^{-at}$$

in which the symbols have the same meaning as before and e is the natural logarithm. Exponential curves have the mathematical property of falling on a straight line when plotted with logarithmic coordinates on the y-axis (but not the x-axis). Researchers have debated which type of equation best represents the true shape of improvement. Power laws and exponential equations generate similar curves, so empirical data that fit one type of equation well tend to also fit the other type equally well, or nearly so. The issue has been debated for the better part of a century.

The curve in Figure 8.2 is an exponential curve, not a power law curve. This is demonstrated in panel (b), which shows that the data points fall on a straight line when the y-axis (but not the x-axis) is plotted with logarithmic coordinates. Hence, error correction does not by itself explain why empirical data so often are found to fit power laws. But according to the Nine Modes Theory proposed in Chapter 6, we should not expect learning from error or any other learning mechanism to provide the complete explanation for the learning curve. The learning curve is a statistical construct that aggregates the effects of a large number of learning events. For example, consider a training study in which 25 subjects learn a skill that requires, on average, 50 learning events for mastery. The total number of learning events behind the resulting learning curve, if plotted in terms of averages across subjects, is then 50 * 25 = 1,250 events. According to the Nine Modes Theory, a person learns in multiple ways during practice, so those 1,250 learning events will be of diverse kinds. Some, but only some, will be error-correction events. Any observed behavioral regularity is a cumulative result of the interactions among all the different learning mechanisms.

To predict the expected shape of change would require a simulation model that learns in all the nine ways described in Chapter 6. No such model exists. However, an approximation can be constructed by focusing on the

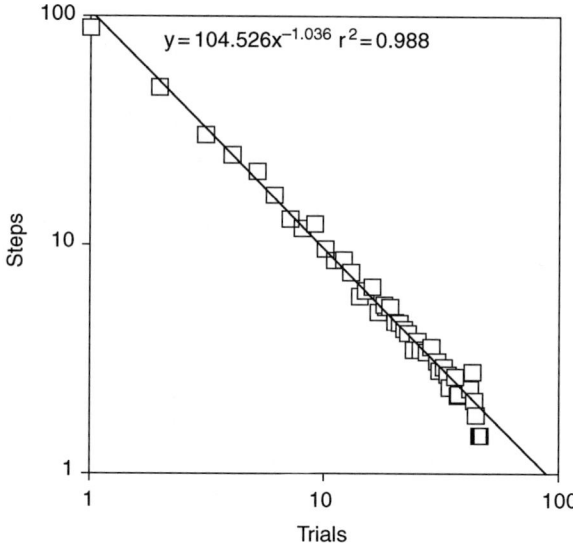

FIGURE 8.3. Learning curve for computer simulation model that learns from both successes and failures. Adapted from Ohlsson and Jewett, 1997, Figure 10, p. 165.

learning mechanisms that are most important during the mastery phase of practice; see Figure 6.2. In the mastery phase, the two most important sources of information are positive and negative feedback generated by the outcomes of the learner's own actions. James J. Jewett and I performed a series of simulation experiments with a computer model that could learn from both successes and failures.[6] We explored the effects of turning one or the other learning mechanism on or off. We found that error correction by itself generates learning curves that fit exponential equations. However, with learning from successes and failures operating in parallel, the behavior of the model was well described by a power law of the same type and shape that is frequently observed in data from human learners; see Figure 8.3. The power law of learning emerged in the interactions between learning from successes and learning from errors. This result does not depend on the internal mechanics of the learning mechanisms. It does not matter at this level of analysis exactly how learners capitalize on successes and correct their errors; it only matters that they are capable of doing so. However, the rate of learning matters. If there are multiple modes of learning, each mode can occur at a higher or lower rate, and the rate parameters can vary independently of each other. The power law fit only appeared for certain settings of those parameters. If those parameters vary from learner to learner, it follows that empirical data will sometimes fit one type of equation better than the other, and sometimes the reverse.

In the end, then, the answer to whether learning curves follow power law equations or exponential equations is "neither." Either type of equation is an equally arbitrary description of the observed behavior. The underlying learning mechanisms are not intrinsically connected to either type of equation, or indeed to any type of equation, and the learning curves they produce if they were to operate in isolation might not be the same as the curve generated by the interactions among the entire set of mechanisms. Furthermore, the learning curve is not a behavior but a statistical construct, created by aggregating data from multiple performances. The exact shape of any one learning curve emerges in the aggregation process, and the outcome depends on the mixture of learning modes and the rates associated with the latter in the particular learning process studied. What remains constant is the negatively accelerated shape of the short-term learning curve.

Multiple overlapping waves
Learning curves like the one in Figure 8.1 are typically obtained in short-term laboratory experiments or training studies. It is not immediately obvious how such short-term practice effects are related to practice in the long term. If a learning curve can reach asymptote within an hour of practice, how can improvements continue for 10 years or longer?

One answer is that strategies are replaced by qualitatively different and more effective strategies. The phenomenon of strategy discovery for already mastered tasks is particularly salient in the study of cognitive development. Since Jean Piaget's monumental contribution, developmental psychologists have struggled to describe the progressive growth of competence through the first 15 years of life.[7] No theorist now subscribes to the sequence of developmental stages that Piaget proposed. Careful empirical studies have shown that children's cognitive competence does not grow in such a lock-step manner.[8] Competence is domain-specific and the rate of growth varies from domain to domain and from child to child, so a child might have reached some level of competence in domain X without being at the same level of competence in some other domain Y. What Piaget called *décalages* and cast as exceptions turned out to be the normal case.

A developmental progression is more likely to consist of a succession of ever more powerful strategies for any one task, with mastery of qualitatively different tasks progressing more or less independently of each other.

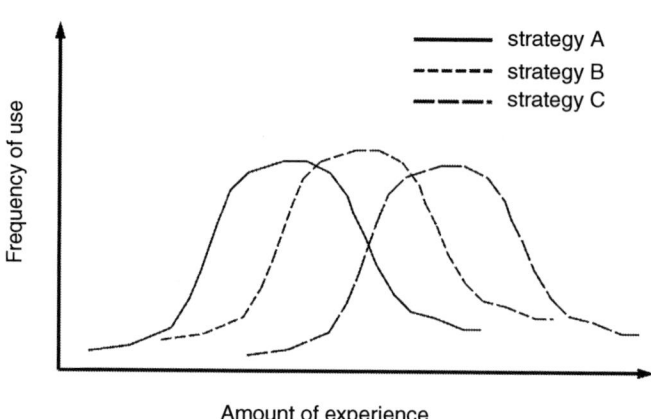

FIGURE 8.4. An in-principle representation of the multiple overlapping waves pattern. After Siegler, 1996, Figure 4.4.

According to developmental psychologist Robert S. Siegler and his co-workers, the relation between the successive strategies for a given task follows a temporal pattern called *multiple overlapping waves*.[9] Each strategy has a life cycle consisting of an initial phase with low probability of use, followed by a period with steady increase in this probability, a peak and a final decline. A graph of the probability of use over time therefore has the shape of a wave. The starting points for different waves differ because the different strategies are discovered at different times. Their peaks vary in height and the time from the discovery of a strategy until it fades can be shorter or longer. At each moment in time, multiple waves are in progress; see Figure 8.4 for an illustration of this concept. In contrast to Figure 8.1, the vertical axis in Figure 8.4 is a measure of the probability or relative frequency of execution of a skill or strategy, not a measure of performance. Each successive strategy is acquired through a negatively accelerated learning curve.[10] The pattern in Figure 8.4 is orthogonal to the shape of improvement of the individual strategies. Although the multiple overlapping waves pattern has only been observed in the first 15 years of life, it is plausible that the same pattern characterizes skill acquisition across the entire life span.

The theoretical challenge posed by the multiple waves pattern is not primarily to understand why a new strategy increases its relative probability of use at the beginning of its life cycle. A new strategy is presumably created for a good reason; it might, for example, enable a task to be performed faster or with less cognitive load. The challenge is to understand why the probability of use drops back toward zero eventually. The obvious hypothesis is that this is due to the competitive evaluation of the new strategy vis-à-vis any previous strategy. If the new strategy is more powerful, in the sense of executing more efficiently, applying more broadly or producing better outcomes, then it will win out during conflict resolution, accrue strength and eventually dominate the prior strategies until some other, yet more powerful strategy is discovered. Each time a new, better strategy is discovered, the gradual increase in its probability of use drives down the probability of use for the prior strategies for that task.

Neither strategy evaluation nor competitive conflict resolution derives directly from the specific properties of any particular mode of learning. The multiple overlapping waves pattern is therefore an example of a long-term pattern in the growth of competence that owes nothing to the internal mechanics of the responsible cognitive change mechanisms. The pattern will appear if new, more powerful cognitive strategies can be discovered (somehow), and if the probability of use is determined (somehow) by competitive conflict resolution. At the level of life-span growth, it does not matter how new strategies are discovered or how conflicts between competing strategies are resolved. The only properties that punch through to the life-span time band are the very capabilities of discovering better strategies and of assessing their relative cognitive utility.

Long-term growth of complexity
Strategy discovery cannot, in practice, continue indefinitely. In some cases, no strategy of higher effectiveness remains to be discovered. This process is only a partial answer to the question of how improvements in performance can continue for 10 years or longer.

A second possible answer is that the bigger the skill, the bigger the learning curve. Greater complexity of the target skill implies a greater value for the B parameter in the power law equation, which implies that learning begins at a higher point on the y-axis and that more practice trials are required to reach asymptotic performance. Simple skills asymptote in a few practice trials; complex skills asymptote only after a long series of trials. The magnitude of the change from the first trial to asymptotic performance is greater in absolute terms for a more complex skill, so the process takes longer.

Some empirical findings support this "big curve" view. I once analyzed the learning curve for writing books, based on data from the late science fiction writer Isaac Asimov, who wrote a total of 500 books in his lifetime.[11] The time to completion for his Nth book turned out to be a power law function of N. A famous study by E. R. F. W. Crossman on cigar rolling in Cuba exhibited power law improvement over millions of trials representing many years of practice.[12] If a skill is complex, the absolute values on the axes are correspondingly greater, but the shape of the learning curve is invariant.

The "big curve" way of scaling from short-term to long-term practice effects overlooks the fact that the large knowledge base of an expert is a set of partially overlapping but distinct skills rather than a single, integrated skill. Consider cooking: Chopping vegetables is a different skill from filleting a fish, and sautéing sea scallops is not exactly the same as scrambling eggs. These skills are complex and there is some overlap in their components: Both chopping and filleting require careful handling of the knife; both sautéing and scrambling depend on keeping the pan at the right temperature. Nevertheless, it is possible to master each of those four skills without mastering any of the other three, so they are distinct. A professional chef has obviously mastered all four. The total competence of the chef consists of hundreds of connected, partially overlapping but nevertheless distinct subskills. The same description applies to the skill sets of coffee shop managers, engineers, fighter pilots and physicians. In general, competence has a clumpy, granular structure. Rules form loosely integrated clusters that encode distinct subskills. A task is likely to exercise some subskills more than others.

The clumpy character of practical knowledge invites the view that the learning curve applies to each subskill separately instead of to the learner's competence as a whole. There is no direct proof of this. But researchers have observed evidence for the closely related fact that when an expert discovers multiple strategies for one and the same subtask, the standard learning curve applies to each successive strategy. So it is plausible that the acquisition of multiple distinct but related subskills moves simultaneously down multiple learning curves, each shaped by how much practice the person experiences on the particular subtask, as opposed to the overall task. That is, the level of mastery of subskill X is a function of how many times the novice has encountered a task that requires that particular subskill, not how much experience he has with the overall task. Skill at chopping only improves when the chef-to-be makes a dish that requires chopping.

The learning curves for the subskills should not be thought of as synchronized. If the target competence takes 10 years to acquire, all relevant subskills are not introduced on the first day of training. The novice faces challenges of gradually increasing complexity. This happens in part because novices migrate from peripheral to central roles in learning-on-the-job contexts and hence assume more and more responsibility, and in part because instructors and trainers deliberately design training sequences so that they lead the novice up the complexity gradient. The musical prodigy first learns to play simple tunes, then moves on to entire concertos; the fighter pilot masters takeoff and landing before he trains the maneuvers of combat; the medical resident learns to take blood samples long before he performs surgery; and so on. As the expert-to-be slides down each of the learning curves for already initiated subskills, he also moves through the curriculum. These two movements impact complexity in opposite ways. The slide down the learning curve renders individual subskills streamlined and less effortful to execute, while the broadening of the skill set renders the overall competence more complex and more difficult to maintain, extend or restructure.

The relations between these opposing tendencies are depicted in Figure 8.5. Time runs along the horizontal axis. Cognitive load, in terms of some measure that decreases with practice such as effort, number of errors or time to task completion, is plotted on the vertical axis. The acquisition of each subskill follows a negatively accelerated learning curve, but at any one time, multiple skills are practiced. Computational mechanisms like constraint-based error correction can explain why the individual subskills improve according to negatively accelerated learning curves but have little to say about the larger pattern. At the longer time band, the details of the individual learning mechanisms are irrelevant. The main change is the broadening of the skill set, a type of change that is driven by the fact that trainees naturally move from simple

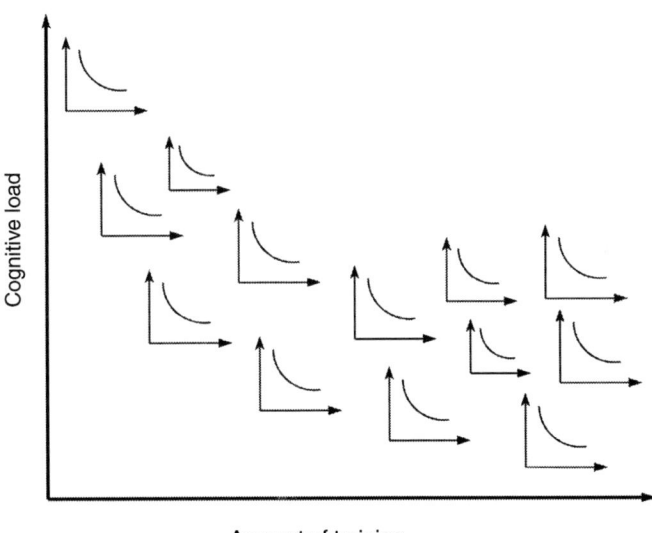

FIGURE 8.5. The multiple-subskill view of long-term practice. Each subskill is learned according to a power law, but the introduction of more subskills broadens the skill set.

to complex undertakings. The complexity of the total skill set – symbolized in the figure by the height of the vertically stacked single-skill learning curves – increases over time. Because the two movements – streamlining individual subskills and broadening the repertoire – push cognitive complexity in opposite directions, it is impossible to derive specific predictions about the time course of complexity in the long-term growth of competence.

In short, competence grows along three dimensions, each with its own shape. The mastery of each individual skill follows a negatively accelerated curve of improvement that is driven both by the elimination of errors and other unnecessary steps and by the optimization and speedup of the remaining steps. The discovery of new, more powerful strategies for individual tasks superimposes the multiple overlapping waves pattern on the learning curves for individual skills. Progress follows the learning curve for each strategy, but the strategies that apply to the same task also succeed each other over time, resulting in the inverted U-shaped pattern in the frequency of use of any one strategy. Finally, the changes in performance on each subtask are embedded within the widening repertoire of distinct but interrelated skills. At the 10-year time band, the growth of competence is not well described as a big learning curve, except in certain special cases. Instead, there is a growth of complexity as more subskills are integrated into the overall competence. The three movements depicted in Figures 8.1, 8.4 and 8.5 do not combine to produce any overall pattern or regularity, as far as we know. The internal mechanics of learning from error impacts the shape of the learning curve for individual strategies but do not punch through to the overlapping waves pattern or the growth of complexity, both of which are due to other factors.

The Anatomy of Competence

The end point of extended practice is expertise. Empirical studies of experts as well as efforts to implement expert systems in Artificial Intelligence have converged on three characteristics of expertise: the large size of the expert's knowledge base, the domain specificity of expert knowledge and the ability of experts to behave flexibly.

Size of knowledge base
Why does it take so long to become expert? The answer is that there is a lot to learn. Simple skills like tying a bowline knot, mastering a new cell phone and finding one's way around an unfamiliar shopping center can be captured in one or two dozen goal-situation-action rules. Not so expertise. We have

no way to count knowledge units (chunks, constraints, rules, schemas, etc.), but rough estimates are available for some task domains. World-class chess players might possess between 10,000 and 100,000 units of chess knowledge, depending on their level of skill.[13] The approximate size of the vocabulary of the average, educated Western adult falls in the narrower range of 30,000 to 60,000 words.[14] Large expert systems in the field of Artificial Intelligence confirm that human-level performance requires thousands of separate pieces of knowledge. In Artificial Intelligence research, this is known as the *Knowledge Principle*: Expert-level problem solving does not reside in the execution of complicated reasoning algorithms but in the application of large amounts of relevant knowledge.[15] A third stream of information comes from work on the implementation of intelligent tutoring systems, instructional software systems that explicitly represent the subject matter that they teach. Systems of this sort usually require several hundred knowledge elements to represent the competence taught in an introductory course in, for example, algebra, computer programming or database use.[16] It is plausible that an expert knows 100 times as much as a beginner, so the expert's knowledge base is likely to be on the order of tens of thousands of knowledge elements. The approximate convergence of these four estimates provides modest confidence in the accuracy of the 10k–100k range.

A computer program can acquire a knowledge base of this size via the diligent typing of knowledge engineers, but human beings have to acquire the knowledge through practice. Estimates of the learning rates of individual learners are few and far between, but they range between 1 and 10 knowledge units (chunks, rules) per hour of practice. If we assume a learning rate of 5 knowledge units per hour, and if we assume that the learner practices 4 hours a day, 5 days a week, 50 weeks per year, then it takes 10 years to accumulate 50,000 knowledge units. In short, it takes years to become an expert because the knowledge base of an expert is large in relation to the rate at which the knowledge is acquired.

Domain specificity
Experienced physicians are better than residents at diagnosing medical patients, but no better at troubleshooting electronic equipment than engineering students, and vice versa. A case could be made that the types of inferences required in the two domains of medical diagnosis and troubleshooting are similar at some level of abstraction, but few medical patients with chest pains would feel comfortable being diagnosed by an electrical engineer. The expert's knowledge is encoded in memory in terms of the concepts that belong

to the relevant domain.[17] The cognitive advantage of an expert over a novice disappears when he is confronted with problems in some other domain. The evidence for this is particularly well established in chess: Chess masters perform orders of magnitude better on a variety of tasks designed to tap into their chess knowledge, but the advantage disappears on analogous tasks with other materials. For example, chess masters are much better than a chess novice at remembering the locations of chess pieces after a brief exposure of a board position, but they are not superior to the average person in remembering a list of random digits; for an expert mental calculator, the relation is the opposite. Similar indications of domain specificity have been observed by researchers in a variety of domains.

The domain specificity of expertise contradicts common sense. The common view is that cognitive competence starts out highly concrete and task specific in childhood, but over time evolves to become more abstract and formal in character as a person matures; in short, children are concrete thinkers while adults are abstract thinkers. Piaget's theory of cognitive development embraced this view. It is frequently expressed in the educational research literature as well as in the popular culture. One reason for this belief is perhaps that "more abstract" tends to be equated with "more powerful." In the realm of declarative knowledge, there is truth in this equality. An abstract concept or principle is powerful in part because it applies to many problems and situations. The matter stands differently with respect to practical knowledge. Efficiency of performance depends on knowledge of exactly when, under which circumstances, each relevant action is to be performed. A jet pilot cannot fly a plane on the basis of the abstract principles of aerodynamics but has to know exactly when to do what. In the course of extended practice, practical knowledge moves from initial, general heuristics to highly detailed and specific procedures.

The domain specificity of the knowledge accumulated through long-term practice is predicted by the constraint-based learning mechanism. The main principle of this mechanism is that errors are unlearned by adding conditions to goal-situation-action rules. The new conditions specialize and refine faulty rules so that they apply only in the set of situations in which the action they recommend is appropriate, correct or useful. The change that occurs throughout practice thus moves practical knowledge from a small initial kernel of very general dispositions to a large knowledge base of highly particular and specific rules with detailed and precise conditions of applicability. This is the type of change generated by constraint-based learning, and its end point is the type of knowledge that researchers believe explains the observable performances of human experts, and also the type of knowledge that Artificial Intelligence researchers believe enables computer programs to mimic expert performance. In this case, the property of the learning mechanism – the fact that it produces increasingly specific knowledge structures – projects onto the long-term time band.

Flexibility
Experts can respond flexibly and intelligently to novel situations and problems that fall within their domain. In the terminology of cognitive psychology, they can *transfer* practical knowledge learned in one situation to another situation within their domain of expertise. Cognitive flexibility is a key feature of expert behavior, but the specialization principle that is at the heart of the constraint-based theory of learning from error appears to make flexibility more rather than less difficult to understand. If skills are morphing from higher levels of generality to greater specificity in the course of practice, the end result should be even less flexible than the starting point. High performance depends on a close fit between skill and task, but better fit to one task necessarily lowers the fit to another, even slightly different task. Effectiveness requires that practical knowledge is specific; flexibility, that it is abstract. We cannot have it both ways, or so it seems.

The rule genealogies and conflict resolution scheme introduced in Chapter 7 resolve this dilemma. The constraint-based specialization theory claims that when new, more specialized versions of rules are added to memory, the previous versions are kept in memory but downgraded in priority. A task will be processed by the most specific rule (or rules) that matches the situation at hand. In the case of a highly familiar task, the most specific matching rules will be the leaf nodes in the relevant genealogies. A completely unfamiliar task will match only against the root rules (i.e., the rules that encode general methods). Between these two extremes lies the succession of rules of intermediate generality that were produced in the course of past learning; see Figure 7.2.

Consider what happens when a person encounters a task that bears some relation to an already mastered task without being identical to it. By hypothesis, the leaf rules in the relevant rule genealogies will not match. However, less specific rules in those genealogies might nevertheless match, precisely because they are less specific. Conflict resolution by specificity causes the novel task to be filtered through the rule genealogy until it encounters intermediate rules that do match. The matching rules will become the initial rule set for the transfer task. Conflict resolution by specificity will automatically pull the most specific prior rules that match out of the total set of rules available. Prior practical knowledge will hence be re-used precisely to the extent that it is applicable to an altered or novel task. The amount of cognitive work needed to transfer the prior skill is a function of how many learning events are required before the rules have been adapted to the new task and stop generating errors.

This explanation for expert flexibility works best at the longest time scale. In the course of 10 years of practice, an expert creates, according to the constraint-based theory, a vast knowledge base of rule genealogies, each containing many rules of varying levels of specificity. When a new situation is encountered, the most specific rules that match are activated. Given widely varied prior experience and 10 years of training, the person's knowledge base will contain tens of thousands of such intermediate rules. Because situations and problems within a domain resemble each other to some degree, the best-fitting subset of prior rules might be almost able to handle the new situation. The versions that fit are likely to be overly general, and hence require some revisions. The issue is how much cognitive work those revisions represent. In situations that exhibit only small differences to previously encountered situations, the amount of cognitive work required to specialize the existing rules to fit the new situation might be minor. If the work required to specialize the rules is a small fraction of the total effort required to perform the task, it will look to an observer as if the expert already knew how to carry out the novel task correctly. A large knowledge base of rule genealogies provides a resource that enables experts to re-specialize their previously learned rules to novel circumstances with a minimum amount of cognitive work, providing the illusion of having mastered the unfamiliar circumstances before they were encountered.

In summary, the constraint-based specialization theory, although originally developed to explain learning from errors in single skills, is compatible with three key features of expertise: The size of the knowledge base is explained by the fact that the repertoire of subskills keeps growing, each new subskill requiring a period of specialization. Although any one subskill can be mastered in a few hours of training, the number of subskills is large, so mastery of the entire skill set continues over a long time. The domain specificity of expertise is predicted by the mode of change implied by the constraint-based theory. If rules start out general or incomplete and become more and more specific, then the ultimate knowledge base consists of highly specific rules. The flexibility of such a knowledge base is explained by the constraint-based transfer mechanism introduced in Chapter 7. The key features of constraint-based error correction are compatible with the cumulative effects of practice over a long time.

ERROR REDUCTION IN COLLECTIVES

Collectives – groups, teams, organizations, populations – are no less error prone than individuals, so a theory of learning from error is potentially applicable at the collective level. In the context of social systems, the study of errors is typically driven by concerns other than those that drive the study in errors in education and training. In the latter contexts, error rates are indices of mastery or lack thereof, clues to how the student or trainee thinks about a subject matter or a target skill. In the context of collectives, errors take on a different and more sinister aspect: They are all too often among the root causes of accidents and disasters.[18] The consequences of an erroneous action can cascade through the collective with disastrous results. The near-meltdown of the Three Mile Island nuclear power plant, the explosion of the *Challenger* space shuttle, the burning of the *Hindenburg* airship and the spectacular capsizing of the Swedish 17th-century warship *Wasa* on its maiden voyage in 1628 have become iconic instances of disasters and failures in sociotechnical systems. The collapse of the walkways in the Kansas City Hyatt Regency Hotel and the failure of the Tacoma Narrows Bridge are equally familiar, at least among engineers. The failure of the Xerox Corporation to exploit its lead in developing the personal computer, and the Allied losses during Operation Market Garden in World War II illustrate the potential for disaster in economic and military affairs.

Since the pioneering works of Jens Rasmussen, Donald Norman and James Reason in the 1980s, safety scientists have pondered the nature of the relation between errors on the part of individuals and accidents, disasters and failures at the collective level.[19] A variety of principles have been proposed. In particular, there have been multiple attempts to classify errors into types as a preliminary step to understanding the origins of errors. Some researchers have focused on the cognitive mechanisms of individual errors, others on operator actions when faced with opaque interactions among multiple simultaneous breakdowns and yet others on the decision-making processes that let a space shuttle take off with leaking O-rings or a commander to launch a battle in the face of intelligence reports that indicate superior enemy forces. It would be rash to claim that any one of these factors, or types of factors, is less than essential for the understanding of collective failure.

However, the list of relevant factors does not provide a theory of the dynamics of collective error rates over time. Do error rates remain constant or fall? If the latter, what is the shape of change? The observation that hierarchical decision-making structures can override counterindicators to an action – the Stupid Boss Theory of collective failure – makes no prediction other than that any hierarchical organization will fail eventually. Similarly, the observation that machinery with many components can malfunction in multiple ways and that it is not possible to foresee all interactions among simultaneously malfunctioning components only predicts that if a complicated technical system operates long enough, a composite breakdown for which the responsible operators are ill prepared will occur. Such assertions, although true, provide little insight into how error rates change over time.

The ability of the individual to learn is one of the factors that contributes to change in the collective. If every operator or participant performs his part of the shared overall task better, we would expect the collective to function better, ignoring for the moment what "better" means in any one context. The question is how individual learning events project onto the collective level. Like individual errors, a collective error can be conceptualized as an action that was taken when it should not have been; indeed, this formulation is almost synonymous with the meaning of error. The observation suggests that the constraint-based perspective applies to the collective itself, regarded as a single entity that learns from its errors.

Constraint-Based Learning in Collectives

It is highly unlikely that any single perspective will cover all aspects of such complicated events as accidents, disasters and collective failures. For the constraint-based perspective to be useful, it is enough if it applies to some significant subset of such events. Three key questions are whether collectives make overgeneralization errors, detect errors via constraint violations and correct errors via the specialization of operating procedures.

The nature of collective errors

Collective errors are, like individual errors, actions taken when they should not have been. There is little point in distinguishing between errors of commission and errors of omission, because when the appropriate action *A* is omitted in a continuously active system, some other action *B* is always performed in its stead; hence, *B* is performed when it should not have been. Every error of omission is therefore also an error of commission. This observation is as valid at the collective as at the individual levels, and it suggests that at least some collective errors can be understood as overgeneralization errors: If the applicability conditions for *B* had been specified in more detail, perhaps *B* would not have been performed and the probability that *A* would have been performed instead would have been greater.

This view gains support from naturalistic corpora of collective errors. Safety scientists have gathered such corpora for several types of collectives, including businesses, clinics and hospitals, military organizations and sociotechnical systems, especially transportation systems (e.g., airlines). The errors described in such corpora exhibit a bewildering variety. However, the variability resides to a large extent in the specifics of the particular events. Narratives of the burning of the *Hindenburg* airship, the collapse of the satellite phone industry and the military losses during Operation Market Garden read like horror stories by very different authors. However, the scripts, as opposed to the events themselves, are not entirely different: In most stories the relevant collective moved in spite of the presence of counterindicators that should have constrained the move. If we abstract from the domain specifics, there is considerable similarity among an airplane crew that takes off in bad weather without de-icing the wings, a corporate management team that becomes gripped by deal fever and completes a financially disastrous merger without adequate review of the financial benefits and a combat force that initiates an attack in the face of intelligence that implies that the battle cannot be won.

For example, consider the corpus of business errors described by Paul B. Carroll and Chunka Mui in their 2008 book about the *Billion Dollar Lessons* that one can draw from "the most inexcusable business failures of the last 25 years."[20] They analyzed hundreds of cases in which the execution of a common business strategy caused a major failure because the strategy was not the right one under the circumstances. They classified their cases into seven types. For brevity, I collapse their classification into four types of strategic business errors. The first is inappropriate extension of an existing business. The move in this case is to expand the business, but the chosen expansion is inappropriate in some way and the result undermines rather than strengthens the business. According to Carroll and Mui, this can happen by overestimation of the benefits of a merger with another company; by overlooking the downsides of rollups and consolidations, that is, attempts to buy up other businesses; and through adjacencies, moves in which a management team expands into an adjacent market for which their business is ill suited or that does not provide any advantage. The lesson taught by these cases is obviously that an expansion of any sort, once thought of and proposed, should be studied carefully for pitfalls and counterindications before the organization charges ahead. The conditions under which different types of expansions are likely to work need to be specified.

The second and third strategy errors are each others' mirror images: To stay the course even though technical inventions are changing the relevant market, and to be too quick to ride an innovation. Carroll and Mui mention Eastman Kodak's lack of response to the digital photography revolution as an example of the former. Xerox's failure to take charge of the personal computer revolution is another. But there are as many cases in which a company invested heavily in an emerging technology that had less commercial potential than first appeared. Carroll and Mui describe the failure of Iridium, the Motorola subsidiary that developed and marketed satellite phones for a brief period before cell phones took over. A very different failure-prone move on their list is overly aggressive "financial engineering," a type of error that requires moral rather than cognitive analysis.

These strategies except the last are legitimate moves that have been carried out with good effect in many cases. Some applications of these strategies turned into failures because they were carried out at the wrong time, under the wrong circumstances. Expansions, continued investment in an established technology and attempts to ride an emerging technology succeed only when specific conditions are met. Carroll and Mui are quite explicit about those conditions, and the thrust of their analysis is that companies need to unlearn these types of strategic errors by adopting stricter conditions for when to apply each business strategy.

Engineering design appears to be a qualitatively different endeavor, but many design errors can also be analyzed as actions taken when they should not have been.[21] For example, the Swedish warship *Wasa* sank in 1628 on its maiden voyage, before leaving Stockholm harbor. Nobody hanged for this disaster, because the fault originated at the top. The Swedish warrior king Gustaf II Adolf had ordered the ship to support his military adventures on the European continent, and the king wanted sufficient firepower to protect his supply lines cross the Baltic Sea and to blockade his enemies. He asked for a second cannon deck, superimposed on a tried and true design for a warship with a single cannon deck. The taller hull and the heavy cannons on the upper deck conspired to elevate the center of gravity and made the ship so unstable that it capsized as soon as the wind hit its sails. The constraint that was violated is simple to state: Do not raise the center of gravity on a ship without testing the effect on its seaworthiness. Examples of constraint violations are equally salient in other fields of activity. World War II is a rich source of errors committed by military organizations, many of them failures to take counterindications into account.[22] These include the inability of the German high command to consider the possibility that their most secret military code, Enigma, had been broken, and to stop sending U-boats to their graves in the North Atlantic. On the other side of the battle, the Allied command launched the disastrous Operation Market Garden against the German front across the Netherlands in September of 1944 in spite of intelligence that German forces had more tanks in the area than originally estimated. The violated constraint is all too obvious: Do not underestimate the enemy.

In short, some collective accidents, disasters and failures can be analyzed in terms of underspecified decision rules, operating procedures that ignore situation features indicating that the action under consideration is not appropriate, correct or useful. If the applicability conditions for the relevant action type had been more precisely specified – when, under which circumstances, is a merger the right move for a corporation? – the disastrous action might have been suppressed, and some other action would have been taken instead. There are no data on prevalence. That is, there is no way of knowing what proportion of all accidents, disasters and collective failures fit this schema. For present purposes, it is enough that some of them do.

The centrality of constraints
Organizations no less than individuals detect errors and impending failures as deviations of experienced outcomes from desired, expected or predicted outcomes. Unintended final outcomes are usually obvious. Falling stock prices, heavy casualties, dead patients and shipwrecks leave no room for doubt that something went wrong. The important question is how the extended process of building wealth, curing patients, operating complex machinery or navigating is judged as being on track versus derailed *before* the final outcome. The more the relevant operators know about the way their system should work, what the system should look like when everything is going well, the higher the probability that they will catch a derailed process before the pre-failure state erupts into unacceptable damage.

To cast the relevant knowledge as consisting of constraints is in many cases straightforward. In fact, safety regulations are particularly clear examples of constraints. The sign "hard hat area" on the gate to a construction site means *if you are walking in this area, you ought to be wearing a hard hat* (or else you have broken the rules); the announcement that "as we prepare to take off, all luggage should be stored under the seat in front of you or in the overhead compartments" can be restructured slightly to say, *if you are in an airplane, and the airplane is about to take off, your luggage ought to be stowed* (or else you are in violation of the safety rules). Some safety rules apply to each participant individually, but there are also safety rules that apply to collectives. A familiar example is the theater sign that says, "occupation by more than N persons in this room is illegal." This constraint applies to the collective as a whole without prescribing any particular behavior on the part of any one individual. Regardless of domain, doing the right thing depends to a considerable extent on knowing what not to do: Do not take off in a snowstorm without properly de-icing the wings; do not underestimate the enemy; do not ignore differences in corporate culture when considering a merger; do not ignore counterindications to the most frequently encountered medical diagnosis; and so on. In general, safety rules are norms, and norms are constraints by another name.

The application of constraints depends on information about the current state of the system, in both individuals and collectives. The unique difficulty that appears at the collective level is that in a complex system, no single operator knows all the constraints, and no single operator has access to all the information about the current system state. How, then, do collectives decide that some constraint has been violated and that the system has slid onto a pre-failure track?

One emergent mechanism at the collective level is that different individuals play different roles, some providing information, others applying constraints. Consider the navigation of a large ship in and out of the San Diego harbor. The harbor is connected to the sea through a long, narrow and winding channel. When a large ship like a military aircraft carrier enters or exits the harbor, the navigating team's need to know the exact position of the ship at each moment in time is acute. If a turn is initiated too late, there is a possibility that the momentum of the massive ship will carry it past the turn and onto the opposite shore. Edwin Hutchins, a cognitive scientist trained as an anthropologist, obtained permission to travel on a U.S. Navy carrier and observe the operation of the navigation team – the Sea and Anchor Piloting Detail in navy terminology – that plotted the successive positions of the ship on a sea chart.[23] The position of the ship on the chart is determined by taking two or three simultaneous compass bearings from the ship to prominent and recognizable landmarks on both sides of the ship, such as a lighthouse or some prominent landscape feature. The bearings are reported to a plotting team inside the bridge, the control and command center of a ship, and drawn as straight lines on the sea chart. The point on the chart at which the lines cross each other (and the line representing the ship's course) is the position of the ship at the point in time when the bearings were taken.

As Hutchins reports in his 1995 book *Cognition in the Wild*, there are multiple possibilities for error. The two seamen on either side of the bridge who take the compass bearings – the pelorus operators – might mistake one landmark for another, fail to read the two bearings at exactly the same moment, read a bearing incorrectly on their instruments or speak it incorrectly when they report it to the plotting team. The members of the plotting team might hear a bearing incorrectly or plot it incorrectly. Nevertheless, aircraft carriers do not run aground. The operating procedures of the Sea and Anchor Detail have evolved over centuries to ensure accurate navigation, and the team members – quartermasters all – are well trained and have long experience. In addition, the team's procedures provide multiple checks on the accuracy of the plot. For example, the bearings are heard by all the members of the plotting team and the plot is visible to the officer of the watch, so errors can be caught quickly. Aircraft carriers do not run aground because the piloting procedures impose a tight set of constraints on the navigation task: If there are different bearings, they should cross each other in a tight box, that is, in the same point on the line representing the course of the ship; the plotted position of the ship has to have a sensible relation to the immediately preceding position; the plotted position has to agree with the depth markings on the chart; and so on. Different team members have different roles in applying these constraints, and Hutchins argues that the roles and the procedures have evolved over a long time precisely to ensure that the team is less error prone than its individual members.

In short, notions of constraints and constraint violations apply to real collectives. Knowledge that operators use to detect errors and pre-failure states can typically be cast as constraints, and the detection of impending disasters depends on information about the system state that allows the operators to decide whether the relevant constraints are violated. The interesting emergent feature is that different individuals can play different roles in a collective systems, some providing information (e.g., the pelorus operators) and others checking for constraint violations (e.g., the plotters). This division of labor has no counterpart in the mind of the individual.

The specialization of operating procedures
How are errors unlearned in collectives? What happens when a complex system encounters an accident, disaster or failure? What change processes are triggered to prevent the same negative outcome from occurring in the future? Can that process be described as a specialization of the relevant operating procedures, at least in a significant subset of cases? One difficulty in answering this question is that we do not possess a corpus of well-documented cases of successful unlearning of errors to complement the corpora of accidents, disasters and failures. It is natural that safety scientists have focused on error types and their origins. The constraint-based perspective does not assign those topics any less importance, but it adds the observation that errors are unavoidable, and that error prevention in the long run therefore depends on unlearning the errors. This requires a change in the relevant operating procedures. Such changes require knowledge about typical system responses to failures, but, paradoxically, to the extent that such responses are successful, they prevent

further errors and hence might attract less attention. Everyone knows that the *Challenger* space shuttle exploded due to a leaking O-ring, but knowledge of how NASA made sure that this will never happen again is less widespread.

In some cases, there is no principled system response. Detected pre-failure errors are passed over in the rush to get work done, and there is no systemwide action. For example, safety scientists who study errors in hospitals report that adverse drug events are quite frequent, in some clinics and hospitals as frequent as one or more such error per patient.[24] But they are handled through local responses and immediate repairs because the nurses who detect them work under severe time pressure and they have to find local solutions that allow them to care for their patients. Amy C. Edmondson, a safety scientist who specializes in the study of adverse drug events, writes that "... healthcare organizations that systematically and effectively learn from failures occurring in the care delivery process are rare."[25] If a collective does not try to learn from its errors, then there is no response to describe. I know of no general description of how collectives respond to errors that is as well grounded in actual cases as the descriptions of the errors themselves.

Common sense suggests that the natural reaction to an accident or a near miss in a manufacturing plant or some other organization is to try to "tighten" – make more explicit and precise – the relevant safety standards. This typically means to formulate more specific prescriptions for how to perform the shared task. In cases of this sort, the specialization principle applies.

The shape of change in collectives
If collectives learn in the same manner as individuals, what patterns or regularities should we expect in the dynamics of error reduction in collectives? To investigate this, we need to separate *populations* from *organizations*. Although the term "population" already has several established usages, it will be used here to refer to a set of more or less independent individuals who communicate with other members of the set but who nevertheless go about their work in an independent manner. There is no division of labor and no organizing center. The set of all pilots that fly commercial airplanes and the population of scientists in a discipline like chemistry or physics are examples.

In general, a collective S can be said to be a population, if the N individuals that make up S are independent, or nearly independent, in the sense that an error on the part of one individual does not affect the probability of error on the part of the other individuals. However, correct behavior on the part of every individual is necessary for S itself to function correctly. Differently put, it is sufficient for a single individual to commit an error for the overall system to have made an error. In this scenario, change in collective performance over time ought to be derivable from the learning of the participating individuals. If a collective S consists of a population of N individual learners $s_1, s_2, s_3, \ldots s_N$, and if each of the latter is accurately described by a learning curve with a gradually and smoothly declining learning curve, then what is the resulting learning curve for S?

The answer is that the aggregated learning curve is of the same shape as the individual curves. For example, Figure 8.6 shows the result of aggregating over 50 independent, simulated agents who were assumed to learn in accordance with an exponential equation. The simulated agents were assumed to have no relevant prior experience (i.e., the E parameter was set to zero) but to vary in cognitive ability. The B parameter – performance on the first trial – was assumed to be normally distributed with a mean of 100 and a standard deviation of 10, while the a parameter – the learning rate – was assumed to be normally distributed with a mean of 1 and a standard deviation of 0.50. The B distribution was chosen arbitrarily but the distribution of the a parameter was guided by empirically found values. The resulting curve is negatively accelerated. Although the individual curves are exponential, the aggregated curve exhibits nearly perfect fit to a power law equation.

Some social systems approximate populations with multiple, nearly independent operators. Transportation industries provide a stock of examples. The occurrence of an error and a subsequent accident in a vehicle moving on land, on the sea or in the air frequently leaves the probability of error in other vehicles of the same type unaffected. Consider the airline system: All pilots (or cockpit crews, if each crew seen as a single agent or operator) who fly commercial airplanes form a population. It is not too gross a simplification to say that each crew executes its flight independently of the other crews and that its errors are its own. The commercial airline system is error free in a given period of time only if every crew flies every flight without error in that period of time. It is sufficient for one crew to make an error – flying too close to another airplane, for example – for the overall system to exhibit at least one error.

How do error rates change over time in air traffic and other transportation industries? Romney B. Duffey and co-workers have made an extensive study of this issue in their 2003 book *Know the Risk: Learning from Errors and Accidents*.[26] They argue that in the case of airlines, the appropriate measure of prior experience is not elapsed time – how many years has a particular airline been in business – but the total number of pilot flying hours. Plotting the number of near misses, a type of error for which extensive quantitative data are available, as a function of experience measured by total flying hours yields the error reduction curve in Figure 8.7. As the figure shows, the curve follows a negatively accelerated

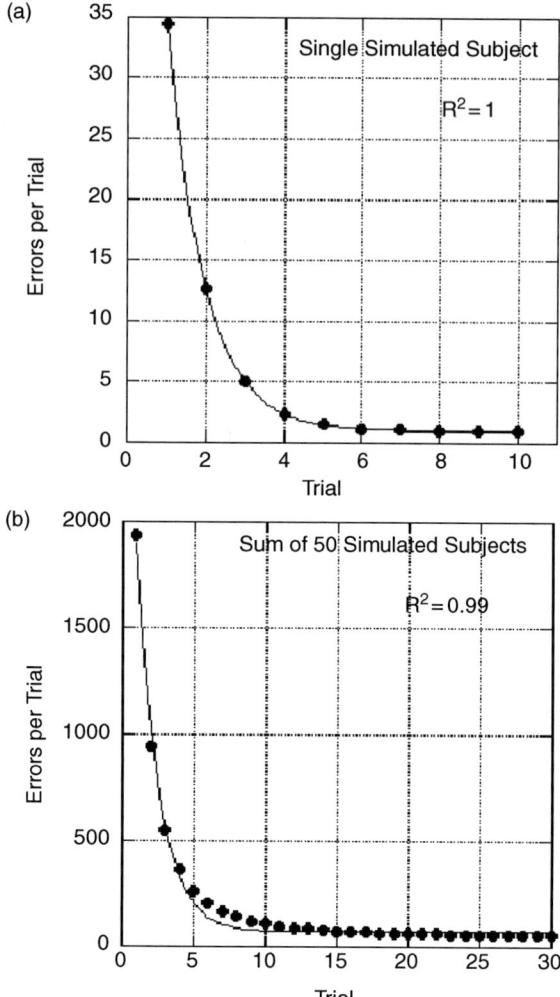

FIGURE 8.6. The effect of additive aggregation on the shape of the error reduction curve. Panel (a) shows a simulated subject with perfect fit to an exponential curve. Panel (b) shows the curve for the sum of the performance of 50 simulated subjects.

curve of the shape we would expect from the prior analysis. Other transportation industries analyzed by Duffey and co-workers conform to the same pattern.

The additive model is applicable to the case of populations, defined here as sets of nearly independent operators. However, this case is oversimplified. It is more common that the agents in a social system interact in ways that

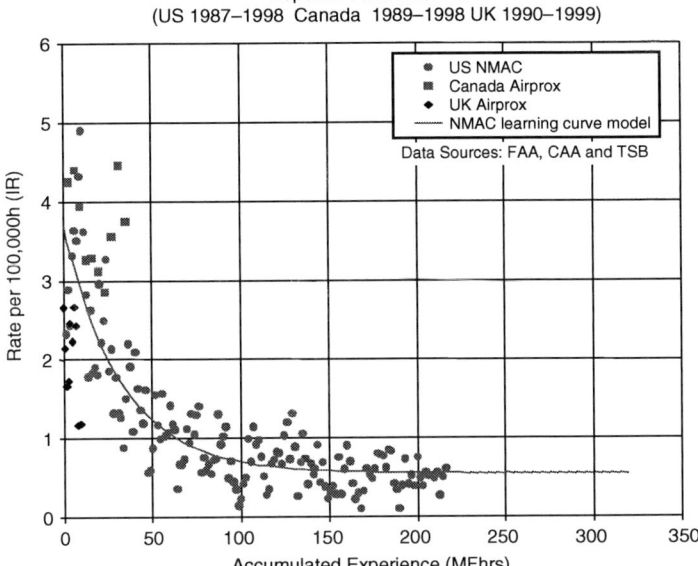

FIGURE 8.7. The error reduction curve in the airline industry, 1987–1999. The errors are events in which one airplane comes too close to another. Reprinted with permission from Duffy and Saull, 2003, Figure 2.6.

change how each one of them operates. For example, the engineers and scientists working at NASA and the employees of a corporation are better thought of as *organizations* than as populations. An organization has a central coordinating agency that imposes a division of labor on its members and assembles their partial solutions into the output of the organization. In organizations, the successful completion of one person's task is typically a prerequisite for the successful completion of another person's task. If so, additive models are insufficient because they do not capture those interactions. So what happens to the shape of change when we move from a population to an organization?

Studies of learning curves in business organizations by economists tend to confirm that learning curves for economic organizations follow the same negatively accelerated curve that characterizes individuals and populations.[27] To the best of my knowledge, there are no empirical learning curves published for manufacturing plants or other types of organizations that depart significantly from the negatively accelerated type of curve. It appears that even when operators are hooked into each other via prerequisite relations, the learning of the collective follows this type of curve. The reason is that even in this case, we can characterize the ongoing change as consisting of both the elimination of steps – the discovery of shortcuts – and the speedup of the remaining steps. The fact that change of this dual sort generates negatively accelerated improvement curves is a level-invariant characteristic.

Summary
A collective – group, team, population or organization – can be regarded as a single entity that learns from error. The abstract principles of constraint-based learning appear to be level-invariant. That is, they apply at the collective level as well, even though the material implementation of the relevant processes is different. A collective fails, perhaps among other ways, by applying underspecified decision rules and operating procedures, thereby performing actions in situations in which they should not have been performed. Errors of this sort are discovered on the basis of error signals that violate constraints on the appropriate, correct or useful system states. When there is an opportunity to learn from such errors, the response is typically to specialize – make more explicit, extensive and precise – the applicability conditions for the relevant decision rules and operating procedures. If the principles of constraint-based specialization are level-invariant, the patterns that characterize collective change over time should be similar to the patterns in individual change. Available data indicate that this is indeed the case. Specifically, learning in collectives follow the same negatively accelerated learning curve that characterizes learning in individuals.

Safety Implications

Although individual error rate curves never fall all the way to zero, it is possible to design collective systems for higher levels of safety than such curves suggest. Safety scientists characterize commercial airlines, the U.S. Navy's nuclear submarines and the European railroads as ultrasafe systems, because the error rates for those systems have fallen so far that the probability of a disastrous accident is 0.0000005 per unit, where a unit is, for example, a unit of time or distance or a passenger, depending on the system.[28] This level of safety requires that errors are caught before they develop into disasters, which in turn requires that the participating individuals are provided with multiple sources of information about the current system state. In technical systems, instruments provide such information. Recommendations in other areas of experience follow the same principle of providing the operators with more dense information and status indicators along the way, so that pre-failure states can be recognized as such before they erupt into disasters. For example, Carroll and Mui recommend that business managers who are considering an acquisition or a merger put together a review board to make an independent review of the relevant factors and to write a report well before the papers are signed. They suggest the appointment of a devil's advocate – once upon a time an honored role in decisions by the Catholic church to confer sainthood – to critique a business deal before it is sealed. Continuous monitors on hospital patients and advance intelligence about the battlefield for soldiers play the same role in those domains of experience.

Providing additional sources of information about system states is useful, but it does not by itself address the generic problem, emphasized by Reason and others, that a complex system can fail simultaneously in more than one way, and it is, in principle, impossible to compute ahead of time all the various consequences of every possible combination of failures on the system indicators. In this case, combinatorics work against us: If there are 100,000 system components, there are $100,000^2$ or 10,000,000,000 possible two-component failure states. It is obviously impossible to list the symptoms of each such failure type ahead of time. A similar situation holds with respect to other complex systems: How many aspects of patient care can go wrong at the same time in a hospital, and how many details are there to be considered in a mega-merger between two corporations? But if the failure states cannot be anticipated or listed ahead of time, how can the operators recognize and interpret them when they occur? The Three Mile Island incident is the type specimen for this problem, but it is potentially a matter of concern for any complex system.

The problem is structurally similar to the problem of automatically diagnosing student misconceptions in intelligent tutoring systems, educational software systems that use Artificial Intelligence techniques to provide individual instruction: The universe of possible misunderstandings is too vast to list all the possible incorrect representations of even a modestly complex subject matter. Constraint-based modeling provides a workable solution to this problem.[29] The constraint base for an intelligent tutoring system does not list possible student errors but states the constraints that specify what is correct for the domain. It thereby indirectly specifies the universe of all possible errors: The latter is the set of all ways in which the constraints can be violated. The analogical situation with a large space of pre-failure states suggests the possibility that constructing a constraint base for a complex system might enable a similar solution: The set of constraints on proper functioning of the system implicitly specifies all the ways in which things can go wrong.

The advantages would be similar to those in the educational context: There is no need to anticipate all possible errors or types of failures. If the expert operator can write down a specification of acceptable functioning in terms of constraints, and if the system provides information that allows continuous monitoring of the constraints, then pre-failure states can be recognized as such even if they were not anticipated. This safety technique is as yet untested.

In short, people manage complex systems better over time. Social practices emerge that allow system designers and operators to learn what not to do. This is error correction writ large. However, safe systems are of little use if the surrounding society crumbles. The question arises whether the ability for collective improvement applies at the highest levels of time, complexity and collectivity.

BIG ERRORS AND THE FATES OF SOCIETIES

The historical perspective on human affairs reveals a punctuated pattern: Nations, societies and entire civilizations come into existence, mature and flourish for some time and then collapse in a period of time that is short compared to the periods of growth and maturity. Applying the notions of error and learning from error to this level of analysis requires some standard of correctness against which observed outcomes can be compared. The purpose of a society is to create and maintain institutions and practices that provide the highest level of prosperity and well-being for its citizens that the historical circumstances allow. At a minimum, institutions and practices should be designed so as to avoid societal collapse. The collapses of which human history provides so many examples cannot have been desired by the people to whom they happened; they must have caused large-scale suffering; and they were caused to some extent by the actions of the leaders and the social practices and institutions the leaders designed. *Sustainable prosperity and well-being for the largest number of average citizens that the material circumstances allow* is the standard against which a nation, society or a civilization can be judged. Deviations from this standard indicate errors in how a society conducts its affairs.

Scholars who focus on big picture history have identified at least three courses of action that yield disastrous results and which therefore deserve to be called errors on the historical scale. The most destructive move of all is to launch a war when other courses of action are available. By the fall of 1944, Hitler and the other central figures of the Nazi government in Germany presumably had second thoughts about going to war against the whole world, although they do not seem to have left behind any written testimony that says this. Whatever their thoughts, the objective truth is that World War II was a war of choice, and it almost wiped Germany off the face of the Earth. Other societies that launched wars of choice have suffered similar fates. What is less obvious is that wars are ruinous for the winners. Wars are the most costly enterprises undertaken by societies, and governments finance them by borrowing money on the international financial markets. Loans have to be repaid with interest, so gigantic loans come with gigantic payments. William J. Bernstein in his 2004 book *The Birth of Plenty* provide data on U.S. payments for World War II: By the time the Vietnam War heated up in the 1960s, the debt burden for World War II, although dropping, was still at approximately 30% of the gross domestic product.[30] The usual reason to launch a war of choice is that a society seeks to enrich itself through plunder. From Roman conquest of fertile farmland and trade routes and Viking raids on prosperous British villages to Nazi looting of French art treasures, the object of war is usually self-enrichment by the extraction of raw materials from the opponent's territory or the expropriation of the products of the vanquished people's labors. Surprisingly but justly, this course of action does not work. Loot is finite and eventually consumed, leaving the conqueror with nothing but the yet-to-be-paid debt on his war effort. Production and trade, not war, are the sources of prosperity. This lesson is naturally formulated as a constraint: Do not wage war unless attacked.

Absence of war does not automatically produce prosperity. What factors differentiate those societies that prosper from those that do not? Bernstein has proposed that there are four factors – four constraints – that determine whether a society prospers or flounders economically. Each factor represents a potential error in the design of a society's institutions and practices. The first constraint is that governments should respect private property. The possibility of improving one's lot is a key driving force behind economic activity, but that incentive goes away if one is not allowed to keep one's gains. Protection of property requires a government of law, laws that constrain the power of the executive branch of government and an independent judiciary that can enforce such laws. The second constraint is that a society should not restrict the focus and scope of scientific inquiry or the development of technology. The results of science are not to be distorted or suppressed to fit ideological, political or religious concepts. This requires freedom of thought and freedom of speech. The third constraint is that governments should not restrict the movement of capital for those who wish to take the risk of engaging in an economic enterprise. The fourth is that governments must allocate resources to maintain and extend the infrastructure that allows goods and services to travel. In short, there are four basic mistakes that nations might commit that will prevent advances toward prosperity: Seize property at the convenience of the executive; suppress science and technology to fit preconceptions; restrict the movement of capital; and neglect the infrastructure. Bernstein provides evidence that wherever these four constraints have been violated, nations languished, but where they were satisfied, nations grew wealthy.

The third type of big error is more fundamental in its consequences than wars of choice and mismanagement of a nation's economic activity: Destruction of the natural environment, especially the natural resources that form the basis of food production, not only leads to poverty but to outright collapse. In his 2005 book *Collapse*, big picture scholar Jarred Diamond has reviewed the depressingly rich repertoire of examples of societal collapse offered by history.[31] From the Viking deforestation of Iceland to unregulated mining and unwise water use in Montana, the tendency not to notice the gradual degradation of natural resources has been a recurring theme in human history and continues unabated in the present overuse of fossil fuels. The operative constraint is simple to state: Do not saw off the branch you are sitting on.

In short, there are three major types of constraint violations at the historical level: wars of choice; suppression of economic activity (through the lack of one or more of the following: property rights, independent judiciary, freedom of thought, free movement of capital and a working infrastructure), and unsustainable use of natural resources. Even at the historical level, there are opportunities to learn from error, if only society leaders could be bothered to do so.

It is important that they be induced to do so, because human history is not about to come to any kind of end. Space stations provide benefits for people living on the Earth, but they also provide a novel place to live. Given the 200,000-year-old itch to move on that drove humans to colonize all of Earth, it would be surprising if space stations did not evolve into cities in space, complete with solar power and chemical food production, not to mention infinite, free real estate. Once near space has been colonized, the step will be short to the colonization of the Moon and the planets. Science fiction authors have begun to imagine the skill sets needed to live an entire life in free fall, and the institutions and practices required to conduct human affairs on an interplanetary scale. Their imaginations will no doubt turn out to be accurate in some respects and inaccurate in others. The future might unfold in many ways, but individuals and societies will continue to improve their skills and practices by translating deviations between expected and observed outcomes into more specific conditions on their operating procedures, another pattern that recurs at each time scale and at every system size.

PART FOUR

CONVERSION

9

The Formation of Belief

Any statement can be held true come what may, if we make drastic enough adjustments elsewhere in the system [of beliefs].

W. V. Quine[1]

To someone standing on the African savannah, walking across a field in the Fertile Crescent or riding across the North American prairie, the evidence of the senses is unequivocal: The Earth is flat. There are local perturbations – valleys and mountains – but they cancel each other over long distances, so the Earth extends in all directions in the horizontal plane. Although it is difficult to prove anything about the beliefs of pre-historic peoples, it would be surprising if they conceived of the Earth in any other way. But the flat Earth generates puzzles: How far does it extend? Does it have an edge? If so, what is beyond the edge? If the ocean extends all the way to the edge, what happens with the water? If it pours over the edge, must not the ocean empty out eventually? Where does the water go? To anyone with the disposition and the opportunity to consider such questions, the lack of intelligible answers must have generated doubt. People living by the sea could make two observations that point to a different conception: Looking out from a high observation point, an observer sees the horizon curve ever so slightly. When a ship approaches, the mast appears over the horizon before the hull.

By the fourth century B.C., Greek philosophers, Aristotle prominent among them, had drawn the right conclusion from these and related observations, and in the third century B.C. the Alexandrian scholar Eratosthenes engaged in an astonishingly successful attempt to estimate the size of what he believed to be a spherical Earth.[2] However, such intellectual exercises were confined to a small portion of the Earth's population, and belief in the spherical shape of the Earth did not become common in Europe until after the Middle Ages. Eventually, astronomy and ocean navigation settled the issue for the elites, and when astronauts returned from space with photographs of a round Earth rotating in space, the knowledge that the Earth is spherical became immediately accessible to everyone. The conversion from a universal belief that the Earth is flat to an equally universal belief that the Earth is spherical happened to the human species as a whole over the course of approximately two and a half millennia.

Individual human beings go through a shorter version of this process. Young children have little doubt that the Earth is flat.[3] Parking lots certainly suggest as much, as do the schoolyard and the local lake. Children gradually come to grips with what adults mean when they say that the Earth is round or when they point to a colored ball in a bookstore or a library and say, "that's the Earth." Empirical studies indicate that in the normal case, the shift from the flat to the round Earth takes several years. In contrast, many adults remember the specific day when they underwent another prototypical case of belief revision: The passage from belief in Santa Claus and his fantastic ability to visit every child on one and the same night to the realization that the man in the red coat is a department store employee. In adulthood, there are many such opportunities to revise beliefs: Does this or that diet, exercise regimen or health practice provide the benefits claimed for it? Has the evidence for global warming reached a point at which it would be prudent to prepare for climate change? Do the political principles that in the past seemed reasonable still deserve allegiance? Do the religious precepts absorbed in childhood still make sense in middle age?

The shared feature of these examples is that they confront a person with alternative and incompatible beliefs. The Earth is either like a pancake or like a soccer ball; as we ordinarily understand those words, we cannot believe both. Likewise, Santa Claus cannot both be the creature of the fairy tale and also a store employee. An exercise regimen either does or does not produce measurable health effects. The average global temperature is rising or decreasing or keeping steady; if it is changing, it moves either upward or downward. To adopt one of these beliefs is to abandon, disbelieve or reject the alternatives. The central question in this and the next chapter is how, by what cognitive processes, a person comes to believe what he previously disbelieved or vice versa, a process variously labeled *belief revision, conceptual change, restructuring* and *theory change* in different niches of the cognitive sciences. The received view claims that people adopt beliefs that are supported by evidence but reject or revise those that are contradicted by evidence. The rejection of that view in this chapter prepares the ground for the different view of belief formation and belief revision proposed in Chapter 10.

THE QUESTIONS OF CONVERSION

Beliefs vary in scope from fundamental to trivial. The former include metaphysical, moral, philosophical, political, scientific and religious principles. As I use the term "belief" it also includes assertions of narrow scope pertaining to the mundane details of everyday life. *There is a subway station at the corner of X and Y streets* is an example. A belief consists of, among other components, a *proposition*, the content of the belief, and its *truth value*.[4] For example, a person may or may not have encoded the existence of a subway station at the X/Y corner into memory; if he has, call his mental representation of this fact P. The person might decide that P accurately describes reality, and so assign it the truth value TRUE.* The resulting memory structure, TRUE (P), is a belief; the proposition P itself, shorn of its truth value, is not. If the person decides that the subway station is located somewhere else, he might assign P the value FALSE instead; FALSE (P) is also a belief. Conversion is a switch in truth value, from TRUE (P) to FALSE (P) or vice versa.

Beliefs tend to be grouped by topic or theme; cognitive scientists prefer the term *domain*. Examples include art, fashion, gardening, health, international relations, law enforcement, money, morals, parenting, pets, politics, relatives, religion, romantic love, sports and the weather, to mention only a few of the domains about which the average person is likely to have at least some beliefs. The set of beliefs about a domain, whether fundamental or trivial, broad or narrow and objectively true or false, is a person's *belief system* for that domain. Although this term usually refers to belief systems of great scope and consequence, with political and religious beliefs as the prototypical examples, I will use the term to cover sets of beliefs about any topic. For example, if someone believes that *coffee contains caffeine*, that *brand XYZ offers the best coffee* and that *coffee grows somewhere far away*, then those three beliefs constitute his belief system regarding coffee, however impoverished it may appear to the knowledgeable caffeine aficionado.

The totality of all his beliefs, regardless of topic or domain, is a person's *belief base*. There is no method for accurately estimating it, but the number of beliefs held by an average educated adult must be in the tens of thousands, probably in the hundreds of thousands. A psychological theory of belief should explain how this vast system is organized and how it grows and changes over time.

A belief can be expressed in discourse to answer a question, communicate information, articulate an argument and for other purposes. However, the

---

* I use small capitals to symbolize subjective truth values.

main use of a belief is to guide action, particularly in unfamiliar situations. If I believe that my destination lies to the left, I am likely to make a left-hand turn at the relevant intersection, even if I have never traveled the intended route before; the action is implied by the belief. Reasoning from belief to action is called *practical inference* or *practical reasoning* in philosophical discourse. It is a high-level process that imposes considerable cognitive load – imagine deciding which actions are implicated by the facts about global climate change – but such reasoning can nevertheless help reduce uncertainty in novel or unfamiliar situations. Beliefs typically have some level of abstraction, so their application involves replacing variables with the objects and events in the situation at hand, which gives beliefs a schema-like character. To be applied, a belief has to be retrieved from long-term memory. The person's representation of the situation or task at hand is the main retrieval probe.

A person's belief base grows over time. The main triggering condition for the formation of a new belief is that new information knocks on the doors of perception and asks to be let in. Opening our eyes automatically triggers perceptual processes that encode what is in front of them. If someone speaks to us in a language we know, it is impossible to will ourselves not to comprehend what the person says. If we see it or hear it, we encode it. In addition, we infer new propositions from prior propositions. Perception, discourse comprehension and reasoning generate a steady flow of new propositions. *The Principle of Ubiquitous Encoding* is a convenient verbal handle for this fact. The new propositions are created in working memory, remain active for some variable amount of time and then fade. A significant subset of those propositions is stored in long-term memory. Research into the psychology of memory has identified some of the factors that control the probability that any one piece of information becomes encoded into long-term memory, but the details are not important here.[5]

Encoding of propositional content is not necessarily associated with assent, but most new propositions do in fact arrive in working memory marked as TRUE. Philosophers write as if doubt is the natural state of mind and as if only a small number of propositions are ever accepted as true, and then only if there are particular reasons to do so. This is a good description of the belief maintenance practice of philosophers. Their lengthy training enables them to overrule the natural disposition of human beings to operate in the opposite way: adopt information as true unless there is reason for doubt.[6]

Consider visual perception. As the proverb has it, seeing is believing.[7] Forming a belief via perception is to construct a mental representation of the relevant state of affairs and also to decide that this representation is veridical.

We are not conscious of any distinction between forming a percept and deciding that it is true; seeing and believing do indeed appear subjectively as a single mental event. The distinction becomes noticeable only when we are faced with some anomaly or illusion. For example, the Ames Room is a weirdly proportioned room that tricks an observer into seeing a person as changing in size when he walks from one side of the room to the other.[8] The observer does not, of course, believe that the person is changing, so in this case seeing is not believing. The acts of encoding (perception in the narrow sense) and assigning a truth value are forced apart by this deliberately contrived illusion. In all but a small number of such cases we automatically and unconsciously trust our visual system. Our attitude to our ears is similar. If we hear a sound, we believe that it has some physical source and we instantaneously form beliefs about its location and nature. If it sounds like the neighbor's dog barking, then we are disposed to believe that it is the neighbor's dog.

Unlike perception, language comprehension is not obviously also believing. Doubting our eyes or ears is difficult, but doubting a writer or speaker comes easily. Nevertheless, everyday human interaction would not work if everybody doubted everything everybody said. In the normal course of events, we tend to believe rather than disbelieve. This habit starts early: Many of our beliefs are imposed on us by our parents while we are still too young to conduct an independent evaluation. In discourse as well as vision, belief is the default and doubt is the exception; as long as new information does not contradict prior beliefs, it is typically accepted as true. This *Principle of Truth as Default* is the reason that April fool jokes work, rumors spread and fiscal markets experience periods of irrational exuberance.

It follows that in the normal case, a belief base grows *monotonically*, through additions and extensions but with no changes in the content or truth value of any prior belief. Everyone undergoes multiple events of this sort every day; indeed, the phrase "you learn something new every day" has achieved proverb status. I refer to this case as *routine* belief formation. The two principles of *Ubiquitous Encoding* and *Truth as Default* plus the standard psychological principles of perception, language and memory that can be found in psychology textbooks are sufficient to understand routine, monotonic belief formation.

The matter stands quite differently when a person receives information that contradicts one or more of his beliefs. The cognitive processes triggered by new but contradictory information cannot be limited to the monotonic processes of encoding its content and accepting it as true. To maintain coherence in his belief system, the person also has to resolve the contradiction.

To achieve this, he might have to abandon or revise prior beliefs, not merely add new ones. For example, children eventually abandon their belief in Santa Claus, and at least some physics students abandon their intuitive, impetus-based beliefs about mechanical motion and replace them with the Newtonian concept of inertia. At the collective level, the human race has abandoned the belief that history cycles through a fixed sequence of eras, among many others.[9] In the fields of politics and religion, people sometimes undergo radical changes of mind, much to the horror of those among their friends who remain believers. Although data on prevalence are lacking, the majority of belief formation events in everyday life must be of the monotonic, routine sort, but *non-monotonic* changes – conversions – fascinate because they are consequential, dramatic and difficult to understand.

Logic appears to provide a straightforward method for non-monotonic belief revision: A proposition that implies a false consequence must itself be false. The relevant inference is called by its Latin name *Modus Tollens*.* If P and Q are two propositions, then Modus Tollens can be rendered as follows:

If TRUE (P), then TRUE (Q).
But, in fact, FALSE (Q).
Therefore, FALSE (P).

The argument, *if the economy is healthy, stock prices rise; but prices have fallen steadily; so the economy is not healthy*, is an instance of this inference rule. The logical validity of Modus Tollens is not in doubt. When beliefs are logically related, Modus Tollens enables a single contradictory fact to produce large-scale change in a belief system: If TRUE (P) is implied by some belief TRUE (O), which itself is implied by yet other beliefs, then the falsification of Q will propagate backward along the implication links and perhaps undermine multiple beliefs.

Both common sense and psychological research suggest that this description of belief revision fares poorly as a psychological theory. Instead, resistance to contradictory information is ubiquitous.[10] People are slow to revise their beliefs and when two people enter into a disagreement, neither of them is likely to convince the other, no matter how many facts or arguments each contributes to the discussion. This is obviously so in religious and political disputes, but resistance to change is present in all areas of experience, including professional and technical domains. Scientists are not necessarily quick to change their favorite theory in response to an inconsistent

---

* The full name is *Modus Tollenda Tollens*, but it is commonly abbreviated.

experimental finding, especially not a finding from some other researcher's laboratory. Louis Pasteur's hypothesis that micro-organisms are involved in fermentation, the out-of-Africa theory of the human colonization of the Earth and the atomic disintegration theory of radioactivity developed by, among others, J. J. Thompson, Ernest Rutherford and Frederick Soddy are only three of the many advances in science that were resisted by scientists at the time.[11] Unlike a logical theory, a psychological theory of belief revision must explain the nature and mechanism of resistance. In the words of Thomas S. Kuhn: "We must ... ask how conversion is induced and how resisted."[12]

Resistance does not prevent conversions, but it makes them more difficult to explain. A theory of non-monotonic belief revision cannot limit itself to describe the processes by which new beliefs are created. It must also explain why contradictory information triggers conversion in some cases but resistance in others.

To summarize, a theory of conversion must answer two interlocked sets of questions: First, how, by what processes, is change resisted? If a person does not respond to contradictory information by revising his beliefs, how does he respond? Second, how, by what processes, and when, under which conditions, is resistance overcome and beliefs revised? A theory of conversion that lacks an account of resistance implicitly predicts that conversion is the common and unproblematic consequence of encounters with contradictory information, while a theory that only specifies the mechanisms of resistance implicitly predicts that conversions never happen. It is possible to explain resistance and conversion by postulating two different processes that produce the two different outcomes, but such dual-process theories require some mechanism that causes a switch between the two. A more elegant theory explains resistance and revision as alternative outcomes of one and the same cognitive mechanism. Furthermore, a theory of conversion needs to specify the factors that determine the direction of a conversion process. Given a large belief base, there are infinitely many possible revisions; which one will occur in each particular case?

Cognitive psychologists, educational researchers, logicians, philosophers of science and social scientists have contributed useful concepts and partial answers to these questions. In the next section I weave those contributions into a theory of resistance to cognitive change in the face of contradictory information. I then review the conversion mechanisms inspired by the history of theory change in science and argue that they fail to explain how resistance is overcome. The strength and weaknesses of the prior theoretical proposals point the way to the rather different theory of conversion proposed in Chapter 10.

THE THEORY OF RESISTANCE

Informal observations of everyday life indicate that encounters with contradictory information are common: Argue with a friend, open a newspaper or read the latest analysis of a moderately familiar topic, and the likelihood of encountering information that contradicts some prior belief is high. If conversions are rare, it is because people do not respond to contradictory information by negating the contradicted beliefs in the logical manner. The question is how people process contradictory information instead. Works by philosophers, psycholinguists, psychologists and social scientists combine seamlessly into a satisfactory theory of resistance, organized around the three core principles of knowledge-dependent processing, center-periphery structure and dissonance reduction through peripheral change.

Knowledge-Dependent Processing

Many of our beliefs are formed in response to discourse: We read or hear something about a topic outside our personal experience. The properties of discourse comprehension are likely to play a central role in belief formation.[13]

Discourse is necessarily incomplete. A text or a speech that tried to be completely explicit would be so studded with asides and explanations, definitions and explications that it would, paradoxically, be unreadable. To sharpen his message, an author or speaker has to leave most of it unstated. This observation applies with particular force to fundamental assumptions. They are rarely stated explicitly. Consider the statement: *Ann is born in January and Bill in December of the same year, so she is older than he is.* The fundamental assumptions behind this statement are that time is linear and that people age as time goes by. However, a storyteller is unlikely to begin, *in a galaxy far, far away, time was linear. ...* Deep principles of this sort are typically left implicit, in part because the writer or speaker might not be fully aware of them, and in part because general principles are assumed to be shared between sender and receiver and so not in need of explicit statement.[14]

The question arises as to what happens when this assumption is not true. If an author writes a text with a particular set of assumptions, what happens to readers who do not share those assumptions? Will readers identify the differences and reflect on them, or will they find the text incomprehensible? Neither of these is the typical outcome. Instead, the reader's prior knowledge will be brought to bear, creating a coherent and connected interpretation of the discourse, but not the one the author had in mind. The intended message is distorted by being assimilated into the reader's prior concepts and beliefs.

Assimilation occurs because discourse comprehension, perception and reasoning are interpretive processes, and interpretation is always a matter of choice. The choices are based on the recipient's prior knowledge. For the sake of brevity, I develop the argument for discourse comprehension only, but it holds equally for perception and reasoning. In discourse comprehension, choices occur at the word, sentence and discourse levels.[15] Consider *lexical access*, the activation of the meaning of a word. A large proportion of words are polysemous; that is, they are used to express multiple meanings. For example, the word "line" can refer to a cashier queue, a fishing tool or something drawn with a pencil, among other things. When the word "line" is encountered, all its meanings are activated in parallel.[16] To identify the intended meaning, the recipient draws as much on knowledge of the world as on knowledge of language. For example, if a word like "river" occurs in the same context, it will support the interpretation of "line" as *fishing line* and suppress the alternative interpretation *cashier line*, while words like "groceries" and "store" would support the latter over the former; see Figure 9.1. What a word is taken to mean depends, in part, on the hearer's prior knowledge, in this case that fishing lines are used near the shores of lakes and that people often stand in line in grocery stores.

Consider next *parsing*, the process of deciding how the words in a sentence are related to each other. It, too, is dependent on world knowledge. Word forms, word order, prepositions and punctuation convey information about how words are meant to be connected, but this information may or may not be sufficient, as illustrated by the following example sentence: *The spy saw the man with the binoculars.* Who owns the binoculars, the spy or the spy-ee? It could be either. Knowledge about how the world works immediately settles this question for the structurally similar sentence, *the bird saw the man with the binoculars.* A bird, lacking the inclination to spy on others, is an unlikely owner of a pair of binoculars.[17] The choice of interpretation depends on knowledge about birds, not about language.

Sentences have to be related to each other for one to make sense out of a discourse. To turn to another stock example of the cognitive lecture hall, if we read that three turtles are resting on a log and that a fourth turtle is swimming below it, we do not hesitate to infer the location of the fourth turtle in relation the first three.[18] The knowledge that is operating in this case is quite abstract: the transitivity of spatial relations like *above* and *below*. Specifically, if X is above Y, and Y is above Z, then X is above Z as well. Implicit bridging

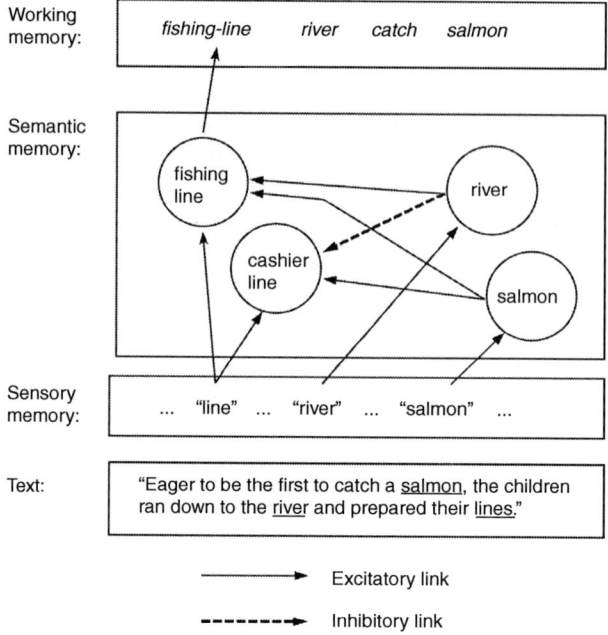

FIGURE 9.1. Meaning disambiguation at the word level. The auditory (or visual) form of the content words appears in sensory memory in the order in which they are encountered. Solid arrows symbolize excitatory relations, the dashed arrow an inhibitory relation.

inferences of this sort are carried out at a high rate while we are reading and listening and they are knowledge dependent.

The strong and necessary role of prior knowledge in discourse comprehension has the peculiar consequence that the recipient of a discourse contributes as much to its meaning as the writer or speaker. The recipient has no direct access to what is in the speaker's or writer's head, so it is the recipient's own prior knowledge that determines the interpretation. This fact spells trouble for the processing of contradictory information: If readers or listeners contribute much to the meaning of the discourse, the message they extract from it will unavoidably be consistent with what they believe. This severely limits the power of discourse to alter a person's beliefs.

As an example, consider the question of the shape of the Earth. If a child believes that the Earth is like a plane surface extending in all directions, and a parent, teacher or other authority figure tells the child, *the Earth is round*, then what happens? It would seem as if the child should take the adult at his word and replace the mental model of a flat surface with the mental model of a sphere. However, research by Joseph Nussbaum, Stella Vosniadou and others on young children's mental models of the Earth has revealed a different outcome: The seemingly simple statement is assimilated to the child's flat Earth model.[19]

To see the mechanism of assimilation operating in this case, consider the options open to the child. What could the adult mean by saying that the Earth is round? The word "round" is ambiguous; it is used to refer to both *circular* (a two-dimensional property) and *spherical* (a three-dimensional property). Which of these meanings will be activated? Unless the child conceives the Earth as extending indefinitely in all directions, the flat Earth must have an edge somewhere, and an edge is a kind of thing that can be circular. The child is likely to conclude that the adult is saying that the flat Earth has a circular edge. In our work with schoolchildren Jason Leigh, Andrew Johnson, Thomas Moher and I often observed that when asked to draw the Earth, the children unhesitatingly drew a circle.[20] When asked which direction is upward with respect to this circle, some children held their pencil perpendicular to their drawing, with the tip of the pencil pointing toward the ceiling. The drawing was not intended as a two-dimensional rendering of a sphere, but as a top-down view of a pancake Earth. In short, if the listener believes that the Earth is flat, the apparently contradictory discourse, *the Earth is round* has no power to teach him or her otherwise, because the listener's prior beliefs hold too much power over its interpretation.

Surely adults succeed in getting through to the child eventually? Holding up a globe and saying, *this is the Earth* ought to settle the issue of circularity versus sphericality. However, Vosniadou and co-workers found evidence for yet another assimilation at a later stage in the child's development: Children who accept that the Earth is a sphere might nevertheless misunderstand the situation in a way that allows them to retain the concept of a flat living space.[21] They documented that some children believe that the Earth is spherical but hollow, half filled with soil and with a hole near the top through which the sun shines. We live inside this hollow sphere, walking about on the flat surface formed by the soil that fills the lower half of the sphere. In this way, the assertion that the Earth is a sphere is assimilated to, and distorted to be consistent with the prior belief that we live on an approximately flat surface.

In short, although writing and speaking seem like straightforward ways to communicate a new idea, close analysis shows otherwise. Comprehension poses multiple interpretive choices at the word, sentence and discourse levels, and the choices depend so heavily on the recipient's prior beliefs that the interpretation of a discourse is almost guaranteed to be consistent with those beliefs. Because new information is interpreted in terms of a person's current concepts and beliefs, such information has little power to change those concepts and beliefs. There is no obvious way to circumvent this assimilation paradox. As we cannot see without our eyeballs, so we cannot understand a discourse without our prior concepts.

Center-Periphery Structure

The conflict between prior beliefs and a current discourse is sometimes explicit, as in an exchange between two persons with different political views, two academics advocating competing theories or two spouses arguing about parenting or family finance. Every disagreement is potentially an opportunity for productive change: There is a chance, however slight, that the other person is right. A detected conflict is likely to trigger other assimilation processes than unconscious interpretive choices.

Clues to how those processes operate emerged in the work of the French philosopher and physicist Pierre M. M. Duhem in the late 19th and early 20th centuries. In his 1914 book *The Aim and Structure of Physical Theory*, Duhem pointed out that the derivation of a testable prediction or a consequence from a hypothesis in physics always assumes the truth of multiple other hypotheses and theories. An experiment might, for example, require multiple measurements, and the measurements obtained with a particular instrument cannot be interpreted without a theory for how that instrument works. If the prediction does not fit the data from the experiment, something is wrong, but it is not clear what: "the physicist can never subject an isolated hypothesis to experimental test, but only a whole group of hypotheses; when the experiment is in disagreement with his predictions, what he learns is that at least one of the hypotheses constituting this group is unacceptable and ought to be modified; but the experiment does not designate which one should be changed."[22] A judgment of accuracy has to compare an entire group of hypotheses to an entire body of experiments.

Duhem's insight was generalized by the American philosopher Willard van Orman Quine and followers to encompass informal as well as scientific belief formation.[23] Like other theorists considered in this chapter, Quine regarded "the characteristic occasion for questioning beliefs" as a situation in which "a new belief, up for adoption, conflicts somehow with the present body of beliefs as a body."[24] His basic observation is the same as Duhem's: "We think loosely of a hypothesis as implying predictions when, strictly speaking the implying is done by the hypothesis together with a supporting chorus of ill-distinguished background beliefs."[25] The consequence is also the same: "When an observation shows that a system of beliefs must be overhauled, it leaves us to choose which of those interlocking beliefs to revise."[26] But Quine follows the train of thought a step further than Duhem: "Just about any hypothesis, after all, can be held unrefuted no matter what, by making enough adjustments in other beliefs."[27] Quine emphasized that facts and observations tend to impinge on a belief system along its periphery, not at its center: "The totality of our so-called knowledge or beliefs ... is a man-made fabric which impinges on experience only along the edges."[28]

Approaching the problem of resistance from the point of view of empirical social science rather than philosophy, Milton Rokeach proposed that belief systems exhibit a *center-periphery structure*.[29] A belief system is normally organized around a core of fundamental and general beliefs. The latter tend to be few in number, and they are often held implicitly. The belief that *individuals differ in their personality traits* is an example. At a slightly lower level of generality, a person might adopt beliefs about particular personality traits; *some people are more outgoing than others, some people are risk takers* and so on. These more specific beliefs are consistent with the core belief but contain additional detail. Belts of increasingly specific beliefs are arranged in concentric rings at successively increasing distances from the core. In each successive ring, the beliefs become not only more specific, but also more numerous and less important. At the periphery of the belief system there are highly particular beliefs such as the claim that *risk takers are drawn to extreme sports* and *risk takers are gamblers*. The center-periphery structure can be seen either as a hierarchy with the core beliefs at the apex and the peripheral beliefs at the bottom – the sideways view, as it were – or as a set of concentric rings with the core beliefs in the center and the peripheral beliefs in the outer circle – the top-down view; see Figure 9.2.

Rokeach hypothesized that resistance to change increases from periphery to center.[30] Peripheral beliefs change relatively easily, but core beliefs remain stable. Like Quine, he emphasized that contradictory information will typically impact a belief system at its periphery, where the beliefs are most specific. For example, a medical study is more likely to show that, for example, *vitamin C is not good for you* (after all) than that *vitamins (in general) are not good for you*. The amount of contradictory information required to overthrow an established belief is therefore a function of the position of that belief within the belief system. Change will happen first at the periphery, overthrowing specific beliefs of narrow scope and little importance. Deeper contradictions might

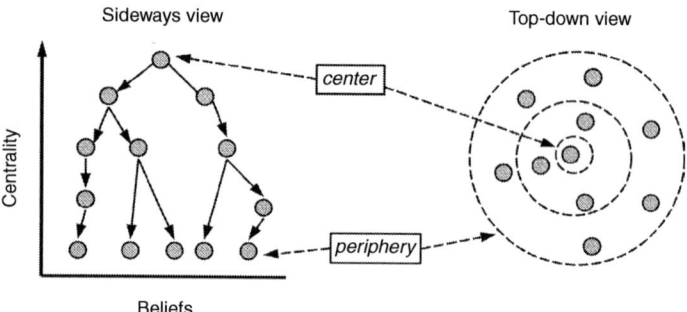

FIGURE 9.2. Rokeach's concept of a center-periphery structure. One or more core beliefs subsume less general or less comprehensive but therefore also more specific beliefs.

affect beliefs of intermediate centrality. Only if the onslaught of contradictory information continues for some time can the change propagate to the center and affect core beliefs. Rokeach's center-periphery principle is discussed further in Chapter 10.

A similar theory of resistance to change was proposed by the philosopher Imre Lakatos.[31] In a critique of the idea that scientists reject theories when they are falsified by observations, Lakatos pointed out that for a fundamental scientific law or principle to make contact with data, the scientist usually has to add auxiliary assumptions.[32] A famous historical example is the attempt by the 16th-century Italian physicist Galileo Galilei to convince his contemporaries of a variety of astronomical phenomena, including that the heavenly bodies have shadows, spots and other imperfections, by inviting them to look through his telescope. They remained unconvinced. Some even refused to look, because Galileo's claims presupposed that the telescope shows an accurate view of the heavens, and they saw no reason to believe this assumption. It seemed more plausible to them that the incomprehensible, unfamiliar and weird contraption produced a distorted view. Lakatos called the set of auxiliary assumptions associated with a set of core principles the *protective belt*. "It is this protective belt of auxiliary hypotheses which has to bear the brunt of tests and get adjusted and re-adjusted, or even completely replaced" to defend the core principles.[33] The auxiliary beliefs are necessary for the core principles to generate predictions about specific situations, but a given set of core principles can be paired with different auxiliary assumptions, so the impact of any contradictory information can be absorbed through changes in the protective belt.

The formulations by Duhem, Lakatos, Quine and Rokeach are variations on a theme: Core beliefs are seldom affected by contradictory information because they are embedded within a system of beliefs of varying centrality and importance, and it is always possible to adjust a belief system in such a way that the new information is accommodated through peripheral changes. To complete this account of resistance, we need to specify the cognitive mechanisms that produce the peripheral changes. Thanks to the efforts of social psychologists, we know what those mechanisms are.

Dissonance Reduction

What kinds of cognitive processes absorb contradictory information with minimal change? This question was studied by the cognitive consistency school of social psychologists in the 1955–1970 period.[34] In a formulation by L. Festinger that has traveled outside academia and become a common phrase, a cognitive conflict sets up a state of mental tension called *cognitive dissonance*. Because dissonance is mildly unpleasant, it triggers mechanisms that aim to eliminate the conflict or at least reduce its intensity.[35] Festinger and other researchers in the cognitive consistency tradition identified multiple candidates for such mechanisms.

When cognitive psychologists and educators turned their attention to the effects of misconceptions on science learning in the 1980s, they re-discovered the problem of how people deal with conflicting information.[36] Unfortunately, they did not reach back to the prior body of research within social psychology, but started over, drawing inspiration instead from the history and philosophy of science. The lists of processes for dealing with contradictory information compiled by Lindley Darden on the basis of the history of science and by William F. Brewer and Clark A. Chinn on the basis of psychological considerations read like updated versions of the corresponding lists of mechanisms compiled three decades earlier by Robert P. Abelson and by Herbert C. Kelman and Reuben M. Baron.[37] This convergence among cognitive researchers and social psychologists inspires confidence in the psychological reality of the proposed mechanisms.

The idea of central interest for present purposes is that a cognitive conflict can be resolved by adding beliefs to a belief system rather than by deleting or revising existing beliefs. In formal terms, when faced with an internally consistent belief base $\{B\}$ and information to the effect that TRUE (P), where $\{B\}$ and TRUE (P) are dissonant, the mind tends to respond by creating a new belief B' such that the conjunction of $\{B\}$ and B' is consistent with TRUE (P).

TABLE 9.1 *Four examples of cognitive dissonance mechanisms, with hypothetical examples of resident beliefs. In Case A, the person is assumed to believe that there is no influenza epidemic, although he is confronted with news reports about the rising number of cases. In Case B, the person is assumed to believe that the world's oil reserves will last indefinitely, although he is confronted with reports about dwindling supplies.*

Dissonance reduction mechanism	Case A: Influenza epidemic	Case B: Oil reserves
Discredit the source	"News media are whipping up hysteria to have something to write about."	"News reports are distorted by pressure from environmentalist fanatics."
Bolster the resident belief	"I've talked to several doctors and they don't see increasing numbers of cases in their waiting rooms."	"Prospectors are investing in new surveys, so they think there are reserves to be found, and they are the experts."
Make an exception	"The cases are increasing in poverty-stricken areas, but not elsewhere."	"Oil fields in the Middle East are running out, but not oil fields in the rest of the world."
Introduce a mediating assumption	"Flu symptoms are similar to allergy symptoms, and the latter always rise this time of the year; so it appears that there are more flu cases than there really are."	"Pumping oil temporarily lowers the level in a well; if the well is left idle for a while, the level is restored; so oil reserves appear lower than they really are."

Different ways of creating the mediating belief B' produce different variants of this mechanism. Festinger outlined two variants that he called *denial* and *bolstering*; because the term "denial" is used in different ways by different theorists in this area, I use the more specific term "discredit the source." In addition, one can extract from Festinger's writings two others mechanisms that I will call *differentiation* and *mediation*; the last is identical to what science-inspired cognitive scientists call *abduction*. Brief summaries suffice to illustrate the idea that contradictions can be resolved without core change by adding new beliefs, if those beliefs are chosen in particular ways. See Table 9.1 for didactic examples.

Discredit the source
The simplest way to reduce dissonance is to form new, negative beliefs about the source (as opposed to the content) of the anomalous information. The crudest response is to decide that the source is dishonest. For example, a person

might decide that a newspaper that reports uncomfortable facts deliberately distorts them to propagandize a particular point of view. This move is readily observable in the public discourse about political and social matters. The wider the scope of such a belief, the more convenient it is: If the entire newspaper staff, not merely a particular journalist, is believed to be systematically biased, then one has given oneself permission to ignore every uncomfortable fact reported by that newspaper. A closely related move is to declare the source to be mistaken. One can admit the honesty of the source and yet claim that the facts are not as stated: The journalist did not interview the right people; the interviewees lied for their own reasons; and so on. Similarly, a research study that produced an unwelcome finding can be dismissed by deciding that it is methodologically flawed. Adding beliefs about the source of the contradictory information rather than about its content allows one to resolve the contradiction without revising prior beliefs and without incorporating the new information into the belief base.

Bolstering
One of Festinger's more interesting proposals was the hypothesis that mental states differ in degree of dissonance and that the dissonance is proportional to the ratio between contradicting and supporting cognitive elements related to the contested belief.[38] In network terms, a belief is a node, supporting arguments or facts are connected to the belief node via links with a positive value and contradicting assertions and arguments are connected via links with a negative value. Festinger hypothesized that the degree of dissonance associated with a belief is proportional to the ratio of the number of negative to the number of positive links. If a belief is contradicted by two arguments and supported by three, the dissonance is of the same strength as if it were contradicted by four arguments and supported by six.

These hypotheses imply that it is possible to reduce the dissonance associated with a conflict by adding supporting evidence, without either revising the content of the contradicted belief or processing the arguments against it. If the strength of the dissonance associated with a belief is 8/4, and we find 8 new arguments in favor, the dissonance is reduced to 8/12. On the basis of this principle, Festinger predicted that a car buyer will tend to spend more time reading consumer reports that praise the car after the purchase than before so that he can deal with any dissonance caused by negative comments or consumer reports about the car.[39] Fifty years of experimental research by social psychologists has supported this and other counterintuitive predictions derived from the bolstering idea.[40] The effects of this mechanism are visible in everyday life. In politics, people tend to access news sources that concur with their beliefs more often than sources that contradict them. A scientist whose favorite theory is falsified by a study from a rival laboratory is more likely to respond by running a series of supporting studies than by changing his theory. Although the addition of new grounds for a belief is a type of growth mechanism – the belief base is extended with new content – bolstering, like discrediting the source, minimizes change because the prior beliefs are not revised and the contradictory information is not accepted as true. Dissonance is not eliminated, only reduced in intensity.

Differentiation/exception
Yet another way to sweep cognitive dirt under the conceptual rug is to differentiate the contradicted belief into a general case and an exception, and then decree that the anomalous information holds only for the exception. This move incorporates the new information into the belief base but minimizes its impact; see Figure 9.3 for a graphical explanation of this process. There are endless variations of this move in reasoning about ethnic groups.[41] Consider a person who holds a negative belief about group X; perhaps he believes that they beat their children. If the person comes into frequent contact with members of group X, he is likely to observe some cases of exemplary parenting behavior. To escape the contradiction between his prejudice and his observations, he can add the auxiliary belief that education, strict law enforcement, religion or some other factor has the power of curing members of X from their child-beating tendencies. If those members of X who are educated, scared of the law or deeply devout are few, the observations of exemplary parenting behavior can be accepted at face value without any change in the belief about X in general. The core belief that (typical) members of X are disposed to beat their children can be kept without revision and without cognitive dissonance. In network terms, differentiation replaces the node that represents the initial belief about X with three nodes: a node representing the overarching concept *all members of group X* and two nodes that represent the two subsets, *typical members of X* and *members of X who are educated* (or law abiding; or religious; etc.). This is a genuine growth mechanism. The new information is incorporated into the belief base and accepted as true. Differentiation nevertheless blunts the impact of the contradictory information by limiting its scope to special cases.

Mediation/abduction
The idea that a contradiction between a belief base {B} and a contradictory piece of information TRUE(P) can be resolved by inventing a mediating belief

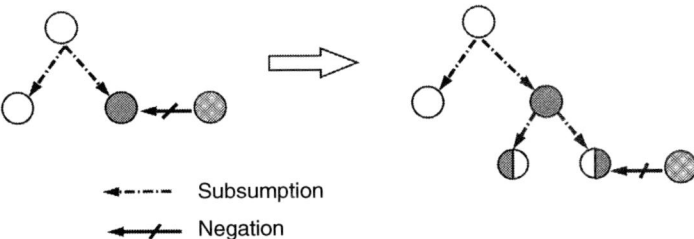

FIGURE 9.3. Dissonance reduction via the creation of an exception. A belief is contradicted by new information. In response, the memory system creates two new subnodes to the corresponding node, and re-attaches the contradicting information to one of the subnodes.

B′ applies more generally. Festinger laid out one example from an anthropological study: The members of the Ifaluk tribe believed that people are basically good-hearted and wish others well. At the same time, they were in a position to observe aggressive behaviors by the young men in their own villages. Taken at face value, these observations constitute evidence that people are not all good, creating dissonance. However, the Ifaluk also believed that evil spirits can take possession of individual human beings and make them perform evil acts. This belief reduces the dissonance between the principle that people are naturally good and the recurring observations of evil behaviors. The accuracy of this description of Ifaluk culture is not the issue here, only the nature of the response to the contradiction: Add a belief that explains how the belief and the seemingly contradictory fact can both be true.[42]

Festinger did not name this mechanism, but in the philosophy of science, an inference from an observation to a possible explanation of that observation is called *abductive reasoning*.[43] Abduction was first codified as a special form of inference by C. S. Pierce in the late 19th and early 20th centuries, but his concept languished in relative obscurity until highlighted by Norwood Russell Hanson in his 1965 book *Patterns of Discovery*. The added belief B′ is in this context thought of as a new explanatory hypothesis or auxiliary assumption. A famous example of abduction occurred in astronomy when the French 19th-century mathematician Urbain Jean Joseph Le Verrier studied perturbations in the observed orbit of the planet Uranus that did not follow from Newton's theory of gravitation.[44] To explain these perturbations, Le Verrier assumed the existence of an as yet unobserved planet with a gravitational pull that accounted for the perturbations. At the time of his proposal, there was no other reason to believe in the existence of this planet, but the truth of this abductive hypothesis was verified when the planet Neptune was observed in 1846. The story repeated itself later in the century when it was discovered that Neptune in turn exhibited perturbations which eventually led to the discovery of Pluto* in 1930 by a young American astronomer, Clyde Tombaugh, working at the Lowell Observatory in Flagstaff, Arizona. Abduction has slowly moved to center stage in the philosophy of science.[45]

The Ifaluk and Neptune cases exhibit the same formal structure: A basic principle (*people are naturally good; planetary orbits are shaped by the law of gravitation*) encounters some contradictory fact (*young men commit evil acts; Neptune's orbit exhibits perturbations*); an auxiliary hypothesis is added to the theory (*people can be possessed by evil spirits; the orbit is distorted by an as yet unobserved planet*); the added hypothesis mediates the conflict and allows the original belief to stand unchallenged. The similarity between dissonance reduction and abductive reasoning has been overlooked because the relevant research communities have approached this process from opposite directions. In the context of dissonance reduction, the purpose of the theorist is usually to explain seemingly irrational behaviors, while in the philosophy of science, the purpose is typically to explain scientific progress. The differences between these two attitudes are irrelevant for the description of belief revision, but the fact that theorists who hold these opposite attitudes have converged on the same type of process should increase our confidence in its psychological reality.

Mediation is a genuine change mechanism, because the contradictory information is incorporated into the person's belief system and becomes represented as a new belief. Unlike the nervous car buyer who continues to believe that he made the right decision in spite of negative consumer reports, the members of the Ifaluk tribe did not deny that their young men engaged in evil acts, nor did astronomers deny that the orbit of Uranus exhibited perturbations. In both cases, the anomalous information was accepted as true. Nevertheless, neither the principle that people are naturally good nor the law of gravitation were affected by the new information. In both cases, the added auxiliary belief protects the challenged core belief, so the change is limited to the periphery of the belief system.

In short, dissonance-reducing mechanisms such as discrediting the source, bolstering, differentiation and mediation (abduction) handle contradictory

---

* In 2006, the International Astronomical Union (IUA) decided that Pluto does not satisfy all the criteria for being a planet. Gravitation is not affected by the change in label, so the explanation for the perturbations of Neptune remains the same.

information by creating new beliefs and in that sense are growth mechanisms. However, the function of the added beliefs is to minimize the impact of the new information. Discrediting the source and bolstering avoid incorporating the contradictory information altogether. Differentiation accepts the new information as true but limits its scope to exceptions. Mediation (abduction) also accepts the new information, but at the price of adding one or more auxiliary, mediating beliefs that may or may not have any independent grounding. A complete theory of these mechanisms would specify exactly how the added beliefs are created, but however fleshed out, they produce peripheral changes that prevent change from propagating up the center-periphery gradient and affecting core beliefs.

Discussion

The empiricist attitude to belief formation is that observations that contradict a belief ought to cause conversion of that belief, but this principle fares poorly as a psychological hypothesis. Fundamental assumptions are often held unconsciously. A reader or listener might not detect a conflict between his own and an author's or speaker's point of view but blithely assimilate the latter's discourse to his own prior beliefs, distorting its message in the process. When the conflict between prior beliefs and new information is detected, the mind can protect core beliefs by calling upon a repertoire of processes that limit the impact of the new information to the periphery of the relevant belief system by introducing auxiliary assumptions or protective distinctions. The epistemological analyses by Duhem, Quine and Lakatos, the center-periphery principle proposed by Rokeach, and the process hypotheses advanced by cognitive consistency theorists like Abelson and Festinger and by cognitive scientists like Darden, Chinn and Brewer combine seamlessly into a coherent, relatively complete and rather satisfactory theory of resistance to contradictory information. The confluence of these diverse contributions would count as one of the great success stories of cognitive science, if only cognitive scientists could be bothered to claim it.

Does the reality of resistance imply that people are irrational? Dissonance-reducing processes sometimes produce veridical extensions to a belief base and sometimes not, but their function is not to increase veridicality but to reduce dissonance. The changes they produce cannot be justified as responses to evidence. Nevertheless, slapping the insult "irrational" on those cognitive moves is problematic. Suppose, for example, that Newton's theory of mechanics is contradicted by the result of an experiment. The rational response is obviously to believe that the experiment was carried out incorrectly, not to reject three centuries of physics. Likewise, should I abandon my belief that a low fat diet is healthy because I read about a single study that did not find any benefit of such a diet? A belief system is the cumulative product of a lifetime of discussing, listening, observing, reading and thinking; it makes little sense to throw it away in response to a single piece of contradictory information.

Dissonance reduction through peripheral change might appear irrational when viewed from a logical perspective, but the latter is merely one perspective among others. It has no special claim on our attention. If we view the cognitive system from a homeostatic perspective instead, then peripheral belief revision appears similar to other processes that keep body and mind in balance by counteracting the impact of external disturbances. As we respond to an increase in ambient temperature on a hot day by sweating, so we respond to contradictory information by minimizing its impact on our worldview.

CONVERSION: SCIENCE AS EXAMPLE

If resistance through peripheral change were the whole truth about belief formation, belief systems could become more detailed, extensive and interconnected, but core beliefs could not change. But people do revise their core beliefs. In particular, the natural sciences have undergone multiple radical conversions – called *scientific revolutions* or *theory changes* – in which fundamental hypotheses were replaced by other, qualitatively different hypotheses. For example, scientists have converted from a flat to a round Earth; from a geocentered to a heliocentered planetary system; from believing that planets necessarily move in circles to the belief that they move in elliptical orbits; from the phlogiston theory to the oxygenation theory of combustion; from the belief that earth, air, water and fire are the fundamental elements to the periodic table of chemical elements; from the hypothesis that mountain formation is due to the cooling and shrinking of the Earth to the belief that mountains form when one tectonic plate crashes into another; from the belief that objects move due to their impetus to the principle that objects remain in rectilinear motion until some force acts on them; from the belief that diseases are due to an imbalance between the body's "humors" (fluids) to the germ theory; and so on.

Philosophers and historians have mined this track record for suggestions about conversion processes. They start from the same assumption as resistance theorists in psychology: Theory change is triggered by contradictory information. But whereas resistance theorists, dismayed by, for example, racial prejudice, tend to emphasize the minimal, even irrational character of such changes, conversion theorists inspired by science de-emphasize resistance and focus primarily on successful conversions. However, resistance cannot be ignored, and it makes the emergence of novel theories harder to understand. A satisfactory explanation must describe the creation of novel theories but also explain why encounters with contradictory information sometimes result in conversion (acceptance of the *contender* theory) and sometimes in resistance (continued acceptance of the *resident* theory). Theorists have proposed several useful concepts and principles, but they do not add up to a satisfactory account of conversion in response to contradictory information, whether in science or in everyday life.

Progress Through Falsification

In the 19th century, philosophers of science emphasized the induction of generalities from data.[46] But induction applies primarily to the initial stages of inquiry in a newly opened field of research. It does not explain what happens when an already established theory encounters contradictory observations. In his 1934 book *Logic der Forschung*, philosopher Karl Popper broke out of the inductive view by arguing that a theory that is contradicted by data is *falsified*.[47] "[A scientific theory] is never inferred, in any sense, from the empirical evidence. There is neither a psychological nor a logical induction. *Only the falsity of the theory can be inferred from empirical evidence, and this inference is a purely deductive one.*"[48] A theory implies certain predictions about how the data from an investigation should turn out; if the predictions turn out to be false, then the theory is false. In his view, falsification is a move from TRUE(P) to FALSE (P) via a Modus Tollens inference

> TRUE (Th) implies TRUE (O)
> FALSE (O)
> So FALSE (Th)

where "Th" stands for a theory and "O" refers to an observation, experimental finding or the like. "... *there is no more rational procedure than the method of trial and error – of conjecture and refutation*: of boldly proposing theories; of trying our best to show that these are erroneous; and of accepting them tentatively if our critical efforts are unsuccessful."[49] Encounters with contradictory information drive science forward because they prompt scientists to abandon their theories and thereby prompt them to seek new and presumably better ones.

Popper was trying to solve the epistemological problem of scientific progress: How can we be sure that scientific knowledge improves over time?

Falsification explains why scientists abandon an established but incorrect theory, but Popper famously declined to speculate on the origin of new theories.[50] But a theory change is typically a change from one theory to another, so without an account of the origin of the alternative theory, an explanation for scientific progress is seriously incomplete. Furthermore, it would be peculiar if the right epistemology of science turns out to be at variance with scientific practice. In Popper's description, scientists appear as logic machines, ready to abandon a well-established theory at the drop of a fact. Historians of science unanimously agree that this is not an accurate description of scientific practice. Researchers in the successful sciences do not strive to disprove their favorite theories. They sometimes test theoretical predictions, but they are overjoyed when those predictions fit their data, however fallacious this reaction might seem to a logician. The ratio of published research articles that claim support for the author's theory to those that report falsification must be 99 to 1 or larger. In 35 years of reading psychological research articles, I have never encountered the latter type of article by an experimental psychologist. Of course, scientists happily publish articles that falsify *somebody else's* theory, a practice better explained by the theory of resistance than by the principle of falsification.

At an abstract level, Popper was of course right. Scientists abandon theories because they are found to be false.[51] But falsification belongs to the sphere of logical forms; it should not be interpreted as a statement about what scientists do as they go about their daily work and even less as a description of their cognitive processes. In A. Newell's terminology, Popper's account of theory change was a *knowledge-level* account; that is, it abstracts from the relevant processes and describes their outcomes in terms of knowledge states.[52] In this interpretation, Popper's falsification principle states that if a scientist knows that his theory implies a particular consequence and if he also knows that the consequence is contrary to fact, then he knows (in an abstract sense) that his theory is false. But this knowledge-level description does not specify how, by which processes, a scientist concludes that a theory is false nor how it is replaced.

The Accumulation of Anomalies

The philosophy of science matured into a distinct subfield of philosophy at the time of the post–World War II expansion of Western university education, and the new field proved popular with students. The number of articles and books about theory change grew rapidly. But the positivist attempts to formalize the relation between theory and data within some logical or mathematical calculus did not attract the new generation. Thomas Kuhn's *The Structure of Scientific Revolutions*, first published in 1962 but better known in its second, 1970, edition, broke with the formal approach.[53] Kuhn's critique of Popper was blunt: "No process yet disclosed by the historical study of [science] at all resembles the methodological stereotype of falsification by direct comparison with nature."[54] This was a declaration that a philosophy of science should be accountable to data from the history of science and describe how episodes of theory change unfold.

Using the Copernican conversion from a geocentered to a heliocentered theory of the planetary system as his main example, Kuhn argued three related theses. First, in the normal case, scientists do not conduct studies to test their theories. Instead, they use those theories to solve problems, explain phenomena, interpret data or answer questions. Kuhn called this activity *puzzle solving*; perhaps his work would have been better received if he had used the less belittling label "problem solving." Although Kuhn's main examples are drawn from physics, it is not difficult to think of examples from other sciences. A chemist who studies a chemical reaction does not usually intend to verify or falsify the atomic theory of matter, the periodic table or the theory of the co-valent bond. He uses those theories to describe how the reaction of interest unfolds. When researchers agree on what constitutes a worthwhile problem and on the criteria for a successful solution, they are engaged in *normal science*.

If scientists normally apply rather than test their theories, how and why do they ever abandon them? Kuhn's second thesis was that scientists sometimes fail to solve the problem they set themselves. The phlogiston theory enabled chemists to solve a good many problems in chemistry, but not all; Jean-Baptiste Lamarck's theory of evolution enabled biologists to understand the fitness between a species and its environment, but not the geographic distribution of species; and so on. An unsolved research problem is a cause for dissatisfaction, but the statement *I believe this theory is true but I have so far been unable to solve problem so-and-so* does not express a logical contradiction. The problem might be (temporarily) unsolvable for other reasons than that the theory is false, including limits on the scientist's creativity or mathematical skills, undetected equipment failures or lack of data. Kuhn did not emphasize (and his many commentators tend to overlook) that his reconceptualization of cognitive conflict injected a pragmatist thread into the study of theory change. The trigger for change is not *falsifying evidence* but *failure to solve a problem*, a very different concept.

Sensitivity to historical data led Kuhn to describe theory change as a protracted affair. An unsolved problem is an anomaly only if it has resisted multiple attacks by several different research teams using different approaches. In addition, a single anomaly is not sufficient reason to abandon a theory. Anomalies have to accumulate before they trigger a search for a better theory. Far from a single Modus Tollens inference, the rejection of a resident theory is a temporally extended, cumulative process.

Kuhn provided a much needed naturalistic turn in the study of scientific theory change, but his account is as incomplete as Popper's. Both accounts focus on successful conversions so they do not explain how falsifying observations or anomalies avoid being swept under the conceptual rug by peripheral change mechanisms. How do anomalies accumulate if each anomaly is dismissed as it arrives? A second problem is that neither Popper nor Kuhn provided any insight into the origin of the alternative theory. Popper stated that this question would remain unanswerable; the title to his book* notwithstanding, there cannot be, he claimed, a logic of scientific discovery.[55] Kuhn took a slightly softer stand: "… how an individual invents (or finds he has invented) a new way of giving order to data now all assembled – must here remain inscrutable and may be permanently so."[56] He did not try to provide a theory of the origin of the alternative theory. But a theory change is typically a change from one theory to another, and it would be surprising if the strengths of the alternative theory were not among the reasons for rejecting the resident theory. By ignoring the second half of the problem of theory change, Popper and Kuhn failed to solve its first half.

The Many Roads Since *Structure*

Kuhn's grand narrative of scientific progress swept through the academic and popular cultures, making "paradigm shift" as much of a household word as "cognitive dissonance."[57] Although his account was met with skepticism among professional philosophers and historians of science, it served as a source of inspiration. The idea of basing theories of cognitive change on patterns extracted from the history of science was, and remains, appealing to cognitive scientists, historians and philosophers.

The story of the post-*Structure* period is one of proliferation, but even when the purpose is to depart from Kuhn, accounts of theory change tend to postulate the same triggering condition as the one Kuhn proposed. For example, in *Human Understanding*, published in 1972, Stephen E. Toulmin set out to create an evolutionary alternative to Kuhn's description.[58] He describes the

---

* *The Logic of Scientific Discovery*

triggering condition for change as the appearance of a scientific problem, and "problems arise ... where our ideas about the world are at variance either with Nature, or with one another: ... Conceptual problems in science emerge from the comparison, not of 'propositions' with 'observations', but of 'ideas' with 'experience.'"[59] A conceptual innovation "calls ... for a collective dissatisfaction with the existing conceptual repertory."[60] Toulmin does not explain how an "idea" being "at variance" with "experience" differs from Kuhn's concept of an anomaly.

The sheer reasonableness of the idea that theory change is driven by conflicting evidence is the strongest argument in its favor. Why would scientists search for a better theory unless they recognize flaws in their current one? But the assumption of cognitive conflict as a driving force brings with it the need to explain how resistance is overcome. Why are the anomalous, contradictory or falsifying data not swept under the cognitive rug via peripheral changes? What enables contradictory information to travel up a belief hierarchy and affect core scientific principles? Although cognitive analyses of science have generated many different proposals regarding the processes of theory change, there is no new and clearly articulated answer to this question. For example, there have been several attempts to propose a Darwinian variation-selection theory of scientific progress. According to Toulmin, the key features of the growth of scientific knowledge are the generation of a population of conceptual variants and their selection for transmission to the next generation of scholars. Presumably, contradictory data and arguments serve the selective function in this application of variation-selection. But why are the data and arguments accepted rather than resisted? A variation-selection account presupposes that negative information about conceptual variants is heeded rather than resisted, but it does not by itself explain how or when, under which circumstances, this happens.

Other theoretical proposals fare no better on this point. Philip Kitcher's 1993 book *Advancement of Science* argues that science moves forward by increasing its explanatory power.[61] In Kitcher's view, a scientific practice is organized around a repertoire of explanation schemas. An explanation schema is a template for how to structure the explanation of a particular type of phenomenon or event. For example, Darwinian variation-selection explanation should identify the ancestor species, describe the heritable variations, explain the relevant selective pressure and calculate its cumulative effect over many generations. To make scientific progress is to improve the repertoire of explanation schemas. Kitcher writes, "Four distinct kinds of processes are at work [in] explanatory progress." They are "the introduction of correct schemata";

"the elimination of incorrect schemata"; "the generalization of schemata"; and finally, "there is explanatory extension" in which an explanatory schema is embedded within a larger schema.[62] These phrases are suggestive of plausible processes, but Kitcher does not explain how any of these processes work. For example, how is a schema eliminated? Presumably, this is triggered by evidence that the schema is inaccurate, but Kitcher provides no explanation of how resistance to such information is overcome. The emphasis on explanatory power is an important contribution, but Kitcher does not propose any new idea about how theory change comes about.

A similar problem adheres to Nancy Nersessians' theory of model-based reasoning.[63] The cognitive basis for model-based reasoning in science is a capacity to build mental models, dynamic knowledge structures that can be executed in the mind's eye to provide an internal simulation of the event, phenomenon or system that those structures refer to. As a simple illustration of the power of running mental simulations, consider the following scenario: A tired traveler returning home leaves his key ring in his travel bag, and in a moment of mindlessness puts the bag in the basement; the next morning, the question arises, *where are the keys?* The inference that *the keys are in the bag and the bag is in the basement, therefore the keys are in the basement as well* is difficult to carry out in deductive logic, but the conclusion is obvious to anyone who visualizes the situation and simulates the sequence of events in the mind's eye. Nersessian identifies five distinct components of model-based reasoning: *visualization, abstraction, modeling, analogy* and *thought experimentation.* Once again, this is a plausible and interesting theory of scientific reasoning. The problem for present purposes is that there is no explicit hypothesis about when and how scientists employ model-based reasoning (as opposed to any other type of reasoning), nor for how model-based reasoning enables a scientist to overcome his resistance to change.

Accounts of theory change tend to implicitly assume that the new, contender theory is better than the resident theory. But new is not necessarily better, so how does the scientist know which of the competing theories to believe? Toulmin asserts that conceptual variants are evaluated by asking, "Given the current repertoire of concepts and available variants, would this particular conceptual variant *improve* our explanatory power *more than* its rivals?"[64] But he provides no details as to how scientists carry out this comparison. A specific explanation is provided by the theory of explanatory coherence developed by Paul Thagard and others to explain the outcomes of cognitive conflicts.[65] That theory applies when there are two competing hypotheses and a set of facts, each of which might be consistent or inconsistent with either hypothesis.

Given a set of quantitative strength values for the links between these knowledge units, algorithms adapted from neural network models enable the resulting network to compute which of the competing hypotheses provides the most coherent account of the given body of facts. This idea has been embodied in a computer model called ECHO that provides intuitively reasonable outcomes for a variety of cases. The emphasis on theory-theory conflicts instead of theory-data conflicts is useful, but the theory only explains why, given two competing explanations for a set of facts, one explanation might be preferred over the other. It does not explain how scientists arrive at a state in which they have two fully developed theoretical proposals to choose between.

Kuhn in the Woodwork

Kuhn's grand narrative of scientific progress, controversial though it was, established a consensus practice for the cognitive study of theory change in science: An account of theory change should be consistent with the practices of scientists as captured in historical case studies and contemporary field studies. Theory change is triggered by cognitive conflicts, interpreted as failures to solve scientific problems. A shift from one theory to another is a temporally extended process, although it is brief compared to the preceding and following periods of relative stability and so deserves the label "scientific revolutions." The source of the novel theories is to be found in the (deliberately unanalyzed) individual and social creativity of scientists. The many descriptions of theory change since the publication of Kuhn's *Structure* do not represent roads away from these ideas but are puzzle-solving efforts within the Kuhnian paradigm of theory change as a response to the accumulation of anomalies.

But any conflict-based narrative of scientific progress requires an account of how resistance is overcome, as well as an explanation of why anomalies sometimes lead to resistance and sometimes to conversion. Neither has been forthcoming. In addition, it is highly plausible that the creation of a contender theory and its acceptance as better than the resident theory are closely related. After all, the contender is constructed with awareness of the weaknesses of the resident theory and with the intent of overcoming those weaknesses. The rejection of the resident theory and the construction of the new theory are not separate processes. Pressing the argument further, it is plausible that the strengths of the contender theory are among the reasons for dissatisfaction with the resident theory. If so, the temporal order implied by conflict-driven theories – anomalies lead to dissatisfaction, which in turn leads to the search for an alternative – is up-ended. Information about the strengths of the contender must be available before the resident is rejected – that is, before the contender has been adopted. How do scientists know what those strengths are before the shift has occurred?

It is also problematic that the proposed processes for the construction of a new theory are specified at such a high level of analysis that they constitute research problems in their own right. Every analysis has to stop somewhere, but an explanation should break down theory change into subprocesses that are already well understood or so simple that their internal structure is unproblematic. In contrast, processes like *conceptual innovation, eliminating an incorrect explanatory schema* and *visualization* are *homunculi*, black boxes that are so complex that they are as difficult to understand as theory change itself. In this sense, the proposed analyses of theory change are largely illusory.

The difficulty of drawing conclusions from the philosophy and history of science regarding the psychology of belief formation is obscured by the ambiguity of the word "science." In the discourse of historians and philosophers, "science" tends to refer to hypotheses, theories or the knowledge content of entire disciplines. The phrase "theory change" then refers to changes in some theory, regarded as an entity that exists in its own right, independently of who believes it. From this perspective, a theory change is described in terms of content and is agnostic with respect to who is changing. But from a naturalistic perspective, theories are held by knowledge-creating agents, human beings, who exist in time and space and who labor under capacity limitations and other material constraints. It is the agent, not the theory, that is changing during theory change. Multiple types of agents are involved: individual scientists, research teams, the set of all scientists who work in a particular discipline at a particular time and the population of all scientists. The identification of the theory as the entity that is changing obscures the differences among the types of agents, especially between the cognitive processes of the individual scientist and the social processes operating in a scientific discipline. Charles Darwin's construction of the theory of natural selection and the adoption of the germ theory by the medical profession become interchangeable examples of "theory change in science." But there is no reason to expect the cognitive processes that operated in the former case to be similar to the social processes that operated in the latter. In general, the cognitive processes of belief formation and belief revision in the individual mind are likely to differ from the processes by which a community of researchers arrives at a new theory. That is, there is no warrant for equating change mechanisms extracted from the history of science with the mechanisms of change in the minds of individual scientists.

CONVERSION: THE CHILD AS SCIENTIST

Cognitive psychologists, developmentalists and educational researchers have explored the idea that everyday conceptual change involves the same processes as scientific theory change. This science-inspired approach is clearly stated by developmental psychologists Alison Gopnik, Andrew N. Meltzoff and Henry M. Wellman:[66] "The central idea of [our] theory is that the processes of cognitive development in children are similar to, indeed perhaps even identical with [sic], the processes of cognitive development in scientists. Scientific theory change is, after all, one of the clearest examples we know of the derivation of genuinely new abstract and complex representations of the world from experience."[67] And again: "In development we see the same kinds of phenomena brought about by radical conceptual change that we see in the history of science."[68] The brains of scientists might not be less prone to resistance than the brains of nonscientists, but the processes of conversion might be more visible in science than elsewhere.

The Theory-Theory

The particular version of this hypothesis that is known as the *theory-theory* retains the assumption that conflict is the driving force behind developmental changes and that belief revision is a matter of evaluating evidence. Gopnik and Meltzoff write: "Theories may turn out to be inconsistent with the evidence, and because of this theories change."[69] And again: "Theories change as a result of a number of different epistemological processes. One particularly critical factor is the accumulation of counterevidence to the theory."[70] With respect to mechanism, the theory-theory claims that change occurs in five stages: encounter with counterevidence; denial; the development of "ad hoc hypotheses designed to account specifically for such counterevidence"[71]; the development of a new, alternative theory, perhaps by developing some idea that is "already implicit in some peripheral part of the earlier theory"[72]; and "a period of intense experimentation and/or observation."[73]

Multiple problems adhere to this list of supposed stages, some of them similar to the problems that plague historical and philosophical science studies. The lack of specification of the relevant processes and the rigidity common to all stage theories are among them. More important for current purposes, there is no explanation in the theory-theory for why there is resistance, nor for how resistance is overcome. Presumably, doubt is generated by contradictory information. But why is that information not swept under the rug via peripheral dissonance reduction? Where does the alternative belief come from? Under which circumstances is it adopted as true?

Ontological Category Shifts

The Ontological Shift Hypothesis developed by Michelene T. H. Chi and co-workers provides a different view of cognitive change.[74] They focus on the role of ontological knowledge in conceptual change. The theory assumes that the learner possesses a small set of high-level categories that specify the types of entities the person believes exist: *event, mental state, object, process, value* and so on. Such ontological categories are defined in terms of the predicates (properties) that are meaningful to assert or deny about the category members.[75] For example, every object has weight but it does not make sense to say that some process, such as rain, weighs 10 kilograms. The problem is not that the statement is false because the true weight is, say, 11 kilograms instead, but that the predicate "weighs X kilograms" cannot be meaningfully asserted or denied about rain or other processes.

When the learner acquires information about some previously unfamiliar phenomenon, that phenomenon gets assigned to whatever ontological category seems appropriate on the basis of easily accessible features. The phenomenon inherits the main features of that category. In particular, the ontological category controls which predicates can be applied to the phenomenon, which in turn has consequences for how new information about the phenomenon is understood. Presumably, assertions that employ predicates that are not meaningful for the assigned ontological category will not make sense to the recipient. Indeed, *the rain today weighed 10 kilograms* can only be understood as referring to the amount of rainwater collected in a particular container, or else in some metaphorical way. If the learner assigns a phenomenon to the wrong category initially, he or she will tend to misunderstand information about it. The cure for this is an *ontological shift*, a re-assignment of the phenomenon to a different ontological category. If the learner already is in possession of the correct ontological category, the relevant processes are to detach the phenomenon from one category and attach it to another. If the learner does not already possess the correct ontological category, that category has to be learned before the shift can occur. Unless the learner is prompted to create the missing category, the misconception caused by its absence is likely to be robust.

The category shift theory implicitly presupposes conflict of a specific sort. In a 2009 article, Chi and Sarah K. Brem emphasized the role of contrast in the triggering of a shift.[76] The learner notices differences between some object, event or phenomenon and the essential features of the ontological category to which it is currently assigned. This weakens the link to that category and presumably triggers the search for a category that provides a better fit. This is a plausible theory, but once again we must ask how resistance is overcome. If the learner notices differences and contrasts between an entity and its current classification, why are they not handled through peripheral changes? A contrasting feature could trigger differentiation, the creation of a special case of the relevant ontological category. For example, a student with a billiard-ball, linear causal conception of gravitation as a one-way force of the Earth upon each individual object could respond to the statement that gravitation is a mutual attraction by creating a special case of linear causation that includes two separate but opposite causal effects, one strong and one weak, which is not a step toward the concept of a gravitational field. In short, the notion of a category shift does not in and of itself provide an explanation for why contrasting features do not trigger peripheral changes instead of the fundamental re-classification envisioned in the ontological shift theory.

The Pedagogical Turn

The anomaly-accumulation view of theory change migrated into pedagogy via the science classroom. A group of educators, including William A. Gertzog, Peter W. Hewson, George J. Posner and Kenneth A. Strike spelled out the instructional implications of the anomaly-accumulation principle: Students must become dissatisfied with their prior, intuitive theory before they are ready to acquire the theory that the science teacher intends to teach.[77] This can be accomplished by presenting them with a sequence of carefully designed anomalies, arguments and laboratory demonstrations that reveal the flaws in their resident misconceptions. For example, a student who believes that heavy objects fall faster than lighter ones might be confronted with the anomaly of equal acceleration in vacuum; a student who believes in the inheritance of acquired characteristics should be asked whether the baby of body-building parents will be born stronger than the babies of couch potatoes; and anybody who believes that the seasons are due to the varying distance of the Earth from the sun should be reminded that when there is winter in one hemisphere, there is summer in the other. Such contradictions presumably create dissatisfaction on the part of the student with his or her view of the matter. Once intellectual dissatisfaction – cognitive dissonance – has set in, the student is presumably ready to absorb the scientific theory.

There is no extensive body of empirical proof that the pedagogical technique of deliberately creating dissatisfaction by confronting students with anomalies is effective in helping students overcome their resistance to change and improve their understanding of counterintuitive scientific subject matters.[78] There have been multiple attempts to implement the strategy, but the outcomes have been mixed. In a 2001 review, Margarita Limón concluded that "the most outstanding result of the studies using the cognitive conflict strategy is the lack of efficacy for students to achieve a strong restructuring and, consequently, a deep understanding of the new information."[79] Consistent with Limón's review, within a decade of the original formulation of the anomaly accumulation pedagogy, researchers began publishing papers that recorded reservations or promoted "revisionist" views. There was a general feeling that conceptual change needed to be "reconceived," "reconceptualized" or "reconsidered"; others disagreed, suggesting instead that conceptual change should be "recast" or even "reframed."[80] In my view, the issue needs to be reconstituted or perhaps restructured.

A Child Is Only a Child

Scientific theory change always was an unpromising source of inspiration for a psychological theory of belief revision. The basic assumption of the science-inspired approach was that "the most central parts of the scientific enterprise, the basic apparatus of explanation, prediction, causal attribution, theory formation and testing, and so forth, is not a relatively late cultural invention but is instead a basic part of our evolutionary endowment."[81] Why should we believe this? If evolution provided the relevant cognitive processes some 200,000 years ago when anatomically modern humans emerged, why did modern science not appear until 300 years ago? Historically, science is indeed "a late cultural invention" that had to wait some 10,000 years after the emergence of urban life before it became an established and recognizable practice. If the relevant cognitive processes constitute "a basic part of our evolutionary endowment," then why did not all societies develop scientific institutions? It is more plausible that science emerged only after millennia and only in a single culture precisely because the processes of explanation, prediction, experimentation and theory formation are not among our basic cognitive processes and had to be invented.

The issue is muddied by a confusion between basic cognitive processes and acquired cognitive strategies. Scientists are professional theorists. They gather data, solve research problems and evaluate theory-data relationships as part of the work they are trained and paid to do. Scientific theory formation is deliberate and supported by cognitive technologies like special-purpose notations and mathematical software; it is also public and guided by codified disciplinary norms and standards. The associated practices are acquired through a lengthy, multi-year training process called "graduate school." Consequently, scientists are aware of how they form theories – there is no end to the stream of books about research methodology – and the tasks of interpreting data and evaluating hypotheses are at the focus of their conscious attention. In contrast, most laypeople could not give a clear account of how they formed any one belief, and even less how they form beliefs in general. Beliefs are formed implicitly, on the run and as a side effect of activities that are undertaken in pursuit of some more pragmatic purpose than to formulate true descriptions of the world.

Given these differences, it is not obvious that the professional practices of scientists hold any clues to the cognitive processes of belief formation and belief revision. Consider an analogy to the voting practices adopted in most Western nations for deciding social and political issues. Voting is clearly an invented practice and we would not expect it to provide clues to the nature of the basic cognitive processes by which people decide what stand to take on social and political issues. Nobody would argue that because political decisions are made by many individuals casting votes, the individual human mind is therefore likely to consist of a population of, say, "evaluation modules," each of which casts a subconscious "vote" for one political stance over another. The distinction between a description of societal voting practices and a psychological theory of individual decision making is obvious. The voting theory of individual decision making could conceivably turn out to be true, but its probability of being true is not increased by its structural similarity to the social practice of voting. But if so, why should we believe that scientific practices provide clues to the psychology of belief formation and belief revision? If the fact that political decisions are made by voting is not sufficient grounds for inferring that voters' minds consist of populations of voting modules, then the fact that scientists evaluate theories by comparing them to evidence is not sufficient to conclude that scientists' minds contain processes for relating beliefs to evidence.

The distinction between the basic cognitive processes of individuals and the acquired methods and practices of scientists is easily blurred because they are described by the same informal vocabulary. As an example, consider the phrase "observing an experimental outcome"; to what does it refer? The highly deliberate, complex and usually mechanized technique of recording, for example, reaction times? Or the mental processes of visual perception? Likewise, "deciding whether claim X is true" is ambiguous between the mental process of belief fixation and, say, the process of running a complex, 10-year longitudinal study to evaluate X. We do not possess two epistemic vocabularies, one for the basic cognitive processes of knowledge acquisition and one for the conscious and acquired activities of deliberate knowledge acquisition; indeed, the very term "knowledge acquisition" spontaneously intrudes itself into both contexts. This terminological ambiguity enables subtle and unnoticed shifts back and forth between the two levels of analysis.

Importing the principles of theory change from the philosophy and history of science into the behavioral sciences was a potentially productive move. Cognitive scientists rightly pride themselves on being interdisciplinary and the cross-disciplinary transfer of principles is a source of progress. But in the case of conversion, the interdisciplinary move did not work. The principles and practices that pertain to scientific theory change do not explain belief revision in children or adults. In fact, the relation is the opposite: The specific features of scientific practice that pertain to theory change constitute phenomena that a psychological theory of the basic cognitive processes involved in belief revision ought to explain. The laudable ambition to be interdisciplinary caused more confusion than clarity by turning that relationship on its head.

FALSIFICATION FALSIFIED

Mismatches between beliefs and reality are guaranteed. We only know the world through a small and necessarily unrepresentative sample of experiences, we often have reasons to move into some unfamiliar task environment, and the world turns, grinding our beliefs into irrelevance. Our minds keep us upright in the stream of anomalies and contradictions by balancing stability and change, resistance and conversion. The principles of knowledge-dependent processing, center-periphery organization and dissonance reduction via peripheral change combine into a plausible theory for how the impact of contradictory information is resisted. The psychological reality of resistance does not prevent conversions, but it makes individual conversions more difficult to explain. A satisfactory theory must not only specify the processes by which change travels up the center-periphery gradient to affect core beliefs but also explain why contradictory information triggers resistance in some situations but conversion in others. If there are processes of resistance, why are they not operating continuously, preventing conversion altogether? If the processes of conversion can overcome resistance, why is conversion rare and perseverance ubiquitous?

There is as yet no theory that resolves this assimilation paradox. Theorists have falsified falsification, made an anomaly out of the accumulation of anomalies, classified ontological shifts under the wrong category and failed to achieve even local coherence. This state of affairs is itself an anomaly that requires explanation. I suggest that the assimilation paradox remains unresolved because it is, in principle, unsolvable. There is no exit, no way to cut the circular relation between old concepts and new information. Experience and discourse are necessarily understood in terms of already acquired concepts and beliefs, so they will be interpreted in ways that make them consistent with those concepts and beliefs. Peripheral change is always possible and always represents the path of least cognitive effort. These insights are stumbling blocks to any current or future theory that postulates that beliefs are based on the evaluation of evidence and that non-monotonic changes in core beliefs are triggered by anomalous, contradictory or falsifying information.

Prior work has nevertheless contributed useful ideas. Kuhn's notion of failing at problem solving puts a pragmatist spin on the discussion about theory change by reminding us that the purpose of a theory is not to be true. In the context of everyday cognition, beliefs and informal theories are not mere possessions, admired for their epistemological beauty, but tools of cognitive trades. Their purpose is to enable us to succeed at various cognitive tasks, including explaining facts, phenomena and regularities; predicting future events; and informing the design of successful artifacts. *Being true* is a helpful attribute that allows a theory to better support those functions, but capturing the truth is a means to that end. Kuhn implicitly promoted the pragmatic view by characterizing normal science as problem solving instead of truth seeking, and by conceptualizing cognitive conflict as a failure to solve a problem that one expected to solve rather than a logical contradiction between theory and evidence.

Other useful contributions include Kuhn's emphasis that theory change is a cumulative, protracted affair. This is one of the main phenomena to be explained: If a single anomaly is insufficient to trigger theory change, why would 10 anomalies suffice? Another fundamental contribution is Chi's principle of category shifts. Because knowledge is hierarchically organized, a person's understanding of a phenomenon can be altered by re-representing it as an instance of a different higher-order knowledge structure. The work by Thagard on coherence adds the important principle that theory change requires a process that compares the relative worth of the resident and contender theories. Theory-theory conflicts rather than theory-data conflicts are the prime movers of theory change. These insights need to be incorporated into the next generation of theories about belief revision. The theory proposed in Chapter 10 proposes a new narrative of conversion that is based on the principle that changes in core beliefs are brought about by success rather than failure.

10

Belief Revision: The Resubsumption Theory

> ... the act of judgment that leads scientists to reject a previously accepted theory is always based upon more than a comparison of that theory with the world. The decision to reject one paradigm is always simultaneously the decision to accept another...
>
> Thomas S. Kuhn[1]

Beliefs can be expressed in discourse (*I believe that ...*; *In my opinion ...*), but they are consequential primarily because they guide action. Only someone who believes that the Earth is round would set sail for China by sailing west from Europe, and only someone who believes that a nuclear chain reaction is physically possible would try to build a nuclear power plant. In everyday life, mundane actions are guided by myriads of beliefs of smaller scope: If you believe that the movie starts at four o'clock, you will try to be at the theater shortly before that time. Beliefs can inhibit action as well as guide it. In the late 19th century, some argued that rockets could not work outside the Earth's atmosphere because the rocket exhaust would have nothing to push against.[2] If this belief had persisted, people would presumably not have built rockets for space travel and there would have been no moon walks.

The outcomes of actions reflect back on the belief or belief system that guided those actions. There can be no better way to become convinced that the Earth is round than by circumnavigating it. The success of the action, the triumphant homecoming, increases confidence in the relevant belief. The relation between action and belief is particularly visible in technology. The main reason for believing in aeronautics is that airplanes fly, and the main reason for believing in nuclear chain reactions is our ability to produce nuclear energy. When beliefs change, actions change accordingly. Investors who become convinced that the stock market is about to fall will move their money to less risky investments. The third contribution of this book is a micro-theory that puts the interaction between truth and utility, between epistemic and instrumental considerations, at the center of belief revision.

BELIEFS, BELIEF SYSTEMS AND COGNITIVE CONFLICTS

Precise specifications of change mechanisms require a description of the entity that is changing, so an explanation of conversion needs to start with a characterization of beliefs and belief systems. This task was begun in Chapter 9. Routine, monotonic belief formation events are assumed to follow the two principles of *Ubiquitous Encoding* (all received information is encoded and some subset is stored in long-term memory) and *Truth as Default* (new information that is consistent with prior beliefs is regarded as true unless there are reasons for doubt). I begin by extending the account from Chapter 9 with additional concepts and distinctions.

The Dimensions of Beliefs

A belief consists of a *proposition* and a handful of *parameters*. The proposition is the content of the belief. A proposition, when expressed in language, corresponds approximately to the meaning of a declarative sentence, like *State Street runs north and south*. Propositions are symbolic structures stored in memory.

The parameters associated with a belief indicate a person's stance toward the relevant proposition. The first parameter of a belief is its *truth value*. To assign a truth value to a proposition is to take a stance as to the veridicality of that proposition. Although the values TRUE and FALSE have received most attention from philosophers, people use many different linguistic markers to specify the status of propositions: "certain," "likely," "plausible," "probable" and their opposites are commonly used, and "don't know," "undecided" and "not sure" should be used more often than they are. For present purposes, the truth value parameter need only take the two values TRUTH and FALSE. A second parameter records the person's level of *confidence* in the belief. If this variable ranges from 0 (no confidence) to 1 (complete confidence), then [P, TRUTH, .90] represents the fact that a person is almost certain that P is true, while [P, FALSE, .25] means that he has tentatively decided that P is false.

Cognitive representations are sometimes referred to as beliefs and sometimes as units of knowledge, but cognitive scientists, laypersons, philosophers and psychologists draw the distinction between belief and knowledge in different ways. In statements like "I don't know for sure, but I believe it is so" and "I don't just believe it, I know it," the distinction appears as one of *degree of certainty*, which makes beliefs and knowledge elements two distinct sets of entities. Philosophers, on the other hand, define knowledge as *justified true belief*, which makes a person's knowledge a subset of his or her beliefs (because not all beliefs are both justified and objectively true). Neither of these usages is the one adopted in this book.

The normative concept employed in philosophy needs to be distinguished from the naturalistic concept of knowledge. In psychology, we routinely refer to what a person thinks is true as that person's knowledge, regardless of its objective truth. For example, developmental psychologists write about children's knowledge of, for example, living things; educational psychologists write about students' prior knowledge about some subject matter; and cognitive analyses of science frequently refer to the knowledge of scientists in antiquity. Once we put objective truth to the side and focus on what a person thinks is true, there is little difference between saying that "he believes that X" and saying that "he knows that X." The terms "knowledge" and "belief" are in this usage interchangeable, as are "informal theory" and "belief system." These observations are not new; I am merely codifying the standard psychological usage.

Cognitive scientists who build Artificial Intelligence systems deviate from these other usages by referring to all mental representations as "knowledge representations." But not all representations encode beliefs. It is not obvious what it would mean to assign truth values to, for example, analogies, goals, images, rules or scripts. In this usage, "knowledge" is a superordinate category, so a person's beliefs constitute a subset of his or her total set of knowledge representations, in direct opposition to the philosophical usage. As an illustration, consider the fact that after close and repeated study of John R. R. Tolkien's volumes about Middle Earth, I know something about that place, its inhabitants and the events surrounding the famous magical rings. My mental representations of these events do not differ in any essential way from my knowledge of the set of events that we refer to as World War II. I can, for example, engage in counterfactual reasoning in either domain (*What would have happened if Frodo had been captured with the ring inside Mordor? What would have happened if the German Luftwaffe had continued to bomb Royal Air Force airfields in 1940 rather than switched to London and other cities?*) Yet my views of the Battle of Helms Deep and the Battle of Britain obviously differ; I believe the latter took place but not the former. It is nevertheless as natural to speak about my knowledge of Middle Earth as to speak about my knowledge of World War II. In the cognitive science usage, my knowledge encompasses all my mental representations, while my beliefs are those knowledge representations that I designate as true, which makes my beliefs a subset of my knowledge.

Neither the everyday practice of using the terms "knowledge" and "belief" to designate degrees of certainty, nor the normative definition of knowledge as justified true belief will play any role in this book. I most often use the term "knowledge" in the cognitive psychology usage, as encompassing a person's beliefs about a topic. Occasionally, I use it in its overarching, cognitive science sense of referring to all mental representations, including nonpropositional representations (e.g., visuals images). The context should suffice to make clear which of the two meanings is intended in each case.

The truth value and the confidence level associated with a belief are distinct from the person's *attitude* toward the belief. Does he view the state of affairs described by the relevant proposition as desirable or as undesirable? Attitudes are, in principle, orthogonal to truth values. Disbelief is not the same as dislike. For example, a stamp collector might believe that the world is switching from physical to electronic mail, and evaluate this state of affairs negatively because there will soon be no more stamps to collect. Another, shrewder stamp collector might have exactly the same belief about which way the world is going but see the development as positive, because he believes that his stamp collection will increase in value as stamps become scarce. The owner of the store who sells stamps to the two collectors might disbelieve that stamps are disappearing, which is a different state of mind from that of the other two.

The role of attitudes in belief formation has received considerable attention from psychologists because common sense suggests and systematic studies confirm that attitudes and subjective truth values are correlated.[3, 4] We tend to accept as true propositions to which we have a positive attitude and doubt propositions that describe states of affairs that we see as negative. In everyday life we call this wishful thinking; in psychology it is called *belief bias*. But we sometimes accept uncomfortable propositions as true, and we sometimes decide that some claim is too good to be true, so the correlation is not perfect; we cannot equate judgments of truth and judgments of desirability. The problem of attitude change – how and why do people come to like what they previously disliked and vice versa – has been studied extensively by social psychologists. The theory proposed in this chapter is not intended to contribute to that field but to clarify the separate problem of how and why people come to believe what they previously disbelieved or vice versa.*

---

* Confusingly, some philosophers refer to facts like "Mary believes that the Earth is flat" as *propositional attitudes*. (Moltmann, 2003, describes the classical view of propositional attitudes in analytical philosophy, critiques it and proposes an alternative.) This usage of "attitude" differs from its psychological use and will be avoided here.

Yet another belief parameter is the *cognitive utility* of a belief. Philosophical discourse tends to presuppose that the striving for truth is desirable in its own right, but people do not generate intuitive theories and belief systems for the sake of knowing something that is true; the latter is a distinctly academic attitude. Truth might be a moral good, but human cognition did not evolve to seek, establish or possess truths. Natural selection in a hunter-gatherer scenario optimizes survival, not amount of good. Even in contemporary life, belief systems and informal theories are not normally held as museum pieces, cherished for their epistemic beauty. Instead, their purpose is to contribute to the successful completion of life's tasks: argumentation, decision making, discourse comprehension, explanation, prediction, planning and so on.

Cognitive utility is a descendant of the concept of utility defined in theories of decision making, which in turn evolved from the utility concept in economics. The latter measures how valuable a good or a service is to somebody. Cognitive utility measures the usefulness of a knowledge representation to the person whose representation it is. The concept was developed by J. R. Anderson in the context of the ACT-R theory.[5] Cognitive utility is a function of both benefits and costs. Both benefit and cost are in turn multidimensional constructs. For example, cost is a function of, at least, cognitive load[6] and time to task completion, while benefit is a function of, at least, frequency of goal attainment and satisfaction with the typical outcome. Perhaps there are other factors that influence cognitive utility as well, but it would be rash to exclude any one of those four.

A belief or belief system does not have to be (objectively) true or consistent with evidence to have high cognitive utility. For example, we operate quite well in everyday life on the basis of something akin to the 14th-century impetus theory of mechanical motion: If you want a ball to travel farther, whack it harder.[7] The impetus theory contradicts Newton's laws of motion and is hence false, but it is nevertheless an effective guide for everyday action. A false or inaccurate belief might generate consequences that are close enough to the facts that actions based on that belief tend to be successful. The utility of a belief system is therefore not directly tied to its truth but measures the extent to which it enables our cognitive processes to run with low cognitive load, fast task completion, frequent goal attainment and high satisfaction.

To summarize, we have to distinguish the content of a belief – the relevant proposition – from the various judgments a person can make about it. The latter can be described as a vector of parameter values. I distinguish between four such parameters: A belief can be judged as true or false, with a higher or lower level of confidence; as desirable or undesirable; and as more or less useful. Veridicality, confidence, desirability, and usefulness are distinct types of judgments. There might be yet other dimensions along which propositions can be judged but these suffice for present purposes.

The Structure of Belief Systems

We have no method for counting beliefs, but we can estimate the size of a person's belief base from the size of his vocabulary. The average educated person in a Western society knows approximately 50,000 words.[8] Some words are synonyms, but many words have more than one meaning; suppose that these factors approximately cancel each other. A person's stock of concepts is then likewise to be estimated at 50,000. Most concepts participate in more than one belief. Consider the concept *dog*: Common beliefs about dogs include *dogs are friendly*; *dogs like biscuits*; *dogs have four legs*; and so on. The total number of beliefs is likely to be an order of magnitude greater than the number of concepts. According to this estimate, a person's belief base contains at least half a million beliefs. A theory of belief formation should explain how this vast system is structured and how it grows over time.

The standard network model of long-term memory invites the view that a belief base is a set of belief nodes linked via binary relations (*implies, contradicts, special case of,* etc.).[9] This view implies that we can only talk about the truth value of a belief system or intuitive theory as shorthand for the truth values associated with its constituent beliefs. This is a misleading side effect of the incompleteness of the network model. Within that model, there is no natural way to represent an area within a network – a subnet – as forming a separate unit, and the network concept provides no tools for assigning belief parameters to such a subnet. But this is a deficiency in the network model of memory rather than a property of memory itself.

Beliefs are grouped in memory by topic or theme into semi-independent belief systems. A belief system is locally bounded in the sense that activation of one belief in a belief system leads with high probability to the activation of the other beliefs in that system (but not necessarily beliefs in neighboring systems). Declarative knowledge is completely interconnected – there is some sequence of links from any belief to any other belief – but it is also structured in the sense that a belief system is a bounded, local and semi-independent area within the overall network. Exactly how the cognitive architecture manages to have it both ways, to maintain local boundaries within the knowledge network without losing complete interconnectedness, is not known.

The present theory borrows M. Rokeach's principle, introduced in Chapter 9, that belief systems exhibit a center-periphery structure.[10] Core beliefs tend to be very general and few in number, and they are often held implicitly. An example is the belief that *diet is important for one's health*. Such core beliefs have a broad *scope*; that is, they cover a wide range of possible instances. Arranged in concentric rings around the core there are belts of successively more specific beliefs of lesser scope. Continuing the health example, the belief that diet is an important determinant of health is more fundamental than any specific beliefs about exactly which foodstuffs are good or bad: *fat is bad for you*; *chocolate is good for you*; and so on. In each successive belt, the beliefs are more specific and more numerous, but also less important. At the periphery of the belief system there are highly particular beliefs of very narrow scope such as the claim that dark chocolate, specifically, is better for one's health than regular milk chocolate.

Specific beliefs are *subsumed* by beliefs closer to the core.[11] That is, the specific beliefs are consistent with the core beliefs but contain additional detail. Educational psychologist D. P. Ausubel stated this clearly: "The major organizational principle [of a person's knowledge] is that of progressive differentiation of trace systems of a given sphere of knowledge from regions of greater to lesser inclusiveness, each linked to the next higher step in the hierarchy through a process of subsumption. It is incorrect, however, to conceive of this mode of organization as deductive in nature."[12]

The center-periphery structure of a belief system is reminiscent of the axiom-theorem structure of formal theories in logic and mathematics, Euclid's axiomatic theory of plane geometry perhaps being the most familiar example.[13] However, subsumption is not logical implication. A peripheral belief is an *instance*, not a deductive *consequence* of the relevant core belief. For example, adopting the belief that *diet affects health* does not logically obligate a person to also believe that a modest consumption of dark chocolate improves health. The core belief does not by itself specify the effects of any particular diet. The core belief is consistent with different, even contradictory specific beliefs: The two beliefs *chocolate is good for you* and *chocolate is bad for you* are both subsumable under *diet affects health* even though they contradict one another, conclusive proof that the relation between subsuming and subsumed beliefs is not logical deduction. A transition along a subsumption link adds additional detail, while deduction only makes explicit what was implicit in the premises. However, once one has adopted the belief that diet affects one's health, one can no longer ignore the question of the health effects of this or that foodstuff without breach of local coherence. The core belief does not enforce adoption of any one belief, but it constrains which specific beliefs one can adopt and remain coherent. The asymmetry of the subsumption relation – beliefs in one belt subsume the beliefs in the next belt out from the core, but not vice versa – imposes a structure, a partial ordering, on the belief system. I refer to such structures as *Rokeach structures*; see Figure 9.2 for a graphical illustration.

Explicit theories in the empirical sciences are sometimes likened to axiomatic theories in logic and mathematics, but I suggest that they are better thought of as Rokeach structures. Newton's laws subsume their applications to particular cases of mechanical motion but they do not logically imply those applications, and Darwin's theory of evolution through natural selection subsumes but does not logically imply any particular Darwinian explanation.

If both informal belief systems and formal theories are structured by subsumption, then it follows that logical reasoning from observational evidence has little power to affect a core belief. If an observed case is subsumed under, rather than logically implied by, a general belief, falsification cannot propagate upstream, from periphery to core, through successive Modus Tollens inferences; the latter are only valid with respect to implication. In the health example, to falsify the general belief that diet influences health one would have to prove that no foodstuff has any effect, a rather more extensive enterprise than merely showing that, for example, dark chocolate has less of an effect than previously thought. Likewise, to reject the notion that, for example, international trade agreements lower the probability of war between nations, a historian would have to show that every trade agreement throughout recorded history left the probability of hostilities unchanged, an impossible task. In short, changes in specific, peripheral beliefs have little impact on the core beliefs that subsume them, because the subsumption relation is tolerant of variability in the subsumed beliefs. Hence, contra Popper, falsification of peripheral beliefs through contradictory observations cannot be the main engine of change in core principles. Subsumption, unlike deduction, does not support the backward propagation of falsification.

If a belief system or informal theory is a cognitive unit in its own right, a person can adopt (or reject, as the case might be) that system as a whole, not only this or that single belief within it. A description of the state of mind created by such an act cannot be reduced to a conjunction of assertions to the effect that the person believes or disbelieves each individual proposition in that system. This view is consistent with the fact that everyday discourse easily accommodates statements like *I believe (do not believe) in the theory of evolution* or *he now believes (no longer believes) in the Marxist theory of history* or *geologists are now firmly convinced that ice ages are (are not) due to astronomic cycles*. In short, an entire belief system, no less than a single belief, is a type of entity to which the mind can attach a truth value. The proof that the truth value of a system is distinct from the truth values associated with the individual beliefs is that all those beliefs need not be associated with the same truth value. It is common among sensible people to recognize strengths in belief systems they reject, as in *I do not believe Karl Marx's theory of history, but I think his analysis of the causes of the French Revolution was largely accurate* or *I am certain that the global climate is warming, but the critics are probably right that the ice core measures are flawed*.

A belief system can enter into relations with other belief systems. In particular, it can appear as a component of another system of more comprehensive scope. Consequently, a person's belief base exhibits a hierarchical structure, with higher-order systems of large scope having multiple belief systems of smaller scope among their parts. For example, a person's beliefs about law enforcement might nestle within his broader system of beliefs about good governance and within his system of beliefs about morals and human nature. The hierarchical structure is clearly visible in the explicit theories of the professions and the sciences. A geologists' theory of earthquakes nestles within his overarching theory of plate tectonics, and the theory of aerodynamics fits within the general theories of physics. In short, a belief system or theory is simultaneously a unit in its own right, a structure that relates units of smaller scope and a component of one or more systems of larger scope.[14]

This Janus-faced character of belief systems does not imply that a belief base branches out from a single starting point, a single *Ur-belief*. A more likely view is that a belief base is anchored in multiple parentless nodes, representing the person's most fundamental beliefs about material reality, life, society and so on. Also, the multiple hierarchies growing from these fundamental beliefs are not freestanding, separate structures, lined up in memory like so many Eiffel Towers standing side by side without touching. A belief can play a role in multiple belief systems. For example, the belief that *cars burn fossil fuels* might play a role in a person's belief systems about climate change, foreign policy and public health. Consequently, the individual's belief base as a whole is not orderly, but a mess of *tangled hierarchies*, a system of center-periphery structures that share components here and there; see Figure 10.1.[15]

The upshot is that we have to distinguish between at least four system levels in the study of belief systems: components of beliefs (propositions and parameters), the beliefs themselves, belief systems and the entire belief base. Change processes can operate on any one of these levels.

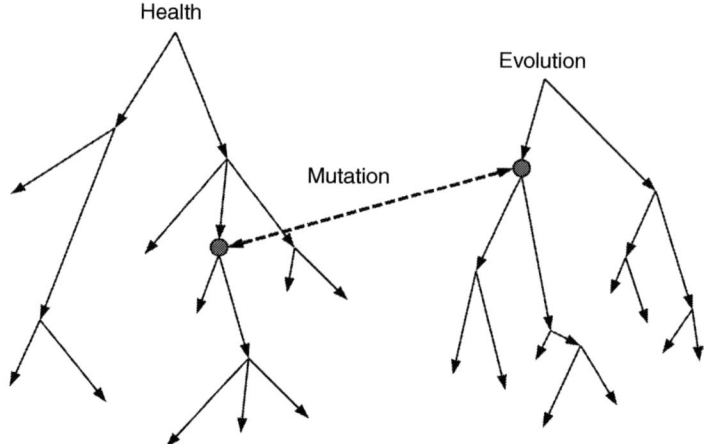

FIGURE 10.1. Two hypothetical center-periphery structures, representing a person's beliefs about health and biological evolution, are tangled by sharing the concept of mutation.

The Components of Conflicts

Cognitive conflicts play an important role in conversion, but a different role from the one envisioned in past theories based on the evaluation of evidence. Due to the operation of the resistance mechanisms described in Chapter 9, theory-data conflicts have less power to drive change than theory-theory conflicts. But the notion of a theory-theory conflict stands in need of clarification.

If all knowledge representations were compatible with each other, then all belief formation events would be monotonic. Belief systems would always grow through additions and extensions. We could believe every state of affairs that we could represent, and once a belief were formed, there would never be any reason to revise it or reject it. But knowledge representations vary in degree of compatibility. In some cases, it is possible to maintain two different representations simultaneously without feeling any cognitive strain. This happens when we see a Saturday street market both as a shopping opportunity and a traffic hassle. The market itself is what it is, and it does not determine or force either conception. We feel no need to choose between them. But when we see an older gentleman and much younger woman stroll through the market arm in arm, we wonder: father and daughter or December-June couple? As we normally use these concepts, the pair cannot be both. Incompatibility recurs in all cognitive processes. Is the Necker cube angled one way or the other?

It cannot be both at the same time. Does the sentence, *they are eating apples* mean that the apples are for eating or that someone is already using them that way? Do the data imply that the global climate is heating up or cooling down? Incompatibility forces the mind to resolve conflict by choosing one representation over the other.

It is not obvious why some alternative representations are mutually incompatible while others are not. What distinguishes pairs of beliefs that are mutually incompatible from pairs of beliefs that are compatible? The shape of the Earth is a case in point. The world has to be in some physical state or another at each moment, but this fact does not imply that our representations of it need to be mutually exclusive. A globe depicts the Earth as spherical while a map depicts it as flat, but we feel no need to choose between globes and maps. We go back and forth between them or use both as circumstances dictate. Why, then, must our *mental* representation of the Earth depict it as *either* spherical or flat?

Sometimes incompatibility is a matter of definition, as in the classical example of a married bachelor. This type of incompatibility is merely a side effect of how certain words are used. In logic, a contradiction is a conjunction of two propositions that assign different truth values to the same proposition, as in "TRUE (P) & FALSE (P)." Neither the definitional nor the logical type of impossibility plays a central role in the theory proposed in this chapter.

In interesting cases of cognitive conflict, the conflicting beliefs specify properties or states of affairs that cannot hold simultaneously.[16] To continue the planetary example, the Earth is both round and heavy; no contradiction there. Why can it not be both round and flat? The sphere and the disc representations of the Earth are incompatible because it is impossible in a material sense for the Earth to be an instance of both. The fact that the Earth cannot be both flat and round is not an assertion about the words "flat," "round" and "Earth," but about shapes and planets. A planet cannot be both flat and round because, briefly put, matter either does or does not occupy a given region of space. Similarly, an animal cannot be both a cat and a dog. This is not because the propositions *X is a dog* and *X is a cat* logically contradict each other; they do not. Instead, an animal cannot be both a cat and a dog because, briefly put, it only has one set of parents, a core piece of our beliefs about mammalian reproduction. The type of conflict that drives cognitive change is not logical contradiction but *material incompatibility*, states of affairs that we believe cannot hold simultaneously.

The source of this type of incompatibility is contextual: It is grounded in our theories about the relevant areas of experience. This observation implies that to perceive a contradiction between two beliefs, we have to have adopted some *background theory* that claims that the states of affairs described by the two beliefs mutually exclude each other. It is because we believe that large, material solids cannot change shape, or simultaneously inhabit two different shapes, that we must choose between different shapes for the Earth. As a second example, our intuitive sense of space and geometry does not allow any compromise between the statements that the Earth is at the center of the planetary system and that the Sun is at its center. In our intuitive theory of three-dimensional space, both states of affairs cannot hold at the same time.

Pairs of representation are more or less incompatible as a function of what the background theory claims. It is not contradictory to believe that certain cancers can be caused either by genetic factors or by some bacterium or virus (but perhaps not both in any one case, except as an unlikely coincidence), because the relevant background theories of physiology allow multiple causes for certain cancers. Similarly, we can look back and forth between two maps of the same area, drawn to different scales, without feeling any conflict, because the relevant background theory – our intuitive understanding of mapmaking – tells us how the two maps relate to each other and explains why one and the same geographic feature looks different in the two maps. When the relevant background theory does not claim incompatibility, the alternative representations are, as we say, different ways of looking at the matter, and we can go back and forth between the two without feeling any need to choose.

In short, for a person to experience a cognitive conflict of the relevant sort, his mental state must include at least the following components. There is some *resident theory* Th1 that the person whose theory it is has adopted as true. The second ingredient is a *contender theory* Th2, also judged as true. For there to be a conflict, the two theories must be incompatible, which implies acceptance of some overarching *background theory* Th0. The background theory implies that Th1 and Th2 cannot both be true, although the person has adopted both Th1 and Th2 as true. So we have the following components in a *conflict scenario* for person S at time t:

$S(t)$: TRUE (Th0)
TRUE (Th0) *implies* INCOMPATIBLE (Th1, Th2)
TRUE (Th1)
TRUE (Th2)

If a person possesses all these knowledge structures, then he is in a state of dissonance and there is a need for change to restore the coherence of his belief base. Cognitive conflicts are not logical contradictions; in particular, they are not contradictions between beliefs on the one hand, and data, observations or experiences, on the other. Instead, a cognitive conflict is a three-way relation between a background theory that subsumes two contending theories for some domain, where "theory" refers to informal, perhaps implicitly held belief systems. A background theory is itself a belief system and hence changeable.

This analysis of cognitive conflict implies that there are three ways for a conflict to be resolved. Local coherence can be restored by changing the truth value of the contender theory to FALSE; this is resistance. Alternatively, it can be restored by altering the truth value of the resident theory; this is conversion. The third possibility is to revise the background theory in such a way that the two theories are seen as compatible. For example, we do not believe that a person can be both a human and a wolf, because in the post-genomic era, we do not believe that living tissue can morph drastically in a short period of time. In medieval times, thinking with a different background theory, we shuttered our windows against werewolfs.[17]

The third type of resolution is clearly visible in science. One of the peculiarities of quantum physics is that it does not assert material incompatibilities where 19th-century physicists expected them: A particle can have both a certain spin and its opposite; a radioactive atom can both have and have not decayed; photons can behave like both particles and waves; and so on. Physicists have proven that these compatibilities are real by exploiting them for practical purposes, as in quantum computers. In this case, the incompatibilities were resolved by revising the relevant background theory to say that something can be both; for example, quantum physicists found a mathematical representation that has both a particle and a wave description of elementary particles as special cases. Abandoning the commonsense background theory that implied these incompatibilities caused a major philosophical debate among physicists and philosophers of science about the nature of physics in the first half of the 20th century.[18] Similarly, some Christian biologists try to reconcile their religious beliefs with their scientific practices by saying, for example, that natural selection is God's way of creating biological species. In this case the relevant background theory is the traditional reading of the Book of Genesis in the Bible as referring to instantaneous creation.[19] The philosophical heartaches that cases like these have caused Western intellectuals indicates that this third type of conflict resolution is uncommon.

A theory of belief formation should explain the origin of cognitive conflicts. Why, how and when does the type of mental state that requires a choice between incompatible beliefs arise? In particular, a satisfactory theory must explain why nascent conflicts are not dealt with through the resistance mechanisms described in Chapter 9. How does a person arrive at a state of mind that contains a theory-theory conflict? If there are multiple modes of resolution, then such a theory also needs to specify the factors that determine which mode will be chosen on any one occasion. Why was the conflict between the wave and particle theories of light resolved by modifying the relevant background theory, while the conflict between phlogiston and oxygen accounts of combustion was resolved by accepting the contending theory? Why are neo-Lamarckian challenges to Darwinism invariably resolved in favor of the resident theory? By what processes can a contender theory ever replace a resident theory?

THE THEORY OF CONVERSION

The theory of conversion proposed in this section explains how a novel belief can be acquired without interference from an incompatible resident belief.* A belief system constructed for one domain of experience by routine, monotonic belief formation mechanisms might be applicable to another, target domain as well. If the former is incompatible with the person's resident theory for the target domain, the latent conflict might go unnoticed due to the lack of global coherence and the division of the belief base into locally bounded subsystems. If the person eventually bisociates the two domains – discovers that the contender can be applied to the target domain – the latent cognitive conflict becomes manifest. The conflict is resolved via competition with respect to cognitive utility. The higher the utility of a belief or a belief system, the higher the person's confidence in it. Conversion – a change in truth value – occurs when the person's confidence in the contender has become greater than his confidence in the resident theory. This point change then propagates through the person's belief base. The extent of the revision is massively contingent on the content and structure of the belief base. Each of these points requires expansion.

Local Coherence and Latent Conflict

Monotonic belief formation is a routine and ubiquitous cognitive process, varying in magnitude and importance from reading in the morning newspaper that there will be rain later in the day to accepting the idea that, for example, the meaning of life is to realize as much as possible of one's creative

---

* This theory is based on Ohlsson (1999a, 2000, 2002, 2009a, 2009b).

potential. Over the life span, a person's stock of beliefs grows vast. To keep his belief base globally coherent, a person would have to test every new belief for consistency against every other belief; indeed, against every consequence of already adopted beliefs; in fact, against every consequence of every possible conjunction of already adopted beliefs. If the number of beliefs is, for example, 500,000, and the person's brain could carry out one comparison per second, it would require a lifetime to test the belief base for global consistency after adding a new belief, and the operation would have to be repeated every time a new belief is created. Maintaining global coherence is impossible and people other than philosophers do not spend a significant proportion of their waking time worrying whether their worldview is coherent.

As P. Thagard has emphasized in multiple articles and books, human cognition is characterized by local rather than global coherence.[20] The striving for coherence operates within tightly interrelated groups of beliefs. This *Principle of Local Coherence* is consistent with the function of declarative knowledge: People activate their beliefs, not to contemplate their epistemic worth, but to perform cognitive tasks, and those tasks arise within particular contexts and situations. An attempt to perform a statistical analysis does not activate my knowledge of SCUBA diving, and an attempt to cook dinner does not activate my knowledge, such as it is, of the mummification practices of the ancient Egyptians (perhaps just as well). Grouping beliefs into interconnected but bounded subsystems facilitates retrieval of beliefs that are relevant for a person's current purpose without also flooding his limited-capacity working memory with marginally relevant beliefs.

Local Coherence implies that a person is likely to remain unaware of conflicts among his beliefs if those beliefs pertain to semantically distant domains or areas of experience. If the concepts and principles of two informal theories Th(A) and Th(B) are never present in working memory simultaneously, and hence never applied to the same event, object or situation at the same time, then any conflict between them remains undetected or *latent*. The conflict between the two theories exists in the eye of an omniscient observer but not yet for the person whose theories they are. Rokeach put it this way: "It may be assumed that in every person's value-attitude system there already exist inherent contradictions of which he is unaware for one reason or another...."[21] In this situation, further growth of the two theories need not be hindered or complicated by dissonance-reducing processes. The question of how we can absorb new information that contradicts prior concepts when that information has to be understood in terms of those very concepts does not arise. The new information can be absorbed without dissonance because it is consistent with the beliefs that are active at the time the information is received, while the beliefs that contradict it are dormant. The resident and contender theories grow separately and in parallel through monotonic belief formation, each within its own context.

Parallel, monotonic growth can result in a latent conflict because surface features are poor predictors of essences. Seemingly distinct and separate phenomena and domains sometimes exhibit deep similarities. Hence, the range of applicability of a belief system cannot be determined by inspecting the beliefs themselves. Building an informal theory for domain A, the person might thereby unwittingly also build a theory of other domains B_1, B_2, B_3, ... that do, in fact, share the same underlying structure, but the act of acquiring a theory for A does not in and of itself reveal those other applications. A person might form a theory that in fact applies to some domain B without being aware that it applies to that domain.

How often might this seemingly unlikely event happen? Recall that a person might possess 500,000 individual beliefs. Belief systems vary in size, but suppose they contain an average of 100 or so beliefs; then a typical person will possess 5,000 distinct belief systems or local theories that guide thinking in particular domains (health, money, sports, etc.). A latent conflict involves two beliefs or belief systems, so the number of possible latent conflicts is approximately $5,000^2$, or 25,000,000. How often does it happen that two domains of experience that seem to be distinct nevertheless are related in such a way that a single theory can apply to both? Intuition suggests that such cases are rare. How rare? If only 1% of all pairs of domains share the same structure, there are 250,000 such pairs in a person's head. In how many of those cases are the two belief systems in conflict, according to some background theory? If only 1% of all pairs of belief systems that apply to the same domains are in conflict, there are 2,500 latent cognitive conflicts waiting to be noticed in the average head. This back-of-the-envelope calculation is not a serious mathematical model, but it illustrates that even though people do not (intentionally) construct multiple theories for the same domain of experience, and even though two belief systems that apply to the same domain are not necessarily in conflict, it is nevertheless reasonable to believe that people carry around with them multiple latent conflicts between their beliefs.

In short, the process that sets the stage for belief revision is that a person responds to some domain of experience A by forming an intuitive theory, Th(A); that Th(A) happens to apply to some other domain B as well; and that Th(A) is incompatible with the person's resident theory Th(B) for that domain according to some background theory Th(o). Due to the impossibility of maintaining global coherence, the person can remain unaware of the conflict between Th(A) and Th(B), so new information about either domain can be absorbed without dissonance via routine, monotonic belief formation processes. The need to choose does not arise as long as the conflict remains latent.

Bisociation and Manifest Conflict

There is no guarantee that a latent conflict is discovered eventually. The parallel, monotonic expansion of two conflicting theories might continue throughout the person's lifetime. The latent conflict becomes *manifest* only if the person becomes aware that theory Th(A), developed to make sense of domain A, applies to domain B as well.

Under which circumstances will a theory that is not normally associated with a domain be retrieved and applied to that domain? How are such semantically remote connections discovered? In his 1964 book *The Act of Creation*, Arthur Koestler called such discoveries *bisociations*.[22] The question of which conditions trigger bisociation falls under the general rubric of memory retrieval: When is any concept or belief activated and applied to the situation at hand? Retrieval occurs via the spread of activation through the memory network, and, briefly put, a concept is retrieved when the sum of activation arriving along its incoming links is above the retrieval threshold.

Applied to the problem of how a latent conflict between two theories Th(A) and Th(B) becomes manifest, the standard principles of memory retrieval imply that this can happen when the person is in a context in which Th(A) is active – that is, he is currently thinking with the concepts of that theory – at the same time that objects and events that belong to domain B are presented to him by the environment. Some external source of information – discourse or observation – can introduce something that belongs to domain B while the person is thinking in terms of Th(A). If we follow Piaget in assuming that cognitive structures strive to apply, then the simultaneous activation of a belief and the occurrence of a potential instance of that belief provide an opportunity to discover that the former applies to the latter; put differently, that the latter can be subsumed under the former.[23]

Since the publication of *The Act of Creation*, the development of theories of analogical mapping has greatly enhanced our understanding of how bisociation might work.[24] Particularly useful are the concepts of *structure mapping*, originally proposed by Dedre Gentner to be the key component of analogical reasoning, and *structural alignment*, discussed by Gentner and

Arthur B. Markman. A structure mapping process constructs a correspondence between the conceptual structure of one knowledge system or representation and the conceptual structure of another in such a way that it is clear which component of one corresponds to which component of the other. Structure mapping can create an analogy between two concrete objects, two situations, two problems and so on, but it can also apply an abstract schema to a concrete situation. Although the bisociation process was an unexplained black box at the time Koestler proposed it, extensive theoretical work on analogical mapping since then has opened that box and shown us multiple views of the cogwheels inside. Researchers have proposed a variety of different computational models of the mapping process, but their details are not needed here.

The discovery that theory Th(A) can subsume domain B causes a link to be created in memory between Th(A) and objects and events in B. Once such a connection has been established, the contender theory Th(A) is no longer semantically remote from events and objects in B. Future encounters with such objects and events will evoke both Th(B) and Th(A), although perhaps not with equal probability or equal activation levels. But once the relevant memory link is formed, Th(A) is evoked by the ordinary process of memory retrieval and the person is in a mental state in which he can think about B in two mutually contradictory ways: in terms of Th(A), which is now better rendered as Th(A+B) to symbolize the extension of its domain of application, and in terms of Th(B). The cognitive conflict between Th(A+B) and Th(B) has become manifest and the person experiences a theory-theory conflict (as opposed to a theory-evidence conflict).

Competitive Evaluation

Once the relevance of the contender theory Th(A+B) for some target domain B has been discovered, the person has a choice as to which theory should determine his behavior or discourse in that domain. The resubsumption theory claims that this choice is not a deliberate act of choosing. Instead, the preference for one theory over the other emerges in a process of competitive evaluation that extends over some period of time. In logic-inspired accounts of theory change, the operative question is, *does the evidence imply that one of these theories is more veridical than the other?* In contrast, the resubsumption principle claims that the operative question is, *which view of the relevant domain has higher cognitive utility?*

Whenever the contender theory Th(A+B) is retrieved and applied to domain B, the person's implicit or intuitive estimate of its utility is updated: Feedback from the environment informs the person about how well the actions derived from the theory work – that is, how good a tool the theory is for solving life's cognitive tasks. Environmental feedback takes different forms in different types of tasks. For example, a poor decision, informed by an inadequate theory of the relevant domain, might lead to an unnecessary waste of time, a type of outcome that cannot be cast as a logical contradiction. If a theory works well – that is, if evoking it enables the person to successfully solve the cognitive tasks he undertakes – then the estimate of its utility increases; if the theory gets the person into trouble, then the utility is decreased. Over time, the feedback generated by task performance converges on a stable estimate of the cognitive utility of the relevant theory.

The contender theory Th(A+B) does not start at zero utility. That theory emerged because it was needed to make sense of domain A and its utility reflects its usefulness in that domain. Hence, the two competitors might start out at comparable utility levels. They might be running neck to neck, as it were, for some time, but if Th(B) generates negative feedback and Th(A+B) generates positive feedback, the advantage of the former will decrease. The person might switch back and forth between them with a gradually increasing awareness that his thinking is incoherent and that a choice has to be made as to what to believe. If the contender theory continues to accrue utility through successful use, it will eventually surpass the resident theory.

If the contender theory is in fact more veridical than the resident theory, its use will tend to increase its estimated utility. At first glance, this state of affairs seems utterly implausible. Why would a theory that arises from an attempt to understand domain B be less useful for dealing with that domain than a theory formed in response to information about some other domain? When we initially become familiar with a domain, we tend to perceive, categorize and remember the domain in terms of perceptual features and simple relations among its surface features. We spontaneously carve the world at the joints as we see them. However, surface validity goes only so far, because surface features are not, in fact, perfect, and sometimes not even good, predictors of underlying mechanisms. Sharks and dolphins look similar but are quite different animals, glass and diamond look similar but are quite different substances and so on. The history of science is a long testimony to the fact that our perceptual systems do not carve the world at its true joints. Effective and accurate theories require that we stand back from the surface appearances and parse reality according to features that might not attract our attention at first. Consequently, a theory that began as an attempt to understand some other area of experience might happen to slice that domain in such a way that when its structure is superimposed on another domain, it provides a better account than the theory initially and spontaneously created for that domain. If a person carries with him some 2,500 latent conflicts, and the contender is superior to the resident theory in only 1% of cases, the person has the potential for 25 deep conceptual discoveries, far more than most people experience in their lifetime.

Competition on the basis of task performance only settles the issue of relative utility. Utility is, in turn, one of the factors that determine a person's confidence in a theory or belief system. The more successful the person is, the more confidence he will have in his theory. Little would change in the resubsumption theory if the two variables of utility and confidence were collapsed into a single variable. Although the theory would gain in parsimony, common sense suggests that confidence in a belief is strongly influenced by other factors over and above its estimated utility. The nature of the source of information affects our confidence; the possibility of formulating a theory mathematically might increase confidence for some; others are more prone to believe in theoretical mechanisms that they can visualize than those they cannot; and so on. For these reasons, to collapse utility and confidence carries too high a theoretical cost, so the two variables are kept separate throughout.

It is plausible that the probability of a switch in truth value is a function of the ratio of the person's confidence in the contender theory to his confidence in the resident theory. Conversion occurs when the confidence levels cross over so that the person's confidence in the contender theory becomes stronger than his confidence in the resident theory. At that point the relation between the two theories has been reversed, so that Th(A+B) has become the standard or default choice in any situation in which both theories apply. But there might be a certain inertia that moves the switching point off-center, so to speak, and there is no guarantee that the relation between the confidence ratio and the disposition to switch truth value is linear. For present purposes, it is enough to hypothesize that the ratio between contender and resident confidence is the main determinant of a switch in truth value and that the former is, in turn, a function of the person's level of success when using either theory to solve everyday cognitive tasks.

According to the resubsumption theory, change is driven by successes rather than by failures. It is the fact that the contender theory turns out to apply to the target domain and that the applications are better or more successful than those of the resident theory that sets the conditions for change. According to this view, a belief might be revised even though it never encounters any anomalous, contradictory or falsifying evidence. Conflict is not produced by flaws and failures but by the creation of an alternative that turns out to be superior. The disposition to convert depends on how well the contender works, not how poorly the resident fares.

A second key feature of the resubsumption hypothesis is that it links intentional and material aspects of a switch in truth value. It situates truth value assignment within real-time cognition instead of leaving it in the Platonic heaven of idealizations and logical relations. Adjusting the utility estimate of a belief is very different from evaluating the strength of evidence. However, utility and truth are linked by the fact that a theory that is true tends to be more useful than one that is false. Actions, judgments or inferences that rely on an inaccurate theory will get a person into trouble more often than those that are based on a more accurate theory. Such epistemic trouble takes many forms: bad decisions, contradictions with other information sources, inability to explain events or regularities, lost arguments, malfunctioning devices, mistaken predictions, rejected journal submissions and so on. Utility is moderated by feedback from the environment about the effectiveness of actions derived from the theory, and effectiveness is in turn a function of veridicality, so utility and truth are linked, if indirectly, via confidence.

Propagation of Change

A shift in the truth value of one belief will tend to propagate through the belief base. In the words of W. V. Quine: "A conflict with experience at the periphery [of a belief system] occasions readjustments in the interior of the field. Truth values have to be redistributed over some of our statements. Re-evaluation of some statements entails re-evaluation of others...."[25]

If the switched truth value is associated with a single, peripheral belief, it will not propagate far and the change will be minor. If the altered truth value is associated with an entire belief system or theory, the switch will have implications for all the beliefs of lesser scope that belong to that theory. There will be a strong tendency to accept the component beliefs as true. The change might roll through the belief system like a wave, presumably giving rise to the subjective experience of conversion. For example, if I should come to believe that *diet does not matter, because a person's health is completely determined by his genes*, this would trigger a wave of changes throughout my belief system for health and diet. The beliefs that *fat is bad for you, chocolate is good for you* and many others would flip from TRUE to FALSE. On the other hand, I would be more disposed to believe in claims about particular links between genes and diseases.

A change in truth value might also propagate upward through the belief base, affecting the truth of any belief system of larger scope that draws on or encompasses the changed belief or belief system. The change that occurs in any one instance is massively contingent on the exact structure and content of the belief base and on the principles by which truth values at different levels influence each other. A point change, a single shift in truth value, might trigger a wave of re-assessments that propagates through the belief base. When the resulting change is limited, it might go more or less unnoticed; when the change is major, it is presumably experienced subjectively as a change of mind. To the extent that the change is expressed in his discourse, it will be perceived as such by others.

Three Vignettes

The purpose of the following three vignettes is to make the resubsumption theory plausible and to illustrate how its concepts and principles apply in different cases. The first two vignettes are didactic; the third is a case from the history of science.

Consider the concept of a feedback circle. An engineering student will encounter this concept in the context of thermostats and other control systems. He might not have noticed that the national economy can be seen as a feedback system as well. For the student to discover this, he has to be in a situation in which the economy comes to mind – through a conversation, news report or other input – but in which the feedback concept has a high enough activation to compete with standard economic concepts like, for example, supply and demand. Suppose the engineering student spends several days studying for an examination on control devices. Afterward, he celebrates with other students at a local watering hole and the conversation turns toward the group members' future prospects and hence to the way the economy is going, which in turn leads them to challenge each others' ideas about how the economy works. In this context, we would not be surprised if our protagonist suddenly tells the group that the economy is a feedback system, perhaps in jest. Once the bisociation has occurred, many applications of feedback concepts to economic phenomena (business cycles, rise of monopolies, stretching of the income distribution, etc.) come to mind. Before the last beer is emptied, the student might be convinced that there is another way to think about the economy than in terms of the equilibrium theorems of classical market economics. The key feature of this hypothetical scenario is the introduction of thoughts about economic events into a situation in which the concepts of control theory already have a high level of activation due to the preparation for the examination.

As a second illustration, consider a person who becomes engaged in local politics for the first time as an adult. Suppose that he initially suffers from what we might call the Civics Theory of politics: Those who stand for election represent the values and principles of the electorate and, once elected to office, their actions, initiatives and votes are consistent with those values and principles. Like any adult, our hypothetical everyman-turned-politico also has an intuitive theory about trade, about buying and selling, about one person offering something that has a certain worth or value to somebody else, who might therefore be ready to offer something of equal value in return. This theory is normally evoked in the context of deciding on a purchase or a sale, not politics. But even modest experience with politics as actually practiced might cause a person to re-conceptualize the work of politicians in terms of trades. Nothing can be accomplished unless a politician is ready to trade favors, and the effective politician knows the political worth of every favor traded and never trades away more than he gains. The veridicality of this view of politics is not the issue here, only the fact that a change from the Civics Theory to the Trade Theory illustrates how a theory formed in the course of everyday activities like buying groceries and shopping for a new car can turn out to provide a better structure for understanding a superficially very dissimilar domain of experience than a theory that was originally formed with reference to that domain.

As an example with scientific subject matter, consider biological evolution via genetic variation and natural selection. Darwin invented this theory to explain the pattern of similarities and differences among living species, their geographical distributions, the fossil record and other features of the living world. As originally stated, his theory was embedded in the biological domain; it was about organisms, species and, after the modern synthesis, genes and mutations. However, the schema of variation and selection, once invented, can subsume other domains as well. At one point, the theory that the immune system develops antibodies that are targeted for a particular virus – which raises the question of how the immune system derives information from the virus in order to concoct the right antibody – gave ground to the idea that antibodies evolve through variation and selection. The immune system issues antibodies of great variety, and it makes more of those antibodies that match foreign particles in the body. In this way, the functioning of the immune system can be resubsumed under the variation-selection principle.[26] The first person who thought of the immune system in this way underwent conceptual change, and given the likelihood that he or she already knew the theory of evolution, this was an instance of resubsuming the facts of immunology under the theory originally developed to explain the history of life.

To verify that this was not an isolated instance, consider two other resubsumptions involving variation and selection. First, Walter G. Vincent has proposed that the variation-selection theory can be applied to the history of aviation: Aeronautical engineers developed a variety of wing shapes, steering mechanisms and other features, and the designs that flew well, met with pilot approval and so forth were carried forward to the next generation of airplanes.[27] In this case, the variation-selection principle can be said to replace a handful of murkier folk ideas about technology; for example, that inventors come up with designs to fill particular needs, that designs are derived mathematically from physics and so on. Second, the variation-selection principle has been applied to the development of fads and fashions in popular culture in the theory of so-called memes: Small snippets of culture – a phrase, a way of wearing a baseball cap, a melody, a slogan, an orthographic rule violation as in eBay, iPod – are constantly generated and they multiply if they catch on; soon variations appear, which in turn may or may not catch on and in turn multiply.[28] My claim is not that these variation-selection theories are correct, but that both Vincent's theory of aviation design and the meme theory of popular culture are examples of resubsumption. In both cases, a domain that at first was thought of in other than variation-selection terms was resubsumed under the already known theory of biological evolution.

Summary

The resubsumption theory postulates complex interactions among five different processes, each with its own set of triggering conditions. The background process is routine, monotonic belief formation in response to new information. Operating on the two principles of *Ubiquitous Encoding* and *Truth as Default*, this process responds to information about domains of experience A, B, C, … by forming multiple belief systems or informal theories, Th(A), Th(B), Th(C), … which encode the person's habitual ways of thinking about objects, relations and events in those domains. Because people operate with *Local Coherence*, the relations between such informal theories tend to escape scrutiny. If Th(A) happens to be applicable to domain B, and if the person possesses an overarching theory Th(o) that implies that Th(A) and Th(B) cannot both be true, then the parallel, monotonic growth of the two belief systems has created a latent theory-theory conflict.

The second process is bisociation, a mental event in which the two contexts A and B intersect, and Th(A) and Th(B) come to be applied simultaneously to some object, event or phenomenon. For bisociation to happen, the concepts and principles of Th(A) must be applicable to B and they must become active at some moment in time when the person is attending to B. This could happen through spontaneous reminding, analogical or similarity-based, of Th(A) in the presence of B; via social interaction that activates Th(A) in a situation in which the person is already thinking about B or vice versa; and in other ways as well. The person is now aware that he has two different ways of thinking about B, in terms of Th(A) and in terms of Th(B), the former now being seen as having a wider scope than previously thought and hence to be better characterized as Th(A+B). If his background theory dictates that Th(A+B) and Th(B) are incompatible, local coherence has been breached. The resubsumption of B under Th(A+B) has made the latent conflict manifest.

The third process is conflict resolution through competitive evaluation. Belief systems and informal theories are tools for dealing with the cognitive tasks a person encounters in the course of life. A person's confidence in a theory will change as a result of his success or failure when that theory is applied. If the learner's cognitive ecology is such that he encounters frequent opportunities to apply the two contending theories, he will gather information about their relative utility. Utility, in turn, drives confidence. If Th(A+B) is in fact a more useful theory for domain B than Th(B), then experience will decrease his confidence in the resident theory and increase his confidence in the contender theory. Eventually, the two confidence levels will pass each other and the person finds himself having greater confidence in the contender than in the resident theory. The successes of the contender, not the failures of the resident theory, drive the shift between the two theories. Figure 10.2 graphically illustrates the emergence of a latent conflict, bisociation and competitive evaluation.

The fourth process is the switch in truth value, belief revision narrowly construed. The theory claims that the two processes of adjusting confidence and switching truth value are independent in the sense that there can be shifts in confidence that are not accompanied by shifts in truth value. The theory claims that the switch in truth value is a function of the relative levels of confidence associated with the competing theories. If the confidence in the resident theory continues to decrease and that of the contender theory to increase, the cumulative consequence will be that the person finds himself believing the latter.

The fifth process is the propagation of the truth value switch, a point change, throughout the belief base. If the change in truth value is associated with a single, peripheral belief, the change might be minor. If the altered belief is a component of a belief system of large scope, the change might propagate downward and upward through the belief base. If the propagation wave affects many beliefs, the person might experience himself subjectively as undergoing a significant change of mind, a conversion.

The five mechanisms of the theory – monotonic belief formation, bisociation, competitive evaluation, truth value switch and propagation through

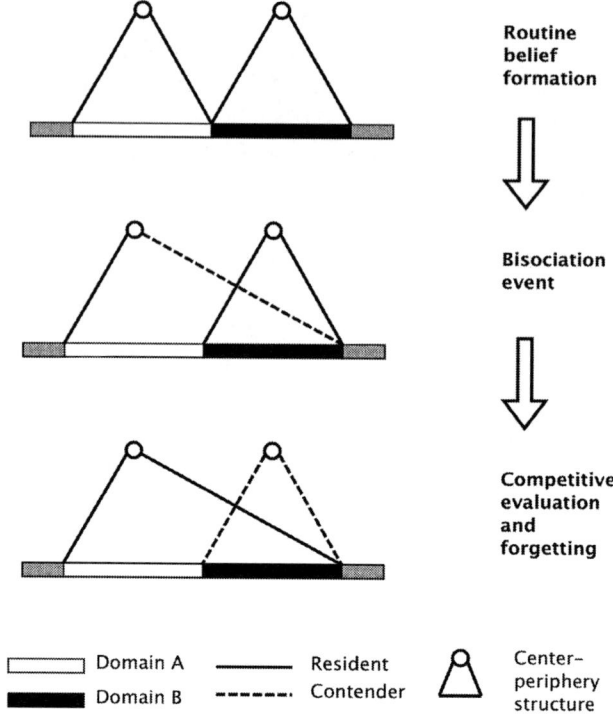

FIGURE 10.2. The flow of events in belief revision.

the belief base – can be decomposed into basic cognitive processes that are neither exotic nor ad hoc. They are frequently postulated throughout the cognitive sciences to explain a wide variety of phenomena and experimental results: memory retrieval through the spread of activation, mapping two knowledge structures via structural alignment, instantiation of an abstraction, implicit quantitative learning and so on. All of these processes have been simulated by computer models, so there is no doubt about our ability to specify them precisely.[29] The contribution of the Resubsumption Theory is to combine these processes in a way that explains how a change in core beliefs can come about in the face of cognitive resistance to contradictory information.

RELATIONS TO OTHER THEORIES

The Resubsumption Theory implies that terms like "belief revision," "conceptual change" and "theory change" are misnomers: It is not so much a belief, concept or theory that is changing but the relation between a knowledge structure and its domain of application. A knowledge structure that was thought to have extension A is discovered to have the wider extension A+B. This is a change in how events, objects and phenomena are grouped rather than in the content of the relevant belief system. Paradoxically, the Resubsumption Theory thus claims that changes in content occur primarily in the course of monotonic belief formation, not during conversion. Conversion is a choice between already formed beliefs.

In this respect, the Resubsumption Theory generalizes the ontological category shift theory proposed by Michelene Chi.[30] She has argued that conceptual change requires that the relevant event, object or phenomenon be re-classified under a different ontological category. The latter are high-level categories that specify the types of entities the world contains: events, objects, processes and so on. When a phenomenon is assigned to an ontological category, it inherits the properties that characterize entities in that category. If the category is inappropriate, the inherited properties might interfere with correct understanding. For example, electromagnetic waves cannot be understood correctly as long as they are thought of as *causal systems* but need to be resubsumed under a *field* category. The resubsumption and ontological shift theories share the idea that change involves disconnecting an area of reality from one higher-order knowledge structure and attaching it to another.

They differ in other respects. Whereas the ontological shift theory singles out ontological knowledge as playing a special role, the Resubsumption Theory treats all knowledge as alike and does not postulate a highest category level. All events, objects, processes, regularities and states of affairs that appear in either direct experience or discourse are subsumed under some concept or intuitive theory. My perception of a particular dog is subsumed under my concept of dogs; a statement about dogs in general is understood in terms of my beliefs about dogs; and so on. Even such mundane assignments and categorizations can sometimes be mistaken and require revision: I might pick up what I think is a ballpoint pen and look for the button that makes the writing tip appear, only to discover that it is a pencil with a missing lead. To re-categorize the object from the category "ballpoint pen" to "pencil" is a resubsumption event (of minimal scope) but it is not an ontological shift. Any concept, belief or theory can subsume new information received through perception or discourse; any piece of information must be subsumed under some concept or another; and every act of subsumption can, in principle, be mistaken and require revision. The ontological shift theory emphasizes the effects of these processes with respect to ontological knowledge,* but I suggest that the power of miscategorization to distort information and the consequent need for recategorization are possibilities associated with any type of knowledge.

These differences notwithstanding, the ontological shift and resubsumption theories share a fundamental assumption: In both, the cure for the initial miscategorization of an experience or a discourse is to recategorize it under some alternative higher-order knowledge structure. Conversion is a process of reorganizing knowledge, not a process of falsification. Both theories imply that the alternative higher-order knowledge representation must already exist for the change to take place and therefore postulate parallel development of such higher-order representations prior to the change. The point cannot be emphasized enough: *According to the Resubsumption Theory, a new theory is not a product of theory change, but one of its prerequisites.*

Unlike theories that tackle the effects of resistance head on, the Resubsumption Theory resolves the question of where the contender theory comes from by designating the presence in memory of an alternative theory as one of the triggering factors for theory change. No special assumptions are needed to explain the origin of the contender theory: It was formed by the same processes as any belief system, because it was not formed *as* an alternative but as part of the person's ongoing efforts to make sense of experience and discourse. The possibility of an alternative is, in part, a fact about the world – domains of experience sometimes share enough structure to be subsumed under one and the same theory – and, in part, a fact about the mind: Due to the layered nature of mental representations, a belief system sometimes turns out to be abstract enough to subsume another domain than the one for which it was created. It is the positive step of creating an alternative theory, in conjunction with a background theory that claims that the two theories are incompatible, that leads to the rejection of the resident theory, not a confrontation with evidence. A theory might replace another without either theory suffering from any contradiction with observations or other types of evidence.

Unlike most theories of conversion, the Resubsumption Theory explains why conversions are rare without invoking the processes of resistance described in Chapter 9. Although the mechanisms of the Resubsumption Theory afford a route to belief revision that circumvents resistance to contradictory information, it does not imply that conversion is common or easy to induce. Conversion occurs only under the simultaneous occurrence of multiple conditions. Even

---

* Chi and Brem (2009) de-emphasize their prior focus on ontological knowledge, but it is not clear how this affects the relation between category shift and resubsumption.

if a person's belief system Th(B) does a poor job of accounting for what happens in domain B, there is no guarantee that he will construct some alternative theory Th(A+B) that does a better job. That is, he may or may not have something to convert to. Even if a potential alternative is present in his belief base, the possibility of applying Th(A+B) to B might go unnoticed for a lifetime. Alternatively, the person might lack an overarching theory that says that these two theories are mutually incompatible. He might cheerfully accept that he has two ways of looking at domain B but not feel any need to choose between them. Also, his environment might not provide a sufficient number of opportunities to apply his contending theory for him to realize that the resident theory has less utility than the contender. Finally, the resident theory might be situated in such a way within his belief base that propagation of a switch in truth value leaves all core beliefs unchanged. All of these conditions affect whether the conversion of a core belief will occur.

In contrast, the ontological shift theory, in its current stage of development, does not come with an explicit formulation of the exact mental triggering conditions for ontological shifts.[31] There is no obvious explanation in the ontological shift theory for why ontological shifts are difficult or have a low probability of occurring. To detach a link between some phenomenon X and a category C_1 and to create a new link between X and some other category C_2 are simple processes that do not seem unduly demanding. Why do we not shift ontological categories at the drop of a hat? The difficulty of conceptual change is attributed by Chi and co-workers to a lack of awareness of the need for such a shift, a lack of the correct target category and "the cognitive demand of re-inheriting all the attributes of a concept based on its new categorical membership." Only the third of these three – the cognitive load associated with conceptual change – applies in the central cases in which a person is aware of a cognitive conflict and is in possession of the correct target category but nevertheless does not shift. In those cases, the cognitive load hypothesis, if taken to be the whole story, predicts that conceptual change will be blocked, and so cannot explain why it happens when it does happen.

A radical difference between resubsumption and other theories of belief revision, conceptual change or theory change is that resubsumption implies that dissatisfaction with a resident theory is neither a necessary nor a sufficient triggering condition for change. The discovery that some other theory provides a different way of looking at something can happen even if one is unaware of any difficulties with one's current beliefs. Spontaneous or opportunistic retrieval in combination with structural alignment do not require doubts about the resident theory. During competitive evaluation, satisfaction and dissatisfaction with outcomes play a role in the adjustment of the relevant confidence levels, but the conversion process is not triggered by doubt but by the conceptual discovery that there is an alternative way of looking at the relevant situation or domain. It is the positive act of extending the reach of a successful conception that sets the stage for theory change, not dismay over the accumulation of anomalies.

Indeed, the Resubsumption Theory implies that the causal sequence between anomalies and conversion is the reverse of that envisioned by Popper, Kuhn and psychologists in the science-inspired tradition. In the presence of a single theory, an anomaly is merely that: yet another anomaly. Because we are never in possession of a belief system that explains everything, we live with anomalies and we deal with them by, briefly put, ignoring them. When a person becomes aware that there is a contender theory, he becomes more motivated to pay attention to anomalies. Anomalies acquire importance only if they become reasons to choose one theory over another, which presupposes that the contender theory has already been constructed by the time the anomalies are seriously considered. Hence, anomalies are not triggers for theory change, although they might guide the direction of such a change.

The main advantage of the Resubsumption Theory over alternative theories is that it resolves the conceptual knot posed by our disturbingly powerful ability to sweep anomalies and contradictions under the conceptual rug. By postulating that the trigger for theory change is the discovery of a previously unheeded conflict between two already acquired belief systems, the theory of resubsumption cuts the circular relation between new information and prior knowledge and resolves the assimilation paradox: Belief revision is possible in the face of resistance to contradictory evidence because theories initially arise in contexts in which they are compatible with the available evidence, and because theory-theory conflicts are not decided on the basis of logical assessment of the strength of the relevant evidence but on the basis of intuitive estimates of relative utility.

THE PRAGMATIC IMPERATIVE

Philosophers tend to discuss belief revision and theory change in terms of logical entities: Theories are conjunctions of propositions, predictions are logical derivations and the key questions are which propositions are true, which predictions follow from which theories and whether theory change is rational. But belief revision happens to people, so every instance of it occurs in somebody's brain. Neuroscientists discuss brain functioning in terms of cause and effect, changes in electrical charges over time and the chemical properties of synapses, and the central questions pertain to the impact of variables like the frequencies of various types of events and the reinforcements, or lack thereof, that accompany them. Logical and physiological descriptions are worlds apart, and yet must in the final analysis be understood as referring to one and the same event. Belief revision engages as perhaps no other issue in cognitive science both sides of the mind-brain duality, and cognitive psychologists are stuck with the task of minting a coin that has intention and cause, meaning and process, as its two sides.

The Resubsumption Theory takes a modest step in this direction by departing from the idea, central to most prior theories, that belief revision is grounded in the evaluation of evidence, and by explicitly linking cognitive utility, a material concept, to the assignment of truth value, an intentional concept. According to the theory, the type of cognitive conflict that drives conversion is incompatibility between already acquired theories or belief systems, not between theory and evidence. Outside academia, the worth of a belief system is a function of its cognitive utility – that is, how successful it allows a person to be when performing whatever cognitive tasks he undertakes. The careful, conscious, explicit and public accounting of the logical relations between hypotheses and observations that characterizes theory change in science is a highly developed and culturally supported practice that does not mirror, process for process, the basic cognitive mechanisms that make conversion possible.[32] Estimation of cognitive utility on the basis of environmental feedback generated by action, not the processing of observations through Modus Tollens, is the key process by which a person adopts one belief rather than another.

Utility and truth are linked because we are disposed to believe that what works is true. Over the long run, people will adopt the beliefs that enable them to be successful, although they might not be aware of this fact, and the adoption of a belief with high utility might occur gradually and outside consciousness. People do not decide to believe in the same way they decide to buy a house. Instead, *they find themselves believing* such-and-such a proposition that has proven useful in multiple contexts. This *pragmatic imperative* is presumably an innate part of our cognitive architecture. After all, we evolved to be hunters and gatherers, not philosophers. Pragmatism might not be a good philosophical theory of truth, but it is a plausible psychological theory of truth value assignment.[33] Perhaps this theory will turn out to work for psychologists, in the sense of generating powerful explanations for cognitive phenomena. If so, psychologists will no doubt come to believe it.

PART FIVE

CONCLUSION

11

Elements of a Unified Theory

> ... the supreme goal of all theory is to make the irreducible basic elements as simple and as few as possible ...
>
> Albert Einstein[1]

> ... condensing of a multitude of laws into a small number of principles affords enormous relief to the human mind ...
>
> Pierre Duhem[2]

The founders of cognitive science found it useful to remind everybody that no benevolent deity has issued psychologists an insurance against complexity.[3] They implied that if the mind is complex, then we should expect theories of mind to reflect that complexity. H. A. Simon and A. Newell wrote that their "... theory posits internal mechanisms of great extent and complexity. ... That is all there is to it."[4] The three micro-theories of creativity, adaptation and conversion proposed in this book conform to this expectation. In each case, the behavioral phenomenon that the theory was designed to explain can be described in one or two paragraphs, but its explanation requires a chapter-length exposition. If the ultimate theory of cognition is a conjunction of many such micro-theories, then that theory is complex indeed.

But the founders might have taken their realism a shade too naively. Scientific theories are human constructions and they are shaped as much by our ambitions, desires and needs as by the reality they explain. Scientists strive for concise principles because they cannot think effectively with complex ones, due to the very limits on cognitive processing that the founders themselves did so much to reveal.[5] The undeniable complexity of reality reappears in the process of articulating abstract principles vis-à-vis particular phenomena, the way the air in a balloon bulges out at the bottom when you squeeze its top.[6] Newton's equations of mechanical motion can be written on a single page, but in the application to the design of a bridge or a rocket those equations generate complex mathematical expressions, as even a brief look at an engineering textbook will confirm. Likewise, a concise statement of Darwin's theory of evolution belies the complexity of variation-selection explanations for particular evolutionary phenomena like flight, kinship selection and vision. In general, simplicity of theoretical expression is gained in return for complexity of articulation, the latter being easier to off-load onto cognitive support systems like paper and pencil, computer software and research assistants.

One approach to complexity, advocated by positivist philosophers of science, is to reduce phenomena at one level of description to phenomena at lower levels, with the levels ordered via part-whole relations:[7] All physical objects are made up of material substances, which are made up of molecules, which are made up of atoms, which in turn are made of elementary particles, which are made up of quarks, which are made of ... we do not yet know what. Once we know, the theory of those ultimate building blocks will be a theory of everything in the reductionist sense. The expectation that the parts and the parts-of-parts will turn out to be simpler than the objects and processes at analytically higher levels has never been fulfilled – there is nothing simple about so-called elementary particles – but analysis into parts is nevertheless a successful research strategy. The substance-molecule-atom-particle and the organism-organ-tissue-cell ladders of parts and parts-of-parts are very useful for understanding nature.

But analysis is not the scientist's only handle on complexity, not even within physics. Simplification is also served by abstract principles that unify large swaths of knowledge by codifying shared patterns. The great conservation laws of physics are the type specimens. Other examples include the unification of terrestrial and celestial mechanics by Newton's principles of mechanical motion and the unification of various radiation phenomena – light, radio waves, X-rays – by the principles of electromagnetic fields.[8] In other natural sciences, the unification of biology by the theory of evolution, the unification of chemical reactions under the principle of reorganization of atoms and the unification of the medicine of contagious diseases under the germ theory are further examples. The key feature of abstract principles is that they are independent of particular objects, processes or mechanisms. They specify constraints that all events of a certain type satisfy. Analysis into parts and the identification of abstract principles are not incompatible research strategies. The two-punch alternation between analysis and abstraction has served the successful sciences well.

Although cognitive psychologists pride themselves on adhering to high standards of rigorous, empirical science, the theoretical goal of research in cognitive psychology is obscure. What does it mean to have a complete theory of human cognition? Behavior differs from situation to situation and from person to person, and it is obviously a function of a person's prior learning history, which in turn is infinitely variable. If so, what kind of statement can serve as a general principle in cognitive psychology? Psychologists with a reductionist mind-set assume that analysis can be pursued all the way down to brain modules and neurons, subsuming mental function under whatever generalizations hold for neural tissue.[9] They overlook the fact that the reduction of mind to brain must cross the mind-brain chasm along the way, and nobody knows what kind of bridge might serve. The majority of cognitive psychologists pursue the analytical strategy but stop short of neural reductionism: High-level cognitive functions like problem solving, memory and decision making are explained through analysis, not into neurons, but into combinations of more basic cognitive processes: Associate two previously unconnected concepts, spread activation from one memory node to another, bind a variable to a particular entity and so on.[10] Newell has suggested that an analytical level of cognition can be specified in terms of its *time band*, the range of the durations of the constituent processes.[11] Newell distinguished between four time bands, but most cognitive psychologists make do with two: The higher-level functions typically studied in psychological experiments execute in minutes or hours, while the basic processes postulated in the explanations of those functions are claimed to execute in seconds or fractions of seconds.

After the cognitive revolution in the late 1950s, it was not yet clear how analysis into basic cognitive processes might serve unification. Researchers published their own flow diagram of whatever cognitive process caught their interest.[12] After two decades of this, it was clear that this research practice was not converging on a general theory.

In two remarkable papers published in the early 1970s, Newell proposed a type of theory that slices cognition into two distinct parts: the infinitely variable and constantly changing knowledge base and the stable machinery that utilizes that knowledge to perform tasks.[13] Although Newell called the second part the "control structure" of the mind, a decade later J. R. Anderson proposed the less engineering-sounding label "cognitive architecture" and the latter caught on. The description of the cognitive architecture can be conceptualized as a blueprint for a particular type of computer, namely, the type of which a human brain is an instance. In this analogy, knowledge plays the role of software. The specification of a cognitive architecture is a classical analytical enterprise: The system as a whole, human cognition, is understood by breaking it down into its parts, and each part into its parts, and so on. The underlying assumption is that the basic machinery of cognition is at least approximately constant across contexts and tasks, shared by all individuals (variations along a few quantitative parameters aside) and stable over time, at least in relation to the duration of individual cognitive processes. The architecture is presumably innate. In this view, variability in task performance across tasks, across individuals and over time is accounted for by variations in the knowledge that is applied in any one performance. Unification is served – and this is Newell's fundamental innovation – by the fact that *the same set of basic processes is used to explain every cognitive phenomenon*. Simplicity is served because the basic processes and their modes of combination can be stated relatively concisely. The complexity that is squeezed out of the basic machinery bulges out in the specification of the knowledge that the cognitive architecture applies to generate behavior. The Soar theory by Newell, J. Laird and P. S. Rosenbloom and the ACT-R theory proposed by Anderson and co-workers are two attempts to propose specific theories of the form that Newell envisioned, but other theorists have proposed models of the cognitive architecture as well.[14] No proposal has won wide acceptance, but the search for the right specification of the cognitive architecture is the only theoretical programme in cognitive psychology that provides a clear vision of what a final theory of human cognition might look like.

The research strategy followed in this book departs from the cognitive architecture programme. The subject of this book is not human cognition. I believe that the latter is too vast and ill-defined a target for theory formation. To illustrate, consider whether dreaming is a cognitive phenomenon. On what grounds would it be excluded? Dreaming appears to be a process of manipulating mental representations, the very stuff of cognition. But if dreaming is included among bona fide cognitive phenomena, then no contemporary theory of the cognitive architecture stands any chance of being even approximately correct. We are too far from understanding the alterations in consciousness during the wake-sleep cycle, let alone the function of dreaming. Similarly, a complete theory of cognition should explain the role of emotions in cognition, the distinction between meaning and reference in language and the digital-to-analogue conversion that presumably occurs somewhere on the path from decision to movement. These and other research problems are so far from being solved that proposing theories of human cognition is premature.

The work reported in this book follows the alternative strategy of focusing on a single, particularly interesting cognitive phenomenon: non-monotonic cognitive change. People demonstrably undergo such changes and the goal of explaining them poses theoretical challenges that are significantly different from those of explaining stable performance or monotonic learning. The first

TABLE 11.1. *The distinctions among routine processing, monotonic (additive) change and non-monotonic change in three cognitive functions.*

Routine processing	Monotonic change	Non-monotonic change
Creativity: Execute the current task strategy.	Follow an unexplored path in the current problem space.	Revise problem space by activating previously unheeded options.
Adaptation: Execute the current task strategy.	Extend strategy by adding rules for previously undecided situations.	Alter strategy by constraining (specializing) existing rules.
Conversion: Retrieve and articulate beliefs.	Form new beliefs that are consistent with prior beliefs.	Revise and propagate the truth values of existing beliefs.

step toward a comprehensive treatment of this type of cognitive change was to identify three subtypes of non-monotonic change – creativity, adaptation and conversion – and to formulate a micro-theory for each. Each such theory is based on a set of assumptions about the routine, steady-state processing that forms the backdrop for cognitive change. Other assumptions describe what happens in monotonic learning. Finally, there are assumptions that explain how non-monotonic changes can occur within a system that satisfies the first two sets of assumptions; see Table 11.1 for an overview of these distinctions.

Each micro-theory conforms to the type of analysis that is standard in cognitive psychology: The relevant behavioral patterns are explained by breaking down the high-level functions (creating, adapting, converting) into component processes, parts and parts-of-parts, that interact to produce those patterns. The three analyses are successful in two respects. First, the component processes are not unique or exotic. On the contrary, the analysis in each case breaks down non-monotonic change into well-known and familiar basic processes that are empirically supported by prior cognitive research. Second, all homunculi have been discharged. In each case, the breakdown ends in basic processes that are not themselves non-monotonic change processes but instead are so simple that there is no doubt that we can specify them precisely; almost all of them have, in fact, been implemented in running computer simulation models.

These successes come at a price: The end points of the analyses, the set of basic processes, differ from micro-theory to micro-theory. Instead of breaking down creativity, adaptation and conversion into one and the same set of basic processes, as in the cognitive architecture approach, I have addressed each type of non-monotonic change on its own terms, so to speak, and proposed a cognitive mechanism that is specifically designed to resolve the questions and issues that pertain to that type of change. In the case of creative insight, the initial problem representation is abandoned in favor of a new one that might break the impasse; in the case of adaptation, the initial, overly general solution method is constrained to apply only to situations in which it does not cause errors; and in the case of belief revision, truth values are converted when the relevant area of experience is subsumed under another, incompatible but more effective belief system. Lined up side by side, these three mechanisms appear unrelated in that they are composed of qualitatively different basic processes.

But a list of unrelated micro-theories does not serve the purpose of unification. It leaves questions unanswered: How does each mechanism relate to the others? What do the three cases of non-monotonic change have in common and how do they differ? The question arises whether deep learning – non-monotonic cognitive change – is a label of convenience, a verbal handle on an arbitrary bundle of research topics shaped primarily by the investigator's interests and personal history. Or is deep learning a natural kind, a type of cognitive change that can be characterized in an abstract, principled way, analogous to, for example, speciation in biology, combustion in chemistry or wave propagation in physics? If deep learning is a natural kind, the explanations for particular instances ought to share certain properties, and unification can be achieved by capturing those properties in a set of abstract principles.

PRINCIPLES OF DEEP LEARNING

The principles proposed in this section specify properties that hold across the processing mechanisms postulated in the three micro-theories of creativity, adaptation and conversion. In conjunction, they constitute a first draft of a unified theory of deep learning; see Figure 11.1. The question whether these properties are necessary, sufficient or both for a cognitive system to be able to override prior experience is discussed after the principles have been stated.

Spontaneous Activity

A human brain is never at rest. At any moment in time, millions of brain cells propagate their signals downstream to other brain cells. Activity is the natural

Elements of a Unified Theory 369

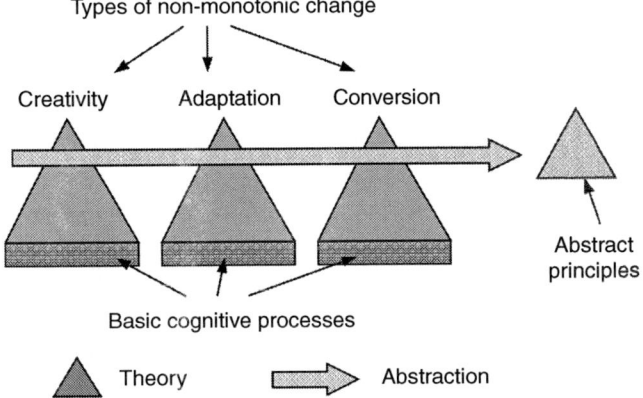

FIGURE 11.1. Structure of the layered research strategy. The micro-theories for creativity, adaptation and conversion are distinct but the abstract principles of the unified theory are instantiated by each.

state of neural matter, or at least neural matter wired the way human brains are wired. Indeed, activity is a prerequisite for neural health. Synapses that do not transmit any signal for a long period of time are pruned from the cortex, and neurons that are not active atrophy and disappear.[15] Because activity is the default state of neural matter, its occurrence has no cause and needs no explanation.

At the cognitive level, it follows that we do not have to explain why cognitive processes occur; that is, we need not explain why, for example, beliefs, concepts, schemas and strategies are greedy for instances and compete to apply. The arrival of stimuli at a sensory surface is sufficient for perceptual processes to engage; a spoken sentence automatically triggers discourse comprehension as well as retrieval of relevant beliefs; and a familiar task automatically activates the relevant strategy. Indeed, the mind does not even need stimulation to be active. While asleep, we dream, and while idle, we daydream. Even stronger evidence is provided by studies of sensory deprivation.[16] People who are awake but placed in a situation where they experience minimal perceptual stimulation do not report a blank mind but streams of thoughts, including visual and auditory sensations and even hallucinations. The generation, activation, application and manipulation of mental representations is the substratum of cognition and it can be assumed in explanations of cognitive phenomena the way the striving of atoms and molecules toward minimal energy states is assumed in explanations of chemical reactions and the universal presence of gravity is assumed in cosmology.

Structured, Unbounded Representations

Mental representations exhibit what psycholinguists call *constituent structure*.[17] A representation consists of components, parts, which themselves are mental representations. Every mental representation at layer N is both a combination of constituents from layer $N-1$ and itself a constituent of some representation of greater complexity or scope at layer $N+1$. The number of layers cannot be determined with any certainty or precision and is likely to vary from one type of representation to another. In perception, many psychological accounts operate with only two layers, visual features and objects, but vision scientists have identified perhaps a dozen distinct layers: features, contours, objects and scenes, with further divisions within each.[18] In the study of discourse comprehension, researchers distinguish between concepts, propositions, text bases and situation models.[19] In the study of cognitive skills, researchers distinguish between actions, individual rules and strategies,[20] and in the study of declarative knowledge,[21] it is necessary to distinguish between concepts, beliefs and belief systems. It matters how the components of a representation are combined. The structure of relations among the components is not imposed *on* the representation, but is an integral part *of* the representation. A representation at layer N can be changed by selecting different elements at layer $N-1$ or by combining them differently.

A repertoire of elements at layer N in conjunction with the rules for how they combine to generate a possibility space at level $N+1$, and the astronomical sizes of such combinatorial spaces guarantee that surprises will never cease. As an example from the material world, the number of different carbon compounds runs into the millions.[22] With respect to the living world, biologists report that there are more ways of making a beetle than one would have thought; taxonomists recognize some 350,000 different species, and that number can only increase over time as evolution throws new species down and naturalists pick them up.[23] In the domain of human creativity, we can ask how many different ways there are to put paint on a canvas: Beetles and painters might be neck and neck with respect to the sizes of their respective possibility spaces. The concept of combination goes a long way toward explaining the diversity and richness of mental representations.

By itself, the concept of a combinatorial space commits us to the counterintuitive conclusion that cognition is bounded in the sense that there is a large but finite and predetermined space of possibilities that we cannot transcend. To reach deeper, we have to recall that the edge of a possibility space is movable, because changes in the underlying layer might generate a different set of elements or new ways of combining them. The projection from layer N to layer $N+1$ creates the space of possibilities at the latter layer, but N is itself created by projection from the preceding layer N-1. Changes in the latter create a different layer N and hence a different possibility space at layer N+1. The linking of at least three layers creates, not a single space of possibilities, but a space of possibility spaces.

A philosopher or a lawyer – specialists in counterarguments – might object that the three-layer model only pushes the problem of a fixed boundary on our cognitive powers one step backward without eliminating it. If the elements and the combination rules at layer N-1 are constant, then the space of possibility spaces is itself finite and bounded. A space of possibility spaces is an awesome construct, providing what for practical purposes might be called infinite variability, especially if we recall that in most cases there are likely to be more than three layers. By the time we work through the combinatorics of, for example, 10 layers, the total set of possibilities might transcend what can be explored in a lifetime, and perhaps in all of human history. Nevertheless, it might seem as if the process of reaching down into the next layer must bottom out at the lowest layer, so, in principle, the total space of possible mental representations is finite and bounded. If the human species survives indefinitely, will we eventually reach a state in which we have formulated every idea that the human brain can conceive?

The conclusion does not follow. First, higher-order layers are feeding back information to lower layers. This means that the elements at the lowest layer, the sense data of positivist epistemology, are not fixed but partially shaped by the higher layers that are built out of them. I know of no reason that a system built on the basis of such circular interactions could not continue to change forever due to its internal dynamics. Second, the processing units at the so-called lowest layer are not fixed but are the result of self-organization among neurons in response to environmental stimulation. Which sensory features we can distinguish in the world depends on which world we live in. As long as the material and social worlds remain turbulent, there will be no fixed lowest layer and hence no limit to change, no principled boundary on our mental representations.

Layered, Selective, Capacity-Limited, Feed-Forward Processing

A processing layer consists of processing units, and each unit in layer N receives inputs from some of the units in layer N-1. Processing layers need not be thought of in physical or spatial terms. They are defined by processing relations: A unit that takes input from another unit is at a higher level than the latter. Choices are made within each unit regarding which operations to execute on its inputs and which computational results to forward to units in the next layer. The key concept is that forward propagation is selective: The results of an operation are only transmitted along some subset of the unit's outbound links. Choices are made on the basis of activation levels that reflect past experience.

In the micro-theory of insight, these concepts are instantiated by the perceptual system. The construction of percepts proceeds through a succession of layers, each layer consisting of processing units – feature detectors, gradient identifiers, contour recognizers, shape extrapolators, movement recorders and so on – which take input from the layer below, manipulate it and, if sufficiently active, pass the result of the manipulation forward to the next layer. The processing units are linked through both excitatory and inhibitory links within each layer. A processing unit is a choice point: A unit is typically linked to more than one successor in the next layer and when a result is fed forward, it might travel along some links but others. The choice in each unit is a function of the activation received from the lower-layer units as well as from surrounding units in the same layer. Each choice point is subject to a capacity limitation; it can only receive so much information per unit of time, it can only perform computations of a certain maximum complexity and it only has so much activation to allocate across its outbound links. Activation is allocated over outgoing links in proportion to their strengths, and when the activation that is allocated to one outgoing link is reduced, that amount is redistributed to the other links, once again proportional to strengths. For the result of a processing unit to be forwarded along an outgoing link, the activation of that link has to be above a certain threshold.

In the theory of cognitive skills, the processing units are goal-situation-action associations, also known as rules. Rules match in parallel, and each rule performs some transformation on the current contents of working memory. The processing is selective because rules compete to fire. The results of executing a rule are fed forward to the next layer of rules by placing those results in working memory. In the theory of declarative knowledge, the elementary unit is a single belief, and the larger structures are arguments, descriptions or explanations. Single beliefs serve as premises for inferences that generate new conclusions, which in turn serve as premises for further inferences.

Ubiquitous Monotonic Learning

A person's knowledge base is continuously extended as a side effect of routine cognitive processing. Perception of an object lays down a trace that makes that very object seem familiar when observed a second time. Repeated performance of a particular task will gradually generate a stock of goal-situation-action associations that encode a habitual response to that task. In routine belief formation, observation and discourse comprehension create a steady stream of novel propositions, most of which are adopted as true and some subset of which are encoded into long-term memory and hence are potentially available for retrieval at a later time. Such monotonic extensions are more automatic than deliberate, virtually continuous and almost effortless. Learning in this sense needs no particular trigger other than the presence of information to be encoded and a modicum of attention and motivation. The probability that the extensions are accessed at some later time is determined by the amount of time between encoding and recall, the amount of intervening memory decay, the type and amount of interference that occurs between encoding and retrieval, the semantic overlap between the original encoding and the subsequent retrieval probe and other variables. The key point is that monotonic cognitive change is continuous, like a mountain stream that never stops flowing. Non-monotonic changes are interruptions, local eddies, that appear here and there in the flow.

Local Coherence and Latent Conflict

The various monotonic extensions of a person's knowledge base are not necessarily consistent with one another. Knowledge structures are accessible only when activated; that is, when they are relevant for the task at hand. A contradiction between a newly created knowledge structure and some prior structure can be discovered only if both are active at the same time. Because the size of a person's knowledge base is very large in relation to the size of his working memory, the probability that two representations will appear in working memory at the same time by chance is minuscule. Capacity limitations also prevent global coherence from being maintained by some special-purpose process. A process that roams over all knowledge structures and inspects every pair of them for conflicts would run for so long that multiple extensions of the knowledge base might have occurred in the meantime, rendering the result of such an inspection obsolete before it is delivered. Cognition operates with local, not global, coherence.

As a consequence, a cognitive conflict can remain latent, that is, undiscovered by the learner himself. The conflict might exist objectively, for an omniscient observer who has access to a complete printout of the person's knowledge base, but not subjectively, for the person himself. For example, categorization processes might create the two categories "government spending" and "incentives for businesses" without the person realizing that both can refer to the same pot of money; skill acquisition processes might create multiple rules that match in the same situations but recommend different, mutually exclusive actions;

and routine belief formation processes might create contradictory beliefs that apply to one and the same domain of experience. Because it is impossible to maintain global coherence, a person's knowledge base is likely to contain multiple conflicts, and such conflicts can remain latent for a long time.

Feedback and Point Changes

Non-monotonic learning requires a mechanism for changing the balance between competing and incompatible processing options. If one option beats its competitors at some moment in time, why does it not continue to do so? If it did, we would be doomed to try and try again the same path that we have tried before, regardless of how unsuccessful it turns out to be. If feed-forward propagation were the sole modus operandi of the cognitive system, as it might be in other mammals and might have been in pre-humans, then we would only be capable of mastering tight contexts that approximate clockwork worlds.

Only change begets change, so a change at one point in the cognitive system must be due to a change elsewhere in the system. What gives creativity, adaptation and conversion their aura of mystery is, in part, that this explanatory principle is circular: If we cannot explain a particular change without referring to a change elsewhere in the system, then we must apparently explain the origin of the latter change in the same way. Consistent with this observation, explanations for non-monotonic changes typically move the change backward one step through the causal links and leave it there: A person breaks out of an impasse by restructuring the perception of the problem – but what caused the restructuring to happen when it did and not earlier or later? What changed? A new idea comes about through a remote connection between two distinct concepts – but why was the person suddenly making a remote connection not made before? What changed? A person forms a new belief in response to anomalous information – but anomalies are always accumulating, so why did this change not happen earlier or later? What changed? Attributing a change to some other change invites the question of how or why the latter change occurred, and this is a problem of the same type and form as the original one and hence has to be dealt with in the same way. There is no obvious way to terminate this regress.

In the present theory, a non-monotonic change at one point in the cognitive system is caused by an altered balance among options at some lower layer. The origin of the latter change lies in the information generated by the activation, articulation and execution of the higher-level knowledge representations. Feedback links carry activation and information from high layers to preceding layers, so that the consequence of a choice at level N will be fed back down to layers N-1, N-2, and so on. Both positive and negative feedback can be passed back down through the processing layers. In the normal case, complex representations send activation down through the layers to keep the simpler representations consistent with themselves. These cases turn up as context effects in psychological experiments: See a drawing as a face and the probability increases that a line in the relevant place is interpreted as a mouth; see a letter sequence as the word "WORD" and the probability of seeing "O" as the letter "O" rather than, say, the digit zero, goes up. Top-down propagation of feedback is usually a stabilizing force.

However, because the choice in each processing unit is massively contingent on the relative levels of activation of the competing options, feedback that propagates down through the system has the potential to tip the balance among the options in some unit. At such tipping points, the top-down feedback might have a destabilizing effect. The perturbation propagates back up through the processing layers and might result in a new representation at some higher level. If the old and new representations are incompatible, then the switch from one to the other looks to an outside observer like a qualitative change of mind. In short, the cause of non-monotonic change is ultimately a change in the balance among competing options at some low-level point in the processing system, caused by the downward propagation of feedback derived from the outcomes of actions.

In the case of negative feedback, a shift in the balance among options occurs because a previously dominant choice is suppressed. In such cases, the key question in understanding the emergence of the new representation is not *how was this new representation accomplished?* but rather, *how and why were the previously active representations inhibited?* All that is needed for something new to appear is that the standard operating procedure, the habitual way of doing or thinking, is suppressed. As Edward Thorndike realized a century ago, in a system that is continuously and spontaneously active, the suppression of one option automatically leads to the execution of some alternative option.[24] A shift in the balance among options can likewise occur by positive feedback that strengthens a previously dormant and hence unexplored option. In such cases, the key question is, *how did such and such an option benefit from the positive feedback being propagated downward through the processing system?* It is possible that many cases of non-monotonic change involve the simultaneous inhibition of prior options and the activation of as yet unheeded ones.

The event that initiates non-monotonic learning is the propagation of feedback – of one sort or the other – through the processing system, and that feedback, in turn, originates in the environment; see Figure 11.2. Feedback is created when the person acts vis-à-vis that environment. The causal chain thus turns back on itself, and the loop is closed without an endless regress. The circular relation between elementary representations, higher-order representations, action and the environment constitutes a dynamic system that never settles.

Amplified Propagation of Point Changes

A change at one point in the cognitive system propagates upward through the layers of processing. The fate of the propagation depends on the exact position of the choice point in the system and how it is linked to other such points. When there is a change at a particular point in the system – a redistribution of activation over alternatives in problem perception, a restriction of range of a single rule of action or an increase in the estimated subjective utility of a belief – that change affects what is forwarded in the propagation process. A change at point X might have little or no consequence, if the difference between the new and the old is absorbed at the next level. A unit X might rise above the relevant threshold and pass its results on to a higher unit Y, but Y itself might remain dormant for lack of activation, so the change at X goes no further. Such *dampened propagation* might cross several layers of processing before it fades. In the normal case, the propagation process supports stability by filtering out perturbations.

In other cases there is *amplified propagation*, popularly known as a butterfly effect. As processing moves forward again after a revised choice at some unit in layer N, it will potentially affect all subsequent layers by feeding each one slightly different inputs than before. A small change at layer N can grow in magnitude at each successive layer. The end product is a qualitatively different representation of the situation or task at hand. In creativity, the point change propagates upward in the perceptual system, possibly resulting in a representational change, but the effects do not end there. A changed representation retrieves different knowledge structures from memory, which in turn means that the search process proceeds through a different space, possibly resulting in a previously unreachable solution. In skill acquisition, a point change – the specialization of a single rule – propagates forward in time: Because the change causes a switch in the sequence of rule firings at some point, the future sequence of rule firings will diverge more and more from the path that the system otherwise would have taken. In belief formation, a switch in a single truth value might start a wave of truth value re-assessments that rolls through the entire belief base.

Elements of a Unified Theory

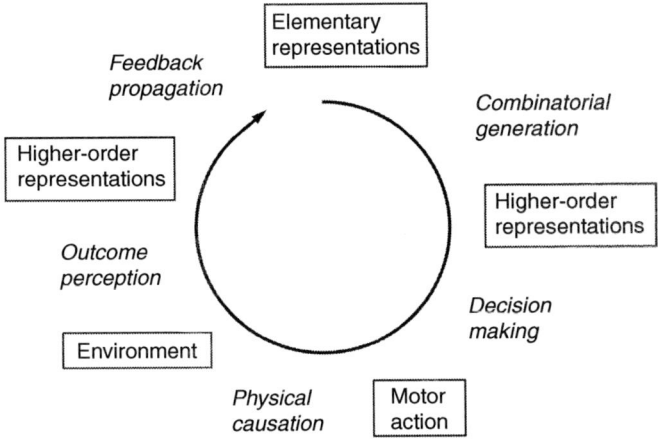

FIGURE 11.2. The deep learning circle.

There might not be any visible effects at the lowest layers; the change becomes noticeable in overt behavior only when it has reached a certain magnitude and begins to affect what the person says and what he does. To the outside observer, this looks mysterious; where did *that* action or *that* utterance come from? Indeed, the person himself might not have conscious access to the layers of representation at which change originated and so might be as surprised as an observer by the effect on his thinking or discourse. The downward propagation of feedback and the upward propagation of a point change work as a team; in conjunction they explicate the phrase *drawing back to leap* into a specific cognitive mechanism.

Whether forward re-propagation from a changed processing unit is dampened or amplified is contingent on the exact distribution of activation levels across the processing system. The construction of a complex mental representation, be it a problem space, a rule set or a belief system, requires a large number of choices, and the choices are made on the basis of the relative activation levels of all the relevant units and links. Activation is in turn an aggregate function of past experience, inputs from lower layers, inputs from excitatory and inhibitory links within the same layer and positive and negative feedback propagating downward from the higher layers. Other factors include the person's goal and the exact distribution of information arriving through perception at each moment in time. The total set of choices behind a particular representation is massively contingent on the exact distribution of action over the entire cognitive system, moment to moment. It is not possible to posses such a detailed map of a person's cognitive system, including the structure and activation of every link and node. Both the occurrence and the magnitude of a non-monotonic change are for all practical purposes unpredictable, and they will remain so even as we increase our understanding of the relevant mechanisms. It does not follow that the study of deep learning cannot be scientific; explanation, not prediction, is the core of science.

Interpretation and Manifest Conflict

Given a rich repertoire of representations, some of which might be incompatible, an object, event, situation or task does not uniquely determine its own interpretation. Its mental representation is co-authored by world and mind. A situation is neither identical to, nor entirely different from previously encountered situations, so it is likely to match each of several representations to some degree but none to perfection. As a result, the situation evokes an array of more or less complete interpretations that might have mutually incompatible implications for action or discourse. Examples include competing interpretations of visual scenes (the Necker cube), alternative ways to parse a sentence (*they are cooking apples*), rules that recommend mutually incompatible actions or subgoals (*left turn, right turn or straight ahead?*), and beliefs that make contradictory claims (*Sun or Earth at the center?*). Such choices are often implicit but become manifest in certain situations such as reversible figures, resource-limited decisions and explicit disagreements.

Competitive Evaluation via Cognitive Utility

Conflicts between multiple incompatible representations of an event, object, situation or task are resolved on the basis of quantitative properties that reflect past experience. The particular quantitative aspects might vary from one processing mechanism to the next. In the context of perceptual processing, alternative interpretations might differ with respect to the levels of activation they receive from the perceptual input, as well as with respect to the strength of the contextual support; how well does the interpretation of an object in a visual scene fit with the overall interpretation of that scene? In the case of skill execution, the production rules in a conflict set might differ with respect to their current relevance, their level of specificity and their cognitive utility. The last is a function of their history of producing successful outcomes. Likewise, competing beliefs and belief systems might over time exhibit higher or lower utility. What remains true across such differences is that choices among alternative, incompatible representations are resolved by the cognitive system on the basis of quantitative properties that reflect past usefulness as well as the current context.

To summarize, the unified theory claims that non-monotonic change occurs through a process that cycles back on itself: Layered, selective and capacity-limited feed-forward processes generate representations that are more or less useful for the tasks a person undertakes. Because there is no mechanism to maintain global coherence, the person might end up creating representations that contradict each other in the sense of depicting materially incompatible states of affairs or recommending mutually exclusive actions. A conflict of this sort might remain latent for some time. It becomes manifest when the conflicting representations happen to be activated at the same time. Selection depends on the relative activation levels among the relevant options. Non-monotonic changes occur when feedback tips the balance among the options available at a particular point in the system. The resulting change is propagated forward through the processing layers. If the propagation is amplified, it might trigger changes of successively greater magnitude at each higher processing layer, until the person finds himself maintaining a different and incompatible problem representation, strategy or belief. The change may or may not take expression in behavior or discourse. See Table 11.2 for brief summaries of the principles. The three micro-theories stated in Chapters 4, 7 and 10 are three different instantiations of these principles for three types of non-monotonic change.

Necessary, Sufficient, or Both?

The question arises whether all the abstract processing principles are necessary conditions for non-monotonic change or whether a cognitive system could be built that only satisfies some of them but nevertheless is capable of non-monotonic change. There is no rigorous way to demonstrate either a positive or negative answer. But if we try to imagine a cognitive system without each of these properties in turn, intuition favors necessity: Without layers of representation, the system is stuck in a single possibility space: If there is no deeper layer to reach into, there is no way to overcome the limitations on the current possibility space. Without selective, feed-forward processing and without feedback links, there is no way of altering the choices made at a lower level. Without the ability to propagate a change through the system, a point change at a lower level might not have any consequences. And so on. Such thought experiments suggest that a cognitive system that can learn from experience must exhibit all the properties described by the abstract principles to be able to override that experience.

TABLE 11.2. *Summary of the deep learning principles.*

Spontaneous Activity:
The cognitive system is continuously and spontaneously manipulating mental representations; activity per se needs no explanation.

Structured, Unbounded Representations:
Representations consist of (less complex) representations. The simplest representations are not fixed but continuously re-shaped by feedback and environmental turbulence.

Layered, Feed-Forward Processing:
Representations are created through a succession of layers, the units in each layer performing certain computations on their inputs and passing their results forward.

Selective, Capacity-Limited Processing:
Each processing unit passes its partial results forward selectively, along some of its outward bound links but not others, due to limits on cognitive processing capacity.

Ubiquitous Monotonic Learning:
The cognitive system is continuously creating new representations in the course of processing and some of those representations are stored in long-term memory.

Local Coherence and Latent Conflict:
The creation of mental representations is not subject to any global coherence check; coherence is only maintained locally. Cognitive conflicts can remain undetected.

Feedback and Point Changes:
Higher processing units feed outcomes of behavior down through the processing layers, possibly tipping the balance among options at a processing unit in some lower layer.

Amplified Propagation of Point Changes:
A change at a single point in the processing system might amplify as it propagates upward through the processing layers, and hence create a new top-level representation.

Interpretation and Manifest Conflict:
Activation of a representation R_A for a domain A in the context of some domain B might reveal that R_A applies to B as well, and thereby makes the R_A-R_B conflict manifest.

Competitive Evaluation and Cognitive Utility:
Conflicts among representations are resolved on the basis of quantitative properties that reflect the past ability of the competing representations to produce successful outcomes.

Are the deep learning principles also collectively sufficient? That is, will a cognitive system that exhibits these properties inevitably undergo non-monotonic change? If such a system lives in a clockwork world in which past experience always and accurately predicts the future, there is no need for non-monotonic change and hence such changes are unlikely to occur. In a turbulent world, on the other hand, the deep learning principles are sufficient to guarantee that a non-monotonic change will occur sooner or later. If negative feedback again and again robs an option of activation, some other, incompatible option must eventually become stronger, given that activity is the natural state of the cognitive system.

The unified theory does not compete with theories of the cognitive architecture. It does not propose an alternative set of basic processes to compete with the processes proposed in various theories of the cognitive architecture. Instead, it places constraints on the latter: If the abstract processing principles in Table 11.2 are indeed both necessary and sufficient for non-monotonic change to occur, then any model of the cognitive architecture, whatever its nature, has to implement those properties, lest it be unable to explain creativity, adaptation or conversion. To the extent that dolphins and chimpanzees are capable of non-monotonic cognitive change, their minds should turn out to instantiate these principles as well. Artificial Intelligence systems and robots, to the extent that we want them to mimic the human capability for non-monotonic change, will have to be built in accordance with the deep learning principles. When space aliens finally land, we should expect their cognitive architecture to instantiate the deep learning principles, unless they borrowed their spaceships from some other species.

EVOLUTIONARY ORIGINS

An explanation for non-monotonic learning, or for any other cognitive function, is stronger if it suggests how that function came into being. How did we acquire the capabilities of creating novelty, adapting to unfamiliar environments and revising our beliefs? In the absence of a hypothesis about origin or source, a computational explanation for a cognitive function is like a rabbit pulled out of a hat. The act of pulling the rabbit out is easy; the trick is to get the rabbit into the hat in the first place. Likewise, a cognitive theory is more plausible if it suggests particular explanations for the origin of the mechanisms it postulates.

A noteworthy feature of the three non-monotonic change mechanisms proposed in this book is that the components of those mechanisms are not themselves non-monotonic processes. That is, the three micro-theories do not hide a homunculus, a black box that carries most of the explanatory burden. There is no "idea generation" box in the theory of insight in Chapter 4, no "flexibility" box in the theory of adaptation from Chapter 7 and no "evidence evaluation module" in the theory of belief revision in Chapter 10. The component processes are either routine processes or monotonic learning processes. They are not exotic and they are not specially designed for the purpose of explaining non-monotonic change. They have typically been proposed to explain a wide range of different cognitive phenomena and they are grounded in prior empirical research. The explanations offered by the micro-theories may or may not be true, but they are complete in the sense of showing how certain subtypes of non-monotonic change can be understood as the emergent result of the interactions among processes that are not themselves non-monotonic change processes.

This observation suggests a particular type of evolutionary explanation: the emergence of new functionality as a side effect of changes in prior structures. This type of explanation is familiar in evolutionary theory, in part due to some long-standing challenges to that theory: What good is half a wing or one-third of an eye? Natural selection is blind to purpose and can only "select" among phenotypes that already exist; it cannot select "for" a function that will be useful to future generations, once that function has grown to sufficient power or versatility. So what drives change during the initial phase of the emergence of a novel adaptation?[25] A common theoretical move for such cases is to assume distinct evolutionary phases in which the emerging adaptation fulfills different functions and hence is subject to different selective pressures. To return once again to the evolution of flight, half a wing might be quite useful as an enlarger of apparent body size, jump stabilizer or thermoregulator. Selective pressure might increase the size of the proto-wing to better fulfill those functions. Once those pressures have provided two-thirds of a wing, the possibilities of, for example, long jumps and glides create a new set of selective pressures that shape the emerging wing to better support flight.

A similar two-stage scenario might have played out with respect to the human capability for cognitive change. The unique evolutionary pathway of human beings – the reliance on learned instead of innate behavior patterns to get through the day – created selective pressures in the direction of increased cognitive ability. If you are going to live by your wits instead of your claws, those wits had better be good. As a result, the different cognitive functions – perception, memory, problem solving, planning and plan execution – increased in complexity and power. As a side effect of this increase in processing power, the mechanisms for routine processing and monotonic learning came to exhibit all the properties specified by the principles in Table 11.2. At that point, non-monotonic change became a possibility. The survival advantages associated with being able to override the imperatives of prior experience in turbulent environments brought new selective pressures to bear that pushed the cognitive system in a new direction. The resulting capability enabled *Homo sapiens* to survive even in environments that changed too quickly and too chaotically for species that rely on innate skills or the monotonic projection of prior experience.

For example, layered processing – the presence of both excitatory and inhibitory links within a layer and the presence of downward feedback links – might have emerged because they improve the accuracy and utility of vision, independent of any need to override prior experience and re-represent unfamiliar situations. But once these features were in place, they provided the possibility of re-perceiving the environment. Likewise, the capability of growing cognitive skills by specializing them might have evolved as a component of the ability to acquire new skills. But once specialization and conflict-resolution mechanisms that are sensitive to specificity were in place, they provided the ability to override an already learned skill as well as creating a new one. Finally, the ability to retrieve declarative representations from memory is useful in a wide range of knowledge-using scenarios, but once this ability was in place, remote associations – bisociations – became possible. For each micro-theory, it is possible to hypothesize selective pressures toward greater capacity that are independent of the need for non-monotonic change but which eventually endowed the relevant cognitive mechanisms with the properties that make such changes possible. This two-phase scenario is speculative but consistent with how complex adaptations evolve.

ON THE DIFFICULTY OF NON-MONOTONIC CHANGE

Scientific theories have many functions. Conceptual advances sometimes support new technologies, but another, equally important function is to help us understand puzzling aspects of life. The most interesting puzzle regarding non-monotonic change is its low probability of occurring. Why are we so eager to push forward but so reluctant to draw back to leap in a new direction? If we are capable, in the sense of possessing the requisite cognitive processes, to see, think, speak and act in novel ways, why do we so often fail to do so when the circumstances call for it? We are stuck on unfamiliar problems – slow to adapt old habits to novel tasks but quick to sweep belief-contradicting information under the cognitive rug. When goal attainment is blocked, our first response is to expand more effort, to execute the tried and true strategies with greater energy, greater attention to detail and higher fidelity to the intended course of action. We push forward before we draw back to leap. Why is this the case, if we evolved a capability for non-monotonic change during the hunter-gatherer era?

The first part of the answer is that the two-stage evolutionary process envisioned in the previous section did not replace monotonic with non-monotonic learning, just as the evolution of vision did not replace the prior senses of smell and touch. The new function was superimposed on top of prior functionality.

The issue of how easy or difficult it is to override past experience is, in part, an issue of balance and priority between monotonic and non-monotonic responses to situations and tasks. Our brains are still designed to prioritize the projection of prior experience, because this cognitive strategy imposes little cognitive load and works well in tight contexts. It is possible that the increase in cognitive ability may have given the human species sufficient control over its survival rate to slow down its own evolution. The capabilities that support routine processing and monotonic learning enabled agriculture, technological innovation, new forms of social interaction, organized protection for children and, eventually, health practices. These factors must have increased the proportion of each generation of humans that lived to reproductive age. Perhaps we are weak non-monotonic learners because evolution toward yet greater capacity for this type of change slowed as the advantages of the already achieved gains in cognitive ability increased the survival rate and hence lowered the selective pressure. Even without this factor, it is likely that the ideal balance between monotonic and non-monotonic change was different for hunter-gatherers who lived short lives under restricted circumstances than it is for people who live through future shock after future shock as the pace of change speeds up.[26] These are speculative but plausible hypotheses. They imply that our cognitive system is biased to prioritize extrapolation over restructuring, projecting past experience over leaping in a new direction.

When we deliberately tackle a project that requires non-monotonic change, we attempt to override this part of our evolutionary programming. But non-monotonic cognitive change is something that happens to a person rather than something he does. It is no easier to control this aspect of brain function with an act of will than it is to exert voluntary control over the operation of the kidneys or the liver. This type of change happens when certain triggering conditions hold and not otherwise, and the probability of non-monotonic change is, in part, determined by the fact that there are multiple such conditions. The relevant cognitive raw materials, the knowledge structures that represent the relevant options, have to have been created by prior monotonic learning and the relevant feedback has to be sufficient to alter the balance among options in one or more choice points. In addition, the distribution of strengths and activation levels across the processing system has to be such that a change at some particular point can propagate through the cognitive system in an amplified way. The probability that all these conditions are at hand simultaneously is low. In short, the built-in preference for monotonic over non-monotonic change, our lack of conscious control over the relevant processes and the dependence of non-monotonic change on the simultaneous occurrence of multiple conditions go a long way toward explaining the low probability of non-monotonic change.

These factors cannot be the whole story, because they affect everyone equally. But some individuals create more than others, behave more flexibly under changing circumstances or show higher willingness to revise their beliefs in the face of new evidence. Such individual differences must be explained by factors that vary from person to person. One traditional approach attributes novelties in thought or action to some unanalyzed power called "creativity," "flexibility," "mindfulness," "tolerance of ambiguity" and so on, or by its opposite (e.g., "perseverance," "rigidity," etc.). Variations in the disposition to restructure are explained by saying that an individual with a long résumé of novel beliefs, ideas or strategies possesses more of this power – however labeled – than individuals with fewer such accomplishments. This way of dealing with individual differences in the disposition for non-monotonic change is circular unless the key explanatory factor – "creativity," "flexibility," "mindfulness" – is analyzed in terms of mental processes and mechanisms.

It is possible that variations in cognitive flexibility – to choose one of the popular terms – can be explained by intrinsic, possibly innate variations in quantitative parameters of the cognitive architecture. For example, people's brains might differ with respect to the total amount of activation that is available to distribute among the relevant cognitive processes. Another possibility is that people differ in the threshold for feed-forward from a processing unit. A high threshold means that only highly activated processing units get to propagate their computational results. This presumably leads to highly effective projection of past experience. A low threshold means that even units with little activation can propagate their results. The consequence might be a high rate of conceptual fluency, ease of making remote connections or other types of behaviors often associated with cognitive flexibility. The size and organization of the various processing systems, especially the density of feedback links, is another factor that might influence the propensity for non-monotonic change. Set the values of such parameters to certain values and the probability of non-monotonic change will turn out to be low; set them to other values and the probability will be higher. There is little reason to expect every brain to be born alike, so the idea that the cognitive architecture exhibits slight quantitative variations from person to person is highly plausible. We do not know how much of the individual differences in the disposition for non-monotonic change might be explained by variations of this sort.

It is consistent with the notion of minor differences in the cognitive architecture that the evidence for the effectiveness of creativity training programs is rather weak.[27] We would not expect innate variations to be directly affected by training. But even if innate differences in the cognitive architecture turn out to be real and influential, it does not follow that the probability of non-monotonic change is fixed or unaffected by what we do. Several aspects of a person's lifestyle that can affect the probability of non-monotonic change are under voluntary control.

To create, adapt or convert, we have to try. In contrast to Picasso's famous comment about finding rather than searching, I claim that deciding to search is a major determinant of the probability of finding.[28] This factor is under voluntary control. We can choose what kinds of projects we undertake, how often we undertake them and how much effort we invest in them. Consistent with this, a recurring feature of the life trajectories of highly creative people is their immense productivity. Creation is hard work. (After six days of it, even a very superior being might feel like taking a day off.) We do not have equally conclusive data with respect to the ability to adapt to novel or changing task environments or the willingness to revise beliefs, but it is plausible that people who change frequently do so because they deliberately seek out situations that require change.

The probability of non-monotonic change is to some extent a function of preparation, the footwork needed to get into a position in which such a change becomes a possibility. For a non-monotonic change to occur, a person has to possess, through prior learning, concepts and skills out of which the novel idea or action can be constructed. To contribute something new to a field of activity, a person has to work long and hard to acquire the requisite building blocks, whether those building blocks belong to the field itself or need to be imported from some neighboring field. Louis Pasteur put this idea succinctly in his famous statement that "in the fields of observation chance favors only those minds which are prepared."[29] This factor is also under voluntary control. We can take Sunday off or we can spend the day reading research articles; we can engage colleagues in small talk or in professionally relevant discussion; we can decide to master new professional tools or we can decide to stick with the known ones; and so on. Building a rich knowledge base is a long-term endeavor and it requires the habits of studying, discussing and practicing.

Closely related to the amount of effort invested in preparation is the variability of personal experience. Some life trajectories go in a circle inside a single environment, while others zigzag from one context to another. We can choose to float easily in the familiar pond or we can subject ourselves to the swells of novel experiences. Sameness creates a narrow range of options, while varied experiences provide a wider range. The experiences we subject ourselves to might not alter our basic cognitive machinery but they supply the content of the knowledge base which in turn determines the range of available options and hence the probability of change. This, too, is under voluntary control.

Everyday discourse makes a sharp distinction between coping with change and initiating change. But from a cognitive point of view, the key feature of either case is the feedback that percolates through the system. Both positive and negative feedback can alter the balance among options. In some cases, positive feedback might elevate a previously unheeded option to win over its competitors. In others, the habitual ways of thought and action might be so entrenched that the person has to subject himself to negative feedback before change can occur. Suppression of past habits, whether of thought or action, has to be strong enough and frequent enough that alternatives are given a chance to demonstrate their cognitive utility. To suffer errors, failures, impasses and other difficulties is for some people an experience to avoid, and the temptation is high to proceed where success comes easy. But we can choose to ignore that temptation and expose ourselves to feedback in general and negative feedback in particular, and we can choose to continue our efforts in the face of repeated and persistent failures and impasses.

In short, choice of projects, level of engagement, time spent in preparation, variability of experience and exposure to negative feedback are five factors that affect the probability of non-monotonic changes and are subject to acts of will. Different individuals make different choices in these respects for reasons that have little to do with the nature of cognition and everything to do with their life situation. Everything else being equal, the person who is born into a situation in which others show little appreciation of, and no support for the intense work required to build a vast knowledge base will be less prepared to undertake creative projects than someone at the opposite end of that dimension. The influence of life trajectory on the disposition for non-monotonic change is better studied with the techniques of the biographer and the novelist than with those of the cognitive psychologist. The important point for present purposes is that differences among individuals in the disposition for non-monotonic change is, in part, due to differences in life trajectories and hence do not necessarily imply deep or intrinsic differences among their cognitive architectures.

Indeed, the relation between variables like "flexibility" and a person's record of creative achievements, successful adaptations and belief conversions is likely to be the opposite of the one commonly supposed: Every person responds to some situations by projecting prior experience and to others by drawing back to leap. When a leap results in a good outcome, we look back over the event and say that the person behaved creatively, flexibly or with an open mind; if the outcome was negative or unproductive, we describe the person in less flattering ways. Non-monotonic change is not caused by some mysterious power called "adaptability," "creativity" or "open-mindedness." The situation is the other way around: It is the occurrence of non-monotonic changes (with positive outcomes) in a person's life trajectory that causes us, as observers, to use such labels. If a person's life trajectory exhibits a sustained streak of non-monotonic changes with positive outcomes, we characterize him in one way; if his life develops in a different way, we describe him differently. The attribution of differences among individuals to differences in unanalyzed powers like "adaptability," "creativity" or "mindfulness" is a post facto characterization, not a cause and hence not an explanation, for differences in the disposition for non-monotonic change.

When we list the factors that affect the probability of non-monotonic change, its low probability of occurrence ceases to be mysterious: Minds are programmed by evolution to push forward before drawing back to leap, the relevant cognitive processes are not under voluntary control and the occurrence of a change requires the simultaneous occurrence of multiple conditions. The latter may be hindered or facilitated by cognitive parameters like working memory capacity and retrieval thresholds. Even with favorable values on the architectural parameters, non-monotonic changes are unlikely unless a person undertakes projects that require such changes, works hard at them, engages in extensive preparations, subjects himself to varied experiences and exposes himself to negative feedback. Taken together, these factors explain why non-monotonic change is difficult even in the presence of cognitive mechanisms that make such changes possible. Alternative theories of deep learning are no doubt possible, but any satisfactory theory must explicate this dialectic between difficulty and possibility.

12

The Recursion Curse

> ... *all inferences from experience suppose, as their foundation, that the future will resemble the past.... It is impossible, therefore that any arguments from experience can prove this resemblance of the past to the future, since all such arguments are founded on the supposition of that resemblance.*
>
> David Hume[1]

> ... *predictions based on some regularities are valid while predictions based on other regularities are not.... To say that valid predictions are those based on past regularities, without being able to say* which *regularities, is thus quite pointless.*
>
> Nelson Goodman[2]

If the deep learning thesis is at least approximately correct, our cognitive processes not only endow us with cognitive mechanisms for learning new knowledge and skills but also allow us to override what we have learned. The three micro-theories of creativity, adaptation and conversion describe cognitive mechanisms that accomplish this. It would be foolish to claim that the micro-theories are exactly accurate. Further research will no doubt force revisions. However, there is no reason to expect the fundamental principle that knowledge is, and must be, defeasible to be contradicted by future research. This feature of cognition is grounded in the ceaseless turbulence of the material and social worlds and in our evolutionary strategy of relying more on acquired skills than on innate behaviors.

The consequence is that we sometimes succeed by projecting the past onto the current situation, but at other times we do better if we override prior experience and generate a novel response to the situation at hand. The choice between extrapolation and drawing back to leap is, in part, under voluntary control and it seems possible that we could become more disposed to override prior experience and consequently experience a higher rate of non-monotonic change. But the paradoxical implication of turbulence is that a higher rate of change will not necessarily be associated with a higher level of success. A stronger disposition to change might not by itself be useful unless we can also learn something about the conditions under which we are better off projecting prior experience and the conditions under which we are better off drawing back to leap. The ideal is not to change with high frequency, but to project prior experience when the situation at hand is like prior situations and hence does in fact lend itself to be handled on the basis of experience, and to draw back and leap when the situation at hand is, in fact, essentially different and requires a novel response.

It is tempting to believe that we can learn to differentiate one class of situations from the other, and hence become more accurate in choosing between extrapolating and leaping. After all, a person's lifetime contains many examples of both types of situations, and the study of history extends that database over generations. If we analyze this accumulated experience from the deep learning point of view, we might be able identify conditions that reliably characterize situations in which we should project rather than leap and vice versa, and so improve the accuracy of our choices.

A moment of reflection reveals the fallacy hiding in this temptation. Our knowledge of the situations in which projection worked well and the situations in which drawing back to leap worked better is itself a strand in our past experience. It is subject to the same turbulence as all experience: We cannot know whether our past experience of when past experience is useful, is itself useful in any future situation. That is, we cannot project whatever experience we have of projecting past experience onto the next situation. Are we better off overriding that experience and making choices as to when to project and when to override in some novel way? The argument against the projectability of past experience applies recursively to our past experience of projecting past experience; similar with our experience of drawing back to leap. In programming terminology, turbulence is recursive; that is, it applies to itself. Hence, we cannot, even in principle, learn from experience when to project prior experience and when to override it.

Philosophers recognize this as a version of "Hume's problem" or "the problem of induction."[3] David Hume asked an epistemological question: How can we know that a regularity induced from past examples is true of the entire set that the examples were drawn from? The problem, said Hume, is that if we apply a principle of inductive inference, what guarantees the validity of that principle? If the principle is itself a generalization over successful past inductions, then the defense of our inductive inferences is circular: They are justified with reference to a principle of inductive inference that is itself the result of induction over past experiences.

There are differences between Hume's formulation of the problem and mine. The point made in this book is not epistemological but psychological. The problem of generalization, of inducing new regularities from particulars, is not as problematic for a psychologist as it was for Hume: It is an empirical fact that people construct generalizations, and the task of the psychologist is primarily to describe how, by what processes, they arrive at those generalizations and only secondarily to comment on their validity. My argument presupposes that a person does in fact possess general knowledge structures and that some of those structures do in fact apply to at least some of the situations in which he finds himself. The psychological question is not whether he ought to apply them but how, by what processes, he decides whether to apply them. Does he conclude that the situation at hand belongs to a tight context in which regularities from past experience can safely be projected, or that there is enough turbulence that the situation needs to be handled by drawing back and leaping in a novel direction? The theory of deep learning is an attempt to explain when and why people take one or the other route, not to evaluate whether their choices tend to be correct.

Another difference between the argument of this book and Hume's problem is that the present argument does not locate the source of the difficulty in epistemic practices or in our cognitive system but in the world itself. Hume did not doubt that there are valid regularities to be discovered. The difficulty, as he saw it, is to identify the valid ones and to know with certainty that the identification is correct. In his perspective, there is hope that a rigorous justification for inductive inferences will one day be found. We do not have one now because we have not thought of it yet. Indeed, in Hume's own words, "... a man is guilty of unpardonable arrogance who concludes, because an argument has escaped his own investigation, that therefore it does not really exist."[4] In the deep learning perspective, the matter stands differently. The world is a turbulent, complex system in which change is the only constant and the laws of change are themselves changing; reality has no rock bottom. The problem of projectability arises out of the characteristic turbulence of reality, so no general, once-and-for-all solution is possible.

The upshot is that as we go through life, circumstances will force us to make judgments about whether to project prior experience or whether to override it, but the decision cannot be reduced to a set of rules. Sometimes we hit it right and sometimes we do not. The best we can do is to remember that turbulence is ubiquitous and thoroughgoing and to be mindful of the need to choose. It helps to stop occasionally on the walk along the river of life, put the backpack down and observe the flow of the water. Notice how the eddies along the riverbank emerge and disappear and re-emerge, but never in exactly the same spot. If you lean closer to observe better, the river sprays water in your face. The bubbling sound you hear is Mother Nature chuckling at her own joke. Change is life.

NOTES

CHAPTER 1. THE NEED TO OVERRIDE EXPERIENCE

1. Heraclitus, fragment 12; Sweet (1995), p. 7.
2. Hume (1777/1910), p. 315.
3. The passage from pre-modern to modern science – the Scientific Revolution, in capitals – in the 16th and 17th centuries has been described many times, e.g., Butterfield (1957), Hall (1956), Henry (2002) and Westfall (1971). Shapin (1998) is recent and highly readable.
4. For different views of the scientific revolution in astronomy, see, e.g., Koyré (1958), Kuhn (1957) and Margolis (1987, 1993).
5. Casper and Noer (1972), Chapters 4–7, Dugas (1955/1988) and Einstein and Infeld (1938), Chapter 1.
6. The search for the chemical elements and the rules by which they combine is described in Brock (1993), Greenaway (1966), McCann (1978), Strathern (2000) and Toulmin and Goodfield (1962).
7. Shapin (1998), p. 32, italics in original. Other historians of science concur: "The ideal of a clockwork universe was the great contribution of seventeenth-century science to the eighteenth-century age of reason" (Butterfield, 1957, p. 150). And again: "The mechanical philosophy saw the workings of the natural world by analogy with machinery; change was brought about (and could be explained in terms of) the intermeshings of bodies, like cogwheels in a clock, or by impact and the transference of motion from one body to another" (Henry, 2002, p. 69). Peterson (1993) associates the clock metaphor with the scientific revolution in astronomy, but Ruse (2002) locates its origin in the works of Robert Boyle.
8. The physics of turbulence is complicated enough to be beyond my mathematical competence; see Nelkin (1994). For present purposes the commonsense concept suffices.
9. There are many attempts to summarize the essence of the complex systems revolution in science for the educated layperson. Gleick (1987) was one of the first and remains one of the best. Lewin (1992) and Waldrop (1992) are very readable. Among serious introductions for people with scientific training, Ford (1992), Laughlin (2005), Nicolis (1992) and Prigogine (1997) focus on physics, while Camazine et al. (2001), Kauffman (1993) and Raff (1996) focus on the biological

sciences. Ormerod (1998) applies complex system concepts to social and economic behavior. Bak (1996) has something to say about all these fields.
10. Weinberg (1977).
11. See Callander (1978) for a review of research on river meandering.
12. The contrast between reversible and irreversible processes is now seen by many scientists as fundamental for understanding nature; see, e.g., Denbigh (1989) for a review of different types of irreversible processes and Prigogine (1997) for a strong statement of the role of irreversibility in the material world. The first physical science in which lack of reversibility played a central role was thermodynamics, although Uffink (2003) has questioned the oft-claimed link between irreversibility ("time's arrow") and the Second Law of Thermodynamics (i.e., the statement that entropy is always increasing). In biology, species have of course been seen as historical entities ever since Darwin. See Gould (2002), Chapter 2, for a reading of Darwin as the inventor of a historical methodology for biology.
13. Regarding the values of physical constants, astrophysicist Neil de Grasse Tyson (2004) writes: "... in recent decades a lot of physicists have been looking for evidence that constants don't hold for all eternity.... there's practically a cottage industry of physicists desperately seeking fickle constants. Some are looking for a change across time; others, for the effects of a change in location; still others are exploring how the equations operate in previously untested domains" (p. 24). For a cosmological theory based on the assumption that the universe, including the basic physical constants, evolves, see, e.g., Smolin (1992).
14. Callander (1978): "Rivers carry the products of erosion as well as water, and in meanders, some sediment is transported by scour and fill. Scour takes place on the outer banks of the bends and deposition on the inner banks ..." (p. 129).
15. "*Self-organization is a process in which a pattern at the global level of a system emerges solely from numerous interactions among the lower-level components of the system* ... the pattern is an emergent property of the system, rather than a property imposed on the system by an external ordering influence ... emergent properties are features of a system that arise unexpectedly from interactions among the system's components ..." (Camazine et al., 2001, p. 8, italics in original).
16. See Bonabeau et al. (1997). Ormerod (1998) compares anthills with human economic and social behavior.
17. For example, a firm is a set of interacting employees and can hence be represented as a network with individuals as nodes and communication channels (face-to-face contacts, e-mail, etc.) as links. But firms interact in the relevant market, so a market (or at least some markets) can be represented as a network with firms as nodes and interactions as links. In this case, an interaction might be that a person leaves one firm and becomes an employee of another. The processes of exchanging E-mails and of exchanging employees are very different in their material details, but they both generate network structures. Particular network phenomena such as the small-world effect (Watts, 1999) might appear at either level, because they are independent of the material properties of the nodes and links. This point was made by von Bertalanffy (1968/1973) in an earlier incarnation of complex systems theory.

18. The observation was first made by Mandelbrot (1967); see Gleick (1987), p. 95, for a nonmathematical exposition. Mandelbrot (1983), Chapter 6, explored many geometrical examples of self-similarity.
19. One side in this debate is represented by S. J. Gould, who argued that species represent one level in a hierarchy of levels and that selection occurs at every level (Gould, 2002, Chap. 8). The other side of the debate is represented by R. Dawkins, who argues that selection applies only at a single level, namely, that of genes (Dawkins, 1976).
20. The idea that the interaction between supply and demand will drive the price of an economic good to a stable level is a basic concept that is covered in any textbook in micro-economics.
21. Koestler (1966); see also Koestler (1964, Book Two) and Koestler (1972).
22. See Alvarez (1998) for a popular account of this hypothesis.
23. Prigogine (1997), p. 26.
24. Peterson (1993), p. 270.
25. Peirce (1878b/1992), p. 193.
26. Hough (2004) provides a summary of what is known about earthquakes. "Seismology is, in many ways, a non-repeatable science ..." (p. 109).
27. Cox (2005).
28. For example, the 15th-century genius Leonardo da Vinci drew the flow of turbulent water, apparently in an effort to understand it better; see, e.g., Plates 241 and 243 in Zöllner (2006). Leonardo's complete paintings and drawings have been collected by Zöllner and Nathan (2003). Many of the drawings can be viewed at *www.universalleonardo.org* and at *www.drawingsofleonardo.org*.
29. See Note 9, this chapter.
30. The first Western works that are widely recognized as works of history in the modern sense are *The Histories* (a.k.a. *The Persian Wars*), a description of the Greco-Persian Wars by Herodotus (484–414 B.C.), and *The History of the Peloponnesian War* by Thucydides (460–400 B.C.). Their works antedate the first works that we now recognize as scientific in the modern sense by 1,500 years.
31. The idea that history passes through a fixed sequence of ages or eras, each age being less happy than the previous one, is stated in Hesiod's poem, *Works and Days*, lines 97–204, written in the eighth century B.C., and in Ovid's *Metamorphoses*, lines 89–150, written in the first decade A.D. This idea has often been combined with the idea that time is cyclic, so that at the end of the sequence, the Golden Age reappears (Lovejoy & Boas, 1935/1997, Chap. 2). This view was held by the Stoics, among others (Whitrow, 1989, Chap. 4). The idea that the Western conception of history has evolved from cyclic to linear is generally accepted but has been disputed by Press (1977). Sciences like climatology, evolution and thermodynamics are firmly on side of linear time.
32. Bernstein (2004), Cheyney (1924), Harris (1968), esp. Chapters 2, 5 and 8, Snooks (2002) and Tainter (1990).
33. The Industrial Revolution is as popular among authors as the scientific one. See, e.g., Ashton (1948/1969), Bernstein (2004), Mokyr (1992, 1993) and Stearns (1998).

34. Lukacs (2001) describes the five desperate days in May 1940 when Churchill's insistence that Britain stand up to Germany was translated from personal stance into national policy. The societal level of analysis that attributes the Allied victory to, among other factors, the ability to mobilize mass production for the war effort, is developed by Overy (1996).
35. Gaddis (2002), p. xi.
36. See Levinson (2006, pp. 272–273) for the quote about shipping containers. Some analysts believe that economic systems like markets exhibit a turbulence of their own; see, e.g., Foster (2005), Mandelbrot and Hudson (2004), Ormerod (1998) and Taleb (2007). For reflections on the unpredictability of events in politics and international relations, see, e.g., Bernstein, Lebow, Stein and Weber (2000), Blyth (2006) and Kuran (1995). Regarding the failure to predict the fall of the Berlin wall in 1987, specifically, see, e.g., Meyer (2009).
37. Exactly what is and what is not innate has been the subject of controversy ever since the publication of Francis Galton's *Hereditary Genius* (Galton, 1892/1962) and Charles Spearman's groundbreaking 1904 article in which he proposed the concept of general intelligence (Spearman, 1904). Recent entries into the debate include the politically inflammatory *The Bell Curve* by R. J. Herrnstein and C. Murray (Herrnstein & Murray, 1994), as well as *The Blank Slate* by Steven Pinker (Pinker, 2002). The evidence for an innate component to general intelligence is thin but consistent. Performance on tests of cognitive ability correlate to a statistically significant degree even when the tests are very different in character; see Carroll (1993). Genetics add another piece of evidence; see Bouchard and McGue (1981) for a review of several hundred studies that relate genetic distance to similarity in IQ test scores, and Posthuma and de Geus (2006) for molecular correlates to IQ test performance. The problem with all studies of this sort is that there is little or no reason to believe that IQ tests measure anything significant. The empirical evidence for innate components is stronger with respect to a small number of specific cognitive domains, primarily language (Crain & Pietrovski, 2002; Laurence & Margolis, 2001), number knowledge (Starkey, Spelke & Gelman, 1990) and, especially, music (McDermott & Hauser, 2005). But the strongest reason to believe in an innate basis for any cognitive ability is not the research evidence but the sheer implausibility of the idea that all brains are born exactly alike; why would they be? Whether innate differences are of such a sort and such a magnitude that they matter for everyday life is a separate question.
38. To highlight the contrast between animal and human learning, compare Moore's (2004) review and synthesis of the mechanisms identified in animal learning with the hypotheses regarding human acquisition of skills proposed to date (Ohlsson, 2008a) and human acquisition of declarative knowledge (Chi & Ohlsson, 2005). See also Tomasello's (1999a, b) attempts to explain the contrasts between animals and humans in terms of the ability of infants to observe, understand and imitate the actions, physical as well as symbolic, of other humans. With respect to the qualitative difference between human and animal language learning, see S. R. Anderson (2004).

39. Tool use, drawing and language emerge naturally and without obvious strain or stress in normal infants. Although behavioral researchers disagree whether tool use is best seen as an extension of perceptual-motor activity (Lockman, 2000) or as a form of problem solving (McCarty, Clifton & Collard, 2001), there is now neuroscience evidence that "behaviors associated with complex tool use arise from functionally specialized [neural] networks" (Johnson-Frey, 2004, p. 71), i.e., that tool use is supported by special features of our brains. Although it might take a team of dedicated cognitive scientists several years to teach 150 words to a chimpanzee, all normal children learn thousands of words spontaneously and seemingly effort-free. There is a long-standing argument, originally formulated by Noam Chomsky and known as *the argument from the poverty of the stimulus*, to the effect that language is supported by special innate capabilities. Crain and Pietroski (2002) show how this argument explains why "language acquisition is a snap." I know of no similar argument with respect to drawing, but the tendency to draw emerges spontaneously; see, e.g., Gardner (1980) and Lambert (2005).
40. For the idea that biological evolution and cognitive change are mechanisms for tracking change in the environment at two different time scales, see Plotkin (1994), especially Chapter 5.
41. Semon introduced the term "engram" in 1904 in a book called *Die Mneme*, written in his native German. Schacter (2001) describes the history of this contribution; see Chapter 7.
42. Describing experiments in which rats first acquired the skill ("habit") of finding their way through a maze, then had a portion of their brain removed and finally were observed as they tried to navigate the maze again, Lashley (1929) wrote, "It is certain that the maze habit, when formed, is not localized in any single area of the cerebrum and that its performance is somehow conditioned by the quantity of tissue which is intact. It is less certain, though probable, that all parts of the cortex participate equally in the performance of the habit …" (p. 107). Neuroscience evidence gathered since then has not confirmed this holographic view of memory at the neural level. The evidence points rather to multiple, separate brain systems (Rolls, 2000). For example, localized lesions sometimes give rise to very content-specific impairment in a person's knowledge (Caramazza & Shelton, 1998).
43. There are many textbooks in cognitive psychology that cover what is known about memory, e.g., Anderson (2004), Goldstein (2008) and Reisberg (2006).
44. The history of the supposed process that cognitive scientists variously refer to as abstraction, generalization and induction stretches across two millennia. Aristotle wrote that multiple perceptions form universal categories (e.g., in the *Posterior Analytics*, Book II, 19: 100a, 1–15). The British empiricist philosopher David Hume (1777/1910) is responsible for posing the problem of justifying inductive inferences in a way that was so intractable as to provide centuries of work for philosophers: To say that inductive inferences have been shown to be accurate in the past and therefore likely to be accurate in the future seems circular, so how can such inferences be justified instead? This formulation of the problem turned out to be so intractable that philosophers eventually decided to abandon it; see Goodman (1954/1983) for an attempt to reformulate the problem. A closely related

issue is how multiple instances support a generalization. Intuition suggests that more instances provide more support, but this notion has also turned out to be intractable. There are many attempts to use probability theory to produce a calculus of corroboration (Hàjek & Hall, 2002), but no such calculus is perceived as successful. In psychology, the idea that people extract commonalities from sets of exemplars is implicitly presupposed by most researchers. One explicit formulation, the prototype theory of concept formation, claims that people compute the mean (or some other statistic) of each relevant dimension across the set of exemplars seen so far. These are assembled into a representation of a typical member of the relevant category; the category is then defined in terms of that prototypical (but possibly fictional) member. Experiments in which people are asked to rate the familiarity of members of a category that they have not, in fact, seen before, shows a strong tendency to rate such members as familiar if they are close to the mean of the set of seen exemplars on the relevant dimensions (Posner & Keele, 1968; Solso & McCarthy, 1981). However, such results are obtained with artificial stimuli that only vary in a small number of dimensions. It is not clear how prototype formation would operate in real life. (What is the average of a sofa and a rug, two instances of the category "furniture"?) The importance attached to prototype theory among experimental psychologists testifies to the enduring appeal of induction. However, the difficulties in understanding how any inductive process could possibly work makes it unlikely that a process of this type plays a central role in human cognition.

45. "…the problem of prediction from past to future cases is but a narrower version of the problem of projecting from any set of cases to others" (Goodman, 1954/1983, p. 83).
46. See Note 43, this chapter.
47. The reader is referred to journals like *Cognition*, *Memory & Cognition*, *Cognitive Psychology*, *Cognitive Science*, *Journal of Experimental Psychology: Learning, Memory, and Cognition*, and dozens of others.
48. Butterworth and Laurence (2005).
49. I have been unable to locate any in-depth treatment or hard data on the role of predator-prey cycles on the evolution of hunter-gatherers during pre-history; research has focused on the impact in the opposite direction.
50. Potts (1996), p. 168. The best theory of human origins says that *Homo sapiens* evolved in Africa, close to the tropics, and later migrated. Hence, there must have been a moment in the history of the human species when humans saw snow for the very first time. The image of them standing on a hilltop and watching in amazement as a snowstorm unfolds is of course grounded in nothing but dramatic license; walking across isolated patches of snow might be more likely, albeit less picturesque. The factual point is that our hunter-gatherer ancestors lived outdoors, so the weather was obviously a factor in their lives. Climate changes typically appear over a long enough time period that they might not be experienced in their entirety by any one person. However, some authors have argued that at least some climate changes might have occurred so abruptly that they might have constituted learning experiences, events to be tracked by cognition rather than by evolution. The attempt to trace the importance and influence

of climate on our evolutionary history is a minor academic cottage industry; see Burroughs (2005), Calvin (1991), Fagan (2005), Potts (1996) and Stanley (1998), among others.

51. Periods of sudden population growth in pre-history are well documented (Bar-Yosef, 1992; Steiner et al., 1999). Warfare has been with us since the beginning of the archeological record (Keely, 1997).
52. The mathematical term "monotonic" applies to a function f, $y = f(x)$, if f is such that every increase (decrease) in the value of x yields an increase (decrease) in the value of y. For example, $y = f(x) = 2x + 3$ is a monotonic function. In contrast, if f is non-monotonic, an increase in the value of x might yield a decrease in the value of y, or vice versa. For example, $y = x^2$ is non-monotonic, because an increase from $x = 2$ to $x = 4$ yields an increase in y from 4 to 16, while an increase from $x = -4$ to $x = -2$ yields a decrease in the value of y, from 16 to 4. In logic, the term "monotonic" is applied metaphorically to a formal logical system in which the inference rules can only add further consequences of already proven propositions. A non-monotonic logical system, in contrast, includes rules for inferring that some previously accepted proposition needs to be rejected in the light of new information. The logical systems developed in the 19th century and first half of the 20th by George Boole, Augustus De Morgan, Gottlob Frege, Bertrand Russell, Alfred North Whitehead and others were monotonic (Kneale & Kneale, 1962/1984). Non-monotonic logics were developed by Artificial Intelligence researchers in the late 1970s and early 1980s (McCarthy, 1980; McDermott & Doyle, 1980; Reiter, 1980). The application of non-monotonic logics to the analysis of human reasoning is recent; see Ford (2005). Applying the term to learning, I refer to learning that augments or extends a person's knowledge base without revision of prior knowledge as *monotonic* and learning that forces revisions in prior knowledge as *non-monotonic*.
53. Kuhn (1977).
54. A. I. Miller (2001), Chapter 4, offers an analysis of how Picasso painted *Les Demoiselles d'Avignon* that highlights the roots of this painting in the intellectual movements within science at the time. Hence, the painting was, in a sense, an adaptation to changes in Picasso's conceptual environment. Once it became widely known, other painters had to adapt to it in some way or another.

CHAPTER 2. THE NATURE OF THE ENTERPRISE

1. Cummins (2000, p. 120).
2. Newell, Shaw and Simon (1958, p. 151).
3. For a history of chemistry, see, e.g., Brock (1993). Regarding the discovery of the structure of DNA, see Oldby (1974/1994). The volume of essays edited by Oreskes (2003) describes the emergence of plate tectonic theory; it should be read in the context of the facts that threaten to falsify that theory (Pratt, 2000).
4. The best summary and overview of the behaviorist approach to learning is Hilgard and Bower's (1966) textbook. The best summary and overview of Piaget's theory of cognitive change is Flavell (1963); see Furth (1968, 1969) for an analysis of Piaget's theory of knowledge.

5. World War II brought the development of what we now recognize as information technologies in the course of code breaking, radar, signal interception, sonar and other information-processing problems. It also brought engineers and psychologists into closer contact. The consequence was the application of information-processing concepts to problems regarding human cognition, the defining feature of modern cognitive psychology. Baars (1986) and Gardner (1985) tell the story in their different ways.
6. See Misiak and Sexton (1973) for a historical review of the phenomenological movement. The approach to cognitive psychology that most directly incorporated phenomenological elements is Gestalt psychology (Köhler, 1976, Chap. 3). Varela, Thompson and Rosch (1993) draw upon phenomenological modes of inquiry in their attempt to reformulate what cognitive science is, or should be, about.
7. For a review of research on tip-of-the-tongue states, see Brown (1991); for an example of a study, see Gollan and Acenas (2004).
8. The reductionist approach aims to solve the conceptual mind-brain knot by cutting it in half and throwing away the mental half. P. M. Churchland (1995, pp. 318–324), has even suggested that once a valid and relatively complete neuropsychological theory is in hand and has been found to be useful in practical affairs, it will spread into the popular culture and ultimately replace the folk psychology based on decisions, memories, thoughts and so on. P. S. Churchland (1996) likewise thinks that it "remains to be seen whether there is a neurobiological reality to sustain notions such as 'belief' and 'desire'" (p. 286). But see Penfield (1975), especially Chapter 20, for a neuroscientist who reached the opposite conclusion. The reductionist perspective has also invaded the self-help literature; see Dispenza (2007), Rock (2006) and others for attempts to go straight from knowledge of the brain to prescriptions for self-improvement while dispensing with mentalistic concepts. An even more radical form of reductionism attempts to understand consciousness in terms of quantum physics (Penrose, 1991; Woolf & Hameroff, 2001). It is ironic that reductionism has gained strength in psychology at the same time that it has fallen out of fashion in the natural sciences; see, e.g., Kauffman (1993), Laughlin (2005), Prigogene (1997) and Raff (1996). Not all scientists share this orientation; Weinberg (2001) is a persistent defender of reductionism in physics. In my opinion, neither reductionism nor anti-reductionism is a valid position. The more fruitful approach is to posit multiple levels of description and figure out how they are related (e.g., Anderson, 2005).
9. Behaviorism was a radical school of psychology that flourished in the first half of the 20th century, conventionally dated as beginning with John B. Watson's (1913) article. The basic principle of behaviorism is that the structure of behavior mirrors the contingencies of the environment, where the contingencies can take the form of contiguity, fixed sequences, conditional probabilities or action-reward relations. Learning consists of forming associative links that encode such environmental contingencies. See, e.g., Schultz (1969, Chaps. 10 and 11), for an overview and Buckley (1989) for a biography of the founder.

10. J. J. Gibson (1966) advocated *an ecological approach* to perception which assumed that there is information in the environment and that the task of our perceptual systems is to identify it and to receive it; no complicated processing is required. For example, ambient light contains information about relative distance in the form of degree of clarity of the retinal image. Close objects have sharp edges while distant objects look fuzzy. Register this information and relative distance judgments follow. This type of analysis applies to auditory perception as well (Gaver, 1993). In a different take on this theme called *rational analysis*, J. R. Anderson (1989, 1990) proposed that if the human mind evolved to be rational, or nearly so, then an analysis of the environment and the tasks that the mind performs is sufficient to predict regularities in behavior. If there is only one best way to perform a task and if our minds evolved to perform it that way, then we should be able to predict behavior by assuming that the mind performs the task in that way. All we need to explain behavior is the right analysis of the task. Some regularities regarding memory can indeed be derived from the assumption that processes such as retrieval conform to statistical regularities in the environment (Anderson & Schooler, 1991, 2000). Pirolli (2005) analyzed information foraging on the Web in this manner. See Oaksford and Chater (1998) for yet other applications of rational analysis. The question is how much insight we gain into the workings of the mind from predictions of behavior, even accurate predictions, derived from environmental regularities. These lines of work are closely related to Artificial Intelligence work on embodied cognition (M. L. Anderson, 2003).
11. See Cole, Engeström and Vasquez (1997) for a collection of papers that explicate and exemplify the anthropological approach to cognition. D'Andrade (1995) has written a history of this line of inquiry. For a statement of the related situated cognition approach to learning, see Clancey (1997) and Lave and Wenger (1991). This approach is not without its critics; see Vera and Simon (1993) and the response by Greeno and Moore (1993).
12. My favorite example is the study of navigation practices aboard U.S. Navy ships by Hutchins (1995).
13. Pylyshyn (1986, pp. 6–7).
14. Varela, Thompson and Rosh (1993) and Clancey (1997) have tried to formulate nonrepresentational theories of cognition. The skepticism regarding representational theories is not new. Furth (1968, 1969) scrutinized the role of representation in J. Piaget's developmental theory and concluded that "... knowing in Piaget's theory is never a mere matter of representation" (p. 150).
15. Visual mnemonic techniques were invented in antiquity (Yates, 1969). The earliest extant description of the technique known as the *system of loci* is by Cicero in *De Oratore* (*On the ideal orator*, II:350–360), completed in 55 B.C. The key idea in this mnemonic technique is to first visualize a series of familiar places or locations (*loci*), to form visual images of objects that correspond to the content to be memorized, and then "place" those images in the locations. To retrieve the content, imagine "visiting" the locations in order and encountering the visual reminder "placed" in each. In the late 16th century, the Jesuit missionary Matteo Ricci gained the confidence and respect of Chinese scholars and civil servants by

demonstrating this and other memory systems, a moment in history when the choice of mental representation might have had a decisive effect on world events (Spence, 1985). For experimental confirmation of the effectiveness of visual mnemonics, see, e.g., Bower (1972), Bower and Reitman (1972), Crovitz (1971), Peters and Levine (1986) and Richardson (1978). The effects of visual mnemonics are robust enough to have educational applications; see Higbee (1979) and Peters and Levin (1986). For a wider perspective on imagery beyond mnemonics, see Finke (1989), Kosslyn (1980) and Richardson (1969).

16. I am exercising a certain amount of poetic license in my portrayal of the tragedy of the moth. Although everyone agrees that (some species of) moths fly toward lights (under certain conditions), even when this leads to their demise, there is no consensus about the mechanism behind this behavior. The most commonly stated idea is that moths evolved to navigate at night by moonlight and that they confuse artificial lights with the moon. By trying to keep a constant angle between the light rays and their flight path, they trick themselves into constant course corrections that result in a spiral path that ends at the light. This view is often stated in online sources; see, e.g., http://e.wikipedia.org/wiki/Moth#Attraction_to_light.

But, as James K. Adams at Dalton State College points out, there is no experimental proof of this explanation, and it does not explain why some moths fly straight at a light; see http://butterflies.freeservers.com/moth_light.html.

Field observations are necessary to resolve this puzzle, but there appears to have been no program of experimental work devoted to ascertaining moth flight paths under controlled conditions since Hsiao (1972, 1973). Direct neural pathways between eyes and the wings should not be taken too literally; the moth nervous system, although small in size, is nevertheless quite complicated. However, in locusts, photoreceptors that are sensitive to the polarization of light feed into a central neural complex that in turn has direct connections to the motor centers that control flight (Homberg, 2004); if so in locusts, perhaps so in moths.

17. See Hebb (1949, 1963) and Bruner (1966). "*Growth is characterized by increasing independence of response from the immediate nature of the stimulus.*" (Bruner, 1966, p. 5, italics in original).

18. Although abstractions have interested philosophers for a long time, there is no widely accepted theory of exactly how abstractions are represented. The most developed candidate is schema theory. The concept of a schema has its origins in British neuroscience between the world wars but was brought into cognitive psychology by Frederic C. Bartlett, who used it as the cornerstone of a theory of long-term declarative memory recall (Bartlett, 1932, pp. 198–202). The concept was picked up or perhaps independently reinvented 30 years later by D. Rumelhart in psychology and M. Minsky in Artificial Intelligence; see Thorndyke (1984) for a history of the concept. It has been employed in research on text comprehension (Schank, 1986) and problem solving (Marshall, 1995), as well as in social psychology; see Brewer and Nakamura (1984) for a review.

19. Markman (1999).

20. Kirkham (1992), O'Connor (1975) and Walker (1989). See Furth (1968, 1969) for the claim that Piaget's theory of knowledge offers a concept of representation that resolves some of the classical issues with respect to representational theories of knowledge.

21. I developed the distinction between an epistemological and naturalistic approach to cognition in Ohlsson (2000). The connections to the naturalistic epistemologies of Dretske (1997) and Kornblith (1995) cannot be developed here; see Kornblith (1985) for other perspectives.
22. The literature on human evolution now encompasses a staggering number of books and articles, but there is relative consensus that the explosion of physical representations in the archeological record 50,000 to 100,000 years ago is associated with the emergence of *Homo sapiens*. Mithen (1996) has made this "big bang of human culture" (p. 151) the cornerstone of his theory of the evolution of human cognition. Other works that emphasize changes in mental representation as key steps in the evolution of human cognition include Donald (1991, 2001) and Tomasello (1999a, 1999b). For the location, content and dating of cave paintings, see, e.g., Chauvet, Deschamps and Hillaire (1996) and Clottes and Courtin (1996); for dates of prehistoric figurines, see McKie (2000, p. 198).
23. Shreeve (1995) and Tattersall and Schwartz (2000, Chap. 7).
24. See Titchener (1912) for the argument that introspection is to psychology what observation is to natural science. Palermo (1971) stated the classical critique: "Each laboratory found, in the introspective reports of its own subjects, the kinds of data which the scientists in that laboratory was looking for to support his theoretical conceptions of the contents of consciousness" (p. 20). See also Ericsson and Simon (1984) for a summary of the introspectionist approach (pp. 48–61). Their book is also the starting point and main defense of the modern cognitive position that verbal reports are behaviors and hence can be used to test theories, but they are not to be taken as observational reports about mind. Like any other type of behavioral data, they have to be analyzed and interpreted. Unfortunately, the distinction between viewing verbal reports as observations and as behavioral data is not always upheld (Jack & Roepstorff, 2002).
25. The basic principle of phrenology is that cognitive functions are localized to specific areas of the brain, and that there is a correspondence between the functioning of brain areas and the outside shape of the skull. Hence, something can be inferred about the former by closely observing the latter. This incorrect theory was invented by Franz Joseph Gall and co-developed with Johann Christoph-Spurzheim. The rise of interest in Victorian science has led to an increased interest in understanding this particular pseudoscience in its historical context (Parssinen, 1974; Simpson, 2005).

    There are multiple online sources:
    http://en.wikipedia.org/wiki/Phrenology,
    http://www.cerebromente.org.br/n01/frenolog/frenologia.htm,
    http://www.whonamedit.com/docor/cfm/1018.html.
26. Anderson (2007), Just, Carpenter and Varma (1999) and Just and Varma (2007).
27. Psychometrics is the science and practice of psychological testing. Alfred Binet in France and L. L. Thurstone and C. Spearman in the United States were among the pioneers. The fundamental idea behind this enterprise is that performance on a test can be attributed to the joint action of a small set of distinct abilities such as numerical, verbal and visual ability, and that the abilities can be identified via

statistical analysis of large numbers of test scores. J. B. Carroll (1993) has summarized the psychometric analysis of mind and its empirical support. H. Gardner's theory of multiple intelligences is a later development of the same concept (Gardner, 1983). For Fodor (1983), a cognitive module is a processing unit with a specialized purpose and a certain independence from the rest of the cognitive system. Modules receive inputs from and deliver their results to other components of the cognitive system, but their internal processing is isolated from the latter. Abilities and modules differ in several respects, but they share the assumption that cognition is accomplished through a set of components that operate relatively independently from each other.

28. Analysis by decomposition into functions needs to be distinguished from what is often termed functional explanation or functional analysis (Hempel, 1959; Nagel, 1961, Chap. 12). The latter is said to be of special importance in the biological as opposed to the physical sciences (but see Hanke, 2004, for a biologist's point of view). A prototypical target of analysis is the statement that *the function of the heart is to pump blood*. The goal of philosophical analysis as usually stated is to grasp why functions are explanatory even though they are not causal, and a typical answer is that they are explanatory precisely to the extent that they can be reduced to some type of causal account. Accepting that explanations that refer to a function or a purpose are irreducible and nevertheless rigorous and scientific was an important step in the cognitive revolution (Boden, 1972; Cummins, 1975, 1983a). Philosophers continue to struggle with the concept of functional explanation (Davies, 2003; Griffiths, 1993; McLaughlin, 2001) and there is now even a psychology of functional explanation (Lambrozo & Carey, 2006). For present purposes, the meaning of "function" as used in the discussion of functional explanation is not the same as its meaning in discussions of functional decomposition. The latter ultimately derives from the mathematical rather than the biological concept of a function: A function maps inputs to outputs and is defined by a set of computations that produce the correct output, given any one input. In the functional decomposition of the cognitive system, functions like *perceiving*, *remembering* and *learning* are not explanatory but targets for explanation; in philosophical parlance, they are explananda rather than explanans. The explanatory task is to demonstrate how a cognitive function is or can be implemented, i.e., to specify the processes that compute that function down to some desired level of detail (Ohlsson, 2007c). This is the sense in which I use the term "function" in this book. It is more closely related to the psychological movement called *functionalism* in the first half of the 20th century (Schultz, 1969, Chaps. 6–8) than to philosophical analyses of functional explanations in biology.

29. For example, a skilled driver might appear to be able to drive and talk on his cell phone at the same time, but Strayer and Johnson (2001) showed that this is not so: The phone conversation affects reaction time when braking and the probability of overlooking traffic signs, indicating that this dual task situation is handled by switching attention back and forth between the two tasks.

30. See, e.g., Alvarez and Emory (2006), Baddeley (1996) and Shanahan and Baars (2005). The term "cognitive architecture" originated with Anderson (1983).

31. The Ego is the structural component that is responsible for a person's adaptation to reality and for compromising between drives and desires, on the one hand, and the constraints of reality, on the other. It was first highlighted in Sigmund Freud's *The Ego and the Id* (Freud, 1923). The concept was later developed further by, among others, A. Freud (1946) and Hartmann (1958). See Marcus (1999) and Wallerstein (2002) for reviews of psychoanalytic ego psychology.
32. For a biography of Alan Turing, see Hodges (1983). For the story of how Turing and others broke the German military code called Enigma, see Kahn (1998) and Sebag-Montefiori (2000).
33. Newell, Shaw and Simon (1958).
34. See Newell (1972, 1973). For the subsequent development of production system models of human cognition, see Neches, Langley and Klahr (1987).
35. Anderson (1983, 1993, 2005, 2007) and Anderson and Lebiere (1998). See Cooper (2006) for a philosophical analysis of the research program behind the ACT-R theory, and Ohlsson (1998) for a reflection on how the cognitive architecture program relates to the traditional psychometric approach to intelligence.
36. Weinberg (1992).
37. The arguments against the Turing-Newell vision have been developed by advocates of the embodied cognition approach; see, e.g., M. L. Anderson (2003). But this supposed alternative is an approach to Artificial Intelligence, not cognitive psychology. There are few if any examples of novel and convincing examples of embodied explanations of standard and well-documented phenomena in human cognition.
38. Pierce and Writer (2005) tell of the discovery of the mechanism of contagion in yellow fever. The corresponding story of cholera is very different (Johnson, 2006), but both are nevertheless stories about breakdowns into component processes. Rosenberg (1992, Chap. 14) contrasts this contamination schema with two other explanatory schemas that focus on configurations of environmental factors and individual predispositions, respectively.
39. Although the electrolysis of water is described in introductory chemistry texts (Brady & Holum, 1988, pp. 696–700; Ebbing & Wrighton, 1990, pp. 774–780), it is still the subject of research; see Wendt and Imarisio (2005).
40. The concept of allopatric (geographic) speciation was first formulated systematically by Ernest Mayr in *Systematics and the Origin of Species from the Viewpoint of a Zoologist* in 1942 (Mayr, 1942/1999). According to this speciation mechanism, the first step is that a population splits into two subpopulations which become geographically and hence reproductively isolated from one another. Each adapts to its geographical area via natural selection. Over time, the accumulated adaptations prevent interbreeding with the other subpopulation, should the two subpopulations happen to be reunited. The change mechanism is adaptation, i.e., the accumulation of beneficial mutations, through natural selection, and the triggering conditions are reproductive isolation due to some geographic barrier. However, there are modes of speciation that achieve reproductive isolation in other ways than via a geographic barrier; see Bush (1975) for a discussion of *parapatric* and *sympatric* speciation. In contrast, the change mechanism

known as the *Baldwin effect* after its originator James Mark Baldwin (1896a, 1896b) claims that the triggering condition for speciation is that members of a species acquire a beneficial behavior or repertoire of behaviors via learning. If the learned behaviors support survival and a high rate of reproduction, then mutations that enable, facilitate, and support those behaviors will be more beneficial than if those behaviors had not been acquired, and hence accumulate over time via natural selection (Simpson, 1953). Consider the chimpanzee habit of poking juicy insects out of holes with help of a straw or thin twig. If a troop of chimpanzees ever became completely dependent on this type of diet, they would obviously undergo selection for precise vision, eye-hand coordination and fine-grained dexterity in hands and fingers. Once again, the change process is the accumulation of beneficial mutations via natural selection, but the triggering condition is completely different in Baldwin speciation than in allopatric speciation, because it consists in the prior existence of a learned behavioral repertoire. Since a pioneering paper by Hinton and Nowlan (1987) demonstrated an impact of learning on evolution in a simulation model, the Baldwin effect has received attention in Artificial Intelligence, machine learning and related fields. See Weber and Depew (2003) for appraisals of the Baldwin effect. The main point for present purposes is that the triggering condition for a change process is a separate piece of theory from the specification of the process itself. It distinguishes ad hoc (merely descriptive) from explanatory accounts and to a large extent determines which phenomena a particular change process can successfully explain.

41. Modern philosophical work on scientific explanation began with Hempel and Oppenheim's (1948) article on the so-called covering law model, which holds that to explain is to subsume a particular event under some scientific law that "covers" it. Four decades later, this model is no longer accepted, but no other analysis of what it means to explain or how scientific explanations differ, if at all, from commonsense explanations has become authoritative (Cornwell, 2004; Keil & Wilson, 2000; Pitt, 1988; Salmon 1989). The philosophical study of psychological explanations, specifically, has expanded the early contributions by Boden (1972), Cummins (1975) and Fodor (1968) in various ways; see, e.g., Cummins (2000). One of the standard themes in this literature is that some explanations explain by decomposing a system into its components and showing how the components produce the system's behavior. The prototypical example is explaining a piece of machinery or a biological system with interacting parts (Bosse, Jonker & Treur, 2006). Cummins (1983b) contrasts componential with transition explanations, the latter showing how a change of state came about by subsuming it under a causal transition law. As I use the term, componential explanations combine elements of both. They are componential (or analytic) because they break down an observed change into a chain of component transitions. In my case, both the explanandum and the explanans are transitions in Cummins's (1983b) sense. A unit change has the same form as what Cummins calls a disposition (*when so-and-so is the case, unit process so-and-so happens, or tends to happen*). Unlike Cummins, I believe an explanation in terms of units of this sort can be genuinely

explanatory even if the units are not causal laws. I do not claim that explanation in terms of chains of component transitions is the only type of explanation, or that this concept resolves all issues in the study of scientific explanation, only that it accurately represents how change is typically explained in science. Empirical data show that it also describes commonsense explanations of biological change (Ohlsson, 2002).

42. Einstein and Infeld (1938) summarized what they called "the mechanical view" in these terms: "In mechanics the future path of a moving body can be predicted and its past disclosed if its present condition and the forces acting upon it are known.... The great results of classical mechanics suggest that the mechanical view can be consistently applied to all branches of physics, that all phenomena can be explained by the action of forces representing either attraction or repulsion, depending only upon distance and acting between unchangeable particles" (p. 67). In chemistry, the main type of change is the formation and dissolution of bonds between atoms: "Dalton's recognition that a chemical reaction is a process in which atoms merely change partners, with reactants one combination of atoms and products another combination of the same atoms, is still the all-pervasive foundation of explanation in chemistry" (Atkins, 2004, p. 112). This is not to deny that at more specific levels of description, the concept of an atomic bond turns out to be quite complex (Silvi & Savin, 1994).

43. I have not been able to locate a single, conceptual review of all types of erosion mechanisms, but Montgomery (2002), Stallard (1995) and Trenhaile (2002) provide windows onto the technical literature.

44. Suggestions for such single, all-encompassing laws of learning are not lacking; see, e.g., Taatgen (2002, 2005).

45. Compare the summary of the Gestalt work in Ohlsson (1984a) with Kaplan and Simon (1990).

46. Compare Abelson's (1959) and Kelman and Baron's (1968) lists of modes of conflict resolution with those of Chinn and Brewer (1993) and Darden (1992). Although these lists do not map onto each other one-to-one, they capture approximately the same concepts. Janoff-Bulman (1992) applied these concepts to the resistance of trauma patients to their altered circumstances.

47. See Anderson and Bower (1973, Chap. 2), for a review of associationism as a psychological theory.

48. Gagné (1965) identified eight types of learning and hence "eight sets of conditions under which changes in capabilities of the human learner are brought about. The implication is that there are eight corresponding kinds of changes in the nervous system which need to be identified and ultimately accounted for" (p. 57). The view in Ohlsson (2008a) is similar. What has changed over time is the conception of the types of learning and (hence) their exact triggering conditions.

49. For two examples of close analyses of individual learning events, see Schoenfeld, Smith and Arcavi (1993) and VanLehn (1991, 1999). D. Kuhn (1995) and Siegler and Crowly (1991) have reviewed the so-called microgenetic method in the context of cognitive development.

50. The concept of punctuated equilibrium was first advocated in paleontology by Eldredge and Gould (1972); see Eldredge (1989) and Gould (2002) for further developments.
51. Imbrie and Imbrie (2002).
52. Callander (1978).
53. For the two-stage theory of the evolution of flight in insects, see Kingsolver and Koehl (1985); for the two-stage theory of the evolution of flight in birds, see Dial (2003) and Sumida and Brochut (2000). For the shrinking-body explanation of the Kiwi bird's large egg, see Gould (1986); notice that this explanation has been challenged by Dickison (2007). For a review of the argument for the kin selection explanation of the evolution of altruism, see Foster, Wenseleers and Ratnieks (2006). The general notion of theory articulation was explicated in Ohlsson (1992b).
54. Cognitive scientists are beginning to tackle this scaling task by running their simulations to mimic long-term learning; see Anderson (2002), Kennedy and Trafont (2007) and Lebiere (1999).

CHAPTER 3. THE PRODUCTION OF NOVELTY

1. Hadamard (1949/1954, p. 29).
2. The story about the failed death ray concept that gave rise to the idea of an airplane detection device is told by Buderi (1996, pp. 52–59).
3. Harman (2001) and Nersessian (1992, 2002, 2008).
4. For a history of the crucial decade in the creation of the impressionist style of painting, see King (2007). For a more sweeping history of the movement, see, e.g., Broude (1994). For a conceptual analysis of how the impressionists contributed to the gradual withdrawal of purely representational art, see Blanshard (1949).
5. Rothenberg and Hausman (1976).
6. Although logic, the systematic study of arguments, was begun in antiquity by Aristotle in his *Prior Analytics* and continued through medieval times (Kretzmann, Kenny & Pinborg, 1988) and beyond (Arnauld & Nicole, 1662/1996), developments in the 19th century brought logic closer to mathematics by depicting deductive arguments as sequences of manipulations on abstract symbols (Boole, 1854/1958). Arguments were said to be valid or invalid solely on the basis of their form, independent of their content. In 1910, the British scholars Bertrand Russell and Alfred Whitehead published *Principia Mathematica*, a complete formalization of logic as it had developed until that time; an abbreviated version of this work is available in Whitehead and Russell (1962). The development of logic up to that point is described in detail by Kneale and Kneale (1962/1984). Russell and Whitehead's formulation is the basis for what is taught in introductory college courses in formal logic, so it is formulated and reformulated in logic textbook after logic textbook (see, e.g., Hurley, 2006; Suppes, 1957). In the course of the 20th century, logicians proved theorems about the Russell-Whitehead logic and expanded the system by incorporating new rules to represent arguments about what is *possibly* the case, what *ought to be* the case, etc. (*modal logic*; see Blackburn, van Bentham & Wolter, 2007; Hughes & Cresswell, 1996) and by introducing rules for what

to conclude when a proposition that was once regarded as true turns out to be false after all (*non-monotonic logic*: see, e.g., Donini et al., 1990 and McDermott & Doyle, 1980). In the second half of the 20th century, logic was vitalized by the creation of computer programs that operate on logical principles (e.g., Amir & Maynard-Zhang, 2004). Logic remains a dynamic field of inquiry after more than two millennia of unbroken, cumulative progress (Gabbay & Woods, 2001).

7. Pythagoras was a sixth-century B.C. Greek philosopher and mathematician. The Pythagorean theorem says that in any right-angled triangle, the square of the hypotenuse, i.e., the side that stands opposite to the right angle, is equal to the squares of the other two sides. No text by Pythagoras himself is extant and very little is known with certainty about him or his life (Riedweg, 2005). Various proofs of the theorem are available at http://en.wikipedia.org/wiki/Pythagorean_theorem.

8. The proof of Gödel's first incompleteness theorem was originally published in an article titled "Über formal unentscheidbare Sätze der Principia Mathematica und verwandter Systeme I" which appeared in the journal *Monatshefte für Mathematik und Physik*, 1931, vol. 38, pp. 173–198. An English translation is available in Gödel (1962/1992) and in the collection of papers edited by Davis (1965/2004, pp. 5–38). Unfortunately, the proof is too complicated and too technical for others than mathematicians to follow. Nagel and Newman (2001) explain the theorem and its proof to nonmathematicians. As one might expect, the application of Gödel's theorem to matters of human cognition is not straightforward; see Lucas (1961) and Slezak (1982). My position is that each human being, when operating in a deductive, symbol-manipulating mode, as in deliberate, conscious reasoning and problem solving, is subject to the Gödel limitation; in that mode, we can, in principle, only reach a subset of all truths. There are two different ways to break out of this box: First, because different individuals view the world in slightly different ways, they can be conceptualized, in their deductive mode, as Gödel-limited systems with slightly different axioms; collectively, they cover a wider range of truths than any single individual. Second, and more fundamental for the theory of creativity, the cognitive processes of a person are not limited to deductive, deliberate thinking. The impact of Gödel's theorem on cognitive psychology is thus to prove the importance of nondeductive processes such as perception, restructuring, subsymbolic learning, etc. for creativity. The micro-theory of creative insight presented in Chapter 4 is consistent with this view.

9. Fodor's argument that one cannot learn a more expressive representational system is developed in more detail than my brief sketch suggests; see Fodor (1976, pp. 79–97).

10. Not all computational mechanisms are capable of performing every computation. If a mental process P maps inputs $I = \{i_1, i_2, i_3, ..., i_n\}$ into some output O, $P(I) = O$, then any theory for that process must be capable of computing the function that P implements, i.e., of producing O when given I (and nothing else). The sufficiency test is a test of the *adequacy* of a psychological hypothesis, not of its *truth*. A sufficiency test does not prove that a theory is true, only that it might, in principle, be true and hence is worth investigating. Theories that do not pass the relevant sufficiency test cannot be true and hence can be set aside

without empirical test. The sufficiency test originated in linguistic work on generative grammars, where it was possible to prove that some grammars cannot, even in principle, produce certain syntactic constructions in English (Levelt, 1974, Chap. 2). Sufficiency testing was introduced into psychology by Newell and Simon (1972a, pp. 13–14). "The emphasis on sufficiency is still rather foreign in psychology. Almost never has it been asked of a psychological theory whether it could explain why man was capable of performing the behaviors in question" (p. 13). Unfortunately, this assessment remains accurate. Theories of creativity in particular have done a poor job of explaining how and why the processes they postulate are sufficient to produce novelty.

11. Hocevar (1980, 1981) and Runco (2004) provide general overviews of creativity research and measures, while Besemer and Treffinger (1981) focus on product measures, specifically. One well-documented product measure is the Creative Product Semantic Scale (CPSS; O'Quin & Besemer, 1989). For examples of applications of product measures, see, e.g., Besemer (1998) and Runco, McCarthy and Svenson (1994). The assessment of the creativity of products has become important for businesses due to the increased emphasis on innovation (O'Quin & Besemer, 2006).

12. See http://nobelprize.org/nobel_prizes/medicine/laureates/2003 for information regarding the prize.

13. "Damadian's camp characterizes Lauterbur's and Mansfield's work as technological refinements of Damadian's central insight, while the Nobel Assembly and other scientists say Lauterbur's and Mansfield's breakthroughs were 'discoveries' in their own right" (Montgomery, 2003).

14. Psychometric measures of creative ability are reviewed in Plucker and Renzulli (1999). The most common measures are based on the idea that creativity consists essentially in divergent thinking. For an example of a psychometric study of divergent thinking, see Seddon (1983); for a critique of divergent thinking tests, see Hocevar (1980, 1981). Psychometric and experimental traditions in the study of creativity show little overlap of findings and measures. In experimental studies, the so-called Remote Associates Test (RAT; Mednick, 1962; Wiley, 1998) is more common than the various divergent thinking measures. See Ford (1999) for real-world application of the RAT. Controversy over measures of creative ability never ceases (Crockenberg, 1972; Kaufmann, 2003).

15. See Baddeley (2007) for an in-depth treatment of this concept.

16. See Ericsson, Charness, Feltovich and Hoffman (2006) for research on the cognitive correlates of expertise.

17. See Sternberg and O'Hara (1999) for an overview of attempts to understand the relation between intelligence and creativity. Although "psychologists still have not reached a consensus on the nature of the relation between creativity and intelligence" (p. 269), there is no uncertainty about the magnitude of the observed correlations between IQ tests (of various kinds) and tests of creative ability: Barron and Harrington (1981) summarized them as ranging from "insignificant negative" to either "weakly positive" or "mildly and significantly positive," depending on the population from which the subjects were drawn (p. 445). Preckel, Holling and Wiese (2006) found the correlations between the

Berlin Structure-of-Intellect Test and four measures of creativity to range from .36 to .54 in a sample of 1,328 German students; when corrected for processing speed, the range was .07 to .24 (p. 164). In a meta-analysis of 447 correlations, Kim (2005, p. 59), found that although the range of values varied between −.41 and .71, the mean correlation was .17 and only a handful of correlations was greater than .41. A correlation of .40 means that 16% of the variation in creativity is accounted for by variation in intelligence, leaving 84% of the variation to be explained by something else. In short, correlational studies show that individual differences in creativity are not explained by individual differences in IQ. The situation is the same for children; see, e.g., Fuchs-Beauchamp, Karnes and Johnson (1993).

18. Harvard scholar David Perkins has developed the interesting notion of *dispositional intelligence* (Perkins et al., 2000; Tishman, Jay & Perkins, 1993). People possess approximately the same cognitive capabilities and capacities, but they are differently disposed with respect to their use. People whom we tend to regard as exhibiting high cognitive ability or unusually high creativity are disposed to engage those capabilities at the drop of a hat. For example, when confronted with a particular set of facts, some people immediately seek to understand their implications. The conclusions they come up with might not require extreme cognitive capacity or complex processing that is beyond the reach of the rest of us. It is the fact that they are disposed to seek such implications that distinguishes them. Applied to the production of novelty, this concept implies that creative individuals are highly disposed to, for example, look for novel ways of doing something.

19. For lifetime creativity studies using a cognitively informed, biography-like approach, see, e.g., Gardner (1993) on Freud and Einstein, Gruber (1974) on Darwin and others. Gruber and Wallace (1999) and Howe (1996) describe the methodology of using case studies in this way. This approach differs from the quantitative approach to lifetime creativity used by Galenson (2006), Simonton (1988, 2004) and others.

20. See Metcalfe (1986) and Metcalfe and Wiebe (1987). Insight problems can also be differentiated from noninsight problems with correlational methodology (Gilhooly & Murphy, 2005).

21. See Bowden and Jung-Beeman (2003), Bowden, Jung-Beeman, Fleck and Kounios (2005), Jung-Beeman et al. (2004), Kounios et al. (2006), Luo and Knoblich (2007) and Luo, Niki and Knoblich (2006).

22. For example, see Kershaw and Ohlsson (2004) and Knoblich, Ohlsson, Haider and Rhenius (1999).

23. To choose 5 objects among 10, pick any 1 among the 10, any 1 among the remaining 9, any 1 among the remaining 8, etc., for a total of $10*9*8*7*6 = 30,240$ different selections. Suppose that the objects can be related to each other via 10 different binary relations, i.e., relations that can be absent or take either one of two values. This provides $3^{10} = 59,049$ different relational structures for each selection of 5 objects. Multiplying these numbers gives us 1,785,641,760 possible configurations.

24. See Miller (1996) for the estimate of vocabulary size.

25. Poincaré's famous and oft-quoted essay, "Mathematical Discovery," appears, among other places, in Poincaré (1908/1952, pp. 46–63).
26. Simonton (1988, p. 7).
27. Finke, Ward and Smith (1992) and Smith, Ward and Finke (1995).
28. The nature and origin of the basic forms is not specified by Finke, Smith and Ward but they could be taken to be the so-called geons of Biederman's (1987) theory of visual perception.
29. Weisberg (1986, p. 50). Weisberg's position is difficult to pin down. Compare the statement that "… there is no convincing evidence for the occurrence of insight during creative thinking" (Weisberg, 1993, p. 67) with the statement that "it should be emphasized that there is no question that all of us have 'aha!' experiences at various times in our lives" (Weisberg, 1986, p. 36). For alternative formulations of the "nothing special" view of creativity and insight, see Kaplan and Simon (1990), Perkins (1981) and Usher (1929/1954).
30. Charles Darwin originally proposed his theory in 1859 in a book titled, *The Origin of Species by Means of Natural Selection, or Preservation of Favored Races in the Struggle for Life*, commonly abbreviated as *The Origin of Species* (Darwin, 1859/2004). For an assessment of the current status of the theory, see Gould (2002).
31. See, e.g., Campbell (1960), Koestler (1966), Pringle (1951) and Vincent (1993) for different approaches to the analogy between evolutionary change and cognitive change.
32. Campbell (1960).
33. There is evolutionary epistemology (Hahlweg & Hooker, 1989; Radnitzky & Bartley, 1987; Wuketits, 1990) as well as evolutionary psychology (Barkow, Cosmides & Tooby, 1992) and "universal Darwinism" (Cziko, 1995; Plotkin, 1994). There are variation-selection theories of artistic and scientific creativity (Koestler, 1966), technological invention (Vincent, 1993), economic progress (Hodgson, 1996; Nelson & Winter, 1982), the immune system (French, Laskov & Scharff, 1989; Gazzinaga, 1992; Jerne, 1967), the history and philosophy of science (Hull, 1990, 2001; Toulmin, 1972), brain function (Edelman, 1987; Sporns & Tononi, 1994), the spread of items – "memes" – of popular culture (Aunger, 2002; Blackmore, 1999; Brodie, 1996; Lynch, 1996) and yet other things (Gazzinaga, 1992).
34. See Amundsen (1989) and Perkins (1994, 1995a).
35. The principle of serendipity, of finding something else than what one was looking for, is well established in creativity research. See Van Andel (1994) for origin, history, examples and patterns of serendipity. Meyers (2007) is a study of serendipity in medical research. Roberts (1989) has compiled a list of examples of serendipity in science, technology and medicine, some more convincing than others. The serendipity principle does not claim that creative people proceed without any goal, only that they did not have the goal of discovering what they in fact discovered. There might nevertheless be a grain of truth in the former idea: Writes wood sculptor David E. Rogers (2001): "Sometimes I begin to carve and the wood itself dictates the form I carve; other times I start with a more independent idea" (p. 53). Within psychology, Finke, Ward and Smith (1992) have proposed a

function follows form principle that highlights the role of exploration of a given material in generating the goal for a creative process.
36. Gruber (1974).
37. Bradshaw (1992) and Wright (1920/1988).
38. Cooper (1992), Hertzmann (1957) and Orenstein (1967). But see Alty (1995) for an application of the heuristic search theory to musical composition.
39. Thorndike (1898).
40. Alexander Bain (1879): "In the full detail of Constructiveness, we shall have to exemplify these three main conditions: – namely, (1) a previous command of the elements entering into the combination; (2) a sense of the effect to be produced; and (3) a voluntary process of trial and error continued until the desired effect is actually produced" (p. 572). And again, C. Lloyd Morgan (1894): "The chick, or the child, in early hours or days of life acquires skill in the management of ... its bodily organs.... The method employed is that of trial and error. What we term the control over our activities is gained in and through the conscious reinforcement of those modes of response which are successful, and the inhibition of those modes of response which are unsuccessful" (p. 213).
41. Thorndike (1898); see bottom of page 105.
42. The cognitive revolution in the 1950s has been the subject of historical (Baars, 1986; Gardner, 1985) and philosophical (Greenwood, 1999) studies as well as personal reminiscences (Mandler, 2002; Miller, 2003; Newell & Simon, 1972b). But the nature of the research and development work that was carried out during World War II and that paved the way for that revolution appears not to have been the subject of a serious historical study (but see Fortun and Schweber, 1993, for such a study of the related case of operations research). One obstacle for such a study is that during the war many of the relevant research and development activities were classified, while after the war they quickly fell too far behind the rapidly moving research front to publish. Hence, the work languishes in forgotten technical reports in military archives. For example, in an interview with Bernard J. Baars (1986), George A. Miller said, "... because of the war ... Smitty (S. S.) Stevens at the Psychoacoustics Laboratory [at Harvard University] hired me to work on voice communications systems for the military.... My special project was the design of optimal signals for spot jamming of speech. It was a top secret project.... At my Ph.D. oral only two people were cleared to read my thesis!" (p. 201). Nevertheless, in their overview of the history of applied cognitive psychology, Hoffman and Deffenbacher (1992) are able to document the importance of the human factors, or human-machine interaction, aspect of the wartime work and the closely related issue of training. During the war, "psychologists were involved in the preparation of training and operations manuals, the design of radar and sonar consoles, gunsights [sic], communications systems, aircraft instrument panels, and many other things" (p. 19). As a result, "there was created a generation of psychologists who specialized in the analysis of training procedures and human-machine interaction" (p. 19). By forcing attention to complex, real-world training problems, this development would by itself have changed cognitive psychology. However, the rise of human-machine interaction as a research topic interacted with the new theoretical perspectives inspired

by the emergence of what we now call information sciences and information technologies. Hoffman and Deffenbacher mention statistical information theory, cybernetics (a.k.a. control theory), signal detection theory and computer programming. They could have added game theory and the theory of decision making. These developments loom large in the reminiscences of the pioneers (Miller, 2003; Newell & Simon, 1972b). Thus, the war effort prompted the cognitive revolution both by presenting new problems to think about and by inspiring new ways of thinking about them.

43. See Conway and Siegelman (2005) for a biography of Norbert Wiener and a history of the rise and fall of cybernetics. Wiener's original work, *Cybernetics* (Wiener, 1948), is too technical for any but mathematically competent readers.
44. Miller, Galanter and Pribram (1960), especially Chapter 2, "The Unit of Analysis." In the authors' own words, they were pursuing "the 'cybernetic hypothesis', namely, that the fundamental building block of the nervous system is the feedback loop" (pp. 26–27).
45. Powers (1973).
46. Newell and Simon (1972a).
47. See Newborn (2003). Newborn (2000) writes: "Deep Blue used a brute force search that was very different than the narrow highly-directed heuristic searches [prominent scientists of the 1950s and 1960s] imagined necessary to avoid the exponential growth of the search space" (p. 28).
48. See Kaplan and Simon (1990). Others have applied the heuristic search theory to explain creativity in more complex domains, e.g., musical composition (Alty, 1995).
49. If two diametrically opposite corner squares are cut off from a checkerboard, can the remaining 62 squares be covered exactly by 31 dominos, if one domino is a rectangle the size of two squares? The answer is negative because the two cut off squares are necessarily of the same color, while a domino the size of two squares necessarily covers one square of each color. Hence, 31 dominoes cannot cover 30 squares of one color and 32 of another.
50. Some authors deny that any special explanation is needed. Weisberg and Alba (1981) write: Empirical studies "seem to indicate that the solution behavior for at least two of [the classical insight] problems can be understood in a straightforward manner: People apply their knowledge to new problems, and if their knowledge is not directly useful, they try to produce something new that will solve the problem through a straightforward extension of what they know. No exotic processes, such as sudden insight, are involved" (p. 189). The same perspective is expressed in Weisberg (1986, 1993). See also Perkins (1981): "What is special about the mental processes that explain sudden insight? The answer seems to be: very little" (p. 71).
51. Newell and Simon (1972a) began modern research on problem-solving strategies by describing strategies for a class of letter arithmetic puzzles (given DONALD + GERALD = ROBERT; which digits should be substituted for the letters to make this a correct addition?), for a class of formal logic problems and for chess. During the following two decades, researchers identified strategies in wide variety of task domains. The fact that strategies are *domain specific*, i.e., that

the strategies of one domain seem to be unrelated to those of other domains, has discouraged a search for a general theory of problem-solving strategies (but see Lenat, 1983, for a promising start). Perhaps due to the difficulty of finding anything general to say, research that primarily aims to identify and analyze problem-solving strategies has waned as a basic research enterprise, but continues to be of interest in applied contexts; see, e.g., Schraagen, Chipman and Shalin (2000). For a strategy-oriented application of search concepts to understanding creativity in Artificial Intelligence, see Buchanan (2001): "Search at the meta-level gives us a means for identifying the choices that are most effective for performing a specific task" (p. 23). This top-down view of (artificial) creativity is almost the opposite of the psychological theory proposed in Chapter 4 of this volume.

52. Hayes and Simon (1974) and Simon and Hayes (1976) did empirical work on the comprehension of problem instructions, but their conclusions fell far short of a theory of the origin of problem spaces. Buchanan's (2001) concept of meta-level search is one vision of such a theory.

53. For a history of Gestalt psychology, see Ash (1995); for many of the original papers, see Ellis (1967); and for a reconstruction of their theory of problem solving, see Ohlsson (1984a).

54. The Gestalt laws are summarized in Goldstein (2008, pp. 72–80). The original texts are Koffka (1922) and Wertheimer (1923).

55. The Necker Cube was first published by the Swiss crystallographer Louis Albert Necker in 1832 in the *London and Edinburgh Philosophical Magazine and Journal of Science* (Necker, 1832) and again the following year in *Annalen der Physik*. While studying line drawings of crystals Necker discovered the tendency of such drawings to flip between two alternative three-dimensional (3D) percepts. How the Necker Cube passed from these science journals into Gestalt psychology I do not know, but it is mentioned in an article on the physiology of vision by Wheatstone (1838, pp. 381–382). The closely related figure-ground distinction and the use of reversible figures to illustrate it are due to the Danish psychologist Edgar Rubin, whose Danish-language book *Synopslevede Figurer* (Copenhagen, Denmark: Gyldendalske, 1915) appears not to have been translated into English. Reversible figures were discussed by the Gestalt psychologists and passed into common knowledge, but knowledge of the original sources was lost along the way. The reversions of the Necker Cube and its relatives continue to serve as symbols or metaphors for representational change in general. For example, Kuhn (1970) drew an analogy between reversible figures and paradigm shifts in science (pp. 111–114). The features of the Necker Cube that continue to fascinate are that a 3D perception of the line drawing is clearly a cognitive construction, and that a shift between the two possible 3D constructions is just as clearly non-monotonic: It is impossible to see the two 3D interpretations of the drawing at the same time. The Necker Cube continues to interest researchers in visual perception as well, now absorbed into a wider research program on "multistability" and "binocular rivalry" (Pearson & Clifford, 2004).

56. Wertheimer (1959/1968, pp. 170–171).

57. Köhler (1972, p. 134).

58. Koffka disagreed with Duncker and the other Gestalt psychologists about the importance of the goal for restructuring. Duncker thought that careful analysis of the goal was one of the forces that drove problem solving (Duncker, 1935/1974, p. 52). But Koffka (1935) wrote: "The reorganization itself must, if it is to be right, depend upon the properties of the field alone, and not upon any field-Ego relationship" (p. 636).
59. Köhler (1924); this book is as yet not translated into English.
60. Piaget (1950): "... the Gestalt theory, although correct in its description of forms of equilibrium or well-structured wholes, nevertheless neglects the reality, in perception as in intelligence, of genetic development and the process of construction that characterizes it" (p. 66). Weisberg has emphasized the dependency of creative work on, and its continuity with, prior experience; see Weisberg (1986, 1993) and Weisberg and Alba (1981).
61. Koffka (1935, p. 636).

CHAPTER 4. CREATIVE INSIGHT: THE REDISTRIBUTION THEORY

1. Köhler (1972, p. 154).
2. Almost any historical account of a creative project with major impact confirms the long durations of such projects; see, e.g., Gruber (1974) for description of Charles Darwin's lifelong work on the theory of natural selection, Westfall (1983) on Newton, Cooper (1992) on Beethoven and so on. Gardner (1993) sketches the life trajectories of Freud, Einstein, Picasso, Stravinsky and other notables.
3. For studies that do just that, see Dunbar (1995, 1997) and Dunbar and Blanchette (2001).
4. DiVesta and Walls (1967) and Maier (1931).
5. Maier (1945).
6. The origin of the Nine Dot Problem is obscure. It is often attributed to Scheerer (1963), but it was probably not invented by him. It was used in a study by Pally (1955), who in turn refers to a psychology textbook by Munn (1946), where it occurs on page 180, but without any source.
7. The B.C. Coin Problem was studied by Schooler, Ohlsson and Brooks (1993). See also Weisberg (1995, Appendix B0).
8. See Metcalfe and Wiebe (1987) and Sternberg and Davidson (1982).
9. Creativity researchers who have critiqued the study of individual insight events include Gruber (1974) and Weisberg (1986, 1993). For Gruber, the issue is that so much more happens in the slow growth of a complex creative project than the appearance of a new idea here and there. For Weisberg, the idea that prior experience is a hindrance is fundamentally wrong; instead, prior experience is the main resource for creative work. This fact is obscured by studying simple problems that do not evoke complex prior knowledge.
10. For example, Metcalf (1986) and Metcalf and Wiebe (1987) showed that people can judge how close they are to solving analytical problems, but not insight problems. Gilhooly and Murphy (2005) did cluster and multiple regression analyses on both insight and noninsight tasks and found support for the distinction between the two types of tasks. Fleck (2008) found that working

memory capacity is related to analytical problem solving but not to insight problem solving.
11. The insight sequence is superficially similar to the four-stage theory of illumination proposed by Graham Wallas (1926). The main difference is that the insight sequence describes problem solving without a pause, while Wallas's stages include an incubation period in which the problem solver rests. Incubation is discussed further at the end of this chapter.
12. See, e.g., Durkin (1937), Fleck and Weisberg (2004), Maier (1931), Metcalfe (1986), Metcalfe and Wiebe (1987) and Ohlsson (1990c).
13. Brain-imaging techniques enable researchers to capture moments of insight; see Bowden and Jung-Beeman (2003); Bowden, Jung-Beeman, Fleck and Kounios (2005); Jung-Beeman et al. (2004), Kounios et al. (2006); Luo and Knoblich (2007); Luo, Niki and Knoblich (2006); and Sandkühler and Bhattacharyya (2008).
14. The classical self-report is Poincaré's autobiographical account of a mathematical discovery, already discussed in Chapter 3 (Poincaré, 1908/1952), but similar events have been reported by many others; see Ghiselin (1952) for a collection of testimonies from artists and writers and Hadamard (1949/1954) for an analysis of self-reports from mathematicians. Examples are mentioned in Chapter 5; see Table 5.1.
15. Using a strict criterion of cessation of all activity to identify impasses, Fleck and Weisberg (2004) found only a single example of the full insight sequence (impasse, restructuring and successful solution) among 34 subjects who attempted to solve Duncker's Candle Problem. However, 13 additional subjects experienced both impasse and restructuring but did not solve the problem within the time limit set by the experimenters. Depending on which number is used, these data estimate the prevalence of the insight sequence as either 3% or 41%; at either frequency, the phenomenon is of interest.
16. The idea that perception is an interpretive process and that consequently there are no theory-free observations – instead, observations are *theory-laden* – was discussed by Hanson (1965), who used the term "theory loaded" as well as "theory laden"; only the latter seems to have survived in philosophical discourse. The concept that observations are theory laden is widely accepted in the philosophy of science. Brewer and Lampert (2001) analyzed this concept from a cognitive point of view. A classical psychological work that emphasizes the complexity of perceptual processing is Neisser (1967). The point is equally visible from an Artificial Intelligence perspective (Marr, 1982).
17. Textbooks on sensation and perception make this abundantly clear (Levine, 2000; Wolfe et al., 2006). See also Biederman (1987) and Marr (1982) for constructive theories of particular aspects of vision.
18. "The whole visual system can be considered a long series of filters, with each stage in the system responsible for extracting a particular aspect of the visual world and passing this aspect on to the next stage" (Wolfe et al., 2006, p. 40).
19. Wolfe et al. (2006, pp. 93–94).
20. Kintsch (1988).

21. "...a fundamental feature of the anatomy of cortical pathways is a feedback of information from higher order cortical areas to areas that are closer to the input from the periphery" (Gilbert, 1998, p. 479). See Felleman and Van Essen (1991) and Gilbert and Sigman (2007) for reviews of the relevant evidence. Researchers are pinpointing the exact brain areas and mechanisms involved in such top-down influences (see, e.g., Grent-'t-Jong & Woldorff, 2007; Ullman, 1995).
22. See Behrens (1987) for an overview of Albert Ames Jr.'s work on visual illusions, and Levine (2000, pp. 262–264) for an explanation. For a recent study of the Ames Room illusion, see Dorward and Day (1996).
23. For the description and origin of these figures, see Note 55 to Chapter 3.
24. Early evidence for parallel activation of multiple meanings was presented by Swinney (1979). The study of lexical ambiguity has since swelled to a research area of its own. There is now neuroscience evidence for the activation of multiple meanings in parallel; see, e.g., Mason and Just (2007).
25. The concept of a situation model was introduced into the psychology of reading by van Dijk and Kintsch (1983, Chap. 10). It has since become a standard conceptual tool for the study of language comprehension (Graesser, Millis & Zwaan, 1997; Zwaan & Radvansky, 1998), with some unexpected applications (Radvansky & Dijkstra, 2007).
26. The average educated adult knows approximately 50,000 words (Miller, 1996), and hence approximately as many concepts. Each concept is likely to enter into more than one knowledge element. The space of possible knowledge elements built out of two concepts (e.g., *dogs are mammals*) is thus approximately 2,500,000,000. We do not know how many of those combinations make sense or are typically acquired by a person in the course of a lifetime, but even if the proportion is one tenth of a percent, the number of two-concept knowledge elements is of the order of a million. Similar calculations would yield even higher numbers for knowledge elements built out of three or more concepts.
27. Anderson (1984), Anderson and Pirolli (1984) and Collins and Loftus (1975).
28. The study of word associations has a long history in psychology (Deese, 1965), and, unlike many other techniques, it is used in both clinical psychology and in basic cognitive research on memory and language. The two basic measures are the probability and the speed with which one word elicits another; see Miller (1996, Chap. 8).
29. This view of long-term memory is due to Anderson (1989, 1990). It is an advance on the more commonly held view that the task of memory is to retain information accurately.
30. Gibson (1977).
31. Newell and Simon (1972a).
32. There is a long line of developmental research on how children make transitive inferences (Donaldson, 1963, Chap. 3; Glick & Wapner, 1968). Transitive inferences are closely related to Piaget's (1952) notion of *seriation* (Murray & Youniss, 1968). Piaget's main work on seriation appears not to have been translated into English [Piaget, J., & Inhelder, B. (1959). *La Genèse des structures logiques élémentaires: classifications et sériations*. Neuchâtel: Delachaux et Niestlé], but see Inhelder and Piaget (1964) for a briefer treatment. Studies with adults, where problems of this

type are called *linear syllogisms* or *three-term series problems*, began with Hunter (1957) and was continued by Clark (1969), DeSoto, London and Handel (1965), and Huttenlocher (1968), all trying to account for the differential difficulty of various three-term series problems. Johnson-Laird (1983, pp. 111–112) and Ohlsson (1984c) concluded independently that people process series problems by building *mental models* of the series and reading off answers by inspecting them in the mind's eye. Johnson-Laird went on to develop the idea of mental models into a general theory of thinking (Johnson-Laird, 2006, pp. 122–126). The concept of a mental model used in these works is closely related to the notion of a *situation model* in theories of language comprehension (Kintsch, 1998) and to the notion of a *problem state* in theories of problem solving (Newell & Simon, 1972a).

33. Although everyone agrees that people are not logical, researchers disagree on the reason for this. Henle (1962) argued that people reach conclusions from given premises that differ from those dictated by logic because they often understand those premises differently than logicians. Others have argued that people operate with a "paralogic" or "psycho-logic" that includes fallacious inference rules such as the conversion of *if* p, *then* q into *if* q, *then* p (Wason & Johnson-Laird, 1972, Chap. 6) or *all A's are B's* into *all B's are A's* (Griggs & Osterman, 1980; Revlin & Leirer, 1978). The notion of invalid inference rules has been applied in clinical psychology to explain pathologies of thought but with only limited success (von Domarus, 1944/1964; Mujica-Parodi, Mataspina & Sackeim, 2000). An alternative type of explanation is that reasoning is primarily determined by nonlogical factors such as attitudes (e.g., Abelson & Rosenberg, 1958). Cheng and Holyoak (1985) have proposed that people reason with pragmatic schemas, patterns of reasoning that are derived from, and hence specific to, an area of everyday experience, e.g., cause-effect relations, obligations or permissions. Cosmides (1989) has attempted to ground particular versions of such schemas in human evolution rather than everyday experience, not without controversy (Buller, 2005). Johnson-Laird (1983, 2006) have proposed that people reason with mental models instead of inference rules or schemas. With the exception of the idea that people do not reason but respond to reasoning problems on the basis of attitudes, these four hypotheses – people understand the premises differently; they reason with a psycho-logic that includes domain-general but logically invalid inference rules; they reason with domain-specific schemas; they reason with mental models – share the goal of describing a mechanism of reasoning that can explain the pattern of errors in human reasoning while also explaining the power of human reasoning.

34. One source of evidence for subgoaling is the scalloped reaction time curves that result when people perform hierarchically organized tasks; see Anderson, Kushmerick and Lebiere (1993, Figure 6.3), Greeno (1974, Figures 3 and 4), and Corrigan-Halpern and Ohlsson (2002, Figure 2). Another type of evidence is that teaching explicit subgoals to students affects how and what they learn from problem-solving practice; see, e.g., Catrambone (1998).

35. Woodworth (1938, p. 823).

36. The modern study of heuristics, rules of thumb that usefully bias choices during search, began with George Polya, a mathematician who tried to codify patterns of reasoning in mathematics for the benefit of students (Polya, 1962, 1968). Newell

and Simon (1972a) proposed a small set of what they called *weak methods*, ways of searching a problem space that depend minimally on the specifics of the problem. There is as yet no general theory of heuristics, but see Lenat (1983) for a promising beginning.
37. Holding (1985, Chap. 6), and Levy and Newborn (1991).
38. The first version of the present theory appeared in Ohlsson (1984b), and it was further developed in Ohlsson (1990c, 1992a), Ohlsson and Kershaw (2003), Knoblich, Ohlsson, Haider, and Rhenius (1999), Knoblich, Ohlsson and Raney (2001) and Kershaw and Ohlsson (2004).
39. Woodworth (1938, p. 823).
40. Matthew I. Isaak and Marcel A. Just analyzed 21 classical problems with respect to the constraints from prior knowledge that need to be overcome to solve them; see Isaak and Just (1995, p. 284, Table 9.1). See Maier (1945) for the classical study of the Hat Rack Problem.
41. Ohlsson (1992a, p. 12).
42. I owe this point to Edward Chronicle, James MacGregor and Thomas Ormerod; see Ormerod, MacGregor and Chronicle (2002).
43. Newell, Shaw and Simon (1962, p. 106).
44. A technical description of the model is available in a conference paper (Ohlsson, 2008b).
45. Koffka (1935), Köhler (1972) and Wertheimer (1959/1968).
46. Baddeley (2007).
47. The limit can be set by finite resources (e.g., activation), rapid decay, storage capacity, and the inability to prevent interference by suppressing irrelevant information (see Baddeley, 2007, Chap. 11).
48. See, e.g., Polk and Seifert (2002) for a collection of representative modeling papers.
49. See a basic psychology text, e.g., Goldstein (2008) or Reisberg (2006).
50. Schwartz (2002).
51. Tulving and Pearlstone (1966) and Tulving and Psotka (1971). Under certain circumstances, a person might even recall more overall at a second, delayed recall attempt (Erdelyi, 1998) than he or she did initially, which strongly supports the reality of failure to retrieve information that is, in fact, in memory.
52. Knoblich, Ohlsson, Haider and Rhenius (1999) and Knoblich, Ohlsson and Raney (2001).
53. Kershaw and Ohlsson (2004).
54. Duncker (1935/1974).
55. See, e.g., Adamson (1952), Birch and Rabinowitz (1951), Duncker (1935/1974), German and Barrett (2005), Glucksberg and Weisberg (1966) and Saugstad and Raaheim (1960). For computational models of functional fixedness, see Greeno and Berger (1987) and Keane (1989).
56. Luchins (1942) and Luchins and Luchins (1959).
57. The Water Jar (or Water Jug) Problem entered psychology with Luchins (1942). In a Water Jar Problem, a person is given three jars or jugs with known volumes (e.g., 3, 5 and 17 units) but otherwise unmarked. There is an unlimited source of water through a faucet, and water can be poured between the jars. The goal is to

obtain a certain amount of water (e.g., 4) through a series of pouring actions. See Atwood and Polson (1979) and Atwood, Masson and Polson (1980) for a process model of how people solve this task.

58. See, e.g., McNeil and Alibali (2005), Smith (1995) and Wiley (1998).
59. Chronicle, MacGregor and Ormerod (2004), Chronicle, Ormerod and MacGregor (2001) and MacGregor, Ormerod and Chronicle (2001).
60. The N-Balls Problem is a generalization of the Coin Problem studied by Schooler, Ohlsson and Brooks (1993). In an N-Balls problem, the task is to determine which of N similar-looking balls is heavier than the rest, using no other tool or resource than a balance beam that can only be used a maximum of X times. For example, to find the heavier ball among 7 balls with 2 uses of the balance beam, first weigh any 3 balls against any of the remaining 3 balls. If the two groups weigh the same, the heavier ball is the one not weighed and no second step is needed. If one group is heavier, it contains the heavier ball. Next compare any two balls in that group. The possible outcomes are obvious, either one of the compared balls is heavier or else the one not weighed is the heavier. The class of N-Balls Problems has been investigated by James MacGregor, Thomas Ormerod and the late Edward Chronicle (MacGregor, personal electronic communication, September 13, 2007).
61. Wallas (1926, pp. 79–82). Although Wallas was first to label it, the incubation concept goes back to the personal testimony of Poincaré, von Helmholz and others (Ghiselin, 1952; Hadamard, 1949/1954).
62. See, e.g., Lubart (2000–2001).
63. Kaplan (1989) and Sio and Ormerod (2009). An unpublished manuscript by R. Dodds, T. B. Ward and S. M. Smith entitled "Incubation in Problem Solving and Creativity" supports the same conclusions as the latter two reviews (personal electronic communication, S. M. Smith, October 3, 2007).
64. Weisberg (1986, p. 30).
65. Simon (1966).
66. The oldest extant version of the Archimedes bathtub story appears in Marcus Vitruvius Pollio, *De Architectura Libri Decem* (*The ten books on architecture*), Book IX, paragraphs 9–12. The paragraphs are available in English translation on line at http://www.math.nyu.edu/~crorres/Archimedes/Crown/Vitruvius.

The full English translation of Vitruvius' text is also available online at: http://penelope.uchicago.edu/Thayer/E/Roman/Texts/Vitruvius/home/html.

Classicists universally agree that there is little reason to believe the story. Vitrivius was not an eyewitness or even a contemporary. He was a Roman who lived in the first century B.C., approximately 200 years after Archimedes. Other authors in antiquity also tell the bathtub story, but they lived even later so there is no way of knowing whether they had independent sources or repeated Vitruvius's story. One strong reason for believing that the story is not true is that the difference between the amount of water displaced by a pure gold crown and a crown of the same weight but made of gold mixed with some lighter metal is so small that it could not have been measured with any accuracy with the tools available to Archimedes; see the calculations on display at http://www.math.nyu.edu/~crorres/Archimedes/Crown/CrownIntro.html.

67. Posner (1973, p. 174).
68. Moss (2002) and Seifert et al. (1995).
69. Yaniv and Meyer (1987).
70. Langley and Jones (1988).
71. Bowden and Jung-Beeman (2003), Bowden, Jung-Beeman, Fleck and Kounios (2005), Jung-Beeman et al. (2004) and Kounios et al. (2006).

CHAPTER 5. CREATIVE INSIGHT WRIT LARGE

1. Koestler (1964, p. 225).
2. Erdoes (1988), Gies and Gies (1991) and Lacey and Danziger (1999) for descriptions of everyday life in medieval Europe.
3. In philosophy, this is known as the problem of induction. See Note 44, Chapter 1, for a brief discussion of this problem.
4. Although Galileo also worked on both astronomy and terrestrial mechanics, historians of science designate Isaac Newton as the person who executed the synthesis of the two fields (e.g., Butterfield, 1957, pp. 163–165; Koyré, 1950).
5. The General Gas Law says that the product of the pressure and volume of a gas sample is proportional to the temperature of the sample, measured on the absolute, or Kelvin, scale: $PV = kT$. The law is an approximation that only holds within a certain range of values. The development of the law began with work of the English 17th-century scientist Robert Boyle, who identified the inverse relation between pressure and volume of a contained sample of air, $PV = k$, one of the three pairwise relations that make up the general law (Shapin, 1998, pp. 96–100).
6. Because adaptive systems shape themselves to the environment in which they are embedded, "only a few, gross characteristics" of the human cognitive architecture "show through to task behavior" (Newell & Simon, 1972a, pp. 788–789); see also Simon and Newell (1971, pp. 148–149). Newell and Simon included among such characteristics the number and character of the memory systems, the read and write times of those systems, the sequential character of central processing and the situation-specific and goal-driven nature of processing (Newell & Simon, 1972a, pp. 791–792).
7. See Chapter 1, Notes 15 (self-organization) and 18 (self-similarity). Gleick (1987) describes the initial creation of the concept of a butterfly effect (also known as sensitive dependence on initial conditions). The term *cascading causation* is from Corrigan-Halpern and Ohlsson (2002).
8. See Baldwin (2001) about the telephone, p. 72; about the lightbulb, Chapter 10; and about the electrical battery, p. 282. Carlson and Gorman (1992) confirm the application of search to the telephone: "... Edison ... realized that he needed a carbon compound that was very sensitive to physical force. Ideally, a small change in the force on the carbon should produce a large change in the resistance, thus amplifying the signal. The task now became one of finding a carbon compound with this electrical property.... [Edison's assistant] Batchelor tested hundreds of carbon compounds and mixtures...." (p. 70).
9. Wentorf (1992, p. 162). For another example of extensive search in the domain of chemistry, see Morgan (1992).

10. See Bradshaw (1992) and Wright (1953/1988). As a second example, Carlson and Gorman (1992) describe Edison as decomposing the design for a telephone into three components, each of which received independent attention, at least initially.
11. Hillier (1992; see pp. 104–105 for the quote, italics in original).
12. Carlson and Gorman (1992).
13. Strathern (2000).
14. Isaak and Just (1995, p. 299).
15. Hillier (1992).
16. Ohlsson and Regan (2001).
17. Chipp (1988).
18. Gruber (1992, p. 17).
19. See Chipp (1988, p. 43 and p. 133) for the dates on which Picasso began and ended work on Guernica. Weisberg (1993, pp. 202–209) has used Chipp's analysis of the creation of Guernica into 10 major steps to argue that creative work proceeds in a gradualist rather than a punctuated manner.
20. Picasso worked on *Les Demoiselles d'Avignon* from the fall of 1906 to July 1907, when the painting was first shown publicly (Miller, 2001, Chap. 4).
21. Olby (1974/1994).
22. Gruber (1974).
23. Bradshaw (1992), and Wright (1953/1988).
24. According to McCann (1978), "Lavoisier's first published results of his speculations on air and the problem of weight gain in calcinations were his 1774 *Opuscules Physiques et Chymiques*. It took several years, however, for these doubts and speculations to converge into a new theory, and the first formal description of the oxygen theory came in papers presented to the Paris Académie des Sciences in 1977" (p. 31, italics in original). Thagard (1990, 1992, Chap. 3) describes Lavoisier's development of the theory from the early 1770s through the early 1780s as a series of semantic networks.
25. Hillier (1992).
26. http://www.en.wikipedia.org/wiki/Fermat's_last_theorem; http://www-gap/dcs.st-and.ac.uk/~history/Biographies/Wiles.html.
27. Gruber (1992, p. 17), italics in original.
28. DeLatil (1954, pp. 25–38), describes the successive inventions that resulted in what we now regard as standard snorkeling equipment (mask, snorkel and flippers) by spear fishermen along the Mediterranean coast of France – the Cote D'Azur – in the 1930s. Cousteau (1953, pp. 8–20), describes the invention of the aqualung (i.e., the "self-contained underwater breathing apparatus," or SCUBA, equipment familiar to all sports divers). The story is retold in Matsen's (2009) biography of Cousteau.
29. The fact that superior creators work on multiple, mutually supporting but semi-independent projects that are pursued more or less parallel is apparent from almost any detailed case study of a creative life; see, e.g., Gruber (1974) on Darwin, Westfall (1983) on Newton, Dubos (1976) on Pasteur, Baldwin (2001) on Edison, Kilmurray and Ormond (1998) on Sargent and Cooper (1992) on Beethoven. See also the collections of papers by Wallace and Gruber (1992) and

Weber and Perkins (1992). I do not know of any study of the tendency to run over deadlines. The bad fit between creatives and bureaucratic organizations is proverbial and supported by case studies of innovations in business; see, e.g., Smith and Alexander (1999).
30. See Wiley (1998) for a laboratory demonstration of this.
31. See Chapter 3, Note 17, regarding the relation between intelligence and creativity.
32. Barron and Harrington (1981), Feist (1999) and Selby, Shaw and Houtz (2005) have reviewed the relation between personality and creativity. Dacey and Lennon (1998, Chap. 5), list 10 character traits of creative individuals that have support in research: tolerance of ambiguity, "stimulus freedom" (the ability to restructure one's perceptions), "functional freedom" (the ability to use common objects in new ways), flexibility, risk taking, preference for disorder, delay of gratification, freedom from sex-role stereotyping, perseverance and courage. Other authors have proposed related but somewhat different lists (Wolfradt & Pretz, 2001). Interestingly, Csikszentmihalyi (1997, Chap. 3), has argued that it is a mistake to look for extreme values on such dimensions. Instead, creative individuals are characterized by the fact that they combine opposites. They combine high levels of energy with habits of quietude and rest, (moderately) high IQ with naivité, playfulness with discipline, fantasy with realism, extroversion with introversion, humility with pride, the masculine with the feminine, rebelliousness with mastery of tradition, passionate commitment with objectivity and suffering with joy.
33. Caprara and Cervone (2000) and Cervone (2004, 2005).
34. In 1979, J. W. Getzels could accurately complain that "there is hardly any systematic work on problem finding" (Getzels, 1979, p. 167). A decade and a half later, Runco (1994) published a series of papers on the topic. The concept has since become accepted as a crucial component of creative work (Jay & Perkins, 1997). There is still no consensus of what makes a good problem finder, but the question is the subject of research all over the world; see, e.g., Lee and Cho (2007), Ramirez (2002) and Suwa (2003).
35. Wild (1992, pp. 123–124).
36. See Chapter 3, Note 35.
37. John-Steiner (2000). The literature on collective cognition is huge. A particularly relevant strand of work consists of so-called network studies; see, e.g., Cowan and Jonard (2003), Schilling and Phelps (2007) and Uzzi and Spiro (2005).
38. Baldwin (2001).
39. Broude (1994).
40. Crane (2002).
41. Buderi (1996).
42. Examples abound in the history of technology. The need for a valve that delivers air at the right pressure from moment to moment during diving has already been mentioned (Cousteau, 1953, pp. 8–20). Finding the right filament for the electrical lightbulb held up Edison's development of a system for electrical light in homes for years (Baldwin, 2001).
43. Rhodes (1989).
44. Margolis (1987, 1993).

45. Larson (2010).
46. Larson (1997, 1998, 2010), Larson, Christensen, Franz and Abbott (1998) and Larson, Foster-Fishman and Keys (1994).
47. Smith and Alexander (1999).
48. Watson and Crick (1953).
49. Pierce and Writer (2005).
50. Oldby (1974/1994) and Watson (1968/1980).
51. See, e.g., Hull's (1990) case study of evolutionary biology. The idea that science makes progress, in part, because scientists critique each other's theories is one of Hull's central themes. This principle is supported by empirical studies of scientists (Dunbar, 1995, 1997).
52. Planck (1949, pp. 33–34).
53. Kunej and Turk (2000), McDermott and Hauser (2005) and Walker (2004). There are regularities in music cognition; see, e.g., Orr and Ohlsson (2001, 2005).
54. The numbers are taken from U.S. Census Bureau occupation data from the year 2000 census. I have taken the liberty of assuming that the numbers have not decreased since 2000. In the category "physicists" I include the Census categories "astronomers," "atmospheric and space scientists" and "other physical scientists."
55. Pacey (1992) and Usher (1929/1954).
56. Rosenberg (1982, p. 8).
57. Baggott (2004) and Einstein and Infeld (1938).
58. See, e.g., Bernstein (2004), Mokyr (1992, 1993) and Stearns (1998).
59. Goldfinch (2000).
60. Margolis (1987, 1993).
61. See *The Extant Fragments*, especially fragment 8(17), in Wright (1981/1995, pp. 166–167). Aristotle, although frequently credited with the four-elements theory, thought that the basic elements or principles were three in number; see Physics (*Physica*), Book I, Chapters 6–7. Strathern (2000) writes: "... the notion of four basic elements ... was to prove one of the biggest blunders in human thought, and its effects were to be a catastrophe for our intellectual development (p. 17).
62. Blanshard (1949) has analyzed the retreat from likeness in painting.
63. Although the Western literary and intellectual traditions continued to change and evolve during the medieval period (Colish, 1997), it is also true that science and technology in the A.D. 400 to A.D. 1400 period progressed at a snail's pace compared to the last 300 years (Pacey, 1992; Usher, 1929/1954).
64. Jansen (2000).
65. Joravsky (1986).
66. Goldfinch (2000).
67. Technological inventions acted as butterfly effects by having strong impact on the outcome of the various battles of World War II. Such inventions include radar, code-breaking techniques, direction finding, the Norden bombsight and, of course, the atomic bomb (Shachtman, 2003).
68. Strathern (2000).
69. Aunger (2002), Blackmore (1999), Brodie (1996) and Lynch (1996).
70. Schick and Toth (1994).

71. The literature of human evolution is by now extensive, with many different ideas and principles proposed as central to the process. Donald (1991) and Mithen (1996) especially emphasize changes in cognitive representation systems.
72. Eldredge (1989), Eldredge and Gould (1972), Gould (2002) and Somit and Peterson (1992). For the quote, see Eldredge and Gould (1972, p. 193).

CHAPTER 6. THE GROWTH OF COMPETENCE

1. Bruner (1970, p. 65).
2. From Gagné. *The Conditions of Learning*, 1E. © 1965 Wadsworth, a part of Cengage Learning, Inc. Reproduced by permission. www.cengage.com/permissions.
3. Furniss (2005, p. 49). See also www.space.com/news/spacehistory/leonov_spacewalk_000318.html.
4. See, e.g., Horai et al. (1995). Cavalli-Sforza (2000), Olson (2002) and Stringer and McKie (1997) provide readable summaries of the relevant evidence.
5. Olson (2002, Chap. 3).
6. Belich (2001).
7. Sténuit (1966) tells the story from the aquanaut's own point of view; additional details are available in Miller and Koblick (1995, pp. 28–30). Three underwater habitats were created and operated by Jacques Costeau's underwater research organization. The Conshelf I experiment is described in Chapter 18 of the popular book, *The Living Sea* (Costeau, 1963); see also Miller and Koblick (1995, pp. 30–33). The second habitat, Conshelf II, was located in the Red Sea and harbored a group of five divers, including Claude Wesley, for one month. Two of the divers lived for six days in a smaller habitat anchored at a depth of 90 feet, breathing an oxygen-helium mixture. The Conshelf II experiment is described and photographically documented in the book *World Without Sun* (Costeau, 1964); see also Miller and Koblick (1995, pp. 33–37). The third habitat, Conshelf III, let six divers live at a depth of 100 meters for three weeks (Miller & Koblick, 1995, pp. 65–71).
8. Two years before Skylab, the Soviet Union launched and manned the space station Salyut, but after three weeks in space, the three-man crew was killed during re-entry to earth's atmosphere. The following Salyut-2 mission was also unsuccessful, so the first successful Salyut mission did not occur until 1974, a year after the Skylab triumph (Furniss, 2005, pp. 98–101). Additional information about Skylab is available at www-pao.ksc.nasa.gov/history/skylab/skylab.html.
9. Questions like how fast people learn or how much they improve while practicing are ill-defined in the general case because the answers depend on the type of task being practiced, the amount of prior learning and other factors. However, we can model improvement in terms of time to task completion by a so-called power law equation, $T_N = T_1 * N^{-a}$, where T_N is the time to task completion on trial number N, T_1 is the time to task completion on the first training trial and a is a parameter that measures the learning rate; see Note 11, this chapter. Newell and Rosenbloom (1981, Table 1.2, p. 25) summarize values for the rate parameter obtained in empirical studies. Unfortunately, the reported values range from .06 to .95, providing little guidance for what to designate as a typical case. Suppose we focus on a task

for which the average time to completion on the first training trial is 10 minutes, or 600 seconds. In this case, if the learning rate parameter a is equal to .25, then it takes approximately 15 training trials to cut the time to task completion in half, to 300 seconds. If the learning rate parameter is instead .75, it only takes 3 training trials to cut the time in half. There are few other task variables that will yield behavioral effects of this magnitude.

10. See Campitelli and Gobet (2005) and Holding (1985, Chap. 3) for cognitive research on chess in general and blindfolded chess in particular. See, e.g., Chase and Ericsson (1981) for a particularly striking case study of a person whose performance improved 10-fold with extended practice on a task that is often considered as measuring a stable characteristic of a person's cognition.

11. The learning curve (or practice curve) is constructed by plotting performance on a task (e.g., time to task completion) as a function of the amount of practice (e.g., number of practice problems completed, total time in the relevant task environment, etc.). The first researchers to display data on the acquisition of a complex skill in this way were probably Edward L. Thorndike (1898) in his study of animals learning how to escape from problem boxes, and Bryan and Harter (1887, 1899) in an influential study of telegraph operators. Ebbinghaus (1885/1964) had displayed data from the memorization of lists of syllables in this way 30 years earlier. Learning curves are typically jagged when plotted for a single learner but become regular when plotted in terms of averages across learners. The shape of the curve emerged early as a research issue. The work by Bryan and Harter (1887, 1899) made researchers search for plateaus, periods during which the learner appears to make no improvements but which are followed by periods of rapid improvement. This supposed phenomenon invited the interpretation that the learner was revising his skill internally, and that the advantages of the revision could not be realized in performance until it was complete. Intriguing as this hypothesis is, subsequent research did not support the existence of plateaus (Keller, 1958). Most researchers have concluded that learning/practice curves exhibit uniform negative acceleration ("Almost any learning curve shows ... a negative acceleration; it flattens out as practice advances; the rate of improvement decreases"; Woodworth, 1938, p. 164), but some are more reluctant to let go of the plateau than others (see, e.g., Stadler, Vetter, Haynes & Kruse, 1996). Interestingly, the learning curve is also a topic of research in economics. Economists discovered that entire factories exhibit such curves when unit cost (a measure of economic performance) is plotted as a function of the length of the production run (a measure of amount of practice). Economists are more prepared to accept different shapes of empirical learning curves (see Note 5, Chapter 8), and they are not as convinced as psychologists that plateaus in the sense of Bryan and Harter are a pseudo-phenomenon (although it should be noted that the word "*plateau*" is often used in economic contexts to refer to the final leveling off of a learning curve, which is properly called the *asymptote*). The difference between psychologists and economists on this point is likely due to the fact that the former typically study learning in one-hour experiments and their learning curves hence describe short-term effects, while the latter study improvement processes in economic organizations that last for months and years and that

involve multiple learners. Obviously, both types of effects have to asymptote at some point, but the appearance of intermediate plateaus is more likely in temporally extended and complex cases.
12. The student was faced with a 5 by 5 matrix, with the letters of the alphabet randomly distributed over the 25 cells. The task was to focus on 12 of the cells in a specified order, notice the letter in each cell and write them down in the specified order. The subset of 12 cells and the order in which they were to be visited were the same from trial to trial, but the distribution of the letters varied.
13. See Notes 40–43, Chapter 7, for background references for the concept of transfer.
14. Bloom (1984), Chi et al. (2001) and Cohen, Kulik and Kulik (1982).
15. See Warren (2006) and Willingham (1998) for theories of motor coordination and motor skill learning.
16. Catrambone (1995, 1998).
17. Corrigan-Halpern (2006) and Corrigan-Halpern and Ohlsson (2002).
18. Empirical evidence for goal hierarchies has been provided by Altmann and Trafton (2002), Anderson (1993, pp. 129-132), Catrambone (1995, 1998), Corrigan-Halpern and Ohlsson (2002, Figure 2), Egan and Greeno (1974, Figures 4.20-4.22), Greeno (1974) and others. The fundamental reasons that complex systems tend toward hierarchical organization have been laid out by Boulding (1961, Chap. 2), Koestler (1972), Simon (1962) and von Bertalanffy (1968/1973, pp. 25ff).
19. See Anderson (1976, pp. 116–119) and Winograd (1975) for early statements of the declarative-procedural distinction, and Ohlsson (1994) for a summary.
20. The cognitive sciences have long pondered how the relation between the declarative, descriptive aspect of knowledge and the action-oriented, prescriptive aspect should be conceptualized; see Ohlsson (1994) for definitions and Ohlsson (2007b) for a historical analysis of the relationship.
21. The term "production rule" stems from the fact that one can view such rules as producing the symbol or symbol structures on their right-hand sides. This notation for describing symbolic computations was invented by the American mathematician E. Post (1943) for the purpose of proving theorems in automata theory. It was imported into cognitive science via Noam Chomsky's (1957/1972) generative grammars. Newell (1966, 1972, 1973) and Newell and Simon (1972a) extended it by implementing the first computer program that could execute a set of production rules and thereby automatically derive the behavior of a set of rules in a given situation or context. For the subsequent development of production system models, see Neches, Langley and Klahr (1987) and for recent developments, see Anderson (2005) and Nason and Laird (2005). The production rule format is as close as cognitive science has come to a lingua franca for describing cognitive processes.
22. Newell (1972, 1973) and Newell and Simon (1972a).
23. Researchers working with the production rule formalism have published a variety of rule sets for tasks ranging from spatial reasoning to geometry; see, e.g., Anderson (1983, 1993), Newell and Simon (1972a), Ohlsson (1990a) and various chapters in Klahr, Langley and Neches (1987). Very simple strategies might be

represented by a dozen rules. For complex strategies, the number is at least an order of magnitude greater.
24. But see Clancey (1985) and Lenat (1983) for two exceptions, as well as the collection of papers in Groner, Groner and Bischof (1983).
25. McDermott and Forgy (1978).
26. The term was introduced by Anderson (1983) and it has come into widespread use as a convenient verbal label for the innate cognitive equipment, that is, the totality of the cognitive structures and processes that are not acquired through learning. See Cooper (2006) for a philosophical discussion of this concept.
27. VanLehn (1991).
28. James (1890, vols. 1 and 2).
29. Thorndike (1898).
30. Bryan and Harter (1897, 1899). This pioneering study has had more impact on micro-economics than on psychology; see, e.g., Jovanovic and Nyarko (1995) and Reis (1991).
31. Ebbinghaus (1885/1964).
32. Watson (1913). Hilgard and Bower (1966) is the classic and most comprehensive review of behaviorist learning theories.
33. See Woodworth (1938) for the summary of complex skill acquisition (pp. 156–175) and for a discussion of the learning curve (pp. 170–173).
34. Woodworth (1938, p. 164).
35. Gardner (1985, Chap. 2). See also the introduction to Wiener (1948, pp. 7–39), the historical observations in Miller (2003) and the historical addendum in Newell and Simon (1972a, pp. 873–889).
36. Wiener (1948); see Conway and Siegelman (2005) and Heims (1991) for the history of the cybernetic movement.
37. Boden (1972, Chap. 4), Miller, Galanter and Pribram (1960), Moray (1987), Powers (1973), Smith (1966) and Smith and Smith (1966).
38. Conway and Siegelman (2005).
39. See Crevier (1993) and Gardner (1985) for the history of cognitive science and Newell, Shaw and Simon (1958) for the original article.
40. Ausubel (1968) and Gagné (1965). See R. C. Anderson (1967) for a review of the period.
41. Fitts (1964) and Welford (1968).
42. Anzai and Simon (1979).
43. Anderson (1982, 1983, 1987) and Anderson, Kline and Beasley (1978, 1979).
44. See Rosenbloom, Laird and Newell (1993) and Rosenbloom and Newell (1986, 1987). The original Soar model learned only by capturing paths to subgoals discovered during problem solving, but Nason and Laird (2005) extended the system with feedback-based (reinforcement) learning.
45. Sun, Merrill and Peterson (2001); and Sun, Slusarz and Terry (2005).
46. VanLehn (1999), VanLehn and Jones (1993), and VanLehn, Jones and Chi (1992). *Cascade* grew out of a prior model of learning from examples in arithmetic (VanLehn, 1990).
47. For a technical review, see Ohlsson (2008a).
48. Bradshaw (1992).

49. The specificity principle was first proposed in Ohlsson (2008a).
50. Fitts (1964).
51. Fitts (1964, p. 261).
52. Neves and Anderson (1981). For a neural network view of the proceduralization of instructions, see Schneider and Oliver (1991).
53. See, e.g., Ohlsson (1987a) for a simulation model that could execute a form of practical reasoning in a very simple spatial task domain. See, e.g., Hiebert (1986) for an analysis of this type of learning from the point of view of mathematics education.
54. Thorndike and Woodworth (1901).
55. See Kieras and Bovair (1986) and Singley and Anderson (1989).
56. Carbonell (1983, 1986), Falkenhainer, Forbus and Gentner (1989), Forbus, Gentner and Law (1994), Holyoak and Thagard (1989a, 1989b), Hummel and Holyoak (1997, 2003), Keane, Ledgeway and Duff (1994) and Veloso and Carbonell (1993).
57. I know of no simulation model of learning from live demonstrations; but see VanLehn (1991, 1999) and VanLehn and Jones (1993) for a model that learns from solved examples.
58. Hilgard and Bower (1966, p. 3).
59. Barrow, Mitrovic, Ohlsson and Grimley (2008) and Ohlsson et al. (2007).
60. The quote is from Thorndike (1898, p. 45). The idea of gradual strengthening was central to the behaviorist notion of learning as the building of stimulus-response connections. After the cognitive revolution, the idea that repeated traversal of a link or repeated application or execution of a knowledge structure causes an increase in the strength associated with that knowledge structure has remained one of the standard tools of cognitive models (Ohlsson, 2008a). The consequences of an increase in strength are typically hypothesized to be that the knowledge structure has a greater probability of being activated, retrieved from memory, applied or executed. The conceptual difficulty inherent in this idea is that once a knowledge structure S_1 has acquired a greater strength than some other structure S_2, it will always win over S_2 in any future situation, which in turn will increase S_1's advantage over S_2, locking the cognitive system into choosing S_1 in any future situation in which both knowledge structures apply. This is not a promising hypothesis if the goal is to explain human flexibility. Thorndike's mentor, William James, saw the problem clearly: "So nothing is easier than to imagine how, when a current [i.e., a neural signal] once has traversed a path [inside the nervous system], it should traverse it more readily still a second time. But what made it ever traverse it the first time?" (James, 1890, vol. 1, p. 109). The introduction of noise into the strength levels or the decision-making process does not go very far toward alleviating this conceptual problem. In the end, this problem cannot be solved unless we also assume that negative feedback has the power to reduce the strength of a knowledge structure.
61. Sun, Merrill and Peterson (2001) and Sun, Slusarz and Terry (2005). In its emphasis on interactions between implicit and explicit learning, the *Clarion* system is a descendant of the instructable neural net model of Schneider and Oliver (1991).

62. There are several different computational models of generalization of practical knowledge; see, e.g., Anderson (1983, 1987), Lewis (1988), Mitchell (1982), Sun, Merrill and Peterson (2001) and Sun, Sluzarz and Terry (2005).
63. Examples of such learning mechanisms are found in, among other works, Elio and Scharf (1990), Jones and VanLehn (1994), Larkin (1981), Neches (1987), Ohlsson (1987b), Ruiz and Newell (1993), Shrager and Siegler (1998) and Siegler and Araya (2005).
64. Altmann and Bums (2005), Gray and Boehm-Davis (2000), Gray, Shelles and Sims (2005) and Schooler and Hertzwig (2005). This form of learning was originally studied by the behaviorists under the label *statistical learning theory* (Estes, 1950) and the main phenomenon was called *probability matching* (Grant, Hake & Hornseth, 1951).
65. Logan (1998).
66. There is a persistent itch among cognitive theorists to reach for a description of cognition at a level of abstraction above that of process models. Indeed, there is a need for a type of description that constrains and specifies the system that a process model is to instantiate and hence explain. Such formulations include Noam Chomsky's distinction between linguistic *competence* and *performance* (Chomsky, 1964; Pylyshyn, 1973); Zenon W. Pylyshyn's distinction between *functional architecture* and *cognitive processes* (Pylyshyn, 1980, 1986); David Marr's distinction between the *computational* and the *algorithmic* levels in vision (Marr, 1982); Allen Newell's distinction between the *knowledge level* and the *symbol level* in the description of an information processing system (Newell, 1982); and John R. Anderson's *rationality principle*, which says that a first approximation model of human cognition can assume that the latter is maximally efficient (Anderson, 1989, 1990). The Principle of Maximally Efficient Learning is a rationality principle of this sort, and it was inspired by these prior formulations but differs from them in its exclusive focus on skill acquisition.
67. Anderson (1989, 1990) and Newell (1990, p. 33).
68. Ohlsson and Jewett (1997).

CHAPTER 7. ERROR CORRECTION: THE SPECIALIZATION THEORY

1. Norman (1981, p. 3).
2. Bruner (1970, p. 67).
3. Cavalli-Sforza (2000), Olson (2002) and Stringer and McKie (1997).
4. These two proverbs regarding learning from error appear in European sources from way back. The Web page http://www.answers.com/topic/a-burnt-child-dreads-the-fire gives sources as far back as A.D. 1250 for the one about dreading the fire, and the Web page http://wwww.answers.com/topic/once-bitten-twice-shy gives multiple 19th-century sources for the second one. The two proverbs appear to have been fused in the American variant *once burned, twice shy*.
5. Thorndike (1927).
6. Thorndike (1898, p. 45).
7. James (1890, vol. 1, pp. 24–27).
8. James (1890, vol. 1, p. 25).

9. The current version of this micro-theory is the descendant of a prior theory that was first published in Ohlsson (1987b). It was re-formulated in Ohlsson (1993a, 1996a, 1996b); see Ohlsson (2007b), Ohlsson, Ernst and Rees (1992) and Ohlsson and Rees (1991a, 1991b) for various applications. The current version is augmented with auxiliary hypotheses about how the error correction mechanism interacts with other learning mechanisms (Ohlsson, 2008a).
10. Allwood (1984), Allwood and Montgomery (1982) and Anderson and Jeffries (1985).
11. See Ohlsson (1994) for the origins and definition of this distinction. It was introduced into cognitive science by Anderson (1976, pp. 116–119) and Winograd (1975). It is ultimately rooted in common sense: There is a clear subjective difference between knowing that something is the case and knowing how to perform a certain type of task. Behaviorally, the distinction is expressed in the fact that the ability to recite from memory a description of a desired task performance does not automatically bring with it the ability to produce that performance without prior practice ("*In order to land a 747 airplane, …*). Neves and Anderson (1981) proposed a computational theory of the translation from a verbal recipe to an executable skill and its application in the domain of geometry. Neuroscience research also supports the distinction between declarative and practical knowledge (Squire, 1987). Indeed, the distinction has turned out to be helpful in understanding the patterns of impairment and ability in diverse classes of patients with brain damage (Eslinger & Damasio, 1986; Glisky, 1992; Timmerman & Brouwer, 1999).
12. Philosophers have explored various ideas about truth, including that truth is the relation between an assertion and a material state of affairs (the correspondence theory, see O'Connor, 1975); that truth consists in an assertion cohering with all other assertions already accepted as truth (the coherence theory; see Walker, 1989); that truth is whatever supports successful action (the pragmatic theory; see Smith, 1978, and Thayer, 1982); and others as well (see, e.g., Kirkham, 1992). The proliferation of theories is sufficient evidence that philosophers do not yet have a theory of truth: "The problem of how to relate truth to human desires, beliefs, intentions, and the use of language seems to be the right one to concentrate on in thinking about truth. It also seems to me this problem is not much nearer a solution today than it was in [John] Dewey's day" (Davidson, 1990, p. 280). Because the attempt at explication has been going on for at least 2,500 years, the lack of success becomes an indictment of the enterprise and suggests that the question is not framed well.
13. Evans (2007), Johnson-Laird (1999) and Shafir and LeBoeuf (2002). But see Rips (1994), especially Table 5.1 (pp. 151–152), for an example of a logic-based theory that predicts certain aspects of logical reasoning with high accuracy.
14. Perkins (1981, pp. 128–129).
15. The dissociation between action and judgment, generation and evaluation, has been observed in a wide variety of behaviors, from pushing buttons in a specified sequence (Kay, 1951) to speech (Mattson & Baars, 1992; Postma, 2000). The developmental experiments regarding number knowledge were done by Gelman and Meck (1983): "The range of set sizes to which the children know that these principles [of counting] apply is much greater than the range that they can successfully count" (p. 357).

16. Botvinick et al. (2001) and Fiehler, Ullsperger and von Cramon (2005).
17. There is a branch of Artificial Intelligence research that builds constraint satisfaction systems. However, the formal definition of a constraint proposed here is different from the one that appears in those models, and constraints are utilized in a different way in the error correction model than in typical constraint satisfaction system. See, e.g., Mackworth (1992), for a review from a computer science point of view and Holyoak and Thagard (1989b) for an application of the traditional constraint satisfaction concept to a cognitive modeling problem.
18. Allwood (1984, p. 415).
19. The hypothesis that cognitive processes are driven by anticipations and expectations have been explored in several areas, including sensory-motor behaviors (Hoffman et al., 2007), text comprehension (Schank, 1982) and memory (Neuschatz et al., 2002). It is possible to experimentally verify the generation of expectations even in the eye movements of babies (Haith, Hazan & Goodman, 1988). Expectations regarding others obviously play an important role in social interactions (Holmes, 2002).
20. Gensler (1987, p. 78).
21. Holmes (1992, p. 57).
22. Bell (2005), McCann (1978) and Thagard (1992, Chap. 3).
23. Brown and Burton (1978), Brown and VanLehn (1980) and Burton (1982).
24. The system does not have to be all that complex before diagnosis becomes difficult; see Burton (1982) regarding the issues in diagnosing errors in arithmetic. The identification of programming errors (Johnson, 1986; Spohrer, Soloway & Pope, 1985), the troubleshooting of complex equipment (Konradt, 1995; Lajoie & Lesgold, 1992; Liu & Liu, 2001; Patrick et al., 1999a, 1999b; Patrick, James, Ahmed & Halliday, 2006) and the diagnosis of sick people (Groopman, 2007; Norman, 2005) are more complicated.
25. Norman (1981), and Reason (1990).
26. Heckhausen and Beckmann (1990), Reason (1990, Chap. 3) and Senders and Moray (1991, p. 89).
27. Laird and Newell (1993), Lenat (1983), Newell and Simon (1976) and Simon (1990).
28. Displacement errors are closely related to the concept of *capture errors*, as introduced by Norman (1981) and Reason (1990). The subtle difference is that the latter notion emphasizes the strength of a rule or action schema, while the notion of displacement emphasizes its generality. Both concepts help explain how a rule grabs control of action even when it should not.
29. Marcus et al. (1992).
30. For example, Anderson and Jeffries (1985) studied errors in problem solving due to loss of information from working memory. Another malfunction view of error derives them from *repairs*, attempts by the cognitive architecture to overcome impasses that happen during the execution of a flawed, incomplete or inconsistent cognitive strategy (Brown & VanLehn, 1980).
31. See Ohlsson and Rees (1991a, 1991b) for the original statement of the constraint-based rule specialization algorithm.

32. "A major lesson from AI [Artificial Intelligence] about generate-and-test situations is that it always pays to transfer knowledge from the test to the generator, so that candidate solutions need never be created at all" (Newell, 1990, p. 100).
33. Langley (1983, 1985, 1987).
34. See Festinger (1957/1962), Piaget (1985) and Schank (1982). Popper's falsificationist philosophy of science has been discussed as a theory of learning from error by Berkson and Wettersten (1984). For action-conflict-change theories in motor learning, see Hoffman et al. (2007).
35. The classic reference is Pauling (1935/1960). Niaz (2001) describes the historical emergence of the co-valent bond.
36. Solomons (1988).
37. See Ohlsson (1993a, 1996b) for more details about the chemistry simulation.
38. The idea that change moves from concrete and specific knowledge structures toward abstract ones has been expressed over and over again in a variety of ways in different cognitive theories that otherwise differ in focus, formulation and intent. Jean Piaget hypothesized that children's cognitive skills advance from sensorimotor skills through a stage of concrete thinking and on to a stage of abstract thinking. (See Piaget, 1950, for an original statement of the stage theory, and Flavell, 1963, for a comprehensive summary.) Contemporary theories of skill acquisition envision a process of generalization that can apply, for example, to production rules to generate more abstract rules (see, e.g., Sun, Merrill & Peterson, 2001, for an example and Ohlsson, 2008a, for a review) and to descriptions to generate more abstract mental representations often called *schemas* (Gick & Holyoak, 1983; Marshall, 1995). This process apparently operates even in implicit learning of such improbable learning targets as abstract grammatical rules embodied in random-looking letter strings (Reber, 1996). The field of category learning has contributed the theory of prototypes, which says that people's representations of categories like "bird" and "fruit" capture the central tendency of the category instances that they have seen. That is, what is acquired in category learning is a representation of the average bird or fruit, a very particular form of generalization. See Rosch (1978) for an early statement of the prototype theory. The literature on later developments is large (Osherson & Smith, 1981; Smith & Minda, 1998; Smith, Osherson, Rips & Keane, 1988). Ashby and Maddox (2005) review evidence, including neuroscience data, on performance of prototype-related categorization tasks. The fundamental principle behind these and many other cognitive theories is that knowledge moves from concrete and specific to abstract and general in the course of learning.
39. Brain-imaging studies have shown that the Specialization Principle applies to other types of learning as well, e.g., category learning (Little & Thulborn, 2006). For the connection to the themes of differentiation and specialization in evolution and ontogenesis, see, e.g., Carroll (2005), Berenbaum (1996), Futuyma and Moreno (1988), Raff (1996) and Wolpert (1992).
40. Like so many aspects of skill acquisition, research on transfer goes back to the work by Edward L. Thorndike. Thorndike and Woodworth (1901) proposed that the amount of transfer from task X to task Y is determined by the overlap or similarity between the two tasks, measured in terms of the number of identical

elements. This formulation leaves open what is to count as an "element." Kieras and Bovair (1986) and Singley and Anderson (1989) have shown that if an element is interpreted as a production rule, then Thorndike's principle predicts the amount of transfer to a high degree. However, rules have to have at least a minimal level of abstraction to apply to multiple situations, so the identical rules interpretation hides within it the second, and older, idea about transfer: Knowledge transfers because it is abstract. This concept has been around since the beginning of systematic thinking about cognition (e.g., James, 1890; see vol. 1, pp. 505–508, and vol. 2, pp. 345–348) and it is still current (Bassok & Holyoak, 1989; Goldstone & Sakamoto, 2003; Ohlsson, 1993b; Ohlsson & Lehtinen, 1997; Reed, 1993; Salomon & Perkins, 1989). A third idea about transfer is that it occurs via analogy (Gentner, 1983; Gick & Holyoak, 1980, 1983; Hummel & Holyoak, 2003; Markman & Gentner, 2000). From a transfer point of view, the main difference between abstraction and analogy is that in the former case, the cognitive work necessary to bridge from the training task to the transfer task – creating the abstraction – is carried out in the context of mastering the training task, while in the analogy case, that work – creating the analogical mapping – is carried out at the time of encountering the transfer task. The transfer mechanism implied by the constraint-based theory strikes a balance between processing for the present and processing for the future, allowing for re-use of previously constructed skill components while also recognizing that re-use typically requires a variable amount of revision; see Ohlsson (2007a). However, it is highly unlikely that there is a single mechanism behind transfer of training (Nokes, 2009). See Detterman and Sternberg (1993), Haskell (2001) and Salomon and Perkins (1989) for useful reviews of transfer research.

41. Detterman (1993) summarized studies that failed to find transfer and pointed out that studies that produce measurable transfer effects tend to provide optimal conditions, including great similarities between training and transfer tasks and strong hints that the training task is relevant to the transfer task, factors that might not be present outside the laboratory. An example is Gick and Holyoak's (1980) study of analogical transfer between two isomorphs of Duncker's classic radiation problem (or *the convergence problem*). Even in a situation in which the two isomorphs follow each other in the course of a short experiment, 59% of the subjects failed to solve the transfer problem without a hint to use the analogue; 24% did not solve it even with the hint (Exp. V, Table 12). However, there is no standard metric and no widely accepted baseline or base rate against which to compare transfer effects: Some experimental subjects will perform a transfer task well even without transfer, so what level of performance is evidence for transfer? Gagné, Foster and Crowley (1948) reviewed a variety of savings measures of transfer – how much less training is required to master the transfer task after mastery of a training task as compared to after no prior training – but recent experimental work on transfer does not typically use such measures (but see Nokes and Ohlsson, 2004, and Singley and Anderson, 1989, for exceptions). In the absence of a standard metric and an accepted baseline for the amount of transfer, claims that transfer effects are great or small are moot. The amount of transfer is also a concern in the design of training in industry and business (Baldwin & Ford, 1988;

Salas & Cannon-Bowers, 2001, pp. 488–489; Yamnill & McLean, 2001). However, training scientists appear to be no further along than laboratory psychologists or educational researchers to settle on standard measures or criteria for assessing transfer effects.

42. Although the term "inert ideas" was used by Alfred North Whitehead in his discussion of the aims of education (Whitehead, 1929/1967, pp. 1–2), the concept of inert knowledge was first given a cognitive formulation and introduced into discussions of transfer by Bereiter and Scardamalia (1985); see Bransford and Schwartz (1999) and Renkl, Mandl and Gruber (1996) for later developments.

43. See Bransford and Schwartz (1999) for the proposal that transfer should be viewed as preparation for future learning. This concept is a close relative to the principle of *transfer-appropriate processing* (Morris, Bransford & Franks, 1977), which says that knowledge applies to a future situation only if it is encoded at the time of learning in a way that makes it relevant for that situation. This principle was already known in the memory literature as *encoding specificity* (Tulving, 1985, Chap. 11; Tulving & Thomson, 1973). Lockhart (2002) has reviewed these concepts.

44. Newell (1990, pp. 102–107) has discussed this in terms of a trade-off between *preparation* and *deliberation*. In computer science, it is more commonly known as the *store-versus-compute trade-off*.

45. Gelman and Gallistel (1978).

46. Ohlsson (1993a, 2007a) and Ohlsson and Rees (1991a).

47. Ohlsson and Rees (1991a).

48. Gelman (2000), Gelman and Gallistel (1978), Gelman and Meck (1983) and Gelman, Meck and Merkin (1986). Although the notion of special cognitive structures for number has been questioned, there is considerable evidence in favor (Wynn, Bloom & Chiang, 2002).

49. The original report of the transfer simulations can be found in Ohlsson and Rees (1991a, 1991b). Further analysis of these data, including a mathematical equation specifying the expected amount of transfer, are reported in Ohlsson (2007a).

50. Bassok (1990) and Bassok and Holyoak (1989).

51. Warren (1965) concluded a review of the comparative psychology of learning by saying that the data "suggest an orderly improvement in the efficiency of learning within the vertebrate series" (p. 110). The review by Moore (2004) provides additional support for this view.

52. Mithen (1996).

53. The view of the relation between instruction and learning that is captured in the Information Specificity Principle emerged out of Ohlsson (1983, 1986, 1988a, 1990b, 1991, 1992g, 1993c, 1996b). See Ohlsson (2008a) for the original statement of the Specificity Principle.

54. See Ohlsson (1992g) and Ohlsson, Ernst and Rees (1992) for the main description of this simulation exercise and Ohlsson (1992c) for some discussion points. VanLehn, Ohlsson and Nason (1994) reviewed this type of application of cognitive models.

55. Leinhardt (1987) and Leinhardt and Ohlsson (1990).

56. Brownell (1947) and Brownell and Moser (1949).
57. Regarding the amount of classroom time required for each subtraction with regrouping, see Leinhardt (1987). Regarding estimates of learning rate, Kurt VanLehn located 11 strategy changes in a 90-minute problem-solving effort, indicating a rate of 1 learning event every 8 minutes (VanLehn, 1991). However, VanLehn (1999) observed a much lower rate of learning in an analysis of 9 students who spent an average of 4.5 hours studying a textbook chapter in physics. Only 28 learning events were identified in the students' verbal protocols, which gives the much lower rate of 1 event per 1.5 hours of studying. It is more likely that a learning event fails to leave any trace in a verbal protocol than that a seasoned researcher thinks he is seeing a nonexistent event, so the higher learning rate is likely to be the one closest to the truth.
58. Researchers who work on intelligent tutoring systems (ITSs) form a community of their own, distinct from the broader field of computer-based education. ITS researchers have their own conferences and their own scientific journals. The ITS field came into its own in the late 1970s; the book edited by Sleeman and Brown (1982) was the defining document. Wenger (1987) reviewed the first wave of work. See Woolf (2009) for a recent appraisal of the field. The technical details of my own approach to ITS design are available in multiple research publications (Buchanan et al., 1995; Fossati, Di Eugenio, Brown & Ohlsson, 2008; Langley, Wogulis & Ohlsson, 1990; Lu et al., 2007; Mitrovic & Ohlsson, 1999; Mitrovic, Ohlsson & Martin, 2006; Ohlsson, 1986, 1987c, 1991, 1992d, 1992h, 1996b; Ohlsson & Langley, 1988; Ohlsson & Mitrovic, 2006, 2007).
59. The first paper on SQL-Tutor was Mitrovic and Ohlsson (1999). For descriptions and analyses of constraint-based tutors, see Mitrovic, Ohlsson and Martin (2006) and references in preceding Note 58 and Note 60 following.
60. See Mitrovic, Suraweera, Martin and Weerasinghe (2004) and Mitrovic, Martin and Suraweera (2007) for general discussions of the database suite. SQL-Tutor is described in Mitrovic, Martin and Mayo (2002), while Suraweera and Mitrovic (2004) and Mitrovic (2002, 2005) cover database design and normalization, respectively.
61. For empirical evaluations of constraint-based tutoring systems, see preceding Notes 58 and 59. For a study of the micro-engineering of a tutor's feedback messages, see Zakharov, Mitrovic and Ohlsson (2005).
62. Conway and Siegelman (2005).
63. Wiener (1948).

CHAPTER 8. ERROR CORRECTION IN CONTEXT

1. Reason (1990, p. 203).
2. From "Prologue: A Tale of Two Farms," from *Collapse: How Societies Choose to Fail or Succeed* by Jared Diamond, copyright © 2005 by Jared Diamond. Used by permission of Viking Penguin, a division of Penguin Group (USA) Inc.
3. Chi, Glaser and Farr (1988), Ericsson (1996), Ericsson, Charness, Feltovich and Hoffman (2006), Ericsson, Krampe and Tesch-Romber (1993), Ericsson and Lehmann (1996) and Feltovich, Ford and Hoffman (1997).

4. The learning curve (or the practice curve) is constructed by plotting performance on a task (e.g., time to task completion) as a function of the amount of practice (e.g., number of practice problems completed, total time in the relevant task environment). The first researchers to display data on the acquisition of a complex skill in this way were probably Edward L. Thorndike (1898) in his study of animals learning to escape from problem boxes, and Bryan and Harter (1897, 1899) in an influential study of telegraph operators. (Ebbinghaus, 1885/1964, had displayed data from the memorization of lists of syllables in this way 30 years earlier.) Learning curves are typically jagged when plotted for a single learner but become regular when plotted in terms of averages across learners. The shape of the learning curve emerged early as a research issue. The results of Bryan and Harter (1897, 1899) made researchers search for plateaus, periods during which the learner appears to make no improvements but which are followed by periods of rapid improvement. This supposed phenomenon invited the interpretation that the learner was revising his skill internally, but that the advantages of the revisions could not be realized in performance until they were complete. Intriguing as this hypothesis is, subsequent research did not support the existence of plateaus (Keller, 1958). Most researchers have concluded that learning/practice curves exhibit uniform negative acceleration ("Almost any learning curve shows ... a negative acceleration; it flattens out as practice advances; the rate of improvement decreases"; Woodworth, 1938, p. 164), but some are more reluctant to let go of the plateau than others (see, e.g., Stadler, Vetter, Haynes & Kruse, 1996). Interestingly, the learning curve is also a topic of research in economics where it was discovered that entire factories exhibit such curves when unit cost – a measure of performance – is plotted as a function of the length of the production run – a measure of amount of practice. Economists are more prepared than psychologists to accept different types of equations as accurate descriptions of the shapes of empirical learning curves, and they are not as convinced as psychologists that plateaus in the sense of Bryan and Harter are a pseudo-phenomenon (although it should be noted that the word "plateau" is often used in economics to refer to the final leveling off of a learning curve, which is properly called its *asymptote*). The difference between psychologists and economists on this point is likely due to the fact that the former typically study learning in one-hour experiments and their learning curves hence describe short-term effects in single individuals, while the latter study improvement processes in economic organizations that last for months and years. Obviously, both types of effects have to asymptote, but the appearance of intermediate plateaus is more likely in temporally extended cases.
5. The search for a mathematical equation for the learning curve began in the first decades of the 20th century (Woodworth, 1938, pp. 170–173). Snoddy (1926) may have been the first person to report that learning curves fit power law equations, but others followed (Stevens & Savin, 1962). The modern formulation of the power law interpretation of the learning curve and a review of some supporting evidence is available in Lane (1987), Newell and Rosenbloom (1981) and Delaney, Reder, Staszewski and Ritter (1998). Although most data sets fit power law equations at least marginally better than other types of equations, there is a long-standing debate whether some other type of equation is

theoretically better motivated. Mazur and Hastie (1978) compared exponential with hyperbolic functions because they suggest that learning is either replacement or accumulation, respectively, and concluded in favor of the latter, but Heathcote, Brown and Mewhort (2000) nevertheless champion the exponential alternative. The debate about the exact shape of the practice curve is complicated by the fact that many published curves were produced by averaging across subjects. Averaging across behavior that do not follow power laws might yield a power law, in which case the law might be a statistical artifact (Estes, 1956). This debate is ongoing (Brown & Heathcote, 2003; Haider & Frensch, 2002; Stratton et al., 2007). It is unclear what the proponents of the artifact view make of data from individual subjects that exhibit near-perfect fit to a power law (Newell & Rosenbloom, 1981, Figure 1.3, Figure 1.5 and Figure 1.6; also Stevens & Savin, 1962). Confusingly, there is a structurally similar debate about power laws in memorization studies (Myung, Kim & Pitt, 2000), but it concerns the shape of forgetting curves for the free recall of memorized lists rather than the improvement curves for skills. One would hardly expect forgetting of, for example, word lists and improvement in, for example, geometry proof finding to depend on the same cognitive mechanism or to generate the same behavioral phenomena, so this second debate is not as relevant for the shape of practice curves as the structural similarity of the arguments suggests. Economic analysts consider a wider spectrum of possible learning curve shapes than do psychologists, perhaps for the reasons stated in the previous note. For example, Uzumeri and Nembhard (1998), following Mazur and Hastie (1978), proposed a hyperbolic function, asserting that it is "known to reflect the way in which individuals learn both conceptual and motor skills" (p. 518); this claim is a surprise to cognitive psychologists who study skill acquisition.

6. Ohlsson and Jewett (1995, 1997).
7. Flavell (1963) is the best summary and overview of Piaget's research and theoretical system. See also Furth (1969). Piaget's own works are so numerous that it is difficult to single out any one text as more central than others; Piaget (1950) and Piaget (1985) are as good as any.
8. See Klahr and Wallace (1976) and Young (1976) for examples of transitional works that took a critique of Piaget's stage theory as the starting point for pioneering an information-processing approach to cognitive development. A decade later, Siegler (1986) summarized this period. Siegler (1987, 1989) performed detailed, response-by-response analyses to demonstrate the variety of strategies used by any one child in the domain of number knowledge, thereby undermining the notion of cognitive stages. There have been later attempts to rescue the idea of cognitive stages by defining them within other formalisms than the pseudo-logic used by Piaget himself – see, e.g., Commons et al. (1998) and van der Maas and Molenaar (1992) – and by being rigorous about the empirical criteria for the existence of stages (Dawson-Tunik, Commons, Wilson & Fischer, 2005). However, it is a fact that children (e.g., Luwel, Verschaffel, Onghena & De Corte, 2003; Ohlsson & Bee, 1991) as well as young adults (Nokes, 2009; Nokes & Ohlsson, 2004, 2005) shift flexibly among multiple strategies within task domains, so it is not clear what meaning can be attached to the notion of cognitive stages.

9. Siegler (1996, Fig. 4.4) and Siegler and Jenkins (1989).
10. Delaney, Reder, Staszewski and Ritter (1998) present evidence that improvement follows a power law both before and after a strategy discovery, but power laws with different slopes.
11. Ohlsson (1992e).
12. Crossman (1959, pp. 153–156).
13. The estimate for number of chess chunks is often stated as 50,000 units, chunks, of chess knowledge, typically supported by a reference to a 1973 paper by William G. Chase and Herbert A. Simon. These two authors published two papers in 1973 that give different estimates. Chase and Simon (1973a, p. 402) give the estimate of 50,000 units, while Chase and Simon (1973b, p. 249) instead advanced the much less precise estimate of 10,000 to 100,000 chunks. The latter estimate is not original but is based on two prior papers by Simon and Barenfeld (1969, pp. 481–482) and Simon and Gilmartin (1973, pp. 38–43). The estimations in these two papers are more thorough than those reported in Chase and Simon (1973a, 1973b). The main method of estimation is to create a chess-playing program with a database of chess chunks, measure its performance as a function of the number of chunks, and then extrapolate how much larger its database would have to be for the program to perform like a world-class player. This method of estimation presupposes that the program plays chess (or performs other chess-related tasks) in at least approximately the same way as the human players; put differently, it assumes that the theory of chess playing embodied in the program is approximately correct.
14. Miller (1996).
15. Felgenbaum(1989).
16. For example, the SQL-Tutor for teaching elementary database skills has more than 600 constraints (Mitrovic, Martin & Mayo, 2002).
17. See Note 3, this chapter, for references.
18. See Martin (1980) and Perry (1984) for blow-by-blow descriptions of the Three Mile Island accident, and Vaughan (1997) for a similarly dense description of the *Challenger* explosion. The analyses of the causes of the *Hindenburg* and the *Titanic* tragedies continue (Bain & van Vorst, 1999; Garzke, Foecke, Matthias & Wood, 2000; Matsen, 2008). See Franzén (1960) and Kvarning and Ohrelius (1992) regarding the warship *Wasa*. Petroski (1992) describes both the walkway collapse at the Kansas City Hyatt Regency Hotel (Chapter 8) and the collapse of the Tacoma Narrows Bridge (pp. 164–171). Smith and Alexander (1999) tell the story of how Xerox fumbled the future. The disastrous Operation Market Garden is described in Ryan (1974). Practice does not necessarily offer protection against errors in handling complex technologies (Youmans & Ohlsson, 2008).
19. Leplat and Rasmussen (1984), Norman (1981) and Reason (1990). "No one *wants* to learn by mistakes, but we cannot learn enough from successes to go beyond the state of the art [in engineering]" (Petroski, 1992, p. 62, italics in original).
20. Carroll and Mui (2008).
21. See Petroski (1992, 2006) for analyses of design errors in a variety of engineering systems. "Past successes, no matter how numerous and universal, are no guarantee of future performance in a new context" (Petroski, 2006, p. 3). See

Franzén (1960) and Kvarning and Ohrelius (1992) for analyses of the warship *Wasa*, specifically; see also the online source http://hem.bredband.net/johava/WASAe.htm#lista.
22. Cohen and Gooch (1991) and Macksey (1998). The disastrous Operation Market Garden is described in the book *A Bridge Too Far* (Ryan, 1974).
23. Hutchins (1995).
24. Edmondson (2004a, 2004b), Firth-Cozens (2001) and Wiig and Aase (2007).
25. Edmondson (2004a, p. ii3).
26. Duffey and Saull (2003).
27. The economic learning curve literature began with a study of the production of B17 Flying Fortress bombers. Mishina (1999) has re-analyzed the data from the original study. For more recent economic studies that use the learning curve as an analytical tool, see, e.g., Mitchell (2000), Uzumeri and Nembhard (1998) and Auerswald, Kauffman, Lobo and Shell (2000).
28. Amalberti (2001, p. 110).
29. Mitrovic and Ohlsson (1999), Mitrovic, Ohlsson and Martin (2006), Ohlsson (1986, 1987c, 1991, 1992d, 1992h, 1996b) and Ohlsson and Mitrovic (2006, 2007).
30. Bernstein (2004, Figure 12.1).
31. Diamond (2005).

CHAPTER 9. THE FORMATION OF BELIEF

1. Quine (1951, pp. 40).
2. The specific arguments given by Aristotle are that (a) if the Earth was created by pieces of earth moving toward the center of the universe (as we would call it now), then a sphere will result; (b) "the fact that the motions of heavy bodies always make equal angles, and are not parallel," an argument that is hard to follow; (c) in eclipses, the outline of the Earth's shadow on the moon is always curved, and only spheres cast curved shadows in all directions; (d) as one moves north or south, the star constellations change; and (e) there are elephants in both "the parts about India," i.e., east of Greece, and "the parts about the pillars of Herculus," possibly areas of North Africa west of Greece, suggesting that these parts are geographically adjacent, as they could be if the Earth were spherical but a lot smaller than it is. Aristotle, *On the heavens* (*De caelo*), II.297a10–298a20. For Eratosthenes' attempt to measure the size of the Earth, see Fischer (1975) and Newton (1980). See also http://en.wikipedia.org/wik/Flat.Earth.
3. See Notes 19, 20 and 21, this chapter, for references to empirical studies.
4. As pointed out in Part III, the propositional theory of knowledge has not succeeded as an epistemological theory, in the sense that there is no consensus among epistemologists as to what a proposition is and what it means for a proposition to be true or false. In this chapter, propositions are whatever knowledge structures encode declarative knowledge in human memory, and "true" and "false" stand for a person's subjective mental state regarding the status of a proposition. See Ohlsson (1994) for a definition of the distinction between declarative and practical (or procedural) knowledge, and Griffin and Ohlsson (2001) for a discussion of the relation between knowledge and belief. The approach to

declarative knowledge in this chapter is an outgrowth of the analyses reported in Ohlsson (1992f, 1993b, 1995a, 1995b, 1999a, 1999b, 2000, 2002, 2007b), Ohlsson and Hemmerich (1999), Ohlsson and Lehtinen (1997) and Ohlsson and Regan (2001).
5. These factors include repetition, depth of processing and prior knowledge. The effects of such factors are covered in any textbook in cognitive psychology, e.g., Goldstein (2008) and Reisberg (2006).
6. Peter Gärdenfors, one of the pioneers of the formal study of belief revision, put it this way: "When we change our beliefs, we want to retain as much as possible of our old beliefs … this heuristic … is called the criterion of *informational economy*" (Gärdenfors, 1988, p. 49, italics in original). Gabbay and Woods (2001) similarly propose a general principle they call the *Ad Ignorantiam Rule*, stated thus: "Human agents tend to accept without challenge the utterances and arguments of others except where they know or think they know or suspect that something is amiss" (p. 150).
7. This proverb goes back at least to 17th-century England. See http://www.greatquotes.com.
8. See Note 22, Chapter 4.
9. The transition from a flat or disc-shaped Earth to a round one is visible in Aristotle, *On the heavens* (De caelo), II.297a10–298a20. The story of how overflow of body fluids and miasmas were replaced by germs as the causes of disease is a riveting tale (Waller, 2002). The idea that history passes through a fixed sequence of eras or ages, each age being less happy than the previous one, is stated in Hesiod's poem, *Works and Days*, lines 97–204, written sometime in the 8th century B.C., and in Ovid's *Metamorphoses*, lines 89–150, written in the first decade A.D. It has often been combined with the idea that time is cyclic, so that at the end of the sequence of ages, the Golden Age appears again (Lovejoy & Boas, 1935/1997, Chap. 2). This view was held by the Stoics, among others (Whitrow, 1989, Chap. 4). The idea that our conception of time has developed from cyclic to linear is generally accepted but has been disputed by Press (1977). Scientific theories like natural selection and plate tectonics are squarely on the side of linear time.
10. See, e.g., Mackie (2006) for a discussion of resistance in everyday contexts and Tavris and Aronson (2007) for a review of what is known about errors and resistance from the point of view of social psychology. The obvious connection between cognitive conservatism and resistance to change in clinical situations is underexplored. Janoff-Bulman (1992, Chap. 2) makes that connection in the special case of reactions to trauma. Interestingly, resistance to contradictory information is even present in the perception of brief visual exposures (Bruner & Postman, 1949).
11. See Dubos (1976) on Pasteur and fermentation, Stringer and McKie (1997) on the out-of-Africa theory and Kragh (2000) about the resistance to the disintegration theory among traditional chemists. Barber (1961) reviewed multiple cases of resistance to scientific advances within science. The existence of such resistance was one of the inspirations behind Lakato's (1980) philosophical theory of a belt of auxiliary assumptions that protect core principles from falsification. More recently, Pratt (2000) has summarized evidence against the plate tectonics theory that would seem sufficient to falsify that theory if Lakatosian processes were not operating. Dunbar

(1995, 1997), Dunbar and Fugelsang (2005), Fugelsang, Stein, Green and Dunbar (2004) and Trickett, Schunn and Trafton (2005) report empirical studies that add detail to the story of how scientists react to unexpected findings. They have found that when evidence contradicts a core hypothesis, scientists do attend to it, largely because they are pushed to do so by their colleagues in the context of laboratory meetings and other public and semi-public interactions. Another finding is that the character of the conflict between theory and data, and the frequency with which the conflict appears both determine the extent and the type of response.

12. Kuhn (1970, p. 152).
13. Major handbooks of psycholinguistics include Gaskell (2007), Graesser, Gernsbacher and Goldman (2003) and Traxler and Gernsbacher (2006). In conjunction, these handbooks cover most aspects of discourse.
14. In a famous article, H. P. Grice (1975) proposed that if conversations are viewed as a form of collaboration, it follows that people strive to moderate the quantity, quality and relevance of what they say, as well as their manner of speaking, so as to be maximally helpful to the listener. This includes saying neither more nor less than what the listener needs to be told, i.e., to state only what is new to him or her. See http://plato.stanford.edu/entries/grice.
15. Gaskell (2007) and Traxler and Gernsbacher (2006).
16. See, e.g., Swinney (1979) for an early paper that supported parallel activation of multiple meanings. As researchers dig deeper, the details become more complicated (Swaab, Brown & Hagoort, 2003). For present purposes, the general idea of parallel activation of more than one meaning, followed by resolution through context (perhaps among other factors), is sufficient.
17. The spy and the bird are visitors from Goldstein (2008, pp. 370–376).
18. The turtles on the log were a gift to psycholinguistics from Bransford, Barclay and Franks (1972). Like other turtles, they have turned out to be long-lived (Jahn, 2004). They demonstrate the ubiquitous presence of bridging inferences in comprehending belief-congruent texts. For an example of the diametrically opposite case, with bridging inferences lacking in the processing of a belief-incongruent text, see Graesser, Kassler, Kreuz and McLain-Allen (1998).
19. Nussbaum (1985), Vosniadou (1994a, 1994b) and Vosniadou and Brewer (1992).
20. Johnson, Moher, Ohlsson and Gillingham (1999), Johnson, Moher, Ohlsson and Leigh (2001) and Ohlsson, Moher and Johnson (2000).
21. Vosniadou (1994a, 1994b) and Vosniadou and Brewer (1992).
22. Duhem (1914/1991, especially pp. 83–88; see p. 187 for the quote).
23. Quine (1951) and Quine and Ullian (1978).
24. Quine and Ullian (1978, p. 16).
25. Quine and Ullian (1978, p. 79).
26. Quine and Ullian (1978, p. 22).
27. Quine and Ullian (1978, p. 79).
28. Quine (1951, p. 39).
29. See Rokeach (1960, 1970). The idea of grouping beliefs or knowledge elements by topic or theme is consistent with the idea that the mind strives for local rather than global coherence. Global coherence is not attainable in a natural system, in part because assessing the coherence of every piece of knowledge

with the rest of the belief base is computationally costly, and in part because living beings, as opposed to ideal systems, sometimes need to maintain inconsistent beliefs. The striving for consistency must in practice be limited to circumscribed domains or topics. The principle that coherence is a matter of degree plays a central role in Paul Thagard's theory of explanatory coherence; see Thagard and Verbeurgt (1998) for a formal definition of coherence and Thagard (1992) for multiple applications to scientific revolutions. The notion that coherence is only locally maintained has been explored by Hoadley, Ranney and Schank (1994), Ranney and Schank (1998) and Ranney, Schank, Mosmann and Montoya (1993).

30. "The more central a belief the more it will resist change" (Rokeach, 1970, p. 23). See Ehrlich and Leed (1969) for a review of relevant empirical studies.
31. Lakatos (1980).
32. Such auxiliary assumptions can take many forms. Sometimes they pertain to the nature of the data. Darwin's famous discussion of the incompleteness of the fossil record as the explanation for why there are so few intermediate forms is in Chapters IX and X of the *Origin of Species*: "[many factors] must have tended to make the geological record extremely imperfect, and will to a large extent explain why we do not find interminable varieties, connecting together all the extinct and existing forms of life by the finest graduated steps" (Darwin, 1859/2004, p. 274). Other assumptions pertain to the nature of the instruments used. For a discussion of Galileo and the assumption that his telescope was accurate with respect to heavenly as well as terrestrial phenomena, and all the reasons to doubt this, see Feyerabend (1975/1988, pp. 84–109) and the response by Thomason (1994). Other auxiliary assumptions are more substantive. Newtonian mechanics predicts that a feather and a marble fall in the same way and at the same rate, a prediction that is directly contradicted by observations unless we take air resistance (friction) into account. Leplin (1982) discusses four historical cases of such auxiliary assumptions: Lorentz's assumption that solid bodies contract in their direction of motion; Pauli's assumption that a previously unknown particle – the neutrino – is ejected from atomic nuclei in radioactive decay; and the assumptions by astronomers that previously unknown bodies accounted for otherwise inexplicable features of the orbits of both Uranus and Mercury.
33. Lakatos (1980, p. 48).
34. See Abelson et al. (1968) for a representative collection of works from the golden age of cognitive consistency research. Abelson (1983) discussed the decline of the cognitive consistency school of research after 1970, while Aronson (1997) provided a retrospective review of the cognitive dissonance theory, specifically. The core principle of the cognitive consistency school was that people have a natural drive toward keeping their beliefs consistent with each other, so the experience of cognitive conflict triggers cognitive processes that have the function of restoring consistency. This principle was articulated in multiple ways. Festinger (1957/1962) coined the term "cognitive dissonance", which has entered the popular lexicon. His version of the cognitive conflict principle has endured (Balcetis & Dunning, 2007; Harmon-Jones & Mills, 1999; Schultz & Lepper, 1996), while several other

formulations that were prominent at the height of the movement (Abelson et al., 1968) have since faded (Abelson, 1983).

35. "The presence of [cognitive] dissonance gives rise to pressures to reduce or eliminate the dissonance" (Festinger, 1957/1962, p. 18).

36. In the early 1980s, studies by Caramazza, McCloskey and Green (1980), Clement (1982), Halloun and Hestenes (1985), McCloskey (1983) and others established that people in general and physics students in particular operate with an intuitive physics that is similar to the physics of the 14th-century scholar Jean Buridan (Clagett, 1959, Chaps. 8–10; Robin & Ohlsson, 1989). Due to the belief that the content of students' intuitive theories impact their learning (Champagne, Gunstone & Klopfer, 1985), identifying their misconceptions in a wide range of science topics became a growth industry in empirical research. For example, Bishop and Anderson (1990), Demastes, Settlage and Good (1995) and Lawson and Thompson (1988) tried to carry out this project with respect to genetics and natural selection; see Driver, Guesne and Tiberghien (1985) for a collection of studies on other subject matters. The enterprise of identifying misconceptions became so popular that the Pfundt and Duit (1991) bibliography contains over 2,000 entries. Comins (2001) provides a readable discussion of misconceptions in the context of science education.

37. Abelson (1959), Chinn and Brewer (1993), Darden (1992) and Kelman and Baron (1968). See also Cameron, Jacks and O'Brien (2002) for a related list of five mechanisms for resisting persuasive communications. Jacks and Cameron (2003) provide some evidence as to the relative prevalence of the different dissonance-reducing mechanisms.

38. The basic concept behind bolstering is that the magnitude of cognitive dissonance is a function of the proportion of dissonant elements. This opens up the possibility of reducing dissonance, not by dealing with the contradiction that gave rise to it but by adding information that changes the relation between the number of consonant and dissonant elements. Although this idea is clearly expressed and exemplified in Festinger (1957/1962), he did not name it or single it out as a special cognitive mechanism. The label "bolstering" appears to have been introduced by Abelson (1959), although he credits Festinger with the concept.

39. Festinger (1957/1962, pp. 48–54).

40. For recent work on bolstering and other resistance mechanisms, see Cameron, Jacks and O'Brien (2002), Jacks and Cameron (2003), and Tavirs and Aronson (2007).

41. Common sense might assume that accurate information about an ethnic or racial group would be sufficient to eradicate incorrect prejudices about the members of that group. The most direct source of information is interaction with members of the group in question. Hence, intergroup contact should be effective in reducing prejudice. This *intergroup contact theory* was codified by Gordon W. Allport in *The Nature of Prejudice*, originally published in the 1950s, and restated in more precise form four decades later by Pettigrew (1998). Social psychologists have studied the exact conditions under which intergroup contact has the expected effect. As the theory of resistance through peripheral change would predict, one of those conditions is that the group member is seen as typical or representative of the group.

If he or she can be seen as atypical, the effect of contact on prejudice is small or nonexistent; see Brown, Vivian and Hewstone (1999) for a relevant empirical study. Allport anticipated this result: "There is a common mental device that permits people to hold to prejudgments even in the face of much contradictory evidence. It is the device of admitting exceptions" (Allport, 1958/1979, p. 23).
42. Festinger (1957/1962, pp. 22–23); Festinger quotes Spiro (1953) as the original source. It should be noted that Festinger's interpretation of the observations that Spiro reported is not identical to Spiro's own.
43. C. S. Peirce wrote about abduction in multiple articles, including "Deduction, induction, and hypothesis" (1878b), "On the logic of drawing history from ancient documents, especially from testimonies" (1901) and "Pragmatism as the logic of abduction" (1903). The text that lifted Pierce's concept into the focus of philosophers of science was Hanson (1965, pp. 85–92). Within philosophy, abduction is typically conceived as an "inference to the best explanation" (Douven, 2002; Harman, 1965, 1968; Lipton, 2004). For recent work from a philosophy of science point of view, see Magnani (2001), Thagard (2007) and Thagard and Shelley (1997). Formal models of abduction have been proposed in Artificial Intelligence and belief revision logics; see, e.g., Josephson and Josephson (1994) and Walliser, Zwirn and Zwirn (2005).
44. See Grosser (1962/1979), Leplin (1982) and Standage (2000).
45. See Lipton (2004) and Thagard (2007).
46. From Francis Bacon in the 17th century to William Whewell in the 19th, the term "induction" has been used to refer to several different concepts, but their shared meaning is that conclusions, generalizations and hypotheses are derived in what we now would call a bottom-up process applied to observations. The only precisely specified process of induction I know of is the extraction of similarities across a set of particulars, and that is the way in which I use the concept in this book. Francis Bacon's *Novum Organum* exists in numerous editions (e.g., Bacon, 1620/1994), while Whewell's central writings on induction are conveniently gathered in one volume by R. E. Butts (1989).
47. Popper (1959/1972).
48. Popper (1969, pp. 54–55, italics in original).
49. Popper (1969, p. 51, italics in original).
50. "The initial stage, the act of conceiving or inventing a theory, seems to me neither to call for logical analysis nor to be susceptible of it" (Popper, 1959/1972, p. 31).
51. Losee (2005) provides a collection of historical examples of falsification.
52. Newell (1982).
53. Kuhn (1970).
54. Kuhn (1970, p. 77). This statement was not an accident: "How could history of science fail to be a source of phenomena to which theories about knowledge may legitimately be asked to apply?" (Kuhn, 1970, p. 9).
55. Popper (1959/1972, p. 31).
56. Kuhn (1970, pp. 89–90).
57. Matthews (2004) and Ohlsson (2000).
58. Toulmin (1972).
59. Toulmin (1972, pp. 150–151).
60. Toulmin (1972, pp. 206–207).

61. Kitcher (1993).
62. The quotes in this paragraph are from Kitcher (1993, pp. 109–111).
63. Nersessian (2008).
64. Toulmin (1972, p. 225, italics in original).
65. For the original descriptions of the ECHO model and the theory of explanatory coherence, see Eliasmith and Thagard (1997), Thagard (1992, especially pp. 71–102) and Thagard and Verbeurgt (1998). The model has inspired empirical research in educational and social psychology; see Ranney and Schank (1998) and Read and Marcus-Newhall (1993).
66. See Gopnik and Wellman (1994), Gopnik and Meltzoff (1997) and Gopnik et al. (2004) for statements of the theory-theory of children's cognition.
67. Gopnik and Melzoff (1997, p. 3).
68. Gopnik and Melzoff (1997, p. 213).
69. Gopnik and Melzoff (1997, p. 39).
70. Gopnik and Melzoff (1997, p. 39).
71. Gopnik and Melzoff (1997, p. 39).
72. Gopnik and Melzoff (1997, p. 40).
73. Gopnik and Melzoff (1997, p. 40).
74. Chi (1992, 1997, 2005, 2008), Chi and Hausmann (2003), Chi and Roscoe (2002), Chi, Slotta and de Leeuw (1994), Chi, Siler, Jeong and Hausmann (2001), Ferrari and Chi (1998), Reiner, Slotta, Chi and Resnick (2000), Slotta and Chi (2006) and Slotta, Chi and Joram (1995).
75. Keil (1979) was the first to notice this interesting feature of ontological categories.
76. Chi and Brem (2009).
77. The science-inspired view was widespread in science education circles in the 1980s, but it was most clearly and explicitly codified in Hewson and Hewson (1984), Posner, Strike, Hewson and Gertzog (1982) and Strike and Posner (1985).
78. Relevant studies include Chan, Burtis and Bereiter (1997), Dreyfus, Jungwirth and Eliovitch (1990) and Jensen and Finley (1995). See Limón (2001) for a review.
79. Limón (2001, p. 364).
80. See Strike and Posner (1992) for "revisionist," Smith, DiSessa and Roschelle (1995) for "reconceive," Dole and Sinatra (1998) for "reconceptualise," Limón and Mason (2002) for "reconsider," Nersessian (2008) for "recast" and Vosniadou, Baltas and Vamvakoussi (2007) for "reframe."
81. Gopnik and Meltzoff (1997, pp. 20–21).

CHAPTER 10. BELIEF REVISION: THE RESUBSUMPTION THEORY

1. Kuhn (1970, p. 77).
2. This misconception about rocketry was not fully laid to rest until the publication of Robert H. Goddard's pioneering article, "A Method of Reaching Extreme Altitudes" (Goddard, 1919).
3. See Bohner and Wänke (2002), Eagly and Chaiken (1993), Fishbein and Aizen (1975) and Kiesler, Collins and Miller (1969).

4. See Evans (2007), Chapter 4, for a review of the evidence regarding belief bias from laboratory studies in cognitive psychology. Belief bias is real enough in everyday contexts as well; see, e.g., Lynn and Williams (1990).
5. The concept of cognitive utility was discussed in Anderson (1990), especially Chapter 5, and it plays a central role in the ACT-R theory (Anderson, 2007).
6. Cognitive load encompasses both the amount of information that needs to be kept active at each moment in time and the amount of cognitive resources allocated to processing that information. It corresponds to working memory load, as measured by, for example, the Operation Span Test (see, e.g., Klein & Fiss, 1999; Turner & Engle, 1989) or Working Memory Span (Baddeley, 2007). Sweller and others have shown that high cognitive load can interfere with learning (Chandler & Sweller, 1991; Sweller, 1988).
7. Evidence of this comes from a variety of empirical studies of students' physics reasoning (Clement, 1982; McCloskey, 1983; Robin & Ohlsson, 1989).
8. Miller (1996, pp. 136–138).
9. Anderson (1984), Goldstein (2008) and Markman (1999, Chapter 4).
10. Rokeach (1960, 1970).
11. The concept of subsumption has two historical roots, each relevant to this chapter albeit in different ways. The earliest is Hempel and Oppenheim's (1948) philosophical proposal that a scientific explanation explains by subsuming particular events under general scientific laws. This proposal has been much criticized and is no longer considered a serious philosophical theory of explanation in the natural sciences (Salmon, 1989). Cummins (1983a, 1983b) has argued that it does not apply to psychology. Although bad philosophy, the subsumption concept might nevertheless be good psychology. Subsumption is central to the theory of meaningful verbal learning proposed by David Ausubel (1963), especially pp. 24–26, and Chapter 4; see also Ausubel (1968). The key idea is that to learn is to subsume new subject matter content under a prior conception, which suggests that learning can be enhanced by providing that prior conception ahead of time in the form of a so-called advanced organizer. This proposal obviously suffers from a circularity problem: How is the learner to absorb the advanced organizer? If he needs an organizer for the organizer, learning is in trouble. Nevertheless, empirical studies tend to support the utility of advanced organizers (Corkill, 1992; Dole, Valencia, Greer & Waldrop, 1991; Luiten, Ames & Ackerson, 1980; Mayer, 1979; Stone, 1983) although there are some exceptions (Barnes & Clawson, 1975; Calandra & Barron, 2005; McDade, 1978). The subsumption theory of learning was generalized beyond advanced organizers into the Elaboration Theory of instructional design (Reigeluth & Stein, 1983; Van Patten, Chao & Reigeluth, 1986), which says that learning is a process of progressive differentiating, elaborating and fleshing out initial concepts. The proposal in this chapter is that subsumption is the relation that structures informal belief systems. This is a hypothesis about representation, not about process. The Resubsumption Theory is not committed to any specific claim about superior learning and retention in the presence of an advanced organizer, because it is not committed to any particular theory of monotonic, routine belief formation.

12. Ausubel (1963, p. 26).
13. The axiomatic format for theories was invented in antiquity. Euclid of Alexandria's axiomatic presentation of geometry, *The Elements*, dates from the third century B.C.; see, e.g., the summary and discussion by Boyer (1985, Chapter 7). An axiomatic theory is specified through two main components: a set of axioms, assertions that are accepted as true at the outset, and a set of truth-preserving inference rules by which new assertions, theorems, can be derived. Euclid's paradigmatic example was clear with respect to the axioms but less so with respect to the inference rules. Developments in formal logic in the 19th century enabled Bertrand Russell and Alfred N. Whitehead to produce a formally specified axiomatic theory of logic in their *Principia Mathematica*, published in three volumes between 1910 and 1913, but available in abbreviated form in Whitehead and Russell (1962). The latter, in turn, was the basis for the first fully functional Artificial Intelligence program, the *Logic Theorist*, by A. Newell, J. C. Shaw and H. A. Simon (Newell, Shaw & Simon, 1958). Although some logicians, mathematicians and philosophers nurture a fascination with axiomatic theories, no serious theory in the empirical sciences was ever initially proposed in this form, nor are working scientists disposed to put their theories on this form.
14. See Chapter 4, Note 34, and Chapter 6, Note 18, for references about the role of hierarchical organization.
15. The concept of tangled hierarchies was introduced into cognitive science by Hofstadter (1999) but is used here in the slightly different sense of Chi and Ohlsson (2005). Two hierarchies are tangled if some node in one is identical to a node in the other. For example, hierarchical classifications of "tools" and "kitchen implements" are tangled by the fact that a "bottle opener" belongs in both, and a person's intuitive theories of health and biological evolution might be tangled because the belief that "random background radiation can cause mutations" appears in both.
16. Leon Festinger tried to separate cognitive conflict from logical contradiction, but did not quite succeed: "I will replace the word 'inconsistency' with a term which has less of a logical connotation, namely, *dissonance*.... The terms 'dissonance' and 'consonance' refer to relations which exist between pairs of 'elements' ... [which refer to] *the things a person knows about himself, about his behavior, and about his surroundings.... two elements are in a dissonant relation, if considering these two alone, the obverse of one element would follow from the other.* To state it a bit more formally, x and y are dissonant if not-x follows from y" (Festinger, 1957/1962, pp. 2–13, italics in original). These terminological twists do not suffice to insert any significant wedge between cognitive dissonance and logical contradiction (i.e., "x and not-x").
17. For a discussion of medieval views of change, see Bynum (2001).
18. The weird aspects of quantum physics – entanglement, the quantized nature of energy, quantum non-locality, wave-particle duality and the uncertainty principle – continue to exercise philosophers (Camilleri, 2006; Cushing, 1991; Putnam, 2005) as well as physicists (Afshar, Flores, McDonald & Knoesel, 2007; Baggott, 2004).
19. The text says: "*In the beginning God created the heavens and the earth.... And God said, 'Let there be light,' and there was light.... And God said, 'Let there be*

an expanse between the waters to separate water from water.' So God made the expanse and separated the water under the expanse from the water above it. And it was so.... And God said, 'Let the water under the sky be gathered to one place, and let dry ground appear.' And it was so.... Then God said, 'Let the land produce vegetation: seed-bearing plants and trees on the land that bear fruit with seed in it, according to their various kinds.' And it was so" (Genesis 1–11, New International Version). This description lacks any causal mechanism. Creation in this sense differs from production through a material process like natural selection. Those who say that natural selection is God's way of creating new species resolve their cognitive dissonance by abandoning the distinction between these two meanings of "create."

20. Ranney and Schank (1998), Ranney, Schank, Mosmann and Montoya (1993) and Thagard (1992).
21. Rokeach (1970, p. 167).
22. Koestler (1964).
23. The repeated application of cognitive schemas to anything in the environment to which they might apply is a theme that runs across Piaget's writings; see, e.g., Piaget (1963).
24. See Gentner (1983) and Markman and Gentner (2000). Key works on analogy include Carbonell (1983, 1986), Falkenheimer, Forbus and Gentner (1989), Forbus, Gentner and Law (1994), Holyoak and Thagard (1989ab), Keane, Ledgeway and Duff (1994) and Veloso and Carbonell (1993). For the idea that structural similarity also provides a mechanism for schema application, see, e.g., Gick and Holyoak (1980, 1983), Holland, Holyoak, Nisbett and Thagard (1986), Ohlsson (1993b), Ohlsson and Hemmerich (1999) and Ohlsson and Lehtinen (1997).
25. Quine (1951, p. 39).
26. Gazzinaga (1992), French, Laskov and Scharff (1989) and Jerne (1967).
27. Vincent (1993).
28. See Aunger (2002), Blackmore (1999), Brodie (1996) and Lynch, (1996).
29. The papers collected by Polk and Seifert (2002) and by Sun (2008) provide examples of a wide range of computer models of cognitive processes.
30. The ontological shift idea was first stated in Chi (1992) and has since undergone considerable evolution (Chi, 1997, 2005; Chi & Brem, 2009; Chi, Slotta & de Leeuw, 1994). It is supported by a literature review (Reiner, Slotta, Chi & Resnick, 2000), laboratory studies (Chi, 2005; Slotta, Chi & Joram, 1995), instructional interventions (Chi & Rosco, 2002; Slotta & Chi, 2006) and by comparisons to historical cases of conceptual change in science (Chi & Hausmann, 2003). For an experimental approach to the study of category shifts, see also Cosejo, Oesterreich and Ohlsson (2009).
31. The difficulty of conceptual change is attributed to a lack of awareness of the need for such a shift (Chi & Rosco, 2002, p. 18), a lack of the correct target category (Chi & Rosco, 2002, p. 19) and "the cognitive demand of re-inheriting all the attributes of a concept based on its new categorical membership" (Chi, 2005, p. 188).
32. D. Kuhn (1989) articulates this argument.

33. Duhem (1914/1991), James (1907/1975), Peirce (1878a), Smith (1978) and Thayer (1982). Writes Pierce: "The essence of belief is the establishment of a habit, and different beliefs are distinguished by the different modes of action to which they give rise" (Pierce, 1878a, pp. 129–130). See Menand (2001) for a history of pragmatic thinking in the United States, as seen in its social context.

CHAPTER 11. ELEMENTS OF A UNIFIED THEORY

1. Einstein (1934, p. 165). Copyright 1934 by the University of Chicago Press.
2. Duhem (1914/1991), p. 21. Copyright 1982 by the Princeton University Press.
3. Miller, Galanter and Pribram (1960) also exemplify this stance: "Arrayed against the reflex theorists are the pessimists, who think that living organisms are complicated, devious, poorly designed for research purposes, and so on.... it seems obvious to us that a great deal more goes on between the stimulus and the response than can be accounted for by a simple statement about associative strengths.... Life is complicated" (pp. 7–9). Other founding documents embodied or expressed a similar attitude (e.g., Neisser, 1967).
4. Newell and Simon (1972a, p. 10).
5. Miller (1956) introduced the concept of limits on the human capacity to process information. See Shiffrin and Nosofsky (1994) for a retrospective review of this famous article.
6. See Ohlsson (1992b) for a discussion of the concept of theory articulation.
7. The idea that we should strive to unify the sciences was championed in the first half of the 20th century by the members and proponents of the philosophical school known as logical positivism. (See Friedman, 1991, for the case that the logical positivists have been misunderstood with respect to their position on this issue.) Otto Neurath was a pioneer and driving force (Neurath, 1937; Reisch, 1994). Unification can be conceptualized in different ways. Neurath and other logical positivists believed that all the sciences could be unified by being reduced to physics, in the sense of adopting a scientific terminology where all terms were reducible to physical descriptions. "The fundamental thesis of our movement is that terms similar to those employed in physics and in our everyday language are sufficient for constructing all sciences" (Neurath, 1937, p. 270). This position, known as *physicalism*, is controversial among philosophers and universally rejected as unworkable, especially by practicing scientists in the behavioral, cognitive and social sciences. In 1998, physicalism was re-invented by the biologist Edward O. Wilson under the label *consilience*. "The central idea of the consilience world view is that all tangible phenomena, from the birth of stars to the workings of social institutions, are based on material processes that are ultimately reducible, however long and tortuous the sequences, to the laws of physics" (Wilson, 1998, p. 266). However, reductionism can be formulated independently of physicalism; see Nagel (1961), Chapter 11, for a classical statement. Reductionism in general has been severely criticized on the basis of both philosophical arguments and the observation that emergent phenomena are commonplace in nature, society and mind (Holland, 1998; Johnson, 2004). (But

see Jones, 2004, for a generally positive assessment of reductionism in science, and Weinberg, 2001, for a persistent defense of reductionism in physics.) A nonreductionist approach to unification is to conceptualize it as a gradual movement toward substantive theories of wider and wider scope (Friedman, 1974). If a theory of phenomenon X turns out to be sufficient to explain phenomenon Y as well, then that theory can be said to unify X and Y. Kitcher (1988) calls this *explanatory unification*. The programme of creating a unified theory of cognition by specifying the cognitive architecture (Newell, 1990) encompasses both explanatory unification, in that one and the same set of principles are supposed to explain a wide range, or even all, cognitive phenomena, and also reductionism, in that higher-order cognitive phenomena are supposed to be explained in terms of more basic cognitive processes.

8. See, e.g., Casper and Noer (1972) for an exposition of the synthesis of terrestrial and celestial mechanics in the theory of gravitation. Kitcher (1988) presents a view of unification as the use of a small number of explanation patterns to explain a large number of diverse phenomena, using the Newtonian and Darwinian revolutions as his primary examples. Evolutionary biologist Theodosius Dobzhansky emphasized the unifying power of Darwinism: "Nothing in biology makes sense except in the light of evolution" (Dobzhansky, 1973, p. 125). James Clerk Maxwell unified electricity, radio waves and, eventually, light into a general field theory (Nersessian, 1992, 2002, 2008). The unification of medicine under the germ theory (Waller, 2002) is only partial, given that there are other causes of illness than germs.

9. See Note 8 in Chapter 2.

10. For example, learning to categorize a set of stimuli might be analyzed into basic processes like noticing a feature, strengthening or weakening a link between a feature and a category, storing an instance in memory and so on, while decision making might be analyzed into some combination of generating options, predicting outcomes and assessing and comparing expected outcomes, and problem solving might be analyzed into goal setting, operator selection, operator execution, outcome evaluation and so on. Examples of this two-level style of theorizing are easy to find on the pages of psychological research journals such as the *Journal of Experimental Psychology: Learning, Memory, and Cognition, Cognitive Psychology, Memory and Cognition* and others.

11. Newell (1990, Figure 3-3, p. 122).

12. It is easy to forget exactly how ubiquitous flow diagrams were in cognitive psychology in the 1950–1970 period. They were used to state models of attention (Broadbent, 1958, Fig. 7, p. 299), concept learning (Hunt, 1962, Figure 8-3, p. 232), long-term memory retrieval (Shiffrin, 1970, Figure 2, p. 382), problem solving (Ernst & Newell, 1969, Figure 11, p. 42) and many other cognitive processes. They are still with us (e.g., Alberdi, Sleeman & Korpi, 2000, Figure 1, p. 80).

13. See Newell (1972, 1973) for the basic concept. Anderson (1983) is the source for the term "cognitive architecture."

14. The best source for the Soar simulation system is the collection of articles edited by Rosenbloom, Laird and Newell (1993, vol. 1 and 2). The ACT project has been presented to the computing public in a series of books as well as numerous articles; see Anderson (1983, 1990, 1993, 2007) and Anderson and Lebiere (1998).

15. Barber and Lichtman (1999), Chechik, Meilijson and Ruppin (1998), Hua and Smith (2004), Huttenlocher, de Courten, Garey and van der Loos (1982) and Purves and Lichtman (1980).
16. Zuckerman and Cohen (1964).
17. For a review of this concept from a linguistic point of view, see Carnie (2008). The arguments for why and how this concept applies to the language of thought were reviewed by Fodor (1976) and Fodor and Pylyshyn (1988). Briefly put, "the constituency relation is a part/whole relation: If C is a constituent of C^*, then a token of C is a part of every token of C^*" (Fodor, 1997, p. 111).
18. See references in Chapter 4, Notes 19 and 21.
19. Gaskell (2007), Graesser, Gernsbacher and Goldman (2003) and Traxler and Gernsbacher (2006).
20. Ohlsson (2008a) and Proctor and Dutta (1995).
21. Chi and Ohlsson (2005).
22. The number 10 million is mentioned on the Web site of the Los Alamos National Laboratory, at http://periodic.lanl.gov/elements/6.html. They in turn refer to the online source *CRC Handbook of Chemistry and Physics*. The exact number does not matter for present purposes, only its order of magnitude.
23. Liebherr and McHugh (2003).
24. Thorndike (1932): "Punishments often but not always tend to shift from [the connections that lead to them] to something else.... They weaken the connection which produced them, when they do weaken it, by strengthening some competing connection" (p. 277).
25. Flight and vision are the two classical challenges of this sort. For the two-stage theory of the evolution of flight in birds, see Dial (2003) and Sumida and Brochut (2000). For a similarly structured theory of flight in insects, see Kingsolver and Koehl (1985). For a discussion of the evolution of vision, see Gregory (2008). Budd (2006, especially pp. 618–619) and Gregory (2008, especially p. 361) propose general principles, including functional shifts and multiple stages with different selective pressures, for the evolution of complex adaptations.
26. The term "future shock" was introduced by Alvin Tofffler in the book with that title (Toffler, 1970). His thesis was that rapid change imposes a strain on the human mind. Bertman (1998) followed up on this thesis 25 years later. The predicted collapse of the human psyche due to too much change appears not to be forthcoming.
27. See Mansfield, Busse and Krepelka (1978) and Scott, Leritz and Mumford (2004). The evidence is not much stronger for training programs that claim to raise a person's intelligence as measured by IQ-tests (Perkins, 1995b).
28. Picasso is often quoted as saying, "I don't search, I find." What he said was, "In my opinion to search means nothing in painting. To find, is the thing." The comment, presumably spoken in either French or Spanish, was recorded by Marius de Zayas, translated into English and published in an article titled "Picasso Speaks" in the New York magazine *The Arts*, May 1923. (Reprinted in Ashton, 1972, pp. 3–6.)
29. Louis Pasteur, in his inaugural lecture as professor and dean, University of Lille, Douai, France, December 7, 1854. English translation in Peterson (1954, pp. 469–474).

CHAPTER 12. THE RECURSION CURSE

1. Hume (1777/1910, p. 316).
2. Italics in original. Reprinted by permission of the publisher from *Fact, Fiction, and Forecast* by Nelson Goodman, p. 82, Cambridge, MA: Harvard University Press, Copyright © 1979, 1983 by Nelson Goodman.
3. Hume's formulation of the problem of induction is set out in Section IV, "Skeptical Doubts Concerning the Operations of the Understanding," in *An Inquiry Concerning Human Understanding* (Hume, 1777/1955).
4. Hume (1777/1910, p. 317).

REFERENCES

Whenever a conference proceeding has both editor and publisher, full conference papers are cited like book chapters.

Whenever an edition other than the first is referenced, the year of the first edition is given first and the year of the consulted edition second, e.g., Darwin (1859/2004).

Names with particles, i.e., "de," "van," "van der," "von," etc., are treated as if the particle is part of the name. For example, publications by VanLehn and Von Domarus are found under the letter V rather than L or D.

Letters with *umlauts* such as å, ä and ö are alphabetized according to the German system of placing them immediately after the underlying vowel. For example, publications by Köhler are placed after other names beginning with Ko-, but before names beginning with Kp-. Names that are customarily written with expanded umlauts, e.g., Koestler, are alphabetized literally.

Classical texts are referenced in the chapter notes by author, title and the label or number of the relevant part (lines, verses, etc.), according to classicist practice. The particular editions of classical works consulted are listed in the first section below.

CLASSICAL REFERENCES

Aristotle (384–332 B.C.)
On the Heavens (*De Caelo*), translated by J. L. Stocks.
In R. M. Hutchins (Ed.), *The Works of Aristotle* (vol. 1, pp. 359–405). Chicago, IL: William Benton and Encyclopedia Britannica, Inc., 1952.
On the Motion of Animals (*De Motu Animalium*), translated by A. S. L. Farquharson.
In R. M. Hutchins (Ed.), *The Works of Aristotle* (vol. 2, pp. 233–252). Chicago, IL: William Benton and Encyclopedia Britannica, Inc., 1952.
Physics (*Physica*), translated by R. P. Hardie and R. K. Gaye.
In R. M. Hutchins (Ed.), *The Works of Aristotle* (vol. 1, pp. 259–355). Chicago, IL: William Benton and Encyclopedia Britannica, 1952.

Posterior Analytics (Analytica Posteriora), translated by G. R. G. Mure.
In R. M. Hutchins (Ed.), *The Works of Aristotle* (vol. 1, pp. 97–137). Chicago, IL: William Benton and Encyclopedia Britannica, Inc., 1952.
Prior Analytics (Analytica Priora), translated by A. J. Jenkinson.
In R. M. Hutchins (Ed.), *The Works of Aristotle* (vol. 1, pp. 39–93). Chicago, IL: William Benton and Encyclopedia Britannica, Inc., 1952.

Marcus Tullius Cicero (106–43 B.C.)
On the Ideal Orator (De Oratore), translated by J. M. May and J. Wisse.
New York: Oxford University Press, 2001.

Empedocles (c. 477–c. 432 B.C.)
The Extant Fragments, translated by M. R. Wright.
Bristol, UK: Bristol Classical Press (2nd ed.), 1995.
Euclid of Alexandria (c. 300 B.C.)
The Elements, translated by T. L. Heath.
The Thirteen Books of Euclid's Elements (3 vols., 2nd ed.). New York: Dover, 1956.

Heraclitus (c. 535–c. 475 B.C.)
Fragments, translated by D. Sweet.
In D. Sweet, *Heraclitus: Translation and analysis*. Lanham, MD: University Press of America, 1995.

Herodotos (484–414 B.C.)
The Histories, translated by G. C. Macaulay, revised by D. Lateiner.
New York: Barnes and Noble Classics, 2004.
An English translation of *The Histories* is also available at http://macams.posc.edu/txt/ah/Herodotus.
Hesiod (8th century B.C.)
Works and Days, translated by M. L. West.
In *Theogony and Works and Days*. London, UK: Oxford University Press, 1999.

Marcus Vitruvius Pollio (c. 80–c. 15 B.C.)
The Ten Books on Architecture (De Architectura Libri Decem), translated by M. H. Morgan. Cambridge, MA: Harvard University Press, 1914. [Re-issued by Dover Books, New York, 1960.]

Ovid (43 B.C.–A.D. 17)
Metamorphoses, translated by D. Raeburn.
London, UK: Penguin Books, 2004.

Thucydides (460–400 B.C.)
The History of the Peloponnesian War, translated by R. Crawley, revised by D. Lateiner.
New York: Barnes and Noble Classics, 2006.
An English translation of *The History of the Peloponnesian War* is also available at http://en.wikisoure.org/wiki/History_of_the_Peloponnesian_War.

OTHER REFERENCES

Abelson, R. P. (1959). Modes of resolution of belief dilemmas. *Journal of Conflict Resolution*, vol. 3, pp. 343–352.
———. (1983). Whatever became of consistency theory? *Personality and Social Psychology Bulletin*, vol. 9, pp. 37–54.

Abelson, R. P., Aronson, E., McGuire, W. J., Newcomb, T. M., Rosenberg, M. J., & Tannenbaum, P. H. (Eds.). (1968). *Theories of cognitive consistency: A sourcebook*. Chicago, IL: Rand McNally.

Abelson, R. P., & Rosenberg, M. J. (1958). Symbolic psycho-logic: A model of attitudinal cognition. *Behavioral Science*, vol. 3, pp. 1–13.

Adamson, R. E. (1952). Functional fixedness as related to problem solving: A repetition of three experiments. *Journal of Experimental Psychology*, vol. 44, pp. 288–291.

Afshar, S. S., Flores, E., McDonald, K. F., & Knoesel, E. (2007). Paradox in wave-particle duality. *Foundations of Physics*, vol. 37, pp. 295–305.

Alberdi, E., Sleeman, D. H., & Korpi, M. (2000). Accommodating surprise in taxonomic tasks: The role of expertise. *Cognitive Science*, vol. 24, pp. 53–91.

Allport, G. W. (1958/1979). *The nature of prejudice* (2nd ed.). Reading, MA: Addison-Wesley.

Allwood, C. (1984). Error detection processes in statistical problem solving. *Cognitive Science*, vol. 8, pp. 413–437.

Allwood, C. M., & Montgomery, H. (1982). Detection of errors in statistical problem solving. *Scandinavian Journal of Psychology*, vol. 23, pp. 131–139.

Altmann, E. M., & Burns, B. D. (2005). Streak biases in decision making: Data and a memory model. *Cognitive Systems Research*, vol. 6, pp. 5–16.

Altmann, E. M., & Trafton, J. G. (2002). Memory for goals: An activation–based model. *Cognitive Science*, vol. 26, pp. 39–83.

Alty, J. L. (1995). Navigating through compositional space: The creativity corridor. *Leonardo*, vol. 28, pp. 215–219.

Alvarez, J. E., & Emory, E. (2006). Executive function and the frontal lobes: A meta-analytic review. *Neuropsychology Review*, vol. 16, pp. 17–42.

Alvarez, W. (1998). *T. rex and the crater of doom*. New York: Vintage Books.

Amalberti, R. (2001). The paradoxes of almost totally safe transportation systems. *Safety Science*, vol. 37, pp. 109–126.

Amir, E., & Maynard-Zhang, P. (2004). Logic-based subsumption architecture. *Artificial Intelligence*, vol. 153, pp. 167–237.

Amundsen, R. (1989). The trials and tribulations of selectionist explanations. In K. Hahlweg & C. A. Hooker (Eds.), *Issues in evolutionary epistemology* (pp. 413–432). Albany: State University of New York Press.

Anderson, J. R. (1976). *Language, memory, and thought*. Hillsdale, NJ: Erlbaum.

———. (1982). Acquisition of cognitive skill. *Psychological Review*, vol. 89, pp. 369–406.

———. (1983). *The architecture of cognition*. Cambridge, MA: Harvard University Press.

———. (1984). Spreading activation. In J. R. Anderson & S. M. Kosslyn (Eds.), *Tutorials in learning and memory* (pp. 61–90). San Francisco, CA: W. H. Freeman.

———. (1987). Skill acquisition: Compilation of weak-method problem solutions. *Psychological Review*, vol. 94, pp. 192–210.

———. (1989). A rational analysis of human memory. In H. L. Roediger & F. I. M. Craik (Eds.), *Varieties of memory and consciousness: Essays in honour of Endel Tulving* (pp. 195–210). Hillsdale, NJ: Erlbaum.

———. (1990). *The adaptive character of thought*. Hillsdale, NJ: Erlbaum.

———. (1993). *Rules of the mind*. Hillsdale, NJ: Erlbaum.

———. (2002). Spanning seven orders of magnitude: A challenge for cognitive modeling. *Cognitive Science*, vol. 26, pp. 85–112.

———. (2004). *Cognitive psychology and its implications* (6th ed.). New York: Worth.

———. (2005). Human symbol manipulation within an integrated cognitive architecture. *Cognitive Science*, vol. 29, pp. 313–341.

———. (2007). *How can the human mind occur in the physical universe?* New York: Oxford University Press.

Anderson, J. R., & Bower, G. H. (1973). *Human associative memory*. Washington, DC: Winston.

Anderson, J. R., & Jeffries, R. (1985). Novice LISP errors: Undetected losses of information from working memory. *Human-Computer Interaction*, vol. 1, pp. 107–131.

Anderson, J. R., Kline, P., & Beasley, C. M. (1978, February). *A theory of the acquisition of cognitive skills* (Technical Report 77–1). New Haven, CT: Yale University.

Anderson, J. R., Kline, P. J., & Beasley, C. M. (1979). A general learning theory and its application to schema abstraction. In G. H. Bower (Ed.), *The psychology of learning and motivation: Advances in research and theory* (vol. 13, pp. 277–318). New York: Academic Press.

Anderson, J. R., Kushmerick, N., & Lebiere, C. (1993). The Tower of Hanoi and goal structures. In J. R. Anderson (Ed.), *Rules of the mind* (pp. 121–142). Hillsdale, NJ: Erlbaum.

Anderson, J. R., & Lebiere, C. (Eds.). (1998). *The atomic components of thought*. Mahwah, NJ: Erlbaum.

Anderson, J. R., & Pirolli, P. L. (1984). Spread of activation. *Journal of Experimental Psychology: Learning, Memory, and Cognition*, vol. 10, pp. 791–798.

Anderson, J. R., & Schooler, L. J. (1991). Reflections of the environment in memory. *Psychological Science*, vol. 2, pp. 396–408.

———. (2000). The adaptive nature of memory. In E. Tulving & F. I. M. Craik (Eds.), *The Oxford handbook of memory* (pp. 557–570). New York: Oxford University Press.

Anderson, M. L. (2003). Embodied cognition: A field guide. *Artificial Intelligence*, vol. 149, pp. 91–130.

Anderson, R. C. (1967). Educational psychology. *Annual Review of Psychology*, vol. 18, pp. 129–164.

Anderson, S. R. (2004). *Doctor Dolittle's delusion: Animals and the uniqueness of human language*. New Haven, CT: Yale University Press.

Anzai, Y., & Simon, H. A. (1979). The theory of learning by doing. *Psychological Review*, vol. 86, pp. 124–140.

Arnauld, A., & Nicole, P. (1662/1996). *Logic or the art of thinking: Containing, besides common rules, several new observations appropriate for forming judgments* (J. V. Buroker, Trans.). Cambridge, UK: Cambridge University Press.

Aronson, E. (1997). Back to the future: Retrospective review of Leon Festinger's "A theory of cognitive dissonance." *American Journal of Psychology*, vol. 110, pp. 127–137.

Ash, M. G. (1995). *Gestalt psychology in German culture, 1890–1967: Holism and the quest for objectivity*. Cambridge, UK: Cambridge University Press.

Ashby, F. G., & Maddox, W. T. (2005). Human category learning. *Annual Review of Psychology*, vol. 56, pp. 149–178.

Ashton, D. (1972). *Picasso on art: A selection of views.* New York: Viking Press.
Ashton, T. S. (1948/1969). *The industrial revolution 1760–1830.* London: Oxford University Press.
Atkins, P. (2004). Ponderable matter: Explanation in chemistry. In J. Cornwell (Ed.), *Explanations: Styles of explanations in science* (pp. 111–124). Oxford, UK: Oxford University Press.
Atwood, M. E., & Polson P. G. (1976). A process model for water jug problems. *Cognitive Psychology,* vol. 8, pp. 191–216.
Atwood, M. E., Masson, M. E. J., & Polson, P. G. (1980). Further explorations with a process model for water jug problems. *Memory & Cognition,* vol. 8, pp. 182–192.
Auerswald, P., Kauffman, S., Lobo, J., & Shell, K. (2000). The production recipes approach to modeling technological innovation: An application to learning by doing. *Journal of Economic Dynamics and Control,* vol. 24, pp. 389–450.
Aunger, R. (2002). *The electric meme: A new theory of how we think.* New York: Free Press.
Ausubel, D. P. (1963). *The psychology of meaningful verbal learning: An introduction to school learning.* New York: Grune & Stratton.
———. (1968). *Educational psychology: A cognitive view.* New York: Holt, Rinehart and Winston.
Baars, B. J. (1986). *The cognitive revolution in psychology.* New York: Guilford Press.
Bacon, F. (1620/1994). *Novum organum* (transl. P. Urbach & J. Gibson). Chicago: Open Court.
Baddeley, A. (1996). Exploring the central executive. *Quarterly Journal of Experimental Psychology,* vol. 49A, pp. 5–28.
———. (2007). *Working memory, thought, and action.* Oxford, UK: Oxford University Press.
Baggott, J. (2004). *Beyond measure: Modern physics, philosophy, and the meaning of quantum theory.* New York: Oxford University Press.
Bain, A. (1879). *The senses and the intellect* (3rd ed.). New York: D. Appleton.
Bain, A., & van Vorst, Wm. D. (1999). The Hindenburg tragedy revisited: The fatal flaw found. *International Journal of Hydrogen Energy,* vol. 24, pp. 399–403.
Bak, P. (1996). *How nature works: The science of self-organized criticality.* New York: Springer-Verlag.
Balcetis, E., & Dunning, D. (2007). Cognitive dissonance and the perception of natural environments. *Psychological Science,* vol. 18, pp. 917–921.
Baldwin, J. M. (1896a). A new factor in evolution. *American Naturalist,* vol. 30, pp. 441–451.
———. (1896b). A new factor in evolution (continued). *American Naturalist,* vol. 30, pp. 536–553.
Baldwin, N. (2001). *Edison: Inventing the century.* Chicago: University of Chicago Press.
Baldwin, T. T., & Ford, J. K. (1988). Transfer of training: A review and directions for future research. *Personnel Psychology,* vol. 41, pp. 63–105.
Barber, B. (1961). Resistance by scientists to scientific discovery. *Science,* vol. 134, pp. 596–602.

Barber, M. J., & Lichtman, J. W. (1999). Activity-driven synapse elimination leads paradoxically to domination by inactive neurons. *Journal of Neuroscience*, vol. 19, pp. 9975–9985.

Barkow, J. H., Cosmides, L., & Tooby, J. (Eds.). (1992). *The adapted mind: Evolutionary psychology and the generation of culture*. New York: Oxford University Press.

Barnes, B. R., & Clawson, E. V. (1975). Do advance organizers facilitate learning? Recommendations for further research based on an analysis of 32 studies. *Review of Educational Research*, vol. 45, pp. 637–659.

Barron, F., & Harrington, D. M. (1981). Creativity, intelligence, and personality. *Annual Review of Psychology*, vol. 32, pp. 439–476.

Barrow, D., Mitrovic, A., Ohlsson, S., & Grimley, M. (2008). Assessing the impact of positive feedback in constraint-based tutors. In B. P. Woolf, E. Aïmeur, R. Nkambou, & S. Lajoie (Eds.), *Intelligent tutoring systems* (pp. 250–259). Berlin, Germany: Springer-Verlag.

Bartlett, F. C. (1932). *Remembering: A study in experimental and social psychology*. Cambridge, MA: Cambridge University Press.

Bar-Yosef, O. (1992). The role of Western Asia in modern human origins. *Philosophical Transactions: Biological Sciences*, vol. 337, pp. 193–200.

Bassok, M. (1990). Transfer of domain-specific problem-solving procedures. *Journal of Experimental Psychology: Learning, Memory, and Cognition*, vol. 16, pp. 522–533.

Bassok, M., & Holyoak, K. J. (1989). Interdomain transfer between isomorphic topics in algebra and physics. *Journal of Experimental Psychology: Learning, Memory, and Cognition*, vol. 15, pp. 153–166.

Behrens, R. R. (1987). The life and unusual ideas of Adelbert Ames, Jr. *Leonardo*, vol. 20, pp. 273–279.

Belich, J. (2001). *Making peoples: A history of the New Zealanders from Polynesian settlement to the end of the nineteenth century*. Honolulu, HI: University of Hawai'i Press.

Bell, M. S. (2005). *Lavoisier in Year One*. New York: Norton.

Berenbaum, M. R. (1996). Introduction to the symposium: On the evolution of specialization. *American Naturalist*, vol. 148, pp. 78–83.

Bereiter, C., & Scardamalia, M. (1985). Cognitive coping strategies and the problem of "inert knowledge." In S. F. Chipman, J. W. Segal, & R. Glaser (Eds.), *Thinking and learning skills* (vol. 2): *Research and open questions* (pp. 65–80). Hillsdale, NJ: Erlbaum.

Berkson, W., & Wettersten, J. (1984). *Learning from error: Karl Popper's psychology of learning*. La Salle, IL: Open Court.

Bernstein, S., Lebow, R. N., Stein, J. G., & Weber, S. (2000). God gave physics the easy problems: Adapting social science to an unpredictable world. *European Journal of International Relations*, vol. 6, pp. 43–76.

Bernstein, W. J. (2004). *The birth of plenty: How the prosperity of the modern world was created*. New York: McGraw-Hill.

Bertman, S. (1998). *Hyperculture: The human cost of speed*. Westport, CT: Praeger.

Besemer, S. P. (1998). Creative product analysis matrix: Testing the model structure and a comparison among products – three novel chairs. *Creativity Research Journal*, vol. 11, pp. 333–346.

Besemer, S. P., & Treffinger, D. J. (1981). Analysis of creative products: Review and synthesis. *Journal of Creative Behavior*, vol. 15, pp. 158–178.

Biederman, I. (1987). Recognition-by-components: A theory of human image understanding. *Psychological Review*, vol. 94, pp. 115–147.

Bishop, B., & Anderson, C. (1990). Student conceptions of natural selection and its role in evolution. *Journal of Research in Science Teaching*, vol. 27, pp. 415–427.

Birch, H. G., & Rabinowitz, H. S. (1951). The negative effect of previous experience on productive thinking. *Journal of Experimental Psychology*, vol. 41, pp. 121–125.

Blackburn, P., van Benthem, J. F. A. K., & Wolter, F. (Eds.). (2007). *Handbook of modal logic*. Amsterdam, the Netherlands: Elsevier.

Blackmore, S. (1999). *The meme machine*. Oxford, UK: Oxford University Press.

Blanshard, F. B. (1949). *The retreat from likeness in the theory of painting* (2nd ed.). New York: Columbia University Press.

Bloom, B. S. (1984). The 2 sigma problem: The search for methods of group instruction as effective as one-to-one tutoring. *Educational Researcher*, vol. 13, pp. 4–16.

Blyth, M. (2006). Great punctuations: Predictions, randomness, and the evolution of comparative political science. *American Political Science Review*, vol. 100, pp. 1–6.

Boden, M. A. (1972). *Purposive explanation in psychology*. Cambridge, MA: Harvard University Press.

Bohner, G., & Wänke, M. (2002). *Attitudes and attitude change*. New York: Psychology Press.

Bonabeau, E., Theraulaz, G., Deneubourg, J.-L., Aron, S., & Camazine, S. (1997). Self-organization in social insects. *Trends in Ecology & Evolution*, vol. 12, pp. 188–193.

Boole, G. (1854/1958). *An investigation of the laws of thought on which are founded the mathematical theories of logic and probabilities*. New York: Dover.

Bosse, T., Jonker, C. M., & Treur, J. (2006). Componential explanation in philosophy, cognitive science and computer science. In R. Sun & N. Miyake (Eds.), *Proceedings of the 28th Annual Conference of the Cognitive Science Society* (pp. 95–100), Vancouver, British Columbia, Canada, June 26–29. Electronic archive at http://www.cognitivesciencesociety.org/conference_past.html.

Botvinick, M. M., Braver, T. S., Barch, D. M., Carter, C. S., & Cohen, J. D. (2001). Conflict monitoring and cognitive control. *Psychological Review*, vol. 108, pp. 624–652.

Bouchard, T. J., & McGue, M. (1981). Familial studies of intelligence: A review. *Science*, vol. 22, pp. 1055–1059.

Boulding, K. E. (1961). *The image: Knowledge in life and society*. Ann Arbor: University of Michigan Press.

Bowden, E. M., & Jung-Beeman, M. (2003). Aha! Insight experience correlates with solution activation in the right hemisphere. *Psychonomic Bulletin & Review*, vol. 10, pp. 730–737.

Bowden, E. M., Jung-Beeman, M., Fleck, J., & Kounios, J. (2005). New approaches to demystifying insight. *TRENDS in Cognitive Sciences*, vol. 9, pp. 322–328.

Bower, G. H. (1972). Mental imagery and associative learning. In L. W. Gregg (Ed.), *Cognition in learning and memory* (pp. 51–88). New York: Wiley.

Bower, G. H., & Reitman, J. S. (1972). Mnemonic elaboration in multilist learning. *Journal of Verbal Learning and Verbal Behavior*, vol. 11, pp. 478–485.

Boyer, C. B. (1985). *A history of mathematics.* Princeton, NJ: Princeton University Press.

Bradshaw, G. (1992). The airplane and the logic of invention. In R. N. Giere (Ed.), *Minnesota Studies in the Philosophy of Science* (vol. 15): *Cognitive models of science* (pp. 239–250). Minneapolis: University of Minneapolis Press.

Brady, J. E., & Holum, J. R. (1988). *Fundamentals of chemistry* (3rd ed.). New York: Wiley.

Bransford, J. D., Barclay, J. R., & Franks, J. J. (1972). Sentence memory: A constructive versus interpretative approach. *Cognitive Psychology*, vol. 3, pp. 193–209.

Bransford, J. D., & Schwartz, D. L. (1999). Rethinking transfer: A simple proposal with multiple implications. *Review of Research in Education*, vol. 24, pp. 61–100.

Brewer, W. F., & Lambert, B. L. (2001). The theory-ladenness of observation and the theory-ladenness of the rest of the scientific process. *Philosophy of Science*, vol. 68, pp. 176–186.

Brewer, W. F., & Nakamura, G. V. (1984). The nature and function of schemas. In R. Wyer & T. Srull (Eds.), *Handbook of social cognition* (pp. 119–160). Hillsdale, NJ: Erlbaum.

Broadbent, D. E. (1958). *Perception and communication.* Oxford, UK: Pergamon Press.

Brock, W. (1993). *The Norton history of chemistry.* New York: Norton.

Brodie, R. (1996). *Virus of the mind: The science of the meme.* Seattle, WA: Integral Press.

Broude, N. (Ed.). (1994). *World impressionism: The international movement, 1860–1920.* New York: Harry N. Abrams.

Brown, A. S. (1991). A review of the tip-of-the-tongue experience. *Psychological Bulletin*, vol. 109, pp. 204–223.

Brown, K. A. (1988). *Inventors at work: Interviews with 16 notable American inventors.* Redmond, WA: Microsoft Press.

Brown, J. S., & Burton, R. R. (1978). Diagnostic models for procedural bugs in basic mathematical skills. *Cognitive Science*, vol. 2, pp. 155–192.

Brown, J. S., & VanLehn, K. (1980). Repair theory: A generative theory of bugs in procedural skills. *Cognitive Science*, vol. 4, pp. 379–426.

Brown, R., Vivian, J., & Hewstone, M. (1999). Changing attitudes through group contact: The effects of group membership salience. *European Journal of Social Psychology*, vol. 29, pp. 741–764.

Brown, S., & Heathcote, A. (2003). Averaging learning curves across and within participants. *Behavior Research Methods, Instruments, and Computers*, vol. 35, pp. 11–21.

Brownell, W. A. (1947). An experiment on "borrowing" in third-grade arithmetic. *Journal of Educational Research*, vol. 16, pp. 161–263.

Brownell, W. A., & Moser, H. E. (1949). *Meaningful vs. mechanical learning: A study in Grade III subtraction.* Durham, NC: Duke University Press.

Bruner, J. S. (1966). *Toward a theory of instruction.* Cambridge, MA: Harvard University Press.

———. (1970). The growth and structure of skill. In K. Connolly (Ed.), *Mechanisms of motor skill development* (pp. 63–94). New York: Academic Press.

Bruner, J. S., & Postman, L. (1949). On the perception of incongruity: A paradigm. *Journal of Personality*, vol. 18, pp. 206–223.
Bryan, W. L., & Harter, N. (1897). Studies in the physiology and psychology of the telegraphic language. *Psychological Review*, vol. 4, pp. 27–53.
———.(1899). Studies on the telegraphic language: The acquisition of a hierarchy of habits. *Psychological Review*, vol. 6, pp. 345–375.
Buchanan, B. G. (2001). Creativity at the meta-level. *AI Magazine*, vol. 22, pp. 13–28.
Buchanan, B. G., & Feigenbaum, E. A. (1978). Dendral and Meta-Dendral: Their application dimension. *Artificial Intelligence*, vol. 11, pp. 5–24.
Buchanan, B., Moore, J., Carenini, G., Forsythe, D., Ohlsson, S., & Banks, G. (1995). An intelligent interactive system for delivering individualized information to patients. *Artificial Intelligence in Medicine*, vol. 7, pp. 117–154.
Buckley, K. W. (1989). *Mechanical man: John Broadus Watson and the beginnings of behaviorism*. New York: Guilford Press.
Budd, G. E. (2006). On the origin and evolution of major morphological characters. *Biological Reviews*, vol. 81, pp. 609–628.
Buderi, R. (1996). *The invention that changed the world: How a small group of radar pioneers won the Second World War and launched a technological revolution*. New York: Simon & Schuster.
Buller, D. J. (2005). Evolutionary psychology: The emperor's new paradigm. *TRENDS in Cognitive Science*, vol. 9, pp. 277–283.
Burroughs, W. J. (2005). *Climate change in prehistory: The end of the reign of chaos*. Cambridge, UK: Cambridge University Press.
Burton, R. R. (1982). Diagnosing bugs in a simple procedural skill. In D. Sleeman & J. S. Brown (Eds.), *Intelligent tutoring systems* (pp. 157–199). New York: Academic Press.
Bush, G. L. (1975). Modes of animal speciation. *Annual Review of Ecology and Systematics*, vol. 6, pp. 339–364.
Butterfield, H. (1957). *The origins of modern science 1300–1800* (revised ed.). New York: Free Press.
Butterworth, A., & Laurence, R. (2005). *Pompeii: The living city*. New York: St. Martin's Press.
Butts, R. E. (Ed.). (1989). *William Whewell: Theory of scientific method* (revised ed.). Indianapolis, IN: Hackett.
Bynum, C. W. (2001). *Metamorphosis and identity*. New York: Zone Books.
Calandra, B., & Barron, A. E. (2005). A preliminary investigation of advance organizers for a complex educational website. *Journal of Educational Multimedia and Hypermedia*, vol. 14, pp. 5–23.
Callander, R. A. (1978). River meandering. *Annual Review of Fluid Mechanics*, vol. 10, pp. 129–158.
Calvin, W. H. (1991). *Ascent of mind: Ice age climates and the evolution of intelligence*. New York: Bantam Books.
Camazine, S., Deneubourg, J.-L., Franks, N. R., Sneyd, J., Theraulaz, G., & Bonabeau, E. (2001). *Self-organization in biological systems*. Princeton, NJ: Princeton University Press.

Cameron, K. A., Jacks, J. Z., & O'Brien, M. E. (2002). An experimental investigation of strategies for resisting persuasion. *Current Research in Social Psychology*, vol. 7, pp. 205–224. Electronic publication available at http://www.uiowa.edu/~grpproc/crisp/crisp.7.12.htm.

Camilleri, K. (2006). Heisenberg and the wave-particle duality. *Studies in History and Philosophy of Modern Physics*, vol. 37, pp. 298–315.

Campbell, D. T. (1960). Blind variation and selective retention in creative thought as in other knowledge processes. *Psychological Review*, vol. 67, pp. 380–400.

Campitelli, G., & Gobet, F. (2005). The mind's eye in blindfold chess. *European Journal of Cognitive Psychology*, vol. 17, pp. 23–45.

Caprara, G. V., & Cervone, D. (2000). *Personality: Determinants, dynamics, and potentials*. Cambridge, UK: Cambridge University Press.

Caramazza, A., McCloskey, M., & Green, B. (1980). Naive beliefs in "sophisticated" subjects: Misconceptions about trajectories of objects. *Cognition*, vol. 9, pp. 117–123.

Caramazzo, A., & Shelton, J. A. (1998). Domain-specific knowledge systems in the brain: The animate-inanimate distinction. *Journal of Cognitive Neuroscience*, vol. 10, pp. 1–34.

Carbonell, J. G. (1983). Learning by analogy: Formulating and generalizing plans from past experience. In R. S. Michalski, J. G. Carbonell, & T. M. Mitchell (Eds.), *Machine learning: An artificial intelligence approach* (pp. 137–161). Palo Alto, CA: Tioga.

———. (1986). Derivational analogy: A theory of reconstructive problem solving and expertise acquisition. In R. S. Michalski, J. G. Carbonell, & T. M. Mitchell (Eds.), *Machine learning: An artificial intelligence approach* (vol. 2, pp. 371–392). Los Altos, CA: Morgan Kauffmann.

Carlson, W. B., & Gorman, M. E. (1992). A cognitive framework to understand technological creativity: Bell, Edison, and the telephone. In R. J. Weber & D. N. Perkins (Eds.), *Inventive minds: Creativity in technology* (pp. 48–79). New York: Oxford University Press.

Carnie, A. (2008). *Constituent structure*. New York: Oxford University Press.

Carroll, J. B. (1993). *Human cognitive abilities: A survey of factor-analytic studies*. Cambridge, UK: Cambridge University Press.

Carroll, P. B., & Mui, C. (2008). *Billion-dollar lessons: What you can learn from the most inexcusable business failures of the last 25 years*. New York: Portfolio.

Carroll, S. B. (2005). *Endless forms most beautiful: The new science of evo devo and the making of the animal kingdom*. New York: Norton.

Casper, B. M, & Noer, R. J. (1972). *Revolutions in physics*. New York: Norton.

Catrambone, R. (1995). Aiding subgoal learning: Effects on transfer. *Journal of Educational Psychology*, vol. 8, pp. 5–17.

———. (1998). The subgoal learning model: Creating better examples so that students can solve novel problems. *Journal of Experimental Psychology: General*, vol. 127, pp. 355–376.

Cattell, R. B. (1963). Theory of fluid and crystallized intelligence: A critical experiment. *Journal of Educational Psychology*, vol. 54, pp. 1–22.

Cavalli-Sforza, L. L. (2000). *Genes, peoples, and languages* (M. Seielstad, Trans.). New York: Farrar, Straus and Giroux.

Cech, T. R. (2001). Overturning the dogma: Catalytic RNA. In K. H. Pfenninger & V. R. Shubik (Eds.), *The origins of creativity* (pp. 5–17). Oxford, UK: Oxford University Press.

Cervone, D. (2004). The architecture of personality. *Psychological Review*, vol. 111, pp. 183–204.

———. (2005). Personality architecture: Within-person structures and processes. *Annual Review of Psychology*, vol. 56, pp. 423–452.

Champagne, A. B., Gunstone, R. F., & Klopfer, L. E. (1985). In L. H. T. West & A. L. Pines (Eds.), *Cognitive structure and conceptual change* (pp. 61–90). New York: Academic Press.

Chan, C., Burtis, J., & Bereiter, C. (1997). Knowledge building as a mediator of conflict in conceptual change. *Cognition and Instruction*, vol. 15, pp. 1–40.

Chandler, P., & Sweller, J. (1991). Cognitive load theory and the format of instruction. *Cognitive Science*, vol. 8, pp. 293–332.

Chase, W. G., & Ericsson, K. A. (1981). Skilled memory. In John R. Anderson (Ed.), *Cognitive skills and their acquisition* (pp. 141–189). Hillsdale, NJ: Erlbaum.

Chase, W. G., & Simon, H. A. (1973a). Skill in chess. *American Scientist*, vol. 61, pp. 394–403.

———. (1973b). The mind's eye in chess. In W. G. Chase (Ed.), *Visual information processing* (pp. 215–281). New York: Academic Press.

Chauvet, J.-M., Deschamps, E. B., & Hillaire, C. (1996). *Dawn of art: The Chauvet Cave. The oldest known paintings in the world*. New York: Harry N. Abrams.

Chechik, G., Meilijson, I., & Ruppin, E. (1998). Synaptic pruning in development: A computational account. *Neural Computation*, vol. 10, pp. 1759–1777.

Cheng, P. W., & Holyoak, K. J. (1985). Pragmatic reasoning schemas. *Cognitive Psychology*, vol. 17, pp. 391–416.

Cheyney, E. P. (1924). Law in history. *American Historical Review*, vol. 29, pp. 231–248.

Chi, M. T. H. (1992). Conceptual change within and across ontological categories: Examples from learning and discovery in science. In R. N. Giere (Ed.), *Cognitive models of science* (pp. 129–186). Minneapolis: University of Minnesota Press.

———. (1997). Creativity: Shifting across ontological categories flexibly. In T. B. Ward, S. M. Smith, & J. Vaid (Eds.), *Creative thought: An investigation of conceptual structures and processes* (pp. 209–234). Washington, DC: American Psychological Association.

———. (2005). Commonsense conceptions of emergent processes: Why some misconceptions are robust. *Journal of the Learning Sciences*, vol. 14, pp. 161–199.

———. (2008). Three types of conceptual change: Belief revision, mental model transformation, and categorical shift. In S. Vosniadou (Ed.), *Handbook of research on conceptual change* (pp. 61–82). Hillsdale, NJ: Erlbaum.

Chi, M. T. H., & Brem, S. K. (2009). Contrasting Ohlsson's resubsumption theory with Chi's categorical shift theory. *Educational Psychologist*, vol. 44, pp. 58–63.

Chi, M. T. H., Glaser, R., & Farr, M. (Eds.). (1988). *The nature of expertise*. Hillsdale, NJ: Erlbaum.

Chi, M. T. H., & Hausmann, R. G. M. (2003). Do radical discoveries require ontological shifts? In L.V. Shavinina (Ed.), *International handbook on innovation* (vol. 3, pp. 430–444). Oxford, UK: Elsevier.

Chi, M. T. H., & Ohlsson, S. (2005). Complex declarative learning. In K. J. Holyoak & R. G. Morrison (Eds.), *The Cambridge handbook of thinking and reasoning* (pp. 371–399). Cambridge, UK: Cambridge University Press.

Chi, M. T. H., & Roscoe, R. D. (2002). The processes and challenges of conceptual change. In M. Limón & L. Mason (Eds.), *Reconsidering conceptual change: Issues in theory and practice* (pp. 3–27). Dordrecht, the Netherlands: Kluwer.

Chi, M. T. H., Siler, S. A., Jeong, H., Yamauchi, T., & Hausmann, R. G. (2001). Learning from human tutoring. *Cognitive Science*, vol. 25, pp. 471–533.

Chi, M. T. H., Slotta, J. D., & de Leeuw, N. (1994). From things to processes: A theory of conceptual change for learning science concepts. *Learning and Instruction*, vol. 4, pp. 27–43.

Chinn, C. A., & Brewer, W. F. (1993). The role of anomalous data in knowledge acquisition: A theoretical framework and implications for science instruction. *Review of Educational Research*, vol. 63, pp. 1–49.

Chipp, H. B. (1988). *Picasso's "Guernica": History, transformations, meanings*. Berkeley: University of California Press.

Chomsky, N. (1957/1972). *Syntactic structures*. The Hague, the Netherlands: Mouton.

———. (1964). *Current issues in linguistic theory*. The Hague, the Netherlands: Mouton.

Chronicle, E. P., Ormerod, T. C., & MacGregor, J. N. (2001). When insight just won't come: The failure of visual cues in the nine-dot problem. *Quarterly Journal of Experimental Psychology*, vol. 54, pp. 903–919.

Chronicle, E. P., MacGregor, J. N., & Ormerod, T. C. (2004). What makes an insight problem? The roles of heuristics, goal conception, and solution recoding in knowledge-lean problems. *Journal of Experimental Psychology: Learning, Memory, and Cognition*, vol. 30, pp. 14–27.

Churchland, P. M. (1995). *The engine of reason, the seat of the soul: A philosophical journey into the brain*. Cambridge, MA: MIT Press.

Churchland, P. S. (1996). Toward a neurobiology of the mind. In R. Llinás & P. S. Churchland (Eds.), *The mind-brain continuum: Sensory processes* (pp. 281–303). Cambridge, MA: MIT Press.

Clagett, M. (1959). *The science of mechanics in the Middle Ages*. Madison: University of Wisconsin Press.

Clancey, W. J. (1985). Heuristic classification. *Artificial Intelligence*, vol. 27, pp. 289–350.

———. (1997). *Situated cognition: On human knowledge and computer representations*. Cambridge, UK: Cambridge University Press.

Clark, H. H. (1969). Linguistic processes in deductive reasoning. *Psychological Review*, vol. 76, pp. 387–404.

Clement, J. (1982). Students' preconceptions in introductory mechanics. *American Journal of Physics*, vol. 50, pp. 66–71.

Clottes, J., & Courtin, J. (1996). *The cave beneath the sea: Paleolithic images at Cosquer*. New York: Harry N. Abrams.

Cohen, E. A., & Gooch, J. (1991). *Military misfortunes: The anatomy of failure in war*. New York: Vintage.

Cohen, P. A., Kulik, J. A., & Kulik, C.-L. C. (1982). Educational outcomes of tutoring: A meta-analysis of findings. *American Educational Research Journal*, vol. 19, pp. 237–248.

Cole, M., Engeström, Y., & Vasquez, O. (Eds.). (1997). *Mind, culture, and activity: Seminal papers from the laboratory of comparative human cognition.* Cambridge, UK: Cambridge University Press.

Colish, M. L. (1997). *Medieval foundations of the Western intellectual tradition 400–1400.* New Haven, CT: Yale University Press.

Collins, A. M., & Loftus, E. F. (1975). A spreading-activation theory of semantic processing. *Psychological Review,* vol. 82, pp. 407–428.

Comins, N. F. (2001). *Heavenly errors: Misconceptions about the real nature of the universe.* New York: Columbia University Press.

Commons, M. L., Trudeau, E. J., Stein, S. A., Richards, F. A., & Krause, S. R. (1998). Hierarchical complexity of tasks shows the existence of developmental stages. *Developmental Review,* vol. 18, pp. 237–278.

Conway, F., & Siegelman, J. (2005). *Dark hero of the information age: In search of Norbert Wiener, the father of cybernetics.* New York: Basic Books.

Cooper, B. (1992). *Beethoven and the creative process.* Oxford, UK: Oxford University Press.

Cooper, R. P. (2006). Cognitive architectures as Lakatosian research programs: Two case studies. *Philosophical Psychology,* vol. 19, pp. 199–220.

Corkill, A. J. (1992). Advance organizers: Facilitators of recall. *Educational Psychology Review,* vol. 4, pp. 33–67.

Cornwell, J. (Ed.). (2004). *Explanations: Styles of explanation in science.* Oxford, UK: Oxford University Press.

Corrigan-Halpern, A. (2006). *Feedback in complex learning: Considering the relationship between utility and processing demands.* Doctoral dissertation. Chicago, IL: Department of Psychology, University of Illinois at Chicago.

Corrigan-Halpern, A., & Ohlsson, S. (2002). Feedback effects in the acquisition of a hierarchical skill. In W. D. Gray & C. D. Schunn (Eds.), *Proceedings of the Twenty-Fourth Annual Conference of the Cognitive Science Society* (pp. 226–231). Mahwah, NJ: Erlbaum.

Cosejo, D. G., Oesterreich, J., & Ohlsson, S. (2009). Re-categorization: Restructuring in categorization. *Proceedings of the 31st Annual Meeting of the Cognitive Science Society* (pp. 573–578). Amsterdam, the Netherlands, 29 July to 1 August, 2009.

Cosmides, L. (1989). The logic of social exchange: Has natural selection shaped how humans reason? Studies with the Wason selection task. *Cognition,* vol. 31, pp. 187–276.

Costeau, J. Y. (1953). *The silent world.* New York: Harper & Brothers.

———. (1963). *The living sea.* New York: Harper & Row.

———. (1964). *World without sun.* New York: Harper & Row.

Cowan, R., & Jonard, N. (2003). The dynamics of collective invention. *Journal of Economic Behavior & Organization,* vol. 52, pp. 513–532.

Cox, J. D. (2005). *Climate crash: Abrupt climate change and what it means for our future.* Washington, DC: Joseph Henry Press.

Crain, S., & Pietroski, P. (2002). Why language acquisition is a snap. *Linguistic Review,* vol. 19, pp. 163–183.

Crane, N. (2002). *Mercator: The man who mapped the planet.* New York: Henry Holt.

Crevier, D. (1993). *AI: The tumultuous history of the search for artificial intelligence.* New York: Basic Books.
Crockenberg, S. B. (1972). Creativity tests: A boon or boondoggle for education? *Review of Educational Research,* vol. 42, pp. 27–45.
Crossman, E. R. F. (1959). A theory of the acquisition of speed-skill. *Ergonomics,* vol. 2, pp. 153–156.
Crovitz, H. E. (1971). The capacity of memory loci in artificial memory. *Psychonomic Science,* vol. 24, pp. 187–188.
Csikszentmihalyi, M. (1997). *Creativity: Flow and the psychology of discovery and invention.* New York: HarperCollins.
Cummins, R. (1975). Functional analysis. *Journal of Philosophy,* vol. 72, pp. 741–765.
———. (1983a). Analysis and subsumption in the behaviorism of Hull. *Philosophy of Science,* vol. 50, pp. 96–111.
———. (1983b). *The nature of psychological explanation.* Cambridge, MA: MIT Press.
———. (2000). "How does it work?" versus "What are the laws?": Two conceptions of psychological explanation. In F. C. Keil & R. A. Wilson (Eds.), *Explanation and cognition* (pp. 117–144). Cambridge, MA: MIT Press.
Cushing, J. T. (1991). Quantum theory and explanatory discourse: Endgame for understanding? *Philosophy of Science,* vol. 58, pp. 337–358.
Cziko, G. (1995). *Without miracles: Universal selection theory and the second Darwinian revolution.* Cambridge, MA: MIT Press.
Dacey, J. S., & Lennon, K. H. (1998). *Understanding creativity: The interplay of biological, psychological, and social factors.* San Francisco, CA: Jossey-Bass.
D'Andrade, R. (1995). *The development of cognitive anthropology.* Cambridge, UK: Cambridge University Press.
Darden, L. (1992). Strategies for anomaly resolution. In R. N. Giere (Ed.), *Minnesota Studies in the Philosophy of Science* (vol. 15): *Cognitive models of science* (pp. 251–273). Minneapolis: University of Minnesota Press.
Darwin, C. (1859/2004). *The origin of species by means of natural selection.* New York: Barnes & Noble Classics.
Davies, P. S. (2003). *Norms of nature: Naturalism and the nature of functions.* Cambridge, MA: MIT Press.
Davis, M. (Ed.). (1965/2004). *The undecidable: Basic papers on undecidable propositions, unsolvable problems and computable functions.* Mineola, NY: Dover.
Davis, R., Buchanan, B., & Shortliffe, E. (1977). Production rules as a representation for a knowledge-based consultation program. *Artificial Intelligence,* vol. 8, pp. 15–45.
Davidson, D. (1990). The structure and content of truth. *Journal of Philosophy,* vol. 87, pp. 279–328.
Dawkins, R. (1976). *The selfish gene.* New York: Oxford University Press.
Dawson-Tunik, T. L., Commons, M., Wilson, M., & Fischer, K. W. (2005). The shape of development. *European Journal of Developmental Psychology,* vol. 2, pp. 163–195.
Deese, J. (1965). *The structure of associations in language and thought.* Baltimore, MD: Johns Hopkins University Press.

DeLatil, P. (1954). *The underwater naturalist* (E. Fitzgerald, Trans.). London: Jarrolds.
Delaney, P. F., Reder, L. M., Staszewski, J. J., & Ritter, F. E. (1998). The strategy-specific nature of improvement: The power law applies by strategy within task. *Psychological Science*, vol. 9, pp. 1–7.
Demasters, S., Settlage, J., & Good, R. (1995). Students' conceptions of natural selection and its role in evolution: Cases of replication and comparison. *Journal of Research in Science Teaching*, vol. 32, pp. 535–550.
Denbigh, K. G. (1989). The many faces of irreversibility. *British Journal for the Philosophy of Science*, vol. 40, pp. 501–518.
DeSoto, D. B., London, M., & Handel, S. (1965). Social reasoning and spatial paralogic. *Journal of Personality and Social Psychology*, vol. 2, pp. 513–521.
Detterman, D. K. (1993). The case for the prosecution: Transfer as epiphenomenon. In D. K. Detterman & R. J. Sternberg (Eds.), *Transfer on trial: Intelligence, cognition, and instruction* (pp. 1–24). Norwood, NJ: Ablex.
Detterman, D. K., & Sternberg, R. J. (Eds.). (1993). *Transfer on trial: Intelligence, cognition, and instruction*. Norwood, NJ: Ablex.
Dial, K. P. (2003). Wing-assisted incline running and the evolution of flight. *Science*, vol. 299, pp. 402–404.
Diamond, J. (2005). *Collapse: How societies choose to fail or succeed*. London: Penguin Books.
Dickison, M. R. (2007). *The allometry of giant flightless birds*. Doctoral dissertation. Durham, NC: Department of Biology, Duke University.
Dispenza, J. (2007). *Evolve your brain: The science of changing your mind*. Deerfield Beach, FL: Health Communications.
DiVesta, F. J., & Walls, R. T. (1967). Transfer of object-function in problem solving. *American Educational Research Journal*, vol. 4, pp. 207–215.
Dobzhansky, T. (1973). Nothing in biology makes sense except in the light of evolution. *American Biology Teacher*, vol. 35, pp. 125–129.
Dole, J. A., & Sinatra, G. M. (1998). Reconceptualizing change in the cognitive construction of knowledge. *Educational Psychologist*, vol. 33, pp. 109–128.
Dole, J. A., Valencia, S. W., Greer, E. A., & Wardrop, J. L. (1991). Effects of two types of prereading instruction on the comprehension of narrative and expository text. *Reading Research Quarterly*, vol. 26, pp. 142–159.
Donald, M. (1991). *Origins of the modern mind: Three stages in the evolution of culture and cognition*. Cambridge, MA: Harvard University Press.
———. (2001). *A mind so rare: The evolution of human consciousness*. New York: Norton.
Donaldson, M. (1963). *A study of children's thinking*. London: Tavistock.
Donini, F. M., Lenzerini, M., Nardi, D., Pirri, F., & Schaerf, M. (1990). Nonmonotonic reasoning. *Artificial Intelligence Review*, vol. 4, pp. 163–210.
Dorward, F. M. C., & Day, R. H. (1996). Loss of 3-D shape constancy in interior spaces: The basis of the Ames-room illusion. *Perception*, vol. 26, pp. 707–718.
Douven, I. (2002). Testing inference to the best explanation. *Synthese*, vol. 130, pp. 355–377.
Dretske, F. (1997). *Naturalizing the mind*. Cambridge, MA: MIT Press.

Dreyfus, A., Jungwirth, E., & Eliovitch, R. (1990). Applying the "cognitive conflict" strategy for conceptual change – some implications, difficulties and problems. *Science Education*, vol. 74, pp. 555–569.

Driver, R., Guesne, E., & Tiberghien, A. (Eds.). (1985). *Children's ideas in science*. Milton Keynes, UK: Open University Press.

Dubos, R. J. (1976). *Louis Pasteur: Free lance of science*. New York: Charles Scribner's Sons.

Duffey, R. B., & Saull, J. W. (2003). *Know the risk. Learning from errors and accidents: Safety and risk in today's technology*. Burlington, MA: Elsevier Science.

Dugas, R. (1955/1988). *A history of mechanics*. New York: Dover.

Duhem, P. (1914/1991). *The aim and structure of physical theory* (P. P. Wiener, Trans.). Princeton, NJ: Princeton University Press.

Dunbar, K. (1995). How scientists really reason: Scientific reasoning in real-world laboratories. In R. J. Sternberg & J. E. Davidson (Eds.), *The nature of insight* (pp. 365–395). Cambridge, MA: MIT Press.

———. (1997). How scientists think: On-line creativity and conceptual change in science. In T. B. Ward, S. M. Smith & J. Vaid (Eds.), *Creative thought: An investigation of conceptual structures and processes* (pp. 461–493). Washington, DC: American Psychological Association.

Dunbar, K., & Blanchette, I. (2001). The in vivo/in vitro approach to cognition: The case of analogy. *TRENDS in Cognitive Sciences*, vol. 5, pp. 334–339.

Dunbar, K. N., & Fugelsang, J. A. (2005). Causal thinking in science: How scientists and students interpret the unexpected. In M. E. Gorman, R. D. Tweney, D. C. Gooding, & A. P. Kincannon (Eds.), *Scientific and technological thinking* (pp. 57–79). Mahwah, NJ: Erlbaum.

Duncker, K. (1935/1974). *Zur Psychologie des produktiven Denkens* (Dritter Neudruck). Berlin, Germany: Springer Verlag. [English version: Duncker, K. (1945). On problem-solving. *Psychological Monographs*, vol. 58, Whole No. 270.]

Durkin, H. E. (1937). Trial-and-error, gradual analysis, and sudden reorganization: An experimental study of problem solving. *Archives of Psychology*, vol. 30, pp. 1–85.

Eagly, A. H., & Chaiken, S. (1993). *The psychology of attitudes*. Belmont, CA: Thomson/Wadsworth.

Ebbing, D. D., & Wrighton, M. S. (1990). *General chemistry* (3rd ed.). Dallas, TX: Houghton Mifflin.

Ebbinghaus, H. (1885/1964). *Memory: A contribution to experimental psychology*. New York: Dover.

Edelman, G. M. (1987). *Neural Darwinism: The theory of neuronal group selection*. New York: Basic Books.

Edmondson, A. C. (2004a). Learning from failure in health care: Frequent opportunities, pervasive barriers. *Quality and Safety in Health Care*, vol. 13 (supplement 2), pp. ii3–ii9.

———. (2004b). Learning from mistakes is easier said than done: Group and organizational influences on the detection and correction of human error. *Journal of Applied Behavioral Science*, vol. 40, pp. 66–90.

Einstein, A. (1934). On the method of theoretical physics. *Philosophy of Science*, vol. 1, pp. 163–169.

Einstein, A., & Infeld, L. (1938). *The evolution of physics: The growth of ideas from early concepts to relativity and quanta.* New York: Simon & Schuster.

Egan, D. E., & Greeno, J. G. (1974). Theory of rule induction: Knowledge acquired in concept learning, serial pattern learning, and problem solving. In L. W. Gregg (Ed.), *Knowledge and cognition* (pp. 43–103). Potomac, MD: Erlbaum.

Ehrlich, H. J., & Leed, D. (1969). Dogmatism, learning, and resistance to change: A review and a new paradigm. *Psychological Bulletin*, vol. 71, pp. 249–260.

Eliasmith, C., & Thagard, P. (1997). Waves, particles, and explanatory coherence. *British Journal for the Philosophy of Science*, vol. 48, pp. 1–19.

Eldredge, N. (1989). *Time frames: The evolution of punctuated equilibria.* Princeton, NJ: Princeton University Press.

Eldredge, N., & Gould, S. J. (1972). Punctuated equilibria: An alternative to phyletic gradualism. In T. J. M. Schopf (Ed.), *Models in paleobiology* (pp. 82–115). San Francisco, CA: Freeman, Cooper and Co. [Reprinted as Appendix to Eldredge (1989), pp. 193–223. Page references are to the reprinted version.]

Elio, R., & Scharf, P. B. (1990). Modeling novice-to-expert shifts in problem-solving strategy and knowledge organization. *Cognitive Science*, vol. 14, pp. 579–639.

Ellis, W. D. (1967). *A source book of Gestalt psychology.* New York: Humanities Press.

Erdelyi, M. H. (1998). *The recovery of unconscious memories: Hypermnesia and reminiscence.* Chicago, IL: University of Chicago Press.

Erdoes, R. (1988). *A.D. 1000: Living on the brink of apocalypse.* New York: Barnes & Noble.

Ericsson, K.A. (1996). *The road to excellence.* Mahwah, NJ: Erlbaum.

Ericsson, K. A., Charness, N., Feltovich, P. J., & Hoffman, R. R. (Eds.). (2006). *The Cambridge handbook of expertise and expert performance.* Cambridge, UK: Cambridge University Press.

Ericsson, K. A., Krampe, R. Th., & Tesch-Romer, C. (1993). The role of deliberate practice in the acquisition of expert performance. *Psychological Review*, vol. 100, pp. 363–406.

Ericsson, K. A., & Lehmann, A. C. (1996). Expert and exceptional performance: Evidence of maximal adaptation to task constraints. *Annual Review of Psychology*, vol. 47, pp. 273–305.

Ericsson, K. A., & Simon, H. A. (1984). *Protocol analysis: Verbal reports as data.* Cambridge, MA: MIT Press.

Ernst, G. W., & Newell, A. (1969). *GPS: A case study in generality and problem solving.* New York: Academic Press.

Eslinger, P. J., & Damasio, A. R. (1986). Preserved motor learning in Alzheimer's disease: Implications for anatomy and behavior. *Journal of Neuroscience*, vol. 6, pp. 3006–3009.

Estes, W. K. (1950). Toward a statistical theory of learning. *Psychological Review*, vol. 57, pp. 94–107.

———. (1956). The problem of inference from curves based on group data. *Psychological Bulletin*, vol. 53, pp. 134–140.

Evans, J. St. B. T. (2007). *Hypothetical thinking: Dual processes in reasoning and judgment.* New York: Psychology Press.

Fagan, B. (2005). *The long summer: How climate changed civilization* (paperback ed.). New York: Basic Books.

Falkenhainer, B., Forbus, K. D., & Gentner, D. (1989). The structure-mapping engine: Algorithm and examples. *Artificial Intelligence,* vol. 41, pp. 1–63.

Feigenbaum, E. A. (1989). What hath Simon wrought? In D. Klahr & K. Kotovsky (Eds.), *Complex information processing: The impact of Herbert A. Simon* (pp. 165–182). Hillsdale, NJ: Erlbaum.

Feist, G. J. (1999). The influence of personality on artistic and scientific creativity. In R. J. Sternberg (Ed.), *Handbook of creativity* (pp. 273–296). Cambridge, UK: Cambridge University Press.

Felleman, D. J., & Van Essen, D. C. (1991). Distributed hierarchical processing in the primate cerebral cortex. *Cerebral Cortex,* vol. 1, pp. 1–47.

Feltovich, P. J., Ford, K. M., & Hoffman, R. R. (Eds.). (1997). *Expertise in context.* Menlo Park, CA: AAAI Press.

Ferrari, M., & Chi, M. T. H. (1998). The nature of naïve explanations of natural selection. *International Journal of Science Education,* vol. 20, pp. 1231–1256.

Festinger, L. (1957/1962). *A theory of cognitive dissonance.* Stanford, CA: Stanford University Press.

Feyerabend, P. (1975/1988). *Against method* (revised ed.). London, UK: Verso.

Fiehler, K., Ullsperger, M., & von Cramon, D. Y. (2005). Electrophysiological correlates of error correction. *Psychophysiology,* vol. 42, pp. 72–82.

Finke, R. A. (1989). *Principles of mental imagery.* Cambridge, MA: MIT Press.

Finke, R. A., Ward, T. B., & Smith, S. M. (1992). *Creative cognition: Theory, research, and applications.* Cambridge, MA: MIT Press.

Firth-Cozens, J. (2001). Cultures for improving patient safety through learning: The role of teamwork. *Quality in Health Care,* vol. 10 (supplement II), pp. ii26–ii31.

Fischer, I. (1975). Another look at Eratosthenes' and Posidonius' determinations of the Earth's circumference. *Quarterly Journal of the Royal Astronomical Society,* vol. 16, pp. 152–167.

Fishbein, M., & Ajzen, I. (1975). *Belief, attitude, intention and behavior.* Reading, MA: Addison-Wesley.

Fitts, P. (1964). Perceptual-motor skill learning. In A. Melton (Ed.), *Categories of human learning* (pp. 243–285). New York: Academic Press.

Flavell, J. H. (1963). *The developmental psychology of Jean Piaget.* New York: Van Nostrand Reinhold.

Fleck, J. I. (2008). Working memory demands in insight versus analytical problem solving. *European Journal of Cognitive Psychology,* vol. 20, pp. 139–176.

Fleck, J. I., & Weisberg, R. W. (2004). The use of verbal protocols as data: An analysis of insight in the candle problem. *Memory & Cognition,* vol. 32, pp. 990–1006.

Fodor, J. A. (1968). *Psychological explanation: An introduction to the philosophy of psychology.* New York: Random House.

———. (1976). *The language of thought.* Hassocks, UK: Harvester Press.

———. (1983). *The modularity of mind: An essay on faculty psychology.* Cambridge, MA: MIT Press.

———. (1997). Connectionism and the problem of systematicity (continued): Why Smolensky's solution still doesn't work. *Cognition,* vol. 62, pp. 109–119.

Fodor, J. A., & Pylyshyn, Z. W. (1988). Connectionism and cognitive architecture: A critical analysis. *Cognition,* vol. 28, pp. 3–71.

Forbus, K. D., Gentner, D., & Law, K. (1994). MAC/FAC: A model of similarity-based retrieval. *Cognitive Science,* vol. 19, pp. 141–205.

Ford, C. M. (1999). Interpretative style, motivation, ability and context as predictors of executives' creative performance. *Creativity and Innovation Management,* vol. 8, pp. 188–196.

Ford, J. (1992). What is chaos, that we should be mindful of it? In P. Davies (Ed.), *The new physics* (1st paperback ed., pp. 348–372). Cambridge, UK: Cambridge University Press.

Ford, M. (2005). Human nonmonotonic reasoning: The importance of seeing the logical strength of arguments. *Synthese,* vol. 146, pp. 71–92.

Fortun, M., & Schweber, S. S. (1993). Scientists and the legacy of World War II: The case of operations research (OR). *Social Studies of Science,* vol. 23, pp. 595–642.

Fossati, D., Di Eugenio, D., Brown, C., & Ohlsson, S. (2008). Learning linked lists: Experiments with the iList system. In B. P. Woolf, E. Aïmeur, R. Nkambou, & S. Lajoie (Eds.), *Intelligent tutoring systems* (pp. 80–89). Berlin, Germany: Springer-Verlag.

Fossati, D., Di Eugenio, B., Brown, C., Ohlsson, S., Cosejo, D., & Chen, L. (2009). Supporting computer science curriculum: Exploring and learning linked lists with iList. *IEEE Transactions on Learning Technologies,* vol. 2, pp. 107–120.

Foster, J. (2005). From simplistic to complex systems in economics. *Cambridge Journal of Economics,* vol. 29, pp. 873–892.

Foster, K. R., Wenseleers, T., & Ratnieks, F. L. W. (2006). Kin selection is the key to altruism. *Trends in Ecology and Evolution,* vol. 21, pp. 57–60.

Franzén, A. (1960). *The warship Vasa: Deep diving and marine archeology in Stockholm.* Stockholm, Sweden: Norstedt and Bonnier.

French, D. L., Laskov, R., & Scharff, M. D. (1989). The role of somatic hypermutation in the generation of antibody diversity. *Science,* vol. 244, pp. 1152–1157.

Freud, A. (1946). *The ego and the mechanisms of defence* (C. Baines, Trans.). New York: International Universities Press.

Freud, S. (1923). *The ego and the id* (J. Riviere, Trans.). Standard Edition, vol. 19, pp. 3–66.

Friedman, M. (1974). Explanation and scientific understanding. *Journal of Philosophy,* vol. 71, pp. 5–19.

———. (1991). The re-evaluation of logical positivism. *Journal of Philosophy,* vol. 88, pp. 505–519.

Fuchs-Beauchamp, K. D., Karnes, M. B., & Johnson, L. J. (1993). Creativity and intelligence in preschoolers. *Gifted Child Quarterly,* vol. 37, pp. 113–117.

Fugelsang, J. A., Stein, C. B., Green, A. E., & Dunbar, K. N. (2004). Theory and data interactions of the scientific mind: Evidence from the molecular and the cognitive laboratory. *Canadian Journal of Experimental Psychology,* vol. 58, pp. 86–95.

Furniss, T. (2005). *A history of space exploration*. London: Mercury Books.
Furth, H. G. (1968). Piaget's theory of knowledge: The nature of representation and interiorization. *Psychological Review*, vol. 75, pp. 143–154.
———. (1969). *Piaget and knowledge: Theoretical foundations*. Englewood Cliffs, NJ: Prentice-Hall.
Futuyma, D. J., & Moreno, G. (1988). The evolution of ecological specialization. *Annual Review of Ecology and Systematics*, vol. 19, pp. 207–233.
Gabbay, D., & Woods, J. (2001). The new logic. *Logic Journal of the Interest Group in Pure and Applied Logics*, vol. 9, pp. 141–174.
Gaddis, J. L. (2002). *The landscape of history: How historians map the past*. New York: Oxford University Press.
Gagné, R. M. (1965). *The conditions of learning*. New York: Holt, Rinehart and Winston.
Gagné, R. M., Foster, H., & Crowley, M. (1948). The measurement of transfer of training. *Psychological Bulletin*, vol. 45, pp. 97–130.
Galenson, D. W. (2006). *Old masters and young geniuses: The two life cycles of artistic creativity*. Princeton, NJ: Princeton University Press.
Galton, F. (1892/1962). *Hereditary genius: An inquiry into its laws and consequences* (2nd ed.). London: Collins/Fontana.
Gärdenfors, P. (1988). *Knowledge in flux: Modeling the dynamics of epistemic states*. Cambridge, MA: MIT Press.
Gardner, H. (1980). *Artful scribbles: The significance of children's drawings*. New York: Basic Books.
———. (1983). *Frames of mind: The theory of multiple intelligences*. New York: Basic Books.
———. (1985). *The mind's new science: A history of the cognitive revolution*. New York: Basic Books.
———. (1993). *Creating minds: An anatomy of creativity seen through the lives of Freud, Einstein, Picasso, Stravinsky, Eliot, Graham and Gandhi*. New York: Basic Books.
Garzke, W. H., Jr., Foecke, T., Matthias, P., & Wood, D. (2000). A marine forensic analysis of the RMS *Titanic*. *Proceedings of the OCEANS 2000 MTS/IEEE Conference and Exhibition*, Providence, Rhode Island, September 11–14 (vol. 1, pp. 673–690).
Gaskell, G. (Ed.). (2007). *Oxford handbook of psycholinguistics*. New York: Oxford University Press.
Gaver, W. W. (1993). What in the world do we hear: An ecological approach to auditory event perception. *Ecological Psychology*, vol. 5, pp. 1–29.
Gazzaniga, M. S. (1992). *Nature's mind: The biological roots of thinking, emotions, sexuality, language, and intelligence*. New York: Basic Books.
Gelman, R. (2000). The epigenesis of mathematical thinking. *Journal of Applied Developmental Psychology*, vol. 21, pp. 27–37.
Gelman, R., & Gallistel, C. R. (1978). *The child's understanding of number*. Cambridge, MA: Harvard University Press.
Gelman, R., & Meck, E. (1983). Preschoolers' counting: Principles before skill. *Cognition*, vol. 13, pp. 343–359.
Gelman, R., Meck, E., & Merkin, S. (1986). Young children's numerical competence. *Cognitive Development*, vol. 1, pp. 1–29.

Gensler, W. J. (1987). Impossibilities in chemistry: Their rise, nature, and some great falls. In P. J. Davis & D. Park (Eds.), *No way: The nature of the impossible* (pp. 73–89). New York: Freeman.

Gentner, D. (1983). Structure-mapping: A theoretical framework for analogy. *Cognitive Science*, vol. 7, pp. 155–170.

German, T. P., & Barrett, H. C. (2005). Functional fixedness in a technologically sparse culture. *Psychological Science*, vol. 16, pp. 1–5.

Getzels, J. W. (1979). Problem finding: A theoretical note. *Cognitive Science*, vol. 3, pp. 167–172.

Ghiselin, B. (Ed.). (1952). *The creative process: A symposium*. New York: New American Library.

Gibson, J. J. (1966). *The senses considered as perceptual systems*. New York: Houghton Mifflin.

———. (1977). The theory of affordances. In R. E. Shaw & J. Bransford (Ed.), *Perceiving, acting and knowing: Toward an ecological psychology* (pp. 67–82). Hillsdale, NJ: Erlbaum.

Gick, M. L., & Holyoak, K. J. (1980). Analogical problem solving. *Cognitive Psychology*, vol. 12, pp. 306–355.

Gick, M. L., & Holyoak, K. J. (1983). Schema induction and analogical transfer. *Cognitive Psychology*, vol. 15, pp. 1–38.

Gies, F., & Gies, J. (1991). *Life in a medieval village*. New York: HarperCollins.

Gilbert, C. D. (1998). Adult cortical dynamics. *Physiological Reviews*, vol. 78, pp. 467–485.

Gilbert, C. D., & Sigman, M. (2007). Brain states: Top-down influences in sensory processing. *Neuron*, vol. 54, pp. 677–696.

Gilhooly, K. J., & Murphy, P. (2005). Differentiating insight from non-insight problems. *Thinking and Reasoning*, vol. 11, pp. 279–302.

Gleick J. (1987). *Chaos: Making a new science*. New York: Penguin Books.

Glick, J., & Wapner, S. (1968). Development of transitivity: Some findings and problems of analysis. *Child Development*, vol. 39, pp. 621–638.

Glisky, E. L. (1992). Acquisition and transfer of declarative and procedural knowledge by memory-impaired patients: A computer data-entry task. *Neuropsychologica*, vol. 30, pp. 899–910.

Glucksberg, S., & Weisberg, R. W. (1966). Verbal behavior and problem solving: Some effects of labeling in a functional fixedness problem. *Journal of Experimental Psychology*, vol. 71, pp. 659–664.

Goddard, R. H. (1919). A method of reaching extreme altitudes. *Smithsonian Miscellaneous Collections*, vol. 71, no. 2. [Reprinted in Goddard, R. H. (2002). *Rockets: Two classic papers* (pp. xiii–80). New York: Dover.]

Goldfinch, S. (2000). *Remaking New Zealand and Australian economic policy*. Victoria, NZ: Victoria University Press.

Goldstein, E. B. (2008). *Cognitive psychology: Connecting mind, research, and everyday experience* (2nd ed.). Belmont, CA: Thomson Wadsworth.

Goldstone, R. L., & Sakamoto, Y. (2003). The transfer of abstract principles governing complex adaptive systems. *Cognitive Psychology*, vol. 46, pp. 414–466.

Gollan, T. H., & Acenas, L.-A. R. (2004). What is a TOT? Cognate and translation effects on tip-of-the-tongue states in Spanish-English and Tagalog-English bilinguals. *Journal of Experimental Psychology: Learning, Memory, and Cognition*, vol. 30, pp. 246–269.

Goodman, N. (1954/1983). *Fact, fiction, and forecast* (4th ed.). Cambridge, MA: Harvard University Press.

Gopnik, A., Glymour, C., Sobel, D. M., Schulz, L. E., & Kushnir, T. (2004). A theory of causal learning in children: Causal maps and Bayes nets. *Psychological Review*, vol. 111, pp. 3–32.

Gopnik, A., & Meltzoff, A. N. (1997). *Words, thoughts, and theories*. Cambridge, MA: MIT Press.

Gopnik, A., & Wellman, H. M. (1994). The theory theory. In L. A. Hirschfeld & S. A. Gelman (Eds.), *Mapping the mind: Domain specificity in cognition and culture* (pp. 255–293). Cambridge, UK: Cambridge University Press.

Gould, S. J. (1986, November). Of kiwi eggs and the Liberty Bell. *Natural History*, vol. 90, pp. 20–29. [Reprinted in S. J. Gould (1991), *Bully for Brontosaurus: Reflections in natural history* (pp. 109–122). New York: Norton.]

———. (2002). *The structure of evolutionary theory*. Cambridge, MA: Harvard University Press.

Gödel, K. (1962/1992). *On formally undecidable propositions of Principia Mathematica and related systems* (B. Meltzer, Trans.). New York: Dover.

Graesser, A. C., Gernsbacher, M. A., & Goldman, S. R. (Ed.). (2003). *Handbook of discourse processes*. Mahwah, NJ: Erlbaum.

Graesser, A. C., Kassler, M. A., Kreuz, R. J., & McLain-Allen, B. (1998). Verification of statements about story worlds that deviate from normal conceptions of time: What is true about *Einstein's Dreams*? *Cognitive Psychology*, vol. 35, pp. 246–301.

Graesser, A. C., Millis, K. K., & Zwaan, R. A. (1997). Discourse comprehension. *Annual Review of Psychology*, vol. 48, pp. 163–189.

Grant, D. A., Hake, H. W., & Hornseth, J. P. (1951). Acquisition and extinction of a verbal conditioned response with differing percentages of reinforcement. *Journal of Experimental Psychology*, vol. 42, pp. 1–5.

Gray, W. D., & Boehm-Davis, D. A. (2000). Milliseconds matter: An introduction to microstrategies and to their use in describing and predicting interactive behavior. *Journal of Experimental Psychology: Applied*, vol. 6, pp. 322–335.

Gray, W. D., Schoelles, M. J., & Sims, C. R. (2005). Adapting to the task environment: Explorations in expected value. *Cognitive Systems Research*, vol. 6, pp. 27–40.

Greenaway, F. (1966). *John Dalton and the atom*. Ithaca, NY: Cornell University Press.

Greeno, J. G. (1974). Hobbits and orcs: Acquisition of a sequential concept. *Cognitive Psychology*, vol. 6, pp. 270–292.

Greeno, J. G., & Berger, D. (1987, July). *A model of functional knowledge and insight* (Technical Report No. GK-1). Berkeley: University of California.

Greeno, J. G., & Moore, J. L. (1993). Situativity and symbols: Response to Vera and Simon. *Cognitive Science*, vol. 17, pp. 49–59.

Greenwood, J. D. (1999). Understanding the "cognitive revolution" in psychology. *Journal of the History of the Behavioral Sciences*, vol. 35, pp. 1–22.

Gregory, T. R. (2008). The evolution of complex organs. *Evolution: Education and Outreach*, vol. 1, pp. 358–389.

Grent-'t-Jong, T., & Woldorff, M. G. (2007). Timing and sequence of brain activity in top-down control of visual-spatial attention. *Public Library of Science Biology*, vol. 5, p. e12.

Grice, H. P. (1975). Logic and conversation. In P. Cole & J. L. Morgan (Eds.), *Syntax and semantics* (vol. 3): *Speech acts* (pp. 41–58). New York: Seminar. [Reprinted in Grice, P. (1989). *Studies in the way of words* (pp. 22–40). Cambridge, MA: Harvard University Press.]

Griffin, T., & Ohlsson, S. (2001). Beliefs versus knowledge: A necessary distinction for explaining, predicting, and assessing conceptual change. In J. D. Moore & K. Stenning (Eds.), *Proceedings of the Twenty-Third Annual Conference of the Cognitive Science Society* (pp. 364–369). Mahwah, NJ: Erlbaum.

Griffiths, P. E. (1993). Functional analysis and proper functions. *British Journal for the Philosophy of Science*, vol. 44, pp. 409–422.

Griggs, R. A., & Osterman, L. J. (1980). Conversion errors in processing artificial set inclusions. *Quarterly Journal of Experimental Psychology*, vol. 32, pp. 241–246.

Groner, R., Groner, M., & Bischof, W. F. (Eds.). (1983). *Methods of heuristics*. Hillsdale, NJ: Erlbaum.

Groopman, J. (2007). *How doctors think*. Boston, MA: Houghton Mifflin.

Grosser, M. (1962/1979). *The discovery of Neptune*. New York: Dover.

Gruber, H. E. (1974). *Darwin on man: A psychological study of scientific creativity*. London: Wildwood House.

———. (1992). The evolving systems approach to creative work. In D. B. Wallace & H. E. Gruber (Eds.), *Creative people at work: Twelve cognitive case studies* (pp. 3–24). New York: Oxford University Press.

Gruber, H. E., & Wallace, D. B. (1999). The case study method and evolving systems approach for understanding unique creative people at work. In R. J. Sternberg (Ed.), *Handbook of creativity* (pp. 93–115). Cambridge, UK: Cambridge University Press.

Hadamard, J. (1949/1954). *An essay on the psychology of invention in the mathematical field* (enlarged ed.). New York: Dover.

Hahlweg, K., & Hooker, C. A. (Eds.). (1989). *Issues in evolutionary epistemology*. Albany: State University of New York Press.

Haider, H., & Frensch, P. A. (2002). Why aggregated learning follows the power law of practice when individual learning does not: Comment on Rickard (1997, 1999), Delaney et al. (1998), and Palmeri (1999). *Journal of Experimental Psychology: Learning, Memory, and Cognition*, vol. 28, pp. 392–406.

Haith, M. M., Hazan, C., & Goodman, G. S. (1988). Expectation and anticipation of dynamic visual events by 3.5-month-old babies. *Child Development*, vol. 59, pp. 467–479.

Hàjek, A., & Hall, N. (2002). Induction and probability. In P. Machamer & M. Silberstein (Eds.), *The Blackwell guide to the philosophy of science* (pp. 149–172). Cambridge, UK: Blackwell.

Hall, A. R. (1956). *The scientific revolution 1500–1800: The formation of the modern scientific attitude*. Boston, MA: Beacon Press.

Halloun, I. A., & Hestenes, D. (1985). Common sense concepts about motion. *American Journal of Physics*, vol. 53, pp. 1056–1065.

Hanke, D. (2004). Teleology: The explanation that bedevils biology. In J. Cornwell (Ed.), *Explanations: Styles of explanation in science* (pp. 143–155). Oxford, UK: Oxford University Press.

Hanson, N. R. (1965). *Patterns of discovery: An inquiry into the conceptual foundations of science.* Cambridge, UK: Cambridge University Press.

Harman, G. H. (1965). The inference to the best explanation. *Philosophical Review,* vol. 74, pp. 88–95.

———. (1968). Enumerative induction as inference to the best explanation. *Journal of Philosophy,* vol. 65, pp. 529–533.

Harman, P. M. (2001). *The natural philosophy of James Clerk Maxwell.* New York: Cambridge University Press.

Harmon-Jones, E., & Mills, J. (1999). *Cognitive dissonance: Progress on a pivotal theory in social psychology.* Washington, DC: American Psychological Association.

Harris, M. (1968). *The rise of anthropological theory: A history of theories of culture.* New York: Thomas Y. Crowell.

Hartmann, H. (1958). *Ego psychology and the problem of adaptation* (D. Rapaport, Trans.). New York: International University Press.

Haskell, R. E. (2001). *Transfer of learning: Cognition, instruction, and reasoning.* New York: Academic Press.

Hayes, J. R., & Simon, H. A. (1974). Understanding written problem instructions. In L. W. Gregg (Ed.), *Knowledge and cognition* (pp. 167–200). Potomac, MD: Erlbaum.

Heathcote, A., Brown, S., & Mewhort, D. J. K. (2000). The power law repealed: The case for an exponential law of practice. *Psychonomic Bulletin & Review,* vol. 7, pp. 185–207.

Hebb, D. O. (1949). *The organization of behavior: A neuropsychological theory.* New York: Wiley.

———. (1963). The semiautonomous process: Its nature and nurture. *American Psychologist,* vol. 18, pp. 16–27.

Heckhausen, H., & Beckmann, J. (1990). Intentional action and action slips. *Psychological Review,* vol. 97, pp. 36–48.

Heims, S. J. (1991). *The cybernetics group.* Cambridge, MA: MIT Press.

Hempel, C. G. (1959). The logic of functional analysis. In L. Gross (Ed.), *Symposium on sociological theory* (pp. 271–307). New York: Harper & Row. [Reprinted in C. G. Hempel (1965), *Aspects of scientific explanation and other essays in the philosophy of science* (pp. 297–330). New York: Free Press.]

Hempel, C. G., & Oppenheim, P. (1948). Studies in the logic of explanation. *Philosophy of Science,* vol. 15, pp. 135–175.

Henle, M. (1962). On the relation between logic and thinking. *Psychological Review,* vol. 69, pp. 366–378.

Henry, J. (2002). *The scientific revolution and the origins of modern science* (2nd ed.). New York: Palgrave.

Herrnstein, R. J., & Murray, C. (1994). *The bell curve: Intelligence and class structure in American life.* New York: Free Press.

Hertzmann, E. (1957). Mozart's creative process. *Musical Quarterly,* vol. 43, pp. 187–200.

Hewson, P. W., & Hewson, M. G. A. (1984). The role of conceptual conflict in conceptual change and the design of science instruction. *Instructional Science*, vol. 13, pp. 1–13.

Hiebert, J. (Ed.). (1986). *Conceptual and procedural knowledge: The case of mathematics.* Hillsdale, NJ: Erlbaum.

Higbee, K. L. (1979). Recent research on visual mnemonics: Historical roots and educational fruits. *Review of Educational Research*, vol. 49, pp. 611–629.

Hilgard, E. R., & Bower, G. H. (1966). *Theories of learning* (3rd ed.). New York: Appleton-Century-Crofts.

Hillier, J. (1992). Electron microscopy and the microprobe analysis: Recalling the ambience of some inventions. In R. J. Weber & D. N. Perkins (Eds.), *Inventive minds: Creativity in technology* (pp. 97–114). New York: Oxford University Press.

Hinton, G. E., & Nowlan, S. J. (1987). How learning can guide evolution. *Complex Systems*, vol. 1, pp. 495–502.

Hoadley, C. M., Ranney, M., & Schank, P. (1994). WanderECHO: A connectionist simulation of limited coherence. In A. Ram & K. Eiselt (Eds.), *Proceedings of the Sixteenth Annual Conference of the Cognitive Science Society* (pp. 421–426). Hillsdale, NJ: Erlbaum.

Hocevar, D. (1980). Intelligence, divergent thinking, and creativity. *Intelligence*, vol. 4, pp. 25–40.

———. (1981). Measurement of creativity: Review and critique. *Journal of Personality Assessment*, vol. 45, pp. 450–464.

Hodges, A. (1983). *Alan Turing: The Enigma.* New York: Simon & Schuster.

Hodgson, G. M. (1996). *Economics and evolution: Bringing life back into economics.* Ann Arbor: University of Michigan Press.

Hoffman, J., Berner, M., Butz, M. V., Herbort, O., Kiesel, A., Kunde, W., & Lenhard, A. (2007). Explorations of anticipatory behavioral control (ABC): A report from the cognitive psychology unit of the University of Würzburg. *Cognitive Processing*, vol. 8, pp. 133–142.

Hoffman, R. R., & Deffenbacher, K. A. (1992). A brief history of applied cognitive psychology. *Applied Cognitive Psychology*, vol. 6, pp. 1–48.

Hofstadter, D. (1999). *Gödel, Escher, Bach: An eternal golden braid.* New York: Basic Books.

Holding, D. H. (1985). *The psychology of chess skill.* Hillsdale, NJ: Erlbaum.

Holland, J. H. (1998). *Emergence: From chaos to order.* Reading, MA: Addison-Wesley.

Holland, J. H., Holyoak, K. J., Nisbett, R. E., & Thagard, P. R. (1986). *Induction: Processes of inference, learning, and discovery.* Cambridge, MA: MIT Press.

Holmes, F. L. (1992). Antoine Lavoisier and Hans Krebs: Two styles of scientific creativity. In D. B. Wallace and H. E. Gruber (Eds.), *Creative people at work: Twelve cognitive case studies* (pp. 44–68). New York: Oxford University Press.

Holmes, J. G. (2002). Interpersonal expectations as the building blocks of social cognition: An interdependence theory perspective. *Personal Relations*, vol. 9, pp. 1–26.

Holyoak, K. J., & Thagard, P. R. (1989a). A computational model of analogical problem solving. In S. Vosniadou & A. Ortony (Eds.), *Similarity and analogical reasoning* (pp. 242–266). Cambridge, UK: Cambridge University Press.

———. (1989b). Analogical mapping by constraint satisfaction. *Cognitive Science*, vol. 13, pp. 295–355.

Homberg, U. (2004). In search of the sky compass in the insect brain. *Naturwissenschaften*, vol. 91, pp. 199–208.

Horai, S., Hayasaka, K., Kondo, R., Tsugane, K., & Takahata, N. (1995). Recent African origin of modern humans revealed by complete sequences of hominoid mitochondrial DNAs. *Proceedings of the National Academy of Science USA*, vol. 92, pp. 532–536.

Hough, S. E. (2004). *Earthshaking science: What we know (and don't know) about earthquakes*. Princeton, NJ: Princeton University Press.

Howe, M. J. A. (1996). The childhoods and early lives of geniuses: Combining psychological and biographical evidence. In K. A. Ericsson (Ed.), *The road to excellence: The acquisition of expert performance in arts and sciences, sports, and games* (pp. 255–270). Mahwah, NJ: Erlbaum.

Hsiao, H. S. (1972). The attraction of moths *(Trichoplusia ni)* to infrared radiation. *Journal of Insect Physiology*, vol. 18, pp. 1705–1714.

———. (1973). Flight paths of night-flying moths to light. *Journal of Insect Physiology*, vol. 19, pp. 1971–1976.

Hua, J. Y., & Smith, S. J. (2004). Neural activity and the dynamics of central nervous system development. *Nature Neuroscience*, vol. 7, pp. 327–332.

Hughes, G., & Cresswell, M. (1996). *A new introduction to modal logic*. London, UK: Routledge.

Hull, D. L. (1990). *Science as a process: An evolutionary account of the social and conceptual development of science*. Chicago, IL: University of Chicago Press.

———. (2001). *Science and selection: Essays on biological evolution and the philosophy of science*. Cambridge, UK: Cambridge University Press.

Hume, D. (1777/1910). *An enquiry concerning human understanding* (Charles W. Eliot, Ed.). Harvard Classics (vol. 37, pp. 289–420). New York: Collier. Available at http://18th.eserver.org/hume-enquiry.html#6.

Hummel, J. E., & Holyoak, K. J. (1997). Distributed representations of structure: A theory of analogical access and mapping. *Psychological Review*, vol. 104, pp. 427–466.

———. (2003). A symbolic-connectionist theory of relational inference and generalization. *Psychological Review*, vol. 110, pp. 220–264.

Hunt, E. B. (1962). *Concept learning: An information processing problem*. New York: John Wiley.

Hunter, I. M. L. (1957). The solving of three-term series problems. *British Journal of Psychology*, vol. 48, pp. 286–298.

Hurley P. J. (2006). *A concise introduction to logic* (9th ed.). New York: Thomson-Wadsworth.

Hutchins, E. (1995). *Cognition in the wild*. Cambridge, MA: MIT Press.

Huttenlocher, J. (1968). Constructing spatial images: A strategy in reasoning. *Psychological Review*, vol. 75, pp. 550–560.

Huttenlocher, P. R., de Courten, C., Garey, L. J., & van der Loos, H. (1982). Synaptogenesis in human visual cortex – Evidence for synapse elimination during normal development. *Neuroscience Letters*, vol. 33, pp. 247–252.

Imbrie, J., & Imbrie, K. P. (2002). *Ice ages: Solving the mystery* (revised ed.). Cambridge, MA: Harvard University Press

Inhelder, B., & Piaget, J. (1964). *The early growth of logic in the child: Classification and seriation*. London, UK: Routledge.

Isaak, M. I., & Just, M. A. (1995). Constraints on thinking in insight and invention. In R. J. Sternberg & J. E. Davidson (Eds.), *The nature of insight* (pp. 281–325). Cambridge, MA: MIT Press.

Jack, A. I., & Roepstorff, A. (2002). Introspection and cognitive brain mapping: From stimulus-response to script-report. *TRENDS in the Cognitive Sciences*, vol. 6, pp. 333–339.

Jacks, J. Z., & Cameron, K. A. (2003). Strategies for resisting persuasion. *Basic and Applied Social Psychology*, vol. 25, pp. 145–161.

Jahn, G. (2004). Tree turtles in danger: Spontaneous construction of causally relevant spatial situation models. *Journal of Experimental Psychology: Learning, Memory, and Cognition*, vol. 30, pp. 969–987.

James, W. (1890). *The principles of psychology* (vols. 1 and 2). London: MacMillan.

———. (1907/1975). *Pragmatism*. Cambridge, MA: Harvard University Press.

Janoff-Bulman, R. (1992). *Shattered assumptions: Towards a new psychology of trauma*. New York: Free Press.

Jansen, M. B. (2000). *The making of modern Japan*. Cambridge, MA: Harvard University Press.

Jay, E. S., & Perkins, D. N. (1997). Problem finding: The search for mechanism. In M. A. Runco (Ed.), *Creativity research handbook* (vol. 1, pp. 257–293). Cresskill, NJ: Hampton Press.

Jensen, M. S., & Finely, F. N. (1995). Teaching evolution using historical arguments in a conceptual change strategy. *Science Education*, vol. 79, pp. 147–166.

Jerne, N. K. (1967). Antibodies and learning: Selection versus instruction. In G. C. Quarton, T. Melnechuk, & F. O. Schmitt (Eds.), *The neurosciences: A study program* (pp. 200–205). New York: Rockefeller University Press.

John-Steiner, V. (2000). *Creative collaboration*. New York: Oxford University Press.

Johnson, A., Moher, T., Ohlsson, S., & Gillingham, M. (1999). The Round Earth Project: Collaborative VR for conceptual learning. *IEEE Computer Graphics and Applications*, vol. 19, pp. 60–69.

Johnson, A., Moher, T., Ohlsson, S., & Leigh, J. (2001). Exploring multiple representations in elementary school science education (pp. 201–208). *Proceedings of the IEEE VR 2001 Conference*, March 13–17, Yokohama, Japan.

Johnson, S. (2004). *Emergence: The connected lives of ants, brains, cities, and software*. New York: Scribner.

———. (2006). *The ghost map: The story of London's most terrifying epidemic – and how it changed science, cities, and the modern world*. New York: Riverhead Books.

Johnson, W. L. (1986). *Intention-based diagnosis of novice programming errors*. Los Altos, CA: Morgan Kauffmann.

Johnson-Frey, S. H. (2004). The neural bases of complex tool use in humans. *TRENDS in Cognitive Sciences*, vol. 8, pp. 71–78.

Johnson-Laird, P. (1983). *Mental models: Towards a cognitive science of language, inference, and consciousness.* Cambridge, MA: Harvard University Press.

Johnson-Laird, P. N. (1999). Deductive reasoning. *Annual Review of Psychology*, vol. 50, pp. 109–135.

———. (2006). *How we reason.* New York: Oxford University Press.

Jones, R. M., & VanLehn, K. (1994). Acquisition of children's addition strategies: A model of impasse-free, knowledge-level learning. *Machine Learning*, vol. 16, pp. 11–36.

Jones, T. (2004). Reductionism and antireductionism: Rights and wrongs. *Metaphilosophy*, vol. 35, pp. 614–647.

Joravsky, D. (1986). *The Lysenko affair.* Chicago, IL: University of Chicago Press.

Josephson, J. R., & Josephson, S. G. (Eds.). (1994). *Abductive inference: Computation, philosophy, technology.* Cambridge, UK: Cambridge University Press.

Jovanovic, B., & Nyarko, Y. (1995). A Bayesian learning model fitted to a variety of empirical learning curves. *Brookings Papers on Economic Activity: Microeconomics*, vol. 1995, pp. 247–305.

Jung-Beeman, M., Bowden, E. M., Haberman, J., Frymiare, J. L., Arambel-Liu, S., Greenblattt, R., Reber, P. J., & Kounios, J. (2004). Neural activity when people solve verbal problems with insight. *Public Library of Science Biology*, vol. 2, pp. 500–510. Available at http://biology.plosjournals.org.

Just, M. A., Carpenter, P. A., & Varma, S. (1999). Computational modeling of high-level cognition and brain function. *Human Brain Mapping*, vol. 8, pp. 128–136.

Just, M. A., & Varma, S. (2007). The organization of thinking: What functional brain imaging reveals about the neuroarchitecture of complex cognition. *Cognitive, Affective & Behavioral Neuroscience*, vol. 7, pp. 153–191.

Kahn, D. (1998). *Seizing the Enigma: The race to break the German U-boat codes 1939–1943.* New York: Barnes and Noble.

Kaplan, C. A. (1989). *Hatching a theory of incubation: Does putting a problem aside really help? If so, why?* Doctoral dissertation. Pittsburgh, PA: Department of Psychology, Carnegie-Mellon University.

Kaplan, C. A., & Simon, H. A. (1990). In search of insight. *Cognitive Psychology*, vol. 22, pp. 374–419.

Kaufmann, G. (2003). What to measure? A new look at the concept of creativity. *Scandinavian Journal of Educational Research*, vol. 47, pp. 235–251.

Kauffman, S. A. (1993). *The origins of order: Self-organization and selection in evolution.* New York: Oxford University Press.

Kay, H. (1951). Learning of a serial task by different age groups. *Quarterly Journal of Experimental Psychology*, vol. 3, pp. 166–183.

Keane, M. (1989). Modelling problem solving in Gestalt 'insight' problems. *Irish Journal of Psychology*, vol. 10, pp. 201–215.

Keane, M. T., Ledgeway, T., & Duff, S. (1994). Constraints on analogical mapping: A comparison of three models. *Cognitive Science*, vol. 18, pp. 387–338.

Keeley, L. H. (1997). *War before civilization.* New York: Oxford University Press.

Keil, F. C. (1979). *Semantic and conceptual development: An ontological perspective*. Cambridge, MA: Cambridge University Press.
Keil, F. C., & Wilson, R. A. (Ed.). (2000). *Explanation and cognition*. Cambridge, MA: MIT Press.
Keller, F. S. (1958). The phantom plateau. *Journal of the Experimental Analysis of Behavior*, vol. 1, pp. 1–13.
Kelman, H. C., & Baron, R. M. (1968). Determinants of modes of resolving inconsistency dilemmas: A functional analysis. In R. P. Abelson, E. Aronson, W. J. McGuire, T. M. Newcomb, M. J. Rosenberg, & P. H. Tannenbaum (Eds.), *Theories of cognitive consistency: A sourcebook* (pp. 670–683). Chicago, IL: Rand McNally.
Kennedy, W. G., & Trafton, J. G. (2007). Long-term symbolic learning. *Cognitive Systems Research*, vol. 8, pp. 237–247.
Kershaw, T., & Ohlsson, S. (2004). Multiple causes of difficulty in insight: The case of the nine-dot problem. *Journal of Experimental Psychology: Learning, Memory, and Cognition*, vol. 30, pp. 3–13.
Kieras, D., & Bovair, S. (1986). The acquisition of procedures from text: A production-system analysis of transfer of training. *Journal of Memory and Language*, vol. 25, pp. 507–524.
Kiesler, C. A., Collins, B. E., & Miller, N. (Eds.). (1969). *Attitude change: A critical analysis of theoretical approaches*. New York: Wiley.
Kilmurray, E., & Ormond, R. (Eds.). (1998). *John Singer Sargent*. Princeton, NJ: Princeton University Press.
Kim, K. H. (2005). Can only intelligent people be creative? *Journal of Secondary Gifted Education*, vol. 16, pp. 57–66.
King, R. (2007). *The judgment of Paris: The revolutionary decade that gave the world impressionism*. New York: Walker.
Kingsolver, J. G., & Koehl, M. A. (1985). Aerodynamics, thermoregulation, and the evolution of insect wings: Differential scaling and evolutionary change. *Evolution*, vol. 39, pp. 488–504.
Kintsch, W. (1988). The role of knowledge in discourse comprehension: A construction-integration model. *Psychological Review*, vol. 95, pp. 163–182.
———. (1998). *Comprehension: A paradigm for cognition*. Cambridge, UK: Cambridge University Press.
Kirkham, R. L. (1992). *Theories of truth: A critical introduction*. Cambridge, MA: MIT Press.
Kitcher, P. (1988). Explanatory unification. In J. C. Pitt (Ed.), *Theories of explanation* (pp. 167–187). New York: Oxford University Press.
———. (1993). *The advancement of science*. New York: Oxford University Press.
Klahr, D., Langley, P., & Neches, R. (Eds.). (1987). *Production system models of learning and development*. Cambridge, MA: MIT Press.
Klahr, D., & Wallace, J. G. (1976). *Cognitive development: An information processing view*. Hillsdale, NJ: Erlbaum.
Klein, K., & Fiss, W. H. (1999). The reliability and stability of the Turner and Engle working memory task. *Behavioral Research Methods, Instruments, and Computers*, vol. 31, pp. 429–432.

Kneale, W., & Kneale, M. (1962/1984). *The development of logic*. Oxford, UK: Clarendon Press.

Knoblich, G., Ohlsson, S., Haider, H., & Rhenius, D. (1999). Constraint relaxation and chunk decomposition in insight problem solving. *Journal of Experimental Psychology: Learning, Memory & Cognition*, vol. 25, pp. 1534–1555.

Knoblich, G., Ohlsson, S., & Raney, G. (2001). An eye movement study of insight problem solving. *Memory and Cognition*, vol. 29, p. 1000–1009.

Koestler, A. (1964). *The act of creation*. New York: Macmillan.

———. (1966). Biological and mental evolution – An exercise in analogy. In P. H. Oehser (Ed.), *Knowledge among men* (pp. 95–107). New York: Simon & Schuster and the Smithsonian Institution.

———. (1972). Beyond atomism and holism – the concept of the holon. In A. Koestler & J. R. Smythies (Eds.), *Beyond reductionism: New perspectives in the life sciences* (pp. 192–232). London, UK: Hutchinson.

Koffka, K. (1922). Perception: An introduction to the *Gestalt-theorie*. *Psychological Bulletin*, vol. 19, pp. 531–585.

———. (1935). *Principles of Gestalt psychology*. London, UK: Routledge & Kegan Paul.

Köhler, W. (1924). *Die physischen Gestalten in Ruhe and im stationären Zustand: Eine naturphilosophische Untersuchung*. Erlangen, Germany: Verlag der Philosophischen Akademie.

———. (1972). *The task of Gestalt psychology*. Princeton, NJ: Princeton University Press.

———. (1976). *The place of value in a world of facts*. New York: Liveright.

Konradt, U. (1995). Strategies of failure diagnosis in computer-controlled manufacturing systems: Empirical analysis and implications for the design of adaptive decision support systems. *International Journal of Human-Computer Interaction*, vol. 43, pp. 503–521.

Kornblith, H. (Ed.). (1985). *Naturalizing epistemology*. Cambridge, MA: MIT Press.

Kornblith, H. (1995). *Inductive inference and its natural ground: An essay in naturalistic epistemology*. Cambridge, MA: MIT Press.

Kosslyn, S. M. (1980). *Image and mind*. Cambridge, UK: Harvard University Press.

Kounios, J., Frymiare, J. L, Bowden, E. M., Fleck, J. I., Subramaniam, K., Parrish, T. B., & Jung-Beeman, M. (2006). The prepared mind: Neural activity prior to problem presentation predicts subsequent solution by sudden insight. *Psychological Science*, vol. 17, pp. 882–890.

Koyré, A. (1950). The significance of the Newtonian synthesis. *Archives Internationales d'Historie des Sciences*, vol. 3, pp. 291–311. [Reprinted in Koyré, A. (1968). *Newtonian studies* (pp. 3–24). Chicago, IL: University of Chicago Press.]

———. (1958). *From the closed world to the infinite universe*. New York: Harper & Row.

Kragh, H. (2000). Conceptual changes in chemistry: The notion of a chemical element, ca. 1900–1925. *Studies in the History and Philosophy of Modern Physics*, vol. 31, pp. 435–450.

Kretzmann, N., Kenny, A., & Pinborg, J. (Eds.). (1988). *The Cambridge history of later medieval philosophy*. New York: Cambridge University Press.

Kuhn, D. (1989). Children and adults as intuitive scientists. *Psychological Review*, vol. 96, pp 674–689.

———. (1995). Microgenetic study of change: What has it told us? *Psychological Science*, vol. 6, pp. 133–139.

Kuhn, T. S. (1957). *The Copernican revolution: Planetary astronomy in the development of Western thought.* New York: Random House.

———. (1970). *The structure of scientific revolutions* (2nd ed.). Chicago, IL: University of Chicago Press.

———. (1977). *The essential tension: Selected studies in scientific tradition and change.* Chicago, IL: University of Chicago Press.

Kunej, D., & Turk, I. (2000). New perspectives on the beginnings of music: Archeological and musicological analysis of a middle paleolithic bone "flute." In N. Wallin, B. Merker, & S. Brown (Eds.), *The origins of music* (p. 235–268). Cambridge, MA: MIT Press.

Kuran, T. (1995). The inevitability of future revolutionary surprises. *American Journal of Sociology*, vol. 100, pp. 1528–1551.

Kvarning, L. A., & Ohrelius, B. (1992). *The Swedish warship Wasa.* New York: Macmillan.

Lacey, R., & Danziger, D. (1999). *The year 1000: What life was like at the turn of the first millennium.* Boston, MA: Little, Brown.

Laird, J. E., & Newell, A. (1993). A universal weak method. In P. S. Rosenbloom, J. E. Laird, & A. Newell (Eds.), *The Soar papers: Research on integrated intelligence* (vol. 1, pp. 245–292). Cambridge, MA: MIT Press.

Lajoie, S. P., & Lesgold, A. M. (1992). Dynamic assessment of proficiency for solving procedural knowledge tasks. *Educational Psychologist*, vol. 27, pp. 365–384.

Lakatos, I. (1980). *Philosophical papers* (vol. 1): *The methodology of scientific research programmes.* Cambridge, UK: Cambridge University Press.

Lambert, E. B. (2005). Children's drawing and painting from a cognitive perspective: A longitudinal study. *Early Years*, vol. 25, pp. 249–269.

Lane, N. E. (1987). *Skill acquisition rates and patterns: Issues and training implications.* New York: Springer-Verlag.

Langley, P. (1983). Learning search strategies through discrimination. *International Journal of Man-Machine Studies*, vol. 18, pp. 513–541.

———. (1985). Learning to search: From weak methods to domain-specific heuristics. *Cognitive Science*, vol. 9, pp. 217–260.

———. (1987). A general theory of discrimination learning. In D. Klahr, P. Langley, & R. Neches (Eds.), *Production system models of learning and development* (pp. 99–161). Cambridge, MA: MIT Press.

Langley, P., & Jones, R. (1988). A computational model of scientific insight. In R. J. Sternberg (Ed.), *The nature of creativity: Contemporary psychological approaches* (pp. 177–201). Cambridge, UK: Cambridge University Press.

Langley, P., Wogulis, J., & Ohlsson, S. (1990). Rules and principles in cognitive diagnosis. In N. Frederiksen, R. Glaser, A. Lesgold, & M. Shafto (Eds.), *Diagnostic monitoring of skill and knowledge acquisition* (pp. 217–250). Hillsdale, NJ: Erlbaum.

Larkin, J. H. (1981). Enriching formal knowledge: A model for learning to solve textbook physics problems. In J. R. Anderson (Ed.), *Cognitive skills and their acquisition* (pp. 311–334). Hillsdale, NJ: Erlbaum.

Larson, J. R., Jr. (1997). Modeling the entry of shared and unshared information into group discussion: A review and basic language computer program. *Small Group Research*, vol. 28, pp. 454–479.

———. (1998). Diagnosing groups: The pooling, management, and impact of shared and unshared case information in team-based medical decision making. *Journal of Personality and Social Psychology*, vol. 75, pp. 93–108.

———. (2010). *In search of synergy in small group performance*. New York: Psychology Press.

Larson, J. R., Jr., Christensen, C., Franz, T. M., & Abbott, A. S. (1998). Diagnosing groups: The pooling, management, and impact of shared and unshared case information in team-based medical decision making. *Journal of Personality and Social Psychology*, vol. 75, pp. 93–108.

Larson, J. R., Jr., Foster-Fishman, P. G., & Keys, C. B. (1994). Discussion of shared and unshared information in decision-making groups. *Journal of Personality and Social Psychology*, vol. 67, p. 446–461.

Lashley, K. S. (1929). *Brain mechanisms and intelligence: A quantitative study of injuries to the brain*. Chicago, IL: University of Chicago Press.

Laughlin, R. B. (2005). *A different universe: Reinventing physics from the bottom down*. New York: Basic Books.

Laurence, S., & Margolis, E. (2001). The poverty of the stimulus argument. *British Journal of the Philosophy of Science*, vol. 52, pp. 217–276.

Lave, J., & Wenger, E. (1991). *Situated learning: Legitimate peripheral participation*. Cambridge, MA: Cambridge University Press.

Lawson, A., & Thompson, L. (1988). Formal reasoning ability and misconceptions concerning genetics and natural selection. *Journal of Research in Science Teaching*, vol. 25, pp. 733–746.

Lebiere, C. (1999). The dynamics of cognition: An ACT-R model of cognitive arithmetic. *Kognitionswissenschaft*, vol. 8, pp. 5–19.

Lee, H., & Cho, Y. (2007). Factors affecting problem finding depending on degree of structure of problem situation. *Journal of Educational Research*, vol. 101, pp. 113–125.

Leinhardt, G. (1987). The development of an expert explanation: An analysis of a sequence of subtraction lessons. *Cognition and Instruction*, vol. 4, pp. 225–282.

Leinhardt, G., & Ohlsson, S. (1990) Tutorials on the structure of tutoring from teachers. *Journal of Artificial Intelligence in Education*, vol. 2, pp. 21–46.

Lenat, D. B. (1983). Toward a theory of heuristics. In R. Groner, M. Groner, & W. F. Bischof (Eds.), *Methods of heuristics* (pp. 351–404). Hillsdale, NJ: Erlbaum.

Leplat, J., & Rasmussen, J. (1984). Analysis of human errors in industrial incidents and accidents for improvement of work safety. *Accident Analysis and Prevention*, vol. 16, pp. 77–88.

Leplin, J. (1982). The assessment of auxiliary hypotheses. *British Journal for the Philosophy of Science*, vol. 33, pp. 235–249.

Levelt, W. J. M. (1974). *Formal grammars in linguistics and psycholinguistics (vol. 1): An introduction to the theory of formal languages and automata*. The Hague, the Netherlands: Mouton.

Levine, M. W. (2000). *Fundamental's of sensation and perception* (3rd ed.). Oxford, UK: Oxford University Press.

Levinson, M. (2006). *The box: How the shipping container made the world smaller and the world economy bigger.* Princeton, NJ: Princeton University Press.

Levy, D., & Newborn, M. (1991). *How computers play chess.* New York: W. H. Freeman.

Lewin, R. (1992). *Complexity: Life at the edge of chaos.* New York: Macmillan.

Lewis, C. (1987). Composition of productions. In D. Klahr, P. Langley, & R. Neches (Eds.), *Production system models of learning and development* (pp. 329–358). Cambridge, MA: MIT Press.

———. (1988). Why and how to learn why: Analysis-based generalization of procedures. *Cognitive Science*, vol. 12, pp. 211–256.

Liebherr, J. K., & McHugh, J. V. (2003). Coleoptera. In V. H. Resh & R. T. Cardé (Eds.), *Encyclopedia of insects* (pp. 209–229). New York: Academic Press.

Limón, M. (2001). On the cognitive conflict as an instructional strategy for conceptual change: A critical appraisal. *Learning and Instruction*, vol. 11, pp. 357–380.

Limón, M., & Mason, L. (Eds.). (2002). *Reconsidering conceptual change: Issues in theory and practice.* Dordrecht, the Netherlands: Kluwer.

Lipton, P. (2004). *Inference to the best explanation* (2nd ed.). London, UK: Routledge.

Little, D. M., & Thulborn, K. R. (2006). Prototype-distortion category learning: A two-phase process across a distributed network. *Brain and Cognition*, vol. 60, pp. 233–243.

Liu, S.-C., & Liu, S.-Y. (2001). An efficient expert system for air compressor troubleshooting. *Expert Systems*, vol. 18, pp. 203–214.

Lockhart, R. S. (2002). Levels of processing, transfer-appropriate processing, and the concept of robust encoding. *Memory*, vol. 10, pp. 397–403.

Lockman, J. J. (2000). A perception-action perspective on tool use development. *Child Development*, vol. 71, pp. 137–144.

Logan, G. D. (1998). Toward an instance theory of automatization. *Psychological Review*, vol. 95, pp. 492–527.

Lombrozo, T., & Carey, S. (2006). Functional explanation and the function of explanation. *Cognition*, vol. 99, pp. 167–204.

Losee, J. (2005). *Theories on the scrap heap: Scientists and philosophers on the falsification, rejection, and replacement of theories.* Pittsburgh, PA: University of Pittsburgh Press.

Lovejoy, A. O., & Boas, G. (1935/1997). *Primitivism and related ideas in antiquity.* Baltimore, MD: Johns Hopkins University Press.

Lu, X., Di Eugenio, B., Kershaw, T., Ohlsson, S., & Corrigan-Halpern, A. (2007). Expert vs. non-expert tutoring: Dialogue moves, interaction patterns and multi-utterance turns. *Lecture Notes in Computer Science*, vol. 4394, pp. 456–467.

Lubart, T. I. (2000–2001). Models of the creative process: Past, present and future. *Creativity Research Journal*, vol. 13, pp. 295–308.

Lucas, J. R. (1961). Minds, machines and Gödel. *Philosophy*, vol. 36, pp. 112–127.

Luchins, A. S. (1942). Mechanization in problem solving: The effect of Einstellung. *Psychological Monographs* (Whole No. 248), vol. 54, pp. 1–95.

Luchins, A. S., & Luchins, E. H. (1959). *Rigidity of behavior: A variational approach to the effect of Einstellung.* Eugene: University of Oregon Books.

Luiten, J., Ames, W., & Ackerson, G. (1980). A meta-analysis of the effects of advance organizers on learning and retention. *American Educational Research Journal*, vol. 17, pp. 211–218.

Lukacs, J. (2001). *Five days in London May 1940.* New Haven, CT: Yale University Press.

Luo, J., & Knoblich, G. (2007). Studying insight problem solving with neuroscientific methods. *Methods*, vol. 42, pp. 77–86.

Luo, J., Niki, K., & Knoblich, G. (2006). Perceptual contributions to problem solving: Chunk decomposition of Chinese characters. *Brain Research Bulletin*, vol. 70, pp. 430–443.

Luwel, K., Verschaffel, L., Onghena, P., & De Corte, E. (2003). Flexibility in strategy use: Adaptation of numerosity judgement strategies to task characteristics. *European Journal of Cognitive Psychology*, vol. 15, pp. 247–266.

Lynch, A. (1996). *Thought contagion: How belief spreads through society.* New York: Basic Books.

Lynn, M. L., & Williams, R. N. (1990). Belief-bias and labor unions: The effect of strong attitudes on reasoning. *Journal of Organizational Behavior*, vol. 11, pp. 335–343.

MacGregor, J. N., Ormerod, T. C., & Chronicle, E. P. (2001). Information processing and insight: A process model of performance on the nine-dot and related problems. *Journal of Experimental Psychology: Learning, Memory, and Cognition*, vol. 27, pp. 176–201.

Mackie, G. (2006). Does democratic deliberation change minds? *Politics, Philosophy and Economics*, vol. 5, pp. 279–303.

Macksey, K. (1998). *Military errors of World War Two.* Reading, UK: Cassell Military Classics.

Mackworth, A. K. (1992). Constraint satisfaction. In S. C. Shapiro (Ed.), *Encyclopedia of artificial intelligence* (pp. 285–293). New York: Wiley.

Magnani, L. (2001). *Abduction, reason, and science: Processes of discovery and explanation.* New York: Kluwer/Plenum.

Maier, N. R. F. (1931). Reasoning in humans: II. The solution of a problem and its appearance in consciousness. *Journal of Comparative Psychology*, vol. 12, pp. 181–194. [Excerpted in Wason and Johnson-Laird (1968), pp. 17–27.]

———. (1945). Reasoning in humans: III. The mechanism of equivalent stimuli and of reasoning. *Journal of Experimental Psychology*, vol. 35, pp. 349–360. [Reprinted in Maier, N. R. F. (1970). *Problem solving and creativity in individuals and groups* (pp. 143–154). Belmont, CA: Brooks/Cole.]

Mandelbrot, B. B. (1967). How long is the coast of Britain? Statistical self-similarity and fractional dimension. *Science*, vol. 156, pp. 636–638.

———. (1983). *The fractal geometry of nature* (updated ed.). New York: W. H. Freeman.

Mandelbrot, B. B., & Hudson, R. L. (2004). *The (mis)behavior of markets: A fractal view of risk, ruin, and reward.* New York: Basic Books.

Mandler, G. (2002). Origins of the cognitive (r)evolution. *Journal of the History of the Behavioral Sciences*, vol. 38, p. 339–353.

Mansfield, R. S., Busse, T. V., & Krepelke, E. J. (1978). The effectiveness of creativity training. *Review of Educational Research*, vol. 48, pp. 517–536.

Marcus, E. R. (1999). Modern ego psychology. *Journal of the American Psychoanalytic Assocation*, vol. 47, pp. 843–871.

Marcus, G. F., Pinker, S., Ullman, M., Hollander, M., Rosen, T. J., Xu, F., & Clahsen, H. (1992). Overregularization in language acquisition. *Monographs of the Society for Research in Child Development*, vol. 57, pp. 1–178.

Margolis, H. (1987). *Patterns, thinking, and cognition: A theory of judgment*. Chicago, IL: University of Chicago Press.

———. (1993). *Paradigms and barriers: How habits of mind govern scientific beliefs*. Chicago, IL: University of Chicago Press.

Markman, A. B. (1999). *Knowledge representation*. Mahwah, NJ: Erlbaum.

Markman, A. B., & Gentner, D. (2000). Structure mapping in the comparison process. *American Journal of Psychology*, vol. 113, pp. 501–538.

Marr, D. (1982). *Vision: A computational investigation into the human representation and processing of visual information*. New York: W. H. Freeman.

Marshall, S. P. (1995). *Schemas in problem solving*. Cambridge, UK: Cambridge University Press.

Martin, D. (1980). *Three Mile Island: Prologue or epilogue?* Cambridge, MA: Ballinger.

Mason, R. A., & Just, M. A. (2007). Lexical ambiguity in sentence comprehension. *Brain Research*, vol. 1146, pp. 115–127.

Matsen, B. (2008). *Titanic's last secrets*. New York: Twelve.

———. (2009). *Jacques Cousteau: The sea king*. New York: Pantheon Books.

Matthews, M. R. (2004). Thomas Kuhn's impact on science education: What lessons can be learned? *Science Education*, vol. 88, pp. 90–118.

Mattson, M. E., & Baars, B. J. (1992). Error-minimizing mechanisms: Boosting or editing? In B. J. Baars (Ed.), *Experimental slips and human error: Exploring the architecture of volition* (pp. 263–287). New York: Plenum Press.

Mayer, R. E. (1979). Can advance organizers influence meaningful learning? *Review of Educational Research*, vol. 49, pp. 371–383.

Mayr, E. (1942/1999). *Systematics and the origin of species from the viewpoint of a zoologist*. Cambridge, MA: Harvard University Press.

Mazur, J. E., & Hastie, R. (1978). Learning as accumulation: A reexamination of the learning curve. *Psychological Bulletin*, vol. 85, pp. 1256–1274.

McCann, H. G. (1978). *Chemistry transformed: The paradigmatic shift from phlogiston to oxygen*. Norwood, NJ: Ablex.

McCarthy, J. (1980). Circumscription – a form of non-monotonic reasoning. *Artificial Intelligence*, vol. 13, pp. 27–39.

McCarty, M. E., Clifton, R. K., & Collard, R. R. (2001). The beginnings of tool use by infants and toddlers. *Infancy*, vol. 2, pp. 233–256.

McCloskey, M. (1983). Naïve theories of motion. In D. Gentner & A.L. Stevens (Eds.), *Mental models* (pp. 299–323). Hillsdale, NJ: Erlbaum.

McDade, C. E. (1978). Subsumption versus educational set: Implications for sequencing of instructional materials. *Journal of Educational Psychology*, vol. 70, pp. 137–141.

McDermott, D., & Doyle, J. (1980). Non-monotonic logic (part I). *Artificial Intelligence*, vol. 13, pp. 41–72.

McDermott, J., & Forgy, C. (1978). Production system conflict resolution strategies. In D. A. Waterman & F. Hayes-Roth (Eds.), *Pattern-directed inference systems* (pp. 177–199). New York: Academic Press.

McDermott, J., & Hauser, M. (2005). The origins of music: Innateness, uniqueness, and evolution. *Music Perception*, vol. 23, pp. 29–59.

McKie, R. (2000). *Ape man: The story of human evolution.* London, UK: BBC Worldwide.

McLaughlin, P. (2001). *What functions explain: Functional explanation and self-reproducing systems.* Cambridge, UK: Cambridge University Press.

McNeil, N. M., & Alibali, M. W. (2005). Why won't you change your mind? Knowledge of operational patterns hinders learning and performance on equations. *Child Development*, vol. 76, pp. 883–899.

Mednick, S. (1962). The associative basis of the creative process. *Psychological Review*, vol. 69, pp. 220–232.

Menand, Louis. (2001). *The metaphysical club.* New York: Farrar, Straus and Giroux.

Metcalfe, J. (1986). Feeling of knowing in memory and problem solving. *Journal of Experimental Psychology: Learning, Memory, and Cognition*, vol. 12, pp. 288–294.

Metcalfe, J., & Wiebe, D. (1987). Intuition in insight and nonsight problem solving. *Memory and Cognition*, vol. 15, pp. 238–246.

Meyer, M. (2009). *The year that changed the world: The untold story behind the fall of the Berlin wall.* New York: Scribner.

Meyers, M. A. (2007). *Happy accidents: Serendipity in modern medical breakthroughs.* New York: Arcade.

Miller, A. I. (2001). *Einstein, Picasso: Space, time, and the beauty that causes havoc.* New York: Basic Books.

Miller, G. A. (1956). The magical number seven, plus or minus two: Some limits on our capacity for processing information. *Psychological Review*, vol. 63, pp. 81–97.

———. (1996). *The science of words.* New York: Scientific American Library.

———. (2003). The cognitive revolution: A historical perspective. *TRENDS in the Cognitive Sciences*, vol. 7, pp. 141–144.

Miller, G. A., Galanter, E., & Pribram, K. H. (1960). *Plans and the structure of behavior.* New York: Holt, Rinehart and Winston.

Miller, J. W., & Koblick, I. G. (1995). *Living and working in the sea* (2nd ed.). Plymouth, VT: Five Corners.

Mishina, K. (1999). Learning by new experiences: Revisiting the Flying Fortress learning curve. In N. R. Lamoreaux, D. M. G. Raff, & P. Temin (Eds.), *Learning by doing in markets, firms, and countries* (pp. 145–179). Chicago, IL: Chicago University Press.

Misiak, H., & Sexton, V. S. (1973). *Phenomenological, existential, and humanistic psychologies: A historical survey.* New York: Grune & Stratton.

Mitchell, M. F. (2000). The scope and organization of production: Firm dynamics over the learning curve. *RAND Journal of Economics*, vol. 31, pp. 180–205.

Mitchell, T. M. (1982). Generalization as search. *Artificial Intelligence*, vol. 18, pp. 203–226.
Mithen, S. (1996). *The prehistory of the mind: The cognitive origins of art, religion and science*. London, UK: Thames and Hudson.
Mitrovic, A. (2002). NORMIT, a Web-enabled tutor for database normalization. *Proceedings of the International Conference on Computers in Education*, ICCE 2002, Auckland, New Zealand, December 3–6 (pp. 1276–1280).
———. (2005). The effect of explaining on learning: A case study with a data normalization tutor. In C.-K. Looi, G. McCalla, B. Bredeweg, & J. Breuker (Eds.), *Proceedings of the 12th Conference on Artificial Intelligence in Education* (pp. 499–506). Amsterdam, the Netherlands: IOS Press.
Mitrovic, A., Martin, B., & Mayo, M. (2002). Using evaluation to shape ITS design: Results and experiences with SQL-Tutor. *International Journal of User Modeling and User-Adapted Interaction*, vol. 12, pp. 243–279.
Mitrovic, A., Martin, B., & Suraweera, P. (2007). Intelligent tutors for all: Constraint-based modeling methodology, systems and authoring. *IEEE Intelligent Systems*, vol. 22, pp. 38–45.
Mitrovic, A., & Ohlsson, S. (1999). Evaluation of a constraint-based tutor for a database language. *International Journal of Artificial Intelligence and Education*, vol. 10, pp. 238–256.
Mitrovic, A., Ohlsson, S., & Martin, B. (2006). Problem-solving support in constraint-based tutors. *Technology, Instruction, Cognition and Learning*, vol. 3, pp. 43–50.
Mitrovic, A., Suraweera, P., Martin, B., & Weerasinghe, A. (2004). DB-suite: Experiences with three intelligent web-based database tutors. *Journal of Interactive Learning Research*, vol. 15, pp. 409–432,
Mokyr, J. (1992). *The lever of riches: Technological creativity and economic progress*. New York: Oxford University Press.
Mokyr J. (1993). *The British industrial revolution: An economic perspective*. Boulder, CO: Westview Press.
Moltmann, F. (2003). Propositional attitudes without propositions. *Synthese*, vol. 135, pp. 77–118.
Montgomery, D. (2003). In a funk over the no-Nobel Prize: Overlooked MRI pioneer lobbies against decision. *Washington Post*, October 10, p. C01.
Montgomery, D. R. (2002). Valley formation by fluvial and glacial erosion. *Geology*, vol. 30, pp. 1047–1050.
Moore, B. R. (2004). The evolution of learning. *Biological Reviews*, vol. 79, pp. 301–335.
Moray, N. (1987). Feedback and the control of skilled behaviour. In D. H. Holding (Ed.), *Human skills* (pp. 15–39). New York: Wiley.
Morgan, L. C. (1894). *An introduction to comparative psychology*. London, UK: Walter Scott. [Facsimile edition issued by Adamant Media Corporation in 2005.]
Morgan, P. M. (1992). Discovery and invention in polymer chemistry. In R. J. Weber & D. N. Perkins (Eds.), *Inventive minds: Creativity in technology* (pp. 178–193). New York: Oxford University Press.

Morris, C. D., Bransford, J. D., & Franks, J. J. (1977). Levels of processing versus transfer appropriate processing. *Journal of Verbal Learning and Verbal Behavior*, vol. 16, pp. 519–533.

Moss, S. A. (2002). The impact of environmental clues in problem solving and incubation: The moderating effect of ability. *Creativity Research Journal*, vol. 14, pp. 207–211.

Mujica-Parodi, L. R., Malaspina, D., & Sackeim, H. A. (2000). Logical processing, affect, and delusional thought in schizophrenia. *Harvard Review of Psychiatry*, vol. 8, pp. 73–83.

Munn, N. L. (1946). *Psychology: The fundamentals of human adjustment*. Boston, MA: Houghton Mifflin.

Murray, J. P., & Youniss, J. (1968). Achievement of inferential transitivity and its relation to serial ordering. *Child Development*, vol. 39, pp. 1259–1268.

Myung, I. J., Kim, C., & Pitt, M. A. (2000). Toward an explanation of the power law artifact: Insights from response surface analysis. *Memory and Cognition*, vol. 28, pp. 832–840.

Nagel, E. (1961). *The structure of science: Problems in the logic of scientific explanation*. New York: Harcourt, Brace & World.

Nagel, E., & Newman, J. R. (2001). *Gödel's proof* (revised ed.). New York: New York University Press.

Nason, S., & Laird, J. E. (2005). Soar-RL: Integrating reinforcement learning with Soar. *Cognitive Systems Research*, vol. 6, pp. 51–59.

Neches, R. (1987). Learning through incremental refinement of procedures. In D. Klahr, P. Langley, & R. Neches (Eds.), *Production system models of learning and development* (pp. 163–219). Cambridge, MA: MIT Press.

Neches, R., Langley, P., & Klahr, D. (1987). Learning, development, and production systems. In D. Klahr, P. Langley, & R. Neches (Eds.), *Production system models of learning and development* (pp. 1–53). Cambridge, MA: MIT Press.

Necker, L. A. (1832). Observations on some remarkable phenomena seen in Switzerland; and an optical phenomenon which occurs on viewing a figure of a crystal of a geometric solid. *London and Edinburgh Philosophical Magazine and Journal of Science*, vol. 1, pp. 329–337. [Excerpt reprinted in Dember, W. N. (Ed.). (1964). *Visual perception: The nineteenth century* (pp. 78–80). New York: Wiley.]

Neisser, U. (1967). *Cognitive psychology*. New York: Appleton-Century-Crofts.

Nelkin, M. (1994). Universality and scaling in fully developed turbulence. *Advances in Physics*, vol. 43, pp. 143–181.

Nelson, R. R., & Winter, S. G. (1982). *An evolutionary theory of economic change*. Cambridge, MA: Harvard University Press.

Nersessian, N. J. (1992). How do scientists think? Capturing the dynamics of conceptual change in science. In R. N. Giere (Ed.), *Minnesota Studies in the Philosophy of Science* (vol. 15): *Cognitive models of science* (pp. 3–44). Minneapolis: University of Minnesota Press.

———. (2002). Abstraction via generic modeling in concept formation in science. *Mind and Society*, vol. 3, pp. 129–154.

———. (2008). *Creating scientific concepts*. Cambridge MA: MIT Press.

Neurath, O. (1937). Unified science and its encyclopaedia. *Philosophy of Science*, vol. 4, pp. 265–277.

Neuschatz, J. S., Lampinen, J. M., Preston, E. L., Hawkins, E. R., & Toglia, M. P. (2002). The effect of memory schemata on memory and the phenomenological experience of naturalistic situations. *Applied Cognitive Psychology*, vol. 16, pp. 687–708.

Neves, D. M., & Anderson, J. R. (1981). Knowledge compilation: Mechanisms for the automatization of cognitive skills. In J. R. Anderson (Ed.), *Cognitive skills and their acquisition* (pp. 57–84). Hillsdale, NJ: Erlbaum.

Newborn, M. (2000). Deep Blue's contribution to AI. *Annals of Mathematics and Artificial Intelligence*, vol. 28, pp. 27–30.

———. (2003). *Deep Blue: An artificial intelligence mile stone*. New York: Springer.

Newell, A. (1966, June). *On the analysis of human problem solving protocols* (Technical Report). Pittsburgh, PA: Carnegie Institute of Technology.

———. (1972). A theoretical exploration of mechanisms for coding the stimulus. In A. W. Melton & E. Martin (Eds.), *Coding processes in human memory* (pp. 373–434). New York: Wiley.

———. (1973). Production systems: Models of control structures. In W. G. Chase (Ed.), *Visual information processing* (pp. 463–526). New York: Academic Press.

———. (1982). The knowledge level. *Artificial Intelligence*, vol. 18, pp. 87–127. [Reprinted in Rosenbloom, P. S., Laird, J. E., & Newell, A. (Eds.). *The Soar papers: Research on integrated intelligence* (vol. 1, pp. 136–176). Cambridge, MA: MIT Press.]

———. (1990). *Unified theories of cognition*. Cambridge, MA: Harvard University Press.

Newell, A., & Rosenbloom, P. S. (1981). Mechanisms of skill acquisition and the law of practice. In J. R. Anderson (Ed.), *Cognitive skills and their acquisition* (pp. 1–55). Hillsdale, NJ: Erlbaum.

Newell, A., Shaw, J. C., & Simon, H. A. (1958). Elements of a theory of human problem solving. *Psychological Review*, vol. 65, pp. 151–166.

———. (1962). The processes of creative thinking. In H. E. Gruber, G. Terrell, & M. Wertheimer (Eds.), *Contemporary approaches to creative thinking: A symposium held at the University of Colorado* (pp. 63–119). New York: Prentice-Hall.

Newell, A., & Simon, H. A. (1972a). *Human problem solving*. Englewood Cliffs, NJ: Prentice-Hall.

———. (1972b). Historical addendum. In A. Newell & H. A. Simon. *Human problem solving* (pp. 873–889). Englewood Cliffs, NJ: Prentice-Hall.

———. (1976). Computer science as empirical inquiry: Symbols and search. *Communications of the ACM*, vol. 19, pp. 113–126.

Newton, R. R. (1980). The sources of Eratosthenes' measurement of the Earth. *Quarterly Journal of the Royal Astronomical Society*, vol. 21, pp. 379–387.

Niaz, M. (2001). A rational reconstruction of the origin of the covalent bond and its implications for general chemistry textbooks. *International Journal of Science Education*, vol. 23, pp. 623–641.

Nicolis, G. (1992). Physics of far-from-equilibrium systems and self-organization. In P. Davies (Ed.), *The new physics* (1st paperback ed., pp. 316–347). Cambridge, UK: Cambridge University Press.

Nokes, T. J. (2009). Mechanisms of knowledge transfer. *Thinking and Reasoning*, vol. 15, pp. 1–36.
Nokes, T. J., & Ohlsson, S. (2004). Declarative transfer from a memory task to a problem solving task. *Cognitive Science Quarterly*, vol. 3, pp. 259–296.
Nokes, T., & Ohlsson, S. (2005). Comparing multiple paths to mastery: What is learned? *Cognitive Science*, vol. 29, pp. 769–796.
Norman, D. (1981). Categorization of action slips. *Psychological Review*, vol. 88, pp. 1–15.
Norman, G. (2005). Research in clinical reasoning: Past history and current trends. *Medical Education*, vol. 39, pp. 418–427.
Nussbaum, J. (1985). The Earth as a cosmic body. In R. Driver, E. Guesne, & A. Tiberghien (Eds.), *Children's ideas in science* (pp. 170–192). Milton Keynes, UK: Open University Press.
Oaksford, M., & Chater, N. (1998). *Rational models of cognition*. Oxford, UK: Oxford University Press.
O'Connor, D. J. (1975). *The correspondence theory of truth*. London, UK: Hutchinson.
Ohlsson, S. (1983). The enaction theory of thinking and its educational implications. *Scandinavian Journal of Educational Research*, vol. 27, pp. 73–88.
———. (1984a). Restructuring revisited I. Summary and critique of the Gestalt theory of problem solving. *Scandinavian Journal of Psychology*, vol. 25, pp. 65–78.
———. (1984b). Restructuring revisited II. An information processing theory of restructuring and insight. *Scandinavian Journal of Psychology*, vol. 25, pp. 117–129.
———. (1984c). Induced strategy shifts in spatial reasoning. *Acta Psychologica*, vol. 57, pp. 47–67.
———. (1986). Some principles of intelligent tutoring. *Instructional Science*, vol. 14, pp. 293–326.
———. (1987a). Truth versus appropriateness: Relating declarative to procedural knowledge. In D. Klahr, P. Langley, & R. Neches (Eds.), *Production system models of learning and development* (pp. 287–327). Cambridge, MA: MIT Press.
———. (1987b). Transfer of training in procedural learning: A matter of conjectures and refutations? In L. Bolc (Ed.), *Computational models of learning* (pp. 55–88). New York: Springer-Verlag.
———. (1987c). Sense and reference in the design of interactive illustrations for rational numbers. In R. Lawler & M. Yazdani (Eds.), *Artificial Intelligence and Education* (pp. 203–237). Norwood, NJ: Ablex.
———. (1988a). Computer simulation and its impact on educational research and practice. *International Journal of Education*, vol. 12, pp. 5–34.
———. (1990a). Trace analysis and spatial reasoning: An example of intensive cognitive diagnosis and its implications for testing. In N. Frederiksen, R. Glaser, A. Lesgold, & M. G. Shafto (Eds.), *Diagnostic monitoring of skill and knowledge acquisition* (pp. 251–296). Hillsdale, NJ: Erlbaum.
———. (1990b). Cognitive science and instruction: Why the revolution is not here (yet). In H. Mandl, E. DeCorte, N. Bennett, & H. F. Freidrich (Eds.), *Learning and instruction, European research in an international context* (vol. 2.1): *Social and cognitive aspects of learning and instruction* (pp. 561–600). New York: Pergamon Press.

———. (1990c). The mechanism of restructuring in geometry. *Proceedings of the Twelfth Annual Conference of the Cognitive Science Society*, Cambridge, Massachusetts, July 25-28 (pp. 237-244). Hillsdale, NJ: Erlbaum.

———. (1991) System hacking meets learning theory: Reflections on the goals and standards of research in Artificial Intelligence and education. *Journal of Artificial Intelligence in Education*, vol. 2, pp. 5-18.

———. (1992a). Information-processing models of insight and related phenomena. In M. T. Keane & K. J. Gilhooly (Eds.), *Advances in the psychology of thinking* (vol. 1, pp. 1-44). New York: Harvester/Wheatsheaf.

———. (1992b). The cognitive skill of theory articulation: A neglected aspect of science education? *Science and Education*, vol. 1, pp. 181-192.

———. (1992c). Simulating the understanding of arithmetic: Answer to Schoenfeld. *Journal for Research in Mathematics Education*, vol. 23, pp. 474-482.

———. (1992d). Constraint-based student modeling. *Journal of Artificial Intelligence and Education*, vol. 3, pp. 429-447.

———. (1992e). The learning curve for writing books: Evidence from Professor Asimov. *Psychological Science*, vol. 3, pp. 380-382.

———. (1992f). Beyond rules and propositions: Reflections on Bereiter's concept of problem-centered knowledge. *Interchange*, vol. 23, pp. 367-378.

———. (1992g). Artificial instruction: A method for relating learning theory to instructional design. In M. Jones & P. H. Winne (Eds.), *Foundations and frontiers in instructional computing systems* (pp. 55-83). Berlin, Germany: Springer-Verlag.

———. (1992h). Towards intelligent tutoring systems that teach knowledge rather than skills: Five research questions. In E. Scanlon & T. O'Shea (Eds.), *New directions in educational technology* (pp. 71-96). New York: Springer-Verlag.

———. (1993a). The interaction between knowledge and practice in the acquisition of cognitive skills. In A. Meyrowitz & S. Chipman (Eds.), *Foundations of knowledge acquisition: Cognitive models of complex learning* (pp. 147-208). Norwell, MA: Kluwer.

———. (1993b). Abstract schemas. *Educational Psychologist*, vol. 28, pp. 51-66.

———. (1993c). The impact of cognitive theory on the practice of courseware authoring. *Journal of Computer Assisted Learning*, vol. 9, pp. 194-221.

———. (1994). Declarative and procedural knowledge. In T. Husen & T. Neville-Postlethwaite (Eds.), *The international encyclopedia of education* (2nd ed., vol. 3, pp. 1432-1434). London, UK: Pergamon Press.

———. (1995a). Epistemic obstacles and the marriage of fantasy to rigor: A response to Suchting. *Science and Education*, vol. 4, pp. 379-389.

———. (1995b). Learning to do and learning to understand: A lesson and a challenge for cognitive modeling. In P. Reimann & H. Spada (Eds.), *Learning in humans and machines: Towards an interdisciplinary learning science* (pp. 37-62). Oxford, UK: Elsevier.

———. (1996a). Learning from performance errors. *Psychological Review*, vol. 103, pp. 241-262.

———. (1996b). Learning from error and the design of task environments. *International Journal of Educational Research*, vol. 25, pp. 419-449.

———. (1998). Spearman's g = Anderson's ACT? Reflections on The Bell Curve and the locus of generality in human cognition. *Journal of the Learning Sciences*, vol. 7, pp. 135–145.

———. (1999a). Theoretical commitment and implicit knowledge: Why anomalies do not trigger learning. *Science and Education*, vol. 8, pp. 559–574.

———. (1999b). Anchoring language in reality: Observations on reference and representation. *Discourse Processes*, vol. 28, pp. 93–105.

———. (2000). Falsification, anomalies and the naturalistic approach to cognitive change. *Science and Education*, vol. 9, pp. 173–186.

———. (2002). Generating and understanding qualitative explanations. In A. Graesser, J. Leon, & J. Otero (Eds.), *The psychology of science text comprehension* (pp. 91–128). Mahwah, NJ: Erlbaum.

———. (2007a). The effects of order: A constraint-based explanation. In F. E. Ritter, J. Nerb, E. Lehtinen, & T. M. O'Shea (Eds.), *In order to learn: How the sequence of topics influences learning* (pp. 151–165). New York: Oxford University Press.

———. (2007b). The separation of thought and action in Western tradition. In A. Brook (Ed.), *The prehistory of cognitive science* (pp. 17–37). New York: MacMillan.

———. (2007c). Psychology is about processes. *Integrative Psychological and Behavioral Science*, vol. 41, pp. 28–34.

———. (2008a). Computational models of skill acquisition. In R. Sun (Ed.), *The Cambridge handbook of computational psychology* (pp. 359–395). Cambridge, UK: Cambridge University Press.

———. (2008b). How is it possible to have a new idea? In D. Ventura, M. L. Maher, & S. Colton (Eds.), *Creative intelligent systems: Papers from the AAAI Spring Symposium* (Technical Report SS-08-03, pp. 61–66). Menlo Park, CA: AAAI Press.

———. (2009a). Resubsumption: A possible mechanism for conceptual change and belief revision. *Educational Psychologist*, vol. 44, pp. 20–40.

———. (2009b). Meaning change, multiple routes and the role of differentiation in conceptual change: Alternatives to resubsumption? *Educational Psychologist*, vol. 44, pp. 64–71.

———. (2010). Questions, patterns and explanations, not hypothesis testing, is the core of psychology as of any science. In A. Toomela & J. Valsiner (Eds.), *Methodological thinking in psychology: 60 years gone astray?* (pp. 27–44). Charlotte, NC: Information Age.

Ohlsson, S., & Bee, N. (1991). Radical strategy variability: A challenge to models of procedural learning. In L. Birnbaum (Ed.), *Proceedings of the International Conference of the Learning Sciences*, Northwestern University, Evanston, Illinois, August 4–7 (pp. 351–356). Charlottesville, VA: Association for the Advancement of Computing in Education.

Ohlsson, S., Di Eugenio, B., Chow, B., Fossati, D., Lu, X., & Kershaw, T. C. (2007). Beyond the *code-and-count* analysis of tutoring dialogues. In R. Luckin, K. R. Koedinger, & J. Greer (Eds.), *Artificial Intelligence in education: Building technology rich learning contexts that work* (pp. 349–356). Amsterdam, the Netherlands: IOS Press.

Ohlsson, S., Ernst, A., & Rees, E. (1992) The cognitive complexity of doing and learning arithmetic. *Journal for Research in Mathematics Education*, vol. 23, pp. 441–467.

Ohlsson, S., & Hemmerich, J. (1999). Articulating an explanatory schema: A preliminary model and supporting data. In M. Hahn & S. Stoness (Eds.), *Proceedings of the Twenty First Annual Meeting of the Cognitive Science Society* (pp. 490–495). Mahwah, NJ: Erlbaum.

Ohlsson, S., & Jewett, J. J. (1995). Abstract computer models: Towards a new method for theorizing about adaptive agents. In N. Lavrac & S. Wrobel (Eds.), *Machine Learning* (pp. 33–52). Berlin, Germany: Springer-Verlag.

———. (1997). Ideal adaptive agents and the learning curve. In J. Brzezinski, B. Krause, & T. Maruszewski (Eds.), *Idealization* (vol. VIII): *Modelling in psychology* (pp. 139–176). Amsterdam, the Netherlands: Rodopi.

Ohlsson, S., & Kershaw, T. C. (2003). Creativity. *Encyclopedia of education* (2nd ed., vol 2, pp. 505–507). New York: Macmillan.

Ohlsson, S., & Langley, P. (1988). Psychological evaluation of path hypotheses in cognitive diagnosis. In H. Mandl & A. Lesgold (Eds.), *Learning issues for intelligent tutoring systems* (pp. 42–62). New York: Springer-Verlag.

Ohlsson, S., & Lehtinen, E. (1997). The role of abstraction in the assembly of complex ideas. *International Journal of Educational Research*, vol. 27, pp. 37–48.

Ohlsson, S. & Mitrovic, A. (2006). Constraint-based knowledge representation for individualized instruction. *Computer Science and Information Systems*, vol. 3, pp. 1–22.

———. (2007). Cognitive fidelity and computational efficiency of knowledge representations for intelligent tutoring systems. *Technology, Instruction, Cognition and Learning*, vol. 5, pp. 101–132.

Ohlsson, S., Moher, T. G., & Johnson, A. (2000). Deep learning in virtual reality: How to teach children that the Earth is round. In L. R. Gleitman & A. K. Joshi (Eds.), *Proceedings of the Twenty-Second Annual Conference of the Cognitive Science Society* (pp. 364–368). Mahwah, NJ: Erlbaum.

Ohlsson, S., & Rees, E. (1991a). The function of conceptual understanding in the learning of arithmetic procedures. *Cognition and Instruction*, vol. 8, pp. 103–179.

———. (1991b). Adaptive search through constraint violations. *Journal of Experimental and Theoretical Artificial Intelligence*, vol. 3, pp. 33–42.

Ohlsson, S., & Regan, S. (2001). A function for abstract ideas in conceptual learning and discovery. *Cognitive Science Quarterly*, vol. 1, pp. 243–277.

Oldby, R. (1974/1994). *The path to the double helix: The discovery of DNA*. New York: Dover.

Olson S. (2002). *Mapping human history: Discovering the path through our genes*. Boston, MA: Houghton Mifflin.

O'Quin, K., & Besemer, S. P. (1989). The development, reliability, and validity of the revised Creative Product Semantic Scale. *Creativity Research Journal*, vol. 2, pp. 267–278.

———. (2006). Using the Creative Product Semantic Scale as a metric for results-oriented business. *Creativity and Innovation Management*, vol. 15, pp. 34–44.

Orenstein, A. (1967). Maurice Ravel's creative process. *Musical Quarterly*, vol. 53, pp. 467–481.

Oreskes, N. (Ed.). (2003). *Plate tectonics: An insider's history of the modern theory of the earth*. Boulder, CO: Westview Press.

Ormerod, P. (1998). *Butterfly economics: A new general theory of social and economic behavior*. New York: Pantheon Books.

Ormerod, T. C., MacGregor, J. N., & Chronicle, E. P. (2002). Dynamics and constraints in insight problem solving. *Journal of Experimental Psychology: Learning, Memory, and Cognition*, vol. 28, pp. 791–799.

Orr, M., & Ohlsson, S. (2001). The relation between complexity and liking in jazz and blue grass. *Psychology of Music*, vol. 29, pp. 108–127.

Orr, M. G., & Ohlsson, S. (2005) Relationship between complexity and liking as a function of expertise. *Music Perception*, vol. 22, pp. 583–611.

Osherson, D. N., & Smith, E. E. (1981). On the adequacy of prototype theory as a theory of concepts. *Cognition*, vol. 9, pp. 35–58.

Overy, R. (1996). *Why the Allies won*. London, UK: Random House/Pimlico.

Pacey, A. (1992). *The maze of ingenuity: Ideas and idealism in the development of technology* (2nd ed.). Cambridge, MA: MIT Press.

Palermo, D. S. (1971). Is a scientific revolution taking place in psychology? *Science Studies*, vol. 1, pp. 135–155.

Pally, S. (1955). Cognitive rigidity as a function of threat. *Journal of Personality*, vol. 23, pp. 346–355.

Parssinen, T. M. (1974). Popular science and society: The phrenology movement in early Victorian Britain. *Journal of Social History*, vol. 8, pp. 1–20.

Patrick, J., Grainger, L., Gregov, A., Halliday, P., Handley, J., James, N., & O'Reilly, S. (1999a). Training to break the barriers of habit in reasoning about unusual faults. *Journal of Experimental Psychology: Applied*, vol. 5, pp. 314–335.

Patrick, J., Gregov, A., Halliday, P., Handley, J., & O'Reilly, S. (1999b). Analysing operators' diagnostic reasoning during multiple events. *Ergonomics*, vol. 42, pp. 493–515.

Patrick, J., James, N., Ahmed, A., & Halliday, P. (2006). Observational assessment of situation awareness, team differences and training implications. *Ergonomics*, vol. 49, pp. 393–417.

Pauling, L. (1935/1960). *The nature of the chemical bond and the structure of molecules and crystals: An introduction to modern structural chemistry* (3rd ed.). Ithaca, NY: Cornell University Press.

Pearson, J., & Clifford, C. W. G. (2004). Determinants of visual awareness following interruptions during rivalry. *Journal of Vision*, vol. 4, pp. 196–202.

Peirce, C. S. (1878a). How to make our ideas clear. *Popular Science Monthly*, vol. 12, pp. 286–302. [Reprinted in Houser, N., & Kloesel, C. (Eds.). (1992). *The essential Peirce: Selected philosophical writings* (vol. 1, pp. 124–141). Bloomington: Indiana University Press.]

———. (1878b). Deduction, induction, and hypothesis. *Popular Science Monthly*, vol. 13, pp. 470–482. [Reprinted in Houser, N., & Kloesel, C. (Eds.). (1992). *The essential Peirce: Selected philosophical writings* (vol. 1, pp. 186–199). Bloomington: Indiana University Press.]

———. (1901/1998). On the logic of drawing history from ancient documents, especially from testimonies. In N. Houser & C. Kloesel (Eds.). (1998). *The essential*

Peirce: Selected philosophical writings (vol. 2, pp. 75–114). Bloomington: Indiana University Press. [Previously unpublished manuscript, dated 1901.]

———. (1903/1998). Pragmatism as the logic of abduction. In N. Houser & C. Kloesel (Eds.), *The essential Peirce: Selected philosophical writings* (vol. 2, pp. 226–241). Bloomington: Indiana University Press. [Previously unpublished manuscript, dated 1903.]

Penfield, W. (1975). *They mystery of the mind: A critical study of consciousness and the human brain*. Princeton, NJ: Princeton University Press.

Penrose, R. (1991). *The emperor's new mind: Concerning computers, minds, and the laws of physics*. London, UK: Penguin Books.

Perkins, D. N. (1981). *The mind's best work*. Cambridge, MA: Harvard University Press.

———. (1994). Creativity: Beyond the Darwinian paradigm. In M. A. Boden (Ed.), *Dimensions of creativity* (pp. 119–142). Cambridge, MA: MIT Press.

———. (1995a). Insight in minds and genes. In R. J. Sternberg & J. E. Davidson (Eds.), *The nature of insight* (pp. 495–533). Cambridge, MA: MIT Press.

———. (1995b). *Outsmarting IQ: The emerging science of learnable intelligence*. New York: Free Press.

Perkins, D. N., Tishman, S., Ritchhart, R., Donis, K., & Andrade, A. (2000). Intelligence in the wild: A dispositional view of intellectual traits. *Educational Psychology Review*, vol. 12, pp. 269–293.

Perry, C. (1984). *Normal accidents: Living with high-risk technologies*. New York: Harper Collins.

Peters, E. E., & Levin, J. R. (1986). Effect of a mnemonic imagery strategy on good and poor readers' prose recall. *Reading Research Quarterly*, vol. 21, pp. 179–192.

Peterson, H. (Ed.). (1954). *A treasury of the world' greatest speeches*. New York: Simon & Schuster.

Peterson, I. (1993). *Newton's clock: Chaos in the solar system*. New York: Freeman.

Petroski, H. (1992). *To engineer is human: The role of failure in successful design*. New York: Vintage Books.

———. (2006). *Success through failure: The paradox of design*. Princeton, NJ: Princeton University Press.

Pettigrew, T. F. (1998). Intergroup contact theory. *Annual Review of Psychology*, vol. 49, pp. 65–85.

Pfundt, H., & Duit, R. (1991). *Bibliography: Students' alternative frameworks and science education* (3rd ed.). Kiel, Germany: Institute for Science Education.

Piaget, J. (1950). *The psychology of intelligence* (M. Piercy, Trans.). London, UK: Routledge & Kegan Paul.

———. (1952). *The child's conception of number* (C. Gattegno & F. M. Hodgson, Trans.). London. UK: Routledge & Kegan Paul.

———. (1963). *The origins of intelligence in children* (M. Cook, Trans.). New York: Norton.

———. (1985). *The equilibration of cognitive structures: The central problem of intellectual development* (T. Brown & K. J. Thampy, Trans.). Chicago, IL: University of Chicago Press.

Pierce, J. R., & Writer, J. (2005). *Yellow Jack: How yellow fever ravaged America and Walter Reed discovered its deadly secrets*. Hoboken, NJ: Wiley.

Pinker, S. (2002). *The blank slate: The modern denial of human nature*. New York: Viking.
Pirolli, P. (2005). Rational analyses of information foraging on the web. *Cognitive Science*, vol. 29, pp. 343–373.
Pitt, J. C. (Ed.). (1988). *Theories of explanation*. New York: Oxford University Press.
Planck, M. (1949). *Scientific autobiography and other papers* (F. Gaynor, Trans.). New York: Philosophical Library.
Plotkin, H. (1994). *Darwin machines and the nature of knowledge*. Cambridge, MA: Harvard University Press.
Plucker, J. A. & Renzulli, J. S. (1999). Psychometric approaches to the study of human creativity. In R. J. Sternberg (Ed.), *Handbook of creativity* (pp. 35–61). Cambridge, UK: Cambridge University Press.
Poincaré, H. (1908/1952). *Science and method* (F. Maitland, Trans.). New York: Dover Publications.
Polk, T. A., & Seifert, C. M. (Eds.). (2002). *Cognitive modeling*. Cambridge, MA: MIT Press.
Polya, G. (1962). *Mathematical discovery: On understanding, learning, and teaching problem solving* (vol. 1). New York: Wiley.
———. (1968). *Mathematical discovery: On understanding, learning, and teaching problem solving* (vol. 2). New York: Wiley.
Popper, K. (1959/1972). *The logic of scientific discovery* (Author, Trans.; revised version). London, UK: Hutchinson.
Popper, K. R. (1969). Science: Conjectures and refutations. In K. R. Popper, *Conjectures and refutations: The growth of scientific knowledge* (2nd ed., pp. 33–65). London, UK: Routledge & Kegan Paul.
Posner, G. J., Strike, K. A., Hewson, P. W., & Gertzog, W. A. (1982). Accommodation of a scientific conception: Toward a theory of conceptual change. *Science Education*, vol. 66, pp. 211–27.
Posner, M. I. (1973). *Cognition: An introduction*. Glenview, IL: Scott, Foresman.
Posner, M. I., & Keele, S. W. (1968). On the genesis of abstract ideas. *Journal of Experimental Psychology*, vol. 77, pp. 353–363.
Post, E. L. (1943). Formal reductions of the general combinatorial decision problem. *American Journal of Mathematics*, vol. 65, pp. 197–215.
Posthuma, D., & de Geus, E. J. C. (2006). Progress in the molecular-genetic study of intelligence. *Current Directions in Psychological Science*, vol. 15, pp. 151–155.
Postma, A. (2000). Detection of errors during speech production: A review of speech monitoring models. *Cognition*, vol. 77, pp. 97–131.
Potts, R. (1996). *Humanity's descent: The consequences of ecological instability*. New York: William Morrow.
Powers, W. T. (1973). *Behavior: The control of perception*. Chicago, IL: Aldine.
Pratt, D. (2000). Plate tectonics: A paradigm under threat. *Journal of Scientific Exploration*, vol. 14, pp. 307–352.
Preckel, F., Holling, H., & Wiese, M. (2006). Relationship of intelligence and creativity in gifted and non-gifted students: An investigation of threshold theory. *Personality and Individual Differences*, vol. 40, pp. 159–170.

Press, G. A. (1977). History and the development of the idea of history in antiquity. *History and Theory*, vol. 16, pp. 280–296.

Prigogine, I. (1997). *The end of certainty: Time, chaos, and the new laws of nature.* New York: Free Press.

Pringle, J. W. S. (1951). On the parallel between learning and evolution. *Behaviour*, 1951, vol. 3, pp. 174–215.

Proctor, R. W., & Dutta, A. (1995). *Skill acquisition and human performance.* Thousand Oaks, CA: Sage.

Purves, D., & Lichtman, J. W. (1980). Elimination of synapses in the developing nervous system. *Science*, vol. 210, pp. 153–157.

Putnam, H. (2005). A philosopher looks at quantum mechanics (again). *British Journal for the Philosophy of Science*, vol. 56, pp. 615–634.

Pylyshyn, Z. W. (1973). The role of competence theories in cognitive psychology. *Journal of Psycholinguistic Research*, vol. 2, pp. 21–50.

———. (1980). Computation and cognition: Issues in the foundations of cognitive science. *Behavioral and Brain Sciences*, vol. 3, pp. 111–169.

———. (1986). *Computation and cognition: Toward a foundation for cognitive science.* Cambridge, MA: MIT Press.

Quine, W. V. (1951). Two dogmas of empiricism. *Philosophical Review*, vol. 6, pp. 20–43.

Quine, W. V., & Ullian, J. S. (1978). *The web of belief* (2nd ed.). New York: Random House.

Radnitzky, G., & Bartley, W. W. III (Eds.). (1987). *Evolutionary epistemology, rationality, and the sociology of knowledge.* La Salle, IL: Open Court.

Radvansky, G. A., & Dijkstra, K. (2007). Aging and situation model processing. *Psychonomic Bulletin & Review*, vol. 14, pp. 1027–1042.

Raff, R. A. (1996). *The shape of life: Genes, development, and the evolution of animal form.* Chicago, IL: University of Chicago Press.

Ramirez, V. E. (2002). Find the right problem. *Asia Pacific Education Review*, vol. 3, pp. 18–23.

Ranney, M., & Schank, P. (1998). Toward an integration of the social and the scientific: Observing, modeling, and promoting the explanatory coherence of reasoning. In S. Read & L. Miller (Eds.), *Connectionist models of social reasoning and social behavior* (pp. 245–274). Mahwah, NJ: Erlbaum.

Ranney, M., Schank, P., Mosmann, A., & Montoya, G. (1993). Dynamic explanatory coherence with competing beliefs: Locally coherent reasoning and a proposed treatment. In T.-W. Chan (Ed.), *Proceedings of the International Conference on Computers in Education: Applications of Intelligent Computer Technologies*, ICCE'93, Taipei City, Taiwan, December 15–17 (pp. 101–106).

Read, S. J., & Marcus-Newhall, A. (1993). Explanatory coherence in social explanations: A parallel distributed processing account. *Journal of Personality and Social Psychology*, vol. 65, pp. 429–447.

Reason, J. (1990). *Human error.* Cambridge, UK: Cambridge University Press.

Reber, A. S. (1996). *Implicit learning and tacit knowledge: An essay on the cognitive unconscious.* New York: Oxford University Press.

Reed, S. (1993). A schema-based theory of transfer. In D. K. Detterman & R. J. Sternberg (Eds.), *Transfer on trial: Intelligence, cognition, and instruction* (pp. 39–67). Norwood, NJ: Ablex.

Reigeluth, C. M., & Stein, F. S. (1983). The Elaboration Theory of instruction. In C. M. Reigeluth (Ed.), *Instructional-design theories and models: An overview of their current status* (pp. 335–381). Hillsdale, NJ: Erlbaum.

Reiner, M., Slotta, J. D., Chi, M. T. H., & Resnick, L. B. (2000). Naïve physics reasoning: A commitment to substance-based conceptions. *Cognition and Instruction*, vol. 18, pp. 1–34.

Reis, D. A. (1991). Learning curves in food services. *Journal of the Operational Research Society*, vol. 42, pp. 623–629.

Reisberg, D. (2006). *Cognition: Exploring the science of the mind* (3rd ed.). New York: Norton.

Reisch, G. A. (1994). Planning science: Otto Neurath and the "International Encyclopedia of Unified Science." *British Journal for the History of the Sciences*, vol. 27, pp. 153–175.

Reiter, R. (1980). A logic for default reasoning. *Artificial Intelligence*, vol. 13, pp. 81–132.

Renkl, A., Mandl, H., & Gruber, H. (1996). Inert knowledge: Analyses and remedies. *Educational Psychologist*, vol. 31, pp. 115–121.

Revlin, R., & Leirer, V. O. (1978). The effects of personal biases on syllogistic reasoning: Rational decision from personalized representations. In R. Revlin & R. E. Mayer (Eds.), *Human reasoning* (pp. 51–81). New York: Wiley.

Rhodes, R. (1989). *The making of the atomic bomb*. New York: Simon & Schuster.

Richardson, A. (1969). *Mental imagery*. London, UK: Routledge & Kegan Paul.

Richardson, J. T. E. (1978). Mental imagery and the distinction between primary and secondary memory. *Quarterly Journal of Experimental Psychology*, vol. 30, pp. 471–485.

Riedweg, C. (2005). *Pythagoras: His life, teaching and influence* (Cornell University, Trans.). Ithaca, NY: Cornell University Press.

Rips, L. J. (1994). *The psychology of proof: Deductive reasoning in human thinking*. Cambridge, MA: MIT Press.

Roberts, R. M. (1989). *Serendipity: Accidental discoveries in science*. New York: Wiley.

Robin, N., & Ohlsson, S. (1989) Impetus then and now: A detailed comparison between Jean Buridan and a single contemporary subject. In D. E. Herget (Ed.), *Proceedings of the First International Conference on the History and Philosophy of Science in Science Teaching*, Florida State University, Tallahassee, Florida, November 6–10 (pp. 292–305). Science Education and Department of Philosophy, Florida State University.

Rock, D. (2006). *Quiet leadership: Help people think better – don't tell them what to do!* New York: HarperCollins.

Rogers, D. E. (2001). Embracing the range. In K. H. Pfenninger & V. R. Shubik (Eds.), *The origins of creativity* (pp. 47–57). Oxford, UK: Oxford University Press.

Rokeach, M. (1960). *The open and closed mind*. New York: Basic Books.

———. (1970). *Beliefs, attitudes, and values: A theory of organization and change*. San Francisco, CA: Jossey-Bass.

Rolls, E. T. (2000). Memory systems in the brain. *Annual Review of Psychology*, vol. 51, pp. 599–630.
Rosch, E. (1978). Principles of categorization. In E. Rosch & B. B. Lloyd (Eds.), *Cognition and categorization* (pp. 27–48). Hillsdale, NJ: Erlbaum. [Reprinted in E. Margolis & S. Laurence (Eds.). (1999). *Concepts: Core readings* (pp.189–206). Cambridge, MA: MIT Press.]
Rosenberg, C. E. (1992). *Explaining epidemics and other studies in the history of medicine*. Cambridge, UK: Cambridge University Press.
Rosenberg, N. (1982). *Inside the black box: Technology and economics*. Cambridge, UK: Cambridge University Press.
Rosenbloom, P. S., Laird, J. E., & Newell, A. (Eds.). (1993). *The Soar papers: Research on integrated intelligence* (vols. 1 and 2). Cambridge, MA: MIT Press.
Roosenbloom, P., & Newell, A. (1986). The chunking of goal hierarchies: A generalized model of practice. In R. S. Michalski, J. G. Carbonell, & T. M. Mitchell (Eds.), *Machine learning: An artificial intelligence approach* (vol. 2, pp. 247–288). Los Altos, CA: Kaufmann.
Rosenbloom, P., & Newell, A. (1987). Learning by chunking: A production system model of practice. In D. Klahr, P. Langley, & R. Neches (Eds.), *Production system models of learning and development* (pp. 221–286). Cambridge, MA: MIT Press.
Rothenberg, A., & Hausman, C. R. (Eds.). (1976). *The creativity question*. Durham, NC: Duke University Press.
Ruiz, D., & Newell, A. (1993). Tower-noticing triggers strategy-change in the Tower of Hanoi: A Soar model. In P. S. Rosenbloom, J. E. Laird, & A. Newell (Eds.), *The Soar papers: Research on integrated intelligence* (vol. 2, pp. 934–941). Cambridge, MA: MIT Press.
Runco, M. A. (Ed.). (1994). *Problem finding, problem solving, and creativity*. Norwood, NJ: Ablex.
Runco, M. A. (2004). Creativity. *Annual Review Psychology*, vol. 55, pp. 657–687.
Runco, M. A., McCarthy, K. A., & Svenson, E. (1994). Judgments of the creativity of artwork from students and professional artists. *Journal of Psychology*, vol. 28, pp. 23–31.
Ruse, M. (2002). Robert Boyle and the machine metaphor. *Zygon*, vol. 37, pp. 581–595.
Ryan, C. (1974). *A bridge too far*. New York: Simon & Schuster.
Salas, E., & Cannon-Bowers, J. A. (2001). The science of training: A decade of progress. *Annual Review Psychology*, vol. 52, pp. 471–499.
Salmon, W. C. (1989). *Four decades of scientific explanation*. Minneapolis: University of Minnesota Press.
Salomon, G., & Perkins, D. N. (1989). Rocky roads to transfer: Rethinking mechanisms of a neglected phenomenon. *Educational Psychologist*, vol. 24, pp. 113–142.
Sandkühler, S., & Bhattacharya, J. (2008). Deconstructing insight: EEG correlates of insightful problem solving. *Public Library of Science*, vol. 3, issue 1, pp. 1–12 (e1459). Available online at www.plosone.org.
Saugstad, P., & Raaheim, K. (1960). Problem-solving, past experience and availability of functions. *British Journal of Psychology*, vol. 51, pp. 97–104. [Excerpted in Wason and Johnson-Laird (1968), pp. 56–64.]

Schacter, D. L. (2001). *Forgotten ideas, neglected pioneers: Richard Semon and the story of memory*. Ann Abor, MI: Psychology Press.

Schank, R. C. (1982). *Dynamic memory: A theory of reminding and learning in computers and people*. Cambridge, UK: Cambridge University Press.

———. (1986). *Explanation patterns*. Hillsdale, NJ: Erlbaum.

Scheerer, M. (1963). Problem-solving. *Scientific American*, vol. 208, pp. 118–128.

Schick, K. D., & Toth, N. (1994). *Making silent stones speak: Human evolution and the dawn of technology*. New York: Simon & Schuster.

Schilling, M. A., & Phelps, C. (2007). Interfirm collaboration networks: The impact of large-scale network structure on firm innovation. *Management Science*, vol. 53, pp. 1113–1126.

Schneider, W., & Oliver, W. L. (1991). An instructable connectionist/control architecture: Using rule-based instructions to accomplish connectionist learning in a human time scale. In K. VanLehn (Ed.), *Architectures for intelligence* (pp. 113–145). Hillsdale, NJ: Erlbaum.

Schoenfeld, A. H., Smith, J. P. III, & Arcavi, A. (1993). Learning: The microgenetic analysis of one student's evolving understanding of a complex subject matter domain. In R. Glaser (Ed.), *Advances in instructional psychology* (vol. 4, pp. 55–175). Hillsdale, NJ: Erlbaum.

Schooler, L. J., & Hertwig, R. (2005). How forgetting aids heuristic inference. *Psychological Review*, vol. 112, pp. 610–628.

Schooler, J., Ohlsson, S., & Brooks, K. (1993). Thoughts beyond words: When language overshadows insight. *Journal of Experimental Psychology: General*, vol. 122, pp. 166–183.

Schraagen, J. M., Chipman, S. F., & Shalin, V. L. (Eds.). (2000). *Cognitive task analysis*. Mahwah, NJ: Erlbaum.

Schultz, D. P. (1969). *A history of modern psychology*. New York: Academic Press.

Schultz, T. R., & Lepper, M. R. (1996). Cognitive dissonance reduction as constraint satisfaction. *Psychological Review*, vol. 103, pp. 219–240.

Schwartz, B. L. (2002). *Tip-of-the-tongue states: Phenomenology, mechanism, and lexical retrieval*. Mahwah, NJ: Erlbaum.

Scott, G., Leritz, L. E., & Mumford, M. D. (2004). The effectiveness of creativity training: A quantitative review. *Creativity Research Journal*, vol. 16, pp. 361–388.

Sebag-Montefiore, H. (2000). *Enigma: The battle for the code*. New York: Wiley.

Seddon, G. M. (1983). The measurement and properties of divergent thinking ability as a single compound entity. *Journal of Educational Measurement*, vol. 20, pp. 393–402.

Seifert, C. M., Meyer, D. E., Davidson, N., Patalano, A. L., & Yaniv, I. (1995). Demystification of cognitive insight: Opportunistic assimilation and the prepared-mind perspective. In R. J. Sternberg & J. E. Davidson (Eds.), *The nature of insight* (pp. 65–124). Cambridge, MA: MIT Press.

Selby, E. C., Shaw, E. J., & Houtz, J. C. (2005). The creative personality. *Gifted Child Quarterly*, vol. 49, pp. 300–314.

Senders, J. W., & Moray, N. P. (1991). *Human error: Cause, prediction, and reduction*. Hillsdale, NJ: Erlbaum.

Shachtman, T. (2003). *Laboratory warriors: How allied science and technology tipped the balance in World War II*. New York: HarperCollins.

Shafir, E., & LeBoeuf, R. A. (2002). Rationality. *Annual Review of Psychology*, vol. 53, pp. 491–517.

Shanahan, M., & Baars, B. (2005). Applying global workspace theory to the frame problem. *Cognition*, vol. 98, pp. 157–176.

Shapin, S. (1998). *The scientific revolution*. Chicago, IL: University of Chicago Press.

Shiffrin, R. M. (1970). Memory search. In D. A. Norman (Ed.), *Models of human memory* (pp. 375–447). New York: Academic Press.

Shiffrin, R. M., & Nosofsky, R. M. (1994). Seven plus or minus two: A commentary on capacity limitations. *Psychological Review*, vol. 101, pp. 357–361.

Shrager, J., & Siegler, R. S. (1998). A model of children's strategy choices and strategy discoveries. *Psychological Science*, vol. 9, pp. 405–410.

Shreeve, J. (1995). *The Neandertal enigma: Solving the mystery of modern human origins*. New York: William Morrow.

Siegler, R. S. (1986). *Children's thinking*. Englewood Cliffs, NJ: Prentice-Hall.

———. (1987). The perils of averaging data over strategies: An example from children's addition. *Journal of Experimental Psychology: General*, vol. 116, pp. 250–264.

———. (1989). Hazards of mental chronometry: An example from children's subtraction. *Journal of Educational Psychology*, vol. 81, pp. 497–506.

———. (1996). *Emerging minds: The process of change in children's thinking*. New York: Oxford University Press.

Siegler, R., & Araya, R. (2005). A computational model of conscious and unconscious strategy discovery. In R. V. Kail (Ed.), *Advances in child development and behavior* (vol. 33, pp. 1–42). Oxford, UK: Elsevier.

Siegler, R. S., & Crowley, K. (1991). The microgenetic method: A direct means for studying cognitive development. *American Psychologist*, vol. 46, pp. 606–620.

Siegler, R. S., & Jenkins, E. (1989). *How children discover new strategies*. Hillsdale, NJ: Erlbaum.

Silvi, B., & Savin, A. (1994). Classification of chemical bonds based on topological analysis of electron localization functions. *Nature*, vol. 371, pp. 683–686.

Simon. H. A. (1962). The architecture of complexity. *Proceedings of the American Philosophical Society*, vol. 106, pp. 467–482. [Reprinted in Simon, H. A. (1970). *The sciences of the artificial* (pp. 84–118). Cambridge, MA: MIT Press.]

———. (1966). Scientific discovery and the psychology of problem solving. In R. G. Colodny (Ed.), *Mind and cosmos: Essays in contemporary science and philosophy* (pp. 22–40). Pittsburgh, PA: University of Pittsburgh Press.

———. (1990). Invariants of human behavior. *Annual Review of Psychology*, vol. 41, pp. 1–19.

Simon, H. A., & Barenfeld, M. (1969). Information-processing analysis of perceptual processes in problem solving. *Psychological Review*, vol. 76, pp. 473–483.

Simon, H. A., & Gilmartin, K. (1973). A simulation of memory for chess positions. *Cognitive Psychology*, vol. 5, pp. 29–46.

Simon, H. A., & Hayes, J. R. (1976). The understanding process: Problem isomorphs. *Cognitive Psychology*, vol. 8, pp. 169–190.

Simon, H. A., & Newell, A. (1971). Human problem solving: The state of the theory in 1970. *American Psychologist*, vol. 26, pp. 145–159.

Simonton, D. K. (1988). *Scientific genius: A psychology of science*. Cambridge, UK: Cambridge University Press.

———. (2004). *Creativity in science: Chance, logic, genius, and zeitgeist.* New York: Cambridge University Press.

Simpson, D. (2005). Phrenology and the neurosciences: Contributions of F. J. Gall and J. G. Spurzheim. *ANZ Journal of Surgery,* vol. 75, pp. 475–482.

Simpson, G. G. (1953). The Baldwin effect. *Evolution,* vol. 7, pp. 110–117.

Singley, M. K., & Anderson, J. R. (1989). *The transfer of cognitive skill.* Cambridge, MA: Harvard University Press.

Sio, U. N., & Ormerod, T. C. (2009). Does incubation enhance problem solving? A meta-analytic review. *Psychological Bulletin,* vol. 135, pp. 94–120.

Sleeman, D., & Brown, J. S. (Eds.). (1982). *Intelligent tutoring systems.* London, UK: Academic Press.

Slezak, P. (1982). Gödel's theorem and the mind. *British Journal of the Philosophy of Science,* vol. 33, pp. 41–52.

Slotta, J. D., & Chi, M. T. H. (2006). Helping students understand challenging topics in science through ontology training. *Cognition and Instruction,* vol. 24, pp. 261–289.

Slotta, J. D., Chi, M. T. H., & Joram, E. (1995). Assessing students' misclassifications of physics concepts: An ontological basis for conceptual change. *Cognition and Instruction,* vol. 13, pp. 373–400.

Smith, D. K., & Alexander, R. C. (1999). *Fumbling the future: How Xerox invented, then ignored, the first personal computer.* New York: toExcel.

Smith, E., Osherson, D., Rips, L., & Keane, M. (1988). Combining prototypes: A selective modification model. *Cognitive Science,* vol. 12, pp. 485–527. [Reprinted in Margolis, E., & Laurence, S. (Eds.). (1999). *Concepts: Core readings* (pp. 355–390). Cambridge, MA: MIT Press.]

Smith, J. D., & Minda, J. P. (1998). Prototypes in the mist: The early epochs of category learning. *Journal of Experimental Psychology: Learning, Memory, and Cognition,* vol. 24, pp. 1411–1436.

Smith, J. E. (1978). *Purpose and thought: The meaning of pragmatism.* New Haven, CT: Yale University Press.

Smith, J. P., III, DiSessa, A. A., & Roschelle, J. (1995). Misconceptions reconceived: A constructivist analysis of knowledge in transition. *Journal of the Learning Sciences,* vol. 3, pp. 115–163.

Smith, K. U. (1966). Cybernetic theory and analysis of learning. In E. A. Bilodeau (Ed.), *Acquisition of skill* (pp. 425–482). New York: Academic Press.

Smith, K. U., & Smith, M. F. (1966). *Cybernetic principles of learning and educational design.* New York: Holt, Rinehart and Winston.

Smith, S. M. (1995). Getting into and out of mental ruts: A theory of fixation, incubation, and insight. In R. J. Sternberg & J. E. Davidson (Eds.), *The nature of insight* (pp. 229–251). Cambridge, MA: MIT Books.

Smith, S. M., Ward, T. B., & Finke, R. A. (Eds.). (1995). *The creative cognition approach.* Cambridge, MA: MIT Press.

Smolin, L. (1992). Did the universe evolve? *Classical and Quantum Gravity,* vol. 9, pp. 173–191.

Snoddy, G. S. (1926). Learning and stability: A psychophysiological analysis of a case of motor learning with clinical applications. *Journal of Applied Psychology,* vol. 10, pp. 1–36.

Snooks, G. D. (2002). Uncovering the laws of global history. *Social Evolution & History*, vol. 1, pp. 25–53.
Solomons, T. (1988). *Organic chemistry* (4th ed.) New York: Wiley.
Solso, R. L., & McCarthy, J. E. (1981). Prototype formation of faces: A case of pseudo-memory. *British Journal of Psychology*, vol. 72, pp. 499–503.
Somit, A., & Peterson, S. A. (Eds.). (1992). *The dynamics of evolution: The punctuated equilibrium debate in the natural and social sciences.* Ithaca, NY: Cornell University Press.
Spearman. C. (1904). "General intelligence," objectively determined and measured. *American Journal of Psychology*, vol. 15, pp. 201–292.
Spence, J. D. (1985). *The memory palace of Matteo Ricci*. London, UK: Penguin Books.
Spiro, M. E. (1953). Ghosts: An anthropological inquiry into learning and perception. *Journal of Abnormal and Social Psychology*, vol. 48, pp. 376–382.
Spohrer, J. C., Soloway, E., & Pope, E. (1985). A goal/plan analysis of buggy Pascal programs. *Human-Computer Interaction*, vol. 1, pp. 163–205.
Sporns, O., & Tononi, G. (Eds.), (1994). *Selectionism and the brain*. New York: Academic Press.
Squire, L. R. (1987). *Memory and brain*. New York: Oxford University Press.
Stadler, M., Vetter, G., Haynes, J. D., & Kruse, P. (1996). Nonlinear phenomena in learning processes. In K. H. Pribram & J. King (Eds.), *Learning as self-organization* (pp. 157–169). Mahwah, NJ: Erlbaum.
Stallard, R. F. (1995). Tectonic, environmental, and human aspects of weathering and erosion: A global review using a steady-state perspective. *Annual Review of Earth and Planetary Sciences*, vol. 23, pp. 11–39.
Standage, T. (2000). *The Neptune file: A story of astronomical rivalry and the pioneers of planet hunting*. New York: Walker.
Stanley, S. M. (1998). *Children of the ice age: How a global catastrophe allowed humans to evolve*. New York: W. H. Freeman.
Starkey, P., Spelke, E. S., & Gelman, R. (1990). Numerical abstraction by human infants. *Cognition*, vol. 36, pp. 97–127.
Stearns, P. N. (1998). *The industrial revolution in world history* (2nd ed.). Boulder, CO: Westview Press.
Steiner, M. C., Munro, N. D., Surovell, T. A., Tchernov, E., & Bar-Yosef, O. (1999). Paleolithic population growth pulses evidenced by small animal exploitation. *Science*, vol. 283, pp. 190–194.
Sténuit, R. (1966). *The deepest days*. New York: Coward-McCann.
Sternberg, R. J., & Davidson, J. E. (1982). The mind of the puzzler. *Psychology Today*, vol. 16, pp. 37–44.
Sternberg, R. J., & O'Hara, L. A. (1999). Creativity and intelligence. In R. J. Sternberg (Ed.), *Handbook of creativity* (pp. 251–272). Cambridge, UK: Cambridge University Press.
Stevens, D., & Savin, H. B. (1962). On the form of learning curves. *Journal of the Experimental Analysis of Behavior*, vol. 5, pp. 15–18.
Stone, C. L. (1983). A meta-analysis of advanced organizer studies. *Journal of Experimental Education*, vol. 51, pp. 194–199.
Strathern, P. (2000). *Mendeleyev's dream: The quest for the elements*. New York: St. Martin's Press.

Stratton, S. M., Liu, Y.-T., Hong, S. L., Mayer-Kress, G., & Newell, K. M. (2007). Snoddy (1926) revisited: Time scales of motor learning. *Journal of Motor Behavior*, vol. 39, pp. 503–515.

Strayer, D. L., & Johnson, W. A. (2001). Driven to distraction: Dual-task studies of simulated driving and conversing on a cellular telephone. *Psychological Science*, vol. 12, pp. 462–466.

Strike, K. A., & Posner, G. J. (1985). A conceptual change view of learning and understanding. In L. West & L. Pines (Eds.), *Cognitive structure and conceptual change* (pp. 211–231). New York: Academic Press.

———. (1992). A revisionist theory of conceptual change. In R. A. Duschl & R. J. Hamilton (Eds.), *Philosophy of science, cognitive psychology, and educational theory and practice* (pp. 147–176). New York: State University of New York Press.

Stringer, C., & McKie, R. (1997). *African exodus: The origins of modern humanity*. New York: Henry Holt.

Sumida, S. S., & Brochut, C. A. (2000). Phylogenetic context for the origin of feathers. *American Zoologist*, vol. 40, pp. 486–503.

Sun, R. (Ed.). (2008). *The Cambridge handbook of computational psychology*. Cambridge, UK: Cambridge University Press.

Sun R., Merrill, E., & Peterson, T. (2001). From implicit skills to explicit knowledge: A bottom-up model of skill learning. *Cognitive Science*, vol. 25, pp. 203–244.

Sun, R., Slusarz, P., & Terry, C. (2005). The interaction of the explicit and the implicit in skill learning: A dual-process approach. *Psychological Review*, vol. 112, pp. 159–192.

Suppes, P. (1957). *Introduction to logic*. Princeton, NJ: D. Van Nostrand.

Suraweera, P., & Mitrovic, A. (2004). An intelligent tutoring system for entity relationship modelling. *International Journal of Artificial Intelligence in Education*, vol. 14, pp. 375–417.

Suwa, M. (2003). Constructive perception: Coordinating perception and conception toward acts of problem-finding in a creative experience. *Japanese Psychological Research*, vol. 45, pp. 221–234.

Swaab, T., Brown, C., & Hagoort, P. (2003). Understanding words in sentence contexts: The time course of ambiguity resolution. *Brain and Language*, vol. 86, pp. 326–343.

Sweller, J. (1988). Cognitive load during problem solving: Effects on learning. *Cognitive Science*, vol. 12, pp. 257–285.

Swinney, D. A. (1979). Lexical access during sentence comprehension: (Re)Consideration of context effects. *Journal of Verbal Learning and Verbal Behavior*, vol. 18, pp. 645–659.

Taatgen, N. (2002). Production compilation: A simple mechanism to model complex skill acquisition. *Human Factors*, vol. 45, pp. 61–76.

———. (2005). Modeling parallelization and flexibility improvements in skill acquisition: From dual tasks to complex dynamic skills. *Cognitive Science*, vol. 29, pp. 421–455.

Tainter, J. A. (1990). *The collapse of complex societies*. Cambridge, UK: Cambridge University Press.

Taleb, N. N. (2007). *The black swan: The impact of the highly improbable*. New York: Random House.

Tattersall, I., & Schwartz, J. H. (2000). *Extinct humans*. Boulder, CO: Westview.
Tavris, C., & Aronson, E. (2007). *Mistakes were made (but not by me)*. Orlando, FL: Harcourt.
Thagard, P. (1990). The conceptual structure of the chemical revolution. *Philosophy of Science*, vol. 57, pp. 183–209.
———. (1992). *Conceptual revolutions*. Princeton, NJ: Princeton University Press.
———. (2007). Abductive inference: From philosophical analysis to neural mechanisms. In A. Feeney & E. Heit (Eds.), *Inductive reasoning: Cognitive, mathematical, and neuroscientific approaches* (pp. 226–247). Cambridge, UK: Cambridge University Press.
Thagard, P., & Shelley, C. (1997). Abductive reasoning: Logic, visual thinking, and coherence. In M.-L. Dalla Chiara, K. Doets, D. Mundici, & J. van Benthem (Eds.), *Logic and scientific methods* (pp. 413–427). Dordrecht, the Netherlands: Kluwer.
Thagard, P., & Verbeurgt, K. (1998). Coherence as constraint satisfaction. *Cognitive Science*, vol. 22, pp. 1–24.
Thayer, H. S. (Ed.). (1982). *Pragmatism: The classic writings*. Indianapolis, IN: Hackett Publishing.
Thomason, N. (1994). The power of ARCHED hypotheses: Feyerabend's Galileo as a closet rationalist. *British Journal for the Philosophy of Science*, vol. 45, pp. 255–264.
Thorndike, E. L. (1898). *Animal intelligence: An experimental study of the associative processes in animals*. PhD dissertation, New York: Teachers College, Columbia University.
———. (1927). The Law of Effect. *American Journal of Psychology*, vol. 39, pp. 212–222.
———. (1932). *The fundamentals of learning*. New York: Teachers College, Columbia University.
Thorndike, E. L., & Woodworth, R. S. (1901). The influence of improvement in one mental function upon the efficiency of other functions. (I). *Psychological Review*, vol. 8, pp. 247–261.
Thorndyke, P. W. (1984). Applications of schema theory in cognitive research. In J. R. Anderson & S. M. Kosslyn (Eds.), *Tutorials in learning and memory* (pp. 167–191). San Francisco, CA: Freeman.
Timmerman, M. E., & Brouwer, W. H. (1999). Slow information processing after very severe head injury: Impaired access to declarative knowledge and intact application and acquisition of procedural knowledge. *Neuropsychologica*, vol. 37, pp. 467–478.
Tishman, S., Jay, E., & Perkins, D. N. (1993). Teaching thinking dispositions: From transmission to enculturation. *Theory into Practice*, vol. 32, pp. 147–153.
Titchener, E. B. (1912). The schema of introspection. *American Journal of Psychology*, vol. 23, pp. 485–508.
Toffler, A. (1970). *Future shock*. New York: Random House.
Tomasello, M. (1999a). The human adaptation for culture. *Annual Review of Anthropology*, vol. 28, pp. 509–529.
———. (1999b). *The cultural origins of human cognition*. Cambridge, MA: Harvard University Press.

Toulmin, S. (1972). *Human understanding.* London, UK: Oxford University Press.
Toulmin, S., & Goodfield, J. (1962). *The architecture of matter.* New York: Harper & Row.
Traxler, M., & Gernsbacher, M. (Eds.). (2006). *Handbook of psycholinguistics.* Philadelphia, PA: Elsevier.
Trenhaile, A. S. (2002). Rock coasts, with particular emphasis on shore platforms. *Geomorphology,* vol. 48, pp. 7–22.
Trickett, S. B., Schunn, C. D., & Trafton, J. G. (2005). Puzzles and peculiarities: How scientists attend to and process anomalies during data analysis. In M. E. Gorman, R. D. Tweney, D. C. Gooding, & A. P. Kincannon (Eds.), *Scientific and technological thinking* (pp. 97–118). Mahwah, NJ: Erlbaum.
Tulving, E. (1985). *Elements of episodic memory.* Oxford, UK: Clarendon Press.
Tulving E., & Pearlstone, Z. (1966). Availability versus accessibility of information in memory for words. *Journal of Verbal Learning and Verbal Behavior,* vol. 5, pp. 381–391.
Tulving, E., & Psotka, J. (1971). Retroactive inhibition in free recall: Inaccessibility of information available in the memory store. *Journal of Experimental Psychology,* vol. 87, pp. 1–8.
Tulving, E., & Thomson, D. M. (1973). Encoding specificity and retrieval processes in episodic memory. *Psychological Review,* vol. 80, pp. 352–373.
Turner, M. L., & Engle, R. W. (1989). Is working memory capacity task dependent? *Journal of Memory and Language,* vol. 28, pp. 127–154.
Tyson, N. de Grasse (2004, November). The importance of being constant. *Natural History,* vol. 113, pp. 18–20.
Uffink, J. (2003). Irreversibility and the second law of thermodynamics. In A. Greven & G. Warnecke (Eds.), *Entropy* (pp. 121–146). Princeton, NJ: Princeton University Press.
Ullman, S. (1995). Sequence seeking and counter streams: A computational model for bidirectional information flow in the visual cortex. *Cerebral Cortex,* vol. 5, pp. 1–11.
Usher, A. P. (1929/1954). *A history of mechanical inventions* (revised ed.). New York: Dover.
Uzumeri, M., & Nembhard, D. (1998). A population of learners: A new way to measure organizational learning. *Journal of Operations Management,* vol. 16, pp. 515–528.
Uzzi, B., & Spiro, J. (2005). Collaboration and creativity: The small world problem. *American Journal of Sociology,* vol. 111, pp. 447–504.
Van Andel, P. (1994). Anatomy of the unsought finding: Origin, history domains, traditions, appearances, patterns and programmability. *British Journal for the Philosophy of Science,* vol. 45, pp. 631–48.
Van der Maas, L. J., & Molenaar, P. C. M. (1992). Stagewise cognitive development: An application of catastrophe theory. *Psychological Review,* vol. 99, pp. 395–417.
Van Dijk, T. A., & Kintsch, W. (1983). *Strategies of discourse comprehension.* New York: Academic Press.
VanLehn, K. (1990). *Mind bugs: The origins of procedural misconceptions.* Cambridge, MA: MIT Press.
———. (1991). Rule acquisition events in the discovery of problem-solving strategies. *Cognitive Science,* vol. 15, pp. 1–47.

———. (1999). Rule-learning events in the acquisition of a complex skill: An evaluation of Cascade. *Journal of the Learning Sciences*, vol. 8, pp. 71–125.

VanLehn, K., & Jones, R. (1993). Learning by explaining examples to oneself: A computational model. In S. Chipman & A. L. Meyrowitz (Eds.), *Foundations of knowledge acquisition: Cognitive models of complex learning* (pp. 25–82). Boston, MA: Kluwer.

VanLehn, K., Jones, R. M., & Chi, M. T. H. (1992). A model of the self-explanation effect. *Journal of the Learning Sciences*, vol. 2, pp. 1–59.

VanLehn, K., Ohlsson, S., & Nason, R. (1994). Applications of simulated students: An exploration. *Journal of Artificial Intelligence and Education*, vol. 5, pp. 135–175.

Van Patten, J., Chao, C.-I., & Reigeluth, C. M. (1986). A review of strategies for sequencing and synthesizing instruction. *Review of Educational Research*, vol. 56, pp. 437–471.

Varela, F. J., Thompson, E., & Rosch, E. (1993). *The embodied mind: Cognitive science and human experience*. Cambridge, MA: MIT Press.

Vaughan, D. (1997). *The Challenger launch decision: Risky technology, culture, and deviance at NASA*. Chicago, IL: University of Chicago Press.

Veloso, M. M., & Carbonell, J. G. (1993). Derivational analogy in Prodigy: Automating case acquisition, storage and utilization. *Machine Learning*, vol. 10, pp. 249–278.

Vera, A. H., & Simon, H. A. (1993). Situated action: A symbolic interpretation. *Cognitive Science*, vol. 17, pp. 7–48.

Vincent, W. G. (1993). *What engineers know and how they know it: Analytical studies from aeronautical history*. Baltimore, MD: Johns Hopkins University Press.

Von Bertalanffy, L. (1968/1973). *General systems theory: Foundations, development, applications*. Norwich, UK: Penguin Books.

Von Domarus, E. (1944/1964). The specific laws of logic in schizophrenia. In J. S. Kasanin (Ed.), *Language and thought in schizophrenia* (pp. 104–114). New York: Norton.

Vosniadou, S. (1994a). Capturing and modeling the process of conceptual change. *Learning and Instruction*, vol. 4, pp. 45–69.

———. (1994b). Universal and culture-specific properties of children's mental models of the earth. In L. Hirschfeld & S. Gelman (Eds.), *Mapping the mind*. Cambridge, MA: Cambridge University Press.

Vosniadou, S., Baltas, A., & Vamvakoussi, X. (Eds.). (2007). *Reframing the conceptual change approach in learning and instruction*. Amsterdam, the Netherlands: Elsevier Science.

Vosniadou, S., & Brewer, W. F. (1992). Mental models of the earth: A study of conceptual change in childhood. *Cognitive Psychology*, vol. 24, pp. 535–585.

Waldrop, M. M. (1992). *Complexity: The emerging science at the edge of order and chaos*. New York: Simon & Schuster.

Walker, R. (2004). Cultural memes, innate proclivities and musical behaviour: A case study of the western traditions. *Psychology of Music*, vol. 32, pp. 152–190.

Walker, R. C. S. (1989). *The coherence theory of truth: Realism, anti-realism, idealism*. London, UK: Routledge.

Wallace, D. B., & Gruber, H. E. (Eds.). (1992). *Creative people at work: Twelve cognitive case studies*. New York: Oxford University Press.

Wallas, G. (1926). *The art of thought*. London, UK: Jonathan Cape.

Waller, J. (2002). *The discovery of the germ: Twenty years that transformed the way we think about disease*. New York: Columbia University Press.

Wallerstein, R. S. (2002). The growth and transformation of American ego psychology. *Journal of the American Psychoanalytic Association*, vol. 50, pp. 135–168.

Walliser, B., Zwirn, D., & Zwirn, H. (2005). Abductive logics in a belief revision framework. *Journal of Logic, Language and Information*, vol. 14, pp. 87–117.

Warren, J. M. (1965). The comparative psychology of learning. *Annual Review of Psychology*, vol. 16, pp. 95–118.

Warren, W. H. (2006). The dynamics of perception and action. *Psychological Review*, vol. 113, pp. 358–389.

Wason, P. C., & Johnson-Laird, P. N. (Eds.). (1968). *Thinking and reasoning*. London, UK: Penguin.

Wason, P. C., & Johnson-Laird, P. N. (1972). *Psychology of reasoning: Structure and content*. London, UK: B. T. Batsford.

Watson, J. B. (1913). Psychology as the behaviorist views it. *Psychological Review*, vol. 20, pp. 158–177.

Watson, J. D. (1968/1980). *The double helix: A personal account of the discovery of the structure of DNA*. New York: Norton.

Watson, J. D., & Crick, F. H C. (1953). A structure for deoxyribose nucleic acid. *Nature*, vol. 171, pp. 737–738.

Watts, D. (1999). *Small worlds: The dynamics of networks between order and randomness*. Princeton, NJ: Princeton University Press.

Weber, B. H., & Depew, D. J. (Eds.). (2003). *Evolution and learning: The Baldwin effect reconsidered*. Cambridge, MA: MIT Press.

Weber, R. J., & Perkins, D. N. (Eds.). (1992). *Inventive minds: Creativity in technology* (pp. 48–79). New York: Oxford University Press.

Weinberg, S. (1977). *The first three minutes: A modern view of the origin of the universe*. New York: Basic Books.

———. (1992). *Dreams of a final theory*. New York: Pantheon Books.

Weinberg, W. (2001). *Facing up: Science and its cultural adversaries*. Cambridge, MA: Harvard University Press.

Weisberg, R. W. (1986). *Creativity: Genius and other myths*. New York: W. H. Freeman.

———. (1993). *Creativity: Beyond the myth of genius*. New York: W. H. Freeman.

———. (1995). Prolegomena to theories of insight in problem solving: A taxonomy of problems. In R. J. Sternberg & J. E. Davidson (Eds.), *The nature of insight* (pp. 157–196). Cambridge, MA: MIT Press.

Weisberg, R. W., & Alba, J. W. (1981). An examination of the alleged role of "fixation" in the solution of several "insight" problems. *Journal of Experimental Psychology: General*, vol. 110, pp. 169–192.

Welford, A. T. (1968). *Fundamentals of skill*. London, UK: Methuen.

Wendt, H., & Imarisio, G. (2005). Nine years of research and development on advanced water electrolysis: A review of the research programme of the Commission of the European Communities. *Journal of Applied Electrochemistry*, vol. 18, pp. 1–14.

Wenger, E. (1987). *Artificial intelligence and tutoring systems: Computational and cognitive approaches to the communication of knowledge*. Los Altos, CA: Kaufmann.

Wentorf, R. H. (1992). The synthesis of diamonds. In R. J. Weber & D. N. Perkins (Eds.), *Inventive minds: Creativity in technology*. New York: Oxford University Press.

Wertheimer, M. (1923). Untersuchungen zur Lehre von der Gestalt, II. *Psychologische Forschung*, vol. 4, pp. 301–350. [Excerpt in English translation titled *Laws of organization in perceptual forms* in Ellis (1967), pp. 71–88.]

———. (1959/1968). *Productive thinking* (enlarged ed. by Michael Wertheimer). Northampton, UK: Tavistock Publications and Social Science Paperbacks.

Westfall, R. S. (1971). *The construction of modern science: Mechanisms and mechanics*. New York: Wiley.

———. (1983). *Never at rest: A biography of Isaac Newton*. Cambridge, UK: Cambridge University Press.

Wheatstone, C. (1838). Contributions to the physiology of vision. Part the first. On some remarkable, and hitherto unobserved, phenomena of binocular vision. *Philosophical Transactions of the Royal Society of London*, vol. 128, pp. 371–394.

Whitehead, A. N. (1929/1967). *The aims of education and other essays*. New York: Free Press.

Whitehead, A. N., & Russell, B. (1962). *Principia Mathematica to *56*. Cambridge, UK: Cambridge University Press.

Whitrow, G. J. (1989). *Time in history: Views of time from prehistory to the present day*. Oxford, UK: Oxford University Press.

Wiener, N. (1948). *Cybernetics, or control and communication in the animal and the machine*. New York: Wiley.

Wiig, S., & Aase, K. (2007). Fallible humans in infallible systems? Learning from errors in health care. *Safety Science Monitor*, vol. 11 (issue 3, article 6), pp. 1–13.

Wild, J. J. (1992). The origin of soft tissue ultrasonic echoing and early instrumental application to clinical medicine. In R. J. Weber & D. N. Perkins (Eds.), *Inventive minds: Creativity in technology* (pp. 123–124). New York: Oxford University Press.

Wiley, J. (1998). Expertise as mental set: The effects of domain knowledge in creative problem solving. *Memory and Cognition*, vol. 26, pp. 716–730.

Willingham, D. B. (1998). A neuropsychological theory of motor skill learning. *Psychological Review*, vol. 105, pp. 558–584.

Wilson, E. O. (1998). *Consilience: The unity of knowledge*. New York: Alfred A. Knopf.

Winograd, T. (1975). Frame representations and the declarative/procedural controversy. In D. G. Bobrow & A. Collins (Eds.), *Representation and understanding: Studies in cognitive science* (pp. 185–210). New York: Academic Press.

Wolfe, J. M., Kluender, K. R., Levi, D. M., Bartoshuk, L. M., Herz, R. S., Klatzky, R. L., & Lederman, S. J. (2006). *Sensation and perception*. Sunderland, MA: Sinauer.

Wolfradt, U., & Pretz, J. E. (2001). Individual differences in creativity: Personality, story writing, and hobbies. *European Journal of Personality*, vol. 15, pp. 297–310.

Wolpert, L. (1992). *The triumph of the embryo*. Oxford, UK: Oxford University Press.

Woodworth, R. S. (1938). *Experimental psychology*. New York: Henry Holt.

Woolf, B. (2009). *Building intelligent interactive tutors: Student-centered strategies for revolutionizing e-learning*. San Francisco, CA: Kauffman.

Woolf, N. J., & Hameroff, S. R. (2001). A quantum approach to visual consciousness. *TRENDS in Cognitive Sciences*, vol. 5, pp. 472–478.

Wright, M. R. (1981/1995). *Empedocles: The extant fragments*. London, UK: Bristol Classic Press.
Wright, O. (1953/1988). *How we invented the airplane: An illustrated history* (F. Kelly & A. Weissman, Eds.). New York: Dover. [Previously unpublished text dated 1920.]
Wuketits, F. M. (1990). *Evolutionary epistemology and its implications for humankind*. Albany: State University of New York.
Wynn, K., Bloom P., & Chiang, W.-C. (2002). Enumeration of collective entities by 5-month-old infants. *Cognition*, vol. 83, pp. B55–B62.
Yamnill, S., & McLean, G. N. (2001). Theories supporting transfer of training. *Human Resource Development Quarterly*, vol. 12, pp. 195–208.
Yaniv, I., & Meyer, D. E. (1987). Activation and metacognition of inaccessible stored information: Potential bases for incubation effects in problem solving. *Journal of Experimental Psychology: Learning, Memory, and Cognition*, vol. 13, pp. 187–205.
Yates, F. A. (1969). *The art of memory*. London, UK: Penguin Books.
Youmans, R., & Ohlsson, S. (2008). How practice produces suboptimal heuristics that render backup instruments ineffective. *Ergonomics*, vol. 51, pp. 441–475.
Young, R. M. (1976). *Seriation by children: An artificial intelligence analysis of a Piagetian task*. Basel, Switzerland: Birkhäuser Verlag.
Zakharov, K., Mitrovic, A., & Ohlsson, S. (2005). Feedback micro-engineering in EER-Tutor. In C.-K. Looi, G. McCalla, B. Bredeweg, & J. Breuker (Eds.), *Proceedings of the 12th Conference on Artificial Intelligence in Education* (pp. 718–725). Amsterdam, the Netherlands: IOS Press.
Zöllner, F. (2006). *Leonardo da Vinci, 1452–1519: Sketches and drawings*. Hong Kong, China: Taschen.
Zöllner, F., & Nathan, J. (2003). *Leonardo da Vinci: The complete paintings and drawings*. Köln, Germany: Taschen.
Zuckerman, M., & Cohen, N. (1964). Sources of reports of visual and auditory sensations in perceptual-isolation experiments. *Psychological Bulletin*, vol. 62, pp. 1–20.
Zwaan, R. A., & Radvansky, G. A. (1998). Situation models in language comprehension and memory. *Psychological Bulletin*, vol. 123, pp. 162–185.

NAME INDEX

Abelson, R. P., 305, 311
Alexander, R. C., 155
Allwood, C. M., 214
Anderson, J. R., 38, 191, 194, 333, 365–6
Anzai, Y., 191
Archimedes, 127
Aristotle, 291
Asimov, I., 265
Ausubel, D. P., 190, 335

Baldwin, N., 134
Baron, R. M., 305
Bassok, M., 243–4
Beckmann, J., 217
Beethoven, L., van, 73
Bell, A. G., 137–8
Bernstein, W. J., 287
Bhattacharyya, S., 154
Blackmore, S., 164
Bower, G. H., 196
Boyle, R., 5
Bradshaw, G., 135–6
Brem, S. K., 323
Brewer, W. F., 305, 311
Broadbent, D. E., 37
Brown, J. S., 216
Bruner, J. S., 30, 37, 169, 205
Bryan, W. L., 188
Burton, R. R., 216

Campbell, D. T., 71–3
Carlson, B., 138

Carroll, P. B., 275–6, 285
Cézanne, P., 54
Chi, M. T. H., 322–3, 327, 355, 357
Chinn, C. A., 305, 311
Chipp, H. B., 140
Chomsky, N., 37
Chronicle, E. P., 125
Churchill, W., 13–14
Collins, A., 37
Columbus, C., 182
Conrad, C., Jr., 171
Corrigan-Halpern, A., 179
Cousteau, J.-Y., 143, 171
Crick, F. H. C., 140–1, 150, 152, 156–8
Crossman, E. R. F. W., 265
Crovitz, H., 141
Cummins, R., 24

Damadian, R., 58
Darden, L., 305, 311
Darwin, C., 71–3, 85, 141, 149, 150, 320, 336, 351, 364
Degas, E., 54
Descartes, R., 5
Diamond, J., 255, 288
Donohue, J., 158
Duffey, R. B., 281–2
Duhem, P. M. M., 302–3, 305, 311, 363
Dunbar, K., 157
Duncker, K., 124

Ebbinghaus, H., 188
Edison, T. A., 88, 134, 137–8, 150, 152
Edmondson, A. C., 280
Einstein, A., 88, 160, 363
Empedocles, 162
Engelbart, D. C., 155
Eratosthenes, 291
Ernst, A., 247

Falco, A., 171
Festinger, L., 228, 305–7, 309, 311
Finke, R. A., 66, 67
Fitts, P. M., 190, 193
Fodor, J. A., 55–6
Franklin, R., 156

Gaddis, J. L., 14
Gagné, R., 44, 169, 190
Galanter, E., 75
Galilei, G., 304
Gallistel, R. C., 237–8
Gelman, R., 237–8, 241
Gensler, W. J., 215
Gentner, D., 345
Gertzog, W. A., 323
Goodman, N., 16, 131, 389
Gopnik, A., 321
Gorman, M. E., 138
Gödel, K., 55–6
Gruber, H. E., 141–2
Gustaf II, Adolf, 276

Hadamard, J., 53
Hanson, R., 309
Harter, N., 188
Hebb, D. O., 30
Heckhausen, H., 217
Heraclitus, 3
Hewson, P. W., 323
Hilgard, E. R., 196
Hillier, J., 137, 139, 141
Hume, D., 3, 389–91
Hutchins, E., 278–9

Isaak, M. I., 138

James, W., 74, 187, 207
Jewett, J. J., 262
Johnson, A., 301
Jones, R., 128
Jung-Beeman, M., 61, 128
Just, M. A., 138

Kaplan, C. A., 79, 126
Kelman, H. C., 305
Kepler, J., 5
Kershaw, T., 122
Kerwin, J. P., 171
Kintsch, W., 95
Kitcher, P., 317–8
Knoblich, G., 121
Koestler, A., 10, 130, 345–6
Koffka, K., 80–1, 84
Köhler, W., 80–4, 87
Kuhn, T. S., 22, 297, 315–6, 319, 327, 329, 358

Laird, J. E., 191, 366
Lakatos, I., 304–5, 311
Lamarck, J.-B., 315
Langley, P., 128, 226
Larson, J. R., Jr., 153
Lashley, K., 16
Lauterbur, P. C., 58
Lavoisier, A., 88, 141, 215
Leigh, J., 301
Leinhard, G., 249
Leonov, A., 169
Le Verrier, U. J. J., 309
Levinson, M., 14
Limón, M., 324
Link, E., 170
Luchins, A. H., 124
Luther, M., 150
Lynch, A., 164
Lysenko, T. D., 162–3

MacGregor, J. N., 125
Manet, È., 54
Mansfield, P., 58
Markman, A. B., 346
Marx, K., 337

Maxwell, J. C., 54
Meltzoff, A. N., 321
Mendeleyev, D. I., 138, 164
Mercator, G., 150, 156, 183
Metcalf, J., 61
Meyer, D. E., 127
Michelangelo, 88
Miller, G. A., 37, 75
Mitrovic, A., 250–1
Moher, T., 301
Monet, C., 54
Moran, N. P., 217
Mozart, W. A., 73, 160, 174
Mui, C., 275–6, 285

Neisser, U., 37
Nersessian, N., 318
Neves, D. M., 194
Newell, A., 24, 37–8, 75, 77, 79, 102, 107, 184, 190–1, 222, 314, 363, 365–6
Newton, I., 43, 120, 131–2, 160, 309, 311, 333, 336, 363–4
Norman, D. A., 37, 205, 217, 273
Nussbaum, J., 301

Ormerod, T. C., 125

Pasteur, L., 297, 386
Pauling, L., 88, 157
Peirce, C. S., 11, 309
Perkins, D. N., 72, 211
Peterson, I., 10
Piaget, J., 25, 84, 228, 263, 270, 345
Picasso, P., 22, 140–1, 150, 386
Pisarro, C., 54
Planck, M., 159
Poincaré, H., 65, 67, 69, 74, 80, 83–5
Polo, M., 182
Popper, K. R., 228, 313–6, 336, 358
Posner, G. J., 323
Posner, M. I., 127
Post, E., 165
Powers, W. T., 75
Pribram, K. H., 75
Priogogene, I., 10
Ptolemei, 162

Pylyshyn, Z. W., 28, 37
Pythagoras, 55

Quine, W. V., 291, 302–3, 305, 311, 349

Rasmussen, J., 273
Ravel, J.-M., 73
Reason, J., 217, 255, 273, 285
Reed, W., 156
Rees, E., 229, 237, 241, 247
Regan, S., 139–40
Reis, P., 138
Renoir, P.-A., 54
Rokeach, M., 303–5, 311, 335–6, 343
Rosenberg, N., 161
Rosenbloom, P. S., 191, 366
Rutherford, E., 297

Schank, R. C., 37, 228
Seifert, C., 127
Semon, R. W., 16
Senders, J. W., 217
Shapin, S., 5
Shaw, J. C., 24, 37, 107, 190
Siegler, R. S., 264
Simon, H. A., 24, 37, 75, 77, 79, 102, 107, 126, 184, 190–1, 363
Simonton, D. K., 65, 67
Smith, D. K., 155
Smith, S. M., 66–7
Soddy, F., 297
Sténuit, R., 170
Strathern, P., 138
Strike, K. A., 323
Sun, R., 191

Thagard, P., 318, 328, 343
Thompson, J. J., 297
Thorndike, E. L., 74, 85, 187–8, 197, 206, 375
Tolkien, J. R. R., 331
Tombaugh, C., 310
Toulmin, S., 316–17
Turing, A., 37

VanLehn, K., 187, 191, 216
Vincent, W. G., 351–2
Vosniadou, S., 301

Wallas, G., 125–6
Ward, T. B., 66–7
Watson, J. B., 188
Watson, J. D., 140–1, 150, 152, 156–8
Watt, R. W., 53
Weisberg, R. W., 70, 84, 126
Weitz, P. J., 171
Welford, A. T., 190
Wellman, H. M., 321

Wentorf, R. H., 135
Wertheimer, M., 80–2, 85
Wesley, C., 171
Wiener, N., 75, 188, 253–4
Wild, J. J., 149
Wiles, A., 142
Wilkins, A. F., 53, 151, 165
Wilkins, M., 156
Woodworth, R. S., 102, 104, 188
Wright Brothers, 73, 135–6, 141, 152, 192

Yaniv, I., 127

SUBJECT INDEX

abduction, 306, 308–11
accumulation, principle of, 70, 78–9, 86
action, analysis of, 177–82
action-conflict-change, principle of, 228
affordance, 100, 103
aftermath, of insight event, 92
analogy, 201, 204, 345–6
analytical thinking, 87, 98, 103–4, 116–17, 133, 135–6, 149
anomaly, 315–16, 323, 327, 348, 358, 374
articulation, of an abstraction, 46, 49, 363–4
assimilation, of new information, 299, 301–2, 327, 358
association, 42, 44
attitude change, 332
auxiliary assumption, 304, 310–11; see also peripheral beliefs and protective belt

background theory, 48, 340–2, 344, 353, 356
behaviorism, 26, 177
belief base, 293–5, 307–8, 334, 337, 340, 342–3, 350, 353, 357, 376
belief bias, 332
belief formation, 294–5, 320, 325, 330, 332, 338, 341–2, 344–5, 352, 355, 373–4, 376
belief revision, 292, 296–7, 310, 312, 320, 324–6, 330, 344, 354, 356–9, 368, 381
belief system, 293, 303, 310–12, 329–31, 333–4, 336–8, 341–2, 344, 348–9, 353, 356, 358–9, 370, 377–8
bisociation, 342, 345, 350, 352–3, 383

bolstering, in dissonance reduction, 306, 311
bottom-up rule generation, 197–8

caching, of search outcomes, 201
cascading causation, 8, 132
center-periphery, in belief systems, 298, 303–4, 311, 326, 335, 337
clockwork, 18, 20, 205
  analysis, 12
  in science, 10–13
  mind-set, 5, 16
  model, 5, 12
  nature, 5
  system, 19
  view, 16–17, 19
  world, 380
cognitive architecture, 37–9, 219, 224, 229, 244, 334, 359, 365–6, 381, 385–7
cognitive dissonance, 305, 307, 324, 340, 343, 345; see also dissonance reduction
cognitive utility, of a knowledge structure, 333, 342, 346–9, 353, 358–9, 378, 387
coherence, 295, 327, 335–6, 340, 342–3, 345, 373–4, 379; see also local coherence
combination, principle of, 66, 86
combinatorial explosion, 64–5, 69, 103, 116
combinatorial process, 64, 67, 370
complex system, 6–7, 11, 13, 19, 205, 216, 256, 278–9, 285–6, 391
componential explanation, 40–1, 46, 48

519

conflict resolution, 37, 103, 186, 225, 236–7, 244, 265, 271, 353
conflict set, 186, 225, 378
constituent structure, 370
constraint, 212–15, 220–2, 226, 231–3, 237–41, 247–51, 254, 257, 276–9, 287
constraint base, 212, 214, 222, 229, 247–8, 250, 285
constraint-based modeling, 250–1, 285
constraint-based theory; *see* specialization
constraint violation, 212, 214, 221–2, 225, 228, 239–40, 247, 250, 254, 274, 278–9, 284, 288
construction-integration process, 95, 97
contender theory, 313, 318–9, 328, 340–2, 344–8, 353, 356–8
context; *see* tight context
control structure, 36–7
conversion, of belief, 293, 297, 326–7, 330, 338, 341–2, 348–9, 355–6, 358–9, 381
core belief, 303–5, 308, 310–12, 317, 326–8, 335–6, 354
creativity
    of individuals, 59–60
    of processes, 61
    of products, 57–8
criteria of adequacy, 49
cybernetics, 188, 190, 196, 253

décalage, in Piagetian theory, 263
declarative knowledge, 182, 210–12, 214–5, 233, 238, 249, 251, 343, 370, 372
deduction, 55
deep learning, definition of, 21
demonstration, in skill acquisition, 195
denial, in dissonance reduction, 306
differentiation, in dissonance reduction, 306, 308, 311
direct impact, 8, 132
direction, of cognitive processing, 62, 65, 69, 79, 83, 117, 297, 358
discrimination, 226–8
displacement error, 218–19;
    see also overgeneralization error
dissonance; *see* cognitive dissonance and dissonance reduction

dissonance reduction, 298, 306, 308, 310–12, 322, 326, 343
distributed model, 36
dual knowledge base, principle of, 210

emergence, 8
empirical inductivism, 17–18, 21
envelope of selectivity, 67, 70
environmentalist approach, 27
error signal, 209, 284
error type, 217–18
excitation, of a knowledge element, 95, 109, 112, 372, 383
execution history, 226–7
expertise, 256, 267–72
explanation; *see* componential explanation
exponential equation, 261–3, 281
externality, 10, 127, 149–50, 157, 171
evaluation function, 76–7, 103
evolution, of humans, 15, 206, 245–46, 324, 381–84

falsification, 313–14, 316, 327, 336, 348, 356
fault, in a task strategy, 216, 255, 257, 259
feedback, in skill acquisition, 75, 96, 98, 109–11, 113, 117–18, 129, 137–8, 148, 157, 159, 188, 190, 196–8, 200, 202, 204, 234, 253, 262, 346–7, 349–50, 359, 371, 374–5, 377, 379, 381, 383, 385, 387

generalization, 16
    of concepts, 43
    of rules, 197–8, 201
generate-and-test, 65, 70–1, 74
gestalt, 80, 83–5, 88, 112, 120, 123–4, 129
goal, 76, 94, 98, 100, 106, 114, 159, 179–81, 184, 210, 229, 377; *see also* subgoal
goal state; *see* problem state

heuristic, 76–77, 79, 103, 116, 135, 195
homunculus, 85, 118, 320, 367, 381

identical elements hypothesis, 243
impasse, 84, 91–2, 104, 106–7, 113–14, 116, 119, 123, 125–9, 143–5, 153–4, 156, 159, 161–2, 165, 374

unwarranted, 91, 104, 106–7, 117, 124–5, 129, 137, 156, 159
incubation, 125–6, 128–9
induction, 16, 234, 313, 390–1
inference rule, 101, 103
Information Specificity, Principle of, 192, 203, 247
inhibition, of a knowledge element, 95, 109, 112, 372, 383
initial state, in problem solving; see problem state
insight, 82, 87–8, 91, 97, 107–8, 110–11, 113–16, 118–20, 125, 130, 133, 136–8, 140–3, 148, 156, 158–9, 163–5, 368, 372, 381
  false, 92, 115
  full, 92, 114
  partial, 92, 114
insight problem, 89–90, 105–7, 115, 120, 133
insight sequence, 92–3, 104, 107, 118, 126, 138
intelligent tutoring system, 249–52, 269, 285
internalization, of a demonstration, 201
introspection, 33

knowledge dependent processing, 298, 326
Knowledge Principle, 269

latent conflict, 342–5, 348, 352–3, 373, 379; see also manifest conflict
Law of Effect, 188, 191, 197, 206
layered approach, 49
learning curve, 45, 175, 188, 257–9, 261–3, 265–8, 281, 283–4
learning event, 45, 47–8, 186–7, 223, 229, 241, 243, 249, 251, 255, 257, 261, 272, 274
learning mechanism, 42, 44, 46–8, 186–7, 191–5, 200–3, 229–30, 246–7, 251–2, 256, 262, 267, 270–1
learning opportunity, 186, 215, 247, 250, 252–3, 259
learning rate, 260, 262
level invariance, 9, 132, 284; see also self-similarity
limitations, of cognition, 63, 70, 79, 117

local coherence, principle of, 343, 352–3; see also coherence
look-ahead, 76–7, 80, 100, 113–14, 118–19

manifest conflict, 342, 345, 353, 378–9; see also latent conflict
massive contingency, 8, 115–17, 146, 159, 241–2, 349, 375, 377
material incompatibility, 339
Maximally Efficient Learning, Principle of, 201, 203
mediation, in dissonance reduction, 306, 308, 310–11; see also abduction
mentalism, 28
model-based reasoning, 318
modeling, in instruction, 195
modes of learning, 190, 252, 262, 265
monotonic change, 21, 295–6, 330, 338, 342, 344–5, 352, 355, 366–7, 373, 381–4, 388; see also non-monotonic change
Multiple Difficulties, Principle of, 122–3
Multiple Mechanisms, Principle of, 187, 203
multiple overlapping waves, 264–5, 268

Nine Modes Theory, 199–201, 203–4, 261
non-monotonic change, 22, 49, 85, 117, 296–7, 327, 366–8, 373–5, 378–87, 390; see also monotonic change

ontological category, 322–3, 327, 355
ontological shift, 322, 327, 355–7
  hypothesis of, 322, 355, 357
optimization, of a strategy, 198, 202
overgeneralization error, 274; see also displacement error

parameter, of a belief, 330, 333–4, 337
pattern, of change, 45, 48
perceive-decide-act cycle, 185
periphery, of belief system, 310–11, 335; see also center-periphery
peripheral belief, 303, 336; see also auxiliary assumption and protective belt
peripheral change, 298, 305, 311–12, 316–17, 323, 326–7
phase, of skill acquisition; see stage

phenomenological approach, 25–6
Piggyback Hypothesis, of instruction, 246–7
possibility space, 137, 370–1; *see also* problem space and solution space
power law equation, 259–63, 281
practical knowledge, 182–3, 195, 210–12, 216–17, 219, 222, 234–7, 253, 259, 266, 270–1
practical reasoning, 194, 201, 294
practice, 172–4, 186–7, 192–4, 198, 202–3, 220, 230, 234, 236, 239, 241, 247, 251, 257, 259, 261, 263, 267–9, 271–2
pragmatic imperative, 359
prediction, 11–12, 14
prescriptive knowledge, 233
prevalence, 47–8, 128, 136, 138, 200, 296
problem finding, 149
problem space, 76, 78, 80, 102, 377;
 see also possibility space and solution space
problem state, 76, 94, 98, 180–1, 229
procedural knowledge, 182;
 see also practical knowledge
proceduralization, 194, 201
process loss, 153–4, 159
processing unit, 94, 107–9, 112, 149, 371–2
Production Systems Hypothesis, 184
projection, of prior knowledge, 16, 21, 103, 131, 133, 382, 384–5, 387, 389, 390–1
propagation, of change, 7, 108, 112–13, 118, 132, 296, 304, 311, 342, 349–50, 353, 357, 375, 377, 385
 amplified, 112, 376–7, 379, 384
 dampened, 112, 376–7
proposition, 293–4, 330, 332–3, 336, 339, 359
protective belt, in belief system, 304;
 see also auxiliary assumption and peripheral belief

reasoning schema, 101, 113
redistribution, of activation, 109, 111, 149, 372
 theory of, 108, 117–20, 129
reductionism, 26, 364–5
relevance criterion, of a constraint, 213–14, 222

replacement, 158–60
representation, 30–3, 38, 42, 80, 340
resident theory, 313, 316, 318–9, 328, 340–2, 344, 347–8, 353, 356–7
resistance to change, 296–8, 303–4, 311–13, 317–19, 321, 324, 326–7, 341, 354, 356, 358
restructuring, principle of, 81, 83–6, 292
resubsumption; *see also* subsumption
 process, 351–3
 theory of, 346, 348–50, 354–9
Rokeach structure, 336; *see also* center-periphery
rule, 183–4, 186, 192, 195, 197–8, 202–3, 218, 220, 222–6, 228–9, 231, 233, 236–40, 243, 257, 259, 266, 271–2, 372, 376, 378
rule genealogy, 223, 225, 236–7, 243–4, 271–2
rule set, 193, 203, 223, 225, 237, 241, 243, 257, 377

satisfaction criterion, of a constraint, 213–14, 222
scale, 46–9, 131–3, 142, 146, 148–51, 153, 159, 163–4, 256, 266, 272, 288;
 see also system level and time band
scientific revolution, 312
scope
 of a belief, 335, 337, 349
 of a goal, 180
 of a representation, 120, 123
search, 76–80, 91, 104, 106, 111, 113, 116–17, 119–20, 134–6, 152–3, 159, 190, 229
self-organization, 9, 83–4, 132, 371
self-similarity, 10; *see also* level-invariance
serendipity, 149
short-cut detection, 199–200, 202
situated cognition, 27
sociocultural approach, 27
solution space, 102–3, 105–6, 108, 153;
 see also possibility space and problem space
solved example, 195, 204
specialization
 of a rule, 220, 224, 229, 235, 239, 242–3, 247, 253–4

theory of, 220, 225, 228–9, 234, 236, 242–4, 253, 257, 271, 284
spread of activation, 98, 118, 128, 149, 345
stage, of practice, 188, 190, 193, 195–6, 198, 200
strategy discovery, 263–5
strategy, for performing a task, 103, 137, 184, 192, 196, 199, 205–6, 208, 218, 220, 223, 229, 231, 234–5, 243–4, 259, 263–6, 268, 276, 370, 379, 384
strengthening, of a knowledge structure, 197
subgoal, 101, 103, 113, 126–7, 134–6, 146, 152, 158, 180, 186; *see also* goal
subsumption, 335–6, 341, 345–6; *see also* resubsumption
system level, 7, 46–8, 131–2, 143, 149, 158; *see also* scale and time band

tangled hierarchy, 337
theory change, 292, 312, 314–21, 324, 326–8, 346, 354, 358–9
theory-theory, the, 321–2
theory-theory conflict, 319, 328, 338, 342, 346, 352, 358
threshold, 108, 110, 111–12, 119, 372, 376

threshold hypothesis, 147
tight context, 12, 103, 117, 253, 374, 384, 391
time band, 365; *see also* scale and system level
transfer, of training, 16, 176, 235–7, 241–5, 271–2
trial, in the context of skill practice, 174, 188, 259
trial and error, 74–5
triangular correlation, 147
triggering condition, for learning, 40–1, 44, 46, 48, 80, 85, 190, 208
Truth as Default, Principle of, 295, 330, 352
truth value, 293, 295–6, 330, 332, 334, 337, 339, 341, 348–50, 353, 357, 359, 368, 376
turbulence, 6, 7, 14, 18–21, 205, 253, 380, 389–92
tutoring, 245, 247, 249, 252

Ubiquitous Encoding, Principle of, 294–5, 330, 352
utility; *see* cognitive utility

variation-selection, principle of, 71–3, 317, 351–2, 364